DEATH IN CHILDBIRTH

Death in Childbirth

AN INTERNATIONAL STUDY
OF MATERNAL CARE
AND
MATERNAL MORTALITY
1800–1950

IRVINE LOUDON

CLARENDON PRESS · OXFORD

Oxford University Press, Walton Street, Oxford OX2 6DP
Oxford New York Toronto
Delhi Bombay Calcutta Madras Karachi
Kuala Lumpur Singapore Hong Kong Tokyo
Nairobi Dar es Salaam Cape Town
Melbourne Auckland Madrid
and associated companies in
Berlin Ibadan

Oxford is a trade mark of Oxford University Press

Published in the United States by
Oxford University Press Inc., New York

British Library Cataloguing in Publication Data
Data available

Library of Congress Cataloging in Publication Data
Loudon, Irvine.
Death in childbirth: an international study of maternal care and
maternal mortality, 1800-1950/Irvine Loudon.
p. cm.
Includes bibliographical references and index.
1. Prenatal care—History—19th century. 2. Prenatal care—
History—20th century. 3. Mothers—Mortality—History—19th
century. 4. Mothers—Mortality—History—20th century. I. Title.
RG516.L68 1992
362.1'982—dc20 92-20160
ISBN 0-19-822997-6

3 5 7 9 10 8 6 4 2

Printed in Great Britain by
Antony Rowe Ltd., Chippenham, Wiltshire

Preface

Faced with the final task of writing this preface, I undertook, on impulse, a brief survey of other people's prefaces. The result was surprising. There seemed to be few conventions. Exceptions foiled almost every generalization. Some were short, some long. Many were dull, and a few were memorable. Some were highly personal, others might have been written by a machine. My publisher's notes to authors, sternly explicit about most things, were silent on the preface. So what did my survey show?

The preface, said Robert Louis Stevenson, is the author's reward for his labours.

When the foundation stone is laid, the architect appears with his plans, and struts for an hour before the public eye. So with the writer in his preface... It is best, in such circumstances, to represent a delicate shade of manner between humility and superiority: as if the book had been written by someone else, and you had merely run over it and inserted what was good.[1]

In short, the author is supposed to put himself on view. Such an opportunity may be welcomed by novelists and journalists, but most authors in the field broadly defined as 'academic' shy away from publicity. Historians in particular should be heard but not seen, so that they can appear detached, impersonal, dispassionate, and invisible. Only in the preface do they exhibit the personal pronoun or give an occasional glimpse of themselves.

My survey of recent works, though slight and riddled with exceptions, suggests that English reticence based on a terror of saying anything that might be embarrassingly private and personal is intensifying. This may explain why some choose the preface to lay bare, not themselves, but the structure or plan of their book. They introduce the reader to themes on which they will expand at a later stage. That, to my mind, is the purpose of the introduction, not the preface.

Others, however, have used their preface quite properly to explain the motives, the origins, or the general purpose of their labours. Macaulay opens his *History of England* with magnificent simplicity: 'I purpose to write a History of England from the accession of James the Second down to a time which is within the memory of men still living.'[2] That he covered only a small part of his self-imposed marathon was unlikely to disturb a man of such supreme

---

[1] Robert Louis Stevenson, *An Inland Voyage* (London, 1878; repr. London, 1929), p. xxi.

[2] Thomas Babington Macaulay, *The History of England from the Accession of James II* (London, 1849).

self-confidence. Some authors explain that they had identified a historical void. 'It is surprising', said Berridge and Edwards in the preface to *Opium and the People*, 'that the vast outpouring of words on the "drug problem" in the last ten years has produced no serious historical examination of the place of narcotics in English Society.'[3] They filled that gap memorably and admirably. Others, like diminutive owners of bull-mastiffs who are taken for a walk by their dogs, fall back on the excuse that the subject took command of the helpless author. An essay, a lecture, or what was originally intended to be a single chapter, grew out of control like a triffid. Engels's *Condition of the Working Class* is an example.[4] Gertrude Himmelfarb's formidable study of Victorian poverty is a work which 'grew—and grew—out of two essays written a dozen years ago'.[5]

But for sheer originality it is hard to beat the preface of Salaman's memorably idiosyncratic *History of the Potato*.[6] When his career as a pathologist had been cut short by illness in 1903, he joined a group who were 'building up the English school of Mendelian inheritance' and wrote pieces about butterflies, mice, guinea-pigs, and poultry. All were 'complete failures'. So he turned for advice to Mr Evan John, his gardener, who suggested the potato because 'I know more about the potato than any man living.' Mr John's omniscient dogmatism proved a mixed blessing, but the study in which the author became 'ever more involved' was his gardener's idea.

Usually a reticent preface precedes a dispassionate history. Passionless history (not quite the same thing) may be dry stuff, but Barbara Tuchman, reviewing her life's work, found that '"think" pieces intended as satire or advocacy, or written from the political passions of the moment' were the ones that had wilted with the passage of time.[7]

The only rough generalization I can offer from my survey is that prefaces to academic studies today are notably impersonal. They consist of little more than a list of people whose help the author acknowledges with courtesy and formality. Indeed, the 'Preface' is fast being replaced by 'Acknowledgements'. The lists, often in alphabetical order, seem to get longer every year, looking more and more like a list of attenders at a memorial service, or subscribers to a supporter's club. Often the only personal touch is a routine expression of 'heartfelt gratitude for the long-suffering devotion of my wife/husband/family during a prolonged and often uphill struggle', as if the author was back from a one-man expedition across the Andes or Antarctica. Medical authors (but not

---

[3] V. Berridge and G. Edwards, *Opium and the People* (London, 1981), p. ix.

[4] F. Engels, *The Condition of the Working Class in England* 1845; 2nd edn., Oxford, 1958), Engels's original preface.

[5] Gertrude Himmelfarb, *The Idea of Poverty* (New York, 1984), p. ix.

[6] R. N. Salaman, *The History and Social Influence of the Potato* (rev. imp., Cambridge, 1985), pp. xxix–xxx.

[7] B. Tuchman, *Practicing History* (New York, 1981), 3. Tuchman's preface is a model of its kind: readable, informative, and not in the least reticent about the author.

historians) have a habit of thanking 'My secretary Deirdre Jones for the skill with which she has turned my illegible manuscript into an immaculate typescript'. The word-processor is putting an end to that.

This brings me to my list of acknowledgements, and also to the fear that the whole process has become so formalized that genuine gratitude is in danger of being mistaken for mere formality. For it is no exaggeration to say I have been astonished by the generosity of colleagues who have shared ideas, provided new insights, and even sent to me valuable material from their own research including unpublished essays, which they have allowed me to use freely. Apart from such conspicuous generosity, some colleagues will not have realized the importance of an off-the-cuff remark: one turned this study from the confines of England and Wales to international comparisons; another aroused my curiosity in the relationship between maternal and infant mortality and was the origin of the last chapter.

I am indebted to the Wellcome Trust without whose support over many years this book would never have been possible. Virtually all the research and a small part of the writing took place when I worked at the Wellcome Unit for the History of Medicine in the University of Oxford. I am deeply grateful to the Directors of the Unit, Charles Webster and his successor Richard Smith who has been immensely helpful with statistical analysis; and also to the Deputy-Director, Margaret Pelling. While working at the Unit, the advice, help, and friendship of Liz Peretz and Anne Summers meant a great deal to me.

When my time as a Research Associate at the Wellcome Unit expired, the Bursar of Green College found room-space for me in the College which proved to be the perfect environment for writing, and for this I express my gratitude to the Warden and Fellows of the College. Others in Oxford to whom I am indebted are the late Professor Sir Alexander Turnbell at the Nuffield Department of Obstetrics and Gynaecology, and Christopher Redman, Obstetric Physician to the Department. I have received a lot of ideas and help from members of the National Perinatal Epidemiology Unit, especially from the Director, Iain Chalmers, and from Alison Macfarlane as well as Miranda Mugford and Lelia Duley. Acting as supervisor to Lara Marks was not only a pleasure; I learnt much from her ideas and her thesis. For the same reason I am grateful to those students who, as part of their pre-clinical course, chose to write a thesis under my supervision on some aspect of the history of childbirth.

Outside Oxford, I am grateful to Patricia Want and Clare Daunton, Librarian and Archivist respectively to the Royal College of Obstetricians and Gynaecologists, for their help, and to the President of the College for permission to see the archives. I have had useful comments and criticism from many people including Sir George Godber, Dr McQuay, Roger Schofield, and S. J. Surtess who wrote to me on the early use of the sulphonamides.

Drs J. Finer, J. D. Fuller, P. Walshe, and Professor E. Blackburn produced a marvellous response to my request (published in the *British Medical Journal*) for information on the 'handywomen' of the past. They and others are thanked in the text. Dr Agnes Greig of Kirkcaldy kindly allowed me to examine in detail her father's records of midwifery practice, and I thank Nora Haines for allowing me to photocopy the ledger from her days as a midwife in the 1930s.

In the USA I received great help from, and would like to thank, the staff of the Countway Library, Boston, Massachusetts, and the History of Medicine Division of the National Library of Medicine in Bethesda, Maryland. In Boston, Luke Gillespie gave me a memorable account of obstetrics in the 1930s, and I am grateful to Leonard Wilson for data concerning maternal mortality in Minnesota. Linda Bryder provided me with valuable data from New Zealand. In the section on Europe I was heavily dependent on outside help, which I received in great and generous measure from Mart van Lieburg, Hilary Marland, L. H. Lumey, and H. I. J. Wildschut in the Netherlands; from Ulf Högberg and Christina Romlid in Sweden; from Signild Vallgårda in Denmark; from Lars Østby, Professor Øivind Larsen, and especially Kristina Kjærheim in Norway; and from C. Savona-Ventura in Malta. In writing Appendix 5, which went through more revisions than any other part of the book, I received stern but immensely helpful criticism from Michael Loudon, and in writing many sections of the book I have been deeply grateful for the sound advice of Jean Loudon. I am especially grateful to the copy-editor for the meticulous care with which he detected and corrected my numerous errors.

I. L.

Green College, Oxford
1991

Contents

List of Figures   xiv

List of Tables   xvii

Introduction   1

PART I: THE MEASUREMENT OF MATERNAL MORTALITY

1. The Measurement of Maternal Mortality   11

    Measuring Maternal Mortality as Total Maternal Deaths
    Measuring Maternal Mortality in Terms of Population
    The Maternal Mortality Rate

2. Problems of Measuring Maternal Mortality   19

    Stillbirths and Multiple Births
    The Length of the Postnatal Period
    The Registration of Births and Deaths in England and Wales
    The Registration of Births and Deaths in other Countries
    Nosology and the International Classification of Diseases
    Associated Deaths
    Associated Deaths and Multiple Causes of Death
    The Proportion of Associated Deaths
    Associated Deaths and International Comparisons
    Hidden Maternal Deaths
    Summary

PART II: THE CAUSES OF MATERNAL MORTALITY

3. The Determinants of Maternal Mortality   43

    Standards of Living and Standards of Care
    The Problem of Poverty

4. Puerperal Fever   49

    Puerperal Fever: Terminology and Fatality
    The Clinical Course of Puerperal Fever
    The Contagiousness of Puerperal Fever
    Charles White of Manchester
    Alexander Gordon of Aberdeen

Some other Accounts of the Contagiousness of Puerperal Fever
Oliver Wendell Holmes and Puerperal Fever
Ignaz Semmelweis and Puerperal Fever
The Neglect of Gordon, Holmes, and Semmelweis
Puerperal Fever and Erysipelas
The Bacteriology of Puerperal Fever
Endogenous and Exogenous Infection
The Importance of the Asymptomatic Carrier
The Treatment of Puerperal Fever

5. Toxaemia of Pregnancy and Eclampsia   85
Early Ideas about the Nature of Toxaemia
Treatment and Prevention
Mortality from Toxaemia

6. Obstetric Haemorrhage   97
Post-partum Haemorrhage
Ante-partum Haemorrhage
Accidental Haemorrhage or Placental Abruption
Ante-partum Haemorrhage: Placenta Praevia
The Mortality from Haemorrhage

7. Abortion   107
Abortion in Britain
Abortion in other Countries: Europe
Abortion in the Soviet Union
Abortion in the USA
Social and Legal Aspects of Abortion

8. Other Causes of Maternal Mortality   130
Contracted Pelvis and Rickets
Surgical Measures in Contracted Pelvis
The incidence of the Rachitic Contracted Pelvis
Puerperal Insanity, Puerperal Mania
Maternal Mortality, Duration of Pregnancy, and Stillbirths

PART III: MATERNAL CARE AND MATERNAL MORTALITY IN VARIOUS COUNTRIES

9. The Importance of International Comparisons   151

BRITAIN

10. Maternal Mortality in Pre-Registration England   158
Women's Perception of Maternal Mortality

11. The Eighteenth Century and the Origins of Man-Midwifery   166

12. Maternal Care in Nineteenth-Century Britain   172

    Who Delivered the Babies in the Nineteenth Century?
    The Nineteenth-Century Midwife
    Childbirth and the Medical Profession in the Nineteenth Century
    Physicians, Surgeons, and the Teaching of Midwifery
    Medical Education and Midwifery in Scotland
    Institutional Care in the Nineteenth Century
    Maternal Mortality in Institutional Deliveries
    The Antiseptic Revolution

13. Maternal Care in Britain, 1900–1935   206

    Midwives Acts, Government Reports, and Public Opinion
    The Royal College of Obstetricians and Gynaecologists
    Midwives and Handywomen
    Obstetrics in General Practice, 1900–1935
    Maternity Hospitals and Medical Education, 1900–1935
    Maternal Care, 1900–1935

14. Maternal Mortality in Britain from 1850 to the Mid-1930s   234

    Maternal Mortality, 1850–1910
    Maternal Mortality, 1910–1934
    Summary
    Regional Variations

15. Maternal Care and Maternal Mortality in Britain, 1935–1950   254

    England and Wales
    The Decline of Puerperal Fever, the Sulphonamides, and the
      Streptococcus
    The Decline in Maternal Mortality and the Second World War
    Abortion, Illegitimacy, and the War
    Conclusions

USA

16. The Geography and Politics of Maternal Care in the USA: 274
    Introduction

    The Politics of Maternal Care in the USA
    Maternal Mortality and the Public Health

17. Home Deliveries and the General Practitioner   281

    The Old Style of Family Doctor
    The Conservative Phase of Obstetric Practice
    Increased Intervention in Home Deliveries
    The General Practitioner and Maternal Mortality
    Rural and Urban Maternal Mortality
    Medical Education and Obstetrics in the USA

18. The American Midwife   298

     The Registration and Education of American Midwives
     The Immigrant Midwives
     Rural Midwifery in the Early Twentieth Century
     The Black Midwives of the Southern States
     The Kentucky Frontier Nursing Service
     Obstetricians against Midwives

19. The American Lying-in Hospital, 1850–1910   327

     The Lying-in Hospitals, 1850–1910
     Antisepsis and Hospital Deliveries
     Maternal Care and the Hospital, 1900–1935
     Out-patient Maternity Services

20. Attitudes to Childbirth and the Problem of Pain   340

     Primitive and Civilized Women
     Pain Relief in Childbirth
     Twilight Sleep
     Pain Relief after Twilight Sleep

21. The Orgy of Interference   351

     DeLee and the Prophylactic Forceps Operation
     The Extent of Interference
     Michigan: A Typical State?

22. Maternal Mortality in the USA   365

     Regional Differences in Maternal Mortality
     Maternal Mortality and Race in the USA
     Poverty and Maternal Mortality amongst Non-White Women
     Secular Trends in Maternal Mortality in Various States
     Conclusions
     Maternal Care and Mortality in Two North American Religious Groups

EUROPE

23. Introduction   398

     Some General Differences

24. European Midwives   402

     The French Midwives
     The Swedish Midwives
     The Dutch Midwives
     The Danish Midwives
     The European Midwives

25. European Lying-in Hospitals and Obstetricians   428

     The Problem of Puerperal Fever
     Tarnier and Puerperal Fever in Paris
     Maternal Mortality and Antisepsis on the Continent

26. Maternal Care and Maternal Mortality in Selected European   445
    Countries

    Genetic, Socio-economic, and Cultural Differences as the Explanation
        of Maternal Mortality Rates
    Trends in European Maternal Mortality
    The Effects of the Second World War

27. AUSTRALIA AND NEW ZEALAND   463

    Australia
    Australia: Standards of Maternal Care in the Inter-war Period
    Abortion in Australia
    The Decline in Maternal Mortality in Australia
    New Zealand

28. Maternal and Infant Mortality   483

    Definition of Mortality Rates
    The Determinants of Infant Mortality
    The Shift of Infant Mortality from Post-Neonatal to Neonatal during
        the Twentieth Century
    Secular Trends in Infant and Maternal Mortality
    The Effects of Social and Economic Deprivation on Maternal and
        Infant Mortality
    International and Regional Comparisons of Infant and Maternal
        Mortality
    Maternal Mortality and Maternal Age and Parity
    Neonatal Mortality and Maternal Age and Parity
    The Direct Causes of Maternal and Infant Mortality
    Prematurity and Pre-term Delivery
    Birth Injury
    Causes in Individuals and in Populations
    Conclusions

    Appendix 1: Hidden Maternal Deaths   518
    Appendix 2: England and Wales: The Classification of Maternal 525
            Deaths
    Appendix 3: Reports on Maternal Mortality in the USA   528
    Appendix 4: Numbers of Births and Statistical Significance   532
    Appendix 5: The Problem of Streptococcal Virulence   534
    Appendix 6: Tables   541

    Select Bibliography   585

    Britain
    United States of America
    Europe
    Australia and New Zealand

    Index   616

List of Figures

1.1 England and Wales, 1851–60 to 1971–80. Total Births and Total Maternal Deaths 12

1.2 England and Wales, 1851–60 to 1971–80. Population of women aged 15–44, Birth Rate, and Maternal Death Rate 13

1.3 England and Wales, 1850–1970. Annual rates of Maternal Mortality 15

1.4 England and Wales, 1850–1980, Maternal Mortality Rates (five-year averages) logarithmic scale 16

4.1 England and Wales, 1865–1900. Showing the trend in Maternal Mortality due to puerperal fever and other causes 73

4.2 England and Wales, 1860–1879. Deaths per million people living, due to scarlet fever, erysipelas, and puerperal fever. Death rates shown as the mean value for the whole period of twenty-five years and as the percentage variation above or below the mean in each year 74

4.3 England and Wales, 1911–1945. Death rates from erysipelas and scarlet fever per 100,000 people of all ages, and the maternal mortality rate per 1,000 births due to puerperal fever 75

7.1 England and Wales 1934, USA 1933. Deaths due to abortion (septic and non-septic) and puerperal sepsis (abortive and non-abortive) shown as percentages of total maternal mortality 113

8.1 Illustration of the female pelvis as seen from above. A is the normal female pelvis. B is a female pelvis with severe distortion caused by childhood rickets 132

9.1 Schematic representation of the trends in Maternal Mortality in various countries, 1889–1950 152

9.2 Trend in Maternal Mortality in the USA, England and Wales, and the Netherlands, 1900–1970. Logarithmic Scale 154

9.3 The percentage of home deliveries in the USA, England and Wales, and Sweden, 1900–1960 155

10.1 Estimates of Maternal Mortality in England, 1650–1870 159

14.1 England and Wales, Scotland, and Ireland. Annual rates of Maternal Mortality, 1850–1950 235

14.2 England and Wales. Annual Rates of Maternal Mortality and the trend between 1870 and 1910 by regression analysis 235

14.3 England and Wales. Annual rates of Maternal Mortality and the trend between 1911 and 1934 by regression analysis 236

14.4 England and Wales, 1870–1910. Annual rates of death due to erysipelas (number of deaths per million persons living) and Maternal Mortality due to puerperal sepsis (Number of Deaths per 10,000 births) 236

14.5 Scotland, 1911–1945. Trend in maternal deaths due to certain causes. Deaths per 10,000 births indexed to 100 in 1911–1945 249

14.6   Maternal Mortality Rates in Administrative Counties of England and
Wales for the decade 1924–1933   253

15.1   England and Wales, 1931–1950. The trends in Maternal Mortality
Rates by cause, indexed to 100 in 1931   255

18.1   USA, 1935–1954. Live births by attendant   299

22.1   USA, 1915–1960. Trend in Maternal Mortality. Annual rates   366

22.2   The periods in which States were admitted to the United States
Death Registration Area   367

22.3   USA 1938–1940. Interstate variations in Maternal Mortality Rates
in terms of four categories of Maternal Mortality   367

22.4   USA, 1938–1940. States ranked according to their level of Maternal
Mortality expressed as a percentage above or below the national
average   368

22.5   USA, 1940. Total non-white births and non-white births attended
by midwives in various states   373

22.6   USA, Massachusetts, 1850–1965. Trend in Maternal Mortality   382

22.7   USA, Minnesota, 1915–1947. Trend in Maternal Mortality   382

22.8   USA, Mississippi, 1920–1970. Trend in Maternal Mortality   383

22.9   USA, Kentucky, 1911–1939. Trend in Maternal Mortality   383

22.10   USA, Virginia, 1928–1947. Trend in Maternal Mortality   384

22.11   Declinc in Maternal Mortality rates in selected States of the USA
and selected countries between 1939 and 1949. Logarithmic scale   390

22.12   United States, 1939–1948. The proportionate reduction in Maternal
Mortality by various causes   392

24.1   Sweden, 1842–1920. Annual number of midwives examined and
authorized to undertake instrumental deliveries   408

24.2   Sweden, 1751–1980. Trend in Maternal Mortality Rate per 100,000
live births. Annual mean, five-year periods   409

24.3   Sweden rural areas, quinquennial periods, 1861–1894. Trend in
Maternal Mortality Rates due to causes other than sepsis, and
percentage of deliveries by trained midwives   411

24.4   Sweden and Norway. Quinquennial periods, 1861–5 to 1900–5.
Trend in Maternal Mortality shown as maternal deaths from all
causes (in the case of Sweden from 1816–21 to 1901–5), maternal
deaths due to puerperal fever, and maternal deaths due to causes
other than puerperal fever   413

25.1   Liège Maternity Hospital, 1860–1910. Maternal Mortality and the
introduction of antisepsis   438

26.1   The Netherlands 1900–1950, Norway 1900–1920, and Denmark
1900–1940. Trends in annual rates of Maternal Mortality   451

26.2   Sweden, England and Wales, and Scotland, 1910–1934. The trend
in direct maternal deaths per 10,000 births due to causes other than
puerperal sepsis and abortion   452

26.3   England and Wales. Secular trends in Maternal Mortality 1905–
1960. Infant Mortality 1910–1960 and Neonatal mortality 1928–
1960   456

26.4   Infant Mortality rates, selected European countries 1925–1965, showing the effects of the Second World War   457

26.5   The trend in deaths from puerperal sepsis in France and England
       and Wales, 1925–1950, showing the effects of the Second World
       War   458

26.6   The Netherlands. Annual trends in Maternal Mortality 1905–1950
       and in Infant and Neonatal Mortality 1910–1960, showing the
       effects of the Second World War   459

26.7   The Maltese Islands. Maternal, Infant, and Neonatal Mortality,
       1924–1960. Showing the effects of the siege during the Second
       World War. Infant Mortality for England and Wales shown for
       comparison   461

27.1   Australia and New Zealand. 1905–1950, Annual trends in Maternal
       Mortality   465

27.2   New Zealand, 1927–1950. Annual rates of Maternal Mortality from
       all causes, from post-partum sepsis, and from septic abortion.
       Logaritmic scale   480

28.1   Diagram showing the definitions of mortality rates as they apply to
       the foetus, the neonate, and the infant   486

28.2   USA, 1954. Infant Mortality by age   487

28.3   England and Wales, 1905–1960. Secular trends in Maternal, Infant,
       and Neonatal Mortality   489

28.4   England and Wales 1905–1985. Secular trends in Post-Neonatal
       and Neonatal Mortality   490

28.5   England and Wales 1905–1985. Secular trends in Early and Late
       Neonatal Mortality   490

28.6   The Netherlands. Infant Mortality, Neonatal, and Post-Neonatal
       Mortality in 1900, 1930, and 1960   491

28.7   New York State, 1936–1938. The effect of parity on the Maternal
       and Neonatal Mortality Rates for mothers of all ages   503

28.8   New York State, 1936–1938. The effect of age on Maternal
       Mortality for mothers of various parities   504

28.9   New York State, 1936–1938. The effect of parity on Maternal
       Mortality Rates for mothers of various ages   505

28.10 Effects of maternal age on Maternal Mortality Rates for first, second,
       and fifth births in New York State 1936–1938 and England and
       Wales, 1976–1984   507

App. 5.1 England and Wales, 1911–1939. Fatality rates of scarlet fever and
       erysipelas   538

List of Tables

1.1 Female Population, Birth Rate, and Maternal Mortality Rate in England and Wales, 1851–1980 14

2.1 Post-natal maternal deaths in Canada, 1927 and 1928, according to the interval between birth and maternal death 22

2.2 Births and Maternal Deaths in England and Wales, 1871–1878 24

2.3 The Assignment of 447 Maternal Deaths according to the Methodology Used in Various Countries 33

2.4 The Effect of Differences in Methodology on the Reported Maternal Mortality Rates in Certain Countries, 1927 34

4.1 Ante-mortem Bacteriological Findings in a Series of 109 Cases of Puerperal Septicaemia, North of England, 1925 53

4.2 Bacteriological Findings in 88 Cases of Puerperal Fever, Aberdeen, 1918–1927 54

4.3 Deaths from Puerperal Septicaemia in Relation to Time of Delivery, Canada, 1927–1928 55

4.4 Deaths from Puerperal Septicaemia in Relation to Days after Delivery, Scotland, 1929–1933 55

4.5 The Maternal Mortality Rate in the Two Clinics of the Vienna Maternity Hospital before and after the Introduction of Semmelweis's Reforms 67

4.6 Maternal Mortality Rates in Norway and its regions, 1866–1877 76

5.1 Medical Treatments for Eclampsia and Pre-eclampsia 89

5.2 Maternal Mortality Rate Due to 'Puerperal Convulsions' and 'Albuminuria of Pregnancy', England and Wales, Scotland, and Ireland, 1912–1920 93

5.3 Deaths Due to 'Puerperal Convulsions' and 'Albuminuria of Pregnancy' Expressed as a Percentage of Total Maternal Mortality in Various Parts of Britain, 1912–1920 93

5.4 Incidence and Maternal Mortality of Toxaemia of Pregnancy in Various Countries up to the Mid-1930s 94

6.1 Cases of Obstetric Haemorrhage, Edinburgh Maternity Hospital, 1844–1846 103

6.2 Maternal Mortality Rates Due to Various Categories of Obstetric Haemorrhage in Various Countries at Various Periods 104

7.1 Deaths Due to Septic and Non-Septic Abortion, England and Wales, 1928–1934 110

7.2 Abortion Deaths of Married, Single, Widowed, and Divorced Women, England and Wales, 1926–1930 111

7.3 Deaths Due to Abortion in Married and Single Women, England and Wales, 1934 111

7.4   Maternal Mortality (Married Women only), according to Social Class of
      Husband, England and Wales, 1930–1932   111
7.5   Deaths from Abortion and Sepsis, England and Wales, 1934, Scotland,
      1931–1935, and Ireland (Eire), 1931–1935   112
7.6   Percentages of Pregnancies that Ended in Live Births, Stillbirths, or
      Spontaneous and Illegal abortions in various American Cities in the
      1920s and 1930s   122
8.1   The Change from Craniotomy to Caesarean Section for the Treatment
      of Severe Cases of Contracted Pelvis, Queen Charlotte's Hospital,
      London, 1890–1909   136
8.2   Estimates of the Incidence and Maternal Mortality associated with
      Contracted Pelvis in Various Countries, 1787–1899   139
8.3   Craniotomy Rates in the Practices of General Practitioners in
      Nineteenth-Century Britain   141
8.4   Duration of Pregnancy in Relation to Cause of Maternal Death,
      Aberdeen, 1918–1927   146
8.5   Puerperal Mortality in Relation to Stillbirths, Aberdeen, 1918–1927   147
9.1   Maternal Mortality Rates in Certain Countries, 1920   153
9.2   Maternal Mortality in the USA, England and Wales, and the
      Netherlands, 1920, 1940, and 1960   154
10.1 Deaths from All Causes, from Phthisis, and from Puerperal Causes,
      England and Wales, 1890–1930   163
12.1 Maternal Mortality in General Practice in the Nineteenth Century   187
12.2 Maternal Mortality in British Lying-in Hospitals before 1880   198
12.3 Maternal Mortality in English Out-Patient Lying-in Charities before
      1880   199
12.4 Stillbirths and Maternal Deaths Recorded by the Eastern District of the
      Royal Maternity Charity, London, 1831–1843   200
12.5 Maternal Mortality at Various London Maternity Institutions following
      the Introduction of Antisepsis in the Early 1880s   201
13.1 The Changing Proportion of Deliveries by Doctors and Midwives in
      Derbyshire between 1910 and 1913   209
13.2 Domiciliary Midwifery Cases Attended by Miss Nora Haines, Queen's
      Nurse and Registered midwife, in 1936 and 1937   215
13.3 Number and Maternal Mortality Rate of Deliveries by Queen's Institute
      Midwives 1905–1931 Compared with Rates for England and Wales   216
13.4 Number, Type, and Size of Hospitals and Related Institutions for the
      Physically Ill in England and Wales, 1891–1931   225
13.5 Maternal Mortality Rates by Cause in Four Lying-in Hospitals,
      1909–1914   226
13.6 The Distribution of Births between Home and Institutions, and
      between Midwives and Doctors in Manchester, 1930–1933   228
13.7 Total Deliveries, Institutional Deliveries, and Home Deliveries by Type
      of Birth Attendant, England and Wales, 1938   231
14.1 Maternal Mortality Due to Puerperal Sepsis from 1870 to 1905, Before
      and After the Introduction of Antisepsis in the 1880s   239

14.2 Maternal Mortality by Gravidity for All Causes and for Various
Categories of Death, Scotland 1929–1933 242

14.3 Maternal Mortality according to Social Class, England and Wales,
1930–1932 245

14.4 Deaths from Puerperal Sepsis and Abortion, England, Wales, and
Scotland, 1930 247

14.5 Maternal Deaths by Cause in Scotland, 1911–1945 248

15.1 Decline in Maternal Mortality by cause, England and Wales, 1935–
1950 256

15.2 Decline in Maternal Mortality by cause, Scotland and Eire, 1935–1950 256

15.3 Live Births in Institutions as a Percentage of Total Live Births, England
and Wales, 1927, 1932, 1937, and 1946 265

15.4 Circumstances of Confinement in Three Selected Occupational
Groups and for All Mothers, England and Wales, 1946 265

15.5 Maternal Deaths from Abortion and Illegitimate Maternities, England
and Wales, 1938–1948 268

16.1 Characteristics of County Groups in the States of the USA Based on
the 1940 Census 276

17.1 Hospital and Home Deliveries in Selected American States, Showing
the Percentage of Hospital and Home Deliveries by Physicians, and
Home Deliveries by Midwives, 1945–1946 284

17.2 A Series of Deliveries in the Private Practice of an American General
Practitioner between 1811 and 1838 288

17.3 Place of Delivery and Birth Attendant at Delivery according to
Economic Status, Cleveland, Ohio, 1931 292

17.4 Maternal Mortality Rates according to Type of Birth-Attendant,
Cleveland, Ohio, 1931 292

17.5 Maternal Mortality Rate (Deaths per 10,000 Births) in Rural and
Urban Areas of Kentucky, 1936–1939 294

17.6 Death Rates from Puerperal Causes per 100,000 Population in Cities
and Rural Districts of the USA and of Certain Selected States, 1926 294

17.7 Maternal Mortality Rates (Deaths per 10,000 Births) in County Groups
of the USA, 1941–1945 and 1944–1948 295

18.1 Authorized and Unlicensed Midwives in Certain States in the USA in
1923 302

18.2 Certain Characteristics of the Midwives of New York and Chicago at
the Beginning of the Twentieth Century 304

18.3 The Birth-Attendants in a Series of Deliveries in Rural Mississippi in
1920 312

18.4 Care by Different Types of Birth-Attendant and the Outcome of
Deliveries, Alabama, 1935 312

18.5 Maternal Deaths by Cause and by Race, South Carolina, 1934–1935 313

18.6 The Proportion of Births Attended by Midwives in Various Countries
and Various States in the USA 314

18.7 Maternal Deaths by Cause, Kentucky, 1932–1936 314

18.8 Maternal Mortality Rates in the USA, 1968–1975 315

18.9 Maternal Mortality Rate of Deliveries Undertaken by the Kentucky Frontier Nursing Service — 320

18.10 Maternal Mortality by Birth-attendant in Various States in the USA, 1914–1928 — 324

19.1 The Maternal Mortality Rates of Lying-in Hospitals in Different Countries and of American Lying-in Hospitals in the 1880s — 328

19.2 Maternal Mortality Rate in New York's Lying-in Hospitals between 1856 and 1876 and the Estimated Rate for Home Deliveries in New York in 1870 — 329

19.3 Boston Lying-In Hospital: The Outcome of In-Patient and Out-Patient Deliveries, 1873–1944 — 331

19.4 The Outcome of Out-Patient Obstetric Services in the USA at Various Periods — 337

21.1 Analysis of 91,000 Deliveries in Iowa for the Years 1930–1932 — 359

21.2 Type of Operation Employed in 10,818 Operative Deliveries in Iowa for the Years 1930–1932 — 361

21.3 Allocation of Maternal Deaths by Place of Delivery, Pontiac, Michigan, 1935–1939 — 362

22.1 Maternal Mortality by Cause of Death in the USA in Five-Year Periods from 1900 to 1920 — 370

22.2 Maternal Mortality Rates according to Colour in States with Few Births and with Many Births to Black Women, 1938–1940 — 374

22.3 Maternal and Infant Mortality Rates in the USA, 1930–1938 — 375

22.4 Maternal Mortality Rate, Percentage Delivered in Hospital, and Percentage Delivered by Physicians in the USA, 1937 — 376

22.5 Maternal Mortality Rates in Fifteen States in the USA in 1934 due to Various Types of Abortion — 386

22.6 Maternal Mortality in Virginia in 1932, 1940, and 1952 by Cause and according to Colour — 387

22.7 Maternal Mortality in the Philadelpha Lying-in Hospital, 1929–37, 1938–45, and 1946–53 — 391

24.1 Population, Total Number of Midwives, and midwives per Million Population in the Netherlands, Denmark, Norway and Sweden, 1929–1930 — 420

24.2 The Number of Midwives and Doctors, and the Proportion of each to Total Population, Norway, 1860–1960 — 420

25.1 Maternal Mortality in Certain European Lying-in Hospitals in the Nineteenth Century — 431

25.2 Home Deliveries and Maternal Mortality in Various European Towns — 432

25.3 Deliveries, Maternal Deaths, and Maternal Mortality per 10,000 Deliveries in Hospital, Home, and Total Deliveries, Paris, 1862 — 432

25.4 Deliveries and Maternal Deaths in the Town and the Maternity Hospital, Amsterdam, 1865–1900 — 440

25.5 Various Towns in the Netherlands: Deliveries and Maternal Deaths from all Causes — 441

25.6   Total Deliveries, Maternal Deaths, and Maternal Mortality in Two
       Groups of Towns, the Netherlands, 1865–1895   441

25.7   Total Maternal Deaths and Deaths from Abortion in the Four Largest
       Towns in the Netherlands, 1865–1900   442

25.8   Maternal mortality in two groups of deliveries, the Netherlands, 1900.
       Group A, deliveries in maternity hospitals and schools of midwifery.
       Group B, home deliveries in the four major towns, 13 secondary towns,
       and 46 small towns.   444

26.1   Maternal Mortality Rates in Scandinavia and in Native White and
       Scandinavian-Born Immigrants in the USA in 1921   448

26.2   Maternal Mortality in Various Countries and Cities in 1875–1879 and
       1900–1904   449

26.3   Deaths Due to Puerperal Fever as a Percentage of Total Maternal
       Mortality in Various Countries, 1920–1924   450

26.4   Maternal Mortality Rates after the Exclusion of Deaths from Abortion
       in Various Countries during the Inter-war Period   453

27.1   Cause of Death of Females Aged 15–49 in Australia in 1923   465

27.2   Maternal Mortality Rates, Deliveries, and Population Density in
       Australia in 1923   467

27.3   Distribution of Maternal Deaths by Cause, Total Births, and Maternal
       Mortality Rate from All Causes, Commonwealth of Australia,
       1920–1923 and New South Wales, 1928–1933   468

27.4   Maternal Mortality Rates from Post-partum Puerperal Sepsis and
       Septic Abortion, Australia, New Zealand, and England and Wales,
       1931–1950   474

28.1   Neonatal and Stillbirth Rates according to whether the Mother
       Survived or Died, New York State (exclusive of New York City),
       1936–1938   484

28.2   Causes of Neonatal and Post-Neonatal Deaths, USA, 1939   487

28.3   England and Wales, 1928–1958. The Decline in Infant and Neonatal
       Mortality   488

28.4   Maternal, Infant, Post-Neonatal, and Neonatal Mortality in the USA in
       1915 and 1929.   492

28.5   Infant and Neonatal Mortality according to Social Class, England and
       Wales, 1911–1932   493

28.6   Infant Mortality by Certain Causes in Social Classes I and V, England
       and Wales, 1921–1932   494

28.7   Maternal Mortality, 1921–1924, and Infant and Neonatal Mortality,
       1924, in Certain Countries   497

28.8   Maternal Mortality Rate per 10,000 Deliveries by Order of Birth
       (Parity) for Mothers of All Ages, New York State (exclusive of New
       York City), 1936–1938   500

28.9   Maternal Mortality Rate per 10,000 Deliveries by Maternal Age for
       Mothers of All Parities, New York State (exclusive of New York City),
       1936–1938   500

28.10 Neonatal Mortality Rates per 1,000 Live Births by Parity and by Age of

Mother, New York State (exclusive of New York City), 1936–1938   501

28.11 The Associations between Age and Maternal Mortality and between Parity and Maternal Mortality, showing that Maternal Age and Parity are Independent Factors in the Determination of the Level of Maternal Mortality, New York State (exclusive of New York City), 1936–1938   502

28.12 Causes of Maternal Mortality and their Relationship to Neonatal Mortality, England and Wales, 1934   514

APPENDIX TABLES

1. England and Wales. Annual Rates of Maternal Mortality, 1847–1945, 1946–1981. Maternal Deaths per 10,000 Births   542

2. The Number of Births, the Number of Maternal Deaths, and the Maternal Mortality Rates for England and Wales for the Years 1872–1878 inclusive, in order to Demonstrate the Extent of the Registration, Effect of the Births and Deaths Registration Act of 1874   546

3. Scotland. Annual Rates of Maternal Mortality, 1856–1950. Maternal Deaths per 10,000 Births   546

4. Ireland/Eire. Annual Rates of Maternal Mortality, 1870–1950. Maternal Deaths per 10,000 Births   549

5. USA. Maternal Mortality in the USA from 1900 to 1920, Based on Data from those States which Comprised the Death Registration Area in 1900   551

6. USA. 1915–1953. Annual Rates of Maternal Mortality by Race, Showing Rates for Total Population, White Population, and Non-White Population   551

7. Sweden. 1756–1950. Maternal Mortality from All Causes. Maternal Deaths per 10,000 Births   553

8. Denmark. Maternal Mortality, 1890–1940. Maternal Deaths per 1,000 Births   555

9. The Netherlands, 1900–1950. Maternal Mortality Expressed as Maternal Deaths per 10,000 Births   555

10. Belgium. 1851–1950. Maternal Mortality from All Causes. Maternal Deaths per 10,000 Births to Nearest Whole Number   557

11. Iceland. 1911–1960. Maternal Mortality Rate per 10,000 Births and Number of Maternal Deaths   559

12. Maternal Mortality in the Commonwealth of Australia and Certain States from 1871 to 1950. Maternal Mortality Rate Expressed as Maternal Deaths per 10,000 Births   560

13. Maternal Mortality in the Commonwealth of Australia, 1931–1950   561

14. New Zealand, 1872–1950. Maternal Mortality Rates. Maternal Deaths per 10,000 Births to Nearest Whole Number   561

15. Amsterdam. 1875–1949. Maternal Mortality Rate for Puerperal Fever and all Puerperal Causes. Maternal Deaths per 10,000 Births   564

16. Paris. 1880–1950. Maternal Mortality Rates. Maternal Deaths per 10,000 Births   566

17. Maternal Mortality in Rural Bangladesh. 1982–1983. Maternal Mortality Rate per 10,000 Live Births   567

18. The Administrative Counties of England and Wales Ranked in Order of their Maternal Mortality Rates per 10,000 Births during the Decennium 1924–1933   568
19. England and Wales. 1921. Causes of Death amongst Women Aged 15–44. Number of Deaths   570
20. England and Wales. 1872–1876. Maternal Deaths by Cause   570
21. England and Wales. 1872–1876, 1930, and 1979–1981. Total Number of Maternal Deaths, Maternal Mortality Rate, and the Percentage of Deaths Due to Certain Causes   571
22. Maternal Mortality at the Dublin Lying-in Hospital under Successive Masterships from 1745 to 1940   572
23. The Dates at which the Various States of the USA were Admitted to the USA Death Registration Area, Arranged in Three Groups   573
24. Land Areas and Population Densities in 1900 and 1980 of Certain Countries and Selected States of the USA   574
25. Maternal Mortality in the USA by State. 1940 and 1960   575
26. USA. 1955. Maternal Mortality, Perinatal Mortality, and Infant Mortality by State   577
27. Distribution of Post-Partum Maternal Deaths by Cause of Death and by Interval between Birth of Child and Death of Mother. New York State (exclusive of New York City), 1936–1938   580
28. Dates from which Vital Statistics First Became Available in Certain Countries   580
29. Maternal Mortality Rate per 10,000 Births, and the Percentage of Deaths Due to Puerperal Sepsis and to other Causes in Certain Countries, 1920–1924   581
30. Rates of Version, Forceps Deliveries, and Craniotomy in Certain European Hospitals. Mid-Nineteenth Century   582
31. Deaths per Million Persons Living: Scarlet Fever, Erysipelas, Puerperal Fever, and Mortality Rate from Puerperal Fever per 1,000 Live Births, 1860–1879. England and Wales   583
32. Some of the Sulphonamides which became Available between 1936 and 1940   584

Introduction

Mrs K, who was born in 1849, was a woman of exceptional talent. In 1873, she won three scholarships to Newnham Hall, Cambridge, where she took a first class with distinctions in the Higher Local Examinations in arithmetic, English, history, English literature, French, Italian, chemistry, geology, botany, and zoology. Women were excluded from taking degrees at Cambridge University, but in 1876, 'while residing at Newnham Hall, she was informally examined in the papers of the Natural Science Tripos, by the kindness of the University examiners, and was declared by them to have attained the standard of a first class'.[1]

On leaving Cambridge she married a German doctor and was appointed in November 1877 to the principalship of a new teacher-training college at a rising salary of £300 a year. She was due to take up this post in Easter 1878 some three months after her first baby was due to be born. She was 29 years old. Arrangements were made for her to be delivered at her home in London by Dr X, the family doctor, who was a licentiate of the Royal College of Surgeons of Edinburgh. A nurse had also been engaged for the occasion.

Mrs K went into labour on Saturday, 12 January 1878. Dr X was called and arrived about 10 p.m. He expected delivery to occur about midnight and said he would be ready at a moment's notice. Leaving the nurse to 'watch the case' he went back to his house, and returned to his patient in time to deliver the baby which was born just after 2 a.m. It was a normal delivery. The husband, standing outside the door, heard the baby cry and his wife say in a firm and cheerful voice: 'O nurse what is it? A girl? O I am so glad. Do give me the darling. Let me kiss it.' He heard her kiss the child and show it to her sister-in-law, saying in German, 'J——, nurse wants you to take the child; isn't it a fine baby?'

An hour and twenty minutes later Dr K heard his wife say to the nurse, 'Wasn't I brave? You will tell my husband, nurse, how brave I was.' But soon afterwards he heard her say, 'O, I am so hot nurse, fan me a little.' Then she complained of pain and asked, 'Am I flooding, doctor? If so you can have ice.' But the doctor said, 'Not at all, only keep quiet, it will soon be over.' Some time later the husband suddenly heard the doctor say (apparently in reference to convulsive twitchings of his wife's face), 'Good gracious, nurse, what is this?' More time elapsed before the doctor rushed out in a very excited state asking

---

[1] Obituary notice of the death of Amy Ogle Kopple, daughter of John Ogle of Bradbourne, St Clare, Sevenoaks, Kent and wife of Dr Kopple, by the Principal of Newnham Hall, published in *Journal of Women's Education Union*, 6/62 (1878), 30–1.

the husband to find some eau-de-Cologne, adding, 'I am afraid your wife is seriously ill; she has suddenly taken a very bad turn.'

It was now 4.30 a.m. The husband was told to run quickly and fetch the doctor's assistant (Mr F). They both arrived back at the house at 5 a.m. 'As we reached the top of the staircase', said the husband, 'and I was about forcing my way to her, I was kept back by Dr X with the remark "only wait one moment".' The doctor entered an adjoining room with the assistant, stayed a few seconds, returned to the bedroom, and then rushed out calling, 'She is dead, she is dead.' In his agony of grief. Dr K entered the bedroom, bent over his wife's body and called her name. He noticed a convulsive movement of her left hand, but Mr F, the assistant, who tried to revive the patient by moistening her mouth with brandy, listened for a heart beat and pronounced her life extinct. The husband heard Mr F say to Dr X, 'Haven't you taken it away? Take it away then and don't let the woman die with it in her.' Dr X then put his hands under the bedclothes and brought out the placenta, throwing it into some vessel and asking the nurse to remove it at once. The nurse reported 'unusual losses and clots of blood'. Soon afterwards Dr X and Mr F left the house, but returned half an hour later, took the nurse into the bedroom, and bandaged the body.

This is not a dramatized account from a Victorian novel. It is a case-history, published in *The Registrar General's Annual Report for the Year 1876* (published in 1878). William Farr, Compiler of Abstracts at the General Register Office, included it in one of his famous series of articles which appeared as appendices to the *Annual Reports* under the title 'Letter[s] to the Registrar General'.[2]

Farr believed that as many as 2,000 out of the over 4,000 maternal deaths a year were avoidable, especially deaths due to haemorrhage of which the death of Mrs K was a dreadful and tragic example. Dr X denied incompetence and protested that the patient 'was a friend of my wife and myself'. He had 'attended promptly and the fine child was born after a short, natural labour. In such another instance he would certainly adopt the same kind of treatment.' Nevertheless, it was eleven days before Dr X could be persuaded to provide a death certificate and when he did he entered the cause of death as '1. Childbirth 2. Extreme exhaustion 3. Anaemia of the heart'. Farr's attention was drawn to the case by the delay in certification and the blatant attempt to cover up the true cause of death. 'Such fearful cases', he wrote, 'should be judged by the Medical Council.'

Maternal mortality is, and always was, terrible in ways that other mortalities are not. Childbirth is a physiological process in which, as an American obstetrician said in the 1850s, death is a 'sort of desecration'.[3] Few women

---

[2] *The Registrar General's Annual Report for 1876* (1878), 248–50.

[3] Charles D. Meigs, *Females and their Diseases: A Series of Letters to his Class* (Philadelphia, Pa., 1848), 576.

died in pregnancy, fewer still in labour. Most lived long enough to see and hold their newborn before dying, often with brutal abruptness, leaving their newborn (and frequently other small children) without a mother, and their husbands without their wives.

I have begun with the story of Mrs K as a reminder that behind the analysis of numbers, trends, causes, and factors lie such tragedies. It would be easy to compile a list of similar case-histories. To do that and nothing else, however, would be an empty exercise, for the story of Mrs K provokes a whole series of questions. Why did she die? Can we accept it as sheer, unavoidable, bad luck, due to the primitive state of obstetric knowledge at the time, and the absence of modern obstetric techniques? Or was it, as William Farr believed, a gross example of medical incompetence? And if it was incompetence what was the reason? Was Dr K simply stupid and careless, or was he the product of an educational system which must bear the blame? If obstetric education was inadequate, was that due to lack of available knowledge, or was it a reflection of a neglect of that part of the curriculum in medical schools? And if the subject was neglected in medical schools (as indeed it was) what does this tell us about the values of medical education and the attitudes of medical men to childbirth and women?

That is one path down which we are led by the death of Mrs K. Another might begin with the fact that Mrs K was an educated middle-class woman, almost certainly able to afford the best medical care available in London. We saw that she had her baby at home, not in hospital, and she was attended by the family doctor and a nurse, not by an obstetrician. Was this usual? And what was the role of the nurse? Clearly she knew something about childbirth because she was left in charge through most of the first stage of labour. Was she a midwife acting as a nurse in middle-class households who also worked as an independent midwife in working-class households? Would she have been a safer birth-attendant than Dr K if she had managed the labour on her own? Were midwife deliveries on the whole safer than deliveries by doctors? Would it have been safer if Mrs K had been delivered in a maternity hospital? Mrs K belonged to what is now classified as social class I. Should we be more surprised that she died than we would have been if she had been a labourer's wife belonging to social class V? What, in other words, was the relative risk of dying in childbirth in different social classes?

It is obvious that these questions are concerned with the concept of 'risk', the risk of dying in childbirth, and the interplay of a wide range of factors including the type of birth-attendant, the quality of the birth-attendant's training and experience, the place of delivery, and the social class of the mother. Yet another series of questions surrounds the date of delivery. As it happens the risk of dying in childbirth in the mid-1870s was unusually high. How much did the risk alter over long periods of time? Was it higher in the eighteenth century than the nineteenth, and in the seventeenth than the eighteenth? When we learn that as recently as the decade 1920–9, some 25,000 women in Britain, and at least a quarter of a million in the USA, died of causes arising from childbirth we cannot fail to enquire how the 1920s compared not only with the past but with the future. When (and how) was the risk of dying in childbirth reduced to its present low level?

Yet another series of questions arises from international comparisons. Would Mrs K have been more safely delivered in another country? If the risk of dying was less in other countries than in Britain, was this a reflection of cultural or racial differences, or was it due to differences in the standards of maternal care provided by the birth-attendants? If Mrs K had been delivered abroad, would she have been delivered by a midwife or a doctor? And if a doctor, would it have been one who specialized in obstetrics or the equivalent of the British general practitioner? And, whether it was a doctor or midwife, would their training have been substantially different from the British?

To answer these questions we need statistical data on populations rather than individual case-histories. How reliable were the statistics? For example, the history of Mrs K revealed an attempt at false certification. This is enough to raise the suspicion that some maternal deaths were concealed and certified as being due to a non-maternal cause. Indeed, this happened and one thing is certain: the published figures of maternal deaths were never exaggerated— they underestimated the true level. This has led some historians to throw their hands up in despair, and declare the statistics hopelessly unreliable. But can we estimate the extent of what I will be calling 'hidden' maternal deaths? Within limits I believe we can. But were maternal deaths hidden to the same extent in different periods and different countries?

It is the identification and analysis of such themes that makes maternal mortality a difficult but extremely fascinating subject containing many puzzling features which cry out for explanations. Why did the graph of mortality climb here, and turn down there? Why was maternal mortality higher in Wales than Wiltshire, in New Zealand than the Netherlands, in Mississippi than Minnesota? In the late nineteenth century it was said of England and Wales that if you drew a line from the Severn estuary to the Wash almost every county above that line suffered an above-average rate of maternal mortality while counties below that line boasted a below-averge mortality. With only minor amendments that differential remained intact at least until the Second World War. The north–south divide in terms of maternal mortality was reversed in the USA where the map of maternal mortality by levels prevailing in the states—deep black for high mortality in the deep south, white in New England and the north-west—remained remarkably constant and still persisted in the 1970s although the absolute rates of maternal mortality had fallen dramatically. Why do such demographic differentials turn out to have been so constant, as if they were deeply ingrained in populations?

These are some of the questions which this study attempts to answer.

To confine ourselves to a statistical analysis of secular trends and regional differences would result in what someone called in a happy phrase 'demography in a thermos flask'. But there is little danger of that. The analysis of maternal mortality can only be achieved by a broad approach. This book is as much if not more a study of various systems of maternal care in different times and different countries than a study of maternal mortality rates. It has to be. Some answers may be found in clinical or pathological factors; others in social or economic changes or in factors which reflect the politics of maternal care or the quality of medical education. The attitudes of doctors to women (reflecting the prevailing ethos), and strongly held views on the deleterious effects of civilization on childbirth, profoundly affected the management of childbirth.

As well as the influence of ideas on childbirth, in some regions it is glaringly obvious that whatever plans were laid to improve the standard of maternal care, they might be defeated by the geographical features of remote and mountainous areas (North Wales, Montana, Northern Scandinavia). Conversely, some countries were able to provide maternal care of high quality partly because they were small, well-organized, and possessed excellent communications (Denmark, the Netherlands).

Although some notable histories of maternal care have been confined to a social-historical or feminist approach with scarcely a statistic, let alone a statistical evaluation, in sight, I believe that without rigorous statistical analysis, the history of maternal care can easily become impressionistic, unreliable, and in the end unsatisfying. If there is the danger that a purely demographic approach may deflect attention from features of central importance which are inherently unmeasurable—attitudes or sentiments for example—there is also the danger that without statistical analysis large conclusions are often based on the shaky foundation of thin evidence and small unrepresentative samples. We cannot escape the fact that if we intend to compare childbirth in different countries at different periods, we require some way in which we can measure the quality (or effectiveness) of maternal care. As the report of a White House conference on child health protection in 1933 pointed out:

With accurate morbidity statistics still unavailable, mortality rates must be the chief criteria by which obstetric practice is judged. Any general improvement in maternity care should be reflected quickly in a reduction of the death rate among mothers, as well as in a lowered incidence of stillbirths and of neonatal deaths. Conversely, stationary rates may be taken to indicate no improvement, and rising rates a falling off in the quality of obstetric practice. Irrespective of our feeling about statistics in general, reliable figures offer the only hope of fair comparison, and deaths are more easily computed than illness.[4]

---

[4] White House Conference on Child Health Protection, *Fetal, Newborn and Maternal Morbidity and Mortality* (New York, 1933), 215.

What I want to emphasize in this introduction is that the history of maternal care and maternal mortality cannot be divided into neat compartments categorized as social, political, economic, demographic, professional, the clinical. Questions bounce back and forth between all these categories. Monocausal explanations are rare. That is why what started as a small study has grown into a large one. Yet, at a time when the history of medicine is growing so fast that it is in danger of splintering into sub-specialities, to spread one's net so wide is to run the risk of being over-ambitious. In the attempt to combine all these approaches in several countries there is bound to be imbalance, and some will feel there is too much emphasis here, too little there. That is inevitable.

As a preliminary step it may be helpful to outline the plan I have followed in writing this book. The text is divided into three parts followed by the appendices and the select bibliography. Part I consists of two chapters on the statistics of maternal mortality. Chapter 1 is a brief and simple description of how maternal mortality is measured. For any reader not already familiar with the subject it is essential for understanding all that follows. Chapter 2 is longer and more complex, being concerned with the statistical problems peculiar to the study of maternal mortality. For readers with a profound antipathy to statistics it is not essential.

Part II starts with a discussion of the meaning of causes and determinants. It then proceeds to deal systematically with the direct clinical causes of maternal deaths: puerperal fever, haemorrhage, toxaemia, and so on. In these chapters I have attempted to trace changing ideas on the aetiology, pathology, and treatment of each condition, and describe their contribution to maternal mortality as a whole.

Part III deals with maternal care and mortality in various countries. It begins with two brief background chapters. Chapter 10 is a discussion of what is known about maternal mortality in England and Wales before 1800, and of women's perceptions of maternal mortality. Chapter 11 is a very compressed account of maternal care in eighteenth-century Britain. The rest of Part III deals systematically with the history of maternal care and maternal mortality in various countries. The order is Britain, the United States, Europe, Australia, and New Zealand. The final chapter (Chapter 28) is in the nature of an addendum. It consists of a discussion of the relationship between maternal and infant mortality, and is a shortened version of a paper published in *Social History of Medicine* in April 1991, with some additional material.[5]

The subjects relegated to the appendices either explore certain points of detail which would have interrupted the flow if embedded in the main text, or they deal with subjects which recur in several chapters and are placed where

---

[5] Reproduced here by the kind permission of the editors of *Social History of Medicine*.

they are to avoid repetition. An example of the latter is Appendix 5 which consists of a discussion of the question of streptococcal virulence which played a very large part in determining patterns of maternal mortality.

Some readers may be more interested in one section of the book than others. Some will turn to the chapters on causes, or the chapters devoted to Britain, or the USA, while others may wish to go straight to the chapters on Europe or Australia and New Zealand. I have therefore tried as far as possible, while avoiding the sin of repetition, to write most of the chapters as separate self-standing essays which can be read in any order after reading this introduction and Chapter 1.

I was tempted to end with a summary statement of conclusions, set out neatly and tidily in sequence. But I rebelled against the idea. There are too many provisos and exceptions to any rules I could formulate, and there are too many questions left hanging in the air. It would have been false to end on a note which pretended anything approaching omniscience, for the more I worked at this study the more I became aware of the huge gaps in our understanding (or mine anyway) of maternal care and maternal mortality in the past. That, I think, is as it should be. 'To communicate what I have tried, and leave the rest to others for farther enquiry, is all my design in publishing these papers.'[6]

[6] Sir Isaac Newton's first advertisement to his *Optics* quoted on the title-page of John Armstrong, *Facts and Observations Relating to the Fever Commonly called Puerperal* (London, 1814).

PART I
The Measurement of Maternal Mortality

1

The Measurement of Maternal Mortality

Before we can come to any conclusions about rates of maternal mortality it is essential to understand the way in which those rates are defined. The process of definition, however, is not quite as simple as may appear at first sight. Measuring rates of maternal mortality is of course measuring the *risk* of a woman dying in pregnancy, labour, or the postnatal period (the puerperium). The measurement of risk is a process of enormous importance in every branch of medicine. Obvious examples are the risk of taking a particular drug, the risk of an anaesthetic, the risk of an operation. Since the eighteenth century maternal risk, measured in terms of maternal mortality, has been used by obstetricians to assess the wisdom of using new techniques, to choose between two alternative techniques, or to compare maternal care in various institutions, towns, regions, or countries.

The problems associated with such measurement are discussed in Chapter 2 but it will be useful if we begin by considering the fundamental question of how you define a maternal death. At first sight it may seem that maternal deaths are the most clearly defined of all deaths. To a large extent this is true. Historical studies of mortality and the calculation of secular trends (changes in death rates over a period of time) are often beset with the difficulties of changing diagnostic categories and the use of vague and uncertain terms. This is a major problem in the study of infant mortality in the eighteenth and nineteenth centuries when deaths were often attributed to 'convulsions', 'debility', 'atrophy', 'marasmus', or 'teething'. For the most part one can only guess what diseases such terms represented, and it can never be assumed such categories were used consistently.

In obstetrics, however, there is much less diagnostic uncertainty. The terms used to describe the complications of childbirth in the late eighteenth century were with few exceptions those which are used today. Continuity of diagnostic terminology and a wealth of clinical descriptions from the past frees the historian of obstetrics from most of the problems of retrospective diagnosis which are encountered with medical diseases. So far, so good; but maternal deaths were not defined in a uniform manner.

Let us take two countries, A and B. Suppose that country A had a consistently lower rate of maternal mortality than country B over a period of several decades. Country A, however, chose to define maternal deaths as those which occurred solely as a result of the complications arising *directly* from pregnancy and childbirth. Country B on the other hand defined maternal deaths as all deaths occurring during pregnancy, labour, or the postnatal period from any cause whatsoever, including deaths from influenza, pneumonia, heart disease, and so on. Was the higher rate in country B partly or solely due to differences in methodology? This very important problem is considered in Chapter 2. For the time being, however, we will assume that the normal methodology is that of country A: namely, that maternal deaths are those which occurred in pregnancy, labour, or the post-natal period and were due to obstetric causes only.

MEASURING MATERNAL MORTALITY AS TOTAL MATERNAL DEATHS

The simplest way to measure changes in the death rate from any cause is simply to count the total number of deaths from that cause that occurred over a chosen period—every year, five years, or ten years, for example. Fig. 1.1

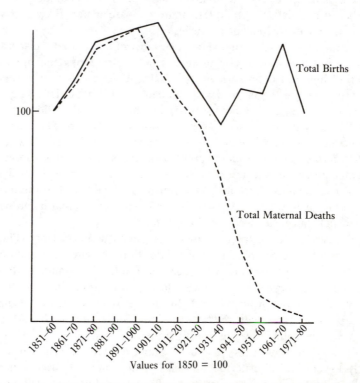

Fig. 1.1 England and Wales, 1851–60 to 1971–80. Total Births and Total Maternal Deaths
Source: Registrar General for England and Wales, *Decennial Supplements*.

shows the total number of maternal deaths in England and Wales in each successive decade from the 1850s to the 1970s, and also the total number of births. (See also Table 1.1.) For convenience, the totals for the 1850s are indexed to 100, and the totals in each of the subsequent decades are calculated by the simple formula:

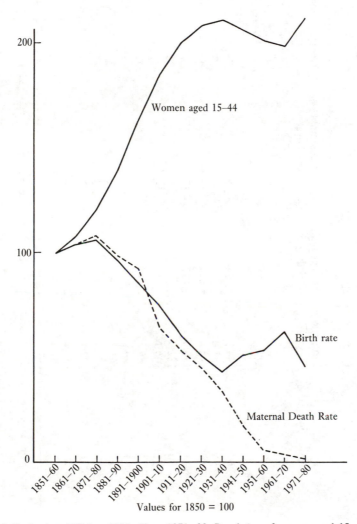

FIG. 1.2 England and Wales, 1851–60 to 1971–80. Population of women aged 15–44, Birth Rate, and Maternal Death Rate
Source: Registrar General for England and Wales, *Decennial Supplements*.

TABLE 1.1 *Female Population, Birth Rate, and Maternal Mortality Rate in England and Wales, 1851–1980*

Decennium	I Female Population aged 15–44 (millions)	II Birth rate[a]	III Average number of births per day[b]	IV Average number of maternal deaths per day[c]	V Average annual maternal deaths per million (women aged 15–44)	VI Maternal mortality rate per 10,000 births
1851–60	4.60	144.8	1,775	8.5	675	47.0
1861–70	4.98	151.0	2,054	9.7	707	47.0
1871–80	5.61	153.6	2,352	11.1	723	47.5
1881–90	6.44	138.9	2,437	11.5	662	47.3
1890–1900	7.50	122.9	2,507	12.0	621	50.9
1901–10	8.55	109.1	2,547	10.2	435	40.0
1911–20	9.22	86.5	2,217	9.0	357	40.7
1921–30	9.64	74.0	1,952	8.0	301	40.7
1931–40	9.73	61.3	1,661	5.9	223	35.8
1941–50	9.56	73.9	1,986	3.0	114	16.8
1951–60	9.27	77.1	1,938	1.1	43	5.6
1961–70	9.18	89.2	2,363	0.59	24	2.5
1971–80	9.77	67.3	1,772	0.23	8	1.2

[a] Average annual birth-rate for the decade expressed as births per 1,000 women aged 15–44.
[b] Average daily births for the decade.
[c] Average daily maternal deaths for the decade.

Sources: Decennial supplements, Registrar General's Reports, and A. Macfarlane and M. Mugford, *Birth Counts* (London, 1984).

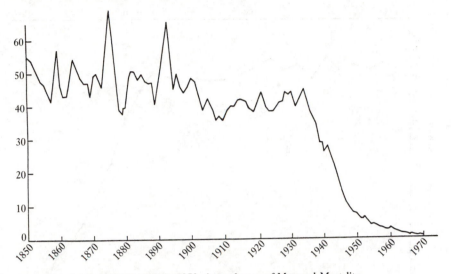

FIG. 1.3 England and Wales, 1850–1970. Annual rates of Maternal Mortality
Source: Registrar General for England and Wales, *Decennial Supplements*.

$$100 \times \frac{\text{total maternal deaths (or births) in each decade}}{\text{total number of maternal deaths (or births) in the 1850s}}.$$

The same method is used in Fig. 1.2 which shows the population of women of childbearing age, total births, and birth rates for each decade with the values for the 1850s expressed as 100.

Fig. 1.1 shows that the total number of maternal deaths in England and Wales rose from the 1850s to the 1890s and then began to fall. The decline in total deaths appears to fall into three phases: first from the 1890s to the 1930s, then more steeply until the 1950s, and finally less steeply from the 1950s to the 1970s.

In round figures, about 31,000 women died in childbirth in the 1850s, 46,000 in the 1890s, and 800 in the 1970s. If these are translated into the average number of maternal deaths per day (which makes them easier to grasp), between 8 and 9 women died daily on average in the 1850s. The daily total rose to a peak of about 12 a day in the 1890s before descending to about 1 a day in the 1950s, and then to the present (1980s) level of about 1 a week. It is probable that the total number of maternal deaths in England and Wales (number, please note, not rate which we come to soon) was higher in the 1890s than any other decade in our history. It is also notable (see column III of Table 1.1) that the total number of births in the 1970s was almost exactly the same as it was in the 1850s. It is, however, uninformative to show deaths

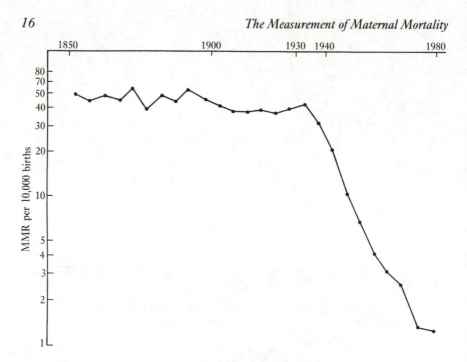

FIG. 1.4 England and Wales, 1850–1980, Maternal Mortality Rates (five-year averages) logarithmic scale
Source: Registrar General for England and Wales, *Decennial Supplements*.

and births simply as totals unless you are concerned with periods of at most a few years because changes in the population must be taken into account.

MEASURING MATERNAL MORTALITY IN TERMS OF POPULATION

The population that is used in the determination of death rates from any cause or groups of causes of death, is the 'population at risk'. Where one is considering deaths from all causes, this is the total population of both sexes and all ages which would probably be used for death rates from diseases such as tuberculosis. In the case of childhood diseases it would be usual to express death rates in terms of the population under the age of 15 rather than total population even though occasional adult deaths occur from such diseases. For the calculation of maternal mortality, the population at risk is not of course the total female population, but only those of childbearing age, usually defined as women aged 15–44, or sometimes as 15–50.

If, instead of showing total maternal deaths as in Figure 1.1, the number of maternal deaths per 1,000 women of childbearing age is shown for each decade, the result can be seen in Figure 1.2. The graph is slightly different. Deaths rose to a peak in the 1870s instead of the 1890s before they began to fall. However, the main feature of this and the previous graph is that the fall in maternal mortality appears to have started in the late nineteenth century and has been continuous ever since. To those familiar with historical trends in infant mortality this suggests there was nothing unusual in the trend of maternal mortality. In fact, there is. The clue lies in Figure 1.2. Although the maternal death rate, expressed as deaths per million women aged 15–44, is indeed falling from the 1870s, so too is the birth rate. The two keep each other company until the mid-1930s when the birth rate begins to rise and maternal deaths keep on falling.

Figure 1.2 is not the right way to show the death rate from maternal causes. The denominator is wrong. The population at risk in maternal mortality is not all women of childbearing age; it is only those women during pregnancy, labour, or the postnatal period. It is obvious that women cannot be at risk of dying from maternal causes when they are not (or have not recently been) pregnant. Moreover, if women are on average having fewer babies, other things being equal the number of maternal deaths per 1,000 women of childbearing age will decline. It is necessary, therefore, to take into account changes in fertility in the calculation of trends in maternal mortality. This brings us to the true measure of maternal mortality—the maternal mortality rate.

THE MATERNAL MORTALITY RATE

Maternal mortality is defined in terms of *the number of maternal deaths per 1,000, 10,000, or 100,000 births*. The number of births used as the denominator is arbitrary. Today, when maternal deaths in developed countries have become rare it is usual to calculate maternal mortality as maternal deaths per 100,000 births; but 10,000 births is the most convenient for historical studies. It will be used throughout this book unless otherwise indicated. The 'maternal mortality rate' can be abbreviated to MMR.

The graph of maternal mortality, using this definition of the MMR (Figures 1.3 and 1.4) provides an entirely different picture. Moreover it is the 'true' picture in the sense that it shows the changing *risk* of dying in childbirth. Figure 1.3 shows the MMR for England and Wales as annual rates from 1850 to 1970. To iron out the annual fluctuations, Figure 1.4 shows the MMR as five-year averages and the scale is logarithmic. A logarithmic scale has the advantage that changes of the same magnitude appear on the graph as changes of the same size. Figure 1.4 shows that far from falling from 1870, the MMR remained more or less on a plateau until the mid-1930s in stark contrast to the steep and sustained fall which followed. The sudden decline in maternal mortality is all the more interesting because it is close to a straight line, showing (because the scale is logarithmic) that for the last fifty and more years maternal mortality has fallen at a remarkably constant rate. Figure 1.3 shows, however, that the pre-1930s plateau was by no means level. There were conspicuous peaks in maternal mortality in 1874 and 1893, a slight but significant fall in the trend between 1880 and 1910, and a slight but significant rise between 1910 and 1934. These details (which in fact tell us a lot about maternal mortality) are considered later. But the broad picture is one of a plateau from 1850 to the mid-1930s, followed by a steep fall.

Clearly we have two major questions to answer. Why was the risk of women in England and Wales dying in childbirth substantially the same in the inter-war period as it was in the mid- to late nineteenth century? and why did it suddenly begin to fall in the mid-1930s and continue to fall at the same rate? Before we can approach these questions we must consider the degree to which the data are trustworthy. This brings us to the problems of measuring maternal mortality.

2

Problems of Measuring Maternal Mortality

Strictly speaking the denominator in the calculation of the maternal mortality rate should be pregnancies; but the number of pregnancies can never be discovered because of the unknown and unrecorded number of abortions and miscarriages, so births are used instead because the data on births are easily available. A purist might argue that the MMR is not therefore really a rate but a ratio; but the use of 'rate' is customary. For practical purposes none of this is of much importance. One author side-stepped these problems neatly by saying: 'The maternal mortality rate can be best interpreted as the *"cost" in mothers' lives of producing 1,000 live births.*'[1]

STILLBIRTHS AND MULTIPLE BIRTHS

Until the introduction of stillbirth registration in 1927 in England and Wales (1939 in Scotland and 1961 in Northern Ireland) 'births' indicated live births only. After 1927 'total births' (live births plus stillbirths) was used as the denominator. The effect of the registration of stillbirths on the MMR was not large. In England and Wales in 1933 the MMR was 45.2 per 10,000 live births and 43.2 per 10,000 total births, a difference of about 5 per cent. The difference in the USA during the inter-war period was of the same order.[2]

When it comes to international comparisons, however, different definitions of a stillbirth can cause difficulties. In some countries during the 1920s a stillbirth was defined as 'a birth of at least twenty weeks; gestation in which the child shows no evidence of life after complete birth'. In most countries, however, a stillbirth was defined as 'the birth of a foetus, after 28 weeks of pregnancy, in which pulmonary respiration does not occur'.[3] This was the definition proposed by the Health Organization of The League of Nations in

---

[1] J. Yerushalmy, 'Infant and Maternal Mortality in the Modern World', *Annals of the American Academy of Political and Social Sciences*, 237 (1945), 134–41.

[2] R. M. Woodbury, *Maternal Mortality*, Children's Bureau Publications, No. 152 (Washington, DC, 1926).

[3] League of Nations, Health Organization, *Memorandum Relating to the Causes and Prevention of Still-births and Mortality during the First Year of Life: Austria, France, Germany, Great Britain, Italy, Netherlands, Norway* (Geneva, 1930). Denmark introduced a rigid system of stillbirth registration as early as 1871, defining a stillbirth as the birth of a dead baby after 28 or more weeks of gestation. Thus the 28-week definition was current in some parts of Europe in the 19th cent. *Report of the Select Committee on Death Certification* (1893), 373. 402, Q. 3034.

1925 and recommended for international usage in 1930. In a few countries, including the USA, if there was evidence that the baby's heart was beating after it had been born, or if there were movements of voluntary muscles, it might be classed as a live birth even if the baby never breathed. In France there was a further complication. By law, all births had to be registered within three days. They were registered either as alive at the date of *registration* (présenté vivant) or dead (mort-né). It was not obligatory to specify whether those entered as 'most-né' were born alive and died in the first three days or whether they were stillborn, but the information was said to be obtainable for statistical purposes.

In the USA interstate differences were even more confusing. Some states defined stillbirths as a dead foetus after twenty-eight weeks of gestation, others after twenty weeks. New York City defined all foetal deaths, regardless of age, as stillbirths. Not surprisingly, it recorded the very high rate of 49.4 stillbirths per 1,000 total births in the 1940s compared with 16.4 in most states. By using the rather unsatisfactory argument that stillbirth and neonatal mortality rates should go hand-in-hand, it was argued that if a state which recorded a high stillbirth rate showed an equally high neonatal mortality rate, the stillbirth rate was probably genuinely high. If the neonatal mortality was low, then the high stillbirth rate was probably a definition anomaly. On this and other evidence it was shown that differences in definition provided a very large part of the interstate differences in stillbirth rates.[4]

Since it became customary in many countries during the 1920s and 1930s to use total births rather than live births in the calculation of MMRs, how much distortion occurred as a result of these differences? In 1935, Elizabeth Tandy, who worked as a statistician at the Children's Bureau in Washington, DC, USA, quantified the effect of such differences on international comparisons.[5] She concluded that even where there were differences in definition, the distorting effect would amount to no more than 0.4 per cent in the denominator. 'The question is evidently not worth consideration in connection with comparability.'

Elizabeth Tandy's work on international comparability appeared in the series of reports published by the Children's Bureau at a time when American doctors were deeply disturbed by the image of obstetrics and prone to attribute their high level of maternal mortality to statistical artefact. Her work, however, was of great importance to statisticians in other countries and to historians today. It was true, she said, that the statistics of maternal mortality could not be taken at face value; but this did not mean they had to be dismissed. It meant they needed careful interpretation and this she set out to

[4] American Public Health Association, Vital Statistics Section, 'Stillbirth and Maternal Mortality Rates', *American Journal of Public Health*, 34 (1944), 889–93.
[5] Elizabeth Tandy, *Comparability of Maternal Mortality Rates in the United States and Certain Foreign Countries*, Children's Bureau Publications, No. 229 (Washington, DC, 1935).

do: 'Many reports in recent years have called attention to the lack of comparability arising from differences in procedure, but none has so far attempted to evaluate the effect of these differences on maternal mortality rates.'[6] She showed that many statistical and methodological differences which at first sight appeared to be large turned out to be insignificant in the context of the scale of international differences in maternal mortality. Definitions of stillbirths was an example. Other problems produced more serious distortions, but the extent of distortion could generally be measured with reasonable accuracy. The essential point was the need to measure, evaluate, and take into account all potential sources of statistical distortion.

This brings us to multiple births and the question of births and deliveries. The birth of twins is one delivery but two births. However, the ratio of twin and triplet births to single births tends to be reasonably constant.[7] In every 1,000 deliveries there will be on average 12 twin births. Triplet births are so uncommon that, for statistical purposes, they can be discounted. 1,000 births is therefore equivalent, on average, to 988 deliveries. An MMR of 50 per 10,000 births would, if we corrected for multiple births, be 50 per 9,875 *deliveries*, giving a corrected MMR of 49.4, a difference of 1.2 per cent. When live births were used as the denominator, failure to take stillbirths into account produced a denominator which was too small by about 5 per cent. Failure to take into account both stillbirths and multiple births produces an error of about 3.8 per cent (5−1.2 per cent). This is small in comparison with the wide range of maternal mortality that was found in practice.

THE LENGTH OF THE POSTNATAL PERIOD

John Clarke remarked in 1806: 'Of those women who die in consequence of uterogestation, it is well known that very few are cut off during the time of pregnancy, and not many during the act of labour.'[8] Most women, in other words, die in the postnatal period, but how is that period defined? Is a death which occurred six months or a year after childbirth, and which a doctor believes can be traced back to childbirth, a maternal death? A few sources show that such deaths were occasionally included in the records of the nineteenth century. In 1870, however, William Farr in the *Annual Report of the Register General for 1870* (p. 408) appears to have settled on one month as the correct period. By the early years of this century, however, it became customary to define the postnatal period as six weeks after delivery, and this

---

[6] Ibid.

[7] A good brief account can be found under the heading 'multiple births' by R. Pressat in C. Wilson (ed.), *The Dictionary of Demography* (Oxford, 1988). Since I am dealing largely with populations of European origin I have assumed a rate of twinning of 1 in 80 deliveries and of triplets of 1 in 80^2, i.e., 1 in 6,400.

[8] J. Clarke, *Practical Essays on the Management of Pregnancy and Labour and on the Inflammatory and Febrile Diseases of Lying-in Women*, 2nd edn. (London, 1806).

TABLE 2.1 *Post-natal maternal deaths in Canada, 1927 and 1928, according to the interval between birth and maternal death*

Period between birth and maternal death	Number of deaths	Percentage	Cumulative percentage
Total for all periods	1,570	100.0	—
under 1 day	480	30.6	30.6
1–6 days	462	29.4	60.0
7–13 days	310	19.7	79.7
14–20 days	132	8.4	88.1
21–7 days	94	6.0	94.1
1–3 months	82	5.2	99.3
3–6 months	7	0.4	99.7
over 6 months	3	0.3	100.0

Source: E. S. MacPhail, 'A Statistical Study in Maternal Mortality', *American Journal of Public Health*, 22 (1932), 612–26.

has remained the standard definition. Evidence from a number of sources shows with remarkable consistency that of women who died after delivery from puerperal causes, 80 per cent died in the first two weeks and very few puerperal deaths occurred after two months (Table 2.1). It is only in recent years when maternal mortality has fallen to a low level that late maternal deaths are of any statistical importance.

Much more important than stillbirths, multiple births, and definitions of the length of the postnatal period are the problems arising from death registration and international differences in the methods of collecting, classifying, and publishing data on births and deaths.

THE REGISTRATION OF BIRTHS AND DEATHS IN ENGLAND AND WALES

Most of the tables and figures in this book are based on published vital statistics. Vital registration was introduced in England and Wales in 1837 (Scotland in 1854). It was not until 1874 that the cause of every death had to be certified by a doctor or, if a doctor had not been in attendance and also in certain categories of death such as suicide or homicide, by a coroner.[9] The dates on which national vital statistics were first published in other countries are shown in Appendix Table 28.

[9] For excellent accounts of vital registration in the 19th cent. see D. V. Glass, *Numbering the People* (London, 1978), esp. app. 4, chap. 4, pp. 181–205, and M. Nissel, *People Count: A History of the General Register Office* (London, 1987).

Between 1837 and 1874 in England and Wales, the onus was placed on the local registrar to ensure that deaths in his area were registered. The registration of the cause of death by medical practitioners was voluntary. Initially, therefore, the causes of death published by the Registrar General were based in part on doctors' certificates and in part on the cause of death reported by the relatives or by other lay witnesses. Nevertheless, as early as 1858, 79 per cent of deaths were registered as to cause by doctors and 4 per cent were registered by coroners. Only 6 per cent had no medical certificate because there had been no medical attendant, while 11 per cent were not certified at all. By 1870, Farr stated, 'The English deaths are not all returned by medical men; but 92 in 100 of them are so returned all over the country, and in London the proportion is 98 in 100.' As for the accuracy of returns on the deaths with which we are concerned, maternal deaths, in 1870 Farr 'scrupulously examined' all deaths in London over a period of six weeks searching for wrongly certified maternal deaths and making 'confidential inquiries' in every doubtful case. Sixty-six maternal deaths were properly returned and only one was not. Since doctors were not paid for certification and had a traditional dislike of 'bureaucracy' and statistics, such completeness of certification is surprising.[10]

The Births and Deaths Registration Act of 1874 was an important advance. It placed the onus of registration on the nearest relative of the deceased instead of the registrar and every registration of a death had to be accompanied by a medical certificate. Although this led to increased diagnostic accuracy, a number of deaths were never registered while the public slowly got used to the idea of compulsory death certification.

For instance, the Select Committee on Death Registration was told in 1893 that although the number of uncertified deaths was decreasing and had fallen to 1.2 per cent in London and 2.7 per cent in England and Wales as a whole, it was still about 6 per cent in North Wales and Scotland, and 24 per cent in Inverness. Unregistered deaths were mainly at the extremes of life (deaths under 1 year or over the age of 80) and occurred most often in crowded working-class areas such as the Glasgow tenements. Infant deaths in some areas were also reduced as a result of many infants being buried as stillbirths when there was good reason to believe they had been born alive.[11] This is clearly important for historians concerned with neonatal mortality. Did the 1874 Act have any impact on the published rate of maternal mortality?

If there was serious under-registration of maternal deaths between 1837 and 1874, the Act of 1874 should have revealed the previous deficit by a sudden rise in the MMR, a rise which could be called a 'registration effect'. Did this occur? There was indeed a rise in the MMR in 1874; but 1874 was

[10] *Annual Report of the Registrar General for 1870*, 408–9.
[11] *Report of the Select Committee on Death Certification* (1893), 373, 402.

TABLE 2.2 *Births and Maternal Deaths in England and Wales, 1871–1878*

Year	Total births	Deaths from puerperal fever	Accidents of childbirth[a]	Total maternal deaths	Maternal mortality rate (per 10,000 births)
1871	797,428	1,464	2,471	3,935	49.3
1872	825,907	1,400	2,403	3,803	46.0
1873	829,778	1,740	2,375	4,115	49.6
1874	854,956	3,108	2,819	5,927	69.3
1875	850,607	2,504	2,560	5,064	59.5
1876	887,968	1,746	2,396	4,142	46.6
1877	888,180	1,414	1,993	3,407	38.4
1878	891,906	1,415	1,885	3,300	37.0

[a] 'Accidents of childbirth' indicates maternal deaths due to all causes except puerperal fever.

Source: Annual reports of the Registrar General for the appropriate years.

too early. A rise due to increased registration would have been expected not in the year the Act was introduced, but in the following year, 1875, and should have increased or at least been sustained through subsequent years. In fact the MMR fell sharply over the four years beginning in 1875, reaching the lowest levels recorded in the nineteenth century by 1878 (Table 2.2). This makes it unlikely that numerous maternal deaths were unregistered before 1874 unless a shortfall in the registration of maternal deaths (the numerator in the equation of maternal mortality), was matched by an equivalent shortfall in birth registration (the denominator). We must examine this possibility.

Before 1874, the onus of birth registration, like death registration, was placed on the local registrar. From 1874, when the onus was transferred to the parents, it was believed that birth registration was more complete. Because the MMR measures maternal deaths in terms of births, if there was a shortfall in both, the one might have cancelled the other out. Is it likely that this happened? The answer is complicated by a statistical anomaly. During a decade when births were rapidly increasing, the number of births registered in 1875 was actually lower than those in 1874 (Table 2.2). The explanation is this. The 1874 Act allowed a longer period to pass between birth and registration. Therefore a substantial number of births which, under previous regulations, would have been registered in 1875, were registered in 1876 swelling the number registered in that year, and decreasing the number of registered births in 1875. This produced a small zigzag in the secular trend of births. To iron out this anomaly, the maternal mortality rates based on the published number of births were compared with the maternal mortality rates based on what was probably the true number of births; and the latter were calculated by the reasonable assumption that there was actually a continuation of the smooth rise in births from 1874 to 1878. The results of this calculation can be seen in Appendix Table 2 which shows the registration effect of the 1874 Act was of minimal importance.

THE REGISTRATION OF BIRTHS AND DEATHS IN OTHER COUNTRIES

In most countries, during the early years of vital statistics, the reports were incomplete and did not include statistics on maternal deaths but only on other selected diseases. When maternal deaths were included they were frequently scattered through the reports rather than shown together, but this is no more than a minor inconvenience for the historian. The methodology of vital statistics in relation to maternal mortality was similar in most European countries (and also in Australia and New Zealand) to that of England and Wales. France published maternal mortality rates in terms of population rather than births, and provided much less detailed information on maternal deaths. Data from the Netherlands, the Scandinavian countries, and Belgium, are amongst the most complete. But the country with by far the most complex system of civil registration was the USA.

Before 1933 the vital statistics of the USA were based on what was known as the 'death registration area'. Some states published vital statistics in the mid-nineteenth century. Massachusetts, for example, introduced death registration in 1842, New York State in 1847, and New Jersey in 1848. But it was not until 1880 that it was decided to amalgamate the statistics from three states (Massachusetts, New Jersey, and the District of Columbia) with the statistics from nineteen cities outside those states, all of which satisfied certain criteria on the completeness of death registration. Together these formed the 'death registration area' and contained about 17 per cent of the population. It was recognized that the states and cities of the death registration area were not representative of the country as a whole, but it was better to rely on a limited number of reliable statistics than a larger number of unreliable ones. As various states satisfied the established criteria they were added to the list so that the 'death registration area' became the 'expanding death registration area'. By 1900, for instance, a further ten states had been added, by 1920 the death registration area consisted of thirty-six states, but it was not until 1933 that all states were included (Appendix Table 23).

There was a similar but less prolonged process for birth registration. In 1890 it was said that no state or city in the USA had a satisfactory system of birth registration.[12] Matters improved because of growing concern over infant mortality. In 1915 the Census Bureau defined the Birth Registration Area

[12] R. H. Bremner (ed.), *Children and Youth in America* (Cambridge, Mass., 1971), 958.

as consisting of 'states or municipalities whose laws and administrative procedures provided for accurate and complete registration of births'. The Birth Registration Area, so defined, was established in 1915 with the initial inclusion of eleven states (Connecticut, District of Columbia, Maine, Massachusetts, Michigan, Minnesota, New Hampshire, New York, Pennsylvania, Rhode Island, and Vermont). All states were included by 1930.

In 1926, Woodbury considered at length the effect of these matters on the statistics of maternal mortality. He showed that many births were still not registered in 1919. For the USA as a whole it amounted to 8.7 per cent of births, but in some states, mostly those in the south with a large black population, it was sometimes as high as 24 per cent. He believed that:

[Maternal] deaths fell short of the true number by as much as 12 per cent . . . births fell short of the true number by 8.7 per cent, and therefore fell short of the number of confinements by about 12 per cent [the additional 3.3 per cent being stillbirths]. Because of the omissions of not far from equal proportions from both the numerator and the denominator . . . the conclusion is perhaps justified that the maternal mortality rate . . . is probably not far from correct.[13]

We return to these problems again in the chapters on maternal mortality in the USA. Here it is only necessary to note that incompleteness of birth and death registration lasted longer in the USA than in most European countries, reflecting the problems of a large and expanding country with many remote rural areas.

NOSOLOGY AND THE INTERNATIONAL CLASSIFICATION OF DISEASES

Classification, the grouping together of things which share certain common features, is an attempt to impose order on chaos. The history of nosology (the classification of diseases) reflects this need for order while recognizing that diseases are concepts, not objects. It is usually said that modern nosology began when Linnaeus, who published his classification of plants in 1751, attempted to impose the same system of classification on diseases in 1763 and grouped them in species, genera, orders, and so on. Boissier de Lacroix (better known as Sauvages) followed a similar plan in his nosology (1768) and subdivided diseases into 10 classes, 295 genera, and 2,400 species. These classifications were succeeded by others such as those of Cullen, Brown, and Pinel. Lacking a firm pathological basis, all these nosologies were ephemeral, although occasional remnants still exist; the modern classification of skin disease, based largely on a Linnean classification of external appearances, was established by the work of Willan and Bateman in the late eighteenth and

---

[13] Woodbury, *Maternal Mortality*, 20. Woodbury provides an exceptionally full and clear account of the errors in estimating maternal mortality in the USA.

early nineteenth centuries. Otherwise, the old nosologies based on anatomy and modelled on natural history, gave way to systems based on the growth of pathology in the first half of the nineteenth century.

As soon as he took up his post as compiler of abstracts at the General Register Office, William Farr saw that no satisfactory nosology existed:

Each disease has in many instances been denoted by three or four terms, and each term has been applied to as many different diseases; vague, inconvenient names have been employed, or complications have been registered instead of primary diseases.[14]

Farr devised a nosology of his own, which was circulated to medical practitioners and coroners in 1845. It remained, with only minor modifications, the Office nosology until he retired in 1880. It was then revised, first in 1881 and again in 1900.

The establishment of national systems of death registration in various countries during the mid-nineteenth century made international comparisons possible. Different nosologies, however, hampered comparisons, and it was clear that an internationally agreed system would be a great advantage. William Farr and the equally famous vital statistician who became a close friend, Adolphe Quetelet of Belgium, became involved in establishing a series of international conferences on the classification of disease.[15] Following a conference in Vienna in 1891, Bertillon of France was charged with drawing up the first international classification. It was based largely on Farr's nosology and published as the first edition of the International Classification of Disease (ICD).[16] It was adopted in the USA, Canada, and Mexico in 1898 and revised editions were published in 1900 and 1910 before Britain adopted the ICD system in 1911. The *Manual of International Statistical Classification of Diseases, Injuries and Causes of Death*, to give it its present title, has been revised regularly, the ninth revision being published in 1975.

What effect did the growth of nosology have on the statistics of maternal mortality? There was one important change. In England and Wales, following the adoption in 1911 of the International Classification of Disease nosology, deaths due to toxaemia, previously allocated to diseases of the kidney, were included amongst puerperal deaths. This is dealt with in Chapter 5. Otherwise, changes in the classification of maternal deaths, which are described in Appendix 2, consisted in large part of subdividing already established categories. They do not create major interpretative difficulties, and there are certainly fewer terminological problems for the historian of childbirth than there are for the historian of other categories of disease.

---

[14] Nissel, *People Count*, 102.

[15] F. Lewes, 'The Letters between Adolphe Quetelet and William Farr', *Bulletin de la classe des lettres et des sciences morales et politiques*, 5th ser., 49 (1983), 417–28.

[16] This first edition of the ICD is often known as the Bertillon classification or the Bertillon edition.

ASSOCIATED DEATHS

Although the problem arising from what used to be called 'associated deaths' and the even more complex problem of what I have chosen to call 'hidden deaths' have attracted very little attention from historians of obstetrics, both were much larger potential sources of error than any we have considered so far.

Associated deaths were those due to a disorder associated with, but not directly due to, pregnancy, labour, or the puerperal state. In modern terminology they are now called 'indirect deaths' while 'true' maternal deaths are known as 'direct deaths'. Most associated deaths were, in practice, due to chronic disorders such as heart disease, tuberculosis, and nephritis. Should such deaths have been counted as maternal deaths? The answer was not always straightforward. If a mother had the misfortune to be killed in a railway accident when she was pregnant, her death would not be recorded as a maternal death. (Today such deaths are listed in the statistics of maternal mortality as 'fortuitous' deaths.) Associated or indirect deaths, however, were quite different.

The underlying notion was that if a woman died in pregnancy from a disease, she may have died because pregnancy reduced her strength and ability to withstand the disease. In such cases, the doctor who certified the cause of death would be expected to show both pregnancy and the disease in question, such as tuberculosis or heart disease, on the death certificate. Which, however, should he put first? This brings us to the general problem of the certification of multiple causes of death.

ASSOCIATED DEATHS AND MULTIPLE CAUSES OF DEATH

The certificates issued at the time of the Act of 1874 were unclear because 'The form of the doctor's death certificate allowed him to enter a number of concomitant or contributory causes of death without complete or adequate guidance as to the causal relation between them.'[17] The wording of the death certificate required the doctor to enter the 'primary' cause of death and, if any were present, the 'secondary' cause(s) of death. Some doctors interpreted 'primary' as being the most long-standing disease, others the last to appear. Each individual death can only be entered once in a list of vital statistics, and the choice of the primary cause determines under which class of diseases that death is entered. It was a problem faced by all countries which published vital statistics.

In an attempt to produce a uniform system so that valid comparisons could be made, a complicated manual of multiple causes of death was published. In

[17] ICD, 4th rev. (1929), introd.

fact more than one manual was produced. The USA, Australia, Scotland, the Netherlands (and sometimes Canada) followed the rules of precedence laid down in the United States Manual of Joint Causes of Death.[18] England and Wales and certain other countries followed the rules of precedence laid out in the Manual of the International Causes of Death.[19] Each manual laid down guidelines which stated that if diseases A and B appeared as concomitant causes of death, A should always take precedence over B or vice versa as the case may be, and a wide variety of possible combinations of causes of death was listed.

It led to a great deal of muddle. Some countries already had their own policies on multiple causes of death and ignored the guidelines of the manuals. In England and Wales the obvious solution—the design of a better death certificate—came in 1927. As a result of the Births and Deaths Act of 1927, two new measures were introduced which affected the recording of maternal mortality. First, stillbirth registration, which had been suggested as long ago as 1893 by the Select Committee on Death Registration, became compulsory; secondly, a new and much less ambiguous death certificate was introduced. Both measures came into operation on 1 July 1927.[20]

As far as maternal mortality was concerned, however, the use of less-ambiguous certification did not solve all the problems of international comparability. The 1918 epidemic of influenza highlighted international differences; regardless of the guidelines in manuals on multiple causes of death some countries included influenza deaths in pregnancy as maternal deaths, others did not. For example, a sharp influenza peak can be found in the records of maternal mortality in the USA, New Zealand, and Scotland but not in Australia or England and Wales. But in spite of the confusion, there are two important questions to which firm answers can be given. The first is concerned with the number of associated deaths compared to true or direct maternal deaths; the second with the extent to which differences in MMRs published by different countries were due to differences in methodology.

THE PROPORTION OF ASSOCIATED DEATHS

In 1881 the Registrar General's Annual Report shows that there were 4,227 deaths attributed directly to childbirth and 1,438 deaths 'of women after

---

[18] Tandy, *Comparability of Maternal Mortality Rates*, 8–9.

[19] RG's Report for 1933.

[20] The new certificate required the doctor to enter: 1. immediate cause of death; 2. antecedent causes, directly related to the immediate cause; 3. concurrent but independent causes and circumstances materially contributing to death. This allowed the RG to have more confidence in asserting that the opinion of the certifier as to the immediate cause of death was to be accepted unless the choice appeared to have been perverse. The certifying doctor's decision was nearly always accepted in certain countries such as Sweden. In the USA, which lay at the other extreme from Sweden, the Bureau of Statistics usually made the final decision. In Switzerland the cause of

childbearing assigned to diseases other than childbirth or puerperal fever'—in other words, associated deaths—and 71 deaths 'in women who were returned as pregnant'. Amongst the last were 7 deaths due to violence which can be excluded as 'fortuitous' deaths in the modern sense, leaving a total of 1,502 (1,438 + 71 − 7) associated deaths. If the Registrar General had chosen to include these as maternal deaths the published figure for maternal mortality in 1881—48 per 10,000 births—would have been inflated to 64. Associated deaths would have amounted to 1,502 out of 5,729, or 26 per cent.

In England and Wales in 1933 there were 2,618 true maternal deaths assigned to 'diseases of pregnancy, childbirth and the puerperal state' and 828 deaths defined as 'not classed to pregnancy but returned as associated therewith'.[21] Thus associated (indirect) deaths amounted to about 25 per cent of the two categories added together, and 31 per cent of true maternal deaths. This was rather larger than usual because of an epidemic of influenza which accounted for 129 of the 828 associated deaths. If influenza deaths are excluded, associated deaths amounted to 27 per cent of 'true' (direct) maternal deaths. After influenza the main causes of associated deaths in 1933 were diseases of the heart (156 deaths), tuberculosis (73), pneumonia (69), and chronic nephritis (55).

Although the Register Office in London was careful to publish 'associated' deaths in a separate table for the purpose of international comparisons, it is not surprising that whenever comparisons were made, countries which included both true and associated deaths in total maternal mortality accused those which did not of dishonesty and attempting to make their statistics look better.[22]

Which method was preferable? Which the more honest? The answer depended on beliefs concerning the state of pregnancy. Some argued that it was a healthy normal state in which there was no increased susceptibility to death from non-puerperal causes. Others described pregnancy as a 'disease of nine months' duration' in which women became more delicate, vulnerable,

death was certified by a doctor specially appointed for the purpose of registering causes of death, with the result that the Swiss vital statistics were often regarded as the most consistent and reliable of any country. *Statistical Handbook Series, No. 12, Official Vital Statistics of Switzerland* (Geneva, 1928).

[21] The RG in 1933 chose to refer to the mortality due to 'true' or direct maternal deaths as the 'puerperal mortality'. He referred to the total of direct and associated/indirect deaths as the 'maternal mortality'. Fortunately this attempt to hijack the term maternal mortality in order to make a special distinction was not used consistently in Britain or anywhere else. It could have caused endless confusion if it had been and it is not a distinction that is used here.

[22] See e.g. R. Marshall Allen, 'Avenues of Progress in Maternal Welfare', Anne Mackenzie Oration for 1936, *Medical Journal of Australia* (1936), 251–8. Allen complained that 'In England two tables are shown, one giving the usual causes and a second those deaths due to diseases associated with pregnancy, such as kidney disease *et cetera*. . . . It is difficult to understand why the incomplete English rate, comprising the first table only, is always compared with our rate from all causes.'

and susceptible to the stresses of life and other diseases, arguing that a pregnant woman who died of an associated cause would probably not have died had she not been pregnant. In 1933 the Registrar General considered these arguments and this is what he had to say about the problem:

Every pregnant woman is exposed to about the same hazards of dying from non-puerperal causes as if she had not been pregnant, and if she does so die the fact of the pregnancy or recent parturition is usually mentioned on the death certificate on the grounds that notwithstanding that normal childbearing is a physiological process it is difficult to assert categorically that in the presence of some serious disease it did not, by diminishing the reserves of strength or by some other means, render recovery more difficult.[23]

By a careful and detailed analysis of the group of associated deaths in pregnant women and deaths due to the same causes in a matched group of non-pregnant women, he showed that the death rates due to the associated diseases in the first group were no higher than they were in the second. There was, in other words, no evidence that pregnancy or labour or the lying-in period increased the risk of death from any of the common causes of associated deaths. Pregnancy was a healthy state. It did not lower the supposed 'reserves of strength'. He concluded this section of the report by saying

This supports the view that the number of deaths which are assigned by the methods applied in England and Wales to 'non-puerperal causes but associated with pregnancy or childbearing' approximately represents the number which ought properly to be so assigned, and that this group of deaths ought not to be laid at the door of childbearing.[24]

This conclusion, however, is not wholly supported by modern research. There is now evidence that cell-mediated immunity is depressed in pregnancy (in teleological terms to prevent the mother's immune system from rejecting the foetus) and that women in the third trimester of pregnancy are more liable to acquire and to die from certain infectious diseases and neoplasms. Conspicuous amongst the diseases are influenza, poliomyelitis, tuberculosis, and smallpox. It has been shown that the risk of acquiring these diseases is between three and seven times as high in pregnant women as in non-pregnant women of childbearing age in the same community.[25] Even if this overturns the conclusion of the Registrar General in 1933, it does not of course affect

---

[23] RG's Report for 1933, 97–8.

[24] Ibid. No one at the time appeared to recognize just how startling this conclusion was. In effect it overturned the deeply entrenched belief that a serious chronic disease was an absolute reason for advising against pregnancy because the woman might well die prematurely as a result of the 'strain' of pregnancy and labour. Indeed, the coexistence of pregnancy and a serious chronic disease was recognized as a 'threat to the life of a woman' and thus as a justification for a therapeutic abortion. There was probably hardly a doctor in England who did not share this view in the 1930s, holding it as a matter of common sense.

[25] E. D. Weiner, 'Pregnancy-Associated Depression of Cell-Mediated Immunity', *Reviews of Infectious Diseases*, 6 (1984), 814–31.

the rates of death due directly to puerperal causes. Associated deaths were always something of a red herring. The purpose of publishing the statistics of maternal mortality was to inform interested people (women, doctors, midwives, and all concerned with maternal health) on the risks *directly attributable to* childbearing and not the incidental risks of coincidental disease which could vary widely from one year to another from such events as influenza epidemics, and give a false impression of wide variations in the risk of death from puerperal causes. As MacPhail said in 1932, vital statistics 'are not compiled merely to satisfy idle curiosity or to bolster some pet theory. Vital statistics, like all statistics, are not worth the time and money spent on them if the usefulness of the facts disclosed does not serve the state.'[26] In my view the Registrar General's system of not including associated deaths in the total, but recording them and showing them separately, was, and still is, the most sensible system.

ASSOCIATED DEATHS AND INTERNATIONAL COMPARISONS

How much did international differences in the inclusion of associated deaths affect international comparisons? Few tried to answer his question until Elizabeth Tandy in the USA published her report in 1935.[27] The method she used was to take a sample of 1,073 certificates of maternal deaths in the USA in 1927, in which the death had been certified by the attending physician as puerperal. From this she then abstracted:

477 certificates, carefully selected so as to include at least one death of every type in the sample. For some of these 477 deaths only one cause of death had been certified, as puerperal sepsis or eclampsia or self-induced abortion, but for by far the greater proportion 2 or even 3 causes were mentioned by the physicians who made out the certificate.

Copies of these 477 certificates (with the names removed) were sent to the bureau of vital statistics in a number of foreign countries, but no information was given regarding the cause assigned in the United States. Each bureau was asked to assign each death either to puerperal causes or to non-puerperal causes according to the methodology they used. The results were shown in a number of different ways in the original publication, but the main findings are summarized in Tables 2.3 and 2.4.

Table 2.4 shows that only Denmark assigned more deaths to puerperal causes than the USA. Most other countries assigned fewer deaths to puerperal causes, with England and Wales and Norway assigning least of all.

---

[26] E. S. MacPhail, 'A Statistical Study in Maternal Mortality', *American Journal of Public Health*, 22 (1932). He was chief of the division of censuses and vital statistics in Ottawa.

[27] Tandy, *Comparability of Maternal Mortality Rates*.

TABLE 2.3 *The Assignment of 447 Maternal Deaths according to the Methodology Used in Various Countries for the Classification of Maternal Deaths*

Country	Puerperal causes (%)	Non-puerperal causes (%)
Denmark	99.4	0.6
USA	92.9	7.1
New Zealand	92.8	7.2
Australia	92.7	7.3
Scotland	92.3	7.7
Netherlands	91.9	8.1
France	82.7	17.3
Sweden	80.5	19.5
England and Wales	78.7	21.3
Norway	76.9	23.1

Source: Elizabeth C. Tandy, *Comparability of Maternal Mortality Rates in the United States and Certain Foreign Countries*, Children's Bureau Publication, No. 229 (Washington, DC, 1935).

In Table 2.4 countries are ranked in order of national MMRs. The first three columns of this table demonstrate the consistency of the rank order in the years 1910, 1920, and 1927. Nineteen twenty-seven was not an atypical year. The final column 1927 (B) shows the mortality rates in each of the countries which would have been recorded had each and every country conformed to the methodology of the USA. In other words, column 1927 (A) shows the published figures while column 1927 (B) shows the published figures after they have been corrected to eliminate differences due solely to differences in methodology. It can be seen that the rates in England and Wales, New Zealand, Norway, and Sweden would have been substantially higher if American methodology had been used, but the rank order was virtually the same. Differences in methodology were sometimes quite large; but in general international differences in MMRs were so great that the methodological element was of relatively little importance. Tandy concluded:

Differences in the method of assignment are insufficient to explain the high maternal mortality rate of the United States as compared with foreign countries. The official figure of the United States, which in the last few years has exceeded that of every country except Scotland, remains high no matter what method of assignment is used . . .

One of Tandy's recommendations was that in future the USA, like England and Wales, should show direct and indirect or associated deaths separately in two tables. This recommendation was not adopted.

TABLE 2.4 *The Effect of Differences in Methodology on the Reported Maternal Mortality Rates in Certain Countries, 1927*

Country	Maternal deaths per 10,000 births[a]			
	1910[b]	1920	1927 (A)[c]	1927 (B)[d]
USA	69	78	65	65
Scotland	57	62	64	64
Belgium	52	61	61	—
Australia	51	50	59	59
New Zealand	45	65	49	59
England and Wales	36	44	41	48
Norway	27	35	24	28
The Netherlands	25	24	29	30
Sweden	25	26	28	32
Denmark	—	24	31	29

[a] To nearest whole number.
[b] Data for 1910 and 1920 are included to demonstrate the constancy of the rank order.
[c] Column 1927 (A) shows the actual MMR published by each country in 1927.
[d] In column 1927 (B) the figures in brackets represent the mortality rates which would have been recorded in each country if the method of assigning maternal deaths which was used in the USA had been applied.

Source: The published vital statistics of various countries and Children's Bureau Publications, US Department of Labor, Washington, DC: Grace Meigs, *Maternal Mortality from All Conditions Connected with Childbirth in the United States and Certain other Countries*. Children's Bureau Publications, No. 19 (1917); R. M. Woodbury, *Maternal Mortality: The Risk of Death in Childbirth and from all the Diseases Caused by Pregnancy and Confinement*, ibid. No. 152 (1926); Elizabeth C. Tandy, *Comparability of Maternal Mortality Rates in the United States and Certain Foreign Countries*. ibid. No. 229 (1935).

HIDDEN MATERNAL DEATHS

I use the term 'hidden [maternal] deaths' for those cases in which a maternal death was certified by a doctor in such a way that childbirth was not indicated and the death was assigned to a non-maternal category. That such mistakes occurred might suggest that the data on maternal mortality are valueless. There are, however, ways in which the historian can, within broad limits, estimate the extent of hidden deaths. The methods by which this can be done are discussed in Appendix 1.

It is a commonplace, easily forgotten, that the reliability of vital statistics in any period depends on the diagnostic accuracy of the certifying doctors, which in turn depends on the training, experience, and the care taken by the whole range of medical practitioners, the good and the bad, the well-informed and the ignorant, the lazy and the conscientious.[28] The use of vague and hopelessly uncertain diagnostic terms in the nineteenth century is a well-known feature of mortality data on deaths amongst infants and children. In the case of maternal deaths, however, vague terminology is rarely a major problem. Deaths were usually obscured for other reasons, sometimes as a result of carelessness, and sometimes because of false certification.

For example, a doctor could certify a maternal death due to puerperal fever simply as 'fever' or as 'peritonitis' because puerperal fever often caused peritonitis. Likewise he could certify a death due to post-partum haemorrhage simply as 'haemorrhage', forgetting to mention childbirth, whether the forgetting was genuine or not. Such cases were often detected by the Register Office and the certificate amended accordingly. Carelessness was common. Deliberate false certification was another matter. It usually arose from one of two motives. Sometimes a doctor's motive was to save the family from embarrassment, as for instance in a death due to induced abortion. More often the reason for concealing the truth was a deliberate attempt by a doctor to avoid blame. Such concealment was a well-known fact, deplored by everyone concerned with the statistics of maternal mortality, but the temptation was strong. Doctors always recognized that if one of their midwifery cases died they were likely to be blamed, especially when the patient died of puerperal fever; so they sometimes attempted to attribute death to a non-maternal cause. The introduction of antisepsis in the 1880s increased the likelihood of blame. In 1892 Dr Rentoul, a general practitioner, told the Select Committee on Midwive's Registration:

It comes to this that practically every doctor who loses a confinement case receives very great blame, no matter whether he deserves it or not, very serious blame indeed; so much so that if one of your confinement cases dies in a particular street, your midwifery practice is almost ruined in that street.[29]

In America, Dr Stanley Warren remarked in 1895 that physicians in private practice often dared not return deaths due to puerperal fever 'through fear of public odium and loss of professional prestige'.[30] Another American doctor remarked in 1925 that:

When a death is recorded as occurring from septicaemia there is no question that this is the true cause of death. For no man will sign a certificate 'puerperal septicaemia' if

---

[28] In addition the RG's office did attempt to identify vague or possibly incorrect certificates. Having written to the doctor concerned certain certificates were altered and errors corrected. But the ability of the office to carry out this function was always curtailed by cost. Nevertheless, it was an important aspect of the problem of hidden maternal deaths and is described in App. 1.

[29] *Report of the Select Committee on Midwives' Registration*, PP 1892, XIV, Q. 466.

[30] S. P. Warren, 'The Prevalence of Puerperal Septicaemia in Private Practice at the Present Time Contrasted with that of a Generation ago', *American Journal of Obstetrics*, 51 (1905), 301–31.

there is any possible opportunity for him to assign the death to any other cause . . . when a patient is found to have died from sepsis, it devolves upon the physician in charge of the case to prove conclusively that he delivered the patient according to good surgical technique.[31]

However, doctors whose aim was to conceal a maternal death, did not enter the first disease that came into their head as the stated cause of death. A gross lie was easily detected by the family, not to mention the Registrar, and could land them in trouble. Instead they used the method of what might be called the 'white lie' or partial truth. If questions were asked the faulty certificate could always be attributed to an oversight or a forgivable diagnostic error rather than a direct lie.

The most common method was to certify a death from puerperal sepsis as being due to another less-opprobrious cause within the class of deaths from childbirth such as haemorrhage. These deceits were the hardest to detect. Although they did not affect the total MMR, they reduced the proportion of deaths assigned to puerperal fever. Arnold Lea remarked in 1910 that:

For many reasons there is considerable reluctance on the part of medical men to attribute death directly to infection, and some of these fatalities are undoubtedly reported under the heading of 'Accidents of childbirth'. Thus abortion and many deaths after operative delivery are included under 'accidents', although in the majority of these the fatal issue undoubtedly arises from infection.[32]

This form of deceit is considered in Appendix 1. Another common method, as in the example given above, was to assign a death from puerperal fever to a non-puerperal cause in such a way that the stated cause was true in all respects except that 'childbirth' was omitted from the certificate. In the 1890s, Dr Bacon of Chicago was well aware that the admission by a physician of such a condition (puerperal fever) in a patient whom he had delivered, would often subject him to a grave reproach.[33] He noted an excess of lying-in women recorded as dying from various 'fevers' that defied belief. 'I have often been told by country practitioners that they never see puerperal fever, but that many find malarial fever quite common in the puerperium.'

Much the most common of all the 'hidden deaths' were those due to puerperal fever which were entered by the certifying doctor as deaths due to peritonitis or septicaemia (commonly called 'blood poisoning') without mention of childbirth. As we will see in Chapter 4, the mode of death from puerperal fever was usually peritonitis or septicaemia or both. The extent

---

[31] G. C. Mosher in *Proceedings of the Fourth Annual Conference of State Directors in Charge of Local Administration of the Maternity and Infancy Act*, Children's Bureau Publications, No. 181 (Washington, DC, 1927).

[32] A. Lea, *Puerperal Infection* (London, 1910).

[33] C. W. W. S. Bacon, 'The Mortality from Puerperal Infection in Chicago', *American Journal of Obstetrics and Gynaecology*, 8 (1896), 429–46.

to which this occurred and the way it can be estimated is described in Appendix 1 which shows that the extent of hidden maternal deaths as a proportion of total maternal deaths was probably highest in the late nineteenth century and decreased steadily through the first three decades of this century to a very low level by 1940. Two processes seem to have been responsible: a better standard of certification and increasing vigilance by the Registrar General.

This raises an obvious question. Was the absence of a significant fall in maternal mortality between, say, 1880 and 1920, a statistical anomaly? Was it due to more accurate and complete certification of maternal deaths? We deal with this in more detail later. Briefly, however, the answer is 'no'. It was a matter closely considered by the Registrar General in 1919.[34] He conceded that doctors tended to be imprecise when it came to certifying deaths due to puerperal fever, and he believed this tendency was decreasing while the rate of detection of 'hidden' deaths was increasing. As a result of his enquiry, however, he concluded that inaccurate certification in the past and subsequent improvement was too slight to explain the absence of the expected fall in mortality. The continuing high level of deaths due to puerperal sepsis could not be dismissed as a statistical anomaly.

It seems likely that the 'hidden death' problem was at least as serious abroad, and probably more so, than it was in Britain. To arrive at something close to the truth, Boxall (a late nineteenth-century obstetrician with a special interest in the statistics of puerperal fever) added one-twelfth to the published statistics of deaths from puerperal fever in England and Wales. Ingerslev in Copenhagen and other Danish cities added 20 per cent. Bacon made elaborate calculations of the under-reporting of puerperal fever deaths in Chicago in the 1890s and felt that adding on 16.5 per cent might bring the total somewhere near the truth.[35]

A similar conclusion was reached in the USA. Grace Meigs of the Children's Bureau wrote in 1917 that:

The statistics due to puerperal septicaemia . . . are without question very incomplete. Many deaths are reported, for obvious reasons, as due to some other condition, such as septicaemia, pyaemia, and the like. This fault in all statistics on the subject has been commented on very frequently both in this country and in foreign countries. It follows that almost never is a case reported as due to infection at confinement when it is really due to some other cause . . . the figures [for puerperal sepsis] though undoubtedly incomplete are reliable as far as they go; they are a statement of the minimum number of cases which have occurred.[36]

---

[34] *Supplement to the 75th Annual Report of the Registrar General* (1919).

[35] Bacon, 'The Mortality from Puerperal Infection in Chicago'.

[36] Grace Meigs, *Maternal Mortality from all Conditions Connected with Childbirth in the United States and Certain other Countries*, Children's Bureau Publications, No. 19 (Washington, DC, 1917), 35–6.

In 1926, Woodbury, also of the Children's Bureau, showed that in cases of maternal deaths in which childbirth was omitted from the certificate, it was sometimes accidental, sometimes deliberate because 'Physicians knew they were often accused, sometimes not without reason, of negligent practice in such cases.' Deaths from puerperal sepsis were hidden, in the USA as in England, in the lists of deaths due to peritonitis or septicaemia.[37]

Clearly, then, 'hidden deaths' was an international problem, and, if it had occurred to exactly the same extent it would have had little effect on international comparisons. How great, in fact, was this inaccuracy? It is impossible to be absolutely sure. The evidence presented in Appendix 1 suggests that in England and Wales in the 1920s and 1930s the published figures for mortality due to puerperal sepsis fell short of the truth by about 5 per cent, or at most 10 per cent. Total maternal mortality probably fell short of the truth by about 3 per cent to 5 per cent. In the latter years of the nineteenth century, the corresponding percentages were probably considerably higher. The same probably applied to other countries.

While treading gingerly on the quicksands of vital statistics, one thing is certain: the number of deaths due to puerperal fever was never exaggerated. No doctor reported a death as due to sepsis if he could attribute it to another cause. There is no justification, however, for rejecting the statistics of maternal mortality as valueless. Certainly, inaccuracy was greatest in the nineteenth century and improved in all Western countries through the first three or four decades of this century. In the context of total maternal mortality, however, the distorting factors were relatively slight. The picture of maternal mortality derived from the published data can be accepted as broadly correct, and there is no support for the supposition that international differences could be attributed to difference in the accuracy of certification. That the extent of inaccuracy can, within broad limits, be estimated and allowed for is the most important conclusion.

SUMMARY

It is easy to become too obsessed by statistical minutiae and fall into the error of placing more weight on estimates of registration errors than the historical data can bear. My conclusions are broad rather than precise. But one further point must be made. In the context of total births maternal deaths were uncommon. Data from a large number of births are needed before we can accept MMRs with confidence. This point is dealt with in Appendix 4.

Having considered such a large number of complex confounding factors, it is worth attempting a broad estimate of the extent to which these factors could

---

[37] Woodbury, *Maternal Mortality*.

have affected the MMR in England and Wales. For this calculation I have chosen, arbitrarily, the year 1925.

In 1925, the official published maternal mortality rate per 10,000 births live births was:	40.8
The maternal mortality rate if allowance had been made for	
stillbirths, would have been:	38.76
and for multiple births as well:	39.60
If we now add the estimated number of hidden maternal deaths the result would have been:	
at a minimum estimate of 3 per cent:	40.88
at a maximum estimate of 6 per cent:	42.10

Thus the likely range of error due to all these factors together is from 40.8 to 42.10, a range of between 3 per cent and 4 per cent. This is the range with which we are concerned when we are considering the data for England and Wales in isolation. When it comes to international comparisons, allowance must be made for associated deaths in some countries.

Thus, if associated deaths had been included in the data for England and Wales in the way they were included in the USA in 1925, the comparable figures for England and Wales would have lain between 47.8 and 49.2. The difference between the official estimate of 40.8 and 49.2 is indeed quite large, being not far short of 20 per cent. Nevertheless, in 1925 the range of mortality rates between the 'best' and the 'worst' Western countries lay between 20 maternal deaths per 10,000 births and around 60. It is clear there was a real gap between the 'best' and the 'worst', even if the width of the gap was somewhat exaggerated by differences in methodology. The saving grace is that to a large extent, the exaggeration can be estimated and the real difference—or something quite close to the real difference—can be calculated.

PART II

The Causes of Maternal Mortality

3

The Determinants of Maternal Mortality

When we discuss the causes of maternal mortality it is essential to distinguish between the immediate or direct causes of death on the one hand, and the causes of mortality levels within populations on the other. It avoids confusion if the term 'causes' is used for the immediate causes of death and 'determinants' for the factors which determined whether the level of mortality in a population at a given time or place was low or high. Before we come to immediate causes of maternal mortality in Chapters 3–8, it is convenient to discuss some general points about the determinants of maternal mortality.

The attempt to discover why a country, a region, or a certain group of the population suffered a particular rate of maternal mortality, and why rates changed with time, is one of the major themes of this study. If we were dealing with infant mortality we would find on many occasions that wide differences in mortality rates between two populations could be attributed to wide variations in a single cause. For instance, the infant mortality rate in Malta was exceptionally high up to the middle of the Second World War; thereafter it fell precipitously. This pattern was almost entirely determined by deaths from infantile diarrhoea and was related largely to the sanitary conditions which prevailed on the Maltese Islands.[1] This is a clear example of a close link between the immediate cause and the determinants.

In maternal mortality, however, it is uncommon to find direct links between causes and determinants. If for convenience we exclude deaths from abortion which were highly variable, the three most common causes of maternal mortality were sepsis (which accounted for between 33 per cent and 50 per cent of all maternal deaths), toxaemia (about 20 per cent of deaths), and haemorrhage (about 15–20 per cent of deaths). This well-known triad of fever, toxaemia, and haemorrhage predominated in the past and is still to be found in some undeveloped countries today. What is both important and surprising is that until the mid-1930s, these percentages were usually independent of the overall maternal mortality rate. The immediate causes of death tended to recur in the same proportion to each other even when the total maternal mortality rates were widely different.

There are exceptions to this rule. For example, the extremely high levels of maternal mortality in nineteenth-century lying-in hospitals were due to an

[1] I. Loudon, 'On Maternal and Infant Mortality', *Social History of Medicine*, 4 (1991), 45–7.

excess of deaths due to sepsis (puerperal fever) where, in epidemic periods, they accounted for 80 per cent or more of total maternal deaths. Abortion is the other main exception, but apart from these the general rule holds. Differences in maternal mortality can seldom be pinned down to a single cause of death. If maternal mortality was high (or low) it was high (or low) for all causes of maternal mortality.

What, then, were the factors which determined that one country or region should have a high rate of maternal mortality, and another a low rate? Broadly speaking there are two views about this. They are often seen as being diametrically opposed to each other, and each view (or more strictly, each set of related views) has had its firm adherents.

STANDARDS OF LIVING AND STANDARDS OF CARE

The first view places most emphasis on clinical standards, suggesting that maternal mortality was determined most of all by the quality of obstetric practice, using the term in a broad sense to include every kind of birth-attendant from the neighbour and the untrained midwife to the specialist obstetrician. High maternal mortality was due to poor obstetric practice, low mortality to good practice, judged by the standards of the time.

That is one view. The other is not quite so simple, but it stems from a rejection of the view that differences in the standards of obstetric care were of overriding importance. Too much emphasis, it is said, has been placed on purely clinical factors, obscuring the real or underlying causes of maternal mortality which can be found in the social and economic conditions of a population and the politics of maternal care. One of the linchpins of this view is the belief that high maternal mortality was due to poor maternal health as a result of social, economic, and nutritional deprivation and so forth.

These are the essential features of the views held by Sir Henry Brackenbury in 1937 and expressed with unusual clarity when the scandal of maternal mortality was at its height and the Ministry of Health's report on the high maternal mortality in special areas was about to be published. In anticipation of the findings of the report he wrote:

I confess that I have misgivings as to the scope and adequacy of that inquiry . . . I cannot believe that in these special areas the skill and care of midwives and general medical practitioners and obstetrical specialists are so different from that shown elsewhere, or the laxities in local administration are so peculiar as to afford an adequate explanation of the exceptional figures of maternal mortality. I cannot help suspecting that, however important such administrative and clinical factors may be, the main explanation may yet be found in those biological, physical, dietetic, sociological, even psychological factors which so far appear to have received insufficient attention.[2]

[2] Sir Henry Brackenbury, 'Maternity in its Sociological Aspects', *Social Service Review*, 18 (1937), 37–47. This assertion would be accepted today with little question if he had been writing about infant mortality.

The same point was made more succinctly by a medical officer of health who wrote with a touch of exasperation in 1937 that what was wanted in South Wales (a well-known maternal mortality black spot) was 'a herd of cows, not a herd of specialists'.[3]

Similarly, Robert Bolt, the Director of the Child Health Association in Cleveland, Ohio, who carried out a detailed enquiry into maternal deaths in 1931, believed that: 'Factors entering into puerperal mortality are so inter-woven with the social, economic, and cultural fabric of the community that it is impossible to evaluate them without a detailed study of each individual case.'[4] These ideas are, in effect, based on the belief that a healthy woman in a healthy frame of mind living and delivering in a healthy environment will have an easy pregnancy and an easy uncomplicated labour; not invariably, perhaps, but in all but a tiny minority of cases. It is the underlying philosophy of what is generally understood by 'natural childbirth' and thus it may be thought of as very modern. In fact, many obstetricians of the late eighteenth and early nineteenth centuries shared a similar faith in the powers of nature.

As Sir Henry Brackenbury realized, his views had very important impli-cations for those involved in the practice of obstetrics. If his views were correct, responsibility for high maternal mortality lay not with the medical and nursing professions, but with politicians and others responsible for the social and economic conditions of the population. A moment's reflection, however, shows that the two sets of views are not mutually exclusive. Poor obstetric care and poor maternal health could interact. For example, a woman who suffered a relatively small post-partum haemorrhage due to clumsy management of the third stage of labour by her birth-attendant might very well die if she was grossly undernourished and anaemic, whereas a healthy woman might survive. In the analysis of maternal mortality, the important question to resolve is therefore the *relative* importance of different deter-minants which fall broadly into the two groups, clinical and non-clinical.

THE PROBLEM OF POVERTY

This brings us to an important theme which recurs at intervals throughout this study: the effect of poverty on maternal mortality. It is discussed in most depth in two chapters: in Chapter 14 in the context of maternal mortality in Britain, and again in Chapter 22 in the context of the high maternal mortality in the black population of the United States. Here it is necessary to consider a few general ideas and stress that 'poverty' is an elusive term when we try to frame definitions which are susceptible to measurement.

Poverty can be defined in a number of ways. Those who have made detailed studies of poverty and welfare tend to distinguish between the subsistence

[3] 'Maternal Mortality in Wales' (leading article), *Medical Officer*, 57 (1937), 215.
[4] R. A. Bolt, 'Maternal Mortality Study for Cleveland, Ohio', *American Journal of Obstetrics and Gynaecology*, 27 (1934), 309–13.

minimum concept and the relative deprivation concept, the first being crude
but relatively easy to measure, the second more sophisticated but much harder
to measure.[5] When we try to measure the effects of poverty on health and the
correlations with mortality rates we turn to the criteria which are available
and measurable: for instance, income levels, occupational status (whether
employed or unemployed and if employed in which category of employment),
quality of housing, water supply and sanitation, nutrition (quantity and quality
of food, and here we must remember the long-term effects of malnutrition in
childhood), and the ability to command resources including the quality of
health care in general and maternal care in particular.

However, when we use one or more of these criteria to construct a measurable poverty line, we may be stressing one aspect of poverty while ignoring
others. Drawing a poverty line has the danger that it lumps together everyone
below that line as if they were a homogeneous mass, labelled as 'the poor'.
We may overlook widely different degrees of poverty. Amongst the poor there
were always hierarchies, well known to the poor themselves. The nineteenth-
century farm labourer, scarcely able to make ends meet and poor by any
standard definition, would have been deeply offended to be bracketed with the
destitutes on the pavement begging for food. The construction of a poverty
line may hide regional differences. We may be examining two regions. A and
B. Both have the same percentage of the population below the poverty line. In
region A, however, it might be that 90 per cent of the poor are only just below
the poverty line. In region B, it might be that only 10 per cent are just below
the line, and more than half are so poor as to be destitute. The point is
obvious, once made.

Apart from problems of definition within a given country, there are other
problems when it comes to international comparisons. What is regarded as
poverty in one country may be seen as sufficiency if not affluence in another.
The poverty line in the black population of the southern states of the USA in
the 1940s was not at all the same as the poverty line in southern England.
Again, this is obvious when stated, but it underlines the fact that poverty is
always relative and poverty lines are artificial constructions. This can be very
important if, as sometimes seems to be the case, mortality is only affected by
relatively severe degrees of poverty. In short, mortality is sometimes a crude
indicator of poverty.

[5] For recent and illuminating discussions of the concept of poverty, see S. Ringen, *The
Possibility of Politics* (Oxford, 1987), 141–65; and A. Sen, *Poverty and Famines* (Oxford, 1981),
9–23. Briefly, minimum subsistence means that a line is drawn which is based on the cost of a
'basket' of commodities essential for survival; all below that line are suffering from poverty.
Relative deprivation is concerned with quality of life as well as mere survival. People are judged to
be suffering from poverty, not only when they are deprived of essentials, but when they are unable
to take part in those activities in a community that are considered normal and universal for all
people. That is a brief if rather over-simplified version of the two concepts, both of which have
been widely used in the measurement of poverty.

What aspect of poverty is most relevant to maternal morbidity and mortality? Those who have written on this subject have usually stressed malnutrition to the exclusion of almost everything else. Few have considered *the ability to command the resources of health care* in relation to areas of deprivation. Women who were unable to command resources in the sense of being unable to pay for a birth-attendant were inevitably dependent on the extent of charitable or governmental forms of maternal care. If such forms of care were unavailable, the poor were forced to turn to untrained midwives, or neighbours, or their family, or even to delivering themselves. Furthermore, even when state-funded maternal care existed, the quality of care might be much lower for the poor than for the middle classes. We will meet examples.

There are other factors too. Maternal preference, for instance. In the United States, for example, maternal care amongst certain early twentieth-century immigrant communities was sometimes determined by the childbirth customs of their country of origin. Some of these communities rejected orthodox maternal care in the form of physician deliveries, not because they were unable to afford the fees, but because they refused to have men in the delivery room. Instead they insisted on their own (trained or untrained) midwives. They were not necessarily worse off as a result; indeed in some of these instances they may have made a wise choice. But they show that the type of care chosen by an individual or a population was not predetermined solely by their poverty or affluence. A particularly interesting example from the 1970s can be found in certain well-fed and prosperous religious communities whose faith insisted on the total rejection of all forms of orthodox medical care. This is described at the end of Chapter 22.

What techniques can be used in the analysis of determinants? How can we sort out the relative importance of poverty on the one hand, and the quality and/or availability of maternal care on the other? One way is to compare populations with widely different levels of poverty in any given period and see if those levels are correlated with differences in maternal mortality. Some useful answers can be obtained this way—for example by examining maternal mortality in terms of social class, income levels, or some indirect measure of relative poverty or affluence such as the rental value of housing.

The other and most useful technique is so simple I almost apologize for mentioning it, but it is absolutely crucial for understanding the evidence I present in later chapters and the conclusions arising from that evidence. In general, if we believe that a mortality rate was determined by two variables, x and y, but we are not sure which was the most important, we can study the trend in mortality when variable x remained constant, but variable y altered— or of course the other way round. It is the equivalent to an experiment in which the experimenter holds one variable constant while the other is raised or lowered so that the effect on whatever it is that is being measured can be observed.

In the case of maternal mortality this means that we should search for historical evidence of periods when the social and economic conditions remained constant, but the quality of maternal care was changing, and note what happened to maternal mortality. Alternatively we can study a population in which the economic and social condition of a population was either improving, or worsening as a result of war, for example, while the standard of maternal care remained more or less constant. In these examples one of the two determinants (the economic status of the population or the quality of maternal care respectively) remains constant while the other one alters. This is on the whole a more useful approach as we will see when we come to specific examples. But first we must consider the immediate causes of maternal mortality.

4

Puerperal Fever

Amongst the causes of death in childbirth, puerperal fever had no rival. It was not only the most common cause, it was also the most terrifying. Charles Meigs warned his students in 1848:

There is a 'word of fear' that I shall pronounce when I utter the name of Puerperal fever; for there is almost no acute disease that is more terrible than this—not even smallpox . . . There is something so touching in the death of a woman who has recently given birth to her child . . . It is a sort of desecration for an *accouchée* to die.[1]

To a much greater extent than any other disease a death from puerperal fever was liable to be attributed to negligence, especially after the introduction of antisepsis in the 1880s. In 1917, an Australian report on maternal mortality described puerperal fever as 'probably the gravest reproach which any civilised nation can by its own negligence offer to itself . . . It should be as rare as sepsis after a surgical operation.'[2]

How many women died of puerperal fever? The proportion of total deaths from the disease which occurred in lying-in hospitals (where, before the 1880s the mortality from puerperal fever was appalling) was, in the second half of the nineteenth century less than 3 per cent. The large majority of deaths from the disease occurred in home deliveries, and a large majority of these after normal deliveries. The experience of doctors and midwives, however, varied widely. Some saw many cases. Others practised for many years, saw few cases or none, and regarded it as a rare disorder. In fact, between 1847 and 1903, 93,342 deaths from puerperal fever were recorded in England and Wales, and this is almost certainly an underestimate of the true total.[3] In 1874, the worst year for puerperal fever on record since death registration began, out of a total of 5,927 maternal deaths, 3,108 (52 per cent) were registered as being due to puerperal fever. Recognizing the extent to which deaths from puerperal fever were under-recorded, Sir William Sinclair

---

[1] Charles D. Meigs, *Females and their Diseases: A Series of Letters to his Class* (Philadelphia, Pa.; 1848). Meigs (1792–1869) was Professor of Obstetrics and Diseases of Women at Jefferson Medical College in Philadelphia from 1841 to 1861.

[2] Commonwealth of Australia Department of Trades and Customs, Committee concerning causes of death and invalidity in the Commonwealth, *Report on Maternal Mortality in Childbirth*. Government Printer for the State of Victoria, 1916 (Melbourne, 1917), C. 7867.

[3] C. J. Cullingworth, *Oliver Wendell Holmes and the Contagiousness of Puerperal Fever* (London, 1906).

stated in 1907, 'We do no violence to statistics if we put down the septic mortality in England and Wales at between 3,000 and 5,000 per annum.'[4] In the decade 1920–9 some 25,000 women in England and Wales and at least a quarter of a million women in the USA died in childbirth, and it is probable that about half died as a direct or indirect result of puerperal sepsis. For a disease which was, in many cases, preventable 'by ordinary intelligence and careful training', these figures were indeed a reproach to civilized nations.

PUERPERAL FEVER: TERMINOLOGY AND FATALITY

For the historian of puerperal fever, one of the problems is the confusing list of nineteenth-century synonyms which reflected the passion for minutely detailed pathological description. They are listed in Appendix 2. In the early reports of the Registrar General for England and Wales puerperal fever first appeared as 'metria', but this obsolete term was soon replaced by 'puerperal fever'. By the end of the nineteenth century, however, the terms 'puerperal septicaemia' (which, strictly speaking, means infection of the bloodstream and was almost always fatal) and 'puerperal sepsis' began to replace 'puerperal fever'. The reason was simple. The term 'fever' was considered to be inappropriate. According to Arnold Lea puerperal fever was 'not a specific form of fever in lying-in women comparable to the exanthematous diseases'. He preferred the term 'puerperal infection', which he used as the title of his book, published in 1910.[5] Although it was to my mind the ideal term, it was, unfortunately, not generally adopted.

The two terms 'metria' and 'puerperal fever' referred solely to postnatal infection, the fever following childbirth or the 'fever of the puerperium'. From about 1900, however, in England and Wales (and in many other countries) 'puerperal sepsis' and 'puerperal septicaemia' came to include puerperal fever in the old sense combined with sepsis following abortion. It was not until 1931, following the adoption by England and Wales of the fourth revision of the International List of Causes of Death, that deaths due to septic abortion were shown separately. Thereafter, deaths due to puerperal fever in the old sense were usually categorized as 'non-abortive sepsis' as opposed to the other category, 'post-abortive sepsis'. I prefer and will for the most part use the terms 'post-partum sepsis' and 'post-abortive sepsis' as they make the distinction crystal clear. Before 1931, however, not only was it impossible to distinguish between the two quite separate conditions, but the very term 'puerperal sepsis' played havoc with notification rates and thus with fatality rates. Let me explain why.

For students of historical epidemiology, records of notification are poten-

---

[4] Sir William Sinclair, *A Plea for Establishing Municipal Maternity Homes* (London, 1907).
[5] Arnold W. W. Lea, *Puerperal Infection* (London, 1910).

tially of immense importance. Unlike mortality statistics, they were intended to record the incidence of a disease, and allow geographical and temporal changes in morbidity to be calculated. If notifications of incidence (morbidity) and deaths (mortality) are both available, fatality rates—the number of deaths per 100 or 1,000 cases—can be calculated. In the absence of effective treatment, changing fatality rates in infective disorders suggest one of two possibilities: changes in the susceptibility or resistance of the population, or changes in the virulence of the infective agent.[6]

Compulsory notification of certain infective diseases was introduced in England and Wales in 1899.[7] Medical practitioners were required to notify each new case of a notifiable disease to the local medical officer of health, and the statistics for the whole country were collated. One of the notifiable diseases was 'puerperal sepsis' which was listed as such without further definition. It caused utter confusion. Instead of notifying every case of puerperal infection, however slight, most doctors interpreted 'puerperal sepsis' as indicating only the most desperate septicaemic cases and many, not knowing what was intended, failed to notify any cases at all. The ridiculous result was that in many areas deaths from 'puerperal sepsis', actually exceeded notifications.

Fothergill calculated that in 1920, when there were about 2,000 deaths from puerperal sepsis, there may have been as many as 80,000 cases, giving a fatality rate of about 2.5 per cent. In ninety-three out of the total of 240 counties and county boroughs, however, there were 310 deaths and only 243 notified cases, giving a fatality rate of 127 per cent. As he rightly commented, 'twenty five years of compulsion has only secured comic figures'.[8]

---

[6] Gibberd suggested in 1931 that 'The "virulence" of an organism and "resistance" of the patient are to some extent reciprocal terms. The product of the two is roughly a constant...'. G. F. Gibberd, 'Streptococcal Puerperal Sepsis', *Guy's Hospital Reports*, 81 (1931) 29–44. The question of the changing virulence of the streptococcus is discussed in Appendix 5.

[7] Following the introduction of death registration in 1837, it soon became apparent that there were no records of the extent of disease—morbidity—although many institutions were collecting records which were, as one author put it, 'wasted records of disease'. Hence the introduction of a system whereby doctors reported, or 'notified', all new cases of certain infectious diseases. This was first introduced by local Acts in Huddersfield in 1876 and Bolton in 1877. In 1889 the Infectious Disease (Notification) Act was introduced on a voluntary basis and was adopted over a period of a few years by most sanitary districts. In 1899 an amending Act extended compulsory notification to the whole of England and Wales. For a brief account of the history of the notification of infectious diseases, see the historical introduction to *Reports of the Local Government Board on Public Health and Medical Subjects*, 'Statistics of the Incidence of Notifiable Infectious Diseases in each Sanitary District in England and Wales during the Year 1911', (London, 1912).

[8] W. E. Fothergill, 'Puerperal Pelvic Infection', *British Medical Journal* (1924), i. 773–4. Fothergill, Professor of Obstetrics and Gynaecology at Manchester, was equally sceptical of the accuracy of notifications of tuberculosis, and even more of notifications of syphilis and gonorrhoea. He may have overstated his case, but his scepticism is a warning against the acceptance of notifications as accurate measures of past morbidity. On the inaccuracy of puerperal fever notifications, see especially G. Geddes, *Puerperal Septicaemia: Its Causation, Symptoms, Prevention and Treatment* (Bristol, 1926).

Even in areas where notifications exceeded deaths, medical officers of health frequently found that numerous cases of puerperal fever which recovered had never been notified at all. As a result of exhortations to notify more cases, notifications increased in some areas but in an irregular and unpredictable fashion which rendered them useless. In Glasgow, for example, the MMR of puerperal fever rose from 20.5 per 10,000 births to 26 between the 1890s and the 1920s, but the fatality rate apparently dropped from 64.1 per cent to 25.3 per cent. This was certainly due not to a huge increase in incidence and thus to a real change in fatality, but to the artefact of an increase in the numbers notified.[9]

Although the inaccuracy and uselessness of notification was recognized as early as 1910, it was not until 1926 that it was decided that for purposes of case notification (but not, of course, for death registration) the term 'puerperal sepsis' would be replaced by the term 'puerperal pyrexia', defined as the presence of fever *regardless of cause* during the postnatal period.[10] As a result, for the calculation of the fatality rate the denominator was deaths due to puerperal sepsis, but the numerator was cases of puerperal sepsis plus cases of fever due to other causes which happened to occur during the postnatal period. And the incidence of these (feverish colds and influenza, for example) could, and did, vary widely with time and place. This unsatisfactory equation was made even worse by another complication which will be considered later in this chapter under the heading 'the bacteriology of puerperal fever'. Puerperal fever (or 'non-abortive sepsis') was unique amongst the notifiable diseases in that, from the bacteriological point of view, it was not one disease but several (see Tables 4.1 and 4.2) for it could be caused by a variety of bacteria. Moreover, the spectrum of bacteria which caused non-fatal cases was quite different from those causing fatalities. Therefore, even if it had been possible to notify all cases of puerperal fever and eliminate cases of pyrexia due to non-puerperal causes, the fatality rates would have been of very limited value. Fothergill's description of the statistics of notification as 'comic' was no exaggeration. Historians frequently have to make do with imperfect data; but the published national data on notification and fatality rates of puerperal fever, before and after 1926, are so unreliable that they are to all intents and purposes useless.

[9] Olive Checkland, 'Maternal and Child Welfare', in ead. and M. Lamb, *Health Care as Social History* (Aberdeen, 1982), 124.

[10] Ministry of Health, circular no. 722 (1926) noted that according to Statutory Rules and Orders 1926, no. 972, Public Health (England), puerperal pyrexia was to be defined as 'Any pyrexia . . . within 21 days of childbirth or miscarriage . . . of 100.4 °F which was sustained during a period of 24 hours or recurred during that period.' Public Record Office, Kew, MH 55/266. Almost exactly the same definition of puerperal pyrexia, with the recommendation that it should be adopted for purposes of notification, was put forward by the North Western Branch of the Society of Medical Officers of Health in 1910. Geddes, *Statistics of Puerperal Sepsis and Allied Infectious Diseases* (Bristol, 1912), 57–8. There were some minor amendments to the definition after 1926, but in substance it remained the same.

TABLE 4.1 *Ante-mortem Bacteriological Findings in a Series of 109 Cases of Puerperal Septicaemia analysed by the Puerperal Fever Sub-Committee of the North of England Obstetrical and Gynaecological Committee in 1925*

	Died	Recovered
Uterus (17 cases examined)		
Streptococci	8	3
Streptococci and Staphylococci	1	0
Streptococci and Colon bacilli	0	2
Staphylococci and Colon bacilli	1	0
Negative	1	1
Blood (54 cases examined)[a]		
Streptococci	31	3
Staphylococci	1	1
Streptococci and Staphylococci	1	0
Colon bacilli	0	1
Doubtful growth	2	0
Negative	9	5

[a] Streptococci were found in the blood in nearly 65% of the 54 cases.

Source: Royal College of Obstetricians and Gynaecologists, Archives. MS report in the Blair Bell papers, sect. S4.

THE CLINICAL COURSE OF PUERPERAL FEVER

In order to avoid confusion, I will, for historical reasons, use the term 'puerperal fever' in this chapter to describe what, after 1931, became known as 'non-abortive' or 'post-partum' sepsis. Puerperal fever is an illness which results from infection of the uterus during or after delivery. Very occasionally it occurred before delivery as a result of premature rupture of the membranes surrounding the foetus, or because of the intra-uterine death of the foetus, or both. But the vast majority of cases which occurred in the past began in the first or second week of the postnatal period. Typically, the uterus was infected during delivery, but the disease only became evident after a latent period, sometimes as short as one or two days, but usually four or five and sometimes longer. Almost all observers agreed the earlier the onset of the disease, the worse the prognosis.[11]

---

[11] 'The sooner after labour the symptoms are manifested, the more serious is our prognosis . . . .' W. Leishman, *A system of Midwifery* (Glasgow, 1876), 779.

TABLE 4.2 *Bacteriological Findings in 88 Cases of Puerperal Fever, Aberdeen, 1918–1927*

	Died	Recovered
1. Results obtained from one or more of the procedures of blood culture, uterine culture, or culture from secondary suppurative processes		
Streptococcus haemolyticus alone or in combination with other organisms	28	26
Staphylococcus		1
Stapylococcus and B. coli		4
Streptococcus viridans and B. coli		1
B. faecalis		1
B. coli		2
Gonococcus		1
B. alkalescens		1
All cultures sterile		22
No bacteriological evidence obtained	1	
Totals	29	59
2. Results of blood culture		
Streptococcus haemolyticus	22	6
Other organisms	0	3
Blood culture sterile	6	50
Blood culture not carried out	1	0
Totals	29	59

Source: Scottish Board of Health; J. Parlane Kinloch, J. Smith, and J. A. Stephens, *Maternal Mortality: Report on Maternal Mortality in Aberdeen, 1918–1927, with Special Reference to Puerperal Sepsis* (Edinburgh, 1928), 52–4.

The time of death could vary quite widely (Tables 4.3 and 4.4). Well over 90 per cent of deaths occurred before the forty-second postnatal day, and death was often dreadfully swift and appallingly distressing. A woman could be delivered on Monday, happy and well with her newborn baby on Tuesday, feverish and ill by Wednesday evening, delirious and in agony with peritonitis on Thursday, and dead on Friday or Saturday. Charles Meigs told his students:

You see gentlemen, there is no occasion to be surprised or astonished when, after having left your patient at ten o'clock in the evening, comfortable and apparently without any untoward symptom or accident, you find her, at six in the morning, a prey to the most unspeakable disorders of innervation, the respiration, and the circulation.[12]

---

[12] Meigs, *Females and their Diseases*, 597.

TABLE 4.3 *Deaths from Puerperal Septicaemia in Relation to time of Delivery, Canada, 1927–1928*

Time in relation to delivery	Number of deaths	% of total deaths	Cumulative percentage
under 1 day	20	3.8	3.8
Over 1 day, under 1 week	116	22.1	25.9
Over 1 week, under 2 weeks	193	36.8	62.7
Over 2 weeks, under 3 weeks	78	14.9	77.6
Over 3 weeks, under 4 weeks	61	11.6	89.2
Over 4 weeks	57	10.8	100.0
Total in which time of death was known	525	(100)	

Source: E. S. MacPhail, 'A Statistical Study in Maternal Mortality', *American Journal of Public Health*, 22 (1932), 612–26.

TABLE 4.4 *Deaths from Puerperal Septicaemia in Relation to Days after Delivery, Scotland, 1929–1933*

Days	Number of cases
1 and 2	0
3	3
4	4
5	5
6	11
7	16
8–14	107
15–21	61
22–28	43
29–35	17
36–42	8
43+	36
not stated	2

Source: C. A. Douglas and P. L. McKinlay, *Maternal Morbidity and Mortality in Scotland* (Edinburgh 1935), 179.

Once the infection had gained entry to the uterine cavity it could spread out into the pelvic tissue causing pelvic cellulitis, the pelvic veins leading to pelvic thrombophlebitis, the peritoneal cavity causing peritonitis. It could also spread into the bloodstream causing puerperal septicaemia. Sometimes the infection was localized in the pelvis, forming a pelvic abscess. But in most fatal cases, the cause of death was septicaemia or peritonitis, and often both together. Death from septicaemia was more merciful that the dreadful death from peritonitis. Meigs had seen patients in Philadelphia: 'who not only suffered intolerable pain, but in whose minds that pain appeared to excite the most unspeakable terror. I think I have seen women who appeared to be awe-struck with the dreadful force of their distress.'[13] Leishman described the course of the illness:

The belly swells further and becomes tense, with great aggravation of the suffering, so that the patient can now no longer bear even the pressure of the bedclothes . . . Low muttering delirium sets in . . . Hiccough, picking of the bedclothes and delirium are the immediate precursors of death.[14]

In 1795 Gordon (whose treatise is described below) described the agony of puerperal peritonitis as 'so excruciating that the miserable patients described their torture to be as great, or greater than, what they suffered during labour'.[15] Occasionally, and mercifully, the intense abdominal pain and rigidity suddenly ceased and the patient became calm. This was often a 'Harbinger of Death', giving false hope to the family.[16]

How common was puerperal peritonitis? I have the strong impression that puerperal peritonitis was more common in the nineteenth century than the twentieth. If true, I know of no explanation, but the impression seems to be supported by two reports. The first was published by Tonnellé at the Paris Maternité in 1830. He found evidence of peritonitis in 193 out of a series of 222 post-mortem dissections.[17] Nearly a century later an analysis of 109 cases of puerperal septicaemia was carried out by the North of England Obstetrical and Gynaecological Society in 1925. They found that clinical signs of peritonitis were present in 20 out of 83 cases which died, and 3 out of the 26 who survived. Post-mortem examination was carried out in 38 cases and evidence of peritonitis was found in 25 cases.[18]

In the nineteenth century the pathological cause of death in puerperal fever was not disputed. What was disputed, often with great ferocity, was the question of the contagiousness of the disease. No subject caused as much dissent as that with which the most famous name in the history of maternal mortality is associated, the Hungarian-born obstetrician Ignaz Semmelweis.

---

[13] Ibid. 596.

[14] Leishman, *A System of Midwifery*, 779–80.

[15] Alexander Gordon, *A Treatise on the Epidemic Puerperal Fever of Aberdeen* (London, 1795), 6.

[16] Ibid., and Meigs, *Females and their Diseases*.

[17] L. Tonellé, *Des fièvres puerpérales observés à la Maternité [de Paris] pendant l'année 1829* (Paris, 1830).

[18] This report can be found in the archives of the Royal College of Obstetricians and Gynaecologists amongst the Blair Bell papers, catalogue no. S.4.

THE CONTAGIOUSNESS OF PUERPERAL FEVER

It is a measure of the importance attached to the subject that in the 1870s the obstetrician Fordyce Barker estimated that in the past twenty years 20,000 pages had been published on various aspects of puerperal fever; and the part of the subject which dominated this vast literature was the question of contagion.[19] Today we tend to associate puerperal fever, if not the whole of maternal mortality, with three authors: Ignaz Semmelweis, Oliver Wendell Holmes, and Alexander Gordon of Aberdeen. All three wrote on the problem of contagion, Semmelweiss and Holmes in the 1840s and 1850s, and Gordon (the least well-known of the three) in 1795.

If priority is to be awarded to anyone it should be Gordon of Aberdeen. Even so, the possibility of contagion had been recognized, albeit dimly, since the seventeenth and eighteenth centuries. Outbreaks of puerperal fever were recorded in hospitals, and also in the form of epidemics which swept through towns such as Leipzig in 1652 and again in 1665. There were recurrent outbreaks in the wards of the Hôtel Dieu in Paris in 1664, and the maternity hospitals of Copenhagen in 1672, and there were epidemics in Rouen and Caen in 1713, in Frankfurt in 1723, and again in Paris in 1736.[20]

In British lying-in hospitals in the eighteenth century there were numerous outbreaks.[21] Gordon wrote of one in which 'none who were seized with it [puerperal fever] survived', and of another lasting thirty-two months in a London lying-in hospital during the 1750s in which almost all who contracted the fever died. He also mentioned an outbreak in the lying-in ward of an Edinburgh hospital in which 'all who were attacked with it in the epidemic season, died'. If we take these fatality rates at face value they are probably the worst on record, for it seems that when puerperal fever was epidemic—a feature which had disappeared by the twentieth century—the fatality rate was extraordinarily high. This, however, was not regarded as proof of contagion.

According to Hirsch, the observation that puerperal fever could be carried by doctors or midwives from one lying-in patient to another was first suggested by Denman in his *Introduction to the Practice of Midwifery* (2nd edn.) in 1788. Conclusive evidence of contagion, however, was first produced by Alexander Gordon of Aberdeen in 1795. What were the current ideas on the cause of puerperal fever before Gordon wrote his treatise?

[19] C. J. Cullingworth, *Puerperal Fever: A Preventable Disease* (London, 1888). See A. Hirsch, *Handbook of Geographical and Historical Pathology* (London, 1885), ii. 450–62, for a comprehensive account of the literature on the contagiousness of puerperal fever up to the 1860s. He summarized over 40 published accounts of the transmission of puerperal fever, and added that he could easily have trebled the number.

[20] J. A. F. Ozanam, *Histoire médicale, générale et particulière des maladies contagieuses et épizootiques* (Lyons, 1835), ii. 13–42.

[21] Hirsch, *Handbook of Geographical and Historical Pathology*. For an outstanding recent account of puerperal fever in the 18th cent., including hospital epidemics, see Margaret DeLacy, 'Puerperal Fever in Eighteenth-Century Britain', *Bulletin of the History of Medicine* (forthcoming).

CHARLES WHITE OF MANCHESTER

This question is most easily answered by reference to the well-known treatise on the management of pregnant and lying-in women written by Charles White, surgeon to the Manchester Infirmary, and published in 1773. White was clear in his own mind about the cause of puerperal fever.[22] It was caused by the carriage of putrid matter from the lower intestines to the womb. During pregnancy 'tight stays and petticoat bindings press the womb... against the lower intestines...' leading to costiveness and the passage of excrementitious matter into the circulation and the womb. Thus the cause of puerperal fever lay partly within the woman herself, and partly in the atmosphere she breathed, for it was customary for the patient to be attended by a crowd of women in a room with a large fire and every door and window closed to ensure she did not 'catch cold'. Curtains were drawn round the bed and pinned together. Every crevice, 'not excepting the key hole' was 'stopped close' creating putrid air and throwing the women into profuse sweats. To make matters worse she was fed hot drinks ('strong liquors, mixed with warm water').

To prevent puerperal fever, White insisted on throwing open the windows, in keeping away the attendant women, and on absolute cleanliness of the lying-in room and the bedclothes. Clean air, clean linen, and correct posture to allow exit of the stools and the lochia were the keys to prevention. Because of White's insistence on cleanliness, some have assumed he had contagion in mind. Nothing could be further from the truth. There is nothing in the whole of White's treatise to suggest the possibility of contagion and absolutely nothing about the cleanliness of the clothes or hands of the doctor in attendance. Where outbreaks of puerperal fever occurred, as in lying-in hospitals, he was sure it was due to the excessive putridity of the atmosphere. Without putridity, no outbreak would occur, a view which was in accordance with current ideas on the causation of fevers. It is against this background that we can understand how disturbing and how startling was the evidence produced only a few years later by an obscure Scottish practitioner in the far north of the country: the evidence of Gordon of Aberdeen.

ALEXANDER GORDON OF ABERDEEN

Alexander Gordon (1752–99), the son of a tenant farmer, attended Marischal College in Aberdeen, graduating AM in 1775. He then studied medicine at Aberdeen, Edinburgh, and probably at Leyden. From 1780 to 1785 he served as a naval surgeon, leaving on half-pay to spend nine months in London

---

[22] Charles White, *A Treatise on the Management of Pregnant and Lying-in Women* (London, 1773).

studying midwifery. When he returned to Aberdeen towards the end of 1785, he was certainly the best qualified if not the only accoucheur in the town. In 1786 he was appointed physician to the Aberdeen Dispensary, and later he instituted courses of instruction for midwives. In 1788 he was awarded the degree of MD by Marischal College.[23]

Puerperal fever was unknown in Aberdeen when a severe epidemic began in December 1789 and lasted until March 1792. At first the epidemic was thought to be no more than the common ephemeral fever known as the 'Weed', which was rarely fatal and for which the accepted regime was cordials, but never bleeding or purging. Gordon, however, recognized the epidemic as the puerperal fever which he had seen in London. By keeping careful and detailed notes he was able to make the crucial observation that the disease appeared to be confined to the practice of a minority of midwives. He was able to predict accurately which the next case of puerperal fever would be, simply by knowing which midwife had attended. He also realized that he himself had unwittingly carried the disease from one woman to another. From these observations he provided irrefutable evidence of what had so far been little more than a faint suspicion: that puerperal fever was a contagious disorder which could be carried by the birth-attendant from one lying-in woman to another. He also showed it was very closely linked with erysipelas.

In both conclusions he anticipated the findings of Holmes and Semmelweis by some fifty years. But he also came to believe that the only chance of cure was early and heavy bleeding and purging which, he said, were 'repugnant to popular opinion'. Partly because of his insistence on bleeding, and partly because he confessed that he himself had carried the disease, the women of Aberdeen turned against him. Hurt by 'the ungenerous treatment which I met with from that very sex whose sufferings I was at so much pains to relieve',[24] he was glad to leave Aberdeen when recalled to active duty in the Navy. Soon, however, he developed pulmonary tuberculosis and was invalided out. An ill man, he returned to his brother James's farm where he died at the early age of 47 on 19 October 1799.

After more than a century of relative obscurity, Gordon's treatise was eventually recognized as a masterpiece of early epidemiology, based on astute clinical observation and written with the clarity of a born writer. Ironically, when Gordon's work was mentioned in the nineteenth century it was to support or refute the idea that bleeding was the only effective remedy. His pioneer work on contagion was scarcely mentioned. Many practitioners were

---

[23] Alexander Gordon, *A Treatise on the Epidemic Puerperal Fever of Aberdeen* (London, 1795); I. H. Porter, *Alexander Gordon, MD, of Aberdeen*, Aberdeen Studies, 139 (Edinburgh, 1958); G. P. Milne, 'The History of Midwifery in Aberdeen', *Aberdeen University Review*, 47 (1978), 293–303; C. J. Cullingworth, *Oliver Wendell Holmes and the Contagiousness of Puerperal Fever* (London, 1906), 33–5.

[24] Gordon, *Treatise*, p. ix.

reluctant to admit the possibility that they themselves might be responsible for spreading the disease in the course of their practice. Nevertheless it would be wholly mistaken to believe Gordon's treatise was ignored. It was part of a steady accumulation of evidence during the fifty or so years that separated Gordon on the one hand from Semmelweis and Oliver Wendell Holmes on the other: evidence which practitioners realized, whatever their private views on contagion, it might be perilous to ignore.

SOME OTHER ACCOUNTS OF THE CONTAGIOUSNESS OF PUERPERAL FEVER

There are many examples of what was rightly regarded at the time as one of the most puzzling features of the contagiousness of puerperal fever. As Dr Armstrong of Sunderland wrote in 1813, 'It is a singular fact, that in whatever place the fever in question occurred, it was principally limited to the practice of one accoucheur in that place.'[25] Roberton found the same in 1831 when he described an epidemic of puerperal fever in Manchester in which the first sixteen cases (who all died) were confined to the practice of one midwife and none occurred in the practice of the other twenty-four.[26] In the same year (1831) Blackmore reported an epidemic in Plymouth in which one practitioner had eighteen cases of puerperal fever in rapid succession while the other practitioners in the town had none.[27] William Hey, Jr. described a similar epidemic in Leeds in a treatise published in 1815.[28]

In the same year as Hey of Leeds, Thomas West, a surgeon-apothecary of Abingdon in Berkshire, published a vivid account of an outbreak of puerperal fever in Abingdon and its vicinity which closely resembles Gordon's account in Aberdeen at the end of the eighteenth century. Starting in spring 1813, cases of erysipelas and puerperal fever began to appear in Abingdon. At first they were few, but they rapidly increased reaching a peak in the spring of 1814 when cases of puerperal fever 'generally commenced about 36 or 48 hours after delivery' (in other words, extremely early) and 'nearly all the cases were fatal'. Many of the midwives who attended lying-in women were attacked with erysipelas. Like Gordon in Aberdeen, West noticed that 'The commencement and termination of erysipelas and puerperal fever were nearly simultaneous . . . since September [1814] I know not of a single instance of these diseases.' West also observed that while many cases of erysipelas and

[25] J. Armstrong, 'Additional Facts and Observations Relative to the Puerperal Fever which Appeared at Sunderland and Several Places in 1813', *Edinburgh Medical and Surgical Journal*, 10 (1814), 444–50.

[26] John Roberton, *Essays and Notes on the Physiology and Diseases of Women* (London, 1851), and id., 'Is Puerperal Fever Infectious?', *Medical Gazette*, 9 (1831–2), 503–5.

[27] E. Blackmore, 'Observations on Puerperal Fever', *Provincial Medical and Surgical Journal*, 9 (1845), 173–8, 210–1.

[28] W. Hey, Jr., *A treatise on the Puerperal Fever* (London, 1815).

puerperal fever took place in some villages, other adjoining villages were totally free from either disease.[29] Scarlet fever was never mentioned in any of these accounts and the importance of this negative evidence is discussed in Appendix 5.

What is especially interesting is that Armstrong of Sunderland, Hey of Leeds, and West of Abingdon, were describing *simultaneous* epidemics of puerperal fever and erysipelas which occurred in 1813. Later we will note that this is one of the unrecognized but most interesting features of such epidemics; that on at least some occasions they broke out simultaneously all over the country. We return to this in connection with the outbreak of 1874. Taken together, these reports show that by the 1830s contagion was widely recognized (but not clearly understood) as one of the features of puerperal fever. In 1833, Robert Lee, a distinguished London obstetrician and author, had no doubt that contagion occurred, especially in institutions. He was one of the first to suggest the closure of lying-in hospitals, and he took great precautions in his own practice against spreading the disease.[30] By the 1830s even practitioners who did not believe in contagion found it politic to take the precaution of washing themselves and changing their clothes after attending a woman with puerperal fever or a case of erysipelas. Campbell of Edinburgh provided an unforgettable anecdote when writing in 1831 about puerperal fever in Edinburgh:

In October 1821, I assisted at the dissection of a woman who died of the disease, after an abortion of the early months; the pelvic viscera, with the external coats were removed, and I carried them *in my pocket* [my italics] to the class-room. The same evening, without changing my clothes, I attended the delivery of a poor woman in the Canongate; she died. Next morning I went in the same clothes to assist some of my pupils who were engaged with a woman in Bridewell, whom I delivered by forceps; she died.[31]

By the 1840s, then, although Gordon's treatise was rarely cited as evidence of contagion, it was widely recognized that if a doctor or midwife attended a case of puerperal fever, or if a doctor attended a case of erysipelas or conducted a post-mortem examination on a woman who had died of puerperal fever, that doctor or midwife could carry the disease to another midwifery case. Moreover, the danger could usually be averted by a complete change of clothes and thorough washing. This was the situation before the work of Oliver Wendell Holmes to whom we come next. But there was no explanation for the puzzling but well-known feature—the tendency for one practitioner to

[29] T. West, 'Observations on some Diseases, particularly Puerperal Fever, which Occurred in Abingdon and its Vicinity in 1813 and 1814', *London Medical Repository*, 2 (1815), 103–5.
[30] Robert Lee, *Researches on the Pathology and Treatment of some of the Most Important Diseases of Women* (London, 1833).
[31] W. Campbell, 'On Puerperal Fever', *Medical Gazette*, 9 (1831), 354.

be dogged by a series of cases of puerperal fever while others no more careful or competent escaped scot-free. That was a total mystery.

OLIVER WENDELL HOLMES AND PUERPERAL FEVER

In the summer of 1842, Oliver Wendell Holmes (1809–94), poet and physician, attended a meeting of the Boston Society for Medical Improvement. The meeting came to an end of its stated business earlier than usual. Dr Condie, a member of the Society and a senior physician in Philadelphia, begged leave 'as there appeared to be no other written communications to be presented' to give an account of 'the prevalence at the present time of puerperal fever of a peculiarly insidious and malignant character'. Puerperal fever was, he said:

A disease which had been found to occur alike in the young and the middle aged—the robust and the delicate—in those surrounded by every comfort and afforded every attention demanded by their situation, as in the poor and the destitute—as well as those who were confined for the first time, as in those who had already borne a number of children—and as well after the most rapid and easy labors, as after those that were protracted and difficult.[32]

Dr Condie did not believe puerperal fever was usually contagious, but it was a disease 'which was capable of being communicated by contagion'. How else, he said, could one explain 'the very curious circumstance' of the disease being confined to the practice of a single physician, 'a Fellow of this College, extensively engaged in obstetrical practice', while there were no cases in the practices of other practitioners in the same district. He was referring to Dr Rutter.

Dr Rutter of Philadelphia, a pupil of Charles Meigs, had a large obstetric practice. From all accounts he was a competent practitioner, as careful and skilled as any in the town. During the 1840s, however, for no apparent reason he found that every midwifery case he attended developed puerperal fever. The effect on his reputation can be imagined, especially when colleagues, no more careful, experienced, or competent than himself, had only sporadic cases in their practices or none at all. Greatly distressed, Rutter ceased practice and quarantined himself for several weeks. He washed frequently and thoroughly. His head and face were shaved. He changed all his clothing and all the equipment he carried with him in his practice, down to the pencil he carried for taking notes. 'Dr Rutter did all this, yet puerperal fever [still] followed him wherever he went, till, worn out and disappointed, he left Philadelphia a disheartened man.'[33]

---

[32] *Transactions of the College of Physicians of Philadelphia*, 1 (1841–6), 50–2.
[33] J. S. Parry, 'Description of a Form of Puerperal Fever', *American Journal of Medical Sciences*, 69 (1875), 46–76.

Sitting in the audience, Holmes's curiosity was aroused and he decided to see for himself 'what experience had to teach in the matter'.[34] The result was his famous paper on the contagiousness of puerperal fever which he read to the Boston Society for Medical Improvement on 13 February 1843. Unfortunately, the paper was published in a journal which had a very restricted circulation and died out within a year, but Holmes republished his work as a pamphlet in 1855.[35] Therefore, before 1855 Holmes's conclusions were not widely known, and after 1855 his growing fame as a poet and writer eclipsed his essay on puerperal fever.

Holmes was 33 when he read his paper and still a relatively obscure young physician. In 1847 he was appointed to the Parkman Professorship of Anatomy and Physiology in the Medical school of Harvard University, which he described as 'not so much a chair as a whole settee', the anatomical portion of which he retained for thirty-six years.[36] Unlike Gordon and Semmelweis, Holmes's work was not based on his own clinical experience or observations. It is an essay based on an extremely thorough search of the literature on puerperal fever, so clear and so beautifully written that it richly deserves its position amongst the classics of medical literature. It is the work of a man who loved writing, who was old enough to marshal his material skilfully but young enough to be passionate and angry and to let these qualities show. His main thesis was this (with the original emphasis): '*The disease known as puerperal fever is so far contagious as to be frequently carried from patient to patient by physicians and nurses.*'[37] He had no idea how it was carried. It might be on the clothes or hands of the physician, or in the atmosphere which surrounded him; but the evidence that it could be carried from one midwifery case to another was overwhelming. He cited many instances which resembled the experience of the unfortunate Dr Rutter. Dr Jackson of Northumberland County, Pa., for instance, who had also suffered a spate of successive midwifery cases who developed puerperal fever, found that: 'Women who had expected me to attend upon them, now becoming alarmed, removed out of my reach, and others sent for physicians residing several miles distant. These women . . . all did well.' Another was Dr Storer of Boston, who deserves mention because he anticipated Semmelweis by several years. Following a similar experience of being dogged by puerperal fever, he decided to wash his hands routinely after every midwifery case in a solution of chloride of lime. He then attended seven women in succession, none of whom developed the disease.[38]

---

[34] Cullingworth, *Oliver Wendell Holmes and the Contagiousness of Puerperal Fever* (London, 1906). This is still probably the best critical account of Holmes and puerperal fever.
[35] Holmes, 'On the Contagiousness of Puerperal Fever', *New England Quarterly Journal of Medicine*, I (1842–3), 503–30; id., *Puerperal Fever as a Private Pestilence* (Boston, 1855).
[36] Cullingworth, *Oliver Wendell Holmes*, 20.
[37] Holmes, *Puerperal Fever as a Private Pestilence*.
[38] Ibid. 43.

In spite of the overwhelming evidence, Holmes could find no explanation for the wide disparity in the incidence of the disease. Many practitioners never saw a case of puerperal fever, or had only one in five hundred or more consecutive deliveries. Other saw them only when called in consultation and not in their own practice, while a few like the unfortunate physicians quoted above might see as many as seventy in a year. Could anything be more mysterious?

In the view of these facts, it does appear a singular coincidence that one man or woman should have ten, twenty, thirty, or seventy cases of this rare disease, following their footsteps like a beagle through the streets and lanes of a crowded city, while the scores that cross the same paths on the same errands know it only by name.

Holmes concluded that any physician who found he had a series of three or more cases of puerperal fever when others had none should regard it as prima-facie evidence that he was the vehicle of contagion.

The time has come when the existence of a *private pestilence* in the sphere of a single physician should be looked upon not as a misfortune but a crime; and in the knowledge of such occurrences, the duties of the practitioner in his profession, should give way to his paramount obligations to society.

His use of the word 'crime' was, perhaps, a tactless indictment of his colleagues. Certainly it was too much for Charles Meigs who, at the age of 51, was a highly experienced and careful obstetrician with a large private practice and a popular and persuasive teacher. Since it is likely that Holmes had little if any practical knowledge of midwifery, it is not surprising that Meigs regarded Holmes as a conceited young upstart.[39] Meigs took deep offence at the suggestion that he or his senior colleagues could have been responsible for spreading such a terrible and agonizing disease. To his dying day he denied the possibility that puerperal fever was a contagious disease. For this he came to be ridiculed, not so much for his denial of contagion—honest differences of opinion were acceptable—as for the offensiveness of his attacks on Holmes. In the end, Meigs's reputation suffered and eclipsed his contributions as a teacher and writer. Ironically, Meigs admired Gordon of Aberdeen because of the latter's advocacy of heavy bleeding in the treatment of puerperal fever, with which Meigs persisted when others were abandoning venesection. Holmes's other great opponent, Professor Hodge, who also held a chair of obstetrics in Philadelphia, was of like opinion. On this subject, Boston and Philadelphia were at odds with each other.[40]

[39] Cullingworth, *Oliver Wendell Holmes*, 2 n.
[40] Meigs was not alone. The few scattered references to Gordon's work in the British medical periodicals of the first half of the 19th cent. are mostly concerned with Gordon's belief in the merits of bleeding. See e.g. *London Medical Surgical and Pharmaceutical Repository*, 18 (1822), 324; *London Medical and Physical Journal*, 50 (1823), 218, 303, 304; and *Medico-Chirurgical Transactions*, 16 (1830), 437, 442.

IGNAZ SEMMELWEIS AND PUERPERAL FEVER

According to the popular notion, Semmelweis was the first person to discover the cause of puerperal fever and the first to show it was a contagious disease. He discovered antisepsis and by doing so abolished puerperal fever in Vienna. But his discovery was ignored and it was only the ignorance and obstinate stupidity of doctors that prevented the abolition of puerperal fever elsewhere. He died a disappointed man from blood-poisoning or disappointment or both. The only true statement in that version is that Semmelweis ended his life in disappointment.[41]

In 1843, when Holmes published his essay on the contagiousness of puerperal fever, Semmelweis had not yet graduated. It was not until 1846 that he was appointed assistant in the Vienna Maternity Hospital and made his first observations on puerperal fever. Semmelweis's work was first published by Hebra in 1847–8 but he did not publish anything himself until 1858. His famous treatise: *The Aetiology, Concept and Prophylaxis of Childbed Fever* was not published until 1861. Surprisingly there is no evidence that Semmelweis knew of the work of Holmes, Gordon, or any of the numerous British authors who had published papers before the 1840s on the contagiousness of puerperal fever.[42]

Ignaz Semmelweis, the son of a grocer, was born in Taban (now part of Budapest) in 1818. Initially he intended to study law but changed to medicine, receiving his doctorate in the University of Vienna in 1844. The hospital to which he was appointed in 1846, the Vienna Maternity Hospital, was enormous. By the 1850s and 1860s it catered for about 8,000 patients a year compared with around 200–300 in the General Lying-in Hospital in London and the Boston Lying-in Hospital in Massachusetts, and around 500 in the New York Lying-in Hospital. No other hospital in the world had such a high reputation for teaching obstetrics. Not only medical students and midwives, but doctors from all over the world came to attend courses of instruction. There was no shortage of cases and pupils had ample opportunity for examining women in labour—a process in which frequent vaginal examinations were considered good practice—and for post-mortem dissection.

In 1833 the Maternity Hospital was divided into two clinics. Medical students and midwives attended both clinics. From 1840 the first clinic was reserved for the instruction of medical students and doctors, the second for midwives. Patients were admitted to the two clinics on alternate days, producing, unintentionally, a system of random allocation. There was no selection of complicated cases for the first clinic and uncomplicated for the second.

---

[41] The main source for this account is Ignaz Semmelweis, *The Aetiology, Concept, and Prophylaxis of Childbed Fever*, ed., trans., and with an introd. by K. Codell Carter, Wisconsin Publications in the History of Science and Medicine (1983). I am much indebted to Codell Carter's excellent and perceptive introduction.

[42] Cullingworth, *Oliver Wendell Holmes*, 2 n.

When Semmelweis was appointed assistant physician it was already well known that the mortality rate from puerperal fever was higher in the first clinic than the second and many explanations were suggested, mostly in terms of differences in the putridity of the atmosphere. It was the death of a colleague following a minor injury during a post-mortem examination that provided Semmelweis with his first insight into the real reason for the difference and showed the connection between post-mortem dissection and puerperal fever. At the Vienna Maternity Hospital it was the custom for medical students to attend post-mortem examinations of women who died of puerperal fever before walking over to the labour wards where they undertook numerous vaginal examinations in labour as part of their routine training. Like Dr Campbell of Edinburgh they saw no reason to wash their hands, and, of course, rubber gloves were not worn. Nor were white coats. Everyone wore their ordinary daytime clothes.[43]

Semmelweis had attended the post-mortem examination of Dr Kolletschka, the colleague who died from septicaemia following the post-mortem dissection, and had been impressed by the similarity of certain pathological lesions to those seen routinely in women dying from puerperal fever. 'Suppose', he wrote, 'cadaverous particles adhering to the hands cause the same disease among maternity patients that cadaverous particles adhering to the knife caused in Kolletschka.' Was this the cause of puerperal fever, and if it was, how could these cadaverous particles be neutralized?[44] The answer was to use a chemical to destroy or render safe the morbid matter. So, from May 1847, he insisted that his pupils washed their hands in disinfectant before attending the labour wards. At first he used *chlorina liquida* and then, when that proved expensive, he used chlorinated lime. The results can be seen in Table 4.5. Maternal mortality in the first clinic fell to a level close to that of the second (midwives') clinic.[45]

The results of chlorine washing were decisive. To Semmelweis they were proof that the etiology of puerperal fever was the transfer of *morbid matter* from the post-mortem room to the maternity clinic. Semmelweis had great

---

[43] Semmelweis wrote: 'Clothing could also cause childbed fever if, for example, the cuffs of one's jacket is contaminated with decaying matter and contacts the genitals during birth'. *Aetiology, Concept, and Prophylaxis*, 150.

[44] Ibid. 89.

[45] In fact, the fall in mortality in the first clinic was even larger than the table suggests. Before Semmelweis's reforms it was the custom in the first clinic to remove some of the ill maternity patients to the general hospital during times of high mortality. When transferred patients died they were entered as deaths in the general hospital rather than the maternity clinic. Thus: 'The reports show reduced mortality [in the first clinic] since only those who could not be transferred because of the rapid course of their illness were included. In the second clinic such transfers were never undertaken, and the transfer of ill patients was greatly reduced after the reforms were introduced. In short, the mortality of the first clinic between 1841 and 1846, high though it was, would have been even higher if the deaths of all the transferred patients had been included, as they should have been.' Ibid. 65.

TABLE 4.5 *The Maternal Mortality Rate per 1,000 Births in the Two Clinics of the Vienna Maternity Hospital before and after the Introduction of Semmelweis's Reforms*

Year	First clinic	Second clinic
1833	52.9	22.6
1834	77.1	86.0
1835	55.5	49.9
1836	74.7	78.4
1837	90.9	69.9
1838	30.4	49.4
1839	50.4	40.5
1840	90.5	20.6
Average 1833–40[a]	65.3	55.2
1841	77.0	35.0
1842	158.0	75.0
1843	89.0	59.0
1844	82.0	23.0
1845	68.0	20.3
1846	114.0	27.0
Average 1841–6[b]	98.0	39.9
1847	50.0	9.6
1848	12.7	13.3
1849	20.6	20.5
1850	10.9	10.6
1851	10.7	30.5
1852	40.0	50.7
1853	20.2	10.9
1854	91.0	61.8
1855	54.1	59.2
Average 1847–55[c]	34.5	29.7

[a] Medical students, doctors, and midwives attending in both clinics.

[b] Medical students and doctors in first clinic; midwives only in second clinic.

[c] Medical students and doctors in first clinic; midwives in second clinic. From May 1847, hand-washing in chloride of lime by all students and doctors attending patients in the first clinic.

Source: Ignaz Semmelweis, *The Etiology, Concept and Prophylaxis of Childbed Fever*, trans. K. Codell Carter (University of Wisconsin Press, 1983), 64 and 131.

difficulty in explaining the connection between puerperal fever and erysipelas until he concluded that erysipelas must produce decaying, and therefore morbid, matter. Once he had made this conceptual step he was able to create his unitary hypothesis, and this, in a way, was his downfall. He criticized English physicians for limiting themselves to erysipelas and failing to understand that morbid matter could come from anywhere. 'Every corpse,' he said, 'no matter what the cause of death, produces matter that can cause childbed fever.' A veterinary surgeon who was also an obstetrician, he said, could transfer childbed fever from dead animals. Every case of puerperal fever was due to the absorption of morbid or decaying matter. There was no other cause.[46]

It may be argued that although Semmelweis came to a false conclusion, at least in practical terms he abolished deaths from puerperal fever. In fact, what he succeeded in doing was to reduce the MMR in the first clinic from the monstrously high levels of 900 and more per 10,000 births to the still very high levels that prevailed in both clinics in the 1850s of about 300 per 10,000 births. A rate of 300 was six times as high as the rate in England and Wales during the same period, and fifteen times as high as the rate achieved by London's Royal Maternity Charity for the period 1842–64, based on 13,783 home deliveries amongst the poor of the East End.[47] This is the context in which his achievement should be seen. Were it not for its prestige as a teaching institution, there would still have been strong arguments for closing the Vienna Maternity Hospital as 'truly an institution of death'.[48]

Semmelweis's work was known in Britain. Simpson had heard of it in 1848,[49] probably from a London doctor named Routh who had worked at the Vienna clinic and kept in touch with Semmelweis after he had returned to England. Routh gave an account of Semmelweis's discovery to the Royal Medico-Chirurgical Society in 1849 when the results of chlorine washing had just become known.[50] There is no evidence it was regarded as an important advance. Indeed, Semmelweis's work had little impact in Britain, Holmes's essay was still 'largely forgotten' even at the end of the nineteenth century, and Alexander Gordon was almost totally forgotten until the twentieth century.[51]

[46] Ibid. 148.

[47] J. Hall Davis, *Parturition and its Difficulties* (London, 1865).

[48] The phrase comes from the comment of a student of Semmelweis who was then working in Pest: 'At one examination the city physician exclaimed that the maternity hospitals are truly institutions of death. I asked a school servant what could have been meant by such a remark. He answered, as if it was the most trivial affair in the world, "Oh well, right now there are a couple more in there on a slab, like fish".' *Aetiology, Concept, and Prophylaxis*, 215.

[49] National Library of Medicine, Bethesda, MS collection. Correspondence between Francis Henry Ramsbotham and James Young Simpson. MC 22.

[50] C. H. F. Routh, 'On the Causes of the Endemic Puerperal Fever of Vienna', *Medico-chirurgical Transactions*, 14 (2nd ser.) (1849), 27–39.

[51] Cullingworth, *Oliver Wendell Holmes*.

THE NEGLECT OF GORDON, HOLMES, AND SEMMELWEIS

Why did the work of these three men have so little impact? All three knew they had made important discoveries. Semmelweis's work has a special appeal to medical scientists today because of his method, pathological observation, and scientific deduction leading to a clinical trial on an unselected group of patients. It feels so modern, so far ahead of its time that doctors today find it hard to understand why his views were not immediately and universally hailed as a major discovery. Semmelweis himself said that his work, if properly appreciated, could have saved as many lives as Jenner's discovery of smallpox vaccination. So what went wrong?

In part Semmelweis was ignored because he took so long to publish his monograph. Those who thought they knew about his work from other sources did not bother to read his long, plodding, and pugnaciously self-justifying book. This, however, was not the only reason. The key to understanding why his work had so little impact lies in the way diseases were described and defined in the mid-nineteenth century.[52]

By the 1840s, Western medical thought was becoming dominated by advances in pathology derived from post-mortem examinations and the correlation of symptoms and signs in life with autopsy findings. Diseases were not defined by cause, but by internal structural lesions which could be established at post-mortem. Most diseases were attributed to multiple and non-specific causes, making aetiology an impossible basis for defining and differentiating diseases. Lobar pneumonia, for instance, was defined in the mid-nineteenth century as a disease of the lungs in which one or more lobes of the lung were inflamed and solidified. If one asked about the causes of pneumonia, the answers would have been many and non-specific; for example, colds, chills, putrid air, the patient's constitution, diet, and so on. All or any of these were potentially causative factors not just of pneumonia but of numerous other diseases.

When the pneumococcus was discovered, however, lobar pneumonia acquired an alternative description. It became known as 'pneumococcal pneumonia'. A single cause had been identified which provided not only a new name but also a precise definition of the disease, allowing doctors to devise logical strategies for prevention or treatment.

So it was with puerperal fever before the discovery and identification of the streptococcus. In the mid-nineteenth century the post-mortem lesions of puerperal fever were established in the most minute detail; but the causes were thought to be many. They included putrid air, epidemic influences, tight stays, difficult labours, overcrowding in hospitals, and so on. That some cases

---

[52] In writing the whole of this section I was influenced by Codell Carter's introduction to his translation of Semmelweis's monograph.

were due to contagion was undeniable. But it was not very important because it was irrelevant to the large majority of sporadic cases occurring in home deliveries. Contagion was therefore an *occasional* cause, but not a *necessary* cause. It seemed futile to suggest that puerperal fever could be attributed to a single cause, yet this is just what Semmelweis was suggesting for puerperal fever when he insisted it was due to the absorption of morbid or decaying matter. In the special case of post-mortem examinations there was no doubt he was right, and in that respect he carried his audience with him. But when he said there must be absorption of decaying matter in *all* cases, and said so without providing a shred of evidence, he lost the support of even his most ardent followers, for he had failed to explain why sporadic cases often followed normal home deliveries, why the disease could occur in epidemics, and why it sometimes dogged the footsteps of some doctors or midwives and not others. It had been known for a long time that puerperal fever could be spread by contagion. There was the work of Gordon, Holmes, Hey of Leeds, Armstrong of Sunderland, and many others, which we have noted above. In this respect Semmelweis had not made an original discovery. And although he was undoubtedly right to insist on disinfection following a post-mortem examination, there was nothing to suggest that disinfecting the hands was of any importance in ordinary everyday obstetric practice. Because Semmelweis's insistence on a unitary hypothesis was unacceptable, his work was judged to be flawed and at best of limited importance. He died a disappointed man, not of septicaemia, but almost certainly of Alzheimer's disease.[53]

PUERPERAL FEVER AND ERYSIPELAS

This is a part of the story of puerperal fever which has largely been neglected. It has the virtue that, like a spotlight in the wings, it provides an indirect illumination, showing features which are easily missed if erysipelas is ignored.

For those unfamiliar with the disease, it should be explained that erysipelas is a wound infection. The wound may be gross and obvious, or it may be a slight nick in the skin at the edge of the mouth, the nose, the shin, the head, or anywhere else, so small as to be virtually invisible. The disease begins as a red flush of the affected area and progresses to a painful swelling of increasing size. The infective organism is always the streptococcus pyogenes, the same organism (and in my opinion the same strains—see Appendix 5) that was the cause of the vast majority of deaths due to puerperal fever. In severe cases the

---

[53] From about 1861 there are clear signs that Semmelweis was suffering from nervous irritability (which may well account for the testiness of the later part of his treatise) which was probably an early sign of the onset of Alzheimer's disease. There is the pathetic story that in July 1865, when he was due to read a report to a faculty meeting, 'He rose, took a piece of paper from his trouser pocket and, to the stupefaction of those present, began to read the text of the midwives' oath.' His colleagues took him home, he was admitted to a mental home, and died on 13 Aug. 1865, aged 47. *Aetiology, Concept, and Prophylaxis*, 56.

disease progresses to produce high fever, septicaemia, and death. This was the disease whose connection with puerperal fever was shown in 1795 by Gordon in a passage of characteristic clarity:

That the Puerperal Fever is of the nature of erysipelas, was supposed by Peautau forty years ago and has been the opinion of Doctors Young and Home of Edinburgh, since that time. I will not venture positively to assert that the Puerperal Fever and Erysipelas are precisely of the same specific nature; but that they are connected, that there is an analogy between them, and that they are concomitant epidemics I have unquestionable proofs. For these two epidemics began in Aberdeen at the same time, and afterwards kept pace together; they both arrived at their *acmè* together and they both ceased at the same time.[54]

As we have seen, Gordon's evidence was confirmed by numerous accounts of deaths from puerperal fever in patients whose medical attendant had attended a case of erysipelas. In 1844 Dr Elkington of Birmingham was called urgently to a case of placenta praevia when he was attending a case of erysipelas. He was forced by the urgency of the case to ' "turn and deliver" without loss of time'. The next day his patient was 'very comfortable' but she was 'attacked with fever' the following day and died three days later.[55] Dr Ingleby of Birmingham also attended a series of confinements after he had treated a case of erysipelas. All developed puerperal fever, and only one survived.[56]

Not everyone was of the same mind, not, at least, about the contagious element. In 1819, Weatherhead published an essay in which he stated that puerperal fever is 'purely an erysipelatous affection'. The choice of the word 'affection' was deliberate, because he did not believe it was contagious. He came to that opinion through an experiment on himself. He abraded the skin of his forearm and then wrapped the abraded area in a moistened bandage which had 'surrounded a lump violently affected with erysipelas'. Call him brave or call him foolish, he was certainly lucky. Nothing happened. He concluded 'the infection is first received into the system by the lungs or otherwise'.[57]

Today, erysipelas is always sporadic, and (with very few exceptions) easily cured with antibiotics. Until the mid-nineteenth century, erysipelas was quite different. It was virulent, and it often occurred in epidemics, sweeping through towns and villages with fatalilty rates of 10 per cent or more. There are well-documented epidemics in the USA from the 1840s to the 1860s, and

---

[54] Gordon, *A Treatise on Epidemic Puerperal Fever*, 55.

[55] F. Elkington, 'Observations on the Contagiousness of Puerperal Fever', *Provincial Medical Journal*, 7 (1844), 287–8. The phrase 'turn and deliver' was a reference to the technique of internal version which was standard (and often effective) practice in cases of placenta praevia.

[56] Ibid. For a list of similar published case-reports, see Hirsch, *Handbook of Geographical and Historical Pathology*, ii. 466–71.

[57] G. H. Weatherhead, *An Essay on the Diagnosis between Erysipelas. Phlegmon, and Erythema, with an Appendix Touching on the Probable Nature of Puerperal Fever* (London, 1819).

many accounts of earlier epidemics.[59] Erysipelas in its epidemic form and also in the form of sporadic cases which could not be attributed to gross or obvious wounds—erysipelas, in other words that appeared to come 'out of the blue'—was known as 'true erysipelas' or '*érysipèle légitime*' to distinguish it from the more common surgical form of erysipelas, a septic complication of an open wound.[59] Through the nineteenth and early twentieth centuries, the age distribution of cases of *érysipèle légitime* changed extensively. In the eighteenth century it appeared to be a disease of all ages. During the nineteenth century it became increasingly a disorder of the extremes of life, a disorder of infancy and old age. By the 1920s, however, cases in infancy were becoming increasingly rare leaving erysipelas as it is today, primarily a disorder of old age.

When epidemics occurred in the past, they were often associated with epidemics of puerperal fever, especially in hospitals where epidemics of erysipelas were the bane of surgical wards. Frequently, an outbreak of erysipelas on a surgical ward was followed by an outbreak of puerperal fever in the lying-in wards in the same hospital because the surgical and lying-in wards were often served by the same staff. It was a powerful argument for building maternity hospitals which were separate from general hospitals.[60] There is, then, a mass of historical evidence pointing to a close link between erysipelas and puerperal fever. We can take this a stage further by using the Registrar General's statistics to see exactly how close this link was. The importance of this will become clear.

The most conspicuous fluctuations in annual death rates from puerperal fever occurred in the late nineteenth century (Fig. 4.1). Figure 4.2 covers the twenty years from 1860 to 1879. It shows mortality rates from puerperal fever, erysipelas, and scarlet fever. Deaths from puerperal fever are shown as deaths per 1,000 births, and also as deaths per million people living to ensure comparability. For each disease the mean death rate for the whole period of twenty years was calculated and is represented as a straight line with the rate at the end. Then the rate for each year was calculated and expressed as a percentage above or below the mean. The result is striking. There is a remarkably close correspondence between the peaks and troughs of puerperal fever and erysipelas, but only a loose correspondence between these two and scarlet fever.[61]

---

[58] Hirsch, *Handbook of Geographical and Historical Pathology*, ii. 389–415.

[59] Ibid. 391.

[60] Ibid. Vol. ii lists a number of concomitant epidemics of puerperal fever and erysipelas. The most important 20th-cent. paper on the problem of lying-in wards in a general hospital is J. B. DeLee and H. Siedentopf, 'The Maternity Ward of the General Hospital', *Journal of the American Medical Association*, 100 (1933), 6–14.

[61] It might be thought that these fluctuations in mortality were simply a reflection of a similar pattern in deaths in women of childbearing age from all causes, but an analysis of this possibility showed it not to be the case. The pattern of peaks and troughs shown in Fig. 4.2 was specific to streptococcal disease. Longstaff (as I was to discover later) had carried out a similar calculation in

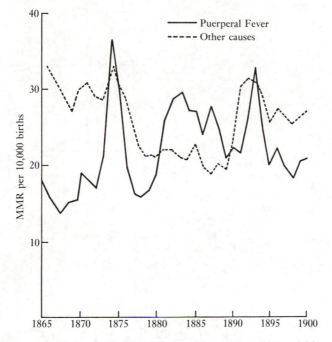

FIG. 4.1 England and Wales, 1865–1900. Showing the trend in Maternal Mortality due to puerperal fever and other causes
Source: Registrar General for England and Wales, *Annual Reports*.

Figure 4.3 shows the trends in annual rates of deaths between 1911 and 1945 for puerperal fever and erysipelas in the upper graph, and for puerperal fever and scarlet fever in the lower one. Once again the close correspondence between puerperal fever and erysipelas is striking, while puerperal fever and scarlet fever followed different paths.[62]

In 1893, Robert Boxall, Assistant Obstetrician to the Middlesex Hospital, surveyed maternal mortality from 1847 to 1892, noted the conspicuous 1874 peak, and found that 'the main element of variation from year to year is attributable to puerperal fever or metria'.[63] He also noted something that has puzzled several observers and can be seen in Figure 4.1: that the trend in maternal deaths from other puerperal causes tended roughly to follow the trend in deaths due to puerperal fever, but did so at a more modest level.

1875. He concluded 'that the curves of [the mortality rates of] erysipelas and puerperal fever are practically identical ... I confess that I find it difficult to avoid the conclusion that they are both due to one poison'. G. B. Longstaff, 'On Some Statistical Indications of a Relationship between Scarlatina, Puerperal Fever and Certain other Conditions', *Transactions of the Epidemiological Society of London*, 4 (1875–81), 421–32.

[62] See App. 5.
[63] R. Boxall, 'On the Mortality of Childbirth', *Lancet* (1892), ii. 9–15.

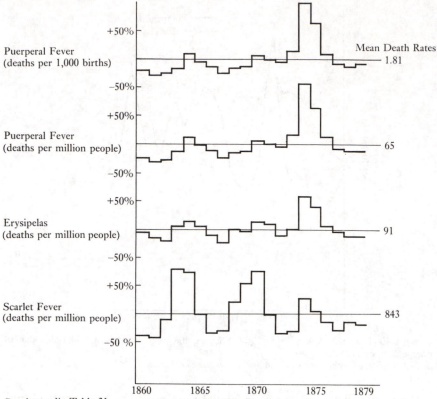

See Appendix Table 31

FIG. 4.2 England and Wales, 1860–1879. Deaths per million people living, due to scarlet fever, erysipelas, and puerperal fever. Death rates shown as the mean value for the whole period of twenty-five years and as the percentage variation above or below the mean in each year
Source: Registrar General for England and Wales, *Annual Reports*.

Boxall's explanation, which had the advantage of being based on direct observation, was:

As many of the cases returned under the head of 'accidents of childbirth' are liable to be complicated by, and to succumb ultimately to, septic mischief, it follows that in those years where the mortality from puerperal fever is greatest, this liability is increased, and *vice versa*.[64]

In other words, a high incidence of sepsis made it more likely that women who were rendered seriously ill by other complications such as haemorrhage would die if they also contracted infection. And if they died under circum-

[64] Ibid.

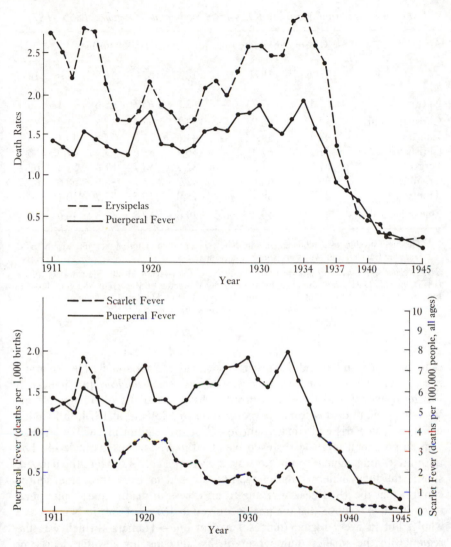

Fig. 4.3 England and Wales, 1911–1945. Death rates from erysipelas and scarlet fever per 100,000 people of all ages, and the maternal mortality rate per 1,000 births due to puerperal fever *Source*: Registrar General for England and Wales, *Annual Reports* and *Statistical Reviews*.

stances in which it was clear, for example, that post-partum haemorrhage and puerperal fever both played a part, most doctors would choose to certify such deaths as being due to haemorrhage in order to avoid the opprobrium attached to deaths from puerperal fever.

Boxall also made another very interesting observation. He noted that the 1874 peak appeared not only for England and Wales as a whole but in just the

TABLE 4.6 *Maternal Mortality Rates in Norway and its regions, 1866–1877*

Area	Maternal mortality rates (deaths per 10,000 births)							
	1866–70	1871	1872	1873	1874	1875	1876	1877
Norway	62.3	67.7	—	62.5	85.6[a]	65.6	70.1	56.4
Christiana Stift	54.1	58.7	—	57.1	83.5	57.8	61.3	37.3
Hamars	42.9	54.4	—	44.6	71.3	75.4	49.1	26.4
Christianasands	71.2	67.4	—	56.4	81.6	63.4	67.9	60.2
Bergens	61.6	81.5	—	82.7	88.7	81.6	85.4	67.4
Trondheim	66.1	62.6	—	62.2	77.9	48.0	68.6	62.7
Tromsø	87.7	88.1	—	78.0	119.5	77.7	10.1	10.6
England and Wales[b]	45.8	49.8	46.0	49.6	69.3	59.5	46.6	38.8

[a] The highest value in each line appears in italics. The peak in maternal mortality was in 1874.
[b] Data for England and Wales are shown for comparison.

Source: *Sundhedstilstanden og medicinal-forholdene: Norge* (Norwegian Health Statistics) C. No. 4 (1877), p. xiii. Data kindly supplied by Lars Østby (Director of Research) and Jens-Kristian Borgan of the Department of Statistics on Individuals and Households, Central Bureau of Statistics, Oslo; *Annual Reports of the Registrar General for England and Wales*.

same way for London and the provinces considered separately. He remarked perceptively that this was *indicative of some widespread influence* [my italics]. It was more widespread than he realized. I have found that there was a conspicuous peak in deaths from puerperal fever in Scotland in 1874, in Sweden in 1874/5, in Paris and Amsterdam in 1875, in Belgium in 1873/4. A high peak in puerperal fever deaths even occurred in Massachusetts in 1874. The most interesting comparison is Norway, shown in Table 4.6. Here the data are shown for total maternal mortality, but other data from the same source confirm that the 1874 peak was due to an excess of deaths due to puerperal fever. Table 4.6 shows that the peak occurred in 1874 not only in Norway as a whole, but in every region (diocese) except one—Hamars—which was the region with the smallest number of births, allowing for a wider degree of random variation; and in this region the peak was in 1875.

It seems most unlikely that such a high peak should appear simultaneously in so many countries by sheer coincidence. Whether the explanation is the transmission of a virulent organism by travellers, or whether it indicates a simultaneous world-wide change in streptococcal virulence (which I suspect is the case although I have no idea how it could have occurred) is unclear; but the data are remarkable.

The close link between puerperal fever and erysipelas is useful as evidence that puerperal fever had the same underlying bacteriological cause in the eighteenth century (and probably in earlier periods) as it did in the late nineteenth century. But the close link can be utilized for another purpose: the calculation of case-fatality rates.

Erysipelas, like puerperal fever, was a notifiable disease. But erysipelas was free from the problems which beset the notification on puerperal fever or 'puerperal sepsis' which I described earlier in this chapter. There is no reason to suspect the case-fatality rates of erysipelas were inaccurate, and the rate rose from 3.9 per cent in 1911 to nearly 7 per cent in 1934. If we assume that the case-fatality rate of erysipelas increased because of increasing virulence of the streptococcus it is probable that the case-fatality of streptococcal puerperal fever rose in a similar manner. If that was the case, it provides one explanation for an otherwise puzzling feature: the international tendency for maternal mortality to rise between 1900 and 1935.

The problem of the virulence (and prevalence) of the streptococcus—or, as an expert on infectious diseases expressed it, the 'epidemic thrust' of the streptococcus[65]—and the epidemiological differences between scarlet fever on the one hand and erysipelas and puerperal fever on the other are complex and not fully understood. They are discussed in Appendix 5. The main conclusion, however, is that changes in the virulence of the streptococcus, rather than changes in maternal care or in the social and economic circumstances of populations, were probably the most decisive factor in determining short-term variations in the trends in maternal mortality in all Western countries until the introduction of the sulphonamides.

THE BACTERIOLOGY OF PUERPERAL FEVER

Although other bacteria could lead to death from puerperal fever, such a large proportion of deaths were due to the organism known as the β-haemolytic streptococcus, Lancefield group A,[66] and also as *Streptococcus pyogenes* or *Streptococcus haemolyticus*, that for most practical purposes it is correct to think

[65] Personal communication, 1 Sept. 1987, A. B. Christie, author of *Infectious Diseases: Epidemiology and Clinical Practice* (1st edn., London, 1969). He writes that he remembers scarlet fever as a serious disease in 1938, but 'scarlet fever began to disappear in the late thirties and early forties. When I reached Liverpool in 1946 it was no longer an epidemic disease—I can't believe this was due to sulphonamides or penicillin. Penicillin was not obtainable, or only with great difficulty, for civilians during the war years so it can be ruled out. . . . I have always put the decline down to the organism losing "its epidemic thrust", though I am not sure what that means . . . I have always been puzzled by the disappearence of scarlet fever. Diphtheria . . . went because of immunisation. But scarlet fever? I still favour "loss of epidemic thrust".'

[66] W. W. C. Topley and G. S. Wilson, *The Principles of Bacteriology and Immunity* (2nd edn., London, 1938). Between 1928 and 1933 Lancefield's work led to the classification of the β-haemolytic streptococci into groups identified by letters of the alphabet. Those in group A corresponded in all respects to the *Streptococcus pyogenes* which was briefly known as *Streptococcus haemolyticus*. Group A streptococci are highly pathogenic to man. Group B and C streptococci are found as pathogens in cattle and other animals but are rarely pathogenic for man.

of puerperal fever as a streptococcal disease.[67] Epidemics of puerperal fever, such as we have described, where wholly streptococcal in origin.

Although it was thought at first that the same organisms predominated in fatal and non-fatal cases, it became clear in the early decades of this century that *Streptococcus pyogenes* was often found in only a minority of non-fatal cases.[68] Of the other organisms found in puerperal fever *Staphylococcus aureus* (the cause *inter alia* of boils and carbuncles) was the one most likely to lead to death while anaerobic streptococci and the coliform bacilli were common causes of non-fatal puerperal fever.[69]

The discovery of the bacterial cause of puerperal fever began in 1864 when Rokitansky demonstrated the presence of organisms in the vaginal discharge of women suffering from the disease. In 1865 Mayrhofer identified these organisms as streptococci and his findings were confirmed by others. In the 1870s, however, only a minority of medical scientists were willing to accept the germ theory. Most believed that the presence of bacteria was accidental, not causative, or that bacteria were generated by putrefaction Finally, however, Pasteur demonstrated in 1879 that the streptococcus could be cultivated in the laboratory from cases of puerperal fever, and shortly afterwards Doléis showed that although the streptococcus was nearly always the causative agent, staphylococci and other bacilli were sometimes present.

When bacteriological methods became established in this century, the identification of the causative organism was based on three techniques: uterine swabs, high vaginal swabs, and blood culture. The results of these techniques are, however, more difficult to interpret than one might imagine. Cultures grown in the laboratory from swabs often revealed a confusingly mixed flora in which the culprit was uncertain. A negative (sterile) culture from a swab could not necessarily be taken as firm evidence that bacteria were

[67] In a recent paper Seligman has drawn attention to the role of anaerobic organisms in non-epidemic puerperal sepsis. It is probable they were most prominent in post-abortive sepsis, and non-fatal cases of post-partum sepsis; but they could also cause death in a few cases of post-partum sepsis, usually after a relatively prolonged illness associated with septic thrombophlebitis. Some of the cases of puerperal sepsis in which bacteriological cultures (see below) were sterile may represent the failure to use techniques suitable for culturing these organisms, amongst which it is now suspected that *Bacteroides* may have been prominent. See S. A. Seligman, 'The Lesser Pestilence: Non-Epidemic Puerperal Fever', *Medical History*, 35 (1991), 89–102.

[68] In the early years of this century, J. Whitridge Williams examined bacteriologically 150 cases of puerperal fever. Culture was negative in 70 cases. Streptococci alone were found in 31 cases (38%), and streptococci with other organisms in a further 12 (15%). Of the remainder, 11 were coliform organisms, 12 unidentified bacteria (8 anaerobic). 4 were staphylococci, and the rest a mixture of probably non-pathogenic organisms. J. H. Burtenshaw, 'The Fever of the Puerperium (Puerperal Fever)', *New York Journal and Philadelphia Medical Journal*, 79 (1904), 1136–7. See also Topley and Wilson, *The Principles of Bacteriology and Immunity*. Lansing and colleagues have recently suggested that Group B streptococci may have played a part in puerperal fever. D. I. Lansing, W. R. Penman, and J. D. Davis, 'Puerperal Fever and the Group B haemolytic streptococcus', *Bulletin of the History of Medicine*, 57 (1983), 70–80.

[69] Topley and Wilson, *The Principles of Bacteriology and Immunity*.

not present. When blood cultures were positive they provided clear evidence of the responsible organism; but blood cultures could be negative even when there was clinical evidence of septicaemia, and it might be necessary to take a series of blood cultures before a positive result was obtained.

To demonstrate these points I have chosen two particularly thorough investigations into the bacteriology of puerperal fever. The first was carried out in 1925 by a committee of gynaecologists in the north of England. The results can be seen in Table 4.1. The second was carried out in Aberdeen on a series of eighty-eight cases of puerperal fever which occurred between 1918 and 1927. The results are presented in Table 4.2.

The Aberdeen investigation showed that in twenty-eight out of twenty-nine fatal cases the infective organism responsible for death was *Streptococcus pyogenes*, which they called by its synonym *Streptococcus haemolyticus*. The remaining fatal case was one in which no bacteriological investigations were carried out. Blood cultures were the clearest guide to the prognosis. *Streptococcus haemolyticus* was grown from blood cultures in twenty-two out of the twenty-nine fatal cases. Of the remaining fatal cases in which the blood culture was sterile most died of peritonitis. This confirms that in fatal cases of puerperal fever the immediate cause of death was either septicaemia or peritonitis, or both; and that *Streptococcus pyogenes*, alone or in combination with other organisms, was responsible. Earlier we cited Fothergill's estimate that the probable case-fatality rate of puerperal fever from all causes in the country as a whole was about 2.5 per cent. That was probably too low an estimate. Even if the true figure was as high as 10 per cent it is likely that the two investigations cited here were based on a selection of severe cases. Thus the overall fatality rate in this series of the Aberdeen series eighty-eight cases was 33 per cent. The fatality rate when *Streptococcus pyogenes* was cultured from a sample of blood, showing that septicaemia had occurred, was 79 per cent.

In the North of England investigation, bacterial investigations were carried out in 71 of the total of 109 cases of puerperal fever. Positive identification of bacteria was obtained in 53 cases. The streptococcus, alone or in conjunction with other bacteria, was found in 49 of these 53 cases; and streptococci were found in 35 of the 38 cases in which a positive blood culture was obtained. Tables 4.1 and 4.2 show that although infection with *Streptococcus pyogenes* was not invariably a death warrant, even when the blood culture was positive for this organism, it was always a sign of great danger.

ENDOGENOUS AND EXOGENOUS INFECTION

By the end of the nineteenth century it was generally accepted that bacteria were the cause and not the mere accompaniment of puerperal fever. The debate on the bacterial origin of the disease was replaced by a new one on the source of the bacteria, in which there were two schools of thought. According to the first (the endogenous school), puerperal fever arose from organisms already present in the vagina of the parturient woman who carried her own source of infection within her when she came to labour. Often it was said that husbands were to blame for vaginal infection by their insistence on sexual intercourse late in pregnancy. It was a cruel and false assertion which added to the misery of husbands already distraught at the death of their wives.

According to the second (the exogenous school), the vagina seldom, if ever, harboured pathogenic organisms. Infection was always acquired from an external source, usually the hands or instruments of the birth-attendant. The endogenous school was attractive because it implicitly exonerated birth-attendants from blame. And the practical consequence of this view was that puerperal fever might be prevented by vigorous sterilization of the vagina before labour using powerful antiseptics. Exogenous infection, on the other hand, laid the blame fairly and squarely on the shoulders of doctors and midwives who were presumed to be guilty until proved innocent.

One of the early reviews of this subject was published in the United States in 1896. The author, Dr Jewett of New York, found that Germany was the stronghold of the theory of endogenous infection and that Frederick Ahlfeld (1843–1929) was the leading advocate. Even in Germany, however, there were dissenting views. Albert Döderlein (1860–1941) believed that the healthy vagina prevented the growth of pathogenic bacteria. He was supported by another prominent German authority, Hans Burkhardt (1862–1932). Moreover, a report from Dresden where douching the normal vagina was used routinely in some years but not in others, showed that douching was more dangerous than doing nothing. Nevertheless, the theory of endogenous infection persisted in Germany for many years.[70]

American and British doctors tended to reject the theory of endogenous infection. Nevertheless, they often acted as if it was true. Disinfection of the vagina with bichloride of mercury, sublimate, or cresol, was widespread in the USA. Some employed douching in normal cases. Others used it only before forceps deliveries. At the end of his paper, Jewett concluded (correctly as it turned out) that all puerperal infection was acquired from external sources and that douching was positively harmful. The debate was still very much alive when Gibberd wrote about it in 1929, saying with a touch of exasperation, that the 'controversy seemed no nearer a settlement'. German authorities persisted in saying that they found pathogenic bacteria in the healthy vagina. American obstetricians denied it and their father-figure J. Whitridge Williams, tongue-in-cheek, added fuel to the flames by saying the difference was easily explained: Americans washed more than Germans.[71]

[70] C. Jewett, 'The Question of Puerperal Self-Infection', *American Gynaecological and Obstetrical Journal*, 8 (1896), 417–29
[71] G. F. Gibberd, 'Streptococcal Puerperal Sepsis', *Guy's Hospital Reports*, 81 (1931), 32–3.

Gradually through the 1930s all but a few accepted that the theory of endogenous infection was dead, although as late as 1936 Colebrook found it necessary when denying the theory of endogenous infection to say 'I know the conception is dear to the heart of some obstetricians and they will not readily part with it'.[72] Historically it was an important debate which not only showed the power of wishful thinking to perpetuate untenable hypotheses, but demonstrated the way that apparently esoteric detail—in this case, whether or not the healthy vagina could harbour pathogenic organisms—had a profound effect on the management of labour.

THE IMPORTANCE OF THE ASYMPTOMATIC CARRIER

Although the bacterial origin of puerperal fever had been demonstrated and the exogenous theory accepted by all but a few die-hards, the mode by which a woman was infected during or after labour was not fully understood until the late 1920s when important advances in understanding how puerperal fever was spread were made due to a number of researchers, notably Lancefield in New York, Smith in Aberdeen, Paine in Sheffield, Nixon and Wright in London, and most of all Leonard Colebrook and his sister and colleague in research, Dora Colebrook. The work of all these people made it possible to identify strains of *Streptococcus pyogenes* with such precision that the source of infection could be traced with certainty.

Leonard Colebrook, who was appointed a member of the scientific staff of the Medical Research Council in 1926 and was joined by his sister in 1930, was appointed as the director of research laboratories established at Queen Charlotte's Hospital in London for the investigation of the causes, prevention, and treatment of puerperal fever. It was common knowledge that the virulent streptococcus caused erysipelas and scarlet fever. Leonard Colebrook showed that in a hospital ward where cases of streptococcal infection were nursed, making the beds could lead to heavy contamination of the air with virulent streptococci. He also demonstrated the extraordinary ubiquity of the streptococcus. What was not appreciated before the late 1920s was that the virulent streptococcus was often present in minor conditions such as tonsillitis, otitis media, sinus infections, wounds, burns, skin infections of all kinds such as whitlows and impetigo, as well as such trivial conditions such as ordinary sore throats, colds, and colds dignified with the name of 'the flu'.

---

[72] L. Colebrook, 'The Prevention of Puerperal Sepsis', *Journal of Obstetrics and Gynaecology of the British Empire*, 43 (1936), 691–714. For the original reports of this work see Public Record Office, Kew, MH 55/263. Leonard Colebrook stated that his primary task in 1933 was 'to assess the danger of infection *from the patient's own throat and nose*'. Ibid. For a textbook view on this subject in the 1930s see Topley and Wilson, *The Principles of Bacteriology and Immunity* (2nd edn.), 1165.

What was even more startling was the demonstration that, on average, 7 per cent of the healthy population were asymptomatic carriers of the streptococcus in the nose and the throat. And when streptococcal infections were prevalent in a region the asymptomatic carrier rate was much higher, sometimes as high as 40 per cent of the population. Those who came into close and frequent contact with cases of streptococcal infection were most likely to become carriers, especially general practitioners whose work brought them into daily contact with the conditions listed above. From a combined investigation of serological and epidemiological data, Dora Colebrook was able to show that in 48 cases of puerperal fever due to the *Streptococcus pyogenes* the probable source of infection was the patient's own nose or throat in 6 cases, a member of the patient's household in 9 cases, the attendant at birth in 24 cases, and uncertain in the remaining 9.[73]

By the 1930s, then, it was clear that the source of infection in puerperal fever was not just the dirty hands, clothes, or instruments of the birth-attendant, although these could certainly spread the disease. Nor was the danger of transmitting the disease confined to the occasions when the birth-attendant had been in contact with a case of puerperal fever or erysipelas. It was enough if the birth-attendant was an asymptomatic carrier. It was more dangerous still if he or she had recently had a cold or sore throat. What was more, the preventive strategies commonly used in domiciliary obstetric practice, which consisted of routine washing and often the perfunctory dipping of hands and instruments in antiseptics, was hopelessly inadequate. Even if masks were worn, which was rare before the Second World War outside hospitals, their construction was such as to make them largely in-effective.[74] A standard of antisepsis and asepsis such as that practised in abdominal surgery was the only effective safeguard; and such standards were rare. Few in ordinary obstetric practice thought it necessary to go to all the trouble of aseptic preparation which they willingly accepted in a surgical theatre.[75]

In 1936, Colebrook came to the conclusion that, 'the danger of invasion by haemolytic streptococci threatens the parturient woman, not from one direction, but from many' and 'the haemolytic streptococci of the respiratory tract constitute the chief menace in maternity work; particularly those strep-

---

[73] Colebrook, 'The Prevention of Puerperal Sepsis'.

[74] Gibberd wrote that it was essential to wear a mask constructed of 16 thicknesses of gauze. Gibberd, 'Streptococcal Puerperal Sepsis', 35. Very few masks in the 1930s came up to this standard, and in domiciliary practice, where the large majority of deliveries took place, it was very uncommon before the Second World War for general practitioners to wear masks when delivering their patients.

[75] The College of Obstetricians in 1929 did, however, recommend for every delivery 'a sterilised gown, a mask and rubber gloves [which] should reach to the elbows. A sterilised oufit should always be provided when poor class women are attended at home.' Royal College of Obstetricians and Gynaecologists, archives, Maternity Commitee minute book, 1929-30, B7.

tococci associated with recent acute infection of the respiratory tract'.[76] Now, at last, certain features of puerperal fever which had seemed so mysterious in the nineteenth century, became clear. Doctors such as Dr Rutter of Philadelphia and all the others, doctors and midwives, who were dogged by a series of cases of puerperal fever in their practice while their colleagues escaped, were almost certainly asymptomatic carriers of a virulent strain of the streptococcus in their throats and noses. Later work (see Appendix 5) suggests that the carrier state could persist for weeks, or even for months.

THE TREATMENT OF PUERPERAL FEVER

When the treatment of puerperal fever was discussed before the mid-1930s, views were held or attacked with a kind of religious fanaticism seldom equalled in other branches of medicine. In 1931, Gibberd referred with exasperation to a method then current which consisted of instillation of glycerine into the uterine cavity, as a method 'which has been "boomed"—no other word is adequate—by Remington Hobbs'.[77] 'Booming' could apply to a very long line of supposedly certain remedies which were extraordinarily varied, often dangerous, and rarely if ever effective. Purging and the administration of antimony and mercury by mouth or inunction were common methods in the early nineteenth century. Bleeding had been advocated since the early eighteenth century, but later most authorities such as Thomas Cooper (1766), Johnson (1769), John Millar (1770), and Henry Manning (1771) advised that bleeding should be used with great caution or not at all.[78] As we have seen, Alexander Gordon of Aberdeen took a different view in 1795. He claimed that during the epidemic in Aberdeen he saw 77 cases of whom 28 died. Those patients subjected to vigorous bleeding all recovered while those who were bled sparingly or not at all, died.[79]

How much it was due to Gordon is uncertain; probably not very much, but there was a swing back to copious bleeding in the treatment of puerperal fever during the early nineteenth century. Even Denman, a naturally cautious and conservative obstetrician who had previously advised against bleeding, changed his mind in 1815. Venesection remained in fashion until about the 1870s when surgical methods came into favour, first with some hesitation, then to an increasing extent during the antiseptic era. The infected uterine cavity was irrigated with douches or treated with packs and pessaries containing iodine, carbolic acid, mercurochrome, or other antiseptics. Intramuscular or intravenous injections, ranging from relatively harmless normal saline to terrifying solutions of formalin and aqueous solutions of silver, were

[76] Colebrook, 'The Prevention of Puerperal Sepsis'.
[77] Gibberd, 'Streptococcal Puerperal Sepsis'.
[78] Burtenshaw, 'The Fever of the Puerperium'.
[79] Gordon, *Treatise on the Epidemic Puerperal Fever*.

freely administered. All these methods were 'boomed' with fervour by their proponents. A few surgeons even recommended hysterectomy as a treatment for puerperal fever, especially if there were remnants of the placenta in the infected uterus. Others, less extreme, employed curretage combined with antiseptic douches.

In 1912, a committee in the USA which investigated the treatment of puerperal fever found that a large majority of American and European authorities would in many cases of puerperal fever 'clean out' the uterus either using a curette, or by using their finger. Only a few employed 'expectant treatment or mild disinfectant douches'. Experience showed later that 'cleaning out the uterus' was rarely successful and often fatal.[80]

From the end of the nineteenth century, high hopes were held for an anti-streptococcal serum invented and used in France by Marmoek (1895) and Charpentier (1896). It was investigated by a committee of the American Gynaecological Society in 1898 and shown to be ineffective.[81] Colebrook began again in the 1920s in the hope of finding an effective anti-streptococcal serum and was still trying when the sulphonamides were introduced. As Gibberd remarked in 1931, 'It is usual to find that the number of different therapeutic measures introduced for combating any disease varies inversely with the efficacy of the treatment.'[82] This is a well-recognized medical truism. As far as puerperal fever was concerned it was an understatement. The uncomfortable truth was that nothing worked. In 1930, towards the end of a life devoted to obstetric practice and research, Whitridge Williams of Baltimore was driven to therapeutic nihilism. The septicaemic cases nearly all die, he said, and the others nearly all recover. Treatment was never effective. In fact, intervention in mild cases of fever does more harm than good. All that could be done for cases of puerperal fever was good nursing to make the woman comfortable and leave the rest to nature.[83]

I am sure Williams was right, and the awful multitude of ineffective remedies stretching back from the 1930s to antiquity was a measure of the anxiety and dread which the condition aroused, and the feeling that to do 'something', anything, was better than doing nothing. Only the very experienced and well-established obstetrician could afford an attitude of total nihilism. The turning-point came with the introduction of the sulphonamides; but we come to this later, in Chapter 15.

---

[80] B. C. Hirst, R. L. Dickinson, and J. B. DeLee, *Report of the Committee on the Treatment of Puerperal Fever*, Paper read to the Section on Obstetrics and Gynaecology of the American Medical Association, Minneapolis, July 1913.

[81] Burtenshaw, 'The Fever of the Puerperium'.

[82] Gibberd, 'Streptococcal Puerperal Sepsis'.

[83] Royal College of Obstetricians and Gynaecologists. Archives. E/06/3. Papers of the 5th Congress of Obstetrics and Gynaecology. These proceedings were published, but not quite in full, in *Journal of Obstetrics and Gynaecology of the British Empire*, 23 (1925).

5

Toxaemia of Pregnancy and Eclampsia

If the cause of a disease is unknown, renaming it not only reflects new theories, but produces an illusion of progress. Toxaemia is a prime example. The disease has been known (in roughly chronological order) as puerperal convulsions, puerperal nephritis and albuminuria, puerperal albuminuria and convulsions, eclampsia, toxaemia, pre-eclamptic toxaemia (or pre-eclampsia), hypertensive disease of pregnancy, pregnancy associated hypertension, and finally by the term currently in use, pregnancy-induced hypertension. I shall use 'toxaemia' for historical reasons.

In spite of the confusing terminology the features of this common disorder are constant and well known. It is a disease of the last trimester (three months) of pregnancy. The first sign is usually a rise in blood pressure, followed by albuminuria and oedema. If symptoms develop such as *malaise*, blurred vision, and severe headache, it has already reached a dangerous stage and may lead to one or a series of *grand mal* convulsions, known as eclamptic fits or eclampsia. Today, the term eclampsia is confined to cases which have progressed to the stage of convulsions. In the past, the term eclampsia was generally used in the same sense, but sometimes it was used to describe toxaemia without convulsions, producing some unavoidable confusion.

In patients who develop toxaemia, progress from early stages to convulsions is usually slow but may be rapid. Very occasionally, eclampsia comes out of the blue without preceding symptoms or signs. Usually, however, there are obvious warning signs for days if not weeks before an eclamptic fit occurs.

Toxaemia of pregnancy is very dangerous. It may cause blindness through retinal haemorrhage. Death can occur as a result of damage to the kidneys or liver or from cerebral haemorrhage. The most common causes of death in the past was an eclamptic fit. Today, the most common cause of death is cerebral haemorrhage but deaths from eclampsia, though rare, still occur.[1] The incidence of toxaemia is higher in first than subsequent pregnancies, in multiple than single pregnancies, and in older than younger mothers. In the 1950s the incidence was estimated as 8.5 per cent in first pregnancies and 4.2 per cent in subsequent pregnancies. It has a tendency to recur.[2] In the United States it

---

[1] C. W. G. Redman, 'Hypertension in Pregnancy', in Sir Alec Turnbell and G. Chamberlain (eds.), *Obstetrics* (London, 1989), chap. 36. See also Redman, 'Eclampsia Still Kills' (leading article), *British Medical Journal* (1988), i. 1209–10.

[2] O. V. Jones, 'Pre-eclamptic Toxaemia', *British Medical Journal* (1957), ii. 1341–3.

is thought to be more common in black than white mothers, but this may reflect more late untreated cases rather than a higher incidence. Usually, the earlier the disease becomes manifest, the worse the outlook, partly because there is a longer time for the disease to worsen. The disease is always resolved by the termination of pregnancy, whether naturally or artificially, although eclamptic fits occasionally occur shortly after delivery.

The incidence of eclamptic convulsions in Britain in the 1970s had fallen to around 4–9 per 10,000 maternities. In New Zealand the incidence was 32 per 10,000 maternities in 1928, and dropped to 8 per 10,000 in 1958. The present low level is largely if not wholly due to better care. Eclampsia can be prevented, toxaemia cannot; and there is no evidence to suggest that toxaemia (hypertensive disease of pregnancy) is less common today than it was fifty or a hundred years ago.[3] What was the incidence of eclampsia in the past?

Lever, to whom we shall return, found that the incidence of eclampsia amongst charity patients delivered in London between 1834 and 1843 was 14 out of 7,400 consecutive deliveries, or 19 per 10,000.[4] These were home deliveries. Reports based on hospital deliveries are apt to be inflated by selection. Therefore, the most useful sources are reports from private practice, many of which were published in the USA. In 1926, Dr Piper in Minnesota collected data on midwifery from twenty-six rural practitioners. The total number of deliveries was 42,390 (an average of 1,630 per practitioner, with a range from 500 to 3,000) and there were 232 cases of eclampsia, giving a rate of 54 per 10,000 deliveries.[5] Here, however, there is strong presumptive evidence that eclampsia was sometimes used by some as a synonym for toxaemia without convulsions. Reports from individual practitioners, in which the same terminological uncertainty often occurs, are in broad agreement with the findings of Piper. Because they were based on small numbers of a thousand or so cases, however, they show wide variations.[6]

Before the mid-1930s, eclampsia differed from puerperal fever in this respect. Deaths from puerperal fever were twice as common in private practice as deaths from eclampsia, but *cases* of puerperal fever were quite differently distributed. Eclampsia tended to be spread evenly throughout the population of childbearing women. Puerperal fever was not. Some doctors saw few or no cases of puerperal fever in ten or even twenty years of active obstetric practice while others saw fifty or more cases in a single year. On the

[3] Redman, 'Hypertension in Pregnancy'; 'Eclampsia Still Kills'.

[4] All 14 cases had convulsions and may be regarded in modern terms as true eclampsia. J. C. W. Lever, 'Cases of Puerperal Convulsions with Remarks', *Guy's Hospital Reports*, NS 1 (1843), 495–517.

[5] W. A. Piper, 'Rural Obstetrics and a Comparative Study of its Relation to Puerperal Mortality Statistics', *Minnesota Medicine*, 9 (1926), 489–99.

[6] There were wide variations in the incidence of eclampsia reported from general practitioners in the USA. For further details see I. London, 'Some Historical Aspects of Toxaemia of Pregnancy: A Review', *British Journal of Obstetrics and Gynaecology*, 98 (1991), 853–8.

other hand, few general practitioners saw no cases of eclampsia, but very few saw as many as ten. On average, American and British general practitioners who delivered between fifty and eighty cases a year would probably have three to four cases of eclampsia in fifteen to twenty years of practice.

EARLY IDEAS ABOUT THE NATURE OF TOXAEMIA

In the early years of the nineteenth century only the end stage of toxaemia, the eclamptic fit, was recognized. The moot question was whether eclampsia was simply ordinary epilepsy in pregnancy or something quite different.[7] The spate of new theories began when J. Lever of London published a paper in 1843 which showed that eclampsia was associated with a large amount of albumen in the urine. By the 1840s, certain signs such as oedema—swelling of the legs and puffy eyelids—blurred vision, and headaches, were recognized as precursors of eclampsia, and Lever was able to show that in these, too, there was albuminuria. Lever was also one of the first to show that eclampsia was much more common in first pregnancies than subsequent ones.[8]

Lever's discovery immediately suggested that eclampsia was related to Bright's disease (nephritis), first described in 1827, which was also characterized by oedema and albuminuria. Uraemia was the end stage of Bright's disease, and it was suggested that eclampsia was due to uraemia. The measurement of blood pressure did not begin until around 1910. Since the earliest sign of toxaemia is a rise in blood pressure, toxaemia in the nineteenth century consisted of what would now be regarded as cases at the advanced stage of oedema, albuminuria, and convulsions. The discovery of albuminuria was regarded as so significant that until 1911 toxaemia deaths in England and Wales were classed in the reports of the Registrar General with diseases of the kidney and placed in the category 'other diseases of the kidney', a dustbin category from which they cannot be extracted. Deaths from eclampsia, however, were classed with maternal deaths, under the heading 'puerperal convulsions'. We therefore have national statistics of deaths from eclampsia before 1911, but not of deaths from pre-eclamptic toxaemia.[9]

This artificial division of toxaemia deaths into two categories was a mistake. Puerperal albuminuria and oedema were recognized as precursors of eclampsia from 1843. The two should have been kept together. Moreover, it soon became obvious that the symptoms of uraemia and eclampsia were quite different. This removed one of the basic tenets from the theory that the

[7] J. Coudon, *An Inaugural Essay on Eclampsia* (Baltimore, Md., 1813).

[8] Lever, in 'Cases of Puerperal Convulsions' and J. B. DeLee, 'Theories of Eclampsia', *American Journal of Obstetrics*, 51 (1905), 325–30 stated that the discovery of albuminuria in eclampsia was first made by Rayer in Paris in 1839. But Lever usually gets the credit.

[9] *Annual Reports of the Registrar General.* Deaths due to non-eclamptic toxaemia were placed in the category 'Other diseases of the kidney'. It is therefore impossible to know the number of deaths due to toxaemia before 1911.

disease was just a form of nephritis somehow connected with pregnancy. In fact, the theory that toxaemia was a disease of the kidney was soon challenged, and new theories proliferated.

In the mid-nineteenth century, some said that eclampsia was due to compression of the ureters, others to a summation of external irritants. A few returned to the idea that it was simply epilepsy. In 1884, Delore believed he had found the cause in a specific bacteria which he named *Bacillus eclampsiae*. To his dismay it was soon identified as the common organism, *Proteus vulgaris*. But the idea steadily grew that toxaemia was due to the existence of specific toxins of pregnancy, or to an over-production of toxins present in the non-pregnant state: hence the name toxaemia. Few were specific about the origin or nature of these toxins, although Ahlfeld in 1894 suggested they were produced in the placenta. But the general idea took hold. DeLee undertook a thorough review of ideas about toxaemia at the beginning of this century and concluded:

You all know the trite expression of Zweifel, that eclampsia is the disease of theories. That I have had more and more proved to me as I waded through the oceans of literature on the causation of eclampsia. As a matter of fact we know practically nothing of the causations of eclampsia. A theory has only to be set up by one investigator to be knocked down by another... only one point seems to be generally conceded, that eclampsia is due to the action of a toxin in the blood upon the nerve centres.[10]

The toxin theory remained dominant for the next few decades. In 1957, Mr O. V. Jones, an authority on toxaemia, noted that the cause of the disease was quite unknown.[11] Although there are some recent theories (which lie outside the scope of this study) the same holds true in the 1980s.

TREATMENT AND PREVENTION

Table 5.1 lists the medical treatments of toxaemia which have been used, singly or in combination, since the first half of the nineteenth century. The length of the list suggests what is in fact the case: none has proved to be more than, at best, partially effective. Because delivery is the only sure way of resolving the disease, surgical methods have always played a large part in the treatment of toxaemia. In the nineteenth century this consisted of induction of labour, usually by artificial rupture of the membranes followed by the insertion of some kind of device (a laminaria tent, a sponge, or a water-bag) into

---

[10] DeLee, 'Theories of Eclampsia'. This is the best short account of the history of ideas on eclampsia that I know and all the better in such an oceanic subject for being succinct. A longer and rather muddled account can be found in W. T. Lusk, *The Science and Art of Midwifery* (4th edn., London, 1899).

[11] Jones, 'Pre-eclamptic Toxaemia'.

TABLE 5.1 *Medical Treatments for Eclampsia and Pre-eclampsia[a]*

Date	Treatment
Pre-1850	Bleeding and purging
1850	Heavy sedation with morphine, chloral, chloroform, etc.
1889	Veratrum Viride
1897	Stroganoff regime
1916	Magnesium sulphate
1922	Intravenous dextrose
1927	Rectal tribromoethanol
1953	Hydralazine
1960	Lytic cocktail and/or diuretics
1968	Benzodiazepines
1970	Oral antihypertensive agents
1990	Low-dose aspirin

[a] I am grateful to Dr C. R. W. Redman, Lecturer in Obstetric Medicine in the University of Oxford, for providing this table.

the lower segment of the uterus to stimulate contractions. It was uncertain and it was unsafe, with a high risk of infection.

In the early years of this century, when Caesarean section became the treatment of choice for obstructed labour (cephalo-pelvic disproportion), it gradually tended to replace induction in severe cases of toxaemia, especially in the USA where it was in full swing by the 1920s. The results were not good, as R. W. Holmes of Chicago pointed out in 1920:

Eclampsia is a disease, as popularly treated, which carries a dual mortality—that incident to the toxaemia and an equal hazard from the surgical intervention. In the preantiseptic days the maternal and fetal mortalities [for eclampsia] were respectively 20.4% and 33.3%: the modern methods exhibited mortalities of 19% and 39.6%: while in cesarean section in the period covered by modern treatment, the deaths were 34.8% and 25.9% respectively. . . . It may be said that the older authorities had no real therapy, yet their results were as good, or even better, than ours. . . . the much lauded cesarean operation shows that approximately one baby is saved at the expense of nearly four mothers.[12]

[12] R. W. Holmes, 'The Fads and Fancies of Obstetrics: A Comment on the Pseudo-Scientific Trend of Modern Obstetrics', *American Journal of Obstetrics and Gynaecology*, 2 (1920), 225–37. The connoisseur of curious stories will not want to miss the account of eclampsia related by Dr Richmond of Newton, Ohio. In 1827, Dr Richmond was called to a woman who was labouring in a log cabin in the backwoods, attended by two midwives. She had suffered a series of eclamptic fits for many hours. After attempting without success to terminate the fits, Dr Richmond proceeded to a Caesarean section, without assistance, and of course without anaesthesia, using only the instruments in his pocket case. He experienced great difficulty from having to cut

Toxaemia, then, was a very dangerous disease in which the cause was unknown, the medical treatments ineffective, and the surgical treatments hazardous. Prevention was the obvious policy and it became fashionable to proclaim that the introduction of antenatal care had made the practice of obstetrics one of the most important branches of preventive medicine. Although antenatal care was seen as the panacea for maternal mortality as a whole, toxaemia was the primary reason for its widespread introduction. It is easy to see why. Of the three main causes of maternal mortality, the reduction of deaths from puerperal sepsis and haemorrhage depended on care provided at or after delivery. Only toxaemia was (in theory) susceptible to prevention through antenatal care.[13]

Although antenatal care was provided on a limited scale before the First World War, it was only in the 1920s that it became a widespread and generally accepted policy in all Western countries that every pregnant woman should attend her doctor or clinic at regular intervals. Such was the faith in antenatal care, that even in countries such as the USA, where private practice reigned and government provision of maternal care was minimal, antenatal clinics for the poor were set up without opposition in cities and rural areas. There are many photographs of such clinics showing the nurse or doctor taking the blood pressure of the patient.[14]

In Britain, voluntary and local authority clinics were established all over the country to provide antenatal care free, or at minimal cost, for women unable to afford the fees of a general practitioner; and, of course, antenatal clinics had become routine in maternity hospitals and departments. First and foremost in the records of these clinics were the columns recording blood pressure and urinalysis. A great deal was said about the virtues of prevention; much less was said about the difficulties of effective prevention so that almost everyone was confident that antenatal care would reduce maternal mortality. Failure to provide comprehensive antenatal care became the cardinal sin of anyone practising obstetrics. This should be remembered when we read the

through the placenta. To make it possible to extract the baby he made a second large transverse incision through the uterus. In spite of all this, the woman is said to have made a good recovery and to have resumed her household duties within three weeks. The report was published in the *Western Journal of Medical and Physical Science*, 3 (1830), 485, and is quoted by J. H. Young, *Caesarean Section: The History and Development of the Operations from the Earliest Times* (London, 1944), 183.

[13] This is not quite true. Antenatal care also provided the opportunity for improving the general health of mothers during pregnancy, and the means of selecting high-risk mothers (first pregnancies, bad obstetric histories, small stature, contracted pelvis, multiple pregnancy, and so on) for hospital delivery; but these were secondary considerations in the early days of antenatal care. In many parts of the Western world in the 1920s, the ability to refer patients to hospitals staffed by skilled obstetricians was the exception rather than the rule.

[14] J. D. Stoeckle and G. A. White, *Plain Pictures of Plain Doctoring: Vernacular Expression in New Deal Medicine and Photography* (Cambridge, Mass., 1985). This is a unique and impressive collection of photographs of primary care medicine in the USA in the mid-1930s, with a well-informed accompanying text.

frequent references to preventable maternal deaths during the 1920s and 1930s. It was often said in Britain and the United States that 40 per cent (or some other figure in that region) of maternal deaths were preventable. In the calculations on which those estimates were based, one of the most frequent categories was 'absence of antenatal care' or 'inadequate antenatal care'. The underlying assumption that a woman who died in childbirth would not have done so had she received adequate antenatal care reflected the unrealistic expectations of the period. For this reason the estimates of preventable maternal deaths are suspect and need careful examination. Certainly many maternal deaths were potentially preventable; but it is likely that the true figure was closer to 25 per cent than 40 per cent.

This is not, of course, to condemn antenatal care as a useless part of obstetric practice. That would be nonsense. But in any period, including the present day as well as the inter-war period, in order for antenatal care to be effective in the prevention of deaths from toxaemia, let alone other complications, certain conditions needed to be fulfilled:

1. The public and the profession needed to be persuaded of the importance of antenatal care and regular attendances, including early booking.
2. The minimum procedures of blood pressure measurement and urinalysis would have to be regularly carried out and recorded. Many general practitioners kept no notes.
3. If toxaemia developed, there had to be effective home treatment or effective procedures for referral to a hospital with competent staff.
4. If a patient developed severe toxaemia and was admitted to hospital, the staff of the hospital needed to have safe and effective ways of terminating the pregnancy and preventing eclampsia.

During the inter-war period it was very rare indeed for all these four conditions to be fulfilled, especially the first two, and here we have the evidence from the records of Dr Greig, a careful, conscientious, and skilled practitioner in Kirkcaldy in Scotland.[15]

Dr Greig's obstetric practice covered the period from 1912 to the 1940s. He delivered on average 20–30 cases a year in the early part of the period, rising to 50–60 in the later part. In 1912, a large majority of his obstetric patients consulted him for the first time at about thirty-five weeks of pregnancy. By 1920 this had fallen to twenty-five weeks, but it was not until 1938 that it had fallen to twenty weeks. Late 'bookings', defined as first attendance after thirty-two weeks, occurred with 60 per cent of his patients in 1912, but

---

[15] The diaries of Dr Greig of Kirkcaldy. The records of this practice were preserved by Dr Greig's daughter, Dr Agnes Greig, who joined and later succeeded her father in the practice. I am grateful to her for allowing me free access to the practice records. Such records are few and most valuable.

fell steadily to 5 per cent by 1938. According to his records he first began to measure the blood pressure and test the urine in 1921. He had three cases of eclampsia (two died) in 1927, 1932, and 1947 respectively. His obstetric cases between 1912 and 1948 numbered 1,482. Thus the incidence of eclampsia was 20 per 10,000 maternities.

For the problem of toxaemia from the consultant obstetrician's point of view we have the evidence of the late Mr O. V. Jones (1907–86).[16] When he arrived in North Wales in 1937 there were no hospital beds and no consultant cover for the large area of Caernarfonshire and Angelsey for which he was responsible, an area containing a scattered population of some 200,000, much of it in remote and mountainous country. There were a few dedicated and able general practitioners, but the general standard of primary obstetric care by midwives and general practitioners was, in his own word, dreadful. Little was done to prevent or treat toxaemia, which Jones discovered was the leading cause of death. A maternity hospital was provided, and Jones adopted a policy of admitting all cases of toxaemia as in-patients. Mild cases were treated by bed rest and sedation, severe by a 'modified Stroganoff regime'.[17] In the treatment of pre-eclamptic toxaemia, skill is needed to judge the optimum time for induction of labour. Too early, and the baby dies of prematurity; too late and the baby may die of placental insufficiency and the mother of eclampsia. Jones used surgical induction, and only rarely resorted to Caesarean section. By the early 1950s he had reduced the mortality due to toxaemia to about one-third of the rate in 1937.

MORTALITY FROM TOXAEMIA

In 1843 John Lever collected data from a number of colleagues, and produced a table showing that 26.5 per cent of mothers who suffered eclamptic fits died as a result.[18] By the mid-1930s, many reports on eclamptic deaths had been published. Few showed any improvement on Lever's findings. In most the mortality rate of eclampsia was around 25–30 per cent. The death rate due to toxaemia as a whole, that is pre-eclamptic toxaemia and eclampsia combined, is more difficult to determine. In 1957, O. V. Jones quoted a

---

[16] This account is based on a meeting and subsequent extensive correspondence with Mr O. V. Jones in 1985 and 1986. His relevant publications are his obituary, *British Medical Journal* (1986), ii. 964; 'Pre-eclamptic Toxaemia', ibid. (1957) ii. 1341–3; 'Thirty Years' Review of an Area Obstetric Service', *Journal of Obstetrics and Gynaecology of the British Commonwealth*, 75 (1968), 754–8.

[17] The main features of the Stroganoff regime were very heavy sedation combined with magnesium sulphate, and the isolation of the patient in a darkened and totally quiet room where she was attended by staff tiptoeing in stockinged feet and peering in the dark. It was based on the theory that stimuli, auditory and visual, were the triggers for eclampsia. The method gained credence because it was so dramatic. The patient was treated as if she was an unexploded bomb. Cynics said the advantage of the regime was that the staff were unable to see in the dark just how bad the patient's condition really was. It was a method used extensively until the 1950s.

[18] Lever, 'Cases of Puerperal Convulsions'. The table can be found on p. 509.

TABLE 5.2 *Maternal Mortality Rate of Deaths Due to 'Puerperal Convulsions' and 'Albuminuria of Pregnancy', England and Wales, Scotland, and Ireland, 1912–1920*

Year	England and Wales	Scotland	Ireland
1912	7.2	10.6	6.6
1913	8.5	11.1	4.6
1914	7.4	9.6	4.8
1915	7.6	8.5	6.1
1916	8.3	8.6	6.5
1917	8.7	9.8	8.6
1918	8.1	10.1	6.8
1919	8.6	10.2	6.9
1920	7.8	9.0	7.8

Source: T. W. Eden, 'Eclampsia', *Journal of Obstetrics and Gynaecology of the British Empire*, 29 (1922), 386–401.

TABLE 5.3 *Deaths Due to 'Puerperal Convulsions' and 'Albuminuria of Pregnancy' Expressed as a Percentage of Total Maternal Mortality in Various Parts of Britain, 1912–1920*

Area	Percentage
London	21.9
Edinburgh	25.0
Dublin	10.3
North of England	24.4
Midlands	25.1

Source: T. W. Eden, 'Eclampsia', *Journal of Obstetrics and Gynaecology of the British Empire*, 29 (1922), 386–401.

widely accepted figure: toxaemia develops in about 10 per cent of all pregnancies, an incidence of 1,000 per 10,000. The data quoted above suggest that eclampsia occurred in between 20 and 50 per 10,000 deliveries, and if about a third of these died, the mortality rate from eclampsia alone would be expected to lie between around 7 and 17 deaths per 10,000.

A rate somewhere between 6 and 10 deaths per 10,000 deliveries is suggested by the statistics published by Eden for the period 1912–20. He combined the deaths under the two headings 'puerperal convulsions' and 'albuminuria of pregnancy'. His data are shown in Tables 5.2 and 5.3. In the

TABLE 5.4 *Incidence and Maternal Mortality of Toxaemia of Pregnancy in Various Countries up to the Mid-1930s*

Country, date, and definition	Maternal mortality rates per 10,000 births		Toxaemia as a percentage of total
	Total	Toxaemia	
England and Wales, 1872–6 (*Puerperal convulsions*)	54.2	6.3	11.6
England and Wales, 1923 (*Puerperal nephritis and puerperal albuminuria and convulsions*)	38.1	6.8	17.8
England and Wales, 1933 (*Puerperal albuminuria and convulsions = 83.5% toxaemia of pregnancy = 16.5%*)	45.1	7.6	16.8
England and Wales, 1930–2 Married women only			
All social classes	41.3	7.9	19.1
Social classes I and II	44.4	8.1	18.2
Social class III	41.1	8.1	19.7
Social class IV	41.6	8.5	20.4
Social class V	38.9	6.8	17.5
(*Definition as for England and Wales, 1933*)			
England, 1871–80. The Lying-in wards of Workhouse Infirmaries			
Provinces	86.8	12.5	14.4
London	88.2	5.6	6.3
(*Puerperal convulsions*)			
Wales, 1929–33			
Special areas	65.0	17.8	27.4
Other areas	54.1	14.1	26.1
(*All toxaemias—see text*)			
Scotland (*Puerperal convulsions and albuminuria*)	61.3	8.5	13.9
Eire (*Albuminuria and convulsions*)	48.2	5.3	11.0
Switzerland, 1922	53.4	6.6	12.4
Switzerland, 1925 (*Toxaemia of pregnancy*)	40.1	5.9	14.7
The Netherlands, 1933 (*Albuminuria and eclampsia*)	31.4	4.2	13.4
Sweden, 1931–5 (*Eclampsia*)	34.5	*c*.5.0	14.5

TABLE 5.4 (*cont.*)

Country, date, and definition	Maternal mortality rates per 10,000 births		Toxaemia as a percentage of total
	Total	Toxaemia	
Canada, 1929	56.0	14.0	25.0
(*Puerperal albuminuria and convulsions*)			
United States death registration area 1921	68.2	18.2	26.7
(*Puerperal albuminuria and convulsions*)			
United States, 1939	40.4	10.1	25.0
(*Toxaemia*)			
Kentucky, USA, 1932–6	50.0	6.5	13.0
(*Toxaemia*)			
South Carolina, USA, 1934–5			
White population	66.2	28.4	43.0
Black population	103.4	37.4	36.2
(*Albuminuria and eclampsia*)			
Maryland, USA, 1930–6	n.a.	n.a.	26.6
(*Eclampsia and chronic nephritis*)			

Source: England and Wales: *Registrar General's Reports*; Ministry of Health, *Report of an Investigation into Maternal Mortality* (London, 1937); Wales: Ministry of Health, ibid.; Scotland: P. L. McKinlay, *Maternal Mortality in Scotland, 1911–1945* (Edinburgh, 1947); Eire: *Annual Reports of the Registrar General* (Dublin); Workhouse Infirmaries: F. J. Mouat, 'Note on the Statistics of Childbirth in the Lying-in Wards of the Workhouse Infirmaries of England and Wales for Ten Years, 1871–1880'; *Transactions of the International Medical Congress of London*, 4 (1881), 392–4 (NB. the patients included a high proportion of unmarried mothers); The Netherlands: Statisteik van de sterfte naar den leeftid en de oorzaken van den dood, Central bureau voor de statisteik (1911–38); Switzerland: League of Nations, Health Organization, Statistical Handbook Series, 12, *Official Vital Statistics of Switzerland* (Geneva, 1928); Australia: *Report on Maternal Mortality in Childbirth*, Dept. of Trades and Customs (Victoria, 1917); Sweden: U. Högberg, *Maternal Mortality in Sweden*, Umeå University Medical Dissertations. NS 156 (Umeå, 1985); Canada: E. S. MacPhail, 'A Statistical Study in Maternal Mortality', *American Journal of Public Health*, 22 (1932), 618; USA (1921): R. M. Woodbury, *Maternal Mortality*, Children's Bureau Publications, No. 152 (Washington, DC, 1926); USA (1939): *Changes in Infant, Childhood, and Maternal Mortality over the Decade 1939–1948*, Children's Bureau Statistical Series, 6, Federal Security Agency, Children's Bureau (Washington, DC, 1950); Kentucky, USA: C. B. Crittenden and Lois Skaggs, *Maternal Mortality in Kentucky: A Study of Puerperal Deaths, 1932–1939*, Kentucky State Department of Health (1939); South Carolina, USA: South Carolina Medical Association, Committee on Maternal Welfare, *Maternal Mortality in South Carolina, 1934–5* (1936), Supplement for 1940–1 (1941); Maryland, USA: C. H. Peckham, 'A Survey of 447 Maternal Deaths Occurring in the Counties of Maryland during the Years 1930–1936 (inclusive)', *American Journal of Obstetrics and Gynaecology*, 36 (1938), 317–30.

United Kingdom, the mortality rate from toxaemia was highest in Scotland, lowest in Ireland, and in-between for England and Wales. The reason is not clear. If the Dublin figures were representative of Ireland, then deaths from toxaemia were not only lower in absolute terms in Ireland, but also in relative terms. In other areas of Britain deaths from toxaemia amounted to between 20 per cent and 25 per cent of total maternal mortality. These findings were, broadly speaking, confirmed by data from other countries which can be seen in Table 5.4.

This table shows that certain difficulties arise from the use of different terminology. As we saw, non-eclamptic deaths from toxaemia were excluded from maternal mortality in England and Wales before 1911; yet the MMR from toxaemia was much the same in the 1930s as it was in the 1870s. This is not altogether surprising. The data for 1933 show that eclampsia accounted for 83 per cent of all deaths due to toxaemia of pregnancy. It should be noted in passing that the English data for 1930–2 do not suggest any obvious association between social class and deaths from toxaemia.[19] The high rate in the 'special areas' of Wales may be a methodological artefact. The figures are based on a definition of toxaemia which included other categories of disease in pregnancy such as pernicious vomiting.

North America appears to have suffered much higher mortality from toxaemia than England and Wales, while Sweden and the Netherlands showed the lowest mortality. It is not clear why the rates in Canada and the USA were so high, nor is it at all clear why Kentucky was an apparent exception, unless it was that Kentucky health authorities do seem to have made a great effort to improve antenatal care in the 1930s. The data for South Carolina show that mortality from toxaemia was higher for the black than the white population, but expressed as a percentage of total maternal mortality it was lower.

In summary, deaths from toxaemia accounted on average for about 20 per cent of maternal mortality, with lower rates in Sweden and the Netherlands and higher for Canada and most parts of the USA; and probably higher in Wales than in England. The decline in toxaemia deaths after the 1930s, will be considered later.

---

[19] In 1958 MacGillivray found that social class and stature did not influence the incidence of toxaemia. I. MacGillivray, 'Some Observations on the Incidence of pre-eclampsia', *Journal of Obstetrics and Gynaecology*, 65 (1958), 536–9. In 1977, however, Baird found that the incidence of pre-eclampsia and the perinatal mortality rate were higher in women of short stature, and short stature was associated with social class. D. Baird, 'Epidemiological Aspects of Hypertensive Pregnancy', *Clinics in Obstetrics and Gynaecology*, 4/3 (1977), 531–47.

6

Obstetric Haemorrhage

The pregnant uterus has a rich supply of large blood vessels. Obstetric haemorrhage can be very sudden, unexpected, and alarmingly copious. Anyone who has witnessed a severe post-partum haemorrhage will testify to the appropriateness of the descriptive term, 'flooding'.

In his review of maternal mortality for the five years 1872–6, William Farr noted that out of the total of 23,051 maternal deaths, 12,805 (55.5 per cent) were due to 'metria' (puerperal fever). Deaths due to puerperal convulsions amounted to 2,692 (11.6 per cent), and deaths associated with obstetric haemorrhage ('Placenta praevia, Retention of the Placenta and Flooding') came to 5,186, or 22 per cent of the total. Haemorrhage, he wrote, was the one major cause of maternal mortality in which women were dying needlessly for want of common skills that every midwife and practitioner should possess.

It is in the cases of ordinary flooding that the skilful midwife saves the mother's life. The authorities agree that the afterbirth is usually expelled in less than 20 minutes; and that where there is delay beyond half-an-hour the utmost care is required. The removal of the placenta by pressure and by gentle mechanical help excites the contractions of the uterus and at once stops the flow of blood. If this is not done, the patient bleeds to death; the heart, no longer filled with the vital fluid, struggles in vain; pangs and syncope follow.[1]

Farr took the trouble to write to two lying-in charities (the Royal Maternity and the Birmingham Lying-in Charity) to see what rules and instructions they gave to their midwives. He found, as he had suspected, that the procedures for preventing haemorrhage in third stage of labour were well recognized. Indeed, the instructions given by these charities were similar to those found in 'books and manuals on midwifery in English and French [which] are now very much at one on this question. It must be so.' It must indeed, because the principles for the management of the third stage of labour (the stage following the delivery of the baby) laid down by Denman in the eighteenth century were widely known. His *Introduction to the Practice of Midwifery* went into several editions and was the standard text for many years.[2]

---

[1] *Annual Report of the Registrar General for the Year 1876*, 241–51. The figures, as Farr admitted, were not wholly accurate; 4,183 death certificates stated the cause of deaths simply as 'childbirth'. Farr added these in proportion to those in which the cause was given. The 1870s as we will see later were unusual in the high percentage of deaths due to puerperal fever.

[2] T. Denman, *An Essay on Natural Labours* (London, 1786) and *An Introduction to the Practice of Midwifery*, 2 vols. (London, 1795).

Nevertheless, many lives were lost through avoidable obstetric haemorrhage. In his evidence to the Select Committee on Medical Education in 1834, Sir Charles Clark, LRCP, President of the Obstetric Society, presented the Committee with a long but memorable lecture on the physiology and pathology of labour and the need to reduce the unnecessary loss of mothers and infants from the hazards of childbirth. It was, in essence, a passionate defence of the speciality of obstetrics at a time when the discipline was often despised.[3] Like Farr forty years later, Clarke stressed the vital importance of the correct management of the third stage of labour: 'A bad practitioner will lose 19 out of 20 of his cases of haemorrhage; a good practitioner will hardly ever lose a case, though he may live to a considerable age.' He illustrated the point by referring to the well-recognized danger of pulling on the umbilical cord in an attempt to drag out the placenta before it was separated from the wall of the uterus. If this was done unwisely, the practitioner:

draws down the uterus itself, making that an external tumor which was an internal cavity [in other words the uterus is inverted like a glove pulled inside out]. It occurs sometimes (and there is an instance upon record of a man who was tried at the Old Bailey for such practice) that the practitioner, not aware of that which he has done, has continued to drag, till he has torn the uterus out of the body, dragging with it the intestines and parts contained within the cavity of the belly; and the patient has died.[4]

This was an extreme and dreadful example. Most deaths from haemorrhage were due to lesser degrees of bad practice. In 1870, Dr Evan Jones of Aberdare in South Wales wrote 'the most pernicious practice among midwives here is that of delivering women on their knees on the floor of the bedroom; much unnecessary haemorrhage takes place . . .'.[5]

Disasters were most likely to occur in women of high parity who, if they had easy previous labours, were lulled into a complacent attitude towards childbirth. This danger, the main complication of what came to be called 'grand multiparity', was not generally recognized until the end of the nineteenth century at the earliest; but there is a memorable case-history from Edinburgh:

In 1873, Agnes Keir of Edinburgh, aged 42 and with a history of twelve previous pregnancies, made no arrangements for the delivery of her thirteenth. 'Owing to a malformation of the vulva in the shape of numerous large polypoid growths, she *never* sought medical aid in any of her previous labours but had been in the habit of delivering herself'. In this pregnancy she delivered herself as formerly, but in attempting to pull the placenta out by the cord, the cord snapped. She continued with housework

---

[3] *Report of the Select Committee on Medical Education*, PP 1834, XIII, pt. 1, Q. 4179–277.

[4] Ibid. Q. 4185. This particular case was widely reported in the medical press. It seemed at the time almost inconceivable that any practitioner could have used such violence were it not that the details were confirmed by a post-mortem examination carried out by John Green Crosse of Norwich, who gave evidence at the trial.

[5] 'Report of the Infantile Mortality Committee of the Obstetrical Society of London', *Transactions of the Obstetrical Society of London*, 13 (1871), 390.

until she fainted from haemorrhage, when a neighbour sent for a medical practitioner. He could not be found so a midwife was summoned who sent her to the hospital, where she died soon after admission.[6]

Most 'unnecessary haemorrhages', however, were due to lack of elementary knowledge by the birth attendant of the physiology of the third stage of labour, and of the simple procedures based on such knowledge.

POST-PARTUM HAEMORRHAGE

Before going further it will be helpful to explain briefly the categories and causes of obstetric haemorrhage. In normal deliveries, when the baby is born the uterus contracts firmly and is reduced to a fraction of its former size. As a result of the contraction the placenta is separated from the wall of the uterus and expelled. Contraction brings the walls of the uterus into apposition. This plays a large part in preventing haemorrhage from the massive blood-vessels which supply blood to the placenta, passing through the gaps in a criss-crossed pattern of uterine muscle fibres. With the contraction of the uterus, these criss-crossed muscle fibres, in an action similar to closing a trellis, clamp off the blood vessels. Obstetric haemorrhage occurs when the uterus is prevented from contracting fully and strongly, either because the placenta has separated from the uterine wall but has not been expelled from the uterus; or because the uterine contraction is feeble, as is the case in grand multiparity when the muscle fibres may be weakened by frequent childbearing.

In a few instances post-partum haemorrhage is due to trauma. In such cases bleeding usually occurs from a torn cervix. But in the large majority of cases (over 90 per cent) bleeding occurs from the placental site. If post-partum haemorrhage is associated with a retained placenta, the need to remove the placenta is urgent. But if there is no bleeding, doctors and midwives have known since the eighteenth century that it is wise to wait for at least a half-hour since the normal physiological processes of the third stage can be slow. Patience has always been the supreme virtue in the management of the third stage of labour. If the placenta was not expelled naturally after a half-hour, various forms of active intervention were described in the nine-teenth century: notably Crédes method, and manual removal where the birth-attendant places his or her hand in the uterine cavity, grasps the placenta, and pulls it out. Manual removal of the placenta is not always an easy procedure. Before blood transfusion and antibiotics were available, it was potentially hazardous, but frequently carried out.

---

[6] Edinburgh, Medical Archive Centre. Records of the Edinburgh Royal Maternity and Simpson Maternity Hospital. Ledgers of complicated obstetric cases. LHB 13 17/1. (From 1870 special ledgers of complicated cases were kept and case-histories were routinely entered by the house-surgeon.)

ANTE-PARTUM HAEMORRHAGE

The other form of obstetric haemorrhage, ante-partum haemorrhage, was placed in two classes by Rigby in 1775. One he called 'unavoidable hae-morrhage'; the other, 'accidental haemorrhage'.[7] His term, 'accidental hae-morrhage' is still used, but the synonyms 'abruptio placentae' or 'placental abruption' are used more often. The term used by Rigby for his first cat-egory—'unavoidable haemorrhage'—was soon replaced by the term 'placenta praevia'.

ACCIDENTAL HAEMORRHAGE OR PLACENTAL ABRUPTION

Accidental haemorrhage or placental abruption is a condition in which part of the placenta becomes detached during pregnancy. Bleeding occurs and is accompanied by abdominal pain and rigidity. Often there is severe shock. Occasionally there is a disturbance of the blood-clotting mechanism which used to be described by the chilling term 'cadaver-blood'. The cause of accidental haemorrhage is unknown. It is accompanied by signs of toxaemia and was until recently said to be due to toxaemia. The present view is that toxaemia is a consequence of placental abruption rather than the cause. The foetal loss is very high: even today it is as high as 30–60 per cent, and the mother's life is at hazard as well. In 1869, Goodell in the USA reported that out of 106 cases, 'fifty-four mothers perished and out of 107 children, six alone are known to have been saved'.[8] Modern data suggest that the condition occurs in about 10 in every 1,000 pregnancies. Like post-partum haemor-rhage it is most common in multiparous patients.[9] In such a dangerous condition many treatments were tried, but most found that simple rupture of the membranes and sedation produced the best results.[10]

---

[7] Edward Rigby, *Essay on Uterine Haemorrhage* (London, 1775).

[8] A. Goodell, 'On Concealed Accidental Haemorrhage of the Gravid Uterus', *American Journal of Obstetrics* (1869), 281 quoted in W. T. Lusk, *The Science and Art of Midwifery* (London, 1899).

[9] S. L. Barron, 'Antepartum Haemorrhage', in Sir Alec Turnbull and Geoffery Chamberlain, (eds.), *Obstetrics* (London, 1989), chap. 32.

[10] Sinclair and Johnson at the Rotunda Hospital in Dublin reviewed a series of cases in 1858 and concluded that rupture of membranes was the treatment of choice. Munro Kerr wrote in the late 1930s, 'I have lived through a period when many different treatments have been advocated and employed, and I have personally had experience of all of them. I have employed plugging, rupture of the membranes, version, meteurynter [the insertion of a rubber bag to dilate the cervix], accouchement forcé, Caesarean section... and I have discarded all except rupture of membranes... and abdominal Caesarean section and hysterectomy in special circumstances.' In 136 cases between 1931 and 1934 Munro Kerr employed Caesarean section only once. Only three mothers died. He also used blood transfusion which was perhaps the greatest single advance in the treatment of placental abrution. J. Chassar Moir, *Munro Kerr's Operative Obstetrics* (6th edn., London, 1956).

ANTE-PARTUM HAEMORRHAGE: PLACENTA PRAEVIA

Placenta praevia was aptly described by James Young Simpson as the condition which aroused more anxiety in the attendant and was of more danger to the mother than any other complication of childbirth. In placenta praevia, the placenta lies so low in the uterus that its lower edge is either adjacent to the internal os (partial placenta praevia), or the placenta lies across and covers the os (central placenta praevia). It is easily missed in pregnancy, although in about one-third of cases warning signs of slight episodes of bleeding occur. But in many cases in the past it was only recognized when labour began with a massive, painless, and often terrifying haemorrhage. The cause of the haemorrhage is easy to imagine. As the cervix dilates and stretches, part of the placenta is stripped away from the placental site which bleeds copiously. Even a simple vaginal examination can precipitate a torrential haemorrhage. The problem is plain: the haemorrhage cannot be stopped until the baby and placenta are delivered, and the placenta stands in the way of delivering the baby.

In the eighteenth and nineteenth centuries placenta praevia was sometimes treated by packing the vagina with cloth or inserting an inflatable bag in the hope of controlling the bleeding. But the most favoured method was to plunge a hand through the placenta, turn the baby in the uterus and pull down both legs to deliver it as a breech. In the 1860s Braxton Hicks recommended turning the baby by external manipulation. This avoided forcible dilatation of the cervix with its attendant dangers, and it was only necessary to pass two fingers through the placenta to grasp one of the baby's legs. If the cervix was not fully open, it was common practice to attach a weight to a cord tied to the baby's leg, and hang the weight over the end of the bed. This pulled the breech down, compressed the bleeding site on the uterine wall, and also acted as a force to dilate the cervix. Often this led to a successful delivery.[11] The obvious alternative was Caesarean section, which was first proposed by Lawson Tait of Birmingham in 1890. His suggestion was 'a bombshell in the obstetric camp' which was bitterly opposed. At the time obstetrics was largely in the hands of physicians who resented such radical advice from a surgeon with a huge practice in gynaecology, but little obstetric experience. Lawson Tait advised amputating the uterus at the time of Caesarean section to avoid sepsis. He carried out such an operation in 1898 but acceptance of the

---

[11] This method, known as plugging with the half-breech was still the preferred treatment for placenta praevia in remote areas such as the Highlands of Scotland in the late 1930s (personal communication, Mr Hamish Chalmers, 1987). It was probably Thomas Denman who should be credited with this idea of compression by the half-breech instead of forcible and immediate breech extraction. Chassar Moir, *Munro Kerr's Operative Obstetrics*, 813.

section for reasons other than gross contraction of the pelvis was very slow.[12] Murdoch Cameron of Glasgow, who pioneered Caesarean section for cases of contracted pelvis, said in 1891 that the suggestion that the section should be performed for placenta praevia was a bad joke. The established method was safe. He himself had treated twenty cases of placenta praevia conservatively without losing a single mother.[13]

The first series of Caesarean sections for placenta praevia were carried out in the USA around 1900 where it became fashionable earlier than in Britain. Before 1920, a few British obstetricians approved Caesarean section for a small number of especially difficult cases of placenta praevia, but most were totally opposed to it. By 1920, opinion was changing fast. More and more papers showed that maternal mortality was lowest when the section was performed. By the mid-1930s, the tide had turned, Caesarean section had become the treatment of choice for virtually all cases of placenta praevia where the facilities were available. The change was based on the statistical evidence. At the beginning of the century, the maternal mortality of Caesarean section in cases of placenta praevia was around 30 per cent or higher. By 1921 it had dropped to 14 per cent and by 1934 to less than 7 per cent.[14]

THE MORTALITY FROM HAEMORRHAGE

Haemorrhage, then, was one of the major causes of maternal mortality. Ante-partum haemorrhage could not be prevented and its treatment required a high degree of skill which, before the Second World War, was usually available only in a few hospitals staffed by specialist obstetricians. Post-partum hae-morrhage, however, could usually be prevented by ordinary skill and judge-ment (which often consisted of waiting patiently) which should have been attainable in home deliveries by midwives and general practitioners.

There are plentiful data on deaths from haemorrhage, but few on the incidence. Table 6.1 is based on the records of the Edinburgh Maternity Hospital for the years 1844–6. It shows that cases of post-partum haemor-rhage were twice as common as cases of ante-partum, and that cases of both kinds of haemorrhage were very common. It also shows that even in such early days, long before blood transfusion, the large majority of women who suffered from an obstetric haemorrhage, survived.[15] This report allows us to calculate

[12] J. H. Young, *Caesarean Section: The History and Development of the Operations from the Earliest Times* (London, 1944).
[13] Murdoch Cameron, 'On the Relief of Labour with Impaction by Abdominal Section as a Substitute for the Performance of Craniotomy', *British Medical Journal* (1891), i. 509–14.
[14] Young, *Caesarean Section*, 171–82 gives a full account of changing attitudes to the use of Caesarean section in placenta praevia.
[15] The incidence and case-fatality rate of post-partum haemorrhage depends, of course, on the definition. Some loss of blood in the third stage is normal. How great does the loss have to be before it is classed as a haemorrhage? Opinions varied, and measurement was uncertain as it was

TABLE 6.1 *Cases of Obstetric Haemorrhage, Edinburgh Maternity Hospital,*
1844–1846

Category of haemorrhage[a]	Number of cases	Rate per 10,000 deliveries
Ante-partum haemorrhage		
Partial placenta praevia	3	21.1
Haemorrhage before labour	12	84.6
Haemorrhage during labour	4	28.2
All ante-partum haemorrhage	19	134.1
Post-partum haemorrhage		
Retained placenta	16	112.9
Post-partum	24	169.4
All post-partum	40	282.3
Obstetric haemorrhage Indefinitely stated	8	56.4
All obstetric haemorrhage	67	472.8

[a] Observed in 1,417 labours. None of the cases was fatal.
Note on the parity distribution of the cases: Parity 1 (27%); 2, 3, and 4 (41%); 5–9 (24%);
10–14 (6%); 15–20 (2%).

Source: J. Y. Simpson, 'Report of the Edinburgh Maternity Hospital, St John's Street', *Monthly Journal of Medical Science*, 9 (1848–9), 329–38.

that the incidence of haemorrhage was 473 per 10,000 (4.7 per cent).[16]

As we move forward from the mid-nineteenth century, it seems reasonable to assume that better training of practitioners and midwives, the introduction of the Midwives Act at the beginning of this century, and the well-established reduction in mortality from Caesarean section for placenta praevia, should have led to a steady reduction in deaths due to haemorrhage by the mid-1930s. Did such a fall occur, and was there a notable difference in death rates from haemorrhage in different countries and regions? Some answers can be found in Table 6.2.

In most Western countries the average rate of maternal mortality from all

common for most of the blood to end up on the floor or soaked up in cotton wool or cloths. It was usually defined as any loss of blood in excess of 1 pint, but the definition was both vague and variable, making estimates of incidence hard to compare with each other.

[16] Two points should be made about this Edinburgh report from the 1840s. First, the high incidence may have been a reflection of a readiness to classify small losses of blood as haemorrhages. Second, it is a report based on a population of hospital cases with a high proportion of women of very high parity. Roughly one-third were in their fifth or over pregnancy. Out of 1,417 cases, there were 11 in their 12th pregnancy, 7 in their 13th, 2 in their 14th, and one each in their 15th, 16th, 17th, and 20th pregnancies. Such high parities would predispose to a high rate of post-partum haemorrhage. Nevertheless, if we allow for high parity and assume that the incidence in populations with fewer women of high parity would have been closer to 300 per 10,000 deliveries, it still means that over 95 per cent of cases of obstetric haemorrhage survived.

TABLE 6.2 *Maternal Mortality Rates Due to Various Categories of Obstetric Haemorrhage in Various Countries at Various Periods*

	Total maternal mortality	Ante-partum haemorrhage		Post-partum haemorrhage and retained placenta			Total Obstetric haemorrhage[a]	Percentage
		Placenta praevia	Accident: haemorrhage	Retained placenta	Post-partum haemorrhage	Both		
England and Wales								
1872–6	54.25	3.07		0.80	8.29	9.09	12.16	22.4
1900	46.60						7.40	15.9
1910	35.50						6.80	19.1
1923	38.10	2.35	0.26	0.73	2.31	3.04	5.65	14.8
1933	43.20	2.26	0.23	0.80	1.13	1.93	4.42	10.2
Scotland								
1931–5	61.30	2.90	2.40			4.0	9.30	15.1
1936–40	48.30	2.00	2.10			4.1	8.20	16.9
Eire								
1934	46.80	2.90				4.4	7.30	15.5
Sweden								
1931–5	32.60	1.70	—	—	—	—	—	
Switzerland								
1925	41.20						15.10	36.6
Netherlands								
1933	31.40	3.10					6.00	19.2
1934	31.60	2.50					4.90	15.5
1935	29.30	1.70					3.80	13.0

Canada 1929					
(Institutional deliveries)	131.00			11.00	8.4
(Non-institutional deliveries)	37.00			7.00	19.0
(All deliveries)	56.00			8.00	14.3
USA					
1921 (Death registration area)	68.20			6.80	10.0
Philadelphia, 1921–33				5.80	10.9
New York State, 1936–8	26.90	1.48	4.25	5.70	21.3
South Carolina, 1934–5					
White	66.20			6.60	10.0
Black	103.40			20.10	19.5
Australia					
1915	45.50			4.70	10.3

a Shown as the rate per 10,000 births and as a percentage of total maternal deaths.

Sources: England and Wales and Scotland: *Registrar General's Reports*, Ministry of Health, *Report of an Investigation into Maternal Mortality* (London, 1937); Eire: *Annual Reports of the Registrar General* (Dublin); Switzerland: League of Nations, Health Organization, Statistical Handbook Series, 12, *Official Vital Statistics of Switzerland* (Geneva, 1928); Sweden: U. Högberg, *Maternal Mortality in Sweden*, Umeå University, Medical Dissertations, NS 156 (Umeå, 1985); The Netherlands: Statistiek van de sterfte naar den leeftid en de oorzaken van den dood, Central bureau voor de statistiek (1911–38); Canada: E. S. MacPhail, 'A Statistical Study in Maternal Mortality', *American Journal of Public Health*, 22 (1932), 618; USA (1921): R. M. Woodbury, *Maternal Mortality*, Children's Bureau Publications, No. 152 (Washington, DC, 1926); New York State: J. Yerushalmy, M. Kramer, and E. M. Gardiner, 'Studies in Childbirth Mortality: Puerperal Fatality and Loss of Offspring', *Public Health Reports*, 55 (1940), 1010–27; South Carolina, USA: South Carolina Medical Association, Committee on Maternal Welfare, *Maternal Mortality in South Carolina, 1934–5* (1936), Supplement for 1940–1 (1941); Philadelphia: Philadelphia County Medical Society, *Maternal Mortality in Philadelphia* (Philadelphia, Pa., 1934); Australia: *Report on Maternal Mortality in Childbirth*, Dept. of Trades and Customs (Victoria, 1917).

causes was, from around 1900 to around 1935, about 50 deaths per 10,000 births (range 35 to 65). Deaths from haemorrhage accounted on average for seven or eight of the fifty deaths or, in round figures, 15 per cent of maternal mortality. But, as the table shows, there were fairly wide variations, although differences in the way that deaths from haemorrhage were classified make detailed comparison difficult and account for the incompleteness of Table 6.2.

The death rate from placenta praevia—2–3 deaths per 10,000 deliveries—stands out because it was remarkably constant in all countries from which data are available, from the late nineteenth century and the mid-1930s. I can think of no maternal complication in which the death rate was so constant and it is interesting that the increasing use of Caesarean section did not reduce the national level of mortality from this condition before 1935. There was, however, a steady fall in deaths due to post-partum haemorrhage in England and Wales between 1900 and 1933, before it could be attributed to blood transfusion. This suggests that birth-attendants (and possibly midwives in particular after the 1902 Act) were becoming more and more skilful in the management of the third stage of labour. If one is searching for statistical evidence of a significant improvement in the standard of maternal care in England and Wales between 1900 and 1935, almost the only example is the reduced mortality from post-partum haemorrhage.

7

Abortion

Of all causes of maternal mortality, abortion stands out as the one which causes the most difficult but also some of the most interesting historical and statistical problems. Sometimes it must be admitted that one sympathizes with doctors in the early part of this century who argued that abortion had no place in the statistics of maternal mortality. They said, quite rightly, that maternal mortality was a matter of public concern. What most people wanted to know was the risks attendant on normal wanted pregnancies. They did not want the field muddied by the illegal and thoroughly distasteful activities of abortionists with their curettes, gum-elastic catheters, and syringes. There was no need, they said, to inflate the statistics with abortion deaths and thereby frighten respectable women. Such were their views.[1]

Nevertheless, abortion is one of the outcomes of pregnancy and it was seldom if ever possible to draw a firm line between 'natural' or spontaneous abortion, and induced abortion, whether therapeutic or criminal. The difficulty of obtaining accurate statistics was obviously due 'in great measure to the desire to conceal an abortion which has been intentionally induced'.[2] Some deaths from abortion were certified as deaths due to some other cause. Shorter has suggested that in England and Wales deaths from criminal abortion were concealed to such an extent that the statistics of maternal mortality due to non-abortive causes were seriously distorted.[3] I think he is

[1] See Professor Strachan of Cardiff in the correspondence columns of the *British Medical Journal* (26 Jan. 1935), 175, and Dr Illingworth of Australia, *Medical Journal of Australia* (30 Mar. 1935), 414. In 1941, the American Public Health Association suggested that in the interests of uniformity, the term 'puerperal fatality rate' should be used to describe all deaths which followed a live or a stillbirth, thus excluding deaths from abortions and ectopic pregnancies. In one notable survey of maternal mortality, J. V. DePorte, *Maternal Mortality and Stillbirths in New York State: 1915–1925* (New York, 1928) abortions were deliberately excluded on the grounds that the total number was unknown.

[2] Ministry of Health, *Final Report of Departmental Committee on Maternal Mortality and Morbidity* (London, 1932).

[3] E. Shorter, *A History of Women's Bodies* (London, 1983). Shorter asserts, without producing the evidence to support the assertion, that the published statistics for England and Wales, which show no significant or sustained fall in deaths from puerperal sepsis before the mid-1930s, are so grossly distorted as to be unreliable. He suggests that deaths from full-term puerperal fever were steadily declining, but were inflated by doctors who, under pressure from the relatives, deliberately falsified death certificates by stating that deaths due to septic abortion were deaths due to full-term sepsis. In I. Loudon, 'Deaths in Childbed from the Eighteenth Century to 1935', *Medical History*, 30 (1986), 1–41, I have stated why I believe it is unlikely that this occurred on a large enough scale seriously to distort the trend in deaths from full-term sepsis without being detected and reported in the numerous investigations into maternal mortality.

wrong, but his assertion highlights the difficulties of the subject and the need for careful assessment of the statistics. We can start by trying to estimate the likely incidence of spontaneous abortion or miscarriage.

Modern estimates suggest that about 10 per cent of conceptions are aborted spontaneously. Although this is based on hospital statistics, it corresponds closely with estimates from various countries earlier this century.[4] The immediate causes of death in abortion were usually haemorrhage or infection. Perforation of the uterus could occur in illegal abortions, therapeutic abortions, and also when curettage was employed following an incomplete abortion. Death could follow a spontaneous abortion, but it was rare. One American study suggested in 1938 that where death followed spontaneous abortion it was usually due to an associated disease in the mother such as pneumonia or influenza. The disease killed the foetus first, which was then aborted, and the mother died from the disease later.[5] Where a woman died after a spontaneous abortion, death from sepsis was so rare that in the absence of firm evidence to the contrary, post-abortive sepsis was an indication that an abortion had been induced, whatever the patient may have said.[6]

In the national statistics of England and Wales (and most other Western countries) deaths due to abortion were split into two separate classes, abortion without sepsis and post-abortive sepsis. Until the early 1930s, 'abortion' or 'abortion without sepsis' formed a separate category in the lists of causes of maternal mortality. Deaths from septic abortion, as we have seen, were buried along with deaths from puerperal fever under the umbrella term puerperal sepsis; they were not shown as a separate category until 1934. There were, of course, problems associated with inaccurate certification. Even in the 1930s,

---

[4] Department of Health, *Report on Confidential Enquiries into Maternal Deaths in England and Wales, 1982–84* (London, 1989), 5 (Table 1.7). Since a small but unknown number of early spontaneous miscarriages are treated at home or never seen by a doctor, the true figure may be above 10%. R. K. Stix and D. G. Wiehl, 'Abortion and Public Health', *American Journal of Public Health*, 28 (1938), 621–8, found that the rate of spontaneous abortion reported in different studies was, with remarkable consistency, close to 10% of all pregnancies. One of the very few reports on the incidence of abortion in the early 19th cent. is by A. B. Granville, 'A report of the Practice of Midwifery at the Westminster General Dispensary during 1819', *Medical and Physical Journal*, 47 (1822), 282–8 and 374–8. He found that over a period of 10 years, out of 515 women questioned, 147 had miscarried at some time during the decade and had suffered in total 372 abortions. Of these he recorded only 12 as being due to 'improper moral and physical treatment of pregnant women' by which one guesses he meant induced abortion. Note that the terms miscarriage and abortion are interchangeable, even though it is often believed that miscarriage denotes a spontaneous termination of pregnancy and abortion an induced termination, whether legal or illegal.

[5] Stix and Wiehl, 'Abortion and Public Health'. In countries such as England and Wales, but not the USA, such deaths would be excluded from the list of deaths due to puerperal or 'direct' causes. They would be entered under 'pneumonia', 'influenza', and so on.

[6] The relative absence of danger in spontaneous abortion was shown by a study of 1,000 successive cases of abortion in New Zealand. In 374 cases in which instrumentation was admitted 49 died of sepsis. In 246 cases of spontaneous abortion there were no deaths. W. H. B. Bull, 'Abortion and Contraception', *New Zealand Medical Journal*, 35 (1936), 39–44. See also n. 11, below.

some deaths from sepsis in England and Wales were reported simply as 'puerperal sepsis' without any statement about the stage of pregnancy, raising the suspicion of a deliberate attempt to hide deaths from induced abortion. However, the Registrar General found in 1934 that no more than 4 per cent of these were deaths due to post-abortive sepsis.[7]

There was another complication. If a death from abortion was reported to the coroner, an inquest was held and the jury decided whether the verdict was manslaughter, murder, suicide, or accident. Such deaths were entered in the class of deaths due to violence. Deaths due to abortion were therefore split into three groups: non-septic abortion, post-abortive sepsis merged with sepsis following childbirth, and 'coroner's cases' or as they were often called, 'inquest cases' of abortion under the heading of violent deaths. Taking all these difficulties into account we can attempt to discover the part played by abortion in maternal mortality.

ABORTION IN BRITAIN

Although it is extremely difficult to estimate the incidence of induced abortion before the Second World War, it seems likely that the incidence and death rate from abortion began to rise in the second half of the nineteenth century and continued to reach a peak in the 1930s. Probably the period of most rapid increase came just after the First World War. Abortion as a serious public health problem was brought to the forefront largely as a result of the 1932 report on maternal mortality. Of course it had been recognized as a serious matter long before, but it was a measure of a new degree of concern that the Registrar General devoted a large section of his 1934 report to abortion. What is the evidence for a rise in abortions during the inter-war period?

Table 7.1 shows certain data on deaths due to abortion in England and Wales between 1928 and 1934 when total numbers and rates of septic abortion were rising. Inquest cases rose as well, but were at most only a fifth of all reported deaths due to abortion, while deaths from non-septic abortion remained more or less level and actually fell between 1933 and 1934.

What do we know of the maternal age, civil state, and social class of women who died from abortion? Some answers are given in Tables 7.2, 7.3, and 7.4. The common idea that most criminal abortions were performed on young

---

[7] In the *Registrar General's Statistical Review of England and Wales for the Year 1934* (London, 1936), 123–4, it is stated that there were '563 sepsis deaths having no statement as to duration of pregnancy in 1934'. If Shorter were correct (see n. 3, above) it would be amongst these one would have expected to find 'hidden' deaths from septic abortion, for doctors could have availed themselves of the opportunity for a 'white lie' by certifying post-abortive deaths as 'puerperal sepsis' with no mention of stage of pregnancy. Yet, on careful enquiry, this was shown not to be the case. What was revealed was a lack of care, a laziness in the certification of deaths, which had been recognized by successive Registrars General since the 1870s, and was the subject of their continual exhortation to greater care in death certification.

TABLE 7.1 *Deaths Due to Septic and Non-Septic Abortion, England and Wales,
1928–1934*

Year	1928	1929	1930	1931	1932	1933	1934
Total deaths due to abortion	405	423	491	426	448	463	494
Deaths due to septic abortion (percentage of total)	224 (55.3)	238 (56.3)	300 (61.1)	229 (53.7)	262 (58.5)	257 (55.5)	295 (59.7)
Deaths due to non-septic abortion (percentage of total)	124 (30.6)	148 (35.0)	124 (25.2)	118 (27.7)	117 (26.1)	121 (26.1)	99 (20.0)
Inquest cases of abortion (percentage of total)	57 (14.1)	67 (15.8)	67 (13.6)	79 (18.5)	69 (15.4)	85 (18.3)	100 (20.2)
Maternal mortality rate due to all puerperal causes[a]	44.20	43.30	44.00	41.10	42.10	45.10	46.00
Maternal mortality rate due to abortion[a]	6.13	6.57	7.56	6.73	7.29	7.97	8.26
Deaths due to abortion as a percentage of deaths due to all puerperal causes	(13.9)	(15.2)	(17.2)	(16.4)	(17.3)	(17.7)	(17.9)
Deaths due to abortion per million women aged 15–44	42	43	50	43	46	47	51

[a] Maternal deaths per 10,000 live births.

Source: Registrar General's Statistical Review of England and Wales for the Year 1934 (London, 1936).

unmarried girls 'in trouble' is clearly mistaken. Eighty-five per cent of abortion deaths between 1926 and 1930 occurred in married women; and the death rate per million married women was much higher than it was for single women. Table 7.4 shows that the death rate from abortion was lowest in social classes I and II, highest in social class V. The difference, however, was not large, and is open to several interpretations. The lower rate in social classes I and II may have been due, not to a lower incidence, but to the ability of these

TABLE 7.2 *Abortion Deaths of Maried, Single, Widowed, and Divorced Women, England and Wales, 1926–1930*

	Age groups							
	15–19	20–4	25–9	30–4	35–9	40–4	45	All ages
Married women	7	150	397	510	498	255	33	1,850
Single, widowed, and divorced	35	97	67	51	44	22	2	318
Death rates per Million women living		65	80	89	88	48		

Source: Registrar Generalis Statistical Review of England and Wales for the Year 1934 (London, 1936).

TABLE 7.3 *Deaths Due to Abortion in Married and Single Women, England and Wales, 1934*

	Deaths of married women per million at ages			Deaths of single women per million at ages		
	15–24	25–34	35–44	15–24	25–34	35–44
Post-abortive sepsis	50	65	35	4	17	—
Non-septic abortion	8	17	19	1	3	—
Criminal abortion	15	17	7	5	12	2
Total abortion	73	99	62	10	32	2

Source: Registrar General's Statistical Review of England and Wales for the Year 1934 (London, 1936).

TABLE 7.4 *Maternal Mortality (Married Women only), according to Social Class of Husband, England and Wales, 1930–1932, per 10,000 Live Births*

	I–II Professional	III Skilled	IV Semi-skilled	V Unskilled
All causes	44.4	41.1	41.8	38.9
Puerperal sepsis	14.5	13.3	12.1	11.6
Puerperal haemorrhage	5.0	4.4	4.8	6.0
Abortion	5.0	5.6	5.6	5.7

Source: Registrar General's Statistical Review of England and Wales for the Year 1934 (London, 1936).

TABLE 7.5 *Deaths from Abortion and Sepsis, England and Wales, 1934, Scotland, 1931–1935, and Ireland (Eire), 1931–1935*

	England and Wales 1934		Scotland 1931–5		Eire 1931–5	
	(per 10,000 births)	(percentage of total)	(per 10,000 births)	(percentage of total)	(per 10,000 births)	(percentage of total)
All puerperal causes	46.0	100	61.3	100	45.3	100
Non-abortive sepsis	15.3	33.3	21.5	35.1	13.4	29.6
Post-abortive sepsis	4.9	10.6	3.7	6.0	1.1	2.4
Total puerperal sepsis	20.2	44.0	25.2	41.1	14.5	32.0
Post-abortive sepsis	4.9	10.6	3.7	6.0	1.1	2.4
Abortion without sepsis	1.6	3.5	1.4	2.3	1.25	2.8
All abortion deaths[a]	6.5	14.1	5.1	8.3	2.35	5.2

[a] Coroner's cases (inquest cases) of abortive deaths are not included in this table.

Source: Registrar General's Statistical Review of England and Wales for the Year 1934 (London, 1936); P. L. McKinlay, *Maternal Mortality in Scotland, 1911–1945* (Edinburgh, 1947); Eire: *Annual Reports of the Registrar General* (Dublin).

social classes to pay for the safest forms of induced abortions, carried out by doctors; or there may have been a lower incidence because of greater use of contraception in social classes I and II; or it may be that women in social classes I and II were able to persuade their doctors to provide false certification. We return to this later.

The link between abortion on the one hand and the desire to limit family size and contraceptive practice on the other has been established by numerous studies. Few death rates are so clearly determined by social attitudes as deaths from septic abortion. The rising rate of abortion following the First World War arose in a period when large families were going out of fashion. It was also a period of growing indifference to the 'morality of parsons' and of a changing climate of sexual liberation: a change which, according to Brookes,

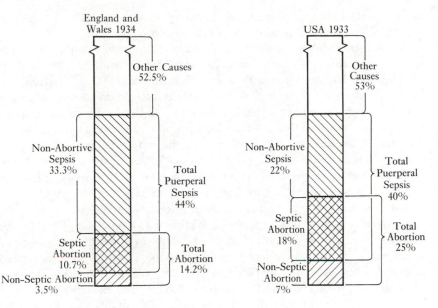

FIG. 7.1 England and Wales 1934, USA 1933. Deaths due to abortion (septic and non-septic) and puerperal sepsis (abortive and non-abortive) shown as percentages of total maternal mortality *Source*: Registrar General for England and Wales, Annual Statistical Reviews; *Maternal Mortality in Fifteen States*, Children's Bureau Publications, No. 223 (Washington, DC, 1934).

had 'made the little footnotes to measure morality look absurd [and] mocked the emptiness of female virtue'.[8]

By the 1930s in England and Wales, abortion caused as many deaths as obstetric haemorrhage. We should notice, however, that the increase in abortion deaths in Britain, although worrying, was quite modest. Table 7.5 shows that in 1934, the year of the highest rate of abortion deaths, for every 10,000 deliveries 46 women died of puerperal causes. Of these, 6.5 (or 14 per cent) died of abortion. Three-quarters of these died from post-abortive sepsis, one-quarter from non-septic pathology, usually haemorrhage.

One of the most difficult questions about maternal mortality before 1930 is the number of puerperal sepsis deaths which were due to abortion and the number due to puerperal fever following full-term delivery. Figure 7.1 shows that post-abortive sepsis in England and Wales in 1934 accounted for about one-quarter of all deaths due to puerperal sepsis and the evidence suggests that the 1934 level represented a peak in the rising tide of abortion deaths.

[8] Dora Russell, *Hypatia, or Women and Knowledge* (New York, 1925) quoted in Barbara Brookes, *Abortion in England, 1900–1967* (London, 1988). Brookes is an excellent source on changing attitudes and those who sought to resist change.

In Scotland, where total maternal mortality was higher, abortion deaths accounted for a smaller proportion of total maternal mortality.

Eire is especially interesting because deaths from septic abortion were, as far as I can discover, the lowest recorded anywhere in the 1930s. The rate for 1931–5 was 1.1 compared with 3.7 in Scotland and 4.9 in England and Wales. It might be thought that for religious reasons there was a greater motive for concealment in Ireland. A high rate of deaths attributed to spontaneous abortions would fuel this suspicion. But the mortality rate due to spontaneous abortion was also lower than in the rest of the British Isles. Also, mortality rates for puerperal sepsis and the proportion of sepsis deaths due to septic abortion were also conspicuously low in Eire. What Eire gained in this respect, however, was offset by high rates from other causes so that total maternal mortality was as high as it was in England and Wales.

An interdepartmental committee on abortion was set up in 1937 by the Ministry of Health and reported in 1939.[9] The members of the committee were people of wide experience, unlikely to be deceived by exaggerated statistics. They estimated that in England and Wales there were between 110,000 and 150,000 abortions a year, of which 60 per cent were spontaneous abortions and 40 per cent illegal abortions. The number of therapeutic abortions was insignificant. In 1936, the year in which the estimate of the total number of abortions was made, if we take the lower estimate of 110,000 abortions, 44,000 were illegal and 66,000 were spontaneous. This leads to the conclusion that 8.9 per cent of pregnancies ended in spontaneous abortion, a rate which corresponds with other estimates of spontaneous abortion.[10]

We come to a major problem, however, when we ask how many abortion deaths would have occurred if it was true that there were 44,000 illegal abortions a year? The answer depends on the estimate of the mortality rate of illegal abortion, and on that there are no sure answers. Nevertheless, a number of estimates were made and suggested a fatality rate of between 3 per cent and 5 per cent in the 1930s.[11]

[9] 'The Abortion Report', *British Medical Journal* (1939), i. 1248–51. *Report of Interdepartmental Committee on Abortion* (London, 1939). Membership of the Committee included T. Watts Eden, Sir Comyns Berkeley, Sir Ewen Maclean, Dr M'Gonigle, and Lady Forber.

[10] In England and Wales in 1936 there were 605,292 live births and 25,045 stillbirths. To these we must add the estimate of 110,000 abortions to arrive at the total of 740,337 pregnancies. 66,000 spontaneous abortions would represent 8.9% of total pregnancies; 44,000 illegal abortions would represent 5.9% of all pregnancies.

[11] Paul Ballard in France suggested that the fatality rate of illegal abortion was 3.5%. *British Medical Journal* (1937), i. 620. A study of abortion in England suggested a mortality for illegal abortion of 4.72%. Ibid. (1936), ii. epitome, para. 317. R. G. Cooke suggested 3% in his paper 'An Analysis of 350 Cases of Abortion', ibid. (1938), i. 1045–7. A report of 1,000 cases of abortion admitted to St Giles Hospital, Camberwell between 1930 and 1934 showed 485 cases of induced abortion with 15 deaths (3.1%) and 246 cases of spontaneous abortion with no deaths. In 269 cases (with 3 deaths) it was not known whether they were spontaneous or induced. See A. Macfarlane and M. Mugford, *Birth Counts: Statistics of Pregnancy and Childbirth* (London, 1984), i. 69 (Table 4.1).

Assuming a 3 per cent mortality rate and 44,000 illegal abortions annually, the expected number of deaths from such abortions would have been 1,320 a year. The actual annual number of registered deaths from abortions in the 1930s rose from (in round figures) 500 to 600 (Table 7.1). This means that around 700 to 800 did not appear as such in the lists of the General Register Office. How can the discrepancy be explained? There are several possibilities.

1. The estimate of total abortions was too high. The interdepartmental committee's estimate of 100,000 to 150,000 a year was based on the estimate of the BMA Committee on Medical Aspects of Abortion (1936) that between 16 per cent and 20 per cent of all pregnancies ended in abortion. While the calculation of the percentage of spontaneous abortion had a reasonably firm foundation, the extra number added on for illegal abortion was guesswork. Nobody knew the true figure.

2. There was false certification on a large scale with many deaths from illegal abortion being certified falsely by a doctor as being due to some other cause. If this was the sole explanation it would have meant that around 7,000 false certificates were provided for abortion cases in the decade 1930–9. It is likely that false certification on such a large scale would have been detected or at the very least strongly suspected; and it would have been publicized if only because it would have provided an explanation for high maternal mortality that would to some extent have exonerated doctors who practised obstetrics. The members of the interdepartmental committee were well aware of the possibility of deception in death certification but there is no hint of deception on such a huge scale in their report or anywhere else.

3. The third possibility is that the estimated fatality rate is too high. The interdepartmental committee found that the risk of death was much reduced when an illegal abortion was carried out by a medical practitioner, and there is no doubt that many were. In a minority report to the Abortion Report, Mrs Thurtle, Labour MP for Shoreditch, recorded her opinion that it was 'not difficult for any woman of moderate means to find a medical man willing to relieve her of an unwelcome pregnancy, regardless of the state of her health'. Fees charged by doctors could be as high as 100 gns. but were usually much lower; unqualified abortionists usually charged between 2 and 3 gns. The estimates of a fatality rate of 3 per cent and 4 per cent were mostly based on hospital statistics in which the patients were a selected group consisting largely of working-class women who were most likely to have been treated by untrained abortionists without the use of antiseptic and aseptic techniques. Moreover they came to the notice of hospital authorities because something went wrong. Pregnancies successfully and rapidly aborted by an abortionist never came near a hospital. If a substantial proportion of illegal abortions were in fact carried out by qualified doctors, and if we remember that hospital cases were a highly selected group, it is likely that the fatality rate was lower than 3 per cent.

It is clear there are many unresolved (and probably insoluble) problems in the attempt to quantify abortion. Probably the disparity between the estimated number of deaths in the 1930s and the recorded number was due to a combination of all three factors considered above, with the first and third—overestimates of the number of illegal abortions and of the fatality rate—being the most important. A similar situation is described in the section on maternal mortality in the USA.

By today's standards, these estimates of induced abortion may seem horrifying. They pale into insignificance compared with our European neighbours, who are considered next.

ABORTION IN OTHER COUNTRIES: EUROPE

Shorter quotes estimates of 8,000 abortion deaths a year in Germany in the 1920s. Just how startling this is becomes clear when one realizes it was more than three times the annual number of deaths from *all* puerperal causes in England and Wales.[12] Eight thousand may be too high. Taussig, from his extensive researches, was more inclined to accept an estimate of 5,300 deaths annually, but even this is more than ten times as many abortion deaths as occurred in England and Wales.[13]

Germany was, however, notorious for its high level of abortion in the inter-war period. The abortions recorded by all 'German Maternities' (maternity hospitals) showed that the number of abortions per 100 births rose from 3 in 1902–4 to 16 in 1929. To what extent this represented a change in admission policies as opposed to an increase in the incidence of abortion is unclear. Likewise, Schottelius is quoted by Taussig as the authority for the assertion that in Hamburg in 1919 the ratio of abortions to confinements was 1:2 (16,779 confinements and 8,707 abortions), but the source of these figures is unclear. Similar levels of abortion were quoted for Berlin. We may distrust points of detail, but virtually all studies suggested that rates of abortion were much higher in large cities than small town or rural areas, a difference that was confirmed by reports from Vienna and from Warsaw in 1912 where it was said there was one illegal abortion to every three confinements.[14]

In France the incidence of abortion during the nineteenth and early

---

[12] Shorter, *History of Women's Bodies*, 194–5.

[13] Taussig, *Abortion, Spontaneous and Induced, Medical and Social Aspects* (London, 1936). Taussig was Professor of Clinical Obstetrics and Clinical Gynaecology, Washington University School of Medicine, St Louis. His book was one of a series on the medical aspects of human fertility, sponsored by the National Committee on Maternal Health. Some of Taussig's prolific data are presented rather uncritically and are open to a variety of interpretations.

[14] The higher urban rates were also found in Britain where, in 1930, deaths due to abortion were substantially higher in London than the County Boroughs, and in the County Boroughs compared with rural areas. James Young, 'Maternal Mortality and Maternal Mortality Rates', *American Journal of Obstetrics and Gynaecology*, 31 (1936), 198–212.

twentieth centuries appears to have been extraordinarily high. It is a point of special interest to demographers because the fertility decline began in France nearly 100 years before it began amongst its European neighbours. This decline and the consequent slow increase in population is generally attributed to contraception, with the main emphasis on coitus interruptus at any rate up to the end of the nineteenth century when the sheath may have become so inexpensive it was widely available across the social spectrum. McLaren, however, makes a strong case for believing that a large component of the fall in fertility was the extraordinarily high incidence of abortion as a means of contraception.[15]

The incidence of abortion in France seems to have climbed rapidly through the second half of the nineteenth and early years of the twentieth centuries. By the end of the nineteenth century small families amongst the bourgeoisie had become the fashion. Abortion as a means of family limitation had become commonplace, even fashionable. It was regarded as a safe procedure. A French doctor remarked in 1909: 'more and more we are struck by the astonishing cynicism with which women—many women and of every social class—talk of such practices [abortion] as the most natural and permissible of acts.'

Although many abortions were carried out by doctors and some by un-trained women, it seems that midwives may have been responsible for the majority. Some midwives were so well known that they had acquired such sobriquets as 'La Mort aux Gosses', 'La Cacheuse'. They enjoyed a degree of notoriety which suggest public acknowledgement if not tacit approval of their actions. It was said that instruments for abortion (including one called the 'canule anglais') were openly on sale in Paris, and it was also believed that antisepsis had made instrumental abortion a safe as well as a sure way of terminating an unwanted pregnancy. In the 1890s, it was said that midwives performed more abortions than deliveries, which may well be true since one abortionist confessed to servicing 2,000 women in 1890, and another in 1891 claimed to have carried out 10,000 abortions—a number which is both hard to believe and impossible to dismiss as pure fiction. In Paris there were strong financial motives. Most babies were born in hospital, leaving some 30,000 home births in 1892 for which 1,000 midwives and 4,000 doctors were competing. To survive economically, midwives turned to abortions.[16]

In addition, it appears that many women attempted self-abortion and then admitted themselves to hospital for the operation to be completed, confessing openly and even expressing pride in their action. According to

[15] A. McLaren, 'Abortion in France: Women and the Regulation of Family Size', *French Historical Studies*, 10 (1978), 461–85, is an excellent source on the social implications of abortion and the connections between abortion and other forms of family limitation, and most of all on the astonishing incidence of abortion in France.

[16] Ibid. 478.

various authorities the percentage of women hospital patients which were abortion cases rose from 7 per cent in 1902 to 30 per cent in 1913. It was also said in 1906 that 100,000 abortions were induced each year in Paris, while government reports after the 1914–18 war referred to between 300,000 and 500,000 abortions a year in France, with one in every two pregnancies ending in an induced abortion.[17]

McLaren warns that such reports may have been exaggerated by those with an axe to grind. Exact figures cannot be known. But the incidence of induced abortion seems to have been higher in nineteenth-century France than any other Western country. There were prosecutions and police reports but only a few. Abortion was, of course, condemned by the church; but legal and religious sanctions seem to have been powerless in the face of abortion as a means of contraception which had become so commonplace that it was socially acceptable. The law and the church made occasional gestures but no real attempt to turn the tide.

In Denmark, Brandstrup found there had been 35,000 abortions treated in hospital, and he estimated the number treated outside hospital was a third of the total. From a careful assessment of 711 hospital cases he concluded only one-fifth of abortions were spontaneous.[18] In Sweden, Lindquivst reported a definite increase in the abortion rate from 1910 to 1927, mainly amongst married women. In Stockholm in 1926 more than half the total maternal deaths were due to septic abortion.[19] Högberg tells us that abortion first became a serious problem in Sweden in the late nineteenth century. Death rates due to abortion climbed in Sweden, as elsewhere, through the 1920s, reaching a peak in the early 1930s when it was estimated that the risk of dying from abortion was 7.65 per 10,000 pregnancies; a figure close to the rate of about 7 deaths per 10,000 *births* in England and Wales, shown in Table 7.1. Because maternal mortality from all causes was lower in Sweden than Britain, abortion was relatively a much larger problem in Sweden. From 1931 to 1935, abortion accounted for 30 per cent of total maternal mortality, compared with 25 per cent in the USA as we will see shortly, and 14 per cent in England and Wales. In the same period, septic abortion accounted for half the total deaths due to sepsis in Sweden, as opposed to 40 per cent in the USA, 24 per cent in England and Wales, 14 per cent in Scotland, and only 7 per cent in Eire.[20]

---

[17] Ibid. 479.

[18] E. Brandstrup, 'Numerical Relationship of Criminal Abortion to other Abortion', *Nord. Med. Tidsskrift* (5 Oct. 1935), 1577. Summarized in 'Epitome of Current Medical Literature', *British Medical Journal* (1935), ii. 90, para. 498.

[19] Taussig, *Abortion*, 364–6, and James Young, 'Maternal Mortality and Maternal Mortality Rates', *American Journal of Obstetrics and Gynaecology*, 31 (1936), 198–212. Balard, reported in *British Medical Journal* (1937), i. 727.

[20] U. Högberg and Ingemar Joelssen, 'Maternal Deaths Related to Abortions in Sweden, 1931–1980', *Gynaecologic and Obstetric Investigation*, 20/4 (1985), reprinted in Högberg, *Maternal Mortality in Sweden* (Umeå, 1985), 85–94.

In other words, in spite of the problems created by the tendency to hide the fatalities due to illegal abortion, there is really little doubt that in many if not all Western countries, rates of abortion and deaths due to illegal abortion were rising from the late nineteenth century. Apart from France where the high incidence happened earlier, the rise was relatively slow through the first two decades of the twentieth century, but accelerated after the First World War. In some countries (notably Germany, Sweden, and the USA), deaths from illegal abortion had risen by the 1930s to heights which could, without exaggeration, be described as very alarming indeed; hence the frequent references to an 'epidemic' in the inter-war period. Nowhere was this more striking than in the Soviet Union, where abortion was legalized.

ABORTION IN THE SOVIET UNION

Abortion was legalized in the Soviet Union in November 1920.[21] The Russian Health Commission had noticed the increase in abortion in Western Europe and asserted, correctly, that attempts to curb abortion by punitive legislation had failed. They had simply driven abortion underground. The Soviet authorities wanted to reduce the birth rate and saw legal abortion as a means to that end and as the only way to abolish the scourge of illegal abortion. It was therefore decided that any woman in the Soviet Union who wanted an abortion could have one, provided it was carried out by a doctor in a hospital. Any other form of abortion carried the liability to imprisonment. No doctor could refuse to carry out an abortion, although he could discourage it if he saw fit.

The result was a demand which was so enormous that by 1924 there was insufficient hospital accommodation. To limit numbers, priority was given to certain groups, namely women with no means of support, and women who, though married and with means of support, already had several children. Unfortunately, this led to an upsurge in illegal abortions. In an attempt to reduce demand, charges were introduced which varied according to ability to pay. Special 'abortaria' were established in the larger cities of the Soviet Union. Moscow had two, each with 250 beds. On the day Taussig himself visited one of these abortaria, fifty-seven abortions were performed. It was said that in 1931 91,000 abortions were carried out in Moscow.[22] Most patients were married women with more than one child. Few were young single women, pregnant from casual sexual encounters. In a series of over 2,000 abortions in Moscow, only 5 per cent of the women were under the age

---

[21] This account is largely based on Taussig, *Abortion*, 405, and Taussig's account of his visit to Russia described in 'An Account of a Visit by American Physicians to the Soviet Union', *American Journal of Obstetrics and Gynaecology* (1931), 134–9.

[22] Taussig, *Abortion*, 405–7.

of 20, 64 per cent were aged 21–30, 30 per cent were aged 31–40, and 2 per cent were over 40.

The legalization of abortion was considered a success from at least two points of view. The birth rate was greatly reduced, and so was the number of illegal abortions and abortion deaths and thus the rate of maternal mortality. One report stated that out of 175,000 abortions carried out legally in hospitals there were only nine deaths, a rate of 5 per 100,000. The death rate of illegal abortions in Moscow in 1926 was 1.2 per cent or 1,200 per 100,000 compared with 29,306 hospital abortions without, it was said, a single death.[23]

What is most striking is the ratio of abortions to births. In Moscow in 1927 the ratio of abortions to births was 1:1.3. In Leningrad in 1928 it was reversed: abortions exceeded births by a ratio of 1.3:1. In the Ukraine in 1927 the ratio of abortions to births was 1:1.2 in large cities, 1:1.4 in small towns, and 1:5.9 in rural areas.[24]

All this was achieved by a system of wholesale abortion carried out under conditions that would not have been acceptable in most of Europe or North America, and not just on moral or religious grounds. In the abortaria, women were operated on with clockwork efficiency, two or more at a time in each operating room, both fully conscious. Visiting American physicians watched as doctors, male and female, using four operating tables simultaneously, carried out fifty-seven abortions between 10.30 a.m. and 1 p.m. On average, one minute was allowed for the patient to get on and off the table, three minutes for preparation, and six minutes in actual curettage. Antiseptics were used, but there were no gowns or sterile drapes, and no patient was given premedication. Few if any were anaesthetized, partly for reasons of economy, partly it was said to reduce bleeding, but mostly to allow mass abortion in a short space of time. The groans of the women sent shivers down the spines of the American physicians who visited these abortaria.[25]

The Soviet physicians were themselves worried by the problems created by the legalization of abortion, and the consequent morbidity in the form of pelvic disorders, endocrine dysfunction, ectopic pregnancies, sterility, and so on that followed even legal abortion in hospital. A campaign to encourage birth-control was therefore instituted in the 1920s.

The implications of the Soviet statistics were profoundly disturbing. They showed that as many as one in every two pregnancies was not only unwanted, but rejected with such dogged determination that women in their thousands were willing to submit to the operation of dilatation and curettage without

[23] While it is reasonable to believe that hospital abortions were safer than illegal ones, the extremely low death rates reported for abortions carried out under the conditions described below and without either blood transfusion or antibiotics are too good to be true. If the women treated in the abortaria had been promptly discharged home, many deaths from sepsis or haemorrhage could have gone unrecorded; but it was said they were kept in hospital for five days.

[24] Taussig, *Abortion*, 410–11.

[25] Id., 'An Account of a Visit by American Physicians to the Soviet Union', 134–9.

anaesthesia. Of course this was Russia. But what if the same demand for abortion existed in other countries where the legalization of abortion on demand was unthinkable, even in Protestant communities, let alone those of the Roman Catholic persuasion? What then? There were, of course, therapeutic abortions in many countries, but they were miniscule in number compared to the productiveness of the Soviet abortaria.

The Soviet Union apart, the 'epidemic of abortion' could be countered by moral or religious exhortation to greater celibacy, by legalization of abortion Russian-style (which was unthinkable), by effective methods of birth-control for everyone, or by the continuation of illegal abortion on a large scale. Where moral exhortation was ineffective and birth-control unavailable or opposed on eugenic or moral grounds, you could be sure to find a high rate of induced abortion. Only occasionally, as in New Zealand in the late 1930s, was the opposition to birth-control lifted because the mounting toll of dead mothers, widower fathers, and motherless children was intolerable. And the population in New Zealand was small enough to make these tragedies starkly visible.

ABORTION IN THE USA

Taussig estimated in 1936 that in the late 1920s the annual rate in the USA was 681,000 abortions and over 8,000 abortion deaths. He believed that the ratio of abortions to births in the USA was 1:2.5 in urban areas and 1:5 in rural. He calculated that the death rate of abortion was 1.2 per cent.[26] There is no doubt that in the USA, as in Europe, there was a growing number of abortions from the beginning of the century, but the rate accelerated, just as it did in Europe, after the end of the First World War.

Table 7.6 shows the outcome of pregnancies in women in a number of American cities. It was based on careful confidential interviews of women attending clinics. New York stands out. Almost 30 per cent of pregnancies ended in abortion, of which only 7 per cent were claimed to be spontaneous. The figures for illegal abortion in the other cities were much lower. If we

---

[26] Id., *Abortion*, 23–7. These estimates were to a large extent based on figures derived from a clinic in New York City, and were probably not representative. Yerushalmy, whose statistical work commands respect, challenged Taussig's estimates. In his investigation of maternal deaths in New York State (excluding New York City) he used Taussig's estimates to calculate the expected number of abortion deaths in New York State. According to Taussig's assumptions there should have been 925 deaths from abortion in New York State. In fact the recorded number was 224. But Taussig also believed that half the deaths from abortion were usually concealed under non-puerperal causes; in other words recorded cases represented 50% of the true figure. There were also 18 questionable cases in Yerushalmy's list of deaths. If these 18 cases were included and the number was doubled to arrive at the supposed true figure for abortion deaths in New York State, the answer was 484 abortion deaths. This was still far short of Taussig's estimate of 925, leading Yerushalmy to the conclusion that either the mortality from abortion was lower than Taussig assumed, or abortions were much less frequent in New York state than New York City. J. Yerushalmy, M. Kramer, and E. M. Gardiner, 'Puerperal Fatality and Loss of Offspring', *Public Health Reports*, 55 (1940), 1013.

TABLE 7.6 *Percentages of Pregnancies that Ended in Live Births, Stillbirths, or Spontaneous and Illegal Abortions in Various American Cities in the 1920s and 1930s*

	New York City	Cincinnati	Baltimore	Minneapolis	Philadelphia
Year of study	1932–3	1935–7	1927–32	1931–5	1925–36
Number of pregnancies	(3,106)	(7,289)	(6,441)	(8,875)	(1,221)
Live births (%)	69.4	81.0	84.4[a]	82.5	82.8
Stillbirth (%)	1.3	2.2	—	1.3	1.2
Spontaneous Abortions (%)	7.2	8.9	10.1	10.7	10.7
Illegal Abortions (%)	22.1	8.0	5.6	5.5	5.2
Total Abortions (%)	29.3	16.8	15.6	16.2	15.9

[a] Live births plus stillbirths.

Source: R. K. Stix and D. G. Wiehl, 'Abortion and Public Health', *American Journal of Public Health*, 28 (1938), 622.

assume that these cities were representative of American cities as a whole, and if we take the figures for illegal abortion at face value (although the likelihood is they were too low) they show, in round figures, that out of nearly 27,000 pregnancies 4,700—about one in six—ended in abortion of which the stated number of illegal abortions was about 2,200 but the real number almost certainly much higher. Assuming a fatality rate of 3 per cent, the expected number of deaths from illegal abortion in 27,000 pregnancies would probably have been at 3 per cent of 2,200, or 66. This might seem to us, as it seemed to the health authorities in the USA, an unacceptable risk. But for women, desperate to end a pregnancy, such a risk may well have seemed well worth while.

In 1933 the Children's Bureau published its study of all maternal deaths in fifteen states in either 1927 or 1928.[27] Few if any studies of maternal deaths, in any country, were carried out with such thoroughness, and none was more devastatingly frank about poor standards of care. The report states:

---

[27] *Maternal Deaths: A Brief Report of a Study Made in Fifteen States*, Children's Bureau Publications, No. 221 (Washington, DC, 1933). This study, usually referred to simply as the Fifteen States' Study, was based on all maternal deaths in 1927 in Alabama, Kentucky, Maryland, Michigan, Minnesota, Nebraska, New Hampshire, North Dakota, Oregon, Rhode Island, Virginia, Washington, and Wisconsin and all maternal deaths in 1928 in California and Oklahoma.

That one quarter of all the maternal deaths in this study followed some type of abortion is probably the most outstanding finding of the study. The further finding that three quarters of the deaths following abortion deaths were due to puerperal septicaemia is equally significant . . . abortion is evidently one of the greatest problems in lowering maternal mortality in this country.[28]

It was found that deaths from sepsis accounted for 40 per cent of total maternal mortality, and sepsis following abortion accounted for 45 per cent of deaths from sepsis. The study also showed that a large number of alleged spontaneous abortions were either febrile on admission to hospital or showed post-mortem evidence of a previous illegal operation, indicating what everyone suspected, that many so-called spontaneous abortions were induced.

Similar reports from New York in 1933[29] and Philadelphia[30] showed that by the decade 1925–34, the USA had one of the highest rates of maternal mortality due to illegal abortion. A majority of these abortion deaths were due to sepsis. Most were due to illegal abortion taking place on an extraordinary scale in the rooms of 'nursing homes', special 'clinics', the offices of physicians, or the bedrooms of pregnant women. The much larger contribution of abortion deaths to total maternal mortality in the USA compared with Britain can be seen in Figure 7.1. This also shows the large proportion of deaths due to puerperal sepsis in the USA which were due to post-abortive sepsis.

SOCIAL AND LEGAL ASPECTS OF ABORTION

There have always been social, cultural, or economic reasons why in certain periods and under certain circumstances, married couples needed to limit the size of their families; and also of course why single women wanted to get rid of a pregnancy or new-born baby. Abortion, infanticide, contraception, and the deposition of unwanted children in foundling homes were alternative strategies, recognized as such by legal or ecclesiastical authorities who saw that even abortion might be a lesser evil than another such as infanticide. The laxness of authorities in enforcing laws against abortion (and the social acceptance of abortion as a means of contraception in certain societies) was often a reflection of this dilemma. The close and complex connections between these methods of family limitation and the way they influenced social

---

[28] Fifteen States' Study, 35–6.

[29] Commonwealth Fund, *Maternal Mortality in New York City* (New York, 1933). The New York Report of 1933 showed that in the years 1931–3, abortion caused 21% of total maternal mortality and had increased by 52% over two years. 73.4% of all abortive deaths followed criminal interference. In New York City, illegal abortions were (in theory) reported to the Department of Health which recorded 1,350 in 1926, rising to 5,197 in 1933.

[30] *Maternal Mortality in Philadelphia* (Philadelphia, Pa., 1934). In Philadelphia abortion was responsible for 44.9% of all maternal deaths and 62% of maternal deaths in illegitimate pregnancies.

attitudes to abortion, have been described with clarity by McLaren in the paper on abortion in France to which we have already referred.[31]

The same sort of inverse relationship between infanticide and abortion was seen in nineteenth-century Britain. In the early part of the century it is thought that induced instrumental abortion was comparatively uncommon and professional abortionists few in number. Infanticide was considered a much more serious problem. By mid-century, many believed that abortionists were on the increase while infanticide was decreasing. A Glasgow physician claimed there were nine abortionists in the city, but others believed there were still very few. By the end of the century, when infanticide seems largely to have died out, abortion, according to one author in the 1890s, had become 'rampant'. Abortionists were said to be on the increase, offering their services in thinly disguised advertisements.[32]

Several authors have stressed the growing importance of abortion to working-class women in the nineteenth century, linking the need for family limitation to female work in factories and mills, partly for the freedom to go to work, and partly because absence at work led to a reduction in the length of breast-feeding and thus to more pregnancies.[33]

It is often said that the growing determination of women to limit the size of their families, which became so prominent in the late nineteenth century, was satistified by birth-control amongst the middle classes and abortion amongst the working classes. It is an assertion based in part on the evidence of the extent to which the working class took abortifacient drugs and the extent to which such drugs were available and often advertised. This is a measure perhaps of the desire for abortion and the market for abortion remedies, but it is not a measure of the incidence of abortion. The number of recommended remedies, ranging from hot baths, jumping downstairs, herbs, drugs, and various poisonous substances, was legion. It is not always realized that there is little evidence that any of them—not even ergot—was effective:

There is no drug and no combination of drugs which, when taken by mouth, will cause a healthy uterus to empty itself unless it is given in doses sufficiently large to endanger seriously, by poisoning, the life of the woman who takes it.[34]

Nevertheless, people had great faith in numerous remedies, not appreciating that in medical matters where there are many remedies it is a sure sign none

---

[31] McLaren, 'Abortion in France'.

[32] R. Sauer, 'Infanticide and Abortion in Nineteenth-Century Britain', *Population Studies*, 32 (1978), 81–93. Keown (see n. 40) would place the recognition of abortion as a social and legal problem a good deal earlier in the 19th cent.

[33] P. Knight, 'Women and Abortion in Victorian and Edwardian England', *History Workshop Journal*, 4 (1977), 57–68; McLaren, 'Women's Work and Regulation of Family Size', *History Workshop Journal*, 4 (1977), 70–81; Sauer, 'Infanticide and Abortion'; N. L. Tranter, *Population and Society, 1750–1940* (London, 1985), 109–10.

[34] W. H. Grace, 'Pathology of Criminal Abortion', *British Medical Journal* (1937), i. 727.

is effective. In any case, faith in a remedy is often sustained by the general principle that one apparent success is remembered where ten failures are forgotten. When we remember that the rate of spontaneous abortion was, in all probability, around 10 per cent of all pregnancies, the chance of a spontaneous abortion in association with (but not caused by) the use of an abortifacient, may not have been a rare event.

Abortion, to be effective, had to be instrumental abortion. In France, the tide of instrumental abortions seems to have occurred earlier and risen to greater heights before the First World War than anywhere else.[35] Elsewhere, it seems that the marked rise in abortion began towards the very end of the nineteenth century and rose to a peak in the 1930s. This is suggested by the data we have discussed for Britain, Europe, Russia, and the USA which suggest there are at least four questions that need to be considered.

1. From which section of the population did the demand for abortion come most of all? Was it mostly young and single girls who had been 'seduced' or married women with families?
2. Why did so many women, especially working-class women, resort to such a dangerous method, not just in Britain but apparently in every Western country?
3. Who carried out most of the abortions?
4. Why was illegal abortion not stopped by legal means?

The first question is easily answered. In every country from which figures were available, a large majority of abortions were carried out on married women, mostly in their late twenties or thirties, and usually with more than one child living. In the USA one survey showed clearly that the rate of illegal abortions increased steeply with increasing parity.[36] Certainly, the young unmarried woman faced with the stigma of unmarried motherhood, was and always had been a prime candidate for an abortion; but abortion was used far more commonly as a method of birth-control amongst married working women designated as 'respectable'. Those who condemned abortion as the resort of prostitutes, 'loose' women, and the young girls led astray by seductive males had the statistics against them.

The simple answer to the second question is that it was a customary form of family limitation primarily because it was cheap and much more certain than contraception. It was only needed occasionally. It required no action or expense between pregnancies any more than it did during or immediately before sexual intercourse. It did not depend on the co-operation of husbands who often hated mechanical methods of birth-control on the grounds that they reduced sexual satisfaction. Carefully considered long-term family planning required a certain degree of social stability, sophistication, and con-

---

[35] McLaren, 'Abortion in France'.
[36] Stix and Wiehl, 'Abortion and Public Health'.

fidence in the future. Abortion, on the other hand, suited families whose long-term needs were so difficult to predict that, living day to day, long-term planning was irrational.[37]

Thus abortion as a means of fertility control had its attractions as well as its dangers; and the data on illegal abortion in American cities, cited above, shows that the risk of dying was smaller than sometimes imagined. Women who obtained their information not from books or government statistics, but from friends and neighbours, were much more likely to hear of success-ful abortions than abortion deaths. And even if the risks of abortion were appreciated, in a society in which 'falling for another baby' was accepted with fatalism as an inevitable consequence of marriage, so too was the remedy of illegal abortion.

Taussig listed the reasons for abortion in the USA during the 1930s. First place went to economic distress and occupational change in the sense of more women going out to work and more wanting to change their jobs. Illegitimacy was no longer the dominant factor it had been a generation earlier. Unhappy domestic relationships (such as a drunken or sexually depraved husband) and fear of confinement were the final reasons in his list.[38] For the whole period from 1900 to the 1930s, it is probably safe to say that in Western countries such as France, Britain, Sweden, the USA, and New Zealand, a rising tide of abortions and deaths from abortion was inevitable when two conditions were fulfilled. First, that there were enough people willing and able to carry out instrumental abortion; secondly, that social and religious restraints had weakened sufficiently to allow many women to accept without fear of con-demnation by their peers what they thought of as a safe and sure means of family limitation.

The question of who carried out the abortions is less easily answered. The sinister 'back-street abortionist' has become a cliché which sometimes suggests they were the main or only source of illegal abortion. In fact a wide range of people were involved in the business. In France, as we have seen, midwives were probably pre-eminent in providing a service and thereby supplementing their income. Many abortions were self-induced. Some who had succeeded on themselves may subsequently have performed the same service for a friend or neighbour. By so doing they could acquire a local reputation, either as an occasional 'amateur' abortionist, or as a 'professional' making a substantial income. In these respects, they had much in common with the neighbour-midwives of the USA and the handywomen of Britain; indeed, it would not be surprising to find they were often one and the same.

Sometimes abortions were performed by midwives and doctors who col-luded and split the fees. A qualified medical man was handy if a woman died

---

[37] Knight, 'Women and Abortion'; McLaren, 'Women's Work'; Tranter, *Population and Society*; Barbara Brookes, *Abortion in England, 1900–1967* (London, 1988).
[38] Taussig, *Abortion*.

after an abortion, to provide a death certificate attributing a death from septic abortion to spontaneous abortion, or to some non-puerperal condition.[39] Taussig believed that in the USA about half the illegal abortions were carried out by physicians, one-fifth by midwives, and the remainder by patients themselves. But there is very little quantitative information on such matters. Those who procured illegal abortions were understandably shy of recording their occupation to satisfy curious historians. What about legal sanctions? In most Western countries, procuring an abortion was a punishable offence. The only exception was a therapeutic abortion carried out openly by a doctor to preserve the life or the health of the mother.[40]

The penalties for procuring an illegal abortion were often Draconian, especially if the woman died, and it was unusual for the crime to be discovered if the woman lived. In the USA the charge varied from manslaughter to first-degree murder and the penalties from at least one to five years in prison (Kansas, Ohio, Philadelphia, and Wisconsin) to life imprisonment or death (Illinois, Louisiana, Kentucky, and Mississippi).[41]

Yet in spite of the seriousness of the crime, indictments were astonishingly few and convictions even fewer. Germany was the only exception. Between 1925 and 1927 there were between 5,000 and 7,000 convictions a year for procuring an abortion. In France, however, where it is thought that illegal abortion was just as common, no more than 300 a year were indicted in the 1920s and only one-third of these were convicted. In England there were on average no more than 1 or 2 convictions a year between 1870 and 1900,[42] but the number of prosecutions doubled between 1900 and 1910, and increased over the next twenty years. In 1919, forty-seven women and thirteen men were prosecuted and forty-two convicted. In 1934 there were thirty-three convictions.[43]

In the USA even fewer indictments were brought or convictions obtained. In the state of Alabama there were forty indictments but only three convictions between 1894 and 1923; the corresponding figures over the same period for Michigan were 156 indictments and forty convictions. In the USA it was almost always women who were prosecuted; according to Taussig men usually got off 'scot-free'.[44]

---

[39] The evidence of such practice can be found in Chap. 18, below.

[40] The most authoritative work on abortion and the law which traces the history of, the numbers of, and criteria for legal abortion is J. Keown, *Abortion, Doctors and the Law: Some Aspects of the Legal Regulation of Abortion in England from 1803 to 1982* (Cambridge, 1988). See also Brookes, *Abortion in England*. Taussig, *Abortion* provides a great deal of information on laws related to abortion in the 1930s in various states in the USA.

[41] Taussig, *Abortion*, 434.

[42] Ibid. 440.

[43] Brookes, *Abortion in England*, 28–9.

[44] In New York, in an unspecified ten-year period in the 1920s or 1930s, only three male abortionists were convicted and all three were promptly pardoned by the State Governor. Taussig, *Abortion*, 438–9.

With the possible exception of Germany, it is difficult to avoid the conclusion that in most countries illegal abortion was to a large degree tolerated. Women saw abortion as a common and convenient, if messy and potentially dangerous, means of family limitation. Those concerned with the scourge of maternal mortality, however, saw it as a scandalous situation because illegal abortion was the only form of maternal mortality which, in theory, was wholly unnecessary and preventable. James Young, an English obstetrician, addressing an audience of American obstetricians in 1936, spoke of:

the terrible havoc which the practitioners of this illicit art are responsible for spreading through our towns, a havoc which, it must be admitted, is beyond the power of legal enactment to control . . . the problem has implications of a moral and religious as well as of a social and economic kind which beset any communal effort of this nature.

He believed an experiment along the Russian lines of legalization would be a disaster, for it would involve 'assuming to ourselves [that is, obstetricians] functions that pertain more to the sociologist and the publicist'. He urged 'the State' to be 'conscious of the gravity of the medical issues'; but he saw no remedy for one of the major causes of maternal mortality.[45] Relatively few were willing to endorse the obvious remedy of birth-control, but the inter-departmental committee on abortion was in favour of increasing access to birth-control advice. In her minority report Mrs Thurtle urged that birth-control information should be provided for all 'who desire to space their families', especially the working class whose only remedy had been recourse to the 'less skilful hands of the non-medical abortionists'.[46]

The main findings of this difficult and often confusing subject can be summarized as follows, with the proviso that data on the incidence and death rate from abortion are by far the most fragile of all the data on maternal mortality.

Most sources suggest that between 7 per cent and 10 per cent of pregnancies ended in spontaneous abortion. Death following spontaneous abortion was uncommon, unless it was due to a severe illness or was treated unwisely by unskilled doctors carrying out curettage.

A large majority of abortion deaths followed illegal abortion, and a large majority of these occurred not in young single women but in married women with several live children.

Apart from France where large-scale abortion occurred earlier, illegal abortion was not perceived as a major public health problem until the late nineteenth or early twentieth centuries when the incidence and death rate due to illegal abortion began to rise. The rise accelerated after the First World

[45] James Young, 'Maternal Mortality and Maternal Mortality Rates', *American Journal of Obstetrics and Gynaecology*, 31 (1936), 211–12.
[46] Ministry of Health, *Report of Interdepartmental Committee on Abortion*.

War to reach a peak in the early 1930s not only in Britain but throughout Europe, the United States, Australia, and New Zealand.

A combination of an increasing desire to limit family size and an increasing willingness to do so by resort to abortion in a climate of sexual liberation were the main factors in the world-wide rise in illegal abortion.

Death rates from abortion were least in Britain, most in Sweden, Germany, the USA, New Zealand, and probably in France although I have not been able to obtain the statistics to test this last assumption.

In all countries deaths from septic abortion formed a significant and some-times a large part of total deaths from puerperal sepsis. The rise in the maternal mortality rate seen in many countries during the inter-war period was associated with a rise in the death rate due to puerperal sepsis but the extent to which this can be attributed to illegal abortion varied widely.

In Britain and the USA (and probably elsewhere) there were discrepancies between the expected number of deaths from illegal abortion and the actual number of recorded deaths from abortion. The likeliest explanation is a combination of three factors: an exaggeration of the true number of abortions, an exaggeration of the fatality rate of illegal abortion, and an unknown amount of false certification whereby deaths due to abortion were certified as being due to some other cause.

A. J. P. Taylor is reputed to have said about birth-control that 'The historian should bear in mind that between about 1880 and 1940 or so he has on his hands a frustrated people.'[47] Thus, in the absence of widely available and effective contraceptive measures or legalized abortion, the twentieth-century rise in illegal abortion and the increasing contribution of abortion deaths to maternal mortality was inevitable.

[47] 'Paul Addison Pays Tribute to A. J. P. Taylor', *London Review of Books* (8 Nov. 1990), 3.

8

Other Causes of Maternal Mortality

CONTRACTED PELVIS AND RICKETS

There is an argument that goes thus. Rickets was very common in the past, causing deformities of the bones and in severe cases dwarfism. Childhood rickets could lead to a deformity of the pelvis known as the rickety flat pelvis. This could cause major complications in labour and therefore must have been a major cause of maternal mortality.

There is no doubt this was true in certain cases, for it is impossible for a vaginal delivery to take place if the baby cannot pass through the pelvis either because the baby is too big or the pelvis too small—the condition known as cephalo-pelvic disproportion. Such cases were often described, but were they rare or common? And if common, how common? Rickets was not the only cause of a small or contracted pelvis, but it was by far the most common cause in the eighteenth and nineteenth centuries and almost the only cause of really gross contraction.[1]

Contracted pelvis and the complications associated with it was the subject of a vast literature. Many supposedly separate forms were described, especially by German authors in the nineteenth century. Indeed, the subject suffered from the nineteenth-century passion for minute classification to such an extent that it got out of hand and had to be simplified. So much was written, however, that it is easy to get the impression that obstetrics used to consist of an endless struggle to drag babies through the pelvis, dead or alive, intact or dismembered. If one looks, for example, at the entry 'Labor, complications of, (distorted pelvis, obstructed labor)' in the first and second series of the catalogue of the Library of the Surgeon General, or at the space devoted to contracted pelvis in nineteenth-century texts with their illustrations of perforators, craniotomy forceps, cranioclasts, cephalotribes, and other instruments designed to 'lessen' the size of the baby and deliver it through a narrow pelvis, it is easy to gain the impression that childbirth consisted of little else, and easy to forget that few papers were published on normal labours. Normal childbirth is passed over quickly at the beginning of textbooks which were designed to teach students how to deal with the abnormal.

---

[1] Contracted pelvis due to other causes, mostly congenital, still exists of course and existed in the past. Now that the contracted pelvis of rickets has disappeared from the West, however, the incidence of contracted pelvis from all causes has greatly diminished.

The condition with which we are concerned, then, is the contracted pelvis that can result from childhood rickets. How common was it? What part did it play in maternal mortality? First of all, what is a contracted pelvis, and how was the complication dealt with?

Pelvic obstruction can occur at the pelvic inlet or outlet. But outlet contraction was rare. The vast majority were the inlet contraction which was characteristic of the rachitic pelvis. The normal female pelvis is heart-shaped rather than oval, because the sacrum at the base of the spine causes a slight indentation. The normal measurement from the front to the back of the inlet (the true conjugate) is about 4½ inches.[2] In severe childhood rickets, what happens is in effect that the pelvis is squashed by pressure applied at the back and the front, reducing the size of the true conjugate. The downward pressure is provided by the weight of the upper part of the body, while the action of muscles tends to pull the front of the pelvis (the symphysis pubis) backwards. In normal children the bones are strong enough to resist these pressures. In children with severe rickets the bones are so soft that the result is a flattening of the pelvis from front to back while the lateral side-to-side measurement is unaffected or even increased. The result is a pelvic inlet which approximates in appearance to the number eight on its side—wide from side to side, but narrow from back to front (Fig. 8.1), especially in the centre. Nineteenth-century obstetricians believed that when the true conjugate was reduced to about 2½ to 3 inches or less a vaginal delivery of a live baby was impossible, and there are records of true conjugates of 1½ inches or less. Occasionally the sacral promontory was pushed so far into the cavity of the pelvis by the deformity that, when a vaginal examination was carried out it was sometimes mistaken for the baby's head and birth was thought to be imminent.

In cases of severe pelvic deformity and in the absence of surgical assistance, the mother would eventually die in labour from ruptured uterus, exhaustion, or shock. Usually, however, surgical assistance was sought, often at an advanced stage of obstructed labour when the head was impacted and jammed firmly in the brim of the pelvis. When that happened the labour had usually lasted for days, the child was usually dead, the woman was exhausted, and repeated attempts at forceps delivery had failed. Under such conditions it required a great deal of skill to deliver the mother and save her life.[3] There is no doubt that many eighteenth- and nineteenth-century obstetricians became

---

[2] Many complex measurements of the pelvis were described in the nineteenth century. In addition to the 'true conjugate' which is the distance between the *top* of the symphysis pubis and the sacral promontory, there is the diagonal conjugate which is the distance between the *bottom* of the symphysis pubis and the sacral promontory, and is the one most easily measured by vaginal examination.

[3] For general discussions of pelvic contraction and its management in the first half of the 19th cent. (the literature is enormous), see especially S. Merriman, *A Synopsis of the Various Kinds of Difficult Parturition* (London, 1814); F. H. Ramsbotham, 'Table of Difficult Cases of Midwifery',

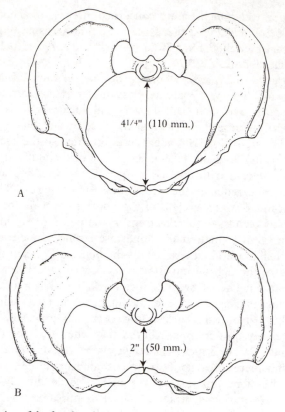

F<small>IG</small>. 8.1 Illustration of the female pelvis as seen from above. A is the normal female pelvis. B is a female pelvis with severe distortion caused by childhood rickets
Source: The author.
The measurement of the width of the pelvic cavity as shown, 4¼ in. or 110 mm. in A and 2 in. or 50 mm. in B, is known as the 'true conjugate'.

extremely skilful in vaginal delivery in cases of grossly contracted pelvis, by the measures described below. With the advent of safe Caesarean section those skills were (thankfully) no longer necessary and have been lost.

SURGICAL MEASURES IN CONTRACTED PELVIS

One way to deal with such a problem was to increase the size of the pelvic inlet by the operation of symphysiotomy.[4] The operation was only carried out

London Medical Gazette, 3 (1829), 284–6; R. Lee, *Clinical Midwifery with Histories of Four Hundred Cases of Difficult Labour* (London, 1842); and id., *Lectures on the Theory and Practice of Midwifery* (London, 1844).

[4] Where the pelvic bones on each side of the body meet at the front, they are joined together (at the symphysis pubis) by a ligament which can be cut with a knife. This is the operation of

if the baby was alive, but few considered that symphysiotomy was a successful method. It was much more common to sacrifice the baby—if it was not already dead—by the operation of craniotomy or 'lessening the head'. If that was not enough, embryotomy might be performed when the baby was dismembered *in utero* and removed piece by piece. The other methods that could be used were Caesarean section, version and breech extraction, the use of the long-forceps which were designed for difficult cases in which the foetal head was above the brim of the pelvis, and finally induction of labour.

The choice of operation was influenced not only by clinical, but also by moral and religious considerations. Induction of labour was a procedure first suggested in the eighteenth century for women in their second or subsequent pregnancies whose first labour had shown clear evidence of gross distortion of the pelvis. To be certain the foetus was small enough, labour was usually induced during the seventh month when the chances of the baby's survival were slim. If the baby died the accoucheur could in theory be held responsible for procuring an abortion or even of committing murder.[5] All this was discussed in 1756 when, according to Denman, there was 'a consultation of the most eminent men in London at that time, to consider the moral rectitude of this practice'. It 'met with their general approbation' and the first induction was carried out the same year.[6]

Nevertheless, there were continuing worries about induction. The French had no experience of it because they condemned it, partly on moral grounds, partly because they claimed it might cause cancers or other diseases of the womb. Much the best account of attitudes to induction can be found in a paper in 1812 by that careful and admirable London accoucheur, Sam Merriman. In his opinion one of the strongest reasons in favour of induction was that many babies otherwise certain to die could be expected to survive provided induction was not carried out too early in pregnancy. He laid down

symphysiotomy which allows the sides of the pelvis to be forced apart slightly, increasing the size of the inlet, but only slightly. The extra space so afforded was bought at the cost of a high risk of mortality, or if the mother survived, of severe morbidity: a life-long urinary fistula was a common result. See Merriman in his *Synopsis of the Various Kinds of Difficult Parturition*, 168–9. Symphysiotomy was introduced by a French obstetrician, Sigault, who performed it for the first time in 1777. It had a brief vogue and died out, but was revived in the late 19th cent. (especially in the United States) when it was often performed until the success of Caesarean section from about 1900 ensured its demise. See J. Chassar Moir, *Munro Kerr's Operative Obstetrics* (6th edn., London, 1956), 610. For accounts of the revival, see W. T. Lusk, *The Science and Art of Midwifery* (London, 1899), 713–48; C. Jewett, 'The Clinical Limitations of Symphysiotomy', *Transactions of the Medical Society for the State of New York* (1893), 126–35; and especially R. P. Harris, 'Which shall we Perform: Craniotomy, Caesarean Section, or Symphysiotomy?', *Medical Press and Circular*, NS 57 (1894), 561–2. Harris maintained that much more space than was generally allowed could result from symphysiotomy. He (quoted in Harris) believed it was still safer than Caesarean section, quoting 3 maternal deaths in 54 Caesarean sections in Italy, 1882–93, against 2 maternal deaths from 54 symphysiotomies in Italy, 1886–93. The difference, of course, is of no significance.

[5] See J. Keown, *Abortion, Doctors and the Law* (Cambridge, 1988), 63–5.

[6] T. Denman, *An Introduction to the Practice of Midwifery* (London, 1795), ii. 395.

several rules for induction which included the following: induction should only be performed on women in whom there was no shadow of doubt that vaginal delivery was impossible; induction should be carried out no sooner than the beginning of the eighth month; and a wet-nurse should be engaged so that the baby could be fed at once. Finally, he emphasized, in italics:

a regard to his own character should determine the accoucheur, not to perform the operation, unless some other respectable practitioner has seen the patient, and has acknowledged that the operation is advisable.[7]

Such were the worries over the legal and moral aspects of induction that in effect a woman had to lose a first baby to the perforator before she qualified for an induction. The only alternatives to induction were craniotomy and embryotomy, and Caesarean section.

In the British Isles, there was little hesitation in using craniotomy, even if the baby was alive, if it was essential in order to preserve the life of the mother. It was very different on the continent of Europe where in the eighteenth and early nineteenth centuries:

it has been made the subject of ecclesiastical discussion, and the doctors of the *Sorbonne*, and the heads of theological schools and colleges have freely given decisions upon it . . . for they assert that it is a deadly sin (*péché mortel*) to perforate the head of a living child in the womb. The clergy are instructed, in the event of the mother refusing to submit to the operation [Caesarean section], to omit no means of persuading her: they are to point out all its advantages, and to intimate that the operation is not so cruelly painful as might be thought: they are directed to speak of submission to it as an act of the greatest love to GOD . . .[8]

The problem, of course, was the baptism of the child. Some had suggested baptism *in utero*, but, as Murdoch Cameron later explained, in countries such as France 'the infant could not be baptised in the uterus, as it should be *natus* before it could be *renatus* by baptism'.[9] British accoucheurs, horrified by such doctrines, accused the French of employing Caesarean section rashly and unnecessarily. The famous French accoucheur, Baudelocque, held the same view and other French accoucheurs defied ecclesiastical authority. Nevertheless there was a profound difference between France and Britain in the techniques employed by accoucheurs in cases of obstructed labour. Where the English tended to carry out about 4–6 craniotomies in every 1,000 deliveries, the French tended to employ craniotomy only once in every 2,000–3,000 deliveries and Caesarean section was performed with much greater frequency

---

[7] See especially, Merriman, 'Cases of Premature Labour Artificially Induced in Women with Distorted Pelvis', *Medico-Chirurgical Transactions*, 3 (1812), 123–45. See also Merriman's section on induction in *Difficult Parturition*.

[8] Merriman, *Difficult Parturition*, 165.

[9] Murdoch Cameron, 'On the Relief of Labour with Impaction by Abdominal Section as a Substitute for the Performance of Craniotomy', *British Medical Journal* (1891), i. 509–14.

in France than England. The French claimed that in a series of 316 sections the maternal mortality rate was just over 50 per cent—almost certainly an underestimate of the true mortality. In England in 1842 there were records of twenty-seven cases of the section performed in Britain. All but two of the mothers died. Lee concluded 'If correctly informed there is no eminent accoucheur now practising in London who has been present at the performance of the operation upon the living body, or who would commend it, if delivery could be effected by the perforator and crotchet.'[10]

Unexpectedly, the introduction of anaesthesia in 1847 had little influence on the incidence of Caesarean section. It was not the agony of the operation that deterred the obstetrician; it was the almost certain death due to the operation until, towards the end of the century, Porro in Italy, Sanger in Germany, and Cameron in Glasgow (who is discussed below) introduced techniques that gradually made the section the treatment of choice for contracted pelvis; not only because it preserved the baby's life, but also because it was soon shown that maternal mortality was less with the section than the perforator. Table 8.1 shows the change in the treatment of contracted pelvis in hospital practice in the two decades 1890–9 and 1900–9. These were the surgical measures used for contracted pelvis. Now we turn to the question of how common the condition was in the nineteenth century.

THE INCIDENCE OF THE RACHITIC CONTRACTED PELVIS

Rickets occurs when the diet is inadequate in vitamin D and exposure to sunlight is diminished. It was most prevalent amongst the poor living in cities. It was of course widespread before the nineteenth century, but many believe there was more severe rickets in the late eighteenth and the nineteenth centuries than in any previous period because of the combination of urban poverty and pollution of the atmosphere associated with the industrial revolution.

In 1792 Osborn in London published the horrendous account of Elizabeth Sherwood, who from infancy had been weak and infirm, was 3 ft. 6 in. tall and unable to stand erect without the aid of a crutch. At the age of 27 she became pregnant, and was four days in labour. On the third day most of the well-known accoucheurs in London were called in consultation for she had the most severely contracted pelvis Osborn had ever seen. She was examined by thirty students before she was finally delivered by Osborn after a long and exceedingly complicated embryotomy. She survived.[11] This was an extreme

---

[10] Lee, *Clinical Midwifery*.

[11] W. Osborn, *Essays on the Practice of Midwifery* (London, 1792), 240–57. A similar history can be found in A. B. Granville, *A Report on the Practice of Midwifery at the Westminster General Dispensary during 1818* (London, 1819). William Osborn practised and taught midwifery in

TABLE 8.1 *The Change from Craniotomy to Caesarean Section for the Treatment of Severe Cases of Contracted Pelvis, Queen Charlotte's Hospital, London, 1890–1909*

	Number	Maternal deaths	Foetal deaths
		1890–99	
Deliveries	10,529		
Cases of Contracted Pelvis[a]	135		
Cases Treated by Caesarean section	7	1	1
Cases Treated by Symphisiotomy	2	—	2
Cases Treated by Craniotomy	28	2	28
Total of Cases Treated	37	3[b]	31[c]
		1900–9	
Deliveries	15,222		
Cases of Contracted Pelvis[d]	259		
Cases Treated by Caesarean section	74	3	8
Cases Treated by Symphisiotomy	1	—	—
Cases Treated by Craniotomy	13[e]	1	13
Total of Cases Treated	88	4[f]	21[g]

[a] Cases in which the true conjugate was of 3½ inches or under.
[b] Maternal mortality 2.9%.
[c] Foetal mortality 23.0%.
[d] Cases in which the true conjugate was of 3½ inches or under.
[e] Of these 13 cases only 3 of the babies were alive when craniotomy was carried out.
[f] Maternal mortality 2.3%.
[g] Foetal mortality 8.0%.

Source: A. Routh, *Caesarean Section in Great Britain and Ireland* (London, 1911), 17.

case, but it seems that such cases, though memorable, were uncommon even in London.

Nineteenth-century Glasgow had the unenviable reputation of having more, and worse, rickets than anywhere else in Britain. Indeed, there was said to be an 'epidemic' of rickets in the mid-nineteenth century which produced a number of rachitic dwarfs with gross contraction of the pelvis who came under the care of the Glasgow obstetrician, Murdoch Cameron. Cameron performed his first Caesarean section on a 4-ft.-tall rachitic patient in April

London with Thomas Denman. Osborn's account of the case of Elizabeth Sherwood was quoted by a speaker at a meeting of the Obstetrical Society in London in the 1870s as an example of the early and 'bad old days' of obstetrics.

1888. Her pelvis was so deformed that the true conjugate was not more than 1½ inches. Cameron was young and had only recently been appointed to the hospital. The operation was undertaken only after consultation with four colleagues. He followed this initial success with a short series of successful Caesarean sections over the next few years. It was the first such series in Britain and briefly earned Caesarean section the name of the 'Glasgow operation'.[12]

In part, Cameron's success was due to his refusal to follow the rule that section should only be performed when forceps had failed, a rule that greatly increased the risk of maternal mortality. He also adopted and improved on Sanger's technique of suturing the uterus. Many obstetricians, however, had become expert at craniotomy. Although the section saved babies, resistance to the operation was powerful, and women were scared of it. Cameron told of a woman who had eleven pregnancies, eight being terminated by craniotomy, and three, under the personal care of Cameron, by induction of labour. He told her that should pregnancy ensue again she must submit to section, adding 'I have had no further trouble on her account.'[13]

Case reports of this kind, however, tell us little except that Glasgow was probably exceptional. How can we estimate the incidence of contracted pelvis? What about pelvimetry, the technique by which it was supposed to be possible to measure the cavity of the pelvis? Pelvimetry by the use of external callipers (external pelvimetry) came into vogue in the late nineteenth century and was practised in the first third of this century, more on the continent of Europe and the USA than in Britain. It fell out of fashion when it was shown to be inaccurate. This is a point of some importance since occasional assertions concerning the incidence of contracted pelvis which were based on external pelvimetry cannot be trusted.

In general there is little information about the incidence of contracted pelvis. There are, however, data of the incidence of, and the mortality associated with, the surgical measures described above. From these, estimates of incidence and mortality of contracted pelvis can be inferred, although it is not an easy or straightforward calculation. One of the problems is that measures such as craniotomy were sometimes used for difficult labours not associated

[12] Cameron, 'On the Relief of Labour'. Cameron's paper contains photographs of the rachitic dwarfs. See also Derek Dow, *The Rotten Row: The History of the Glasgow Maternity Hospital, 1834–1984* (Carnforth, 1984), 59–70. That Glasgow really was exceptional is shown by a letter written 7 years after Cameron's paper by Dr R. Jardine, physician to the Glasgow Maternity Hospital, which was published in the *British Medical Journal* (1898), ii. 748–9. In the context of the excellent teaching opportunities in Glasgow he said: 'In most maternity hospitals contracted pelves are rare, with us they are so common we are never without cases under treatment. Last year about 10% of the indoor cases were of this nature. Within the last few years considerably over fifty Caesarean sections have been done [for contracted pelvis].'

[13] Cameron, 'On the Relief of Labour', i. 509. See also J. C. Edgar, 'Embryotomy: Its Prognosis and Limitations', *Transactions of the Medical Society of the State of New York* (1893), 110–21.

with contracted pelvis but with other conditions which made speedy delivery of the patient essential. If we use the incidence of craniotomy as an indirect measure of the incidence of contracted pelvis clearly there may be an error from the inclusion of cases where craniotomy was used for other reasons. The resultant error, however, will be to exaggerate rather than underestimate the incidence of contracted pelvis.

There is also the problem that many of the statistics were derived from hospitals where, by the second half of the nineteenth century, cases included a varying proportion of specially selected high-risk cases and emergency admissions amongst which there was an excess of cases of contracted pelvis. (This applies especially to Queen Charlotte's Hospital in Table 8.1.) Thus the use of hospital data may exaggerate the calculation of incidence of contracted pelvis. None the less, what we deduce from the frequency of such operations may give us some guide to the incidence of pelvic contraction and of the associated maternal mortality in the context of total maternal mortality. Tables 8.2 and 8.3 represent an attempt to estimate these values.

In some of the reports on which Table 8.2 is based, a careful record was kept of all cases of gross contraction in a long series of deliveries. These provide direct estimates. In others, incidence is inferred from the descriptions of the number and type of operations employed, namely craniotomy, embryotomy, Caesarean section, long-forceps delivery, and induction together with deaths recorded as being due to obstructed labour or rupture of the uterus.

The data from the Royal Maternity Charity are unusually detailed and the authorship (Ramsbotham) inspires confidence. Here, the incidence of contracted pelvis is based on the report of twenty-two deliveries with the long forceps, thirty-eight craniotomies, eight cases of ruptured uterus, twenty cases of induced premature labour, and no Caesarean sections. The data from the Lying-in Hospital in Dublin are especially important because they recorded labours as 'ordinary', 'tedious', and 'laborious', the last being defined as 'such as are protracted beyond 24 hours, and where the disproportion between the head of the foetus and the pelvis is so great' that craniotomy had to be performed. Baudelocque's report from Paris is also likely to be reliable. It was based on thirteen cases which were:

extracted by the *crotchet* after perforation, on account of mal-conformation of the *pelvis*; in these the death of the child was first ascertained. The Caesarean section was performed in two cases, the diameter of the *pelvis* being only one inch and six lines from *sacrum* to *pubes* [and] in one, the section of the *symphysis pubis* was performed, the diameter of the *pelvis* being only two inches and a quarter.[14]

The Vienna figures are based on the number of craniotomies; but it is important to remember that craniotomy was an operation subject to the

---

[14] Quoted in Merriman, *Difficult Parturition* (1820).

TABLE 8.2 *Estimates of the Incidence and Maternal Mortality associated with Contracted Pelvis in Various Countries, 1787–1899*

Source and date	Number of cases	Number of cases of contracted pelvis	Incidence of contracted pelvis (per 1,000 cases)	Total maternal deaths	Deaths due to contracted pelvis
1. Dublin Lying-in Hospital 1787–93	10,387	49	4.7	199	16 (8%)
2. Baudelocque, Paris Lying-in Hospital 1799–1809	17,308	41	2.3	n.a.	n.a.
3. Royal Maternity Charity, London 1831–43	35,743	88	2.5	166	19 (11%)
4. Merriman, private practice early nineteenth century	2,497	8	3.2	14	1 (7%)
5. Collins, Dublin early nineteenth century	16,654	79	4.8	n.a.	n.a.
6. James Young Simpson, Edinburgh Maternity Hospital 1844–8	1,459	1	0.7	n.a.	n.a.
7. James Wilson, Glasgow Lying-in Hospital and Dispensary 1851–2	900	1	0.9	4	1

TABLE 8.2 (cont.)

Source and date	Number of cases	Number of cases of contracted pelvis	Incidence of contracted pelvis (per 1,000 cases)	Total maternal deaths	Deaths due to contracted pelvis
8. Guy's Hospital, London 1854–63	14,874	18	1.2	n.a.	n.a.
9. Paris, Maternité, 1853–62	22,504	57	2.5	1,553	n.a.
10. Maternity Hospital, Vienna, second clinic 1861–2	1,127	4	3.5	150	1 (0.7%)
11. Registrar General's Report 1869	n.a.	n.a.	n.a.	3,412	56 (1.6%)
12. Queen Charlotte's Hospital 1890–9	10,520	135	12.8	n.a.	n.a.

Note: n.a. = data not available.

Sources: 1, 2, 4: S. Merriman, *A Synopsis of the Various Kinds of Difficult Parturition* (London, 1814); 3: F. H. Ramsbotham, 'The Eastern District of the Royal Maternity Charity', *London Medical Gazette*, NS 2 (1843–4), 619–23; 5: J. Braxton Hicks and J. J. Phillips, 'Remarks on Tables of Mortality after Obstetric Operations', *Transactions of the Obstetrical Society of London*, 13 (1870), 55–87; 6: J. Y. Simpson, 'Report of the Edinburgh Royal Maternity Hospital, St John's Street', *Monthly Journal of Medical Sciences*, 9 (1849), 329–38; 7: James Wilson, 'Report of the Glasgow Lying-in Hospital for the Year 1851–52 with an Address to the Students Attending the Hospital', *Glasgow Medical Journal*, 1 (1853), 1–3 (based on craniotomies only); 8, 9, 10: Léon Le Fort, *Des maternités* (Paris, 1866); 11: *Annual Report of the Registrar General for 1867* (London, 1869); 12: see Table 8.1, above. Note that the cases of contracted pelvis reported here included minor degrees in which craniotomy or Caesarean section were not needed. This, together with the selection of complicated cases by the hospital, explains the unusually high incidence of contracted pelvis of 13.1 per 1,000 deliveries.

TABLE 8.3 *Craniotomy Rates in the Practices of General Practitioners in Nineteenth-Century Britain*

	Total number of deliveries	Cases of Craniotomy (rate per 1,000 deliveries)
Francis Toogood[a] Bridgewater (*c.*1800–17)	1,135	5.2
Robert Dunn London (1831–50)	4,049	2.2
Charles Godson Barnet (*c.*1842–60)	2,203	1.3
Anderson Smith (*c.*1830–58)	1,300	2.0
H. W. Bailey Thetford (1808–58)	6,476	2.3

[a] Dr Toogood was a physician with a large consultant practice in which he was called in to complicated cases by other general practitioners in his area.

Source: J. Toogood, 'On the Practice of Midwifery with Remarks', *Provincial Medical and Surgical Journal*, 7 (1844), 103–8; R. Dunn, 'On the Statistics of Midwifery from Private Practice', *Transactions of the Obstetrical Society of London*, 1 (1859–60), 279–97; C. Godson, 'Midwifery Statistics of Thirty-five Years of Obstetric Practice', ibid. 18 (1876), 23–38; Anderson Smith, '1300 Midwifery Cases Attended in Private Practice', *Lancet* (1859), i. 481; H. W. Bailey, 'Statistics of Midwifery', *Transactions of the Obstetrical Society of London*, 2 (1860), 299–307; W. T. Greene, 'A Synopsis of One Thousand Five Hundred Consecutive Labours', ibid. 19 (1877), 204–17.

vagaries of fashion. Collins, when Master of the Rotunda (the name given to the Dublin Lying-in Hospital after the conspicuous circular building had been added to it), was prone to resort to forceps and craniotomy. He reported 79 craniotomies out of 16,654 deliveries, an incidence of 4.8 per 1,000. The Edinburgh series of cases was small, but meticulously recorded by James Young Simpson and it is worth noting in passing that the same hospital in 1937 reported an incidence of contracted pelvis of 1.2 per 1,000 deliveries and no deaths associated with the condition. The Guy's Hospital series was largely outdoor cases, and is based on the number of craniotomies. The data from the Registrar General's report for 1869 simply record the deaths due to rupture of the uterus (41 deaths), deformed pelvis (10), craniotomy (1), and Caesarean section (4). Finally, Table 8.3 shows the incidence of craniotomy in general practice in the nineteenth century.

Table 8.2 is based on deliveries amongst the poor of various cities in which the incidence of rickets would have been higher than in rural areas. Even if quite a large margin of error is allowed, it seems that the incidence of gross contracted pelvis was quite low, ranging from about 1–5 in every 1,000 deliveries. Moreover, the contribution of contracted pelvis to maternal mortality was likewise small, varying from a maximum of 11 per cent to 1 per cent or less. One study which took particularly careful note of deaths in which contracted pelvis could be implicated was the Fifteen States' Study in the USA covering 1,176,303 deliveries in the years 1927–8. Out of 7,537 deaths only 145 (2 per cent) were associated with contracted pelvis.[15]

One of the striking features of all these calculations is the consistency of the estimates of incidence, coming as they do from widely different sources, whether they were derived from direct observation or inferred from operative procedures. There is no suggestion that the incidence of contracted pelvis was as high as 10 per cent or even 5 per cent. The data all suggest an incidence of less than 1 per cent except for the data from Queen Charlotte's Hospital where it was known that this hospital selected a large proportion of cases of contracted pelvis. Therefore, gross distortion of the pelvis in parturient women in the nineteenth century was uncommon. Perhaps the most important point, and one which needs to be stressed most of all, is that although contracted pelvis was a cause of maternal mortality it was an uncommon cause. Out of every twenty women who died in childbirth in the nineteenth (and most probably in the eighteenth) centuries, eighteen or nineteen if not more died of causes not connected with contracted pelvis.

There is, however, another suggestion which is extremely difficult to prove or disprove. This is the suggestion that minor degrees of contracted pelvis due to rickets led to long labours and sometimes to forceps deliveries in which the risk of maternal mortality was increased, chiefly by predisposition to puerperal fever. In such cases contracted pelvis would not usually be mentioned in the records of mortality. Without records containing detailed accounts of hundreds if not thousands of labours, free from selective bias, no verdict can be given. But it has been suggested that regional differences in maternal mortality due to puerperal fever may reflect regional differences in the incidence of rickets and thus of long and difficult labours. The suggestion may be correct. Nevertheless there is no evidence that long difficult labours were more common in the mid-nineteenth than the mid-twentieth century. It is, of course, difficult to be sure since the classification of a labour as short or long, difficult or easy, is usually subjective, but there is some evidence to hand.

In 1850 the London obstetrician, Fleetwood Churchill, defined a normal labour as:

---

[15] *Maternal Deaths: A Brief Report of a Study Made in Fifteen States*, Children's Bureau Publications, No. 221 (Washington, DC, 1933); and *Maternal Mortality in Fifteen States*, ibid. No. 223 (Washington, DC, 1934).

one in which the head presented and descended regularly, the process being un-complicated and concluded by natural powers within twenty four hours with safety to mother and child, and the placenta was expelled spontaneously in due time.[16]

From the records of six famous and experienced eighteenth- and nineteenth-century accoucheurs he found that out of every 1,000 labours the number that was entirely normal ranged from a minimum of 914 to a maximum of 990; the mean was 943. This makes it unlikely that long difficult labours from moderate degrees of contracted pelvis (degrees, that is, which allowed vaginal delivery to occur eventually) were common.

Although rickets was comparatively common and contracted pelvis from rickets certainly occurred, contracted pelvis probably made only a small contribution to maternal mortality. Nevertheless, the relative absence of rickets was invoked as an explanation for the low maternal mortality in the Netherlands and Scandinavia during the early years of this century and this is discussed at some length in the first section of Chapter 26. The interested reader may care to turn to this chapter for further evidence on contracted pelvis.

PUERPERAL INSANITY, PUERPERAL MANIA

There were a few other causes of maternal mortality, each appearing regularly in the lists of causes of maternal mortality. Most were not in the least controversial or mysterious. Deaths due to ectopic gestation, for example, usually accounted for 1 per cent or less of all maternal deaths. Phlegmasia dolens and 'sudden death' (especially when it occurred around the tenth postnatal day) can be translated into modern terminology with a reasonable degree of confidence as deep-vein thrombosis and pulmonary embolus. When prolonged bed-rest after delivery, the period of 'lying-in', was the rule, the risk of pulmonary embolus was increased. Nevertheless, it is uncommon to find that such deaths accounted for more than 2–3 per cent of all deaths. But there is one category of maternal death that seems to have been much more common in the nineteenth than the twentieth century, which is far from easy to interpret. This was the category known as 'puerperal mania', or sometimes as 'puerperal insanity'. In the Registrar General's report on maternal mortality in England and Wales for the period 1872–6, out of a total of 23,051 maternal deaths 573 (3 per cent) were ascribed to 'puerperal mania'[17] (see Appendix Table 20). Thus it was a rare cause of maternal mortality but one which raises some interesting questions.

[16] Fleetwood Churchill, *On the Theory and Practice of Midwifery* (London, 1850). The authorities he quoted were Smellie, Bland, Leake, Clarke, Merriman, and Lever.

[17] I have written in some detail on this condition in I. Loudon, 'Puerperal Insanity in the Nineteenth Century', *Journal of the Royal Society of Medicine*, 81 (1988), 76–9. This is a brief summary of that paper.

The interpretation of the terms 'puerperal insanity', 'puerperal mania', and 'puerperal melancholia' can be confusing. All three were used. 'Puerperal insanity' was usually regarded as synonymous with 'puerperal mania', but mania and melancholia were recognized as the opposite poles of the same affective illness. Nowadays it is debatable whether puerperal depression and puerperal psychosis are specific affective disorders with distinctive features and an aetiological connection with childbirth, or whether the association with childbirth is fortuitous. But there is no doubt that the predominant form today is depression. Mania occurs very rarely. Not so in the nineteenth century when it seems cases of mania exceeded cases of melancholia by a ratio of at least 4 : 1.

There was a striking uniformity in descriptions of puerperal mania. In its acute form it began suddenly in the first or second postnatal week. The patient's behaviour was described as 'highly excitable', 'elated', 'irritable', 'furious madness', or 'wildly incoherent, raving and very difficult to control'. Extreme restlessness, violence, and total inability to sleep were characteristic. Often food was totally rejected. Many patients soiled or destroyed their bedding. Even women of highly respectable backgrounds, clergymen's wives for example, were apt to produce an astonishing barrage of aggressively obscene and erotic remarks which left everyone wondering where on earth they had heard such things. This feature, called 'erotomania', was one of the hallmarks of puerperal mania. It is not difficult to imagine the extreme distress of a family when the birth of a much wanted baby was followed by such terrible and inexplicable behaviour in a mother noted for her former gentleness and modesty; especially when it became clear that the baby itself was in danger from the homicidal tendencies of the mother. Family practitioners, hardened to the tragedy of maternal deaths from haemorrhage or puerperal fever, were horrified by this terrible, incomprehensible, disorder. 'It was dreadful for a woman to be bereft of reason at such a time.'[18]

The records of lunatic asylums in the nineteenth century often display an apparently large number of cases of insanity attributed to puerperal causes. At the Warwick County lunatic asylum 154 females were admitted between 1886 and 1888. Ninety were women of childbearing age, of whom seventeen were

---

[18] For accounts of puerperal insanity in the nineteenth century, see D. Tuke, 'On the Various Forms of Mental Disorder', *Journal of Mental Science*, 8 (1856), 460–4; id., 'Cases Illustrative of Puerperal Insanity', *Edinburgh Medical Journal*, 12 (1867), 1083–101; Lee, *Three Hundred Consultations in Midwifery* (London, 1864); R. Gooch, *An Account of some of the Most Important Diseases Peculiar to Women* (London, 1831); J. C. Bucknill and D. Tuke, *A Manual of Psychological Medicine* (London, 1858); Churchill, 'On the Mental Disorders of Pregnancy and Childhood', *American Journal of Insanity*, 7 (1850–1), 297–317; J.-É.-D. Ésquirol, 'De l'aliénation mentale des nouvelles accouchés et des nourrices', *Annuaire Médico-Chirurgical des Hôpitaux de Paris*, 1 (1819), 600–32; L. V. Marcé, *Traité de la folie des femmes enceintes, des nouvelles accouchés et des nourrices* (Paris, 1868). In Britain Gooch and Tuke were amongst the leading 19th-cent. authorities on puerperal insanity. Ésquirol in Paris was one of the first to describe puerperal mania.

thought to have puerperal insanity, thirteen suffering from mania, two from melancholia, and two from dementia. An examination of the records, however, showed that puerperal insanity was a fashionable diagnosis. The doctor in charge of admissions was required to find a 'cause' for insanity and enter it in the appropriate column of the admissions ledger. Sometimes 'puerperal' was chosen as the appropriate label when months or years had passed since childbirth. On other occasions it was clear that the patient was physically ill, probably with puerperal fever, and delirious. The delirium of fever was labelled as 'puerperal mania'. Such cases often died.

How much confusion of this sort occurred in the lists of causes of maternal mortality derived from private and hospital practice is difficult to determine. Certainly puerperal mania occurred. Certainly in some instances of great severity, mania alone could lead to death from exhaustion, lack of sleep, and lack of food. Gooch wrote: 'There can be no doubt that a very large proportion of cases of diseased mind in lying-in women and nurses [i.e. nursing mothers] ultimately recover, but it is equally certain that some of them die . . .'.[19]

Just as certainly some cases of delirium due to fever were mistaken for, or at least labelled as, cases of puerperal mania. In the records of the Simpson Memorial Hospital in Edinburgh for 1873 a postnatal patient with a fever of 103° F tried to jump out of the window. She was restrained, but she died in delirium and her death was ascribed to puerperal mania. A post-mortem, however, showed pus in the peritoneal cavity—clear evidence of puerperal sepsis. Such explicit evidence is rare, but there are other examples of violent behaviour and delirium in the records of lying-in hospitals in which it is impossible to be sure whether the disease was mania or the delirium of fever.

Deaths ascribed to puerperal mania or some other category of mental disorder associated with childbirth still appear in the records of the twentieth century, but in steadily diminishing numbers. The report of the Registrar General for England and Wales in 1934, for example, shows that out of 2,748 maternal deaths only 21 (0.76 per cent) were ascribed to puerperal insanity— a rate of about one-quarter of the level in the 1870s. The profound fall in maternal mortality during the second half of the twentieth century might have led to a large relative increase in deaths due to puerperal psychosis. In fact there were 268 direct and indirect (i.e. associated) maternal deaths in 1979– 81 of which 9 indirect deaths (3.3 per cent) were attributed to 'mental disorders'. Although the population had increased considerably there were in round figures only three maternal deaths a year due to puerperal mental disorders in the 1970s compared with twenty a year so attributed in the 1930s, and over 100 a year in the 1870s.

Even quite a brief study of puerperal insanity in the nineteenth century

---

[19] Gooch, *Account of some of the Most Important Diseases Peculiar to Women* (1831).

leaves a strong impression that although it is a muddled area with many uncertainties, there was a central core of cases and deaths from puerperal mania that rapidly diminished through the twentieth century. But puerperal psychosis was always a rare cause of maternal mortality.

MATERNAL MORTALITY, DURATION OF PREGNANCY, AND STILLBIRTHS

The end of this section on the causes of maternal mortality is a convenient place to consider two features of maternal mortality that have not yet been mentioned. First, the proportion of maternal deaths that occurred from various stated causes according to the time of birth, as when:

- there was no birth (delivery);
- delivery was very premature: under 7 months;
- delivery was premature, but between 7 and 9 months;
- delivery took place at or after full-term.

Secondly, we must look at the MMRs from various causes which were associated with stillbirths compared with live births.

TABLE 8.4 *Duration of Pregnancy in Relation to Cause of Maternal Death, Aberdeen, 1918–1927*

Cause of death	Number of deaths[a]			
	Deaths during pregnancy (no delivery)	Premature delivery under 9 months	Premature delivery over 7 months under 9 months	Full-term delivery
Sepsis	—	—	5	48
Septic abortion	—	14	—	—
Abortion other than septic	—	13	—	—
Albuminuria, convulsions	11	—	9	19
Haemorrhage	2	3	6	15
Other causes	12	4	31	57
Totals	25	34	51	139

[a] Total births: 37,984; total maternal deaths: 249.

Source: J. Parlane Kinloch, J. Smith, and J. A. Stephen, *Maternal Mortality: Report on Maternal Mortality in Aberdeen, 1918–1927, with Special Reference to Puerperal Sepsis*, Scottish Board of Health (Edinburgh, 1928), 41–2.

TABLE 8.5 *Puerperal Mortality in Relation to Stillbirths, Aberdeen, 1918–1927*
Live births: 36,372; stillbirths: 1,552.

Cause of death	Live births		Stillbirths	
	Number of deaths	Deaths per 1,000 births	Number of deaths	Deaths per 1,000 births
Sepsis	49	1.3	6	3.9
Albuminuria, convulsions	18	0.5	10	6.4
Haemorrhage	11	0.3	10	6.4
Other causes	65	1.8	24	15.5
All causes	143	3.9	50	32.2

Source: J. Parlane Kinloch, J. Smith, and J. A. Stephen, *Maternal Mortality: Report on Maternal Mortality in Aberdeen, 1918–1927, with Special Reference to Puerperal Sepsis*, Scottish Board of Health (Edinburgh, 1928), 41–2.

Tables 8.4 and 8.5 to which we turn for answers are based on a report of maternal deaths in Aberdeen between 1918 and 1927 compiled with unusual care and attention to detail.[20] Many of the deaths included in Tables 8.4 and 8.5 as deaths from 'other causes' were due to non-puerperal causes, and unfortunately the data do not allow the associated deaths to be separated from the puerperal. That the population was generally unhealthy is suggested by the finding that out of the 252 women who died, 141 were recorded as having been in an 'unsatisfactory' state of health during pregnancy.

The main findings are that 10 per cent of maternal deaths occurred in women during pregnancy in which no birth took place and here the most common cause was toxaemia. Maternal deaths associated with premature delivery accounted for 33 per cent of all maternal deaths and here the association was almost entirely with abortion in the very premature group, and with haemorrhage and 'other causes' in the group who delivered between seven and nine months. This latter group is conspicuous for a large number of deaths (31) due to 'other causes'. The implication is that these were largely deaths late in pregnancy due to pre-term delivery in women who themselves died of non-puerperal causes, conditions such as chest infections or heart disease. Although a few deaths from sepsis occurred when delivery took place between seven and nine months (and probably these were close to term), the

[20] J. P. Kinloch, J. Smith, and J. A. Stephen, *Maternal Mortality: Report on Maternal Mortality in Aberdeen, 1918–1927, with special reference to puerperal sepsis* (Scottish Board of Health, Edinburgh, 1928). It is important to note that this report followed the Scottish custom of including associated (indirect) causes of maternal mortality.

large majority of sepsis deaths occurred with births at full term. If associated deaths are excluded it is broadly true to state that the majority of mothers who died after delivery but before full term, died either of the complications of an abortion or of toxaemia.

As far as stillbirths are concerned, the MMR associated with stillbirths was greater than that associated with live births by a factor of 8.2. That is not an unexpected finding. Indeed it was confirmed by many surveys of maternal mortality and I found none in which this large differential was not demonstrated. You can see in this survey that the overall MMR of all mothers of all births, live and stillborn, was 66.3. The MMR of the mothers of live births, however, was only 39 per 10,000, whereas the MMR of mothers of stillbirths was 322 per 10,000 births. The importance of this for pre-registration studies of maternal mortality based on parish records, where maternal deaths associated with stillbirths are likely to be missed, is mentioned in Chapter 10.

Tables 8.4 and 8.5 show that the mothers of stillbirths died of a wide variety of causes. The rate was higher in deaths due to toxaemia by a factor of 12.8, haemorrhage by a factor of 21.3, and other causes by a factor of 8.6. Only in deaths due to sepsis was the maternal risk of an associated stillbirth relatively slight: here the risk factor was 3.0. The number of maternal deaths, however, was relatively small; too much attention should not be paid to the exact values attached to these risk factors. Most surveys showed that the strongest association between increased maternal risk and stillbirths occurred in maternal deaths due to toxaemia, but the general conclusion is an important one. Where a maternal death occurred in association with a stillbirth a wide variety of disorders could be responsible for the death of both the mother and the foetus.[21]

---

[21] Occasionally a misunderstanding has arisen which should be mentioned. Before stillbirths were registered and included in the denominator in the calculation, some have assumed that a maternal death associated with a stillbirth was also excluded from the total of maternal deaths. This was not of course the case. Had it been the case it would indeed have led to a serious underestimate of the number of maternal deaths.

PART III

Maternal Care and Maternal Mortality in Various Countries

9

The Importance of International Comparisons

In the rest of this study (with the exception of Chapter 28) I will be taking a number of countries in turn. In most chapters the general plan is to begin by examining their systems of maternal care and then to consider the relationship of these systems of maternal care and other factors to their trends in maternal mortality. In essence there is little difference between regional and inter-national comparisons except for scale, and the use of regional comparisons in a wide range of historical studies is now well established. In the history of childbirth, however, there are some specific ways in which international comparisons can illuminate features which could easily be missed by confining the study to a single country. The most obvious example is the comparison of trends in maternal mortality.

We saw in Chapter 1 (Figures 1.3 and 1.4) that the two major features of the trend in maternal mortality in England and Wales were the high plateau from 1850 to the mid-1930s and the subsequent steep decline. Were these features confined to England and Wales, or were they part of an inter-national trend? The importance of the question is obvious. If they were found throughout the Western world it suggests they were due to international rather than parochial determinants. A superficial glance at Figures 9.1 and 9.2 suggests that a similar pattern was found in all Western countries. On closer examination, however, certain differences can be seen. For example, between 1880 and around 1910, there was a steep fall in maternal mortality in some countries such as Sweden and the Netherlands. In others such as Britain, Australia, and New Zealand, maternal mortality either failed to decline or the decline was very modest. Some of these differences can be seen in Figure 9.1 which is a broadly diagrammatic representation of the international trends.

The most striking feature is that between 1910 and the mid-1930s the failure of maternal mortality to decline was universal. Indeed, in virtually every Western country there was an upward trend, sometimes very slight (as in England and Wales), sometimes quite marked (as in Scotland, the USA, and Sweden). Moreover the rank order of countries in terms of maternal mortality, as shown in Table 9.1, was for all practical purposes unaltered, with the graph of the trends running like parallel railway lines. When we remember that this was a period in which mortality in general and infant mortality in particular were declining throughout the West, and when we realize that systems of maternal care let alone social, economic, climatic, and geographical con-

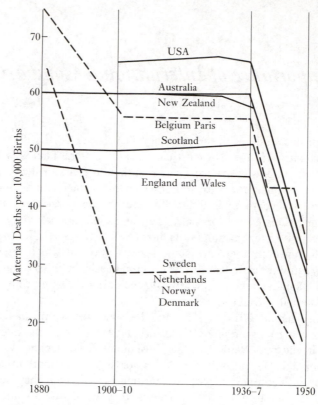

Fig. 9.1 Schematic representation of the trends in Maternal Mortality in various countries, 1889–1950

ditions, varied widely between these countries, we might well have expected that their trends in maternal mortality would have followed quite different paths, criss-crossing each other as the rate fell in one country and rose in another. Instead they stayed where they were, widely separated but static, as if frozen and immovable apart from a slight general tendency towards deterioration. The change which took place after the mid-1930s was just as remarkable.

In all Western countries the decline in maternal mortality has been steep, continuous, and virtually constant each year from 1935 to 1980. The wide international differences of the 1930s had virtually disappeared by the 1960s. From 1900 to 1960 the analogy which comes to mind is a long-distance race in which, during the early stages, there is some sprinting and jostling for position. But soon the athletes become separated and strung out along the track, holding their relative positions on the track for a long series of laps. Then, towards the end of the race, they rapidly converge, coming shoulder to

TABLE 9.1 *Maternal Mortality in Certain Countries, 1920*

Country	Maternal mortality all causes (per 10,000 live births)
Denmark	23.5
The Netherlands	24.2
Sweden (1918)	25.8
Norway (1919)	29.7
Uruguay	33.8
Japan	35.3
Finland	36.0
Italy	36.7
Union of South Africa	41.0
England and Wales	43.3
Spain	50.1
Australia	50.1
Germany (1919)	51.5
Ireland	55.3
Belgium	60.9
Scotland	61.5
New Zealand	64.8
France	66.4
Chile	74.8
United States	79.9

Source: R. M. Woodbury, *Maternal Mortality*, Children's Bureau Publications, No. 15 (Washington, DC, 1926), 57.

shoulder as they breast the tape. This can be seen in Figure 9.2, and the extent of convergence is vividly shown by Table 9.2. By 1960 the MMR in the three countries which occupied the highest, the lowest, and the intermediate positions in the league table of maternal mortality during the inter-war period—that is the USA, England and Wales, and the Netherlands—were virtually identical. No one in 1935 could have forecast such a change would take place in the next twenty-five years.

What were the factors which made it so much safer to have a baby in Scandinavia or the Netherlands than the USA before the Second World War? and what were the changes that wiped out that differential so soon after the war had ended? Without international comparisons the question would not arise.

International comparisons also allow us to focus on cultural differences that surround childbirth. Immigrant groups are especially interesting. Landing in a strange country, they often preserved their sense of identity by living together in tight-knit communities, speaking their native language and clinging to

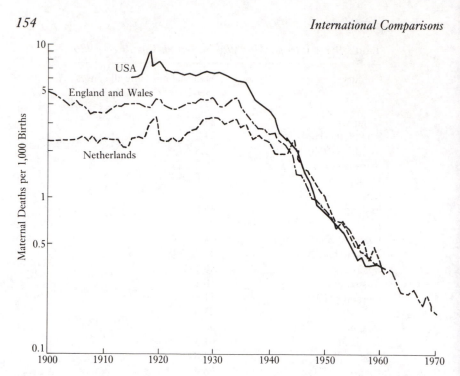

FIG. 9.2 Trend in Maternal Mortality in the USA, England and Wales, and the Netherlands, 1900–1970. Logarithmic Scale

TABLE 9.2 *Maternal Mortality in the USA, England and Wales, and the Netherlands, 1920, 1940, and 1960*

	1920	1940	1960
USA	68.9	37.6	3.7
England and Wales	43.3	26.1	3.9
The Netherlands	24.0	23.5	3.7

Source: Published vital statistics of England and Wales, the Netherlands, the USA. See Appendix Tables 1, 6, and 9.

a wide range of the traditions of their country of origin including their own traditions of childbirth. After a few generations they usually became assimilated, adopting the traditions of their new country at any rate as far as medical care and childbirth were concerned. We will come to examples in the chapters on the United States, and will note that certain religious groups followed a similar pattern.

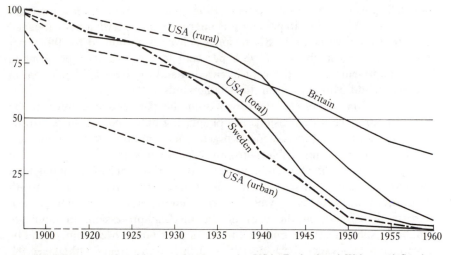

FIG. 9.3 The percentage of home deliveries in the USA, England and Wales, and Sweden, 1900–1960
Source: These are estimates based on a wide variety of sources.

My third and final example of the advantage of international comparisons is the question of where the majority of deliveries took place, whether in home or in hospital. A question which is frequently discussed by historians of maternal care is the role of maternity hospitals. Is there a connection between the relative proportions of home and hospital deliveries and the mortality rates when countries are compared?

In almost every country included in this study there has been a general trend throughout the twentieth century to move away from home deliveries by midwives and general practitioners and towards delivery in hospitals under the care of full-time obstetricians. Figure 9.3 shows that the pace at which this has occurred has varied widely. The half-way mark (that is, the date when home confinements had fallen to 50 per cent of all deliveries) was reached in the USA as a whole about 1940, in urban areas around 1920, but in rural areas not until about 1945–7. New Zealand moved in this direction even faster, reaching the half-way mark by 1926 with hospital deliveries increasing rapidly over the following fifteen years.[1] In Sweden, the half-way point came between 1935 and 1940; by 1950 home deliveries had already been reduced to less than 5 per cent.[2] In Britain it was shortly before 1950. The Netherlands persisted longer than any other country with a policy of home deliveries by midwives. Hospital deliveries accounted for only 26 per cent of

---

[1] P. M. Smith, *Maternity in Dispute: New Zealand, 1920–1939* (Wellington, 1986), 118.
[2] I am grateful to Dr Signild Vallgärda for providing data on home deliveries in Sweden. See also U. Högberg and J. Joelsson, 'The Decline in Maternal Mortality in Sweden, 1931–1980' in Högberg, *Maternal Mortality in Sweden* (Umeå, 1985).

total deliveries in 1957, 33 per cent in 1965, and they were still less than half (47.4 per cent) in 1970.[3] In passing it is interesting to note what has happened recently. By the years 1979–81, hospital deliveries accounted for 98–9 per cent of all births in the USA, 98.6 per cent in the UK, 99.5 per cent in France and Denmark, 99 per cent in Sweden and the USSR, 71 per cent in Yugoslavia, and 64.6 per cent in the Netherlands.[4]

The question of hospital delivery has in the past and continues in the present to produce wide divisions of opinion, not only amongst those providing maternal care (midwives, general practitioners, and obstetricians), but also amongst women having babies, groups concerned with women's place in society and the right of women to make their own choices, and not least amongst historians of maternal care. Some historians have seen the growth of maternity hospitals as a symbol of the determination of obstetricians to increase their status in the eyes of the medical profession, to dominate childbirth, subordinate the midwife, increase their power over women, and by these means to advance their specialty and their own careers. Others see the development of the maternity hospital as a benign and inevitable process of evolution. Obstetrics has developed into a highly scientific and rapidly advancing specialty in which, while acknowledging the importance of maternal satisfaction, hospital delivery is essential to ensure the safety of the mother and child. Anyone who has attended conferences in which such opposing views are discussed will know that this is a subject highly charged with emotion and one in which, by selection, both camps are able to produce a wealth of statistics to defend their views. In historical discussions what is often forgotten is that maternity hospitals were far from homogeneous; they were extremely diverse.

In the USA during the early decades of this century, maternity hospitals ranged at one extreme from the back-room of a physician's office with a couple of beds but without even a wash-basin, let alone a labour ward, and so-called maternity homes which were little more than abortion factories. At the other extreme were well-equipped maternity departments in teaching hospitals staffed by specialist obstetricians and junior staff under training.

In Britain there were separate maternity hospitals, some dating from the eighteenth century, and obstetric departments in general hospitals, staffed by trained midwives and obstetric specialists. Under the broad cover of 'maternity institutions', however, there were also nursing homes of widely varying efficiency, small general hospitals which mixed up maternity cases with surgical ones, cottage hospitals with a few beds in a side-room designated as maternity beds, old workhouse premises turned into Poor Law maternity hospitals, and rural voluntary hospitals staffed by local general practitioners of

[3] *Verslag van des Geneeskundig Hoofdinspecteur van de Volksgezondheld* (various years).
[4] S. Houd and A. Oakley, 'Alternative Perinatal Services: Report on a Pilot Survey', in J. M. L. Phaff, *Perinatal Health Services in Europe* (London, 1986).

varying ability. The range in terms of facilities, type of birth-attendant, and specialized care was enormous. Moreover, by the middle of this century, countries had developed widely different policies. Some admitted all or nearly all women to hospital for delivery regardless of parity or obstetric history. Others followed a policy of selection. Primipara, 'grand multipara', and multiple pregnancies as well as women with a history of previous obstetric complications were selected for hospital admission while others were encouraged to have their babies at home. It was possible for American authorities in 1960 to assert that their low rate of maternal mortality of just over $3\frac{1}{2}$ deaths per 10,000 births was a triumphant vindication of their policy of total hospital delivery. Their counterparts in the Netherlands could make the same claim for the same reduction in maternal mortality as a vindication of their policy of home deliveries.

Enough, then, has been said to demonstrate the danger of assuming that in comparing hospital deliveries in one country with hospital deliveries in another one is comparing like with like. The statistics of hospital delivery must be handled with great care, for when it comes to assessing standards of maternal care it was not the place of delivery—however imposing the reputation and façade of an old-established lying-in hospital—that mattered so much as the quality of the staff. This of course brings us to the question of the type of birth-attendant and thus to the division of deliveries between midwives and doctors. Once again there were wide international differences which can be seen in Table 18.6. Behind those statistics there were even wider differences in the quality of midwife training, the status of the midwife, and the attitudes towards midwives. The purpose of this study is to try to answer a range of questions, such as those raised in this chapter, by the study and comparison of a number of Western countries.

10

Maternal Mortality in Pre-Registration England

Although the chronological boundaries of this study are 1800 to 1950, it is worth looking briefly at the level of maternal mortality that prevailed during the previous 150 years. Some important work has been carried out in recent years which forms the background to the following chapters.

The estimation of maternal mortality rates before civil registration is a difficult task. Data are usually sparse. A frequent problem in estimating levels of maternal mortality is the need for a large number of records of births/baptisms and deaths to obtain significant numbers.[1] Estimates in England depend to a large extent on Bills of Mortality and parish registers. The difficulties of the London Bills are well known, especially the dependence of the historian on causes of death decided by the searchers rather than by medical practitioners. Childbirth, however, was such an obvious condition that deaths in childbed were probably recorded with a relatively high degree of accuracy.

In the case of parish records the methodology of family reconstitution makes use of baptisms as a proxy for births. The death of a woman during a chosen period after the baptism of her infant is assumed to be a death due to puerperal causes. If the chosen period is too short, late puerperal deaths may be missed; if too long, deaths from non-obstetric causes may be unwittingly included as puerperal deaths during periods of high general mortality. Other problems include the variable interval between birth and baptism, and the question of stillbirths and deaths in pregnancy with an unborn child. Stillbirths were seldom recorded in parish records and a maternal death associated with a stillbirth may be missed. This is important, not because stillbirths were common, but because maternal mortality was much higher following a stillbirth than a live birth. These and other problems, and the ways in which they can be dealt with, are explained with clarity in an important essay by Schofield to which the interested reader is referred.[2]

---

[1] See App. 4.

[2] R. Schofield, 'Did the Mothers Really Die? Three Centuries of Maternal Mortality in "The world we have Lost"', in L. Bonfield, R. Smith, and K. Wrightson (eds.), *The World we have Gained: Histories of Population and Social Structure* (Oxford, 1986), 231–60. I am indebted to this essay and grateful to Dr Schofield for permission to cite his chapter.

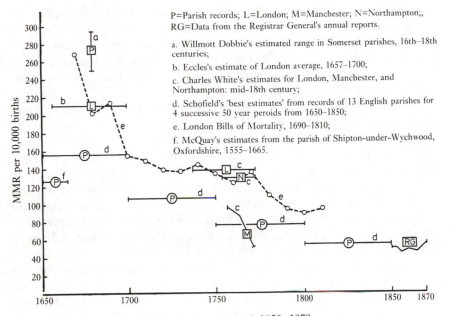

P=Parish records; L=London; M=Manchester; N=Northampton;,
RG=Data from the Registrar General's annual reports.

a. Willmott Dobbie's estimated range in Somerset parishes, 16th–18th centuries;

b. Eccles's estimate of London average, 1657–1700;

c. Charles White's estimates for London, Manchester, and Northampton: mid-18th century;

d. Schofield's 'best estimates' from records of 13 English parishes for 4 successive 50 year peroids from 1650–1850;

e. London Bills of Mortality, 1690–1810;

f. McQuay's estimates from the parish of Shipton-under-Wychwood, Oxfordshire, 1555–1665.

FIG. 10.1 Estimates of Maternal Mortality in England, 1650–1870

Figure 10.1 brings together a number of estimates of maternal mortality between 1650 and 1870. Willmott Dobbie estimated the MMR in three Somerset parishes from the sixteenth to the eighteenth centuries as 244–94 maternal deaths per 10,000 baptisms. It is the highest estimate, at least for a rural area.[3]

Schofield's estimates of the rates in thirteen English parishes are the most thorough and convincing. McQuay, however, was fortunate in finding in Shipton-under-Wychwood, in Oxfordshire, parish records containing exceptional, if not unique, data for the calculation of maternal mortality in early modern England since cause of death was included. Figure 10.1 shows only the tail-end of McQuay's estimate of an average rate of maternal mortality of 127 per 10,000 births between 1565 and 1665.[4] Schofield's estimates of maternal mortality for 1550–99 and 1600–49 which are not shown in Figure 10.1 (they were 93 and 116 respectively) were close enough to McQuay's estimate for 1565–1665 to reinforce confidence in their validity.

Eccles's estimates were based on the London Bills of Mortality and the

[3] B. M. Willmott Dobbie, 'An Attempt to Estimate the True Rate of Maternal Mortality, Sixteenth to Eighteenth Centuries', *Medical History*, 26 (1982), 79–80.

[4] T. A. I. McQuay, 'Childbirth Deaths in Shipton-under-Wychwood, 1565–1665', *Population Studies*, 42 (1989), 54–6.

registers of a London parish (St Botoph without Aldgate). The basis for
Charles White's eighteenth-century estimates of maternal mortality in
London, Northampton, and Manchester is uncertain.[5] The continuous series
of data marked 'e' on Figure 10.1 are based on decennial totals of childbed
deaths taken from the London Bills of Mortality.[6] The figure ends with the
Registrar General's data from 1850 to 1870.

Taking all these estimates together, there is broad agreement. It seems
there was a continuous and substantial decline in maternal mortality in
England from the second half of the seventeenth century to the first half of
the nineteenth. Rates were consistently higher in London than the provinces,
as one might expect; but the decline occurred to much the same extent in
both town and country. Maternal mortality fell from a level of around 150–60
per 10,000 births in the provinces and 210 in London during the second half
of the seventeenth century, to a level close to 50 by 1850. This is a considerable fall which was not matched by a similar fall in total mortality. If crude
death rates are used as an indication of total mortality, there was a decline of
about 30 per cent between 1700 and 1850, but it was much more modest than
the fall in maternal mortality.[7] This suggests that the decline in maternal
mortality must be explained largely in terms of factors specific to childbirth
rather than in terms of factors likely to have impinged on mortality from all
causes. Thus it is unlikely such a fall in maternal mortality was solely or
even largely due to improved economic conditions and better nutrition.
Indeed, as Wrigley points out, 'In the eighteenth century, as before, there
is scant evidence of any link between living standards and mortality.'[8] Of
course, childbirth may be a special case. Maternal mortality may have declined
because of a fall in the incidence and/or the severity of childhood rickets. But
for reasons given in Chapter 8 it is most unlikely that rickets as the cause of
contracted pelvis was more severe in the early eighteenth century than it was
in the early nineteenth, or indeed that rickets was a major cause of maternal
mortality in either century. Likewise, the decline in maternal mortality might
be attributed to a fall in the virulence of *Streptococcus pyogenes*, but I know of no
reason to believe that was the case. Such evidence as there is—for example,
the severe epidemics of puerperal fever in the eighteenth century lying-in
hospitals—makes it unlikely.

Some would attribute the fall in maternal mortality to the increasing

[5] Charles White, *A Treatise on the Management of Pregnant and Lying-in Women* (London, 1772).
It seems likely that his London figures were based on the Bills of Mortality.

[6] I have used the data from the London Bills extracted and published in 1811 by 'Obstetricus',
'Proportion of Deaths in Child-bed to Births', *London Medical and Physical Journal*, 25 (1811),
213–15. The identity of the author is uncertain, but I believe it to be probably Francis Henry
Ramsbotham or possibly Samuel Merriman. Both were exceptionally able London accoucheurs
with a deep interest in statistics.

[7] The crude death rate in 1700 was 32.3; in 1850 it was 21.0. E. A. Wrigley and R. S.
Schofield, *The Population History of England, 1541–1871: A Reconstruction* (London, 1981), 531–5
(table A3.3).

[8] Wrigley, *People, Cities and Wealth* (Oxford, 1987), 234.

involvement of medical practitioners in childbirth, but the chronology is wrong. The period when a substantial number of medical practitioners (as opposed to a few city accoucheurs) began to undertake midwifery on a significant scale was the second half, or even the last third, of the eighteenth century. By that time the greater part of the fall had already occurred. A related factor to be mentioned only to be dismissed, is the obstetric forceps. Although I believe their introduction and use from around the 1740s was on balance a benefit which saved the lives of mothers and babies, it was a factor too slight, on too limited a scale, and too late to account for the major part of the decline we are discussing. In short, man-midwifery may have played a significant role in lowering maternal mortality, but not before the late eighteenth century. Only then had obstetric education become popular with young aspiring surgeon-apothecaries because midwifery had become a standard part of routine medical practice.

I think this leaves one probable candidate: a significant rise in the number, status, skill, and efficiency of English midwives.[9] It may be difficult to believe that the untrained (in the formal modern sense) midwife of the early eighteenth century was significantly better than no midwife at all, but it must be remembered that the only alternative to a midwife for the large majority of the population in England before 1750 was delivery by a neighbour or a member of the family. That this was potentially lethal is suggested by evidence from remote areas of Britain in the nineteenth century and certain parts of the USA in the twentieth. We come to this later.

Unfortunately we have no knowledge of the number of women (especially in rural areas) who were delivered in pre-industrial England by family, neighbours, or friends with no pretence to the title 'midwife'. If, however, more women took up midwifery as an occupation during the late seventeenth and early eighteenth centuries, if midwives became more skilled and careful, and if the occupation of midwife became increasingly respected by the recruitment of respectable women who took pains and pride in their work, it is possible that the decline in maternal mortality was related both to an increasing proportion of midwife deliveries and to a higher standard of midwifery.[10]

This brief survey of pre-registration maternal mortality brings us to a

---

[9] That such a rise occurred is implied by Jean Donnison, *Midwives and Medical Men* (London, 1977), and also by the rescue of the eighteenth-century midwife from her Sarah Gamp image by D. N. Harley, 'Ignorant Midwives—A Persistent Stereotype', *Bulletin of the Society for the Social History of Medicine*, 28 (1981), 6–9. Most compelling is the evidence of the character, training, authorship, and abilities of such well-known midwives of the late seventeenth and first half of the eighteenth centuries as Sarah Stone, Elizabeth Blackwell, Mrs Draper, and Elizabeth Nihell: see J. Donnison (1977) and J. H. Aveling, *English Midwives* (London, 1872). In prestige and probably in their pride in their job, such women seem to have stood head and shoulders above their nineteenth-century successors.

[10] Harley, 'Ignorant Midwives', argues persuasively that eighteenth-century midwives were often literate and respectable, even affluent. Many were the wives of prosperous merchants and yeomen and sometimes of surgeon-apothecaries.

subject which it is convenient to discuss at this point; the perception by women of maternal mortality and their consciousness of the risk of dying in childbirth.

WOMEN'S PERCEPTION OF MATERNAL MORTALITY

An expectant mother today, learning that a woman like herself in the 1930s suffered a risk of dying in childbirth that was forty to fifty times greater than the risk to which she was exposed, would reasonably conclude that it must have been frightening to have a baby in the 1930s. And she would probably imagine that in the distant eighteenth century, it must have been ten times worse, with terrified women dying in childbirth like flies. It is a wide-eyed open-mouthed view of childbirth in the past that is shared by some historians. It appears, for example, in Porter and Porter's book on medicine and disease from the patient's point of view during the 'long eighteenth century' and the same sort of view can be found in Gélis's recent work.[11] In Porter and Porter's view, 'even a natural event such as childbirth terrorized a mother's heart' and 'birth itself was *extremely dangerous* for both mother and child' [my italics] because 'innumerable mothers died in childbed'. With this kind of thing in mind, Schofield chose as the arresting title for his essay 'Did the Mothers Really Die?'; and he looked at maternal deaths against the background of total mortality.

In pre-industrial England deaths in childbirth were only a relatively small proportion of deaths amongst women of childbearing age. Even for mothers in the age of maximum childbearing, 25–34, maternal deaths accounted for only one in every five deaths in that age group.[12] Moreover, as maternal mortality was declining faster than mortality from other causes in the eighteenth century, the relative risk of dying in childbirth decreased. What was the relative risk in the nineteenth and early twentieth centuries?

In towns of moderate size where news spreads easily by word of mouth, the perception of the danger of dying in childbirth was shaped by the number of local women dying in childbirth, not by abstract concepts such as the MMR. The most important thing to remember, however, was that *the risk of dying in childbirth was perceived within the context of total mortality*. If deaths due to disease or accidents amongst women aged 25–34 in the 1890s had been as rare as they are today, the prospect of dying in childbirth might have been terrifying. The 1890s, it will be recalled, was the decade in which *total* maternal deaths in England and Wales probably reached the highest point of any historical period (see Fig. 1.1). The maternal mortality per million women

[11] R. Porter and D. Porter, *In Sickness and in Health: The British Experience 1650–1850* (London, 1988); J. Gélis, *A History of Childbirth: Fertility, Pregnancy and Birth in Early Modern Europe*, trans. R. Morris (Cambridge, 1991).
[12] Schofield, 'Did the Mothers Really Die?', 258 (table 9.7).

TABLE 10.1 *Deaths from All Causes, from Phthisis and from Puerperal Causes, England and Wales, 1890–1930*

	1890	1930
Women aged 15–44		
Total deaths from all causes	47,720	34,363
Deaths due to phthisis/pulmonary TB	15,269	9,547
Maternal deaths	4,195	2,854
Maternal deaths as percentage of total deaths	8.8	8.3
Women aged 25–34 (1890) and 25–44 (1930)		
Total deaths from all causes	16,021	23,452
Deaths due to phthisis/pulmonary TB	5,782	5,655
Maternal deaths	1,936	2,348
Maternal deaths as percentage of total deaths	(12.1)	(10.0)

Source: Annual Report of the Registrar General for the Year 1890; Registrar General's Statistical Review for the Year 1930.

aged 25–34 in 1890 exceeded the death rate from all causes per million women aged 25–34 in 1990. But deaths from causes other than childbirth were much more common in the 1890s. Table 10.1, for instance, shows maternal deaths in relation to total deaths for women of childbearing age and deaths due to phthisis or pulmonary tuberculosis.

In the 1890s, when maternal deaths accounted for 8.8 per cent of total deaths in women of childbearing age and 12.1 per cent in women aged 25–34, on average just over eleven women died every day in childbirth. But 120 women of childbearing age died daily of other causes, 42 of them from phthisis. By the 1930s one might have expected these statistics would have altered profoundly. Mortality from phthisis and many other common causes had declined quite steeply while maternal mortality remained on a plateau. But the decline in the birth rate meant that total deaths from childbirth were declining as well (Fig. 1.1). In 1933, puerperal mortality came fourth in the list of causes of death in women of childbearing age, being overtaken by deaths due to tuberculosis, circulatory disease, and cancer. In women aged 25–35, however, the most common age of childbearing, puerperal deaths came second, exceeded only by deaths from tuberculosis.[13]

The importance of seeing maternal mortality against the background of a high rate of general mortality led Schofield to the conclusion that in pre-industrial England, 'women will have known of others who died giving birth to a child; but they may also have considered it such a rare event that there was

[13] Ministry of Health, *Report of an Investigation into Maternal Mortality* (London, 1937), Cmd. 5422, 14 (diagram 1).

little risk that the tragedy would befall them.' He concluded, 'Childbearing in "the world we have lost" turns out to have been a rather less mortal occasion than we may have been inclined to believe.'[14]

In all historical periods people tend to adapt to diseases and causes of death which were a familiar and unchanging part of everyone's experience and with which they grew up. Only sudden crises in mortality, especially when they bear a foreign label (French pox, Asiatic cholera, Spanish flu), inspire terror. In the case of childbirth, it was not only background mortality that reduced the visibility of childbed deaths, but the low relative risk in the context of total deliveries. A maternal mortality rate as high as 200 per 10,000 births (as in London around 1700) meant that 98 women survived childbirth for every 2 who died. By the 1890s, 99 survived for every 1 who died.

Nevertheless, childbirth is a common event. In Western countries in 1990, few people have personal knowledge of a maternal death. This represents a radical change. Until the mid-1930s a majority of women in their childbearing years had personal knowledge of a member of her family, a friend, or a neighbour in a nearby street who had died in childbirth. So, today, most of us have a similar experience of deaths in road accidents. But few of us ride our bicycles or drive our cars with the dread that perhaps we ought to feel. The appalling fact is that we have adapted to road deaths to such an extent that preventive legal action is often opposed on the grounds of personal inconvenience. If we remember this we may be in a better position to understand the apathy in the past to preventable maternal deaths.

Yet in spite of all this, deaths in childbirth were always different from other deaths. Childbirth was the only major cause of mortality that was not a disease, and in that way it stood apart. It was always a tragedy. When a maternal death occurred it was swift, unexpected, and a sudden and brutal disruption of a family. Time and again, medical practitioners hardened by the hundreds of illnesses they were unable to cure and which ended in death, testified to the special and dreadful quality of a maternal death. They were the deaths which, in a lifetime of medical practice, they never forgot.[15] The death of a mother was not the same as the death of an infant or child. Within recent memory old women would recall their children in such a phrase as 'I had ten and brought up seven' or 'I had eight and lost three', saying so with a mixture of sadness and pride. This is not surprising when one recalls that in their youth for every 1,000 births four or five mothers might die but 100 or more

---

[14] Schofield, 'Did the Mothers Really Die?', 260.

[15] It was the special tragedy of a maternal death and the growing realization that many such deaths were preventable that led William Farr to exclaim against 'this deep, dark and continuous stream of mortality' and ask 'how long is this sacrifice of lives to go on?'. Letters to the Registrar General in *Annual Reports of the Registrar General* (1875), 234; and (1876), 242.

infants perished. To have brought up more than half of a large family in circumstances of hardship and poverty was an achievement, and they knew it. But never for one moment did they recall a maternal death and dismiss it as lightly as the death of an infant.

11

The Eighteenth Century and the Origins of Man-Midwifery

It is a historical commonplace that the eighteenth century saw the change from the old style of childbirth to the new as a result of extensive changes in the type of birth-attendant, the way childbirth was conducted, the understanding of the nature of the mechanisms of normal and abnormal, the teaching of medical practitioners and midwives, and the publication of obstetric texts. It was in the eighteenth century that not only the foundations, but a large part of the superstructure of modern maternal care were laid. All I shall do in this chapter is describe very briefly those features of eighteenth-century midwifery that form the essential background to understanding maternal care and maternal mortality in the nineteenth century.

The key feature of the eighteenth century was the growth of man-midwifery; that is the growing involvement of medical practitioners in the management of childbirth, both normal and abnormal. The word 'management' encompasses ideas of power and control. Leavitt has described childbirth before the advent of man-midwifery as the era when:

Within their own homes, birthing women controlled much of the experience of childbirth. They determined the physical setting for their confinements, the people to attend them during labor and delivery, and the aids or comforts to be employed. Midwives traditionally played a non-interventionist, supportive role in the home birthing rooms.[1]

The appearance of man-midwifery in Britain in the eighteenth century can be traced back to the seventeenth century on the continent of Europe. Jean Astruc, who was appointed lecturer in midwifery by the Royal Faculty of Physicians of Paris in 1745, placed the beginning of man-midwifery in France in the year 1663. It was a fashion which started with the aristocracy, filtered down to the people, and then crossed the frontier to other countries. France

---

[1] J. Leavitt, *Brought to Bed: Childbearing in America, 1750–1950* (New York and Oxford, 1986), 37–8. Some historians have seen the appearance of the man-midwife in the eighteenth century as the end of the golden age of childbirth as a result of what is usually called the 'medicalization of childbirth', a term I detest because of its ugliness. Leavitt, however, concedes that 'Despite the very positive aspects of social childbirth, a romantic image of childbirth in this early period would be misleading.' In her view the rot set in not when men started delivering babies in the eighteenth century, but when a rapidly increasing number of women were delivered in hospital in the twentieth century, and women were delivered 'alone amongst strangers'.

led the way when, in 1663, Madame de la Valerie set the fashion by sending for Julian Clement, a surgeon of high reputation, who delivered her in conditions of great secrecy. It was a novel and successful venture, which was repeated when Clement was engaged by Madame de la Valerie to attend her subsequent labours. This venture:

brought men-midwives into repute, and put the princesses (who had previously employed only midwives) into the fashion of making use of surgeons for this occasion; and as it soon became the fashion, the name of *accoucheur* was invented to signify this class of surgeons. Foreign countries were not slow in adopting this custom, and in adopting it, they adopted also the name of *accoucheurs* although they had no such word in their language. It is true they have rather chosen in England to call them midwives.[2]

It is certainly an entertaining story, even if it is too pat, too neat to be convincing. It is much more likely that Clement's attendances on Madame de la Valerie reflected a growing interest and involvement of medical practitioners in childbirth that had been going on for some years. However, the story has the merit that it contains the essence of the difference between the ancient regime of childbirth and the modern.

Under the ancient regime, it is said, 'whenever a confinement took place the women of the family or the neighbourhood seemed to fulfil a social function'.[3] Indeed, the whole ethos of childbirth was that of a social rather than a medical occasion. For her 'confinement' a woman surrounded herself by her chosen group of friends and a midwife whose role was part servant, part expert. Her 'confinement' and 'lying-in' were in a sense a retreat, as the word 'confinement' suggests. Indeed, Laget stresses the importance of feminine modesty as an essential element of the customs of the old regime:

The fear of being indecent, the fear of being dishonoured, the fear of being seen in the throes of suffering—these great ageless concerns were at the core of debate over 'the indecency of having men deliver women'. By the eighteenth century the surgeons, having formed an increasingly powerful guild, had acquired a certain competence in difficult cases and were often called to attend women in childbirth—reluctantly, yet with great faith.[4]

The only exceptions to the rule that men were rigidly excluded were the occasions when there was a major complication such as obstructed labour. Then, to save the mother's life, a surgeon had to be called, but at the cost of destroying the traditional milieu of childbirth. Wilson provides a similar description of seventeenth-century childbirth in England. Women were attended by a midwife who:

[2] J. Astruc, *Elements of Midwifery*, trans. S. Ryley, surgeon (London, 1766).
[3] M. Laget, 'Childbirth in Seventeenth- and Eighteenth-Century France: Obstetrical Practices and Collective Attitudes', in R. Forster and O. Ranum (eds.), *Medicine and Society in France* (Baltimore, Md., 1980), 137–76.
[4] Ibid.

was only one of several women invited to the birth. For this was an important social occasion, and it seems that perhaps six or more women typically attended. . . . Men on the other hand were conspicuously absent . . . every account of childbirth takes this exclusion of men for granted . . . birth was a female affair.[5]

Although Wilson has argued that the term man-midwife was widely used and midwifery was a routine part of surgical practice in the seventeenth century, it seems clear that at least in the provinces medical practitioners were involved in very few deliveries during the early eighteenth century.[6] The absence in country places of anyone but a country midwife was confirmed by a well-known midwife, Sarah Stone, herself the daughter of a midwife. When she began her career in Bridgwater and Taunton between 1702 and 1730, there were no men-midwives at all. But when she moved to Bristol around 1730 she found that 'every young MAN who hath served his apprenticeship to a Barber-Surgeon, immediately sets up for a Man-Midwife although as ignorant, or indeed much ignoranter than the meanest Woman of the Profession.'[7] In the 1720s John Maubray, and in the 1730s Sir Richard Manningham, had begun classes in midwifery in London. In a text, probably by the latter and probably published *c.*1740, it was clearly stated that only recently had men been admitted to the practice of midwifery. This innovation was necessary because of 'Men being more skilful in Anatomy, and better disposed to find out help in unforseen cases'. The author added, 'Until now knowledge of the practice of Midwifery could not be easily obtained without going into foreign countries.'[8] What is notable is the rapidity with which man-midwifery was taken up and incorporated into the routine practice of the rank-and-file

[5] A. Wilson, 'Participant or Patient? Seventeenth-Century Childbirth from the Mother's Point of View', in R. Porter (ed.), *Patients and Practitioners: Lay Perceptions of Medicine in Pre-Industrial Society* (Cambridge, 1985), 129–44, and cf. 'Childbirth in Seventeenth- and Eighteenth-Century England', unpub. thesis (University of Sussex, 1984). It is clear that the custom of attendant women in the lying-in room continued after the introduction of man-midwifery into the late 18th cent. and probably into the 19th cent. Thus, Charles White in 1772: 'When the woman is in labour she is often attended by a number of her friends in a small room with a large fire, which, together with her own pains, throw her into profuse sweats.' C. White, *A Treatise on the Management of Pregnant and Lying-in Women* (London, 1773), 2. See also the evidence from Richard Paxton, n. 12, below. Leavitt in *Brought to Bed: Childbearing in America* implies that the custom of 'women-support groups' at a confinement was still common in the USA in the mid-19th cent.

[6] There is a slight but interesting document which illustrates this point. In Jan. 1724 Mrs Frances Dryden received a letter from her father in which he warmly congratulated his daughter on the news of her pregnancy, but went on to protest, 'I am amazed when at the same time you tell me you have no thoughts of coming to Town but of going early into Lincolnshire . . . you ought not especially now in your first child to run the hazard of a Country Midwife in a Country Place where upon extraordinary occasion no other help could be had . . . you should not once think of lying in anywhere but in London.' Northamptonshire Record Office. Letters of Lady Dryden. D (CA) 988.

[7] Sarah Stone, *A Complete Practice of Midwifery* (London, 1737).

[8] Anon., *From the Charitable Infirmary for the Relief of Poor Women Labouring of Child and during their Lying-in: Next door to Sir Richard Manningham's in Jermyn Street. St James, Westminster* (n.d.).

practitioners throughout England, and by a number of physicians and surgeons in the cities, especially London. By the 1750s, London had started to provide lying-in hospitals and dispensaries and courses of instruction in midwifery for young practitioners.[9]

In London and the provinces a growing number of surgeon-apothecaries were eager for their share of the trade in midwifery and found themselves in bitter competition with the midwives, many of whom had built up high reputations and lucrative practices amongst the middle classes, the rich, and the aristocracy. But the tide was turning. From about the 1740s, and to a rapidly increasing extent, medical practitioners succeeded in establishing themselves as the proper attendants at all complicated labours and at as many normal ones as they could get. By the end of the century it is likely that in town and country a large majority of surgeon-apothecaries (the direct predecessors of the general practitioners) were practising midwifery on a regular basis. London might still be considered the best place for a lady of quality to be confined, but the art or science of man-midwifery spread rapidly throughout the provinces.

Richard Kay (1716–51) came down from Lancashire to London in 1744 to attend two courses of instruction in midwifery given by William Smellie before returning to Baldingstone where he practised in partnership with his father as a surgeon-apothecary and man-midwife until he died in an epidemic of fever, probably typhus, in 1751.[10]

The Pulsfords, Benjamin (1716–84) and his nephew William (1737–65), who practised as surgeons in Somerset in the 1750s, close to Sarah Stone's original territory, routinely delivered women in their practice, both privately and as part of their duties as parish doctors.[11]

Richard Paxton's career as a medical practitioner covered almost the whole of the second half of the eighteenth century. He practised near Maldon in Essex. When he retired he wrote his memoirs. The cases which stand out are his midwifery cases and the complications that occurred. Paxton and his partner were ordinary country surgeon-apothecaries, and each had a busy

The tract is interesting as it recommends the provision of lying-in hospitals for 'all sorts of women promiscuously, for among the unhappy wretches of ill-fame, there are doubtless many real objects of compassion'. Without such a hospital women would die from want of assistance. If necessary the legislature should provide such a hospital.

[9] The first lying-in hospital in London was the General Lying-in Hospital, established in 1739. The first out-patient lying-in charity to be founded which later became famous as the Royal Maternity Charity was founded in 1757. Maubray and Manningham were teaching midwifery in the 1720s and 1730s, and the most famous teacher of all, William Smellie, arrived in London and immediately started teaching in 1739. By the end of the century there were numerous teachers offering courses of midwifery whose comprehensiveness varied according to the fees charged.

[10] W. Brockbank and F. Kenworthy (eds.), 'The Diary of Richard Kay (1716–1751) of Baldinsgstone near Bury', *Chetham Society*, 16 (1968).

[11] Somerset County Record Office, Taunton, ledger of William Pulsford, surgeon of Wells, DD/FS Box 48.

midwifery practice which they cultivated in competition with local midwives. On many occasions they were called to deal with complications in midwife deliveries.[12]

Matthew Flinders (1755–1802) practised in the second half of the eighteenth century as an ordinary provincial surgeon-apothecary in the small Lincolnshire town of Donington. In 1775 he attended forty-three deliveries, two of which in close succession led to the complaint that he had 'not been in bed or my boots off for forty hours'. It was his custom to wait beside his midwifery cases from the onset of labour until they were safely delivered and tucked up in bed. Labours were described in his ledger as 'easy', 'normal', or 'excellent', or at worst as 'lingering labours'. None of the mothers died. Flinders often fretted as he thought of lost fees from patients who called at his home and found him away at a midwifery case, and in any case he found midwifery as an occupation both tiring and tedious. But he had no doubt of its central importance in building and maintaining his practice, and he was terrified of competition from local midwives. Indeed, he seldom left home for fear of losing a midwifery case to a midwife. Attendance at normal deliveries was a leading part of his, and most of his contemporaries', stock-in-trade.[13]

It is clear that during the second half of the eighteenth century, an increasing number of women chose to engage medical practitioners to attend them in their confinement. 'Engaged to attend' is the key phrase for two reasons. First, because frequent attendance at normal labours was the only way in which medical practitioners could learn to distinguish the normal from the abnormal and become proficient. Secondly, because it indicates that the choice was determined by women. They decided during pregnancy whether they would prefer a medical man or a midwife to attend them at their delivery. Why the custom changed and medical men were chosen so often is extremely difficult to answer. It takes us into the hidden territory of women's attitudes to childbirth. Laget complains that 'the greatest difficulty for anyone who tries to understand [childbirth in the past] is the total lack of firsthand testimony'.[14] Certainly we lack basic information not only on the reasons why men became acceptable as birth-attendants in the eighteenth century, but also on the numbers and status of women delivered by midwives on the one hand and

---

[12] London, Wellcome Institute Library, casebook of Richard Paxton of Maldon, Essex (1753–99), MS 3855. In one case Paxton gives a graphic and gruesome account of a complication in a room which contained not only the midwife but also a group of attendant women, as described for deliveries in the 17th cent.

[13] Lincoln Archives Office, ledgers of Matthew Flinders, surgeon of Donington, Lincs. (1755–1802). I have written at greater length about the Pulsfords, Richard Kay, Richard Paxton, and Matthew Flinders in I. Loudon, *Medical Care and the General Practitioner: 1750–1850* (Oxford, 1986).

[14] Laget, 'Childbirth in Seventeenth- and Eighteenth-Century France'.

medical men on the other, and how those features varied at different times and in different regions during the eighteenth century.[15]

Although such details are unresolved, certain main features are clear. There can be no doubt that the eighteenth century was a period of phenomenal growth in obstetric knowledge, teaching, and practice. The contributions of men in London such as William Smellie, William Hunter, John Leake, Thomas Denman, and William Osborn not to mention Charles White of Manchester and Alexander Gordon of Aberdeen, were outstanding. Translations of standard treatises from France and the Netherlands by authors such as François Mauriceau, Hendrik van Daventer, Jean Astruc, Paul Portal, Pierre Amand, and Pierre Dionis were available and widely read in England. Around 1750, however, the centre for the publication of texts on midwifery moved from Paris to London (see Chap. 23).

By the end of the eighteenth century the anatomy of the gravid uterus was understood. So too was the mechanism of normal labour, the mechanics of malpresentations, and the proper indications for forceps delivery. Instead of a reliance on tradition and assertion, a beginning had been made in the collection of statistics by which obstetric procedures could be evaluated. The nature and management of the major complications such as placenta praevia and post-partum haemorrhage were largely understood. The contagiousness of puerperal fever had been demonstrated by Gordon, although his views were neither widely known nor necessarily accepted. Certain bad and dangerous practices of the past had been recognized and condemned; for example, accouchement forcée and pulling on the cord to deliver the placenta. All these advances in knowledge were available to practitioners in the texts of midwifery which appeared in growing numbers. The best of them, those by Smellie and especially Denman's works, were of astonishing maturity for their time and served the needs of students and practitioners well into the nineteenth century. None of this existed before 1730. In the seventy years to the end of the century, midwifery had advanced so quickly that it could reasonably claim a position as an academic discipline on a par with physic and surgery; a claim, however, which as we will see was resisted by leading physicians and surgeons.

---

[15] It has sometimes been suggested in the past that the rise of man-midwifery was due to the introduction of the obstetric forceps because the two more or less coincided in Britain. There is no longer serious support for this view. Forceps delivery played a very small part in 18th-cent. obstetric practice, and less still in influencing women to choose men-midwives rather than traditional midwives to attend them at their confinements. See I. Loudon, *Medical Care and the General Practitioner*, 85–99.

12

Maternal Care in Nineteenth-Century Britain

Accoucheurs who were old enough to have seen the rapid growth of obstetrics since the 1750s, had every reason in 1800 to be optimistic about the future. They knew their discipline was small by comparison with physic and surgery, but it was young, vigorous, and enthusiastic. It had made huge strides. They would have found it hard to believe that the nineteenth century would turn out to be more a period of stagnation than progress in maternal care. While remarkable advances were taking place in medicine, surgery, and especially pathology, the practice of obstetrics—that is the clinical management of pregnancy and normal and abnormal labours—was virtually the same in 1870 as it had been in 1780 except for the introduction of anaesthesia in 1847.

The root of the trouble was the status of obstetrics. From the academic point of view it stood apart from mainstream medicine instead of growing up to stand proudly alongside physic and surgery. Teaching and practice were marred by intense bickering amongst the medical institutions, showing the snobbery of the Royal Colleges of Physicians and Surgeons at its worst. On the one hand the Colleges asserted their right to control the practice of midwifery; on the other, they declined to have anything to do with the teaching or practice of a subject so far below their dignity. As an obstetrician observed in 1830:

Here in a department of the medical profession, the practice of which involves at the same time the existence of two individuals, that practice is left without any control whatsoever and there are no means of ascertaining the qualifications of the persons who take it in charge.[1]

It may seem that stagnation is too harsh a word to describe nineteenth-century obstetrics. There was, after all, an immense obstetric literature, and a multitude of new obstetric instruments named after the obstetricians who invented them. These alone can easily produce an illusion of a vigorous and progressive specialty. There was also a handful of physicians and surgeons (and it really was little more than a handful) who made notable contributions to the improvement of obstetrics: men such as Francis Ramsbotham, Sam

---

[1] A. B. Granville 'Political Condition of Midwifery in the Metropolis', *Lancet* (1830–1), i. 301–2. Augustus Bozzi Granville, whose father (Bozzi) was Italian and mother (Granville) was English, trained in midwifery in France and was appointed physician-accoucheur to the Westminster General Dispensary in London.

Merriman, Robert Lee, Robert Barnes, A. B. Granville, J. H. Aveling, Robert Braxall, Braxton Hicks, and C. J. Cullingworth. Almost without exception they were members of the Obstetrical Society of London, rightly described in mid-century as the only organized body with an interest in obstetrics and gynaecology, and a society which, *faute de mieux*, played the part of a quasi-college of obstetricians.[2]

One of the Society's great virtues was that it drew its membership from a broad base. In the 1880s, when the Society was at its most active, less than 8 per cent of its members held a hospital appointment and could be considered as consultants in the modern sense, and almost all of these worked in London as surgeons or physicians. None practised midwifery alone. 'If anyone tried to do so I think it would kill him very soon', said Dr Aveling in 1892. The rest of the membership of the Society was made up of general practitioners from all over the country.[3]

Apart from the Obstetrical Society there was (in England and Wales but not in Scotland or Ireland) no body, no institution, no medical college which took an interest in obstetrics as a branch of medicine. In the medical schools it was a despised subject. During the period of medical reform it was neglected. Until the Medical Act Amendment Act of 1886 English students could, and often did, qualify and become registered as medical practitioners without any obstetric education whatsoever. The blame lies fairly and squarely on the shoulders of the élite physicians and surgeons of the medical schools whose malign influence on obstetrics is a theme we can trace right up to the 1930s. They saw obstetrics as a messy and unscientific activity divided between ignorant, illiterate, unskilled, untrained midwives and the lowest level of medical men, the general practitioners. Such attitudes were held in spite of the fact that by ordinary simple skills it was possible for a medical practitioner to preserve the lives of literally thousands of mothers and babies when, relatively speaking, he could do little for medical and surgical cases. Training in obstetrics should have taken first, not last place in the medical curriculum.[4]

The situation as far as midwives were concerned was worse. Almost nothing was done to introduce formal training and regulation for midwives. A series of bills was introduced in the second half of the century, but none reached the statute book until the twentieth. It is also significant, that where we can identify advances in obstetric practice, it is usually a case of the

[2] The Obstetrical Society was founded in 1825 but faded out from lack of support in 1830. It was re-founded in 1858. The present Royal College of Obstetricians and Gynaecologists was not founded until 1929.

[3] The membership lists published in the *Transactions of the Obstetrical Society of London* show the names and positions held by the Fellows of the Society. Aveling's remark can be found in *Report of the Select Committee on Midwives' Registration*, PP 1892, XIV, Q. 340–1.

[4] I have written at some length on the status of the general practitioner and his role in midwifery in *Medical Care and the General Practitioner, 1750–1850* (Oxford, 1986). Jean Donnison's *Midwives and Medical Men* (London, 1977) is an excellent source on this subject.

adoption of a technique developed in some other branch of medicine; for examples, anaesthesia, bacteriology, antisepsis, and advances in surgical techniques which made Caesarean section a safe operation. Apart from anaesthesia, all these advances came at the end of the century. The general picture of nineteenth-century obstetrics is, therefore, rather gloomy. To find out why, the first question is who delivered the babies? what was the relative proportion of deliveries by midwives and doctors? and what was the role of maternity institutions in the provision of maternal care?

WHO DELIVERED THE BABIES IN THE NINETEENTH CENTURY?

That so simple a question should be so difficult to answer may come as a surprise. But the truth is that while a great deal is known about nineteenth-century medical practitioners, our knowledge of the midwives is based on slender evidence and dominated by fictional portraits such as Sarah Gamp. Reliable data on the number of midwives and the proportion and distribution of women they delivered are scarce. The first national census in 1801 attempted, very imperfectly, to provide information on occupation. But it was not until 1841 that individuals' occupations rather than family occupations were recorded; a process which was refined in subsequent censuses.[5]

In 1841 the census returns showed that in England and Wales there were about 17,000 medical practitioners and just over 700 midwives. By 1851 the numbers were 19,000 and 2,204 respectively and by 1881, 19,000 and 2,600. The estimates of medical practitioners were probably quite close to the truth, but the estimates of midwives were known to be very inaccurate. The apparent trebling of midwives between 1841 and 1851 is certainly spurious. One authority in 1892 put the number of midwives in England and Wales at between 10,000 and 15,000 and another estimated a total between 7,000 and 9,000. Neither had a firm basis for their estimates.[6]

Confusion arose partly because many women practised in an itinerant sort of fashion, attending only one or two cases, or delivered babies as a sideline to other occupations such as nursing or field labour, while others made a regular living as midwives. However, even those who shunned manual labour were usually known by their neighbours not as 'the midwife' but as 'the woman who goes about nursing' and probably gave their occupation on the census

---

[5] For an account of the problems of recording social class and occupations in the national censuses, see M. Nissel, *People Count: A History of the General Register Office* (London, 1987).

[6] Evidence of Dr Aveling, Consulting Physician to the Chelsea Hospital for Women and author of the *History of English Midwives*, in *Report of the Select Committee on Midwives' Registration*, PP 1892, XIV, Q. 251 and evidence of Mr Napier, Q. 20–1.

forms as 'nurse' or some other occupation such as 'housewife' rather than 'midwife'.[7] The census returns are therefore of little use.

A private survey carried out in 1805–6 by Dr Edward Harrison gives a few data for the early nineteenth century.[8] He received several reports of persons in various occupations such as a blacksmith who undertook man-midwifery as a sideline. A practitioner in Cambridge reported a 'failed grocer turned man-midwife and bone-setter', and the Medical Society of Liverpool reported many irregular midwives in the city without defining 'irregular'.[9] Harrison's correspondent from Nottingham was much more informative, writing to say there were in the town 4 physicians, and 15 surgeon-apothecary men-midwives in competition with 11 midwives 'all uninstructed'. In the country, within a fifteen-mile radius of the town, there were 35 surgeon-apothecaries all of whom undertook midwifery and no fewer than 123 midwives 'all uninstructed'.[10] In Durham there were 5 practitioners all practising surgery, midwifery, and pharmacy and 2 midwives.[11] From Suffolk came the information that 'all apothecaries in this county are accoucheurs. Few of the poor, comparatively speaking, are delivered by women.' But there were, most unusually, three midwives who had all 'commenced business after hearing a course of lectures on the subject in London. They are therefore better qualified than many in other places but they are the first females who heretofore ever received any regular instruction.' That was 1805 and it is worth noting.[12]

From a variety of such sources it seems likely that in the first decade of the nineteenth century midwives flourished in the country rather than the towns. Apart from physicians, a large majority of practitioners, whether they called themselves surgeon, apothecary, surgeon-apothecary, or surgeon-apothecary and man-midwife (these terms were for all practical purposes interchangeable at the time and the term 'general practitioner' had not yet been invented)

[7] *Report of the Select Committee on Midwives' Registration*, Q. 20–1 and evidence of Miss Paget, Q. 151 and Q. 692. In 1871 the census showed 3,349 midwives and 31,180 women were returned as nurses. There is a strong likelihood that many of the latter acted as midwives. Farr, *Annual Report of the Registrar General for 1876*, 250.

[8] Edward Harrison (1766–1838), MD Edinburgh, of Horncastle in Lincolnshire was persuaded by the Lincolnshire Benevolent Medical Society to undertake an investigation into the state of medical practice in England. He published a report entitled *Remarks on the Ineffective State of the Practice of Physic in Great Britain with Proposals for its Future Regulation and Improvement*. The answers to a questionnaire sent to medical practitioners in various parts of the country were published in the short-lived periodical the *Medical and Chirurgical Review* (which ran to 16 volumes published between 1794 and 1807), 12 (1805)–15 (1807). (This periodical should not be mistaken for the *Medico-Chirurgical Review* which was first published in 1824.)

[9] Ibid. 13 (1806), pp. xlii and lxix.

[10] Ibid. pp. ci–ciii. Since most midwives lived in villages this fits in with evidence from the 1870s, discussed below.

[11] Ibid. pp. cviii–cix.

[12] Ibid. p. xxxv.

practised midwifery.[13] A well-known example was the distinguished provincial surgeon, John Greene Crosse of Norwich who, in the first half of the nineteenth century, earned a large income from 'a large general practice in medicine, surgery and midwifery' and consultations in midwifery for 80–100 doctors a year.[14] Midwifery, in other words was undertaken routinely by virtually all general practitioners, and in the provinces by some surgeons and physicians with consultant practice and hospital appointments.

Moving forward to the mid-nineteenth century, the most important attempt to answer the question 'who delivered the babies?' was undertaken by the Obstetrical Society of London. In the 1860s, William Farr of the Registrar General's Office asked the Society to 'obtain information as to the treatment and management of infants in this country with a view to ascertaining the extent and causes of infant mortality . . . His request was at once acceded to.' A committee was established for the purpose and its report, which was based on 'a series of questions [which] was drawn up and a copy sent to each Fellow', was published in 1870.[15]

The first question 'related to the proportion of births attended by medical men and by women respectively . . .'. The replies showed that the proportion of midwife deliveries varied widely. In villages the percentage varied from about 40 per cent to over 90 per cent. In small non-manufacturing towns with a population of between 6,000 and 10,000, midwife deliveries formed a much smaller proportion, seldom exceeding 5–10 per cent, but there were exceptions. In Long Sutton (population 6,124) it was 26 per cent and in the market town Altrincham, in Hampshire, it was 53 per cent of all deliveries.

In large manufacturing towns such as Birmingham, Leeds, Sheffield, and Bury the majority of deliveries were by midwives: in Glasgow 75 per cent, in Coventry 90 per cent. In Wakefield (population 23,000) midwife delivery was the rule amongst the Irish, but English-born mothers in 'nearly every case were attended by medical men'. In Edinburgh midwife deliveries were said to occur only to 'a trifling extent'. London showed a clear division between the East End where 30–50 per cent of the poor were attended by midwives, and the West End and surburbs such as Wimbledon where midwife deliveries were seldom higher than 5 per cent. In short, midwife deliveries predominated in villages and working-class areas of large manufacturing towns and cities, while general practitioner deliveries predominated in small non-manufacturing towns, suburbs, and affluent areas of large towns and cities.

---

[13] For an account of the problems surrounding the terminology used by medical practitioners to describe themselves and the adoption of the term 'general practitioner', see I. Loudon, *Medical Care and the General Practitioner*.

[14] John Greene Crosse of Norwich (1790–1850), FRS 1834, FRCS 1843. His notebooks can be found in the manuscript collection of the Wellcome Institute Library, London, MSS 1916 and 1917.

[15] 'Report of the Infant Mortality Committee', *Transactions of the Obstetrical Society of London*, 13 (1870), 132–49; ibid. 14 (1871), 388–403.

For all that it is based on shaky evidence, it is worth attempting an estimate for the 1880s, when the average annual number of births in England and Wales was around 890,000 and about 1 per cent of deliveries took place in Poor Law hospitals and 0.3 per cent in voluntary hospitals. This left some 878,000 home births. In a few remote areas deliveries took place without either midwife or doctor, but they can be discounted.[16]

There were about 19,000 medical practitioners in the 1880s of whom some 18,000 practised midwifery. If they undertook on average fifty deliveries a year they would have accounted for the whole 878,000 births and more. While it is certain that a number of general practitioners delivered as many, if we allow for young practitioners still trying to establish a practice, and some of the older ones who were able to abandon midwifery, as well as those who had lost many cases to midwives, the average may have been closer to twenty-five cases a year. In that case, deliveries by general practitioners would account for 450,000 deliveries a year, leaving 428,000 for the midwives. If Aveling's lower estimate of 10,000 midwives in England and Wales was correct (see above) each midwife would have had on average about forty-three deliveries a year.[17] The estimate that about half the deliveries were undertaken by midwives and half by medical practitioners is probably not far from the mark, although the social and geographical distribution of midwife and doctor deliveries certainly varied widely. If anything it probably underestimates the deliveries by midwives.[18]

But how were these confinements distributed? We often assume that the landed gentry employed obstetricians, the middle classes general practitioners, and the working classes midwives. The first two of these assumptions may well have been broadly true; the third is a pitfall of potential errors. As Thompson has shown so vividly, the diversity within the working classes went far beyond such simple divisions of skilled and unskilled labourers.[19] Within this diversity do we find the choice of birth-attendant reflected the hierarchies between and within occupational groups? In the railway industry did the wives of the Swindon 'carriage finishers and upholsterers . . . a class in themselves'

---

[16] *Report of the Select Committee on Midwives' Registration*, app. 4, p. 13.

[17] This would accord with Farr's opinion in 1876, that 'In towns, a midwife in full practice may attend 100 cases a year . . . but one case a week will be a fair average.' *Annual Report of the Registrar General* (1876), 250.

[18] Until he looked into it, the reliable and perceptive obstetrician C. J. Cullingworth believed that a majority of confinements were attended by doctors. When he obtained returns from 'a number of trained midwives throughout the country and from over 800 mothers of the pauper class, or the class immediately above' he found he was mistaken. These returns came from 'agricultural centres, mining centres, from factory towns and from various parts of London'. They showed that 62% of 4,000 confinements were attended by midwives. He concluded 'from one half to three quarters of the confinements in England and Wales are attended by midwives and not by doctors'. Cullingworth, *The Registration of Midwives* (London, 1898; reprinted from the *Contemporary Review* (Mar. 1898)), 3–4.

[19] F. M. L. Thompson, *The Rise of Respectable Society: A Social History of Victorian Britain, 1830–1900* (London, 1988).

and the wives of the footplatemen and signalmen, the 'aristocrats' of railway workers, choose a doctor to deliver their wives, while the 'porters, shunters, cleaners, loaders, carters and the like who were unskilled' chose a midwife? Take the printers, piano-makers, engine fitters, and lathe operators, and in textiles the hand-combers before the advent of the wool-combing machine; did these employ doctors while the wives of tenters, and the multitude of pick-wielders, barrow-pushers, and sweeper-uppers employed midwives?[20] In other words, did the members of the higher ranks of working-class groups underline their social position in the town or street by their choice of birth-attendant? It would not be surprising if they did, for it is certain that general practitioners delivered large numbers of women who, however they are described, came below the level of the middle classes, both upper and lower; and the choice of doctor or midwife must have been determined by some internal logic, however complex. The division of deliveries between midwives and doctors was probably determined by geographical location, sometimes by ethnic origin like the Irish women in Wakefield, often probably by the local reputations of midwives and doctors, sometimes by membership of sick clubs and friendly societies, and very often by available income. What we can assert with reasonable confidence is that competition for cases was keen and the fears of general practitioners that well-trained midwives might erode their share of a highly competitive occupation was understandable. There was no shortage of birth-attendants in the nineteenth century. On the contrary, there was an excess.

As far as general practitioners were concerned, competition for cases meant lower fees and increased disgruntlement at having to undertake a tiring and time-consuming occupation which was poorly paid. This goes some way to explain what we will come to later: the increasing tendency from about 1870 for general practitioners to intervene with their forceps to get a midwifery case over and done with as quickly as possible.

THE NINETEENTH-CENTURY MIDWIFE

If, as we have suggested, about half of all births during the nineteenth century were attended by midwives, it is clear they must have played a large part in determining the level of maternal mortality. What kind of women were they, and what was the quality of care they provided?[21]

---

[20] Ibid. 216–19, 242–3.

[21] The main sources here are J. Donnison, *Midwives and Medical Men* (London, 1977), and J. Towler and J. Bramall, *Midwives in History and Society* (London, 1986). An important early source is J. H. Aveling, *English Midwives: Their History and Prospects* (London, 1872), republished with an introduction and biographical sketch of the author by J. L. Thornton (London, 1967). Important primary sources include the *Transactions of the Obstetrical Society of London*, various volumes between 1870 and 1891, and the *Report of the Select Committee on Midwives' Registration*, especially the evidence of Dr Aveling, Mr Robert Rentoul, Mrs Zepherina Smith, Miss Rosalind Paget, Mrs Martin, Miss Rebecca Gill, and Mr Drage.

The low status of the midwife in Britain stood in contrast with many European countries. The generally low standard led to an increasing demand for state-controlled training and regulation. Although there were careful and experienced midwives, few had attended any sort of course of training, formal or informal. Most had probably served some sort of informal apprenticeship in the sense of learning by accompanying an experienced woman on her rounds. Sometimes it was mother and daughter or some other family relationship; but whether it was a family business or not, the hit-and-miss quality of such a system was obvious. Training was also provided for midwives by lying-in institutions; but this produced a very small number of trained midwives, some of whom went into independent practice while a few became private tutors.[22]

William Farr commented on this unsatisfactory state of affairs and we should note in passing that the word 'nurse' was often used loosely to mean midwives or nurses or women who were both.

Midwifery is as well understood in England . . . as the other parts of surgery; but errors in practice are sometimes committed; and though excellent nurses, considering their education, are sometimes met with, medical precepts are too often set at nought by the nurses and old women in attendance, who have peculiar views of their own, which they lose no opportunity of announcing and carrying into effect, with the best intentions in the world but the worst consequences. . . . It is true that a medical man can be called in where the danger is imminent; but, to discover the danger a knowledge of its sources is required; and those who have come in contact with midwives and 'monthly nurses' are well aware that ignorance does not diminish self-confidence. . . . If schools for the education of nurses and midwives were established in the metropolis, and the large towns, under medical supervision, and some distinction were conferred upon those who proved attentive, kind, and skilful, such schools would probably be frequented. A highly useful profession would be thrown open to women, who now have so few fields of profitable employment. . . . The nurses of hospitals acquire a practical knowledge of their art, and get employment out of doors; but as a general rule, hospital nurses are under-paid, and the consequence is that they are often a very inferior class of women, who can get no other engagement. . . . I may state that the want of good, educated, trustworthy nurses is felt in the highest circles, as well as in the middle ranks of society. The nurse is always present with the patient, the medical man only occasionally . . .[23]

---

[22] The facilities for training in hospitals was limited. In the voluntary hospitals, annual admissions were small so that for teaching purposes student midwives were in competition for cases with medical students. The Poor Law hospitals could have provided the opportunity for training on a large scale, but only a few agreed to do so. There were schemes for training midwives in some provincial Poor Law Infirmaries; in Liverpool, for example. But the Kensington Poor Law hospital was the only one in London to undertake formal training in midwifery. Opposition to training often came from the Poor Law Guardians who considered it unnecessary. *Report of the Select Committee on Midwives' Registration*, Q. 157–242.

[23] *Annual Report of the Registrar General for 1841* (London, 1843), 380–2. Some years later he returned to the subject because nothing of substance had been done, and wrote: 'Until lately it was assumed that midwives were born, not made; their professional education was wholly neglected, or left to chance; and it still rests on an unsatisfactory footing, although efforts have been made to impart systematic instruction in some quarters', *Annual Report of the Registrar General for 1870*, 407.

Plans for training and regulating midwives were, broadly speaking, supported by consultant obstetricians who had nothing to fear and much to gain if midwives in lying-in hospitals became more skilled and reliable.

General practitioners, however, had good reason to fear competition, especially amongst middle-class patients, and especially if middle-class women joined the ranks as trained midwives. One such, however, who had a large experience of superintending midwifery in country districts was emphatic in her evidence to the Select Committee on Midwives' Registration that trained midwives actually increased the amount of midwifery work for general practitioners because trained midwives were much more willing to send for a doctor than the untrained midwife.[24] The attitudes of mothers to the training of midwives was also mixed. Although there is little evidence that the middle classes wanted to be delivered by a midwife rather than a doctor, the middle classes liked a well-trained woman, preferably of middle-class origins, to attend their lying-in. Amongst the poor, however, for whom expense was dominant, the most common birth-attendants were the multitude of untrained and largely illiterate women who also did nursing, laying-out, and other jobs in steady demand. The dangers of such women were emphasized by doctors and senior trained midwives who had seen their work at close hand. Many of these midwives were unable either to detect or deal with ordinary complications. It was said they buried as stillborn 'many that were nothing of the kind'.[25] Their unwillingness to send in time for medical help was well known; if such a summons was unnecessary, the midwife was condemned for her ignorance; if necessary, she was condemned for mismanagement.[26] Untrained midwives, for instance, rarely sent for a doctor to repair a torn perineum, leaving women with gross birth injuries and sometimes with permanent fecal incontinence.[27]

Poor women chose the untrained midwife because she was cheap. She could deliver the baby and then visit for a week or so and help with housework. If a doctor was engaged to attend, he had to be paid, and a woman had to be engaged to care for the mother during the lying-in period—which could cost as much as a shilling a day. When, in the late nineteenth century, a few trained women were employed as district midwives, it was found that one trained midwife could manage all the deliveries with ease where previously there may have been as many as six part-time untrained midwives. But the trained midwife would not, of course, spend much time in the house or do the housework, so trained midwives were a mixed blessing. The trained

---

[24] Evidence of Mrs Martin, *Report of the Select Committee on Midwives' Registration*, Q. 702.
[25] Evidence of Miss Paget, ibid. Q. 133.
[26] Evidence of Mrs Martin, ibid. Q. 710.
[27] 'A very large proportion of ruptured perineums occurred and were concealed. The midwife is obliged to call in a physician to undertake the repair, and very frequently (and naturally) ignores its existence, lest the rupture should be considered due to her want of skill. Evidence of Mr Drage, ibid. Q. 718.

midwife could, however, help the mother to wash, 'which the untrained nurse had never done; it is not considered proper for untrained nurses to wash a patient'.[28]

The reform of the midwives was tediously slow, showing little of the vigour and speed we tend to associate with Victorian reform. That it occurred in the end, and in spite of the opposition of general practitioners and members of parliament that were lobbied, was largely due to a small group of people: William Farr at the Register Office, members of the Obstetrical Society of London, and a small number of energetic and high-minded middle-class women such as those who founded the Midwives Institute, the forerunner of the College of Midwives in 1941, which became the Royal College in 1947.[29]

Amongst the obstetricians in favour of the reform of midwives, Cullingworth stood out.[30] The Obstetrical Society had provided an important precedent. Midwives had been instructed, examined, and registered by the Society since 1872.[31] Although the number of women who presented themselves for examination was small in relation to the total number of midwives, this initiative was accompanied by deputations from the Obstetrical Society which tried to persuade the government to introduce legislation. Eventually, in 1902, the Midwives Act was passed.

Finally, we must mention the monthly nurse, who played an important part in midwifery. Although she had some knowledge of midwifery, her role was confined to working under the directions of the doctor. She sat with the patient through the first stage of labour; she kept an eye on things if the doctor was busy elsewhere; she assisted the doctor with the delivery, and

---

[28] Ibid. Q. 708.

[29] Mrs Zepherina Smith was a good example of the reforming women. The daughter of a parson, she was impressed as a young girl, when she went parish visiting, by the number of women who dated ill health from a confinement. She decided midwifery must be improved and midwives drawn from a high social class. She herself trained as a nurse and midwife, and in January 1873 passed the examination of the Obstetrical Society. Members of the Rural Nursing Association and a Workhouse Nursing Association were also active in the reform of midwives.

[30] See Cullingworth, *The Registration of Midwives*. Cullingworth, who worked first in Manchester before moving to St Thomas's Hospital in London, was a realist. He had no doubt of the need for universal training and certification, but he could see that 'no British Parliament would give its sanction' to a penal clause, so the old untrained midwife would still exist for the poor. However, people who chose an untrained midwife in the future would do so with their eyes open. 'The race of ignorant and unskilful women in whose hands the practice now so largely rests, would gradually disappear.' He added that the Obstetrical Society had trained and certified midwives 'for not a farthing', although malicious critics have accused it of 'selling bogus diplomas'. Such opposition was misplaced. It was not the intention to have midwives replace general practitioners.

[31] *Transactions of the Obstetrical Society of London*, 33 (1891), 59. The numbers applying to take the examination increased rapidly in the late 1880s when it seemed likely a bill would soon be passed and a certificate from the Obstetrical Society would ensure admission to the register. By December 1890, 1,130 candidates had taken the examination, 197 had failed, 13 'did not present themselves', and 2 were struck off for misconduct.

she undertook all the routine nursing of the mother and the baby during the month of lying-in. For families and family doctors, monthly nurses were important people; so much so, that in the late nineteenth century some hospitals trained and provided certificates for monthly nurses.[32]

In practice, however, where the patient could afford to do so, doctors often recommended the employment of a midwife as the monthly nurse because of her greater ability to deal with an unexpected emergency. Thus there were: first of all, independent midwives taking full responsibility for a delivery and sending for a doctor only in an emergency; secondly, women who practised both as an independent midwife and as a monthly nurse as the occasion demanded; thirdly, the monthly nurse, working under the direction of the doctor, who never practised as an independent midwife.

By the end of the nineteenth century some progress had occurred. The day when all future midwives would be trained and certificated was only a short way off, and there was already the rudiments of a midwifery service provided by a few charities in various parts of the country. But even at the very end of the century the vast majority of midwife deliveries were carried out by untrained women who, as Farr had said, 'had peculiar views of their own which they lose no opportunity of carrying into effect, with the best intentions in the world but the worst of consequences'.

CHILDBIRTH AND THE MEDICAL PROFESSION IN THE NINETEENTH CENTURY

Throughout the nineteenth century obstetrics was much more a branch of general practice than a speciality, even within institutions. In most of the dispensaries, in the Poor Law hospitals, and in virtually all the non-teaching provincial voluntary hospitals—not only in the nineteenth century, but well into the twentieth—the posts of accoucheur or obstetrician were held by local general practitioners who acquired their appointment through seniority, experience, reputation, and not uncommonly a touch of nepotism.

In the first half of the nineteenth century, so few were the medical men who resembled consultants in anything like the modern sense and so concentrated were they in the metropolis, that if you took away London, you would be hard put to it to find thirty elsewhere. Take away Edinburgh, Glasgow, Dublin, Manchester, and Birmingham as well and there would be scarcely enough to count on the fingers of one hand. In 1850 (and quite possibly in 1900), you could have travelled west from London through Reading, Oxford, Gloucester, Cheltenham, Bath, Bristol, and Exeter to Plymouth without finding a single physician- or surgeon-accoucheur who was the equivalent of such London

---

[32] There is an illustration of such a certificate from St Mary's Hospital in Manchester, dated 23 Apr. 1887, in J. Towler and J. Bramall, *Midwives in History and Society*, 147.

practitioners as Francis Ramsbotham, Sam Merriman, John Lever, and Robert Lee. You would, however, have met hundreds of general practitioners all busily engaged in the practice of midwifery, some of them cursing it, some of them loving it, but most of them acknowledging that without it their practices would wither away.

An analysis of 2,000 randomly selected entries in the *Medical Directory* for 1847 showed that only 24 medical practitioners (1.2 per cent of the sample) professed in any sense to specialize in obstetrics; and of these, 21 practised in London. Four described themselves as 'GP-accoucheur', 1 of whom held the unexpected qualifications MD (Cantab.) MRCP; 5 were 'surgeon-accoucheurs' and 15 were 'physician-accoucheurs' including one LRCP, one MRCP, one FRCP, and MDs from a variety of universities.[33]

The predominance of physicians should be noted. From the eighteenth century and through the whole of the nineteenth century it was physicians rather than surgeons who held the teaching posts and formed the élite. Most of the leading obstetricians of the eighteenth century were physicians. The first professor of midwifery in Britain was Dr Joseph Gibson who was appointed in Edinburgh in 1726. When the Glasgow chair was established in 1815, Dr James Towers was appointed, and a physician, W. Montogomery, was appointed to the University of Dublin chair in 1827. The first Professor of midwifery at University College London—and the first to be appointed in England—was a physician, Dr David D. Davis.[34]

As late as the 1880s and 1890s, Champneys and Matthews Duncan were at St Barthomolew's Hospital, Charles Cullingworth had come down from Manchester to St Thomas's Hospital, Robert Barnes was at St George's, James Aveling was at the Chelsea Hospital for Women, Robert Boxall was at the Middlesex, and W. S. Playfair held the chair in obstetrics at King's College. All were physicians, and all except one Fellows of the London College. The authors of almost all the important obstetric publications in the nineteenth century were physician-accoucheurs rather than surgeons. By the end of the century, however, obstetrics began to change and become a surgical speciality. It was a change of emphasis with far-reaching consequences.

Obstetricians, whether they were general practitioners or practitioners who specialized in the subject and taught in medical schools, had practised and preached a remarkably conservative approach to the management of labour from the 1780s to about the 1870s. When labours were slow, they were ready—possibly too ready—to wait for nature to take its course. Then, quite

---

[33] The result of this analysis, but not the detail presented here, was published as Loudon, 'Two Thousand Medical Men in 1847', *Bulletin of the Society for the Social History of Medicine*, 33 (1983), 4–10.
[34] Eardley Holland, 'The Medical Schools and the Teaching of Midwifery', in J. M. Kerr, R. W. Johnstone, and M. H. Phillips, *Historical Review of British Obstetrics and Gynaecology* (London, 1954), chap. 30.

suddenly, they became much more interventionist. Within little more than a decade, many had swung to the other extreme. 'Operative obstetrics', with its surgical overtones, became fashionable, especially when Caesarean section— previously so unsafe as to have been virtually banned in England—became a standard technique by the end of the century. This swing towards a more surgical approach to childbirth came from, and in part was due to, the emergence of gynaecology as a new and rapidly growing speciality in the last third of the nineteenth century.

Gynaecology offered the obstetricians the possibility of expanding their territory even more in a surgical direction. It was an attractive proposition. Gynaecology was a new speciality which attracted high fees. Most of all, it had the potential to place the obstetrician-gynaecologist on a par with the general surgeon. General surgeons, however, resisted the change, claiming gynaecology as their department. In London, where this professional rivalry was most conspicuous and bitter, surgeons banned obstetricians from performing gynaecological operations at general hospitals. Obstetricians, they said, could diagnose gynaecological disorders and prescribe medical treatments—in other words they could behave as physicians—but they could not operate.[35]

Most of the physician-accoucheurs, who had never seen themselves as belonging to a surgical speciality, were not disposed to quarrel with the surgeons. But those who were surgically inclined fought hard for the possession of gynaecology. Young practitioners in the early twentieth century with an eye to a career in obstetrics, took the wise approach of obtaining both the MRCP and the FRCS. They saw which way the tide was flowing and they fought, and eventually won, the territorial campaign for gynaecology. By the 1920s there were still general surgeons who undertook hysterectomy and ovariectomy, if only because there were so few obstetrician-gynaecologists; but the link between obstetrics and gynaecology was forged and the obstetric-physician was fast dying out.

This, however, is jumping ahead. Why was midwifery so closely linked to general practice? and why, when there was an abundance of midwives, did general practitioners take up this arduous form of practice with such apparent enthusiasm?

To answer the last question first, it was not simply the fees. Money was important, but midwifery was an underpaid activity. A busy practitioner was able to earn more (and wear himself out less) by confining himself to the practice of physic, surgery, and pharmacy than he could by spending hours at the bedside of a woman in labour. Many would have liked to abandon midwifery but only those who were well established dared to do so. Apart

---

[35] The ban imposed on obstetricians by general surgeons applied specifically to ovariotomy, which played a crucial role in the early development of gynaecology.

from money, however, there was a certain 'job-satisfaction' that is inherent in obstetrics, and there was always the motive that general practitioners believed they were safer birth-attendants than ignorant untrained midwives. Most of all, however, general practitioners took all the midwifery they could get because of the conviction that 'the successful practice of midwifery... at the outset of life as surely establishes a professional man's reputation as the contrary retards his progress'. Without midwifery 'it is vain to expect employment in the country and not very easy in the metropolis'.[36]

'Deliver the babies and you will have the family as patients for the rest of your life' became an article of faith with general practitioners from the late eighteenth to the mid-twentieth century. In short, midwifery was the linchpin of general practice and the essence of the concept of the 'family doctor'.[37]

But it was not an easy way to make a living. Richard Smith (1772–1843), a Bristol surgeon and perceptive observer of medical practice, believed that

The man-midwife... cannot be compensated at all by the mere lying-in fee, unless it leads to other business. I know of no surgeon who would not willingly have given up attending midwifery cases provided he could retain the family in other respects—but that is unprofitable, as every accoucheur knows... midwifery destroys those who practise it.[38]

Midwifery was exhausting and demanded judgement, skill, and quick thinking. A general practitioner said in 1892:

I have no hesitation in saying, after more than thirty years' experience as student and practitioner that midwifery is the most anxious and trying of all medical work, and to be successfully practised calls for more skill, care, and presence of mind on the part of the medical man than any other branch of medicine.[39]

When general practitioners wrote about midwifery, they usually stressed the trials and anxieties of the abnormal. It may therefore be useful to describe the average home delivery by a doctor around 1870.

The middle classes were always delivered at home. It was extremely rare for them to be sent to hospital, even in an emergency. Whether the doctor was a general practitioner or a specialist in obstetrics with a hospital appointment, he (and only rarely was it 'she') would have seen the patient during pregnancy, but antenatal care in the modern sense was unknown. When it came to the delivery, he would not have worn a gown, gloves, or a mask. He delivered the baby in his ordinary day clothes. To remove his jacket would have been seen

---

[36] Jonathan Toogood, 'On the Practice of Midwifery with Remarks', *Provincial Medical and Surgical Journal*, 7 (1844), 103–8.

[37] Loudon, 'The Concept of the Family Doctor', *Bulletin of the History of Medicine*, 58 (1984), 347–62, and id., 'Obstetrics and the General Practitioner', *British Medical Journal*, 301 (1990), 703–7.

[38] Bristol Record Office, Bristol Infirmary Biographical Memoirs, ii. 157–9.

[39] *Report of Select Committee on Midwives' Registration*, Q. 1660. Evidence of Mr Brown, MRCS LSA, general practitioner.

as a vulgar habit, but he would roll up the long cuffs which were the fashion. He would carry a midwifery bag containing forceps, a breech hook, instruments for craniotomy, a silver catheter, scissors, needles and thread for repairing the perineum, and a bottle of chloroform together with a clean linen handkerchief which he could roll into a cone to administer the anaesthetic according to the method described by Simpson in 1848. The instruments might be clean but they would not be sterilized.

When he arrived, unless birth was imminent, he would carry out at least one and probably a series of vaginal examinations to check the progress of labour, using a lubricant which was unsterile and contained no antiseptic agent. While he waited with all the patience he could muster, he would think of his other patients on whom his income and practice depended. He was a busy man, tempted to 'hurry things up' in a slow labour and often urged to do so by the patient's family saying 'For heaven's sake, can't you do something doctor?' This doctor might be as careful and conscientious as anyone could wish. If he had attended a case of erysipelas or another lying-in patient with puerperal fever he might have washed carefully and changed his clothes. Otherwise the danger of contagion would never occur to him. He would wash his hands in a perfunctory manner because it was a gentlemanly thing to do, but not in the prolonged and thorough fashion with a nail brush that later became surgical routine. When streptococcal disease was prevalent in his practice the chances of this doctor transmitting the disease to his patient must have been high, even if he never used instruments. There were many ways in which he could have infected his patient unwittingly in the course of a normal delivery. There were the vaginal examinations, the jar of unsterilized lubricant, his daytime clothes, his instruments if he used them, and above all something no one knew until the 1920s: the possibility that he was a nose or throat carrier of the streptococcus. All these were potential sources of infection.[40]

Yet, in spite of all these dangers, some general practitioners were able to achieve low rates of maternal mortality in general practice. A selection can be seen in Table 12.1 but it must be stressed that they cannot be regarded as a representative sample. They all practised in non-industrial areas. The total number of deliveries was small for each individual, allowing chance to play a large part in determining the mortality rate. And they were a self-selected literate group, motivated to publish by their good results. Practitioners whose records would have shown high levels of maternal mortality above the national average, whether through bad luck or bad management, would have been unlikely to publish the fact.

---

[40] For an account which makes these points in greater detail and even more forcibly than I have, see W. S. Playfair, 'Introduction to a Discussion on the Prevention of Puerperal Fever', *British Medical Journal* (1887), ii. 1034–6.

TABLE 12.1 *Maternal Mortality in General Practice in the Nineteenth Century*

Author and date of publication	Practice area	Period in which the deliveries took place	Number of deliveries	Forceps rate (%)	Maternal mortality rates (per 10,000 deliveries)
E. Copeman 1841–2	Norfolk	1835–41	840	—	23
J. Waddington 1843–4	Margate	1788–1844	2,159	0.1	9
J. Toogood[a] 1844	Bridgwater	c.1810–17	1,135	1.3	70
C. Earle 1846	Norfolk	1800–46	4,320	—	39
Anderson Smith 1859	—	—	1,300	2	8
Robert Dunn 1859–60	—	1831–50	4,049	5	7
Mr Rigden 1870	Canterbury	1860s	4,390	—	2
H. W. Bailey 1860	Thetford	1818–58	6,476	1.7	2
S. Lawrence 1862–3	Montrose	—	1,000	—	5
Dr Thompson 1867–8	Wanbury Cheshire	1850–68	2,200	—	9
H. C. Rose 1876	Hampstead	—	1,250	0.7	16

[a] Dr Jonathan Toogood of Bridgwater had a large consulting as well as general private practice in obstetrics. His paper includes the mortality of all his cases, private and consulting, which largely explains his relatively high rate of maternal mortality.

Source: E. Copeman, 'Report on Midwifery in Private Practice', *Provincial Medical and Surgical Journal*, 3 (1841–2), 131–2; J. Waddington, 'Statistics of Midwifery', *London Medical Gazette*, NS 2 (1843–4), 144–5; J. Toogood, 'On the Practice of Midwifery with Remarks', *Provincial Medical and Surgical Journal*, 7 (1844), 103–8; C. Earle, 'Report of Obstetric Cases Occurring in Private Practice', ibid. 7 (1846), 261–3; Anderson Smith, '1,300 Midwifery Cases Attended in Private Practice', *Lancet* (1859), i. 481; R. Dunn, 'On the Statistics of Midwifery from Private Practice', *Transactions of the Obstetrical Society of London*, 1 (1859–60), 279–97, quoted in *Report of the Registrar General for 1870*, 410; H. W. Bailey, 'Statistics of Midwifery', *Transactions of the Obstetrical Society of London*, 2 (1860), 299–307; S. Lawrence, 'Statistical Report of One Thousand Midwifery Cases', *Edinburgh Medical and Surgical Journal*, 8 (1862–3), 712–24 and 800–14; Dr Thompson, 'A Few Notes on a Country Obstetric Practice', *Edinburgh Medical Journal*, 13 (1867–8), 69–71; Henry Cooper Rose, 'A Contribution to the Statistics of Midwifery in General Practice', *Transactions of the Obstetrical Society of London*, 18 (1876), 147–59.

How well the generality of medical practitioners practised this difficult part of their profession reflected the extent and quality of medical education in obstetrics. The profound importance of medical education not only in imparting facts and theories, but also in instilling attitudes, is what we consider next.

PHYSICIANS, SURGEONS, AND THE TEACHING OF MIDWIFERY

In the first half of the nineteenth century when the territory of various practitioners was becoming more sharply defined, midwifery stood apart because it was practised by all types of practitioner, although the general practitioners undertook the lion's share of non-midwife deliveries. To which branch of medical practice did obstetrics really belong, as a physician asked in 1825?

The present question . . . is, to which branch of medicine, *physic* or *surgery*, does the act of *midwifery* belong? or does it belong to either? One would imagine not, since it appears to be disavowed by both. Surgeons, who aim at eminence in the higher walks of their art, hold it in contempt. The pharmaceutic branch, as a body, disclaim it. The College of Physicians refuse their sanction to it, and hold no communion with those who practise it. No public provision, in this country, is made for teaching it; nor is any test of ability required from those that practise it, by either college or corporation.[41]

The attitude of the College of Physicians, and its concern with its own dignity, was shown in the evidence of the President, Sir Henry Halford, to the Select Committee on Medical Education in 1834 when he tried to defend the indefensible. A licentiate of the College, as opposed to a fellow, could, he said, practise as an accoucheur and deliver as many babies as he wished. No one engaged in the practice of midwifery, however, could become a fellow of the College. 'Knowledge of the diseases of women and children is expected of us', said Sir Henry, but 'midwifery is rather a manual operation . . . a manual labour' which would 'discredit men who had been educated at universities' and 'disparage the highest grade of the profession'.[42]

The position of the College of Surgeons was similar. It was a new establishment, replacing the Company of Surgeons and desperate to defend the new high status of surgery, as John Abernethy explained in the early years of the nineteenth century:

There was a time when surgeons were considered as mere appendages of physicians, the mere operators to be put in motion by their directors: but times are changed, and surgeons are changed too . . . and in consequence have got a kind of information which puts them on a par with others of the profession.[43]

[41] Miscellaneous intelligence, 'Society of Physicians', *London Medical Repository*, NS 3 (1825), 84. Later in this article the author refers to obstetrics as an 'art involved in mystery. It practises in the dark. Its operations are all disgusting and demoralising . . .'. It was uncommon to find a physician express his distaste for childbirth so explicitly, although such views were widely held.

[42] *Report of the Select Committee on Medical Education*, PP 1834, 13. Evidence of Sir Henry Halford, PRCP, Q. 223–34. In the opinion of Wakley, editor of the *Lancet*, Halford's evidence on midwifery showed 'the folly, the absurdity and the narrow-mindedness of the President of the Royal College of Physicians'. He was unworthy to be named in the same page as the many famous licentiate physician-accoucheurs. *Lancet* (1833–4), ii. 906.

[43] Royal Society of Medicine, London. The notebooks of John Greene Crosse of Norwich. MS. 285.g.11.

Surgeons who practised pharmacy or midwifery were excluded from Council of any other office in the College. If a member of Council was found to be practising either, he was promptly expelled.[44] James Guthrie, President of the College of Surgeons in 1833, 1841, and 1854 explained to the Select Committee on Medical Education in 1834 that midwifery was permissible for the young surgeon at the beginning of his career, struggling to make a living, because 'Mrs Such-a-one will send for anyone as a man-midwife, who is known to be of respectable character. But persons do not go to a surgeon on such an understanding.' The public, he said, would lose faith in senior established surgeons if they did not devote their lives solely to surgery, adding 'I must say I would be exceedingly sorry to see the first accoucheur in this town president. I do not think it would lead to the advancement of the science.'[45]

Against this solid wall of prejudice from the leading medical corporations, the lone voice of Sir Charles Clark, a distinguished accoucheur and the first president of the Obstetrical Society of London, tried to convince the committee of the need for educating all practitioners in midwifery. He treated the committee to a long (and in fact excellent) lecture on normal and abnormal parturition, stressing the difficulties and dangers of childbirth. He had neither the need nor the stomach to attack the views of the presidents of the two Royal Colleges. He was more concerned with refuting those who regarded midwifery as women's work from which men, except on very rare occasions, should be excluded, and who believed there was:

nothing more unnecessary or unmanly than for a surgeon or physician to neglect his patients, to sit beside a lady's bedside for hours together in a natural labour which any female of prudence could manage.[46]

This was an argument on a different level. The objections put forward by the Colleges of Physicians and Surgeons were based on the preservation of their status and dignity. But there was another school of thought, or rather a range of opinions, which opposed the idea of man-midwifery of any kind. The extremists, a sort of lunatic fringe, claimed that all obstetric complications were created by men-midwives. The mere presence of a man in the lying-in room, they said, was enough to induce a baby at the moment of birth to retreat back into the womb in terror. In any case, they said, disgusting erotic motives were the real reason why medical men chose to practise midwifery.

[44] The evidence of James Guthrie to the Select Committee on Medical Education in 1934 is slightly muddled, but it suggests there were 200 'pure' surgeons, practising surgery only and 7,800 general practitioners holding the MRCS. *Report of the Select Committee on Medical Education*, Q. 4731–3.

[45] Ibid. Q. 4801. Inconsistency never worried Guthrie, because elsewhere in his evidence he admitted that he, like all London surgeons, treated as many medical cases as surgical.

[46] T. Champney, *Medical and Chirurgical Reform* (London, 1797).

Man-midwifery was an immoral activity.[47] Sir Anthony Carlisle, a fashionable surgeon and a dreadful snob, gave an air of spurious respectability to such views and established an institution for the delivery of upper-class women run entirely by midwives, because:

I consider it derogatory to any liberal man to assume the office of a nurse, of an old woman; and that it is an *imposture* to pretend that a medical man is required at a labour. The craft therefore involves imposture, mischievous interference, and gross indecency. Not only is it beneath our dignity, but it is not within our province. I do not consider the delivery of a woman as a surgical operation; it is a natural operation. The men-midwives have recourse to surgical operations to make themselves in request, and to make it believed the parturition is a surgical act . . .[48]

Although these extremists and their salacious comments have attracted the attention of historians, in my opinion they had little influence on the development of obstetric care. None the less, they represented the extreme end of a general contempt for the practice of midwifery which had such a malign effect on teaching.

With the formalization of medical education following the Apothecaries Act of 1815, there was initially no attempt to include midwifery in the syllabus. The logical body to teach and examine in the subject was the College of Surgeons. But it flatly refused to do so until, under pressure from the Obstetrical Society in London, the College introduced a licence in midwifery in 1852. Candidates were required to have attended two courses of lectures and to have conducted twenty labours. The examination was an oral one. Few candidates for the examination appeared and the licence was discontinued over the problem of the admission of women, the women in question being Elizabeth Garrett Anderson and Sophia Jex-Blake.[49]

In 1827 the Society of Apothecaries made attendance at a course of lectures on midwifery and diseases of children one of the requirements for sitting for the LSA; but a planned examination in midwifery was never introduced on the grounds that no suitable examiners could be found. Without an examination few candidates took midwifery seriously and the 400 to 500 who took the LSA each year (with an 80–90 per cent pass rate) did so with virtually no instruction in the subject. During the first half of the century, neither Oxford nor Cambridge examined students in midwifery. The examination for the degree of Bachelor of Medicine in the University of London did, however, insist on proper instruction in midwifery and included a

---

[47] See e.g. 'Medical Practitioner', *An Important Address to Wives and Mothers on the Dangers and Unsuitability of Man-Midwifery* (London, 1830).
[48] *Report of the Select Committee on Medical Education*, Q. 5975. See also a debate on the necessity for man-midwifery by Dr Kinglake of Taunton in a series of articles and replies in the *London Medical and Physical Journal*, 36 (1816), 3–9, 96–100, 176–87, 288–92, 365–7.
[49] See Zachary Cope, *The Royal College of Surgeons of England: A History* (London, 1959), and the excellent biography by Jo Manson, *Elizabeth Garrett Anderson* (London, 1965).

paper and oral examination devoted solely to midwifery. In this respect, London University was alone.[50]

When the Medical Act of 1858 was introduced, a medical student could qualify and register with the General Medical Council as a medical practitioner on the basis of a single qualification in medicine or surgery. In practice a large majority passed examinations in both; but not in midwifery. In 1885, the conjoint examination of the Colleges of Physicians and Surgeons (first suggested in 1859) was introduced and included an examination in midwifery. It was only after the Medical Act Amendment Act of 1886 that medical students were required to pass an examination in all three subjects before qualifying and registering. Even then the quality of teaching in midwifery was often appalling.

Evidence to the Select Committee on Midwives' Registration in 1892 showed there were not enough maternity cases in hospitals in the 1890s for teaching medical students even at the low level demanded so that 'the present training of the medical student in midwifery is dangerously defective'. The requirement that each medical student attend twelve labours and conduct three was sometimes met by the student sticking his head through the door of the labour room and saying 'How do you do' to the woman before signing the register as having been present. The introduction of a compulsory examination in midwifery made little difference. In fact it was said 'there has been a distinct retrograde movement for a number of years... 30 years ago [the] medical man was better trained in midwifery and better able to practise it'.[51]

We are so used to the idea that the nineteenth century saw huge strides in medical education, that it may be difficult to adjust to the notion that the apprentice or young practitioner in the eighteenth century who chose to attend a private course of midwifery in London (paying handsomely for the privilege), may have been better motivated and better fitted to practice midwifery than his successor a hundred years later. After the 1815 Apothecaries Act the medical student was wholly concerned with physic, surgery, pharmacy, materia medica—and Latin, in which most failures occurred. These, not midwifery, were the hurdles between the student and the coveted qualification MRCS LSA, known colloquially as 'the College and Hall'. In general the

---

[50] The University of London was created by a charter granted by the Crown in 1836 which empowered the new university to grant degrees in the arts, law, and medicine, after examination, for candidates who had completed a course of instruction at University College, King's College, and such institutions as might thereafter be approved for the purpose. H. Hale Bellot, *University College, London. 1826–1929* (London, 1929). In 1851 the regulations for the MB in the University of London showed that candidates were examined in physiology; general pathology, general therapeutics, and hygiene; surgery; medicine; midwifery; and forensic medicine. The time allocated for examining in midwifery was the same as it was for the other subjects. See app. B in E. A. Gray, *By Candlelight: The Life of Arthur Hill Hassall 1817–94* (London, 1983).

[51] *Report of the Select Committee on Midwives' Registration*, Q. 365, 374, 378, and 455. Evidence of Mr Rentoul. On his own Rentoul is not necessarily to be trusted, but here he echoed the views of many.

teaching of midwifery in England in the nineteenth century was grossly inadequate. Many fresh young general practitioners embarked on their career with a degree of ignorance about normal and abnormal labours that hardly bears thinking about. But this was England; Scotland was different, and we must consider briefly the differences in terms of general and obstetric education.

MEDICAL EDUCATION AND MIDWIFERY IN SCOTLAND

There were four universities which granted medical degrees in Scotland: Edinburgh, Glasgow, Aberdeen, and St Andrews. There were also colleges of physicians and surgeons, but no society of apothecaries, the apothecary being virtually unknown in Scotland. In the eighteenth and early nineteenth centuries, the Universities of Aberdeen and St Andrews granted the degree of MD on the basis of two letters of recommendation from established physicians and a fee. No attendance or examination was required, and Scottish degrees as a whole were unjustly scorned by the English on that account.

The scorn was misplaced. There are many occasions in the eighteenth and nineteenth centuries, and some in the twentieth, when it is difficult to avoid the conclusion that as far as medical education and the organization of the medical profession were concerned they did things more sensibly and often more thoroughly in Scotland than they did in England. Certainly from the mid-eighteenth to the mid-nineteenth centuries the medical doctorates of Edinburgh and Glasgow and the licences of their colleges of physicians and surgeons represented the highest standard of medical education that could be obtained in Britain. Many young men travelled from other countries to acquire a Scottish medical education. The degree of MD (Edin.) was a very common qualification amongst English physicians (especially dissenters who were barred from entry to the Universities of Oxford and Cambridge) as well as general practitioners.[52]

Scotland was remarkably free from the distinctions and dissensions of medical practitioners in England. In Scotland, medical practitioners:

be they graduates of any university, fellows or licentiates of either of the colleges of surgeons, are in point of fact, the physicians, surgeons and accoucheurs of their respective patients... The regulations of these [Scottish] institutions imply what, in point of fact, is the case, that the general practitioner exists everywhere; that the distinctions of the profession are in many situations unnecessary or impracticable; and where they are practicable, they leave it to circumstances and the choice of the individual, whether he is to restrict himself to one department, or act in all.[53]

---

[52] Loudon, *Medical Care and the General Practitioner*, and id., 'Two Thousand Medical Men in 1847'.

[53] Review of the *Transactions of the Associated Apothecaries* in *Edinburgh Medical and Surgical Journal* (22 July 1824), 162–3.

In Edinburgh both fellows and licentiates of the College of Physicians of Edinburgh were permitted to practise surgery and midwifery. There was no college of midwifery, 'the practitioners of which, therefore, take refuge either in the College of Physicians or in that of Surgeons'.[54] English obstetricians admitted the superiority of obstetric education in Scotland. In his presidential address to the Obstetrical Society of London in 1878, W. S. Playfair complained:

I am supposed to teach a mass of young men the entire subject of midwifery and the diseases of women and children in a short summer course of something under forty lectures ... the result is that students leave our schools more ignorant of obstetrics than of any other subject ... [while] ... universities in Scotland insist on a course of one hundred lectures.[55]

The Edinburgh College of Surgeons required the study of midwifery, *materia medica* and pharmacy, anatomy, and surgery. For the general practitioner, the LRCS (Edin.) represented the most comprehensive medical education available in Britain. Until the foundation of London University, it had no rival in terms of breadth. In short, if a student wanted a thorough grounding in midwifery in the nineteenth century he could find it in Edinburgh, Glasgow (or Dublin at the 'Rotunda' lying-in hospital), but not in England.

INSTITUTIONAL CARE IN THE NINETEENTH CENTURY

Institutional maternal care was provided on a regular basis for the poor, supported by charity or public funds, and existed in two forms. Deliveries in the patient's own home (out-patient care), or deliveries in the wards of hospitals and infirmaries (in-patient care).[56] In both forms of care the majority of deliveries were undertaken by midwives who had received some training; but also, and to a varying degree according to the type of institution, by student midwives and medical students. One or more obstetricians were appointed to the institution (usually honorary, sometimes paid) to teach and to deliver complicated cases. The obstetrician might be a complete or partial specialist in obstetrics, or a local general practitioner.

The Poor Law maternity systems provided for the larger number of deliveries in the nineteenth century with an increasing number taking place in Poor Law institutions. Before the new Poor Law Act of 1834, Poor Law maternal care was 'outdoor'. Midwives and practitioners were employed and paid by the parish to deliver women in their homes. On the whole it was a

---

[54] Ibid.

[55] W. S. Playfair, *Transactions of the Obstetrical Society of London*, 21 (1879), 29–372.

[56] Because it can cause confusion, it should be noted that whereas today the word 'admission' is used to describe admission to hospital as an in-patient, in the 18th and 19th centuries 'admission' was used for both in- and out-patients, meaning admission to the care of the charity.

system which worked well, at least in rural areas in the late eighteenth and early nineteenth centuries, not least because payments to practitioners were often quite generous and appointments as parish surgeon were sought after.

The main thrust of the 1834 Act, as is well known, was the abolition of outdoor relief and the substitution of the harsh regime of the workhouse to deter the able-bodied from applying for public assistance. Even the most ardent supporter of the 'less eligibility' rule, however, was unlikely to feel it was a principle which applied to childbirth. Nevertheless, when the work-houses developed their sick wards and these evolved into separate Poor Law infirmaries, first in London in 1867 and then in the provinces, they scooped up midwifery cases. Outdoor maternal care under the Poor Law virtually disappeared in the cities although it persisted in rural areas.[57]

Out-patient care, however, continued to be provided by the maternity departments of dispensaries whose main concern was medical and surgical cases. Only a minority of general dispensaries possessed maternity depart-ments; most out-patient maternal care was provided by separate lying-in charities. The most famous was the Royal Maternity Charity in London which was 'set on foot' in March 1757, and appears to have been based on a similar institution in Newcastle upon Tyne.[58] After a poor start with a difficult and inefficient accoucheur, Dr Ford was appointed accoucheur to the Charity in 1764.[59] The Royal Maternity Charity was the most successful of all the nineteenth-century lying-in institutions (see Table 12.4), but out-patient midwifery was provided in the second half of the nineteenth century by some of the voluntary hospitals. The main purpose was to provide 'good teaching material' for medical students who were 'sent on the district' with minimal instruction and little supervision.

In-patient care, which formed the mainstay of teaching, was sometimes provided in the form of lying-in wards in general hospitals, but more often in separate lying-in hospitals. Instruction of midwives was carried out in a few of the workhouse infirmaries established under the Poor Law Amendment Act

[57] After 1834 there was an interim period in which indoor and outdoor midwifery coexisted. Dr Leete, medical officer to the Union of Thrapston in Northamptonshire in the 1850s, was paid 10 s. for attendance of each midwifery case 'in the union house' [i.e., the workhouse] and £1 for outdoor cases. He attended four 'union house' cases and two outdoor cases in 1850. Complicated cases were paid at the rate of £1. 10s. 0d. Northampton County Record Office. Day-books of Dr Leete of Thrapston. See final pages of day-book 'Leete IX/1'.

[58] Royal College of Obstetricians and Gynaecologists. Records of the Royal Maternity Charity. See also S. A. Seligman, 'The Royal Maternity Charity: The First One Hundred Years', *Medical History*, 24 (1980), 403–18.

[59] The Library of the Royal College of Obstetricians and Gynaecologists, London. Records of the Royal Maternity Charity. Minutes of 27 Jan. 1764. There was also a large number of minor lying-in charities which did not provide medical care but confined themselves to providing food, clothing, and coals for women during pregnancy and the lying-in period. They should be mentioned in passing, but here we will only be concerned with institutions which provided midwives and medical practitioners for the delivery of women.

(the 'new poor law') of 1834.[60] It has been suggested that lying-in hospitals were founded in the eighteenth century as a deliberate strategy to legitimize the professional aspirations of men-midwives and strengthen their image in their competition with midwives.[61] That such a motive played a part, consciously or unconsciously, is possible, but the assertion is based on speculation rather than evidence. It ignores the stated views of those involved in providing charitable obstetric care and overlooks the fact that the initiators and founders of such charities were usually lay men and women rather than accoucheurs. Even if one allows for the transformation of disreputable motives into respectable ones by the process of rationalization, William Farr's explanation is more convincing:

Seeing how destitute of comforts, means, and medical appliances many women are, the thought occurred to some benevolent persons that they might be received and delivered in hospitals. It was the extension of the hospital system to midwifery cases, which have some analogy with wounds and injuries for which hospitals had been used since the date of their foundation. Contrary to expectations, the advantages these institutions offered were over-balanced by one dread drawback; the mortality of mothers was not diminished; nay, it became in some instances excessive; in other instances appalling.[62]

By the second half of the nineteenth century, the number of deliveries undertaken by the out-patient charities exceeded those undertaken by the hospitals; and the number of women delivered in workhouse infirmaries exceeded those delivered in voluntary hospitals. In 1889, for example, the Royal Maternity Charity had the highest annual number of deliveries: 3,331; Queen Charlotte's Hospital, the Mecca of obstetrics in London, delivered 995 women as in-patients and 1,179 as out-patients (total 2,174); the General Lying-in Hospital delivered 484 as in-patients and 1,091 as out-patients (total 1,575); St Mary's Hospital in Manchester delivered only 25 as in-patients and 782 as out-patients (total 807).

In the context of total births, institutional deliveries, especially in-patient deliveries, played a very small part. The following are estimates in round numbers of the extent of institutional maternal care in the 1880s when the average annual number of live births in England and Wales was 890,000.[63] The average annual deliveries in institutions in the 1880s was as follows:

---

[60] Maternity wards in general hospitals were much more common in Paris than London, and indeed, in France as a whole than England.

[61] See e.g. M. A. Versluysen, 'Medical Professionalisation and Maternity Hospitals in Eighteenth Century London', *Bulletin of the Society for the Social History of Medicine*, 21 (1977), 34–6.

[62] *Report of the Registrar General for 1870* (1872), 407.

[63] My sources here are app. 4 in the *Report of the Select Committee on Midwives' Registration*, and the authors listed in Table 12.2. The list on which the estimates are based may be incomplete, but checking them against the lists of hospitals and dispensaries published by Burdett in 1902, suggests the error is not large.

In-patient deliveries:

Voluntary hospitals	2,700 (0.3%)
Workhouse infirmaries	29,000 (3.2%)
Total	31,700 (3.5%)
Out-patient deliveries	36,000 (4.0%)
Total institutional care	67,700 (7.5%)

One of the reasons for making this calculation is that in the next section of this chapter I will be discussing the rates of maternal mortality in institutional deliveries. Whether those rates were exceptionally high or exceptionally low, the numbers of births and maternal deaths in institutions were so few that they would have had only a marginal effect on the trend in maternal mortality in England and Wales as a whole.

MATERNAL MORTALITY IN INSTITUTIONAL DELIVERIES

Farr's description of the mortality of lying-in hospitals, quoted above, was no exaggeration. From their earliest days, their wards were subject to periodic waves of puerperal fever. In the eighteenth century, so great was the mortality in some years that the hospital authorities were rumoured to have buried two women in one coffin to conceal the size of the slaughter. In 1769–70, when the fever raged in the Westminster Lying-in Hospital, out of 63 women delivered, 19 had the fever and 14 died. In Edinburgh at the end of February 1773, puerperal fever appeared in the wards of the lying-in hospital. 'Almost every woman, as soon as she was delivered, was seized with it; and all of them died', but the disease was not seen in the town.[64] The same dreadful mortality continued until the last two decades of the nineteenth century. Indeed it was often worse in the nineteenth than the eighteenth century. It occurred 'in all hospitals, in all maternity institutions, in all climates, in the south of France as it does at St. Petersburg, in Dublin as in Vienna, in London as in Moscow'.[65] It was not that puerperal fever was confined to run-down or inefficient institutions. On the contrary, Queen Charlotte's Hospital and the Rotunda in Dublin had the highest reputations; yet the MMR at the former was often between 110 and 200 per 10,000. In 1849 it rose to the staggering level of 932 while the MMR at the Rotunda in 1861 was 519.

An obvious suspicion, that the rate of puerperal fever in lying-in hospitals was directly linked to the frequency of obstetrical operations, proved to be at best a partial explanation. A very large majority of cases occurred after

---

[64] John Clarke, *Practical Essays on the Arrangement of Pregnancy and Labour and on the Inflammatory Diseases of Lying-in Women* (2nd edn., London, 1806).

[65] Florence Nightingale, *Introductory Notes on Lying-in Hospitals* (London, 1876), 24, the most vivid and striking source on the problems of 19th-cent. lying-in institutions. See also Léon Le Fort, *Des maternités* (Paris, 1866) which she was quoting here and which I have used extensively.

non-instrumental deliveries. Nor was it due to a high rate of admission of complicated cases from the community.[66] Nor could it be tied to social class or illegitimacy. The prevalence of puerperal fever depended 'neither on the social condition of the women, nor on the moral conditions under which delivery may occur'.[67]

Searching for an explanation, Florence Nightingale quoted many European authorities. It is interesting that although she was, as always, extremely well-informed, she never mentioned Semmelweis and although she conceded the possibility of contagion, she placed more emphasis on 'foul air, putrid miasmas, and predisposition to malignant inflammatory action'. She concluded that the larger the hospital the worse the miasmatic influence and the higher the rate of maternal mortality. Crowding and frequency of deliveries were the key:

however grand, or however humble a home may be in which the birth of the child takes place, there is only one delivery in the home at the time ... In many London workhouses the number of deliveries yearly is so small that, so far as concerns annual deliveries, they approach more closely to dwelling houses ... than they do to lying-in hospitals properly so-called.[68]

We now turn to Tables 12.2, 12.3, and 12.4 which reveal one of the most striking and well-known features of maternal mortality in the nineteenth century. The rate of maternal mortality in the wards of lying-in hospitals was horrific. Maternal mortality in the charities which delivered the poor in their own homes, however, was not only much lower than it was in the hospitals, but was frequently lower than national levels although they delivered only the poorest members of society in some of the worst urban housing. This finding

---

[66] This was shown convincingly by J. E. Burton, 'Out-door versus In-door Maternity Charities', *Medical Press and Circular* (1882), ii. 150–1, 172–3. The only institutions in which it is likely that low mortality rates in out-patient deliveries and high rates in in-patient care were in part due to the transfer in labour of a large proportion of complicated cases under out-patient care to the parent hospital, were the teaching hospitals such as Queen Charlotte's Hospital.

[67] Nightingale, *Introductory Notes*. It was often pleaded by Queen Charlotte's Hospital that their high rate of maternal mortality was due to their policy of admitting unmarried mothers, in whom it was known the mortality was high. But the proportion of unmarried mothers delivered in workhouse infirmaries was even higher, amounting to three-quarters of all deliveries, and the mortality rate in the workhouses was significantly lower than it was in Queen Charlotte's Hospital. See F. J. Mouat, 'Note on the Statistics of Childbirth in the Lying-in Wards of Workhouse Infirmaries of England and Wales for Ten Years, 1871–1880', *Transactions of the International Medical Congress of London*, 4 (1881), 393–5.

[68] Nightingale, *Introductory Notes*, 25–8. The reasons for the high level of maternal mortality in Florence Nightingale's own maternity ward in King's College Hospital were discussed by C. R. Rowling, 'The History of the Florence Nightingale Lying-in Ward, King's College Hospital', *Transactions of the Obstetrical Society of London*, 10 (1869), 51–6. The author blamed miasmatic influences due to siting a lying-in ward in a general hospital. In the subsequent discussion Dr Barnes agreed, saying: 'He did not suppose that any physician in this town would now advocate the establishment of a lying-in ward in a general hospital.' Interestingly, the paper—published in 1869—never mentions the work of Gordon, Oliver Wendell Holmes, or Semmelweis.

TABLE 12.2 *Maternal Mortality in British Lying-in Hospitals before 1880*

	Number of deliveries	Percentage of deaths due to puerperal fever	Maternal mortality rate (per 10,000 deliveries)
England and Wales (1855–67)	1,714,706	33.3	48.3
King's College Hospital (1862–7)	780	88	333.0
Queen Charlotte's Hospital (1828–68)	9,626	73	253.0
Queen Charlotte's Hospital (1860–4)	1,746	—	420.0
Queen Charlotte's Hospital (1865–9)	1,918	—	182.0
British Lying-in Hospital (1749–96)	24,079	—	160.0
British Lying-in Hospital (1858–68)	1,741	—	143.0
City of London Lying-in Hospital (1859–68)	4,966	—	109.0
Rotunda Hospital, Dublin (1857–61)	6,521	—	260.0
Liverpool Lying-in Hospital (1864–73)	1,948	—	159.1
Glasgow Maternity Hospital (1873)	312	—	250.0
40 London Workhouse Infirmaries (5 years)	11,870	66	78.0
Liverpool Workhouse Infirmary (1858–70)	6,396	61	90.6
8 Military Lying-in Hospitals (12 years)	5,575	53	73.0

Source: Anon., *An Account of the British Lying-in Hospital for Married Women in Brownlow Street* (London, 1797); A. B. Granville, 'A Report of the Midwifery Department of the Westminster General Dispensary', *Medical and Physical Journal*, 44 (1820), 231; id., 'Phenomena, Facts and Calculations...Derived from Eleven Years' Experience of Two Lying-in Institutions', *Transactions of the Obstetrical Society of London*, 2 (1860), 139–96; F. H. Ramsbotham, 'The Eastern District of the Royal Maternity Charity', *London Medical Gazette*, NS 2 (1843–4), 619–23; J. Hall Davis, *Parturition and its difficulties* (London, 1865); A. B. Steele, *Maternity Hospitals, their Mortality, and What should be Done with them* (London, 1874); Florence Nightingale, *Introductory Notes on Lying-in Hospitals* (London, 1876); F. J. Mouat, 'Note on the Statistics of Childbirth in the Lying-in Wards of the Workhouse Infirmaries of England and Wales for Ten Years, 1871–1880', *Transactions of the International Medical Congress of London*, 4 (1881), 392–4; T. H. Bickerton, *A Medical History of Liverpool* (London, 1920).

was not confined to Britain. It was found in all Western countries, as we will see in Chapter 19 (the United States) and Chapter 25 (the Continent of Europe). In virtually all lying-in hospitals, whether in Britain, Europe, or the United States, the MMR nearly always exceeded 100 maternal deaths per 10,000 births, and often exceeded that figure by a large amount. By comparison, the national level of mortality in England and Wales was just under 50 per 10,000 births. It was calculated that the MMR in 934,781 home deliveries in the 1860s in London, Edinburgh, Paris, and other European centres was 47 per 10,000 births. The MMR in 888,312 hospital deliveries in

TABLE 12.3 *Maternal Mortality in English Out-Patient Lying-in Charities before 1880*

	Number of deliveries	Maternal mortality rate (per 10,000 deliveries)
England and Wales (1855–67)	1,714,706	48.3
Westminster General Dispensary, London (1849–60)	7,717	22.2
Benevolent Institution, London (1848–59)	4,761	16.0
Royal Maternity Charity, London (5 years)	17,242	30.0
Royal Maternity Charity, Eastern District (1831–43)	35,743	44.6
Royal Maternity Charity, Western District (1842–64)	13,783	19.6
Liverpool Ladies' Institution (early 1800s)	6,101	13.0
Birmingham Lying-in Charity (1876–80)	4,806	14.5
Newcastle upon Tyne (1879–81)	1,304	15.3
St George's Hospital, London (1864–70)	?	32.8
Guy's Hospital, London (1853–60)	11,928	30.2
Guy's Hospital, London (1869)	1,929	25.9
St Thomas's Hospital, London (1858–64)	3,512	25.6
St Mary's Hospital, Manchester (1879–81)	7,621	26.2
Glasgow Maternity Hospital (1879–81)	2,969	87.5

Source: Anon., *An Account of the British Lying-in Hospital for Married Women in Brownlow Street* (London, 1797); A. B. Granville, 'A Report of the Midwifery Department of the Westminster General Dispensary', *Medical and Physical Journal*, 44 (1820), 231; id., 'Phenomena, Facts and Calculations ... Derived from Eleven Years' Experience of Two Lying-in Institutions', *Transactions of the Obstetrical Society of London*, 2 (1860), 139–96; F. H. Ramsbotham, 'The Eastern District of the Royal Maternity Charity', *London Medical Gazette*, NS 2 (1843–4), 619–23; J. Hall Davis, *Parturition and its difficulties* (London, 1865); A. B. Steele, *Maternity Hospitals, their Mortality, and What should be Done with them* (London, 1874); Florence Nightingale, *Introductory Notes on Lying-in Hospitals* (London, 1876); F. J. Mouat, 'Note on the Statistics of Childbirth in the Lying-in Wards of the Workhouse Infirmaries of England and Wales for Ten Years, 1871–1880', *Transactions of the International Medical Congress of London*, 4 (1881), 392–4; T. H. Bickerton, *A Medical History of Liverpool* (London, 1920).

the same cities was 342.[69] The only consistent exceptions to high hospital mortality in England were not the famous lying-in hospitals, but the workhouse infirmaries and military hospitals.

No statistical tests are required to see that the differences in maternal mortality between the in-patient institutions and the out-patient charities

[69] Le Fort, *Des maternités*, 49.

TABLE 12.4 *Stillbirths and Maternal Deaths Recorded by the Eastern District of the Royal Maternity Charity, London, 1831–1843*

	Number of cases	Maternal mortality rate (per 10,000 live births)
Total number of deliveries	35,743	
Live births	33,868	
Stillbirths	2,263 (6.3%)	
Total maternal deaths	166	49.0
Puerperal (direct) maternal deaths	126	44.6
Associated (indirect) maternal deaths	40	
Puerperal (direct) maternal deaths by cause		
Haemorrhage	56	
Puerperal sepsis	34	
Other	36	
Associated (indirect) deaths		
Phthisis	15	
Pneumonia	6	
Typhus	6	
Asiatic cholera	4	
Other disease	9	
Deaths in the group 'other' which might have been associated with contracted pelvis		
Ruptured uterus	8	
Deaths after craniotomy	6	
Deaths after forceps deliveries	3	
'Exhausted after lingering labour'	1	
Total	18	

Source: F. H. Ramsbotham, 'The Eastern District of the Royal Maternity Charity', *London Medical Gazette*, NS 2 (1843–44), 619–25.

(differences in the MMR between 100 or more and 30 or less) were highly significant. Table 12.4 shows deaths by cause in deliveries undertaken by the Royal Maternity Charity. It should be noted that out of 166 maternal deaths only 34 (20 per cent) were due to puerperal sepsis. In the hospitals, the very high mortality was almost entirely due to an excess of deaths due to puerperal sepsis which accounted for at least 80 per cent of total mortality, the large majority following normal, not instrumental, deliveries.

The evidence leaves little doubt that until the final ten to fifteen years of the nineteenth century, the safest way for a woman in London to be delivered, *regardless of social class*, was at home by a trained member of the staff of the

TABLE 12.5 *Maternal Mortality at Various London Maternity Institutions Following the Introduction of Antisepsis during the early 1880s*

	Number of deliveries	Direct maternal deaths	Maternal mortality rate	Total maternal deaths	Maternal mortality rate (per 10,000 births)
Queen Charlotte's Hospital					
1860–4	1,746				424.0
1865–9	1,918				182.0
1870–4	2,228				220.0
1875–9	2,201				268.0
1880–4	3,401				105.0
1885–9	4,564				42.0
1890–4	4,894				59.0
1895–9	5,638				42.0
1900–2	3,738				45.0
General Lying-in Hospital					
1838–60	5,833				308.0
1861–79	3,773				170.0
1880–7	2,585				62.0
1888–92	2,364				38.0
St Bartholomew's[a]	4,999	4	8.0	6	12.0
St Thomas's[a]	6,816	13	19.1	15	22.0
Guy's[a]	10,100	24	23.7	24	23.7
Middlesex[a]	3,210	5	15.5	6	18.7
Charing Cross[a]	917	4	43.6	4	43.6
King's College[a]	1,955	2	10.2	3	15.3
Total	27,997	52	18.5	58	20.7

[a] Outdoor departments, 1895, 1896, and 1897.
Source: C. J. Cullingworth, *Puerperal Fever: A Preventable Disease* (London, 1888); W. Williams, *Deaths in Childbed* (London, 1904); Elizabeth Garrett Anderson, 'Deaths in Childbed', *British Medical Journal* (1898), ii. 839–40.

Royal Maternity Charity or a trained midwife. The next safest was to be delivered at home by a private doctor and the next in the wards of a workhouse infirmary. The most dangerous by a long measure was in the wards of a prestigious hospital such as Queen Charlotte's where the mortality was ten or more times as high as the Royal Maternity Charity. Since this was known to all involved in maternal care, what possible excuse was there for allowing inpatient care to continue?

That very question was raised by Robert Lee, a distinguished London practitioner, in the 1830s,[70] and by Evory Kennedy, Master of the Rotunda, whose suggestion in the 1860s that lying-in hospitals, as then constituted, should be closed provoked a storm of protest on both sides of the Atlantic.[71] James Young Simpson in Edinburgh believed it would be as well to abolish the 'medical, surgical and obstetric palaces' and replace lying-in hospitals with small separate buildings made of iron.[72] What, then, should be done? Close the Rotunda and Queen Charlotte's Hospital and turn them into out-patient dispensaries? It seemed unthinkable. The superintendent of Glasgow's lying-in hospital echoed the feelings of many when he wrote in 1853:

But what are we to do with those poor unfortunates who have not even these insalubrious places of filth and squalor to live in? Are we to shut our hospitals, infirmaries and fever houses against them? . . . Hospitals are necessary evils . . . There may be reasons for shutting hospitals, but not because deaths occur in them.[73]

This view was not shared by Florence Nightingale who had used a large sum of money, raised by her friends and admirers, to establish a lying-in ward 'where young women, properly recommended, could be instructed in midwifery'. It was a plan close to her heart and the ward was opened in 1862 in King's College Hospital. From the outset it was dogged by puerperal fever, the worst year being 1867. Without a moment's hesitation she closed the ward at the end of 1867. Childbirth, she said, was not a surgical condition. No institution which supposedly existed for the benefit of poor lying-in women, had any right to continue if the risk of mothers dying in their wards was greater than would have been if they had been delivered in their own homes. Nightingale's crisp decisiveness, which informs every page of her *Notes on Lying-in Hospitals*, stood in contrast to the indecision of the physician- and surgeon-accoucheurs. Soon, however, the urgency of the problem was recognized. For example, Dr Steele of Liverpool was influenced by the record of the Liverpool Ladies Charity to which he was the consultant physician:

---

[70] Robert Lee, *Researches on the Pathology and Treatment of some of the Most Important Diseases of Women* (London, 1833).

[71] E. Kennedy, *Hospitalism and Zymotic Diseases as More Especially Illustrated by Puerperal Fever or Metria . . . Also a Reply to the Criticisms of Seventeen Physicians upon this Paper* (2nd edn., London, 1869).

[72] J. Y. Simpson, 'Report of the Edinburgh Royal Maternity Hospital, St John's Street', *Monthly Journal of Medical Science*, 9 (1848–9), 329–38. Presumably Simpson had corrugated iron in mind. It was available in the 1840s as a building material which could be easily washed down and was not so liable to absorb putrid vapours as wood or plaster. The evidence that corrugated iron was available can be found in Philip Cox and Wesley Stacey, *Rude Timber Buildings in Australia* (London, 1969). Apparently ship-loads of iron sheeting were sent out to Australia in the both halves of the 19th cent, and a patent had been taken out for using zinc for galvanizing corrugated sheets of iron for building purposes.

[73] James Wilson, 'Report of the Glasgow Lying-in Hospital for the Year 1851–52 with an Address to the Students Attending the Hospital', *Glasgow Medical Journal*, 1 (1853), 1–10.

In the Ladies Charity of this town, about 1,500 women are delivered annually at their own homes; the death rate so far as it can be accurately ascertained, is so small as to be almost practically nil... puerperal fever has never occurred in epidemic form... during three years and three months there have been 5,035 deliveries and 15 deaths none of which, except for one case of phlegmasia dolens, were from puerperal disease.

He took the original step of writing to fifty 'leading accoucheurs' to ask them: 'Do you consider it conducive to the welfare of married women of the class just above pauperism that they should be delivered in a Lying-in Hospital, or at their own homes, skilled attendance being in either case available.' Thirty replied and all but two said 'at their own homes'.[74]

Between 1800 and 1880, when hospitals were expanding and medical and surgical admissions were rising, the number of patients delivered in lying-in hospitals tended to diminish. This was a tacit admission that lying-in hospitals were dangerous institutions. Some of them simply reduced their intake—St Mary's at Manchester, for example—but a few such as Birmingham were actually closed down.[75] The disastrous record of the lying-in hospitals stood in stark contrast to the success of hospital medicine and surgery. Obstetricians were seen to be helpless. Nothing except temporary closure reduced the dreadful waves of puerperal fever. In the 1870s, just when accoucheurs were faced with the possibility of abolishing all forms of in-patient maternal care, the future was suddenly transformed by the discovery—or rather, remembering Semmelweis—the rediscovery, of antisepsis.

THE ANTISEPTIC REVOLUTION

The antiseptic revolution was, of course, a product of bacteriology. As far as puerperal fever was concerned, 'The discovery of the active part played by micro-organisms in the production of septicaemia', said Cullingworth in 1888,

furnished the key to the whole situation. Everything was accounted for. The propagation by personal contact, the manner in which the disease dogged the footsteps of individual practitioners and became the scourge of the lying-in hospitals... all these facts were now easily explained.[76]

Bacteriology provided the pathological basis, and surgery provided the practical application of antisepsis.

Sir James Simpson had drawn attention to the close pathological similarity between surgical sepsis and puerperal sepsis and the morbid lesions produced by both. He likened the bare surface of the uterus where the placenta was

---

[74] A. B. Steele, *Maternity Hospitals, Their Mortality, and What should be Done with them* (London, 1874). See also J. E. Burton, 'Out-door versus In-door Maternity Charities'.
[75] Steele, *Maternity Hospitals*.
[76] Cullingworth, *Puerperal Fever: A Preventable Disease* (London, 1888), 14–15.

attached, and injuries to the cervix or vagina sustained in childbirth, to surgical wounds through which bacteria could gain access.[77]

The analogy between puerperal sepsis and surgical wound infection was an important observation. It underlined the surgical approach to obstetrics and the importance of the work of Joseph Lister who first published the results of the use of antisepsis in surgery in 1867.[78]

More than a decade passed before Lister's principles were fully accepted, and antisepsis was used for the first time in obstetric practice in the lying-in hospitals of various countries between 1879 and 1884. The results were extremely impressive. Maternal mortality fell from levels well above the national average to the same or even to lower levels. 'Puerperal fever has been almost entirely banished'; wrote Cullingworth only eight years after its introduction; and he was echoed by the author of an editorial in the *British Medical Journal* in the same year who forecast that very soon death from puerperal septicaemia would be measured in 'fractions per thousand'.[79] Professor Playfair said in 1887:

From being hotbeds of death and disease in which no woman could be confined without running a serious risk, sometimes hardly less grave than that of a capital surgical operation, in the majority of well-managed lying-in hospitals a woman is now actually as safe, if not safer, than if she was confined in a large and luxurious private house, with nurse, physician, and all that money can now procure.[80]

The reason for such a claim can be seen in Table 12.5. The fall in mortality in Queen Charlotte's Hospital and the General Lying-in Hospital in London was spectacular. Mortality was reduced to between one-fifth and one-tenth of the level of the 1860s and 1870s and the abrupt fall coincided with the introduction of antisepsis. In the obstetric out-patient departments of general hospitals the fall was less spectacular. They had already achieved low levels of maternal mortality. But if the rates shown in the third section of Table 12.5 are compared with those in Table 12.2 it can be seen that a fall, albeit a small one, did occur.

It might be argued that other reasons could be suggested to account for the fall in mortality. Perhaps there was a general improvement in the standard of care. Perhaps there was a change in admission policies which led to a larger number of low-risk mothers being admitted. There is nothing to support such views. The only material change in obstetric practice was the use of antisepsis. And the most conclusive evidence will appear later: a similar fall in the mortality of lying-in hospitals was seen throughout the developed world.

[77] Ibid.

[78] Lister used carbolic acid which he had stumbled on by chance. It was not until 1883 that he heard for the first time of Semmelweis's work and his prior use of the same chemical. F. H. Garrison, *Introduction to the History of Medicine* (4th edn., Philadelphia and London, 1929).

[79] Cullingworth, *Puerperal Fever*; editorial, *British Medical Journal* (1888), ii. 1457.

[80] Playfair, 'Introduction to a Discussion on the Prevention of Puerperal Fever', *British Medical Journal* (1887), ii. 1034–6.

In Britain and on the Continent, there was a great deal of discussion on the best antiseptic agent. In the early days of antisepsis it was generally agreed that carbolic acid was much less effective than sublimate of mercury. The latter, however, was toxic and could be fatal if used repeatedly for vaginal douching. However, vaginal douching was soon shown to be not only unnecessary, but harmful; and the aptly named corrosive sublimate in a strength of 1 in 1,000 was considered the ideal solution for the disinfection of the hands and instruments of the birth-attendant.[81]

In conclusion, there is no doubt that the introduction of Listerian antisepsis and its later combination with asepsis was the most important development that had ever occurred in obstetric practice. The results reported by the hospitals produced a sense of euphoria. Many believed that the scourge of maternal mortality would soon be defeated. It is against this background that one can understand why the continuation of a high level of mortality after the introduction of antisepsis was more than a disappointment; within the profession it was regarded as a scandal.

---

[81] A good brief account of the details of early antiseptic practice in midwifery can be found in Cullingworth, *Puerperal Fever*, 26–30.

13
Maternal Care in Britain, 1900–1935

For the large majority of mothers of all social classes in nineteenth-century Britain, maternal care depended on private arrangments made by mothers with handywomen, midwives, or medical practitioners. Care provided by charities and the Poor Law accounted for less than 10 per cent of all births. By contrast, the salient feature of maternal care in Britain in the twentieth century was the increasing involvement of authorities, medical and lay, charitable and governmental, in the care of mothers and children. The terms 'maternal and child health' and 'maternal and infant welfare', which are now so familiar, were twentieth-century innovations which symbolized what is often called the politics of maternal care: a subject which has recently attracted the attention of many scholars to whose work the interested reader is referred.[1]

Although the roots of maternal politics can be traced to the late nineteenth century and the work of William Farr, three statistical trends at the turn of the century came to be seen as alarming in their implications: high infant mortality, high maternal mortality, and a falling birth rate. The consequent prospect of demographic decline brought maternal and child health firmly into the field of politics.

Initially, however, there seemed grounds for guarded optimism. The birth rate had fallen from 127.6 (births per 1,000 women aged 15–44) in 1890 to 100.6 in 1910, but infant mortality had fallen as never before. It was 105 per 1,000 births in 1910 compared with 163 in 1899 and 154 in 1900. Moreover, maternal mortality reached the lowest ever recorded level of 35.5 per 10,000 births in 1910 compared with the peak of 65.1 in 1893. It seemed that the

---

[1] Amongst the works to which I am much indebted are: J. Lewis, *The Politics of Motherhood* (London, 1980); R. Dingwall, A. M. Rafferty, and C. Webster, *An Introduction to the Social History of Nursing* (London, 1988), especially chap. 8; C. Webster, 'Healthy or Hungry Thirties?', *History Workshop Journal*, 13 (1982), 110–29, and 'Health, Welfare and Unemployment during the Depression', *Past and Present*, 109 (1985), 204–30. Also J. Lewis, 'Mothers and Maternity Policies in the Twentieth Century' in J. Garcia, R. Kilpatrick, and M. Richards (eds.), *The Politics of Maternity Care: Services for Childbearing Women in Twentieth-Century Britain* (Oxford, 1990), 15–29; J. Kitzinger, 'Strategies of the Early Childbirth Movement: A Case-Study of the National Childbirth Trust', ibid. 92–115; and E. Peretz, 'A Maternity Service for England and Wales: Local Authority Maternity Care in the Inter-War Period in Oxfordshire and Tottenham', ibid. 30–46; Jean Donnison, *Midwives and Medical Men* (London, 1977); J. Towler and J. Bramall, *Midwives in History and Society* (London, 1986).

improving survival of mothers and children would at least compensate to some extent for the decline in fertility.

However, while infant mortality continued to fall after 1910, maternal mortality began to rise, reaching 35.5 in 1910, 38.7 in 1911, and 41.7 in 1914. This upturn was totally unexpected. Fear of depopulation, and eugenic fears that 'the wrong sort' had the largest families and the 'right sort' would dwindle away, increased in 1918 following the slaughter of young men in the trenches of the First World War.

While the First World War stimulated advances in certain branches of medicine such as surgery and bacteriology, obstetrics was not one of them. Farquhar Murray remarked in 1936 that

The profession, like the community, had emerged from the great war, and that part of their professional work which their training and war service had least prepared them for, maternity work, naturally suffered. They could not, and did not, see what was happening.[2]

It was therefore inevitable that maternal and child welfare would occupy a prominent position when the Ministry of Health was created and took over the numerous activities of the Local Government Board. In retrospect the Ministry may have achieved less than was expected of it as far as health is concerned, partly because it was also responsible for housing and the Poor Law. Nevertheless, it symbolized a post-war determination to deal with problems of health in general and maternal and child health in particular. To deal with the latter Dr Janet Campbell, a woman of great energy and capability, was appointed. From the start she recognized the importance of the persisting high level of maternal mortality.[3]

MIDWIVES ACTS, GOVERNMENT REPORTS, AND PUBLIC OPINION

Of all the legislative milestones between 1900 and the National Health Service in 1948, the Midwives Act of 1902 was the most important as far as maternal care was concerned. It was followed by the Midwives Acts of 1918 and 1936 in England and Wales and the Midwives Act (Scotland) 1937.[4]

Under the Midwives Act of 1902 (which became operative in 1903), the Central Midwives Board was created as the examining and supervising body

---

[2] E. Farquhar Murray, 'Whither Midwifery?', *British Medical Journal* (1936), ii. 375–7. An interesting paper in spite of its banal title. Farquhar Murray was Professor of Obstetrics at Newcastle upon Tyne and the first to introduce the concept of the maternity 'flying squad' for treating obstetric emergencies at home.

[3] See e.g. Janet Campbell, 'Maternity Homes', *Lancet* (1921), ii. 162–4, in which the failure of maternal mortality to decline is the central feature of the paper.

[4] One of the most perceptive analyses of this subject is chap. 8, 'Midwifery', in R. Dingwall, A. M. Rafferty, and C. Webster, *An Introduction to the Social History of Nursing* (London, 1988). See also J. Towler and J. Bramall, *Midwives in History and Society* (London, 1986), 226. Note that

and a roll of midwives was established. It was illegal after 1903 for anyone to practise as a midwife unless she was on the roll although the 'handywoman-midwife'—to whom we will return—continued to exist in the poorest areas until the 1930s.

The Central Midwives Board recognized three categories of midwife. Those who were enrolled 'by virtue of bona fide practice' who were nick-named the 'bona fides'; the 'certificated midwives' who had obtained a certificate from one of a variety of institutions such as lying-in hospitals and the Obstetrical Society of London and were enrolled 'by virtue of prior certification'; and the new recruits and the great hope for the future—those who had taken and passed the CMB examination. In 1908, out of 27,234 midwives on the roll, 11,636 (43 per cent) were 'bona fides', 9,964 (36 per cent) were certificated midwives, and 5,934 (21 per cent) held the CMB certificate.[5]

The last group, those who held the CMB certificate, increased as the other groups dwindled, but there were still bona fide midwives in practice as late as the early 1930s. For various reasons, the introduction of the trained midwife was by no means as smooth as expected. One factor was the considerable number of general practitioners who were hostile to the Act, believing trained midwives would rob them of midwifery cases.[6] That their fears were not groundless is suggested by Table 13.1.[7] This table shows that between 1909 and 1913 there was a large fall in doctor deliveries, mostly to trained midwives—just as general practitioners had forecast in their evidence to the *Select Committee on Midwives' Registration* in 1892.[8] Consequently, co-operation between general practitioners and midwives varied from friendly and efficient in some areas to mutual hostility in others with doctors complaining they often received no fee when called out by a midwife, and some even refusing to attend midwife cases under any circumstances.[9]

In an attempt to improve the availability of trained obstetric care, under the terms of the National Health Insurance Act of 1911 a maternity benefit allowance of 30*s.* was introduced to allow more women to employ doctors for

the College of Midwives was not established until 1941, having evolved from the Midwives Institute which in turn had evolved in 1881 from a number of midwife associations such as the Matron's Aid Society. For the somewhat complicated history of midwives' associations, see Donnison, *Midwives and Medical Men.*

  [5] *Report of the Departmental Committee Appointed by the Lord President of the Council to Consider the Working of the Midwives Act, 1902*, PP 1909, XXXIII.

  [6] *Report of the Department Committee*, 1909. In Oxford City, Dr Rivers said his work had fallen from 80–90 deliveries a year to around 20, and a young partner had not been able to build up a large midwifery practice. Q. 6527–37 and Q. 1690.

  [7] This table is based on Derbyshire. Although there were wide differences between counties, most reported a change in the division of births along the Derbyshire lines.

  [8] *Report of the Select Committee on Midwives' Registration*, PP 1892, XIV. See especially the lengthy evidence of Dr Robert Rentoul, Q. 345–689.

  [9] Ibid. QQ. 54 and 545.

TABLE 13.1 *The Changing Proportion of Deliveries by Doctors and Midwives in Derbyshire between 1910 and 1913*

	1909	1910	1911	1912	1913
Births registered	16,152	15,936	15,440	14,561	14,703
Percentage of total births delivered by:					
Doctors	42.4	35.1	29.5	26.3	25.1
Midwives (total)	57.6	64.9	70.5	73.7	74.9
untrained	47.9	49.8	52.5	53.1	51.4
trained	9.7	15.1	18.0	20.6	23.5

Source: Janet Lane-Claypon, 'The Economic Aspects of Midwifery', in *Local Government Board, 44th Annual Report, 1914–1915*, Supplement on Maternal Mortality, PP 1914–16 xxv, Cd, 8085, p. 92.

their delivery. For two reasons it was not an immediate success. First, the response of the independent midwives and general practitioners was to raise their fees, the former to around 15s. (range 10s.–21s.) and the latter to around 30s. Second, although the allowance was enough for most women to be able to employ a general practitioner, it left them with the problem of nursing care during their lying-in which the employment of the untrained handywoman-midwife did not. To a certain extent this explains the perpetuation of the 'bona fides' and the handywomen. Only the well-off could afford to employ both a doctor and a midwife as a maternity nurse.

The Midwives Act (1918) required local authorities to pay 'medical aid' fees to doctors called in by a midwife, which helped to remove the mutual hostility between midwives and general practitioners.[10] The Maternal and Child Welfare Act of the same year required local authorities to provide free antenatal clinics. The Midwives Act (1936), however, was a major advance, revolutionizing the prospects for midwives. Some have said that the decades following this Act were the golden age of district midwifery. This Act, which was mandatory, required local authorities to provide a salaried midwifery service 'adequate to the needs of their area'. It not only provided much better prospects for midwives; it was symbolically important, for it gave substance to the official view that domiciliary midwifery would remain the backbone of a national maternity service.

While the work and status of the midwife was being upgraded, a series of

---

[10] The medical aid fee was only provided for families unable to pay; and even then there was a sting in the tail, because local authorities were encouraged to recover the fee from the family whenever possible.

official reports drew attention to the problem of maternal mortality. The first appeared as a supplement to the annual report of the Local Government Board in 1914.[11] When the Ministry of Health was established there was a notable series of reports arising from the work of Dr (later Dame) Janet Campbell and her colleagues.[12] In 1932 the Ministry of Health produced a report on maternal mortality and morbidity in England and Wales (preceded by an interim report in 1929). Another much more thorough report on maternal mortality in England was published in 1937 acompanied by a separate report on maternal mortality in Wales in the same year. Together, they provide the most comprehensive account of maternal mortality ever produced in Britain.[13] A report on maternal mortality in Scotland appeared in 1942 and one on Northern Ireland in 1943. At the same time public health departments in counties and county boroughs, urged on by the Ministry, paid increasing attention to maternal and child welfare, especially after the First World War, as one can see in their annual reports. While it is clear that the Ministry of Health and local health authorities were deeply concerned over the extent of maternal mortality, to what extent was maternal mortality a matter of concern?

It is never easy to judge the true extent of public concern in the past. Banner headlines and government statements are often poor indicators. It is unlikely that death in childbirth was a common subject for discussion in pubs, clubs, or at dinner tables.[14] Nevertheless, there were many who believed at the time that women, if not their husbands, were deeply concerned. General practitioners constantly complained that their patients were being 'scared to death'. Public concern was shown by the establishment of unofficial but powerful maternal mortality committees consisting mostly of lay women. The Ministry of Health took them very seriously, and also came under pressure from the Labour Party and various trade unions.[15]

---

[11] *Local Government Board, 44th Annual Report, 1914–1915*, PP 1914–16, xxv, Cd. 8085.

[12] These included: Campbell, 'The Training of Midwives', *Reports of Public Health and Medical Subjects*, 21, Ministry of Health (London, 1923); ead., 'Maternal Mortality', *Reports of Public Health and Medical Subjects*, 25, Ministry of Health (London, 1924); ead., Isabella D. Cameron, and Dilwys M. Jones, 'High Maternal Mortality in Certain Areas', *Reports on Public Health and Medical Subjects*, 68, Ministry of Health (London, 1932); and a private publication ead., *Maternity Services* (London, 1935).

[13] Ministry of Health. *Interim Report of Departmental Committee on Maternal Mortality and Morbidity* (London, 1930); *Final Report of Departmental Committee on Maternal Mortality and Morbidity* (London, 1932); *Report of an Investigation into Maternal Mortality* (London, 1937), Cmd. 5422, PP 1936/37, xi; *Report on Maternal Mortality in Wales* (London, 1937), Cmd. 5423, PP 1936–7, xi.

[14] In this broad general public sense, Fox, who has denied that maternal mortality was ever a scandal, is right. But in the narrower sense of the attitudes of those concerned with maternal welfare the evidence suggests she is mistaken. E. Fox, 'Powers of Life and Death: Aspects of Maternal Welfare in England and Wales between the Wars', *Medical History*, 35 (1991), 328–52.

[15] Public Record Office, Kew, Records of Maternal and Child Health, Ministry of Health. See MH 55/265 on the Labour Party's campaign on maternal mortality, MH 55/679 on the Maternal Mortality Committee set up by Mrs Tennant in 1937, and MH 55/217 for the reaction of the Ministry of Health to criticism from the Weymouth Trades Union Congress in 1934.

In 1930, Sir George Newman, the Chief Medical Officer of Health to the Ministry wrote that 'The question of maternal mortality is now engaging the anxious consideration of the Cabinet.'[16] And maternal mortality was the subject of a number of leading articles and correspondence in the columns of *The Times*.[17]

In July 1934, *The Times* reported a speech by Mr Chamberlain (he was Chancellor of the Exchequer at the time) who said that in spite of all that had been done the statistics showed no improvement whatever. He felt deeply the need for improving these dreadful figures, and he was puzzled and baffled by the failure to achieve progress.[18] In 1935 the Minister of Health, Sir Kingsley Wood, referred to maternal mortality as 'The great blot on public health administration'. At a meeting of the Ancient Order of Foresters the Chief Ranger, Mr C. E. Prust, spoke of 'The persistent scandal of maternal mortality . . . We have it on the highest authority that a majority of these lives could be saved and if they could, they must be.'[19]

Certainly, then, there was public disquiet at the continuing high toll of maternal deaths. It was, of course, something obstetricians had recognized for a long time; and it was an important impetus in the establishment of the College of Obstetricians and Gynaecologists in 1929.

THE ROYAL COLLEGE OF OBSTETRICIANS AND GYNAECOLOGISTS

To deal effectively with maternal mortality, obstetricians saw that it was essential to put an end to the tendency for hospital obstetrics and gynaecology to be seen simply as a sub-speciality of general surgery, practised as a side-line by general surgeons.[20] Thus the primary purpose of the College was

---

[16] Public Record Office, Ministry of Health, MH 55/271.

[17] See 'Maternal Mortality' (leading article), *The Times* (5 Mar. 1928), 13. See also Dr Donald Roy, 'Maternal Mortality' (correspondence), ibid. 15 May 1930; *The Times* (28 Oct. 1930), 11; 'Maternal Mortality' (leading article), ibid. (28 Oct. 1930), 15.; 'Maternal Mortality' (leading article), ibid. (23 June 1934), 13.

[18] *The Times* (4 July 1934), 10.

[19] Ibid. (7 Aug. 1934), 7. Of the numerous reports in the press, most were rightly critical. An exception appeared in 1937 when the Chief Medical Officer of the Ministry of Health, Sir Arthur McNalty, was quoted as saying that in spite of the damning evidence of the 1937 reports on maternal mortality, there was really no cause for concern. He compared the MMR in Edinburgh Maternity Hospital for 1823–44 and the rate for England and Wales for 1935, claiming there had been a steady decline in maternal mortality between these points. Whether this was gross historical and statistical ignorance or downright dishonesty is uncertain. 'Maternal Mortality' (leading article), ibid. (29 Apr. 1937), 17.

[20] This brief account of the early attitudes and policies of the Royal College of Obstetricians and Gynaecologists is based on the minute books and archives of the college from its commencement to the late 1930s. I am most grateful to Council of the college for allowing me access to their archives, and for the help I obtained from Patricia Want, the college librarian, and the college archivist, Claire Daunton.

to establish a corpus of doctors trained as specialists in obstetrics and gynaecology. It was the only way the College could command a seat at high table alongside its sister institutions, and the only way to improve lamentably low standards. That was the view of the founders of the College. In putting their ideas into practice, the College of Obstetricians met an astonishing degree of resistance from the Royal Colleges of Physicians and Surgeons who, in a manner reminiscent of the early 1800s, believed their autonomy was threatened and did their best to strangle the new College at its birth.

The attitude of the College towards maternal care in general, and the practice of general practitioners and midwives in particular, was mixed. It is true that it introduced a diploma in obstetrics for general practitioners and endorsed the official view of the Ministry of Health in the 1930s that the midwife and the general practitioner formed the 'backbone' of British obstetrics. But it recognized that its authority did not extend to the independent general practitioners (stoutly supported by the British Medical Association) or the midwives (controlled and supported by the Central Midwives Board). In short, domiciliary midwifery lay outside the authority of the College which appreciated the danger of becoming involved in non-specialist obstetrics, and of treading on toes in the process. Indeed, the College in the 1930s had more than enough on its hands fighting for recognition. Inevitably, it had to concentrate on establishing itself as the institution which created a new speciality through education, examination, and accreditation; and by doing so to see that hospitals were staffed with fully trained obstetricians. It thus ensured that hospital admissions would be reserved for high-risk and complicated cases with sufficient normal ones for teaching of medical students and midwives. Deliveries under the care of midwives and general practitioners was not their province. As for policies on maternal care as a whole, while the Royal College of Obstetricians and Gynaecologists became extremely influential after the Second World War, it had relatively little influence in its first few years when maternal mortality was at its height.

This brief survey of official aspects of maternal care—Act of Parliament, Institutions, Government reports and policies, and the extent of public concern—is a necessary preliminary to the real matter of this chapter: the provision of maternal care at the bedside, whether in home or hospital, by a variety of birth-attendants. We begin with midwives and handywomen.

MIDWIVES AND HANDYWOMEN

Although the Midwives Act (1902) led to a transformation of the standard of midwife care, it was singularly unsuccessful in establishing a contented and well-paid profession.[21] In the early years following the Act an independent midwife in large towns might just be able to attend over 200 cases a year, but to do so she would require 'phenomenal endurance'. A realistic maximum was about 150; fewer than 150, and employment as a maternity nurse was welcomed as an additional source of income. Assuming no bad debts, at best a midwife could earn about £112 a year out of which she had to meet considerable expenses—apparatus, drugs, clean dresses, help in her home (for which she would have neither time nor energy) would leave her with about £90 a year or just under £2 a week. Even so, there was no guarantee that a large list of patients would be obtained. 'Some midwives may be overworked, others have no cases at all.' Indeed, if midwives had been evenly distributed in England and Wales, 'no single midwife could earn a living'.[22]

Midwife practice in rural areas was worst of all, providing no more than forty to fifty cases a year for each of which the average fee was often much lower (around 5*s.* to 7*s.* per case), and employment as a maternity nurse was rare. A rural midwife would be lucky to earn £25 a year if she confined herself to midwifery.[23] Most midwives settled in large urban areas where the untrained midwife was tending to disappear and work was plentiful. Rural areas were so badly served that:

As the present generation of untrained midwives passes away, the necessity for every rural district to be served by a district nurse-midwife, with a living guaranteed, will become imperative. Where there is no midwife the next-door neighbour does service.[24]

Even when she combined general nursing and midwifery (which was usual) the rural nurse-midwife was rarely able to make ends meet from private practice.[25] Most were therefore employed by County Nursing Associations which usually consisted of an affiliation of a large number of small local charities, each supporting one or two midwives or nurse-midwives.[26]

By the 1920s, when most midwives were working for voluntary organizations or local authorities, the plight of the minority in independent practice was no better in 1920 and 1930 than it had been in 1910. Lady Forber (Dr

---

[21] My main source in what follows is Janet Lane-Claypon, 'The Economic Aspects of Midwifery', *Local Government Board, 44th Annual Report, 1914–1915*; Supplement on Maternal Mortality, 85–101, a mine of information and a model of clarity.

[22] Supplement, 91.

[23] Ibid. 89.

[24] Ibid. Evidence of the County Medical Officer of Health of Bedfordshire (Annual Report, 1913), 80–90.

[25] Ibid. 97–8.

[26] The Essex County Nursing Association in 1913 consisted of 57 local associations employing 60 midwives who, on average, delivered 25 cases a year each. The Sussex County Nursing Association consisted of 61 affiliated societies employing 81 midwives who delivered, on average, 18 cases a year each. The usual salary paid by a County Association was about £70–£80 a year. The patient was required to pay towards her care. The cost to the County Associations was met in part by these fees and in part by charitable donations. Ibid. 98–9.

Janet Lane-Claypon), who became their champion, showed that in spite of their professional status, they worked for less than 1*s*. an hour which was less than the rate for a shorthand typist. Annual incomes of those in regular employment ranged from £50 to £100 a year.[27] The independent midwives were hamstrung by competition with general practitioners. To get employment they needed to charge less than local doctors. If they raised their fees they lost practice. As a consequence some sought salaried employment (when they could find it), some left the profession, and others became health visitors not from choice but solely to earn a larger salary.

It is not surprising that the distribution and employment of midwives was very uneven. Janet Campbell found in 1923 that out of 11,814 rural parishes, 63 per cent were provided with trained midwives, 3.5 per cent with 'bona fides' midwives still in practice, and the remaining one-third were 'entirely unprovided' with the services of a registered midwife.[28]

What, then, was the standard of care provided by midwives in the mid-1930s, when all but a very few of the 'bona fides' had disappeared? An organization which employed a large number of district nurses and nurse-midwives, and was renowned for its high reputation, was the Queen Victoria's Jubilee Nursing Institute (Queen's Institute) founded in the 1800s with the object of promoting district nursing and midwifery services throughout the country.[29]

Miss Nora Haines was a 'Queen's nurse-midwife', and rightly proud of it. She practised in the 1930s and 1940s in Gloucester, Hereford, Farnham Royal, and Warnham (outside Corsham). Like all registered midwives she was required to keep a register which she has preserved and from which we can build a picture of the work of a district midwife.[30] Her duties were midwifery and general nursing. 'As a Queen's nurse, we were responsible for all from 0 yrs. to the grave.' Table 13.2 summarizes the results of an analysis of all her midwifery cases in 1936 and 1937. Out of the total of 129 cases, 23 were 'booked', meaning that the doctor delivered the baby and Miss Haines acted as the maternity nurse. In such cases she attended the patient through the long first stage of labour, called the doctor when birth was imminent, and was responsible for the largest part of postnatal care.

The remaining 106 cases were delivered by Miss Haines on her own. In 66 cases delivery was normal. In 40 cases she sent for a doctor under the

---

[27] Lady Forber (Dr Janet Lane-Clayton), 'The Independent Midwife', *British Medical Journal* (1935), i. 490; ead., 'The Economic Conditions of Midwifery Practice', ibid. ii. 862–3.

[28] Campbell, 'The Training of Midwives'.

[29] Donnison, *Midwives and Medical Men*, 107 The Queen's Institute provided nurses but not midwives in the cities. In rural areas, however, they provided nurse-midwives.

[30] In 1987 Miss Haines kindly lent her register to Dr Anne Summers and myself when we were both working at the Wellcome Unit for the History of Medicine in Oxford. She wrote to me about her practice, giving me permission to photocopy the ledger and use her data for publication 'provided the privacy of my patients is respected'. I am very grateful.

TABLE 13.2 *Domiciliary Midwifery Cases Attended by Miss Nora Haines, Queen's Nurse and Registered Midwife, in 1936 and 1937*

	Number	Total
Confinements attended in 1936 and 1937		129
Attended in labour solely by midwife		66
Cases attended by doctor and midwife		23
Cases in which the doctor was booked to attend		
Forceps used	11	
Forceps not used	12	
Medical aid cases[a]		40
Stitching of torn perineum	12	
Forceps used	15	
Forceps not used	7	
Manual removal of placenta	1	
Transferred to hospital	5	

[a] Cases in which the midwife sent for medical aid during labour or after delivery, and the doctor's fee was paid by the local authority under the terms of the Midwives Act (1918).
Source: The ledger of Miss Haines's midwifery cases, by kind permission.

medical-aid scheme, most commonly to stitch a torn perineum. One case was a retained placenta, removed by the doctor under chloroform anaesthesia. In 5 medical-aid cases a serious or potentially serious condition led to the patient's admission to hospital. Of the remaining 22, all safely delivered at home, 15 were forceps deliveries, almost always for 'delay in the second stage'. There is no record of a maternal death in the whole ledger (although the outcome of cases admitted to hospital is unknown) and no record of a case of puerperal fever.

The relationship between Miss Haines and the general practitioners with whom she worked was amicable: 'One phoned a doctor night or day. Of course they varied in their ability—don't we all? but I never found any enmity.'[31] It is clear that Miss Haines enjoyed and valued her work as a midwife. The ledger conveys a strong impression of a high standard of careful and skilful home midwifery backed up by a system of medical aid and hospital admission which worked well. That the record of Miss Haines was typical and in keeping with that of Queen's Institute midwives as a whole, is suggested by the data in Table 13.3 which show a consistent mortality rate in Queen's Institute deliveries of around 50 per cent or less than the national level; and there are good reasons for believing these mortality rates were accurate.[32]

[31] Personal communication, Miss Haines (Apr. 1987).
[32] All maternal deaths were included in Queen's Institute statistics, regardless of where they occurred. 'Every maternal death amongst cases taken by our midwives, in which no doctor has been engaged for the confinement, is counted wherever it occurs—whether in hospital, in the

TABLE 13.3 *Number and Maternal Mortality Rate of Deliveries by Queen's Institute Midwives 1905–1931 Compared with Rates for England and Wales*

Year	Queen's Institute deliveries		England and Wales
	number of deliveries	maternal mortality rate (per 10,000 live births)	maternal mortality rate (per 10,000 live births)
1905	4,500	25	42
1906	6,592	23	40
1907	8,904	17	38
1908	10,498	9	36
1909	13,537	18	37
1915	23,453	19	42
1916	23,659	21	41
1917	22,382	18	39
1918	27,880	33	38
1919	35,266	22	44
1920	49,080	19	43
1923	54,544	15	39
1924	55,828	16	41
1925	47,926	22	41
1926	56,868	15	41
1927	55,828	13	44
1928	65,077	19	43
1929	63,131	21	44
1930	66,003	20	39
1931	66,570	17	40

Source: Queen's Institute statistics, J. M. Munro Kerr, *Maternal Mortality and Morbidity* (Edinburgh, 1933), 244–5; England and Wales, Registrar General's statistics.

If midwives like Miss Haines provided an extraordinarily high standard of care, what about the other extreme—the totally untrained handywomen? They were another matter. Hardly any doctors or health officials had a good word to say for the handywomen. They were seen as a legacy from the worst sort of midwifery in the nineteenth century and became one of the scapegoats for

patient's home, or elsewhere; and cases have occurred where the death did not take place till three months or more after the confinement.' Evidence of Miss Peterkin, quoted in J. M. Munro Kerr, *Maternal Mortality and Morbidity* (Edinburgh, 1933), 245. It should also be noted that associated deaths were included in the mortality statistics of the Queen's Institute (hence the high rate in 1918 due to deaths from influenza), but excluded in the data for England and Wales in Table 13.3 so that the difference was even larger than shown. Had associated deaths been included for the national data, the mortality rates would, on average, have been 15% higher. Table 13.3 also shows the increasing work of Queen's Institute nurse-midwives who by 1931 were responsible for more than 10% of all deliveries in England and Wales.

high maternal mortality. Unfortunately, we know little about their practice as midwives. We know they were found in urban slums, small towns, and villages where poverty was greatest or access to trained care was hard to obtain. We know they were frequently employed as layers-out of the dead and providers of a kind of home-help and rudimentary nursing service for neighbours, receiving payment in kind or a small fee. It was often difficult to draw the line between a full-time handywoman and a kind and helpful neighbour to whom many in the same street or village turned as a matter of course. If they delivered babies they were acting as midwives and breaking the law. Nevertheless there were cases of handywomen delivering women at home without notifying a registered midwife or doctor, and some were prosecuted for doing so.[33] It may be, however, that 'back-street' deliveries by handywomen were much less common than their role as assistants at deliveries carried out by general practitioners when the mother was unable to afford the cost of both a doctor and a trained midwife or monthly nurse.

Dr Finer of Essex has vivid memories of this, and roundly condemns the handywomen as

extremely dangerous and ill-informed; but during those years there was really no alternative ... I started in general practice as an assistant in Stalybridge in 1931. At that time unemployment was virtually 100% and the usual procedure for pregnant women was to book with municipal midwives ... [which] ... saved the patient any expense. In that practice 'handywomen' were not required. After four months I took an assistantship in Dagenham where the procedure was completely different. There the patient booked with the doctor for home delivery or with Salvation Army midwives. If the former, the patient was attended by handywomen or 'gamps' ... completely unqualified and used to do other duties such as laying out the dead, etc.

In 1932, Dr Finer started his own practice in Dagenham:

I then accepted bookings for home deliveries [and] the patient arranged her own handywoman. There was absolutely no ante-natal attendance whatsoever but when labour commenced the handywoman and doctor concerned were summoned. These handywomen were mainly ignorant, their duties being to cover the bed with old newspapers and to keep water boiling. Because they knew virtually nothing about parturition the doctor would be called out several times because the stages of labour were not properly understood ... Altogether from 1932 to 1948 I delivered about 1000 babies at home. I must say I despaired of this arrangement and much preferred the cases which had booked with the Salvation Army and later the Local Authority Midwives who did all the normal deliveries and called one in on a medical aid form in case of difficulty.[34]

[33] See J. Towler and J. Bramall, *Midwives in History and Society* (London, 1986), 192. The prosecution reported here was in 1910. See also Lewis, *Politics of Motherhood*, on the handywomen.
[34] Personal communication, Dr Finer, Chigwell, Essex, Oct. 1990. I am most grateful to Dr Finer, and also to Drs Fuller and Walshe, and Professor Blackburn, whose evidence appears below and who wrote in response to a notice in the *British Medical Journal* in Sept. 1990 requesting information on handywomen.

Dr Finer's evidence shows that whether they liked it or not, general practitioners often had to work with handywomen. Some, however, remember
handywomen with some affection. Professor Blackburn recalls being told that
when he was born in 1918 his mother was attended (at home) by the family
doctor and a Mrs Green who was known locally as the 'woman-what-does'.
She had coped well, it was said, with the early stages of labour before the
doctor arrived and she was known for working with doctors in her area.[35]

Likewise, Dr Fuller of Thorney in Cambridgeshire recalls that when he
started in practice in the 1950s there was a handywoman who had worked
with the local doctor for many years. From his student days 'on the district' in
Dublin just after the Second World War, Dr Walshe has fond memories
of handywomen who 'could recognise complications which we as students
(though accompanied by a recently qualified colleague) were slow to recognize
and [with which we were] ill-equipped to deal'. Certainly they made life easier
for the Dublin medical student during his initiation into the art of home
deliveries, but there is no information on what they got up to (if anything) on
their own.[36]

Although handywomen were sometimes rough and ready, and always a
possible source of puerperal infection, there is no direct evidence that handywomen were an important cause of maternal mortality. They were often
maligned, but they undertook certain menial but essential services for the poor
at a time when publicly provided nursing and midwifery care was chaotic and
patchy.

OBSTETRICS IN GENERAL PRACTICE, 1900–1935

The characteristic feature of general practice obstetrics from the late nineteenth century to the late 1930s was lack of change. As Victor Bonney
observed in 1919, 'Taking the conduct of labour in general, not much more
than a bowl of antiseptic stands between the practice of today and the practice of the [eighteen] sixties.'[37] And not only conduct, but attitudes. From
the 1870s to the 1930s one finds the same passionate belief that midwifery was the linchpin of general practice, the same ambivalent feelings
towards a branch of practice which brought intense satisfaction on a good
day and irritated exhaustion on a bad one, the same (and often astonishing)
self-confidence in the face of major obstetric complications, and the same
impatience of doctors who attended a delivery at midday knowing they still
had a visiting list as long as your arm before an evening surgery of thirty or

---

[35] Personal communication, Emeritus Professor E. K. Blackburn, Sheffield, Sept. 1990.

[36] Personal communication, Dr P. Walshe, ships' surgeon; Medical Officer, NATO Forces
Europe, Oct. 1990.

[37] V. Bonney, 'The Continuing High Mortality of Childbearing', *Proceedings of the Royal Society
of Medicine*, 12/3 (1918–19), 75–107.

more patients, and the prospect of retiring to bed only to be called out in the early hours to yet another delivery. Small wonder, perhaps, that general practitioners so often chloroformed their patients and slipped on the forceps at the earliest opportunity. Speed, they said, was essential.

Speed, and the ability to deal with anything no matter what the surroundings. Here is Dr Dale Logan, writing in 1934 on midwifery in a working-class general practice in Lanarkshire, where his patients lived in such inadequate housing that often there was little but 'two box beds in the room', one for the parents, one for the children.

Success as a practitioner follows efficiency in midwifery. The psychological effect of the presence of friendly and sympathetic people in familiar surroundings on a woman . . . cannot be overestimated. This is entirely overlooked by public health authorities and specialists. I believe that a woman is more sympathetically and kindly treated and as efficiently looked after in her own home, if she is in the hands of an experienced and capable general practitioner as she would be in any institution. I have frequently carried out difficult obstetric manipulations with the patient under chloroform, and at the same time tried my best to pacify little ones in the only other bed.[38]

Dale Logan used chloroform routinely to 'keep the patient "on the borders of dreamland"', was sparing in the use of forceps, but happy to deal with such alarming complications as placenta praevia, manual removal of an adherent placenta, version, and high and low forceps deliveries—while pacifying the little ones. He took pride in his skill.

I have only very rarely sent a patient to hospital. The dangers and difficuties of general midwifery practice have been magnified out of all proportion by specialists and public health officials. They are doing their best to frighten the general practitioner from having anything to do with midwifery work . . . The publicity maternal mortality is getting in the press has put the fear of death into many expectant mothers [and] our daily newspapers are full of all sorts of terrible tales about puerperal fever and how much the general practitioner has to do with its causation . . . In Mid-Lanark many of us have attended hundreds of cases of midwifery cases in the most appalling slums and under the worst possible conditions and during that time had no cases of puerperal fever, while it appears in the best houses under the best possible nursing conditions.[39]

In March 1906 the *British Medical Journal* published a paper by Peter Horrocks, a consultant obstetrician at Guy's Hospital. Its title was 'Midwifery of the present day', and the paper presented a carefully reasoned case for a

---

[38] Dale Logan's report was submitted to the Committee on Scottish Health Services entitled 'Contract Medical Practice in Lanarkshire during the Past Thirty Years: A Plea for the General Practitioner'. It was published in the *Lancet* (1934), ii. 1141–3, under the title 'The General Practitioner and Midwifery'.

[39] According to Dale Logan, between 12% to 35% of his patients never paid and other general practitioners who charged no more than 15*s*. to 30*s*. to attend a delivery found that more than a third of their patients did not pay. Midwifery was a poorly paid occupation. Ibid. 1142.

conservative non-interventionist approach to midwifery, with the use of strict antisepsis and asepsis in every case, normal and abnormal.[40] The response was an explosive self-revelation of attitudes to midwifery in general practice.[41]

Ferdinand Rees, MD of Wigan opened the attack with a scathing letter attacking the 'elaborate aseptic ritual drawn out over a period of twenty minutes' and the unwillingness to intervene. The author, he said with heavy sarcasm, 'would be a great success as a general practitioner!' Did he not realize that 'the more civilised women become, the more frequently they need assistance ... What is the value of medical knowledge and skill unless we are going to apply it to the maximum?' Dr Wynne of Leigh agreed that 'the civilised woman is not in a normal environment and cannot vie with the independence displayed on these occasions by the Indian squaw or the Esquimaux mother'. He thought the idea of asepsis in general practice was hopelessly impractical, while Dr Thomas of Boscombe went so far as to accuse Dr Horrocks of advice which was 'almost a return to the barbarism of the Middle Ages. The modern middle-class educated woman neither can nor will bear pain as her mother did. They see no necessity for it, and, after all, why should they?' Dr Mears of North Shields described Horrocks's conservatism as 'Antediluvian ... civilisation, injudicious breeding and modes of dress and occupation' made normal delivery no longer possible and 'midwifery must come to the rescue':

I use chloroform and the forceps in every possible case, and have done so for many years. The whole proceeding occupies from *15 to 40 minutes* [my emphasis] ... antiseptics are worse than useless ... Do not wear rubber gloves if you can help it. Wash the hands at the patient's house before examining. Having observed these rules do not bother about micro-organisms ... If anything savours of being 'almost criminal' it is the turning out on the public of young doctors who have never used the forceps.

As the debate continued, one of the most revealing of the thirty or so letters came from Dr Leeson of Twickenham, written with the exasperation of a man who sees that no one has tackled the real issue. If there was unnecessary intervention it was due to the hurried life and low fees.

This waiting midwifery, this scientific midwifery, cannot be done at the price and the public must be taught this. We cannot dance attendance upon a case for a day and a night and neglect all our other work and knock ourselves up with fatigue for miserably inadequate fees ... [which are] ... probably a fraction of what a cabman would obtain for waiting at the gate. It is midwifery that takes the life out of us, and yet it is the foundation of family practice and upon it few of us dare turn our backs.

---

[40] P. Horrocks, 'An Address on Midwifery of the Present Day', *British Medical Journal* (1906), i. 541–5. The paper was an address to the local branch of the British Medical Association.
[41] The correspondence in response to this paper can be found in *British Medical Journal* (1906) i. 549, 634, 712, 773, 831, 892, 949, 960, 1012, 1073, 1132, 1199, 1255, 1259, 1324, 1383, 1448, and 1572; and ibid. ii. 399, 452, and 460.

Between about 1870 and the late 1930s, a substantial number of general practitioners were using forceps and anaesthesia (often with inadequate antiseptic and aseptic techniques) with a frequency that today seems shocking.[42] 'We did approximately 250 cases a year', says Dr Finer, writing of general practice in 1931, 'mostly with chloroform and forceps and my principal said that it allowed us to get to bed quicker.'[43]

The most common indication for forceps delivery in general practice obstetrics has always been 'delay in the second stage of labour' or 'prolonged labour'. The interpretation of 'delay' and 'prolonged' has been subjected to the wildest swings of fashion. In the early nineteenth century, when forceps rates of 1 per cent were commonplace, delay in the second stage was commonly defined as '*at least six hours*'.[44] By the 1950s and 1960s it was usually defined as between half an hour and an hour depending on the force and frequency of contractions, and a forceps rate of 5 per cent or less was usual in general practice. Before the Second World War, however, a high rate of intervention with forceps rates of 50 per cent or more reflected hospital teaching and habits instilled in young practitioners by their senior partner, and was based on the apparent belief that anything except a swift short second stage demanded instant intervention. It was commonplace. It was not considered bad practice.[45]

It is important to remember, however, that many general practitioners were careful, skilled, conscientious and not in the least prone to unnecessary intervention. Their virtues go unrecorded. The cases which received publicity were the 'failed forceps', which ended in the patient being sent to hospital, often with appalling injuries after prolonged and inappropriate attempts at a forceps delivery at home. Some accounts of such failed forceps are horrifying. In one series of 100 cases of admission to hospital for 'failed forceps', 12 mothers died and 19 were described as 'survived but morbid'. Only 38 of the infants survived. In one case the doctor put on forceps four times without anaesthetic before admitting her to hospital. It was reported the woman's screams awakened the entire neighbourhood.[46]

It was often said that general practitioners failed to keep up to date. There was little postgraduate education in the modern sense, and what there was

[42] For further discussion of forceps rates in general practice, see I. Loudon, 'Deaths in Childbed from the Eighteenth Century to 1935', *Medical History*, 30 (1986), 1–41 (esp. table, p. 35).

[43] Personal communication, Oct. 1990. Dr Finer, Chigwell, Essex.

[44] S. Merriman, *London Medical and Physical Journal*, 24 (1810), 362.

[45] The records of Dr Greig of Kirkcaldy in Scotland, a most careful and conscientious general practitioner, show he used forceps between 1921 and 1923 in 55% of cases. (Records in the private possession of Dr Greig's daughter, Dr Agnes Greig, who kindly allowed me access to her father's notebooks.) A high rate of forceps delivery was employed by doctors who worked with the midwife Nora Haines, as we can see in Table 13.2.

[46] M. D. Crawford, 'The Obstetric Forceps and its Use', *Lancet* (1932), ii. 1239–43. The most vivid account I know of mismanaged labours (from Liverpool).

consisted almost entirely of meetings of branches of the British Medical Association which usually had small audiences. While most general practitioners were aware of the high rate of maternal mortality, it is doubtful if many had read the reports on the subject. When the Secretary of the Medical Research Council wrote to the head of His Majesty's Stationery Office in 1932, suggesting that the recent report on maternal mortality should be made available to all practitioners, he received a memorably dusty answer:

Even the panel doctor must buy some reading matter, although it does not usually extend beyond the Daily Mail and the Evening Standard. Had this report been a book of obscene reminiscence it would have been a best seller. We shall have to sell 1,000 copies out of nine or ten thousand to cover the cost and we shall be amazed if we do ... Excepting only the lack of interest shown by farmers in research for their benefit, there is nothing in the Stationery Office experience more disappointing than the lack of interest in the medical profession in the public health. In one medical man's house there is a stack of Lancets and British Medical Journals all unopened in their wrappers. He is 'much too busy'. He plays bridge five nights a week, belongs to every local club that can possibly attract business, and lectures to girl guides on first aid. Some girl guides are quite pretty. In his spare time he plays golf and reads the Sketch. The terrible thing about this latest Maternal Mortality Report is the revelation of the lives which might be saved not by advanced technique, but by the simplest aseptic precautions that one would have expected medical men to observe on their own initiative.[47]

For many reasons, there was a steady erosion of home deliveries by general practitioners, especially in large towns and industrial areas. In 1936 an investigation by a team from the Ministry of Health made the following pertinent observation which to a large extent explains the high rate of intervention by general practitioners:

As the greater part of midwifery in the patients' homes is conducted by midwives, the doctors undertake, with few exceptions, little midwifery in their private practices. Even this limited domiciliary practice is being encroached upon by the increased use of maternity homes and hospitals. Unless a doctor in private practice has a special interest in midwifery or is of repute for his obstetric skill, his maternity practice tends to be restricted to supplying medical aid in midwives cases. His experience is thus limited; he treats only cases with some degree of abnormality; he loses touch with the normal.[48]

By the mid-1930s, a substantial number of general practitioners undertook no midwifery, others were largely confined to medical-aid cases, and relatively few were undertaking home deliveries of their private patients. Some were active in nursing homes, local authority hospitals, and in some of the

---

[47] Medical Research Council, London, Archives. Reply by Mr Scrogie to Sir Walter Fletcher, 13 Oct. 1932. MRC 2060/2. The report referred to was the *Final Report of the Departmental Committee on Maternal Mortality and Morbidity* (1932).

[48] Public Record Office. Report of investigation into areas with specially high rates of maternal mortality. MH 55/264.

provincial voluntary hospitals where the honorary obstetrician was often a local general practitioner with a special interest in midwifery. But the slow erosion of GP deliveries did not begin, as many believe, after the introduction of the National Health Service, but earlier, in the 1930s.

MATERNITY HOSPITALS AND OBSTETRIC EDUCATION, 1900–1935

The first four decades of the twentieth century saw an acceleration of the nineteenth-century expansion of hospitals and related medical institutions throughout the Western world. Maternity hospitals, however, were a special case, and all kinds of undercurrents influenced the way they developed in different countries.

In Britain, although there was the dramatic fall in lying-in hospital mortality by 1900, enthusiasm for in-patient obstetric care on a large scale was tempered by memories of the disasters of the nineteenth century. After the First World War, however, there was a growing demand for hospital delivery for several reasons.

In part it was a question of public demand. The Women's Co-operative Guild, which demanded trained midwives in 1914 and a trained midwife and easy access to a doctor in 1917, campaigned for sufficient hospital beds for women from poor homes in 1918.[49] There was also a growing demand by middle-class women for hospital or nursing-home delivery to obtain the services of specialists and modern methods of anaesthesia and analgesia, including Twilight Sleep.[50]

These demands were in harmony with the wishes of consultant obstetricians who regarded obstetrics as a surgical activity which belonged to the hospitals. Victor Bonney, for instance, saw delivery as a surgical operation and spoke of the uterus after delivery as a surgical wound to be managed by surgical measures.[51] Hospital delivery was not only an ideal to be pursued for its own sake as a new branch of surgery, but the only way to reduce the level of maternal mortality.[52] The only question about hospital delivery in the inter-war period was how far it could be extended; and money rather than obstetric policies provided the answer. For financial reasons total hospital delivery, even if it was desirable, was out of the question, and few, in fact, advocated such an

---

[49] Lewis, 'Mothers and Maternity Policies'.

[50] 'Twilight Sleep', the new and ephemeral fashion in obstetric analgesia, played a large part between about 1910 and 1918 in the switch from home to hospital delivery in the USA where it will be discussed. Although it played a smaller part in Britain it lasted well into the 1920s.

[51] V. Bonney, 'The Continued High Mortality of Childbearing', *Proceedings of the Royal Society of Medicine*, 12/3 (1918–19), 75–107.

[52] Ibid. The conclusion that increased hospital delivery would lower maternal mortality was reached by the Section on Obstetrics and Gynaecology of the Royal Society of Medicine at a meeting in 1919.

extreme measure, even as a distant goal. So, for the time being at least, women delivered in hospital would have to be strictly limited to 'Those who show some abnormality, and those whose domestic conditions are unfavourable.'[53] Although the expansion of hospital deliveries during the inter-war period was, by the standards of some other countries (Sweden, the USA, and New Zealand, for instance) limited and unimpressive, it was the inter-war period which saw the beginning of the trend which led without interruption to the present position of virtual total hospital delivery.

Did the increase in hospital deliveries lead to safer childbirth? It is a simple question, but there is no simple answer: for the way the question is framed implies, as we saw earlier, a degree of homogeneity which did not exist; and it implies that the place of delivery was the important determinant of the standard of care.

As Webster has said, the hospital service in the inter-war period consisted of an extraordinary collection of heterogeneous institutions.[54] Eardley Holland spoke in 1935 of the 'hundreds of little hospitals giving local practitioners the opportunity of performing Caesarean sections and other obstetric operations'.[55] Because it was feared that large maternity units would encourage outbreaks of puerperal fever, there was a deliberate policy of promoting small maternity units with small wards for one to three patients.[56] This policy is reflected in Table 13.4, where you can see that a large increase in the number of maternity hospitals and related institutions was accompanied by a fall in their average size.

An illustration of the complexity of analysing hospital performance comes from a report on the performance of six maternity institutions during the years 1909–1914.[57] The main findings are summarized in Table 13.5, and the enormous differences in MMRs are obvious. What is the explanation? Were there really such large differences in the standard of care?

A and B were large metropolitan hospitals. Hospital A ran an out-patient service (E). C and D were two provincial lying-in hospitals; D (but not C) ran an out-patient department (F). The lowest rates of mortality occurred in the *out-patient* departments of two lying-in hospitals (E and F). The next best results occurred in two London lying-in hospitals (A and B) and the worst in

[53] This was the official view of the Ministry of Health and of most obstetricians. See leading article, 'Safety and Comfort in Childbed', *Lancet* (1920), i. 506.

[54] Charles Webster, *The Health Services since the War*, i (London, 1988), chap. 1.

[55] He asserted that many of these Caesarean sections were extremely dangerous because they followed failed forceps deliveries and were partly responsible for high maternal mortality. Eardley Holland, 'Maternal Mortality', *Lancet* (1935) i. 936–7.

[56] Campbell, 'Maternity Homes'. In Wiltshire, for example, the idea of one large maternity department for the whole county was rejected. Instead, it was decided to establish five small units in Salisbury, Swindon, Calne, Malmesbury, and Corsham.

[57] Isabella Cameron, 'Maternal and Infant Mortality in Maternity Hospital Practice', in *Local Government Board, 44th Annual Report, 1914–1915*; Supplement, 104–17.

TABLE 13.4 *Number, Type, and Size of Hospitals and Related Institutions for the Physically Ill in England and Wales, 1891–1931, with figures for number of beds*

Type of hospital	1891 No.	Beds	1911 No.	Beds	1921 No.	Beds	1938 No.	Beds
Teaching (voluntary)	24	301	24	345	25	383	25	504
General (voluntary)	385	39	530	41	616	48	671	68
General (public)	18	677	76	539	74	511	133	398
Maternity (voluntary)	16	13	8	39	14	39	235	15
Maternity (public)	—		—		1	12	18	36
Chronic and unclassified (voluntary)	12	56	47	45	50	47	40	62
Chronic and unclassified (public)	1082	85	1404	128	1914	133	1882	126

Notes: The increase in the number of voluntary maternity institutions between 1921 and 1938 was largely due to the establishment of numerous registered maternity homes with only a few beds; hence the fall in average number of beds from 39 to 15 between 1921 and 1938. The large number but small size of the general voluntary hospitals reflects the cottage hospitals, most of which had 20 or fewer beds.

Source: R. Pinker, *English Hospital Statistics* (London, 1966), based on table VII (p. 57) and table VIII (p. 58).

the two provincial hospitals (C and D). Hospital C, however, was a provincial lying-in hospital with no out-patient services which admitted an exceptionally high proportion of serious cases from outlying districts. None was refused admission if beds were available and only a small proportion of admissions were normal cases. Hospital D likewise admitted a high proportion of abnormal cases. Each was providing a service heavily weighted with high-risk and emergency admissions. It is clear that comparisons between these institutions in terms of maternal mortality are virtually meaningless without a detailed breakdown of the number and mortality rate of various types of admission—low-risk normal cases, high-risk booked cases, and cases admitted as emergencies during or after labour—and cases admitted after an instrumental abortion had gone wrong. Such data are rarely available.

Munro Kerr has much to say on this aspect of assessing the mortality rates of hospitals. In those such as the Glasgow Royal Maternity, where a high proportion of admissions were emergencies, many were moribund on admission, sometimes as a result of 'failed forceps', many were sick women suffering from serious incidental disease, and others were cases of septic abortion. These categories alone accounted for a third of all maternal deaths in the Glasgow Maternity which, because of its situation and admission policies, inevitably incurred a high rate of maternal mortality. Thus the MMR

TABLE 13.5 *Maternal Mortality Rates by Cause in Four Lying-in Hospitals, 1909–1914*

	Hospital in-patients 1909–14		Hospital out-patients 1909–14		England and Wales 1913[f]
	A and B[a]	C[b]	D[c]	E[d] and F[e]	
Total births	10,205	2,553	1,722	14,294	881,138
Total maternal deaths	48	145	51	12	3,492
Maternal mortality rates[g], all causes	47	568	296	8	40
Maternal mortality rates, Puerperal fever	8	54	34	1	13
Percentage of total	17	9	11	12	32
Maternal mortality rates, Eclampsia	10	127	57	1	9
Percentage of total	21	22	19	12	22
Maternal mortality rates, Haemorrhage	7	96	46	2	6
Percentage of total	15	17	15	25	15

[a] Two metropolitan lying-in hospitals.
[b] Provincial lying-in hospital.
[c] Provincial lying-in hospital.
[d] Out-patient department attached to metropolitan hospital A.
[e] Out-patient department attached to provincial hospital D.
[f] Corresponding maternal mortality rates for England and Wales as a whole in 1913 given for comparison.
[g] Shown as maternal deaths per 10,000 births.

Source: Isabella Cameron, 'Maternal and Infant Mortality in Maternity Hospital Practice' and other sources in *Local Government Board, 44th Annual Report, 1914–1915*, Supplement containing a Report on Maternal Mortality in Connection with Childbearing and its Relation to Infant Mortality, PP 1914–16, xxv, Cd. 8085.

in this hospital from 1925 to 1929 was 280 per 10,000 deliveries, and from 1930 to 1934 it was 200 per 10,000 deliveries when in Scotland as a whole it was around 50 per 10,000 births.[58]

There were, however, other hospitals which achieved very low levels of maternal mortality. The most famous was the East End Maternity Hospital in London which admitted relatively few emergencies and no abortions, and was known for its high standard of antenatal care and practice of asepsis. Here,

[58] Kerr, *Maternal Mortality and Morbidity*, 256–65. See also D. Baird, 'Maternal Mortality in Hospital', *Lancet* (1936), i. 295–8.

almost all deliveries were by midwives, and rates of surgical intervention were exceptionally low. This hospital delivered large numbers of poor patients in the East End of London in the 1920s and 1930s with an impressively low MMR. In the early 1930s the MMR from all causes in this hospital was less than ten when it was nearly forty in the country as a whole and the MMR from puerperal sepsis was just over two when it was around sixteen for England and Wales. Unfortunately almost nothing is known of the MMRs of the multitude of small hospitals and nursing homes.[59] It is therefore impossible to generalize about the standard of maternity hospital care as a whole in the absence of detailed records of admissions and outcomes. There is, however, another and indirect approach to the problem.

Since there were wide regional variations in the proportion of hospital deliveries in the 1930s, is there any evidence of a correlation between the extent of institutional delivery and the level of maternal mortality? Take the case of Manchester which, in the early 1930s, had one of the highest proportions of institutional deliveries in Britain. Table 13.6 shows that a half of all deliveries were institutional; 43 per cent were delivered as in-patients and 8 per cent were delivered by a hospital out-patient service. Thirty-nine per cent of patients were delivered at home by midwives, and only 10 per cent of these were booked home deliveries by a doctor. Yet the maternal mortality in Manchester was virtually the same as it was in England and Wales as a whole.

Now compare Manchester with Birmingham which had shown a consistently low rate of maternal mortality. In 1930 the MMR in Birmingham was 27.3 compared with 43 in Manchester. The percentage of home deliveries by doctors in Birmingham was similar (11 per cent), but there were many fewer in-patient deliveries and many more home deliveries by midwives. What was conspicuous in Birmingham, however, was an exceptionally well-integrated maternity service, organized by Dr Ethel Cassie, the Medical Officer of Health for maternal and child services.[60]

This suggests what I believe is a key observation. As far as the risk to the mother was concerned, the place of delivery, whether it was home or hospital, was not a matter of great importance except for cases with serious complications. What mattered most was the morale and the standard of co-operation and integration between all concerned with maternal care. Indeed, Birmingham—an industrial area where a high mortality might have been expected—can be contrasted with the maternity services in the mainly rural countries of Devon

---

[59] A survey of 50 selected small maternity homes in 1920 (with a total of 9,108 admissions) showed an overall MMR of 62 (above the national level) and an MMR due to puerperal sepsis of just over 10 (below the national level). Campbell, 'Maternity Homes', 164.

[60] Public Record Office, Ministry of Health, MH 66/442. In the series of reports on maternal and child welfare in various counties and county boroughs, carried out in the 1930s by medical officers from the Ministry of Health, the most glowing report (by Dr J. H. Turnbull) was concerned with the maternity services in Birmingham.

TABLE 13.6 *Distribution of Births between Home and Institutions, and between Midwives and Doctors in Manchester, 1930–1933*

	Numbers	Percentage	Maternal mortality rates (per 10,000 births)
Notified births in Manchester, 1930–3	53,537	100	—
Domiciliary cases, 1930–3			
attended solely by midwives	20,896	39	—
(doctor called in by midwives)	(11,061)	(21)	—
attended by doctor and midwife as maternity nurse	3,687	7	—
attended by doctor alone	1,502	3	—
total attended by doctor	(5,189)	(10)	—
total domiciliary deliveries	26,085	49	—
Institutional deliveries, 1930–3			
confinements in hospitals and nursing homes	22,932	43	—
attended by out-patient service of St Mary's Hospital	4,520	8	—
total institutional deliveries	27,452	51	—
Maternal mortality rates, 1930–3			
Sepsis			
Manchester	—	—	14
England and Wales	—	—	17
Non-septic causes			
Manchester	—	—	29
England and Wales	—	—	25
Total maternal mortality rate			
Manchester	—	—	43
England and Wales	—	—	42

Source: R. Veitch Clark (MOH for Manchester), 'Report of Meeting of Royal Sanitary Institute', *Lancet* (1935), i. 936–7.

and Gloucestershire in what is usually thought of as the favoured South. In both counties the proportion of home deliveries was high, hospital provision was slight, scattered, and inefficient, and such maternity services as existed were poorly integrated. In the early 1930s there were twenty-four consultant obstetricians in Lancashire and ten in Birmingham. In Gloucestershire there was none and general practitioners who encountered major complications preferred to call on an experienced colleague rather than a general surgeon at Bristol or Gloucester whose knowledge of obstetrics would be slight. In 1932 when the MMR for England and Wales was about 40, in Manchester about 43, and in Birmingham about 27, it was 49.8 in Devon and 56.2 in Gloucester.[61]

In short, there is little to support the view that increased hospital deliveries either worsened or improved the risk of dying in childbirth. Certainly the failure of maternal mortality to decline cannot be attributed to increased hospital delivery. If the maternity services of the inter-war period had any conspicuous failures, they lay in such factors as under-funding and a conspicuous lack of integration, co-ordination, and leadership.

However, even the best-designed services would have failed if the training of the birth-attendants was deficient; and although there were occasional exceptions, the general standard of obstetric education for medical students before the Second World War was dreadful.

In 1898, Elizabeth Garrett Anderson had said:

It is unfortunately true that the puerperal mortality all over England is higher than it ought to be. The responsibility for this rests in great measure with the examining bodies. When they recognise that a sound and extensive knowledge of practical midwifery is infinitely more important to a practitioner than a minute acquaintance with organic chemistry and the refinements of physiology there will be a chance of improvement but not till then . . .[62]

If anything, the standard degenerated, and obstetrics remained the Cinderella subject of the medical curriculum. In 1911, an Edinburgh obstetrician stressed the remarkable progress of gynaecology as a branch of surgery in the teaching hospitals, where the surgeons were prima donnas, regarded with awe and admiration by the students.[63] Compared with gynaecology, however, little development had taken place in obstetrics or obstetric education because of the scorn with which surgeons regarded childbirth. Indeed:

the average surgeon takes a pride in his ignorance of obstetrics . . . No advance has been made. The student is merely required to be present at a number of so-called cliniques [*sic*], and attend personally a given number of cases, or, as an alternative, attend personally twenty-five cases of labour . . . to gain a certificate in practical midwifery. More than likely he may, in these cases, never see an abnormality [and] it must be remembered that the essence of obstetric practice is to be able to conduct abnormal cases. If all confinements were normal, obstetrics as an art would cease to exist, and be practised by nurses and neighbours.[64]

---

[61] Public Record Office, Ministry of Health, Maternal and Child Health, Gloucester, MH 66/90, 91, 92. Devon, MH 66/58, 66, 88.

[62] Elizabeth Garrett Anderson, 'Deaths in Childbed', *British Medical Journal* (1898), ii. 839–40 and 927.

[63] F. W. N. Haultain, 'A Retrospect and Comparison of the Progress of Midwifery and Gynaecology', *Edinburgh Medical Journal*, NS 6 (1911), 17–37. The model for the gynaecologist/surgeon was Lawson Tait, described by Haultain as a man of 'intrepid fearlessness, an almost ruthless manner and marvellous dexterity'. See also Anon., 'The Address in Obstetrics', *British Medical Journal* (1906), ii. 445–6 and Sir J. Halliday Croom, 'The Teaching of Obstetrics to Undergraduates', *Edinburgh Medical Journal*, 21 (1918), 268–300.

[64] Haultain, 'A Retrospect'.

Obstetric instruction, such as it was, often consisted of ward-rounds in the lying-in wards to see patients already delivered. As Haultain said, 'The parade of the puerperal wards, so far as true clinical instruction is concerned, is a farce, and might be as thoroughly conducted at Madame Tussaud's.'[65]

But Edinburgh was relatively advanced. The distinguished obstetrician Sir Eardley Holland remembered that at his medical school in 1901, 'getting your Midder done and out of the way', as the Dean put it, consisted of one month on the 'Extern. district', unsupervised and with no in-patient midwifery teaching whatsoever. The equally distinguished Sir Dugald Baird, recalling his student days in the 1920s, said that clinical instruction consisted of watching their teachers perform Caesarean sections from a distance in an amphitheatre, and conducting domiciliary deliveries 'on the district', unsupervised, with no practical instruction, and without being allowed to give drugs to relieve pain or stop bleeding.[66]

A doctor who recalled his student days at the London Hospital around the time of the First World War, says he was expected with little previous experience to deliver fifty-four patients on the district on his own in a fortnight. 'I lost all sense of time. I did not know whether it was yesterday, today or tomorrow. It sounds absurd but it was true. The month we spent on maternity was itself enough to undermine the stoutest constitution.'[67]

Indeed, these and many other accounts of the gross inadequacy of obstetric education may sound exaggerated but they were not. Sending uninstructed students out on the district was a process of toughening them up by 'throwing them in at the deep end' without a moment's thought that the person who risked death by drowning was the patient, not the student.

This so-called teaching was an unsavoury and disgraceful exploitation of the poor in the districts adjoining teaching hospitals. It instilled bad habits and scorn for 'midder'. It is not surprising that many doctors practised midwifery in a careless manner, for they had been brought up to do so. Therefore, many general practitioners abandoned midwifery if they could, or delegated it to a young and inexperienced partner or assistant. It is salutary to remember that most of these students were destined to deal with major obstetric complications in their practices on the basis of such totally inadequate training, sometimes in areas where there was no possibility of calling in an obstetrician or transferring a woman in labour to a hospital. If I was asked to pick out one factor above all others as responsible for the high maternal mortality in the first thirty-five years of this century, it would be the standard of obstetric education in the medical schools.

---

[65] Ibid.

[66] Baird, 'The Evolution of Modern Obstetrics', *Lancet* (1960), ii. 557–64, 609–14.

[67] R. N. Salamann, *The Helmsman takes Charge* (unpub. memoirs, n.d.). My thanks to Dr Lara Marks for drawing my attention to this. It is fair to say that during the 1920s the London Hospital reformed this deplorable state of affairs.

TABLE 13.7 *Total Deliveries, Institutional Deliveries, and Home Deliveries by Type of Birth Attendant, England and Wales, 1938*

	Total births (000s)	Percentage of total
Total births in England and Wales in 1938	621	100
Institutional births	155	25
Home births	466	75
Midwife births		
Local authority	205	44
Independent midwives	57	12
Total	262	56
Midwife as maternity nurse with doctor		
Local authority	75	16
Independent	19	4
Total	94	20[a]
Total births with which the midwife was involved	356	76
General practitioner delivery without midwife	110	24
General practitioner and midwife as maternity nurse	94	20[a]
Total general practitioner births	204	44

[a] Note that the 94,000 births attended by general practitioner and midwife acting as maternity nurse appears twice under the headings midwife births and general practitioner births.

Source: E. Grebenik and D. J. Parry, 'The Maternity Services in England and Wales before the War', *Agenda*, 2 (1943), 133–46; Jane Lewis, *The Politics of Motherhood* (London, 1980); A. Macfarlane and M. Mugford, *Birth Counts* (London, 1984), ii. 1–3. See footnote in text.

MATERNAL CARE, 1900–1935

We have reviewed the institutions and people—midwives, general practitioners, consultants—who provided maternal care. What was their relative contribution by the late 1930s? An answer is provided in Table 13.7 which represents an estimate of total births in England and Wales in 1938, according to place of delivery and birth-attendant.[68]

What this table conceals, however, is the most prominent feature of maternal services before the Second World War, namely the immense diversity. We have seen several examples: the varying proportion of hospital deliveries and

[68] In Table 13.7 deliveries are rounded up to the nearest thousand because it is based on estimates rather than exact figures. The proportion of institutional deliveries is a best estimate from the data available. The data on midwives are probably quite accurate. In compiling this table, it was assumed that deliveries undertaken by handywomen were so few that they can be discounted, an assumption that would be dangerous for the period before 1920, but may be justified for 1938. It was also assumed that the doctors undertaking home deliveries were all general practitioners. A few home deliveries were undertaken by consultant obstetricians. In short the table gives a broad rather than a precise picture.

the wide variation in hospital mortality and in the level of integration of maternity services. The preconception that maternity services were poor in the industrial north and west, and good in the favoured south and east, does not bear close examination. We have noted the poor services of Gloucester and Devon. Two other areas, Tottenham and Oxfordshire, both relatively prosperous southern areas, showed immense differences. In 1938 Tottenham provided 50 per cent hospital deliveries and high quality maternity services by the standards of the time. Oxfordshire's services were inadequate and only 10 per cent of deliveries took place in hospital.[69] Examples of such diversity were commonplace. In fact, the more closely maternity services are examined, the more often one finds there was wide diversity, even within the boundaries of a county or county borough.

Diversity, then, was the outstanding feature of maternity services during this period. Another was the establishment of institutions of considerable influence and power such as the Central Midwives Board, the Midwives Institute, the Ministry of Health with an active Maternal and Child Welfare Division, the (Royal) College of Obstetricians and Gynaecologists, numerous charitable organizations and committees concerned with maternal care, and the growing involvement of public health departments in maternal and child health. All these were twentieth-century innovations. All were expected to have a beneficial effect on maternal care.

What, then, was the result of all these innovations? Was there a substantial improvement in the quality of maternal care? Were the mothers of the inter-war period substantially better served than their predecessors in the late nineteenth century? Diversity precludes a simple answer. Here and there (for example the work of the Queen's Institute midwives) there was vast improvement. Overall, however, by the harsh judgement of the statistics of mortality, the answer must be not very much except in the sense that some of the groundwork was laid for improvements during and after the Second World War.

The diverse, uncoordinated, ramshackle maternal care of the first third of this century was largely a consequence of three main features: the deplorable standard of obstetric education in the medical schools; the fragmented system divided between the occasional old-style handywomen, midwives, general practitioners, medical officers of health, and hospital consultants; and finally the feebleness and indecision with which policies were implemented. Although the high level of maternal mortality cried out for imaginative leadership, apart from some shining exceptions men and women of the necessary energy and persuasiveness were rarely found in the medical schools, the corridors of the Ministry of Health, or public health departments. The

---

[69] See Peretz, 'Maternity Services for England and Wales', a model of a local study which exemplifies many of the features outlined in this chapter.

medical officers of health who were responsible for co-ordinating maternity services in their areas, were, to put it mildly, seldom perceived as formidable figures of authority. In any case, they were answerable to local authorities which, with an eye to the rates and the next local election, only too often responded to initiatives such as the Maternal and Child Welfare Act (1918) by attitudes described as the 'last word in a despairing effort to avoid obligations'.[70]

Another factor was lack of funds through public parsimony; but there is yet another that is easily overlooked. Although many had strong views and were all too ready to identify this or that as the prime factor, no one was really sure about the cause or cure of high maternal mortality. Thus there is no guarantee that if a central state-controlled body with draconian powers had existed—and no such system was conceivable in Britain at the time—it would have produced a substantial improvement in maternal care. As we will see in the next chapter, there was no simple answer to the problem of maternal mortality.

[70] A phrase quoted in C. Webster, *The Health Services since the War* (1988), 9.

14

Maternal Mortality in Britain from 1850 to the Mid-1930s

In this chapter we turn to an analysis of the trend, causes, and determinants of maternal mortality, starting not at 1800, but at 1850 when detailed national data on maternal deaths first became available in England and Wales (the corresponding dates in Scotland and Ireland were 1856 and 1870 respectively).[1]

If we visualize the graph of maternal mortality from 1850 to the present as a view of a mountain range, from a long distance it would be seen as a high plateau ending on the right with a steep downward slope. This is exactly how it looks if five-year averages are plotted on a logarithmic scale, as in Figure 1.4. The closer we get, however, the more we see that the plateau, far from being flat, consists of a complex series of peaks and hollows. We will also see that the lowest point in the plateau is 1910, with a general tendency to slope downwards from 1850 to 1910, and upwards from 1911 to 1934. These features are visible when annual rates are plotted, as in Figure 14.1 which shows the trends in maternal mortality in England and Wales, Scotland, and Ireland, and Figures 14.2 and 14.3 which show the trend in maternal mortality (by regression analysis) in two segments: from 1850 to 1910 and 1911 to 1934 respectively. In practice it is convenient to use the low point, 1910, as a way of dividing this chapter into two parts.

MATERNAL MORTALITY, 1850–1910

The most notable feature of the first period is the exceptional peak of maternal mortality in 1874 when maternal mortality reached the highest level ever recorded in English national statistics. This was followed by a deep hollow. Indeed, the huge swing from an MMR of 69.3 in 1874 to 37 in 1878 is the largest short-term fluctuation in the whole period. After a ten-year gap of relative calm there is a second but lower peak of mortality in 1893. After that, the trend is downwards until 1910. It is notable that from 1850 to 1910 the fluctuations were not symmetrical. The greatest disturbances were surges above the normal level, mortality crises, in fact: a point to which I will return.

[1] For annual rates in the UK see Appendix Tables 1, 3, and 4.

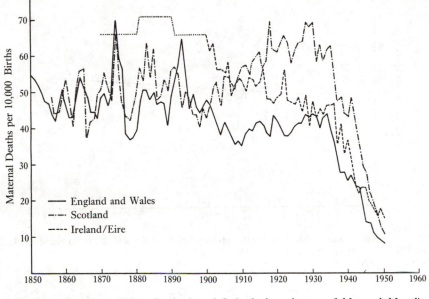

FIG. 14.1 England and Wales, Scotland, and Ireland. Annual rates of Maternal Mortality, 1850–1950
Source: Appendix Tables 1, 3, and 4.

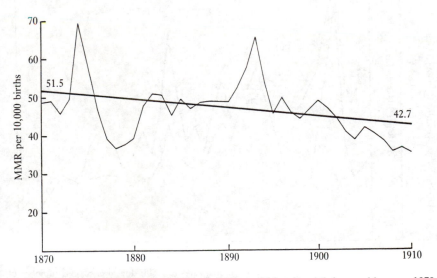

FIG. 14.2 England and Wales. Annual Rates of Maternal Mortality and the trend between 1870 and 1910 by regression analysis
Source: Appendix Table 1.

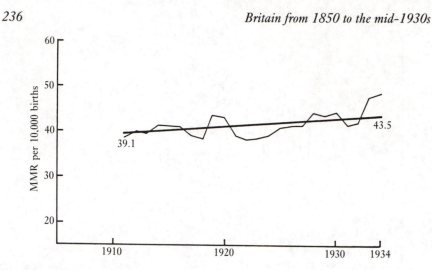

FIG. 14.3 England and Wales. Annual rates of Maternal Mortality and the trend between 1911 and 1934 by regression analysis
Source: Appendix Table 1.

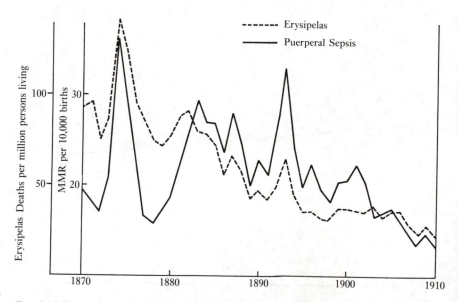

FIG. 14.4 England and Wales, 1870–1910. Annual rates of death due to erysipelas (number of deaths per million persons living) and Maternal Mortality due to puerperal sepsis (Number of Deaths per 10,000 births)
Source: Registrar General for England and Wales, *Annual Reports*.

The trend and fluctuations in Scotland were remarkably similar to those in England and Wales until 1900. Thereafter their pathways diverged.

Why did such large annual fluctuations in maternal mortality occur? We noted in Chapter 4 that some features such as the 1874 peak and the trough on either side of it were constant features not only in Britain as a whole but also in various regions and indeed in other countries. Some general widespread process seems to have been in operation. The hectic landscape of maternal mortality during this period cannot be correlated with fluctuations in social or economic factors or with changes in the type, quality, or availability of obstetric practice. Nor can we argue that changes in the accuracy or completeness of death registration were significant, for the general trend from 1850 to 1910 was downwards in spite of compulsory notification of death from 1874 which might have been expected to produce a post-1874 rise as a registration effect.

In Chapter 4 we also noted the close relationship between the trend in deaths due to erysipelas and the trend in maternal mortality, suggesting that the fluctuations in maternal mortality were to a very large extent governed by the death rates of puerperal fever which, in turn, reflected changes in streptococcal virulence (see Appendix 5). In Chapter 4 we also noted that the tendency for deaths from other causes to follow the pattern of deaths from puerperal fever (Figure 4.1) was due to the increased number of deaths from non-septic causes because of concomitant infection.

The peak, or mortality crisis, of 1874 was, as we have seen, a general phenomenon seen in London, in the provinces, in Scotland, and in certain other countries. In Norway (Table 4.3) it appeared in every region except one, where the crisis was spread over the two years 1874 and 1875. The 1893 peak was quite different. It was more localized. In Scotland there was a peak in 1891 but not 1893, and there are no convincing signs of a peak during the 1890s in other countries. In England and Wales, however, the 1893 peak, like the 1874 peak, was found both in London and the provinces. In Wales it was found in most counties and interestingly it was most conspicuous in the mining valleys with high population densities and heavy industry. It was least conspicuous or absent in northern counties which were mountainous, sparsely populated, non-industrial, and notable for poor communications.[2]

Why the 1874 and 1893 crises in maternal mortality should have been so different is something I do not understand. But the 1893 crisis could be explained in terms of local person-to-person spread of a virulent strain of the streptococcus, and a high carrier rate in the population. At the beginning of this century, George Geddes was a general practitioner in rural Scotland where he rarely saw any cases of puerperal fever. When he moved to indus-

[2] W. Williams, *Deaths in Childbed* (London, 1904), 20, 21, 24, and 32. In Merthyr Tydfil, a coal and iron town in Glamorgan, the average maternal mortality between 1891 and 1900 was 31 per 10,000 births; in 1893 it rose to exactly three times the average.

trial Lancashire, what struck him most forcibly was the very high rate of this disease in industrial areas, and he asked himself why? He concluded in 1912 that wherever people were crowded together in industrial areas and the rate of industrial injuries (and thus of septic wounds) was high, the streptococcus thrived and the likelihood of a mother being infected and developing puerperal fever was also high. It is a plausible hypothesis, although Geddes's attempt to provide statistical proof was flawed by his use of notification rates which, as we have seen and as he himself conceded, were grossly unreliable.[3]

I believe we can postulate that *the dominant feature of maternal mortality in the nineteenth century was puerperal fever. The high level and wide annual fluctuations in the mortality from puerperal fever reflected changes in the virulence of the streptococcus in the community, and the transfer of streptococci to lying-in mothers.* Nothing else had anything like so strong an effect in determining the trend in maternal mortality. If that hypothesis is accepted, what was the effect of antisepsis on the trend in maternal mortality?

Figure 14.2 shows that the most conspicuous part of the downward trend between 1850 and 1910 occurred in the last fifteen years, from 1895 to 1910. Antisepsis and asepsis were introduced into obstetric practice around 1880. The techniques were adopted first in the hospitals, where as we have seen, the results were sometimes dramatic. There was, as we would expect, a delay in the use of these techniques in general practice. Therefore a delay in the decline in maternal mortality until 1895 or thereabouts is reasonable. From 1895 to 1910 antisepsis seems to be the prime candidate for explaining the declining rate of maternal mortality. However, Figure 14.4 shows that deaths from erysipelas also declined in the years preceding 1910, and at much the same rate as deaths from puerperal fever.[4] The feature shared by puerperal fever and erysipelas was the *Streptococcus pyogenes*. Antisepsis cannot have had any effect on the incidence or mortality from erysipelas. This suggests that maternal mortality declined between 1895 and 1910 not because, or not only because, of antisepsis, but rather because of a fall in the virulence of the streptococcus.

The most conclusive evidence comes from international comparisons. Table 14.1 shows the mortality rate for puerperal sepsis in various countries at five-year intervals from 1870 to 1905, spanning either side of the quinquennium 1880–1885 when antisepsis was introduced. For each country there are two lines of figures. The upper line for each country gives the MMR due to puerperal sepsis (expressed as deaths per 10,000 births) and the lower line

---

[3] G. Geddes, *Statistics of Puerperal Sepsis and Allied Infectious Diseases* (Bristol, 1912), and id., *Puerperal Septicaemia: its Causation, Symptoms, Prevention and Treatment* (Bristol, 1926). In spite of the flawed statistics I find Geddes's convincing.

[4] For erysipelas the actual decline was from around 35 deaths per million living in 1895 to about 25 in 1910.

TABLE 14.1 *Maternal Mortality Due to Puerperal Sepsis from 1870 to 1905, Before and After the Introduction of Antisepsis in the 1880s*

	1870	1875	1880	1885	1890	1895	1900	1905
England and Wales	18	28	18	26	22	20	21	18
1870	100	155	100	144	122	111	116	100
Scotland	17	30	14	29	26	19	17	18
1870	100	176	82	170	160	112	100	106
Ireland	23	31	26	31	23	29	22	18
1870	100	134	113	135	100	126	96	78
Norway	28	31	24	26	25	14	16	9
1870	100	111	104	93	89	50	57	32
Sweden	31	32	24	22	12	13	8	12
1870	100	103	77	71	39	42	26	39
The Netherlands	13	16	11	14	12	9	9	7
1870	100	123	85	107	92	69	69	54
Amsterdam	—	36	26	28	12	8	4	2
1875	—	100	72	77	33	22	11	5
Switzerland	—	—	41	52	31	25	20	26
1880	—	—	100	127	76	61	49	63

Source: F. W. N. Haultain, 'A Retrospect and Comparison of the Progress of Midwifery and Gynaecology', *Edinburgh Medical Journal*, NS 6 (1911), 17–37; *Amsterdam Statistical Bulletins* (various years).

shows those values indexed to 100 in the first year for which values could be obtained to facilitate comparison. Between 1870 and 1905 there was no fall in mortality due to sepsis in England and Wales or Scotland. There was a modest fall in Ireland. In certain European countries, however, the decline was striking, especially in Norway, Sweden, and the Netherlands. The most impressive fall occurred in Amsterdam. In all of these the fall is much too large to be explained solely in terms of a fall in streptococcal virulence. It is, at the very least, highly probable that antisepsis reduced these national levels of mortality due to puerperal sepsis to a very considerable extent.[5]

It is ironic that of all the countries in north-west Europe, Britain, where (*pace* Semmelweis) antisepsis was first introduced, was the odd one out. Why was there so little response to antisepsis in Britain compared with our Continental neighbours? What was the essential difference? The answer may be the low standard of antiseptic practice in home deliveries in Britain. In the Netherlands and Scandinavia it is likely that antisepsis was used effectively in

[5] The most important source on this is U. Högberg and G. Brostrom, 'The Impact of Early Medical Technology on Maternal Mortality Rate in late 19th Century Sweden', *International Journal of Obstetrics and Gynaecology*, 24 (1986), 251–61.

home confinements because a substantial majority of deliveries was under-taken by midwives who were trained and closely supervised, ensuring that a new technique such as antisepsis was used as it should be.

MATERNAL MORTALITY, 1910–1934

Compared with the previous sixty years, in this period the trend was quite different. Figure 14.3 shows it as a slightly irregular upward slope from an MMR of 39.1 in 1911 to 43.5 in 1934. Gone are the high peaks and wide fluctuations of the nineteenth century to be replaced by a relatively smooth rise ending at the beginning of the steep post-1935 fall in mortality. The epidemics of puerperal fever and erysipelas which swept through towns and communities in the eighteenth and early nineteenth centuries and were still found occasionally after 1850, had disappeared by the twentieth. This is a point of some demographic importance.

Demographers who have studied historical trends in mortality in European countries distinguish between the old demographic regime of mortality and the new, and the period of transition between the two.[6] The characteristic feature of the 'old' demographic regime was the recurrent mortality crises which can be seen as tall peaks rising high above the underlying trend. This pattern gave way to the 'new' regime in which the crises have diminished or disappeared and the graph has smoothed out.

It used to be argued that it was the mortality crises which acted as 'regulators', preventing the population from increasing. That view is now discarded. But the point I am concerned with here is the timing of the transition. In mortality from all causes in England and Wales, the transition from the old regime to the new took place between the end of the seventeenth century and the beginning of the nineteenth.[7]

In the case of maternal mortality, however, it looks as if the transition from the old regime with its recurrent mortality crises due to puerperal fever, to the new regime when puerperal fever became endemic, took place at the very end of the nineteenth century. The same is probably true of erysipelas and scarlet fever—in other words of streptococcal disease as a whole. Of course it is possible that before 1850 the mortality crises in puerperal fever were much larger than they were in the second half of the nineteenth century, and that the transition began much earlier. We only have published national figures since the introduction of vital registration, and what they show may be the attenuated tail-end of a long process of transition. Some patchy

---

[6] See R. Schofield, D. Reher, and A. Bideau, *The Decline in Mortality in Europe* (Oxford, 1991), esp. the chaps. by R. Schofield and D. Reher ('The Decline of Mortality in Europe'), and A. Perrenoud ('The Attenuation of Mortality Crises and the Decline of Mortality').

[7] The timing varied in different European countries, the most extreme example being Finland where the old regime persisted until the end of the nineteenth century. Perrenoud, ibid.

evidence of very high fatality rates in the eighteenth century makes this a serious possibility, although I doubt if sufficient data could be obtained to test that hypothesis. But the trends in maternal mortality suggest the interesting possibility that the transition from the old demographic regime to the new may have occurred at different periods for different diseases and different mortalities.

From 1910 to 1934 the important question is why did maternal mortality not only fail to decline in the face of all that was being done in the field of obstetrics and maternal care, but actually increased? It was a question constantly asked by authorities not just in Britain but in other countries which suffered a similar experience. Amongst the factors which have been suggested to explain the pattern of maternal mortality are the following:

1. That the rise was an artefact due to greater completeness and accuracy of death registration and changes in the International Classification of Diseases.
2. That the fall in the birth rate led to a proportionate rise in high-risk first deliveries—in other words the effect of increasing primiparity.
3. That high mortality was due to a decline in the health of mothers as a consequence of poverty, malnutrition, and poor housing, all of which increased maternal susceptibility to death from various puerperal causes.
4. That the cause was a lack of improvement if not decline in the standard of obstetric care as a whole, associated with increased interference and the employment of surgical measures in normal and moderately difficult labours.
5. That the increase in deaths due to septic abortion was the major reason for the rise in maternal mortality, with the corollary that the exclusion of abortion deaths from the calculations would have revealed a downward trend in maternal mortality.
6. That there was an increase in the virulence of the streptococcus.

Registration Effects

These can be dismissed as relatively unimportant. False certification—deliberate or accidental—had become relatively trivial by 1910. Successive Registrars General considered the possibility that the rise in maternal mortality was a statistical artefact only to dismiss it. The 1937 report on maternal mortality in England and Wales (which was based on data from the late 1920s) concluded that improved registration did not affect the trend during this period.[8] The 1911 classification of diseases did, however, include one important change: the removal of deaths due to toxaemia from diseases of the kidney to diseases of childbirth. This led to a rise in the rate for non-septic

---

[8] Ministry of Health, *Report of an Investigation into Maternal Mortality* (London, 1937), Cmd. 5422.

TABLE 14.2 *Maternal Mortality by Gravidity for All Causes and for Various Categories of Death, Scotland, 1929–1933*

Cause of death	Gravidity (percentages)[a]					No. of deaths
	1	2	3	4	5+	
All causes	32	15	12	8	33	2,465
Puerperal sepsis after spontaneous delivery	25	21	15	9	30	306
Puerperal sepsis after interference	60	11	8	3	18	238
Abortion	13	10	14	15	48	150
Eclampsia	83	14	2	0	1	145
Placenta praevia	14	14	10	10	52	105
Post-partum haemorrhage	20	16	18	18	28	87
Accidental haemorrhage	14	8	10	8	60	62

[a] Deaths in each cell expressed as percentages of total deaths (final column).

Source: C. A. Douglas and P. L. McKinlay, *Maternal Morbidity and Mortality in Scotland* (Edinburgh, 1935), 215.

maternal deaths from 21.9 in 1910 to 24.4 in 1911. Thereafter, however, the graph drawn according to the post-1911 classification lay so close to that constructed on the pre-1911 classification that the difference is of minimal significance.[9]

The Effect of the Fall in Fertility

The second proposition—increasing primiparity due to the falling birth rate— has always been a serious contender. The effects of parity and maternal age on maternal risk are described in Chapter 28. Maternal risk in first births (primiparity) is high, in second and third births it is low, and then from fourth births onwards (referred to as 'grand multiparity') the risk begins to rise steeply, soon reaching levels in excess of first births. Table 14.2 shows maternal deaths by gravidity (number of pregnancies) and by cause in Scotland for the years 1929–33. It shows that about one-third of maternal deaths occurred during first pregnancies, and about one-third in fifth and subsequent pregnancies. What is also clear is that the distribution of deaths according to gravidity differed widely according to cause. The risk of dying of puerperal sepsis after interference and of eclampsia was highest in women having their first baby. Deaths due to haemorrhage and abortion, however, tended to be more common in women in their fifth and subsequent pregnancies.

[9] The two graphs can be seen in A. Macfarlane and M. Mugford, *Birth Counts: Statistics of Pregnancy and Childbirth* (1984), i. 197 (Fig. 10/1).

When the birth rate falls, as it did in this period, first births with their relatively high mortality increase as a proportion of total births. Could this have accounted for the rise in maternal mortality? Probably not, because the proportion of fifth and subsequent births, also associated with high mortality, were steadily decreasing. This was the subject of much detailed statistical analysis. The general conclusion was that because the increase in primiparity was balanced by the decrease in grand multiparity, parity changes due to the falling birth rate could not account for the rise in maternal mortality during the period with which we are concerned.[10] Munro Kerr believed that the advantage due to decreased grand multiparity more than compensated for the extra mortality associated with increased primiparity; if anything the fall in the birth rate should have produced a fall in maternal mortality. The most careful and detailed examination of the effect of parity change can be found in the 1937 report on maternal mortality. It concluded that increased primiparity accounted for at most 1 per cent of puerperal mortality for every ten years during the previous three decades.[11]

Social and Economic Factors

The proposition that high maternal mortality was predominantly due to poverty and malnutrition has provoked the liveliest debate, for there can be no doubt that women who are grossly undernourished and anaemic are more likely to die from a complication of childbirth than well-fed healthy women. The point at issue, however, is the *relative* importance of such factors in the maintenance of high maternal mortality. Some believed the general standard of living and the health of mothers was the most important determinant. We quoted Brackenbury to this effect in Chapter 3 where this question was discussed in a general way. Others supported the socio-economic side of the debate with varying degrees of fervour.[12]

[10] There is, however, one proviso. If a population changes over a relatively short period from having moderately large families starting young, to having much smaller families starting late—and this has been a tendency in recent years in Britain—an adverse parity and age effect would be likely to reach significant levels.

[11] For detailed discussion of these points, see T. A. Coghlan, *Childbirth in New South Wales* (Sydney, 1900). Dame Janet Campbell, 'Maternal Mortality', *Reports of Public Health and Medical Subjects*, 25, Ministry of Health (London, 1924); H. E. Collier, 'A study of the Influence of Certain Social Changes upon Maternal Mortality and Obstetrical Problems, 1834–1927', *Journal of Obstetrics and Gynaecology of the British Empire*, 37 (1930), 27–47; J. M. Munro Kerr, *Maternal Mortality and Morbidity* (Edinburgh, 1933), 25; Ministry of Health, *Report of an Investigation into Maternal Mortality* (London, 1937), 88–111.

[12] See M. I. Balfour and J. C. Drury, *Motherhood in Special Areas of Durham and Tyneside* (London, 1935); J. Campbell, I. D. Cameron, and D. M. Jones, 'High Maternal Mortality in Certain Areas', *Reports on Public Health and Medical Subjects*, 68, Ministry of Health (London, 1932); R. Titmuss, *Poverty and Population: A Factual Study of Contemporary Social Waste* (London, 1938); Lady Williams, 'Malnutrition as a Cause of Maternal Mortality', *Public Health*, 50 (1936–7), 11–19; C. Webster 'Healthy or Hungry Thirties?', *History Workshop Journal*, 13 (1982), 110–29. I have discussed the evidence on this point in I. Loudon, 'Obstetric Care, Social Class and Maternal Mortality', *British Medical Journal* (1986), ii. 606–8.

It has been suggested, for instance, that the rise in maternal mortality between 1929 and 1934 was a direct consequence of the economic depression. A brief glance at long-term trends in maternal mortality, however, shows there had been many similar rises in the previous fifty or sixty years which failed to show any connection with economic circumstances. To argue that the rise in maternal mortality from 1911 to 1935 reflected increasing poverty runs counter to the prevailing belief that the demographic downturn in mortality from the end of the nineteenth century can in large part be attributed to a rising standard of living. But there is direct evidence that socio-economic factors were weak determinants of maternal mortality.

If poverty was a crucial factor, maternal mortality should have been highest amongst the poor. That the reverse was true was discovered, usually with surprise bordering on disbelief, by almost everyone who investigated this proposition. As early as the eighteenth century Robert Bland suspected that the affluent classes were more likely to die in childbirth than poor women in the meanest of tenements. He put it down to the stuffy overheated bedrooms of the well-to-do and the gaping broken windows and draughts of fresh air the poor had to put up with. Definite evidence of what may be called (to contrast it with infant mortality) the 'reverse social-class gradient' of maternal mortality, was produced by Roberton in Manchester in 1851. In 1898 Cullingworth found to his surprise that maternal mortality was lowest in the poorest parts of London and highest in the affluent districts. This London differential was rediscovered by Dudfield in 1934. Fairbairn showed the same phenomenon in Leeds in the 1920s where the MMR for the city as a whole was 44.9 but the rate was 59.3 in the middle-class areas, and 30.1 in the parts inhabited by the working classes. Kerr found the same in Glasgow, and confirmed the underlying suspicion that the differential depended on the person attending the birth. He showed that where it was a doctor (mostly the middle classes) the MMR for the years 1929–31 was 50.4, but where it was a midwife (mostly the working classes) it was 26.0. The same was found in Aberdeen in 1928. In 1931, the Registrar General showed that maternal mortality was higher in social classes I and II than in IV and V (Table 14.3).

The 1937 report on maternal mortality in England and Wales examined very closely the correlation between areas of unemployment and areas of high maternal mortality and concluded there was no association in the country generally, but on the contrary there was a negative correlation with unemployment in some areas. The 1935 report on maternal mortality in Scotland did not divide maternal deaths by social class, but noted that in deaths from puerperal sepsis all social classes were affected and the authors 'gained the impression' that the rate was highest in the upper classes.[13]

[13] R. Bland, 'Midwifery Reports of the Westminster General Dispensary', *Philosophical Transactions*, 71 (1781), 355–71; J. Roberton, *Essays and Notes on the Physiology and Disease of Women* (London, 1851), 434–7; C. J. Cullingworth, 'On the Undiminished Mortality from

TABLE 14.3 *Maternal Mortality according to Social Class, England and Wales, 1930–1932*

Causes	Social Class			
	I and II	III	IV	V
All causes	44.4	41.1	41.6	38.9
Abortion	5.0	5.6	5.6	5.7
Sepsis	14.5	13.3	12.1	11.6
Haemorrhage	5.0	4.4	4.8	6.0
Toxaemia	8.1	8.1	8.4	6.8

Source: *Registrar General's Annual Statistical Review for England and Wales for 1934*, 131.

There is more important evidence still, based on the general principle that if there are two independent variables influencing a trend in the same direction and it is uncertain which is the more important, the problem can be solved by holding one variable and altering the other. In effect this was done in what became known as the 'Rochdale experiment', a well-known episode in the history of maternal mortality.

Rochdale is an industrial town in Lancashire which was hard hit during the depression. In 1930, when the town had 'the very unenviable distinction' of the highest rate of maternal mortality in Britain (it was just under 90 deaths per 10,000 deliveries) Dr Andrew Topping was appointed as the Medical Officer of Health. He found an appalling standard of maternal care: 'little short of murder' was how he described some of the deliveries. Being a man of unusually vigorous character, he 'used the pulpit, the press and the public platform', and reformed the standard of maternal care in the town, reducing the rate of maternal mortality to 17.5 by 1935. He managed this remarkable transformation during the worst years of the depression without any alteration in the social or economic circumstances of the mothers.[14] Oxley and his colleagues concluded that the high maternal mortality in Rochdale:

Puerperal Fever in England and Wales', *Transactions of the Obstetrical Society of London*, 40 (1898), 91–114; R. Dudfield, 'A survey of the Mortality due to Childbearing in London from the Seventeenth Century', *Proceedings of the Royal Society of Medicine*, 17 (1924), 59–72; Kerr, *Maternal Mortality and Morbidity*; J. Kinloch, J. Smith, and J. A. Stephen, *Maternal Mortality in Aberdeen* (Edinburgh, 1928); Ministry of Health, *Report of an Investigation into Maternal Mortality* (London, 1937), 75–81; Charlotte Douglas and Peter L. McKinlay, *Report on Maternal Morbidity and Mortality in Scotland*, Department of Health for Scotland (Edinburgh, 1935).

[14] A. Topping, 'Maternal Mortality and Public Opinion', *Public Health*, 49 (1936), 342–9.

Could not be attributed to economic disabilities from which as a highly industrialised community this borough in common with its neighbours was naturally suffering during the years of the investigation ... [but to] the existence of obstetrical factors, which, in many instances, were capable, with considerable justification, of being regarded as preventable.[15]

To all this evidence we can add the low rates of maternal mortality achieved by the out-patient lying-in charities discussed in the previous chapter. The important conclusion is not that poverty and malnutrition had no effect on the risk of dying in childbirth, but rather that the effect was surprisingly slight compared to the effect of the standard of maternal care and the type of birth-attendant. In due course I will produce evidence from the USA which is closely similar and points to the same conclusion.

The Remaining Propositions

The three remaining propositions—poor obstetric practice, the rising rate of abortion, and increasing streptococcal virulence—all require the analysis of cause-specific trends. For reasons which will appear, the most comprehensive source for these trends is Scotland, and there were certain differences in the trend in maternal mortality in Scotland compared with England and Wales.[16]

The MMR in Scotland was not only higher than in England and Wales; it rose more steeply from 1910 to 1930 and fell slightly from 1930 to 1935 (Figures 14.1 and 14.5). The rise in England and Wales was more gentle and continued without significant interruption to 1934. The rise in maternal mortality in Scotland was largely confined to deaths due to post-partum sepsis and abortion. The death rate from all causes other than sepsis remained more or less level throughout this period; and the contribution of abortion deaths to total maternal mortality was smaller in Scotland than England and Wales (Table 14.3).[17]

In Scotland until 1931, unlike England and Wales, it was customary to include associated deaths in the published rates of maternal mortality. In the 1935 report on maternal mortality in Scotland, which was based on a detailed investigation of all maternal deaths between October 1912 and early 1933, there were 2,527 maternal deaths. Of these, 62 were fortuitous deaths (and can be excluded) and 420 were associated deaths as defined in Chapter 2. Thus the number of direct or 'true' maternal deaths was 2,045. Associated deaths accounted for 17 per cent of total maternal mortality. About half the

---

[15] W. H. F. Oxley, M. H. Phillips, and J. Young, 'Maternal Mortality in Rochdale: An Experiment in a Black Area', *British Medical Journal* (1935), i. 304–7.

[16] The main Scottish sources are Douglas and McKinlay, *Report on Maternal Morbidity*; McKinlay, *Maternal Mortality in Scotland, 1911–1945* (Edinburgh, 1947).

[17] Note that in Fig. 14.5 abortion deaths are not shown separately but constitute the large majority of the deaths in the category 'other diseases of pregnancy'.

TABLE 14.4 *Deaths from Puerperal Sepsis and Abortions, England, Wales, and Scotland, 1930*

Cause of death	England and Wales, 1930 (per 10,000 births) (percentage total maternal mortality)	Scotland 1930 (per 10,000 births) (percentage total maternal mortality)
Total puerperal sepsis	19.2 (43.6)	26.6 (38.3)
Non-abortive sepsis	14.6 (33.2)	23.3 (33.6)
Septic abortion	4.6 (10.5)	3.3 (4.7)
Non-septic abortion	1.9 (4.3)	c.0.4 (0.5)
Total abortion deaths	6.5 (14.8)	3.7 (5.3)

Source: C. Douglas and P. I. McKinlay, *Report on Maternal Morbidity and Mortality in Scotland*, Department of Health for Scotland (Edinburgh, 1935).

difference between the English and the Scottish levels of maternal mortality can be attributed to the inclusion of associated deaths and half to a higher level of all direct maternal deaths. The fall in maternal mortality in Scotland between 1930 and 1935, which looks odd when you compare it with England and Wales, was entirely due to the reclassification of maternal deaths and the exclusion of associated deaths. This can be seen in the last line of Table 14.5 where the MMR due to 'other puerperal conditions' (this is where associated deaths were placed) fell from 58 in 1926–30 to 11 1931–5.[18]

There is one small difference of considerable interest but only minor statistical importance. Although they were only a minor cause of maternal mortality, there was a large increase in Scotland during the inter-war period in deaths due to 'uncontrollable vomiting of pregnancy' (hyperemesis gravidarum). This can be seen in Table 14.5 and Figure 14.5. In 1930, deaths due to this cause accounted for 5.5 per cent of Scottish maternal mortality compared with 1.3 per cent in England and Wales where there was no corresponding rise in this category. In Scotland the fall in the rate of such deaths by 1940–5 was as dramatic as the rise in the late 1920s.[19] No one has provided a convincing explanation of this anomaly, but it was noted that the women who died of this disorder were largely poor and usually had a history of a severely deficient diet, and especially protein deficiency. It is probably the only category of maternal mortality strongly associated with social class and nutritional deficiency. Why this complication of pregnancy was so conspicuous in Scotland is a mystery. A much more important cause of maternal mortality was poor obstetric care, judged by the standards of the time.

[18] Douglas and McKinlay, *Report on Maternal Morbidity*.
[19] McKinlay, *Maternal Mortality in Scotland*, 97–104.

TABLE 14.5 *Maternal Deaths by Cause in Scotland, 1911–1945*

Causes of death	Five-year periods						
	1911–15	1916–20	1921–5	1926–30	1931–5	1936–40	1941–5
All Causes	58.4	61.8	62.8	67.2	61.3	48.3	37.0
	100	106	107	115	105	83	63
Causes other than sepsis	42.3	46.2	44.1	45.8	39.8	36.3	29.9
	100	109	104	108	94	86	71
Puerperal sepsis[a]	16.2	15.6	18.7	24.1	21.5	12.0	7.1
	100	96	115	149	133	74	44
Other diseases of pregnancy	1.6	1.7	2.6	2.2	3.0	2.5	1.8
	100	106	162	137	187	156	112
Puerperal haemorrhage	8.3	8.1	7.7	7.9	7.0	6.1	5.0
	100	97	93	95	84	73	60
Toxaemia and eclampsia	10.3	9.7	10.2	11.4	10.6	9.5	7.6
	100	94	99	111	103	92	74
Uncontrollable vomiting of pregnancy	1.6	1.2	2.2	3.1	2.7	2.3	0.7
	100	75	137	194	169	144	44
Other puerperal conditions[b]	49	109	72	58	11	6	7
	100	222	147	118	22	12	14

Note: The first of each pairs of lines of values shows the maternal mortality rate per 10,000 live births, and the second shows mortality rates in each five-year period as a percentage of the rate in 1911–15.

[a] In Scotland as opposed to England and Wales, deaths from septic abortion were excluded from the category 'puerperal sepsis' and included in 'other diseases of pregnancy'.

[b] Other puerperal conditions contained deaths due to 'associated diseases' (indirect maternal deaths until 1931).

Source: P. L. McKinlay, *Maternal Mortality in Scotland, 1911–1945* (Edinburgh, 1947), 12.

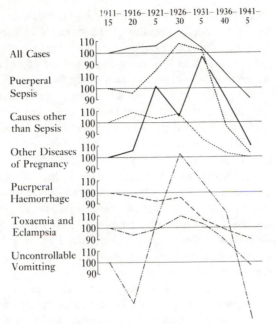

Fig. 14.5 Scotland, 1911–1945. Trend in maternal deaths due to certain causes. Deaths per 10,000 births indexed to 100 in 1911–1945
Source: P. L. McKinlay, *Maternal Mortality in Scotland, 1911–1945* (Edinburgh, 1947).

The authors of the 1935 report on maternal mortality in Scotland believed that 60 per cent of maternal deaths were due to avoidable causes. This figure, however, should be accepted with caution. It included every death in which antenatal care had been absent or inadequate, even if there was no obvious link between the cause of death and the standard of antenatal care. It also included all deaths due to abortion, and it included cases which they labelled as 'negligence' on the part of the patient. The latter included cases in which a mother allowed herself to come into contact with one of her children who had recently suffered from a septic condition. How she could have avoided doing so was not explained.

The category of avoidable deaths which cannot be dismissed, consisted of cases in which it was found there had been 'unsatisfactory obstetrics at the delivery and errors of judgement during the postnatal period'. This label was attached to one-third of all maternal deaths, and that seems a realistic figure for avoidable deaths. Most were the result of hurry and impatience leading to unnecessary interference. They were most frequent in 'the artisan and semi-professional classes' who employed a doctor and were often delivered in small hospitals where forceps rates as high as 40 per cent were recorded. Out of 532 deaths from puerperal sepsis (which excluded septic abortion) 219 followed a surgical procedure such as forceps delivery or version. Two-thirds of the latter (142) were associated with 'unsatisfactory obstetrics or errors of judgement by the attendant'. In addition there were 101 deaths due to 'failed forceps'. Therefore, at least 203 deaths were due to unnecessary or inefficient surgical deliveries—a terrible indictment of the standard of care provided by doctors, and the authors did not hesitate to say so.[20] Similar data for England and Wales are not available, but it is likely that a similar proportion of deaths due to poor obstetric practice occurred south of the border.

The contribution of abortion to maternal mortality is the most difficult to assess. It has been suggested by Shorter, for instance, that there were many 'hidden' abortion deaths and that the data on puerperal sepsis in Britain were grossly distorted.[21] His suggestion is based on the unprovable assertion that families and their famly doctors conspired very frequently to certify un-respectable abortion deaths as respectable deaths due to puerperal fever. Although I have found no evidence of a single instance, that such a cover-up occurred occasionally—perhaps when a young unmarried girl from a re-spectable middle-class family 'got into trouble' and died from the services of an abortionist—is certainly plausible. That it occurred on such a scale that the statistics were seriously distorted and nobody noticed or commented, is not.[22]

The various reports on maternal mortality, and especially the 1935 Scottish report, inquired most minutely into individual maternal deaths and were highly critical. The membership of the committees which drew up these reports contained men and women with an intimate and practical experience of the realities of public health and obstetric practice at all levels. No evidence of a large-scale cover-up of abortion deaths by certification as deaths due to puerperal fever was ever discovered, nor was it reported by the Registrars General, or by those concerned with maternal welfare at the Ministry of Health. It is unlikely that these bodies would have failed to detect and report any large-scale conspiracy to hide deaths from septic abortion under the heading of post-partum sepsis. Indeed, they might have welcomed evidence which pointed in this direction when the rising rate of deaths due to post-partum sepsis showed the medical profession in such a bad light. Shorter's assertion cannot be disproved, but it is unlikely to be true. More serious difficulties arise from the way abortion deaths were presented.

In Chapter 5 we noted the confusion that arose from placing deaths from post-abortive sepsis and post-partum sepsis together in the single category 'puerperal sepsis'. Fortunately, this method was not followed in Scotland where, until 1930, all deaths from abortion, septic and non-septic, were combined in one category, and deaths from post-partum sepsis was kept apart in a separate category. Thus we know that the rising mortality rate in Scotland due to puerperal sepsis was not due to a rising rate of abortion, but to post-partum sepsis or puerperal fever in the old terminology. In England and

---

[20] Douglas and Mackinlay, *Report on Maternal Morbidity*, 11.

[21] E. Shorter, *A History of Women's Bodies* (London, 1982), chaps. 5, 6, and 8.

[22] I have discussed this assertion in Loudon, 'Deaths in Childbed from the Eighteenth Century to 1935', *Medical History*, 30 (1986), 25–6.

Wales, although we cannot be certain, it seems probable that between 1910 and 1930 the MMR due to post-partum sepsis remained level or rose very slightly. The greater part of the rise in the rate in puerperal sepsis was due to a rise in deaths due to post-abortive sepsis.

We are left, then, with seeking an explanation for a marked rise in the rate of deaths due to post-partum sepsis between 1910 and 1935 in Scotland, and a probable slight rise in England. One of the factors responsible was probably a rise in the virulence of the strains of the streptococcus implicated in deaths due to post-partum sepsis. For the evidence behind this assertion the reader is referred to Appendix 5.

SUMMARY

It is clear that a wide range of factors were responsible for the rising trend in maternal mortality in Britain between 1910 and 1935. The standard of care provided by midwives almost certainly improved, but the major part of the improvement was probably delayed until the 1930s. As far as deliveries by doctors were concerned, poor obstetric education led to unacceptable obstetric practices in which inadequate antisepsis was combined with an unnecessary degree of interference in normal labours. It is impossible to say whether the standard of care provided by general practitioners actually worsened during this period, but there is little to suggest that it improved. Increased streptococcal virulence and a rising rate of abortion were also important factors, and rising death rates from comparatively rare conditions such as hyperemesis gravidarum made a small contribution. Lack of an adequate number of specialist obstetricians and of specialized facilities may have played a part, but the rising trend cannot be attributed to worsening social and economic conditions, to a rising proportion of first births, or to statistical artefacts. The number of avoidable deaths is a matter of opinion; it all depended on the criteria used in allocating maternal deaths to one of the two categories—avoidable and unavoidable. Some of the published estimates of avoidable deaths were exaggerated, but it is likely that at least one-third of maternal deaths during this period were due to careless obstetric practice and therefore potentially avoidable.

REGIONAL VARIATIONS

One of the most striking and least understood features of maternal mortality was the wide regional variations. I have left them to last because although they appear to offer important clues, in fact they provide little new evidence. In Scotland regional differences defy explanation. Counties with high levels of deaths from puerperal fever often had low levels from other causes and vice versa. Where areas of high total maternal mortality were identified for one period, they had changed completely in the next. There was no consistency. Sometimes the borders showed the highest levels; at other times it was the highlands or the central belt.[23] The probable explanation is random variation due to small numbers. The only moderately consistent finding was that deaths from puerperal fever were usually highest in urban areas.

In England and Wales, the regional variations were much more consistent suggesting they represented 'real' rather than chance variations. Figure 14.6 shows that maternal mortality was high in the north and west (especially Wales), and low in the south and east—the division of the country along a line from the Severn to the Wash which still appears so often in maps of rates of morbidity and mortality (for details see Appendix Table 18). This picture was broadly consistent from the 1880s to the 1930s. Usually large cities with efficient centres of obstetrics and organized maternity services (London, Edinburgh, Manchester, Liverpool, Birmingham) tended to show lower rates of mortality than other urban areas. When regional variations are shown separately for puerperal fever and other causes, the same general north-west–south-east divide remains more or less intact, but there are interesting exceptions.[24]

The highest rates of death due to puerperal fever were mostly the industrial and heavily urbanized areas such as South Wales mining valleys, almost the whole of the North of England except Cumberland, Westmorland, and Northumberland, and large parts of the Midlands. No predominantly rural counties showed high rates for puerperal fever except for Cambridgeshire, Anglesey, and the Isle of Wight. This fits quite neatly with the theory put forward by Geddes (and discussed above) that the areas with the highest mortality from puerperal fever were just those parts of the country where high density of population and frequent septic wounds associated with a high rate of industrial accidents may have generated conditions favourable for the spread of streptococcal infection. The standard of obstetric care may also have been lower in industrial towns. Puerperal fever and possibly poor standards of care tended to go together with urbanization and heavy industry.

On the other hand the highest rates of deaths due to nonseptic causes were found mostly in the more remote rural areas, parts of North Wales, Cumberland, Westmorland, and Cornwall, for instance. In such areas there were difficulties in obtaining trained birth-attendants. North Wales, where deliveries by family or neighbours persisted long after they had disappeared elsewhere, is the classic instance.[25] These conclusion were confirmed by that acute observer, Dame Janet Campbell: high maternal mortality was usually found in areas with heavy industry or in remote rural areas.[26]

[23] See Douglas and MacKinlay, *Report on Maternal Morbidity*, 47–52.

[24] See maps for the years 1921–30 in Kerr, *Maternal Mortality and Morbidity* (Edinburgh, 1933), 10.

[25] Williams, *Deaths in Childbed*.

[26] Campbell, 'Maternal Mortality'.

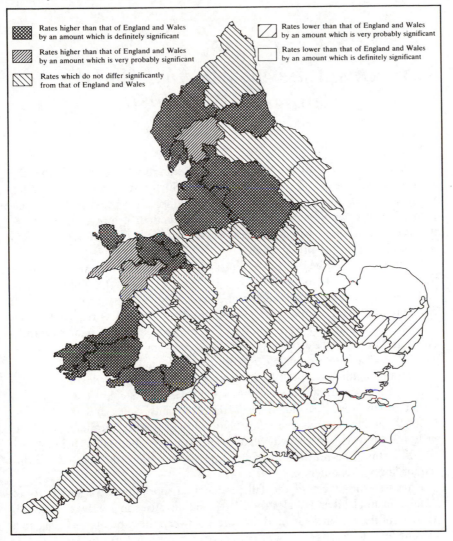

FIG. 14.6 Maternal Mortality Rates in Administrative Counties of England and Wales for the decade 1924–1933
Source: Ministry of Health, *Report of an Investigation into Maternal Mortality* (London, 1937).

15

Maternal Care and Maternal Mortality in Britain, 1935–1950

In this brief period of fifteen years, maternal mortality fell so steeply that the 1950 rate was only a fifth of the rate in 1935. Such a steep and sustained fall in maternal mortality had never occurred before. It represented a demographic change without parallel in the mid-twentieth century, all the more impressive because it has continued at virtually the same rate and without interruption up to the present time.[1]

When the decline began, those who had been involved in maternal care in the 1920s and 1930s found it hard to believe that it would continue. There had been so many false dawns in the past when a downturn in maternal mortality over two or three years was followed by a relentless rise back to the previous level, that they were haunted by the prospect of a similar pattern in the near future. At best, they thought, maternal mortality would flatten out when it reached an irreducible minimum of unavoidable deaths. Some estimated this minimum would be in the region of 1 maternal death per 1,000 births, or 10 per 10,000. In fact, this point was reached much sooner than expected—in New Zealand in 1947, England and Wales and the USA in 1948–9, the Netherlands in 1950, Belgium in 1951, and Australia in 1951–2. By 1960 the MMR in virtually all Western countries had fallen below 4 per 10,000 births. The purpose of this chapter is to explore the reasons for this extraordinary phenomenon.

What was the extent of the fall in maternal mortality in various parts of Britain? In England and Wales the MMR for all causes in 1950 was about 20 per cent of the rate in 1935, and the trend between these points was close to a straight line. In Scotland it was virtually the same. In Eire the fall was less impressive, the 1950 rate being around 36 per cent of the 1935 rate. What is remarkable is that the decline in maternal mortality as a whole seems to have been unaffected by the war which had neither an unfavourable nor a favourable influence on the risk of women dying in childbirth. Figure 15.1 shows, however, that the trend between 1935 and 1950 was quite different for various categories of maternal mortality. This suggests that the sudden and profound decline in mortality was not due to a single factor but to several

---

[1] See App. Table 1.

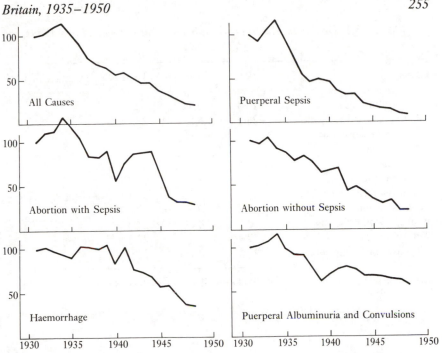

FIG. 15.1 England and Wales, 1931–1950. The trends in Maternal Mortality Rates by cause, indexed to 100 in 1931
Source: Appendix Tables 1 and 1A.

which came into operation at different periods. The most important of these factors can be listed as follows:

1. The introduction of the sulphonamides and penicillin.
2. A steep decline in the virulence of the streptococcus.
3. The introduction of ergometrine, blood transfusion on a large scale, and the growth of obstetric flying-squads, all three playing a large part in the prevention and treatment of obstetric haemorrhage.
4. Improved obstetric care in general, notably in the standard of care provided by midwives in the early phase and in hospital care in the later phase; and also a greater degree of co-operation between all concerned with maternal services and a greater degree of availability of maternal services to all the population.
5. An improvement in the standard of living and the nutritional state of the population as a whole.
6. Improvements in obstetric education.

The contribution of these factors to the fall in maternal mortality will become clear when we examine the decline in various categories of maternal deaths shown in Tables 15.1 and 15.2, and Figure 15.1.

TABLE 15.1 *Decline in Maternal Mortality by Cause, England and Wales,*
1935–1950

Cause	1935	1950	1950 as a percentage of 1935
Post-partum sepsis	10.4	0.4	3.8
All other causes than post-partum sepsis and abortion	23.7	6.8	28.7
Toxaemia	7.8	2.6	33.3
Haemorrhage	4.7	1.1	23.4
All causes excluding abortion	34.1	7.2	21.1
Septic abortion	5.2	0.9	17.3
Abortion without sepsis	2.2	0.6	27.3
Total abortion	7.4	1.5	20.3
All causes including abortion	41.5	8.7	21.0

Note: Maternal mortality rates per 10,000 births. Rates for 1950 shown as a percentage of the rates for 1935.

Source: A. Macfarlane and M. Mugford, *Birth Counts: Statistics of Pregnancy and Childbirth* (London, 1984), ii. 276–7.

TABLE 15.2 *Decline in Maternal Mortality by cause, Scotland and Eire,*
1935–1950

Cause	1935	1950	1950 as a percentage of 1935
Scotland			
Total sepsis including septic abortion	20.2	2.0	9.9
All other causes including non-septic abortion	42.8	11.0	25.7
All causes	63.0	13.0	20.6
Eire			
Total sepsis including septic abortion	15.3	2.2	14.4
All other causes including non-septic abortion	31.4	13.4	42.7
All causes	46.7	15.6	33.4

Note: Maternal mortality rates per 10,000 births. Rates for 1950 shown as a percentage of the rates for 1935.

Source: Appendix Tables 2 and 3, below.

ENGLAND AND WALES

In England and Wales deaths from haemorrhage had declined by 1950 to a rate which was 23 per cent of the 1935 rate; but the decline was not smooth and continuous. Between 1935 and 1942 the rate fell only slightly, most of the decline occurring between 1942/3 and 1950. There are two reasons for the commencement of the fall in the 1940s. First, Chassar Moir's work on ergometrine. This came into general use in the 1940s, and its widespread employment, especially the technique of intravenous ergometrine with the delivery of the anterior shoulder, greatly reduced the incidence and mortality due to post-partum haemorrhage.[2]

Secondly, blood transfusion became widely available to the civilian population as a result of wartime measures. (Blood transfusion was employed in obstetric haemorrhage before the war, but only on a limited scale.[3]) Deaths from haemorrhage still remained unnecessarily high until 1955 when the Ministry of Health advised that in cases of haemorrhage in home deliveries, the patient should be transfused at home by the flying-squad before being moved to hospital. The mortality rate from post-partum haemorrhage promptly fell from 6 to 3 per 100,000 total births.[4]

Between 1935 and 1950 deaths from toxaemia of pregnancy (puerperal albuminuria and convulsions) declined least of all. There was a relatively slight decline before the outbreak of war, possibly due to an improvement in antenatal care. During the war, deaths from toxaemia remained high. This may have been linked to the rise in illegitimate births, which is discussed below. Unmarried mothers as a whole probably received a lower standard of antenatal care.[5] Toxaemia remained the most intractable problem. Deaths in this category generally occupied second place in the list of causes until the 1930s, when, with the rapid fall in deaths due to sepsis, toxaemia became the most common cause of maternal mortality and has remained in that position. This leaves us with the decline in deaths from puerperal fever and abortion. In Scotland the decline in maternal mortality was so similar to that in England and Wales that there is no need to consider it separately.

[2] J. Chassar Moir, *Munro Kerr's Operative Obstetrics* (6th edn., London, 1956), 50, 86, 857.

[3] Most of the fall in haemorrhage deaths occurred in post-partum rather than ante-partum haemorrhage. The decline in the death rate for ante-partum haemorrhage fell from 1.8 per 10,000 births in 1939 to 0.6 by 1950, the latter figure being 33% of the former. The rate for post-partum haemorrhage, however, fell from 28 in 1939 to 5 in 1950, the latter being about 18% of the former. A. Macfarlane and M. Mugford, *Birth Counts: Statistics of Pregnancy and Childbirth*, ii (London, 1984).

[4] Personal communication, Sir George Godber. Sir George was Chief Medical Officer of Health at the Ministry of Health at the time and was responsible for the instruction.

[5] The distress that could be caused by illegitimate pregnancies under wartime conditions is described by S. Ferguson and H. Fitzgerald, *History of the Second World War: Studies in the Social Services* (London, 1954). See chap. 3 as a whole and pp. 99–102 in particular. They show that it is entirely plausible to suggest that social constraints made continuous and effective maternal care very difficult indeed for many unmarried mothers during the war.

THE DECLINE OF PUERPERAL FEVER, THE SULPHONAMIDES, AND THE STREPTOCOCCUS

In the decline in maternal mortality, puerperal fever (non-abortive sepsis) led the way. More than 80 per cent of the fall in *total* maternal mortality between the peak of 1934 and 1940 was due to a reduction of deaths from non-abortive sepsis. Only 20 per cent was due to a reduction in all other categories. There seems little doubt that the introduction of the antibiotics, first the sulphonamides, and then, after 1945, penicillin, was the reason.[6] When were the sulphonamides introduced?

Early in 1935, Professor Domagk in Germany was demonstrating the process of phagocytosis to students. He showed that if living streptococci derived from infected humans were injected into the peritoneal cavity of mice, they all died; but if the streptococci were injured by heat or chemicals before injection, some of the mice survived. He then thought of trying the experiment of administering a series of chemicals to mice just after injecting them with live streptococci. Out of the series of chemicals he used, one, chosen almost at random, was a red dye called prontosil rubrum. Twenty-six mice injected with streptococci died; a further twelve which had received a single dose of prontosil after being injected with the same strain of streptococci recovered. None of the other chemicals had any effect.

It was an astonishing result. Although the experiment was repeated elsewhere, no other scientist achieved a 100 per cent recovery rate, but the results were good enough to justify a trial of prontosil in human beings with serious streptococcal illnesses. The first few reports from Germany on the therapeutic use of prontosil in streptococcal infections were not very convincing. The most important evidence came from the work of Leonard Colebrook.[7]

Colebrook's interest in puerperal fever originated in 1926 when the wife of a close friend died of the disease. At first he worked at St Mary's Hospital until, as the reader may recall, he was appointed in 1930 as the director of the special Medical Research Council isolation block at Queen Charlotte's Hospital to investigate the prevention and treatment of puerperal fever. When he arrived at Queen Charlotte's he found it was not customary for the staff to wear gloves or masks, or even for obstetric instruments to be sterilized.[8]

---

[6] I use the term antibiotics to include the sulphonamides. The habit of referring to the sulphonamides as 'chemotherapy' and penicillin and its derivatives as antibiotics is now outmoded.

[7] The main sources for this account are L. Colebrook and M. Kenny, 'Treatment with Prontosil of Puerperal Infections due to Haemolytic Streptococci', *Lancet* (1936), ii. 1319–22; Colebrook, 'The Story of Puerperal Fever: 1800–1950', *British Medical Journal* (1956), i. 247–52; and V. Colebrook, 'Leonard Colebrook: Reminiscences on the Occasion of the 25th Anniversary of the Birmingham Burns Unit', *Injury: The British Journal of Accident Surgery*, 2/3 (1971), 182–4.

[8] V. Colebrook, 'Reminiscences', 182

Colebrook promptly introduced strict aseptic procedures throughout the hospital. This is of some importance because it cannot be argued that subsequent events in 1936 can be attributed to a change in aseptic procedures.

In 1935 Colebrook heard by chance of Domagk's work and managed with difficulty to get hold of some prontosil. He was at first reluctant give the drug to patients because of evidence of kidney damage when it was given to mice. Finally he decided to use it when a patient was admitted with puerperal septicaemia and a fever of 104 °F who was so desperately ill she seemed certain to die.[9] Prontosil was given to this patient late that day, and the staff watched her anxiously all night. Next morning her temperature was normal, and she made a full recovery. The same occurred with the next seriously ill patient whose fever of 106 °F not only came down rapidly to normal, but whose blood cultures rapidly became negative. 'This was something we had never seen before in ten years' experience', wrote Colebrook. It showed that 'the drug was being kept in the bloodstream and was absolutely restraining the growth of the streptococci and killing them without interfering with the normal defence mechanism of the body'.[10] A trial of the drug in the treatment of puerperal fever was planned and began in May 1936. The results were published in December 1936.[11]

Colebrook and Kenny showed that in the previous five years the fatality rate of cases admitted under their care (they tended to be selected severe cases) had ranged from 16.6 per cent to 31.6 per cent, with an average of about 25 per cent. The fatality rate of the patients treated with prontosil in the trial was 4.7 per cent. Other reports published in 1937 confirmed the effectiveness of sulphonamides in the treatment or prevention of puerperal fever in hospitals in London, Edinburgh, Glasgow, Belfast, and Liverpool in 1936 and 1937 showing that other obstetricians and surgeons had obtained supplies of prontosil in 1936. It is certain that sulphonamides were widely used in hospitals in 1937, and it is known they were prescribed in general practice during the same year.[12]

In 1935, scientists at the Pasteur Institute in France made what turned out to be an important observation. They suggested that prontosil rubrum was broken down in the body into a much more simple chemical, *p*-aminobenzene sulphonamide (also known as sulphanilamide) which had been known for

---

[9] Ibid.

[10] L. Colebrook, 'The Story of Puerperal Fever', 250.

[11] Colebrook and Kenny, 'Treatment with Prontosil'. Meave Kenny was Colebrook's house-surgeon at the time. A trial of prontosil album in Glasgow in 1937 was equally successful, reducing the fatality of puerperal fever from 13.4% to 1.4%. M. A. Foulis and J. B. Barr, 'Prontosil Album in Puerperal Sepsis', *British Medical Journal* (1937), i. 445–6.

[12] The evidence for these statements can be found in I. Loudon, 'Puerperal Fever, the Streptococcus and the Sulphonamides, 1911–1945', *British Medical Journal* (1987), ii. 485–90.

many years, and that in fact proved to be the case.[13] Sulphanilamide was simple to manufacture, it was cheap, and because it had been known as a chemical for a long time, it was not patented. Drug firms were quick off the mark to add it to their lists of products. As early as spring 1937, only four months after Colebrook and Kenny's paper was published, sulphonamides were available on prescription and could be used by general practitioners to treat their patients. By the end of 1937, at least twelve brands were available, although the one produced by May and Baker which became a household name as 'M & B 693' or just 'M & B' (it was sulphapyridine) did not appear until 1938 (Appendix Table 32).

Until they were upstaged in the 1940s by penicillin, there is no doubt the sulphonamides were regarded as 'miracle drugs'. They were not only extremely effective in puerperal fever. Another Medical Research Council trial in 1937 showed they were equally successful in erysipelas.[14] They were also effective in the treatment of pneumonia, meningococcal meningitis, middle-ear and mastoid disease, gonorrhoea, urinary infections, and many other conditions.[15] Interestingly, the sulphonamides were 'disappointing' in the treatment of scarlet fever, although penicillin was highly effective (see Appendix 5).[16] Hawkins and Lawrence came to the conclusion, endorsed by Taylor and Dauncey in 1954, that the introduction of the sulphonamides was 'one of the rare situations which endorse the identification of an agency of major importance as contributory to a statistical trend'.[17]

Not everyone, however, was convinced the credit should go to the sulphonamides. Some argued the sulphonamides could not have been available for general use as early as 1937, but we have shown this was not true. Others pointed out that puerperal fever mortality had already begun to fall in 1935 and 1936. They argued that this showed the virulence of the streptococcus was declining after 1934, and this, rather than the sulphonamides whose introduction at this time was coincidental, explained the fall in puerperal fever deaths.

The latter argument was based on a short-term analysis of the trend from 1930s. The long-term trend, however, shows that from the 1850s to the 1930s the trend in deaths due to puerperal fever was a series of peaks and troughs. The unusually high peak of 1934 would, on historical evidence, have been followed by a swing downwards. Thus the levels of puerperal fever

---

[13] L. Colebrook, 'The Story of Puerperal Fever'.

[14] W. R. Snodgrass and T. Anderson, 'Prontosil in the Treatment of Erysipelas: A Controlled Trial of 312 Cases', *British Medical Journal* (1937), ii. 101–4.

[15] L. Colebrook, 'The Story of Puerperal Fever', 250.

[16] H. S. Banks, *Modern Practice in Infectious Fevers*, 2 vols. (London, 1951).

[17] F. Hawkins and J. S. Lawrence, *The Sulphonamides* (London, 1950); W. Taylor and M. Dauncey, 'Changing Patterns of Mortality in England and Wales: II. Maternal Mortality', *British Journal of Preventive and Social Medicine*, 8 (1954), 172–5.

mortality in 1935 and 1936 were predictable, rather than exceptional. There was interesting evidence on this from the USA where they, too, suffered a high peak of streptococcal deaths in 1934. In the maternity department of Cook County Hospital in Chicago there was an unusually high peak of deaths due to sepsis in 1934, followed by a fall similar to that in Britain, in 1935 and 1936. In 1937, however, when the mortality in Britain had fallen to a new low level, in Chicago it began to rise again. It was not until 1939 that the trend was reversed and it should be noted that sulphonamides were not used as early in the USA as they were in Britain. Thus the authors say they 'had some sulfanilamide in 1938, and penicillin was available to the wards in 1945 in limited amounts'.[18]

Nevertheless, the argument based on a sudden and unprecedented decline in streptococcal virulence was hard to counter. It greatly concerned Colebrook in 1936, and he dealt with it at some length when he wrote his paper.[19] There is no doubt that streptococcal disease was undergoing a change. From about 1950 (and possibly a little earlier) scarlet fever became a trivial illness and had been declining in severity since the 1880s when it was deadly.[20] But for reasons explained in Appendix 5, the epidemiology of scarlet fever was quite different from the epidemiology of puerperal fever and erysipelas.

From 1937 the availability of the sulphonamides made it impossible to differentiate between a fall in streptococcal virulence and a fall due to therapy. The most striking evidence in favour of the sulphonamides, however, has been quoted above. Even when virulence of the streptococcus was declining (and there is little doubt that it was), there were still many cases of streptococcal disease—cases of puerperal fever and erysipelas—who were so ill that almost certainly they would have died before 1937, and those who recovered would have done so after a long and extremely anxious illness. When such cases were treated with the sulphonamides, however, what was new and almost unbelievable at the time, was the speed of recovery and conversion of positive blood cultures into negative ones. If sulphonamides were widely used in 1937, and we have evidence they were, they could indeed have brought about a 'demographic downturn'. Between 1935 and 1950, although declining streptococcal virulence played a part in lowering mortality from puerperal fever, it was a relatively small part compared with the use of antibiotics. Of the two factors, the antibiotics were the most important.

---

[18] J. E. Fitzgerald, A. Webster, 'Nineteen-Year Survey of Maternal Mortality at Cook County Hospital', *American Journal of Obstetrics and Gynaecology*, 65 (1953), 528–33.

[19] Colebrook and Kenny, 'Treatment with Prontosil'.

[20] There had been previous periods when scarlet fever had been a mild illness—the 1830s, for example—but the general feeling remained that by the 1950s the streptococcus has lost much of its venom, and it is undeniable that in Western countries rheumatic fever and acute nephritis, previously common, were rare by the 1960s. Whether the antibiotics were responsible for this change has been hotly debated, but the weight of evidence is against that hypothesis.

THE DECLINE IN MATERNAL MORTALITY
AND THE SECOND WORLD WAR

In the first part of this chapter we noted that the decline in maternal mortality by cause of death revealed different patterns which are shown in Figure 15.1; and we discussed the decline in deaths from haemorrhage and toxaemia. Apart from changes due to straightforward clinical advances however, there were changes in the provision of maternal care; and these were intimately bound up with events in the Second World War.

In the final years of the 1930s there was some improvement in maternity services, and in social and economic conditions compared with the depression years. Increasing concern through the 1930s over the poor quality of maternity services was rammed home by the series of reports on maternal mortality, especially the 1937 report which was much more thorough and disturbing than its predecessors.[21] Care provided by midwives probably improved most of all as a consequence of the Midwives Acts of 1936 (England and Wales) and 1937 (Scotland). More maternity beds were provided and an increasing number of specialist obstetricians were being trained, largely because of the activities of the Royal College of Obstetricians and Gynaecologists; but the overall scale of improvement was slight.

The network of maternity services which covered the country at the outbreak of war had one primary characteristic: it was strong in some places, weak in others . . . Country districts were often badly served . . . Even within towns, where the services were numerically adequate, quality varied from one district to another . . . One of the most disquieting features of all was the maldistribution of obstetric skill. In some parts of the country specialist advice in childbirth was almost unobtainable.[22]

Perhaps the worst feature of all was the fragmentation of the maternity services.

The health visitor, the domiciliary midwife and the hospital, all supposed to work hand in hand, were often responsible to different authorities and boards. The medical officer at the local clinic was cut off from the institutional services and never saw a confinement. The general medical practitioner, unless he was called in privately, or happened to be employed by a local authority, did not come into the picture at all, except in domicilary emergency cases, if he was prepared to attend them. More often than not, when he was called in by a midwife, he saw the patient for the first time and knew nothing about her history.[23]

This description of general practice obstetrics may have been true of London, but it was inaccurate elsewhere; there was still a substantial amount of

---

[21] This report, although published in 1937, was based on maternity during the period 1929–34. The introduction of the sulphonamides was barely mentioned and there was no confidence that maternal mortality was about to decline.

[22] Ferguson and Fitzgerald, *History of the Second World War*, 29.

[23] Ibid. 72–3 (app. III).

deliveries by general practitioners in small towns and country areas, some taking place in cottage hospitals. But it is at least partially true that the hallowed belief in midwifery as the linchpin of general practice was dented. General practitioners grumbled about the low fees, the time involved at the bedside, and the anxiety and effort. There were signs of a tendency for senior and experienced practitioners to abandon midwifery as soon as they could afford to do so, or leave it to assistants and junior partners. Antenatal care had been a disappointment. It failed to reduce maternal mortality. Much had been expected, but little had come of all the efforts to establish clinics. It was suggested the reason was either a poor standard of antenatal care, or a failure of patients to attend in early pregnancy, or both.[24] In fact, what was lacking was continuity of care. Antenatal care is rarely effective when maternity services are fragmented.

Such was the state of affairs in August 1939, a few days before the outbreak of war when the emergency maternity service was established in the 'late-summer days of 1939 [and] feats of improvisation were achieved which bordered on the impossible'. In the end it was indeed a remarkable service.[25] It has been said that 'War is good for babies.' Was the Second World War good for mothers? The brief answer is yes, on the whole; provided your country was not occupied by the enemy. In Britain the war led to a number of changes in maternal care which would have occurred eventually but not as rapidly as they did. Blood transfusion is an example we have mentioned. Another is nutrition. It may seem to be a paradox that shortage of food and rationing led to improved nutrition, but improved economic conditions from war work together with rationing ensured a more equable supply and a more balanced diet for women whose diet had been poor partly from poverty, partly from tradition. The Scottish women who died from hyperemesis gravidarum, as described above, are an example. Further, expectant mothers were provided with vitamins and iron as well as extra milk. The number of pregnant women with moderate or severe iron-deficiency anaemia fell as a result, and some attribute the fall in deaths due to post-partum haemorrhage during the war to this factor.[26]

There were other more subtle consequences. The acceptance in war of a degree of regimentation, such as identity cards and the need to register and apply to authorities for ration cards and food and mineral supplements, encouraged women to 'put themselves under supervision early in pregnancy'. In large part it established a habit of early antenatal care and taking iron tablets which was standard by the end of the war.[27] The war also led to an

---

[24] Royal College of Obstetricians and Gynaecologists and Population Investigation Commitee, *Maternity in Great Britain* (London, 1948), chap. 4.

[25] Ferguson and Fitzgerald, *History of the Second World War*, chap. 2.

[26] *Maternity in Great Britain*, 36.

[27] Ibid.

unprecedented expansion of hospital beds. It was estimated that there were some 10,000 maternity beds in England and Wales in 1938 and over 15,000 in 1945. Very little of this expansion was in voluntary hospitals or nursing homes; nearly all of it was in local authority institutions and emergency maternity homes.[28]

The emergency maternity service had been established in 1939 in the expectation of early and heavy bombing. Arrangements were made to evacuate expectant mothers at the outbreak of war. Evacuated they were, in large numbers, but there was an anticlimax when the expected bombing did not occur. Many mothers (especially those who had left their children behind when evacuated) simply turned around and went back home, leaving empty beds behind them.

To preserve the maternity units that had been created with such effort and amazing speed, a 'trickle scheme' was introduced. Instead of evacuation *en masse*, small numbers of mothers were persuaded to travel to emergency maternity homes a few weeks before their baby was due. This kept the scheme open and flexible for the time when it was really needed, when the 'blitz' began. From then on there were few vacancies in maternity beds. Moreover, when the 'blitz' was over, the authorities were surprised by the continuing demand for these beds.

This was not evacuation in the accepted sense of the term ... The women who registered [for evacuation] did not seek safety but maternity beds ... The emergency homes, which had been useful as an insurance against air attack, had become an indispensable extension of social services ... The 2,800 beds in the emergency homes, sufficient for roughly 56,000 births annually (an average of twenty confinements per bed per year), had become an asset more precious than had been foreseen by the planners and organisers in 1939.[29]

The excess could not be managed as home deliveries. There was a desperate shortage of domiciliary midwives who were already overworked to a worrying extent. The increasing demand for maternity beds was met by shortening the long lying-in period that had been customary.

Although the emergency maternity homes were dismantled by 1947, the experience gained by mothers and the authorities from the emergency maternity service instilled new habits and aroused new expectations. The old tradition in the poorest areas of little or no antenatal care and delivery at home by a handywoman, which was of course dying through the 1930s, was totally abolished. Hospital delivery came even higher on the list of women's demands than it had been before the war. Tables 15.3 and 15.4 show the extent to which this demand had been met. Most important of all was the way the

[28] Ferguson and Fitzgerald, *History of the Second World War*, 72–3 (app. III).
[29] Ibid. 40 and 46.

TABLE 15.3 *Live Births in Institutions as a Percentage of Total Live Births, England and Wales, 1927, 1932, 1937, and 1946*

	1927	1932	1937	1946
England and Wales	15.0	24.0	34.8	53.8
South East	23.7	33.7	46.8	—
Midlands	11.4	18.6	26.7	—
South West	11.0	17.4	24.9	—
North	8.2	11.6	19.1	—
Wales	4.6	8.2	17.0	—

Note: The data for 1927 to 1937 are based on births for the whole of each year; those for 1946 on all births in the week 3–9 Mar. 1946.

Source: *Registrar General's Statistical Review 1937*, 217; *Maternity in Britain* (1948).

TABLE 15.4 *Circumstances of Confinement in Three Selected Occupational Groups and for All Mothers, England and Wales, 1946*

	Wives of			All mothers
	Professional and salaried workers	Manual workers	Agricultural workers	
Number	1,127	8,926	567	13,514
Home (percentage)	23.8	49.9	55.2	46.2
Hospital				
Booked (percentage)	26.7	40.0	33.6	38.6
Unbooked (percentage)	1.0	2.0	4.0	2.2
Private ward (percentage)	9.6	1.4	2.0	2.5
Nursing home (percentage)	39.0	6.8	5.2	10.6

Source: Based on *Maternity in Great Britain* (1948), 54.

emergency medical service had provided specialist care in areas where none had existed, leading to a determination that the uneven distribution of specialist services, including maternity, should not be allowed to return to the pre-war state when the war had ended.

If the health of mothers and the standard of obstetrics improved throughout the war, it was due to planning inspired by a sense of urgency and freed from the financial constraints imposed in the 1930s. Food rationing with special supplements and the work of the emergency maternity service contributed to the sustained fall in maternal mortality and in retrospect became part of the foundations of a National Health Service system of comprehensive maternal care.

The only remaining cause of maternal mortality to be considered is abortion. Within the context of maternal mortality it was a major cause of death, but it stood alone as something which was often illegal, which most people found distasteful, and many considered immoral. Abortion tended to raise in the 1930s, as it still does today, violent emotion and prejudice; and partly for this reason it is the most complex part of this chapter.

ABORTION, ILLEGITIMACY, AND THE WAR

We should begin by recalling three features of abortion. First, a large majority of cases with complications occurred in married women. In a survey of 2,665 cases of abortion admitted to hospital between 1935 and 1950, 2,350 were married women, 303 were single, and 12 were widows.[30] Secondly, a large majority of these were induced abortions. Where abortion was accompanied by fever it was considered proof that abortion was induced. It was estimated in the above series of abortions that 90 per cent of all cases admitted to St Giles and Dulwich Hospitals in London were either self-induced or induced by someone else.[31] The third point is that the organisms found in fatal cases of septic abortion were quite different from those found in deaths from post-partum sepsis. A large majority of the latter were due to *Streptococcus pyogenes* against which the sulphonamides were highly effective. In septic abortion, however, there was a much wider and more varied bacterial spectrum. Only a minority of cases were infected with *Streptococcus pyogenes* and only some of the other organisms were sensitive to sulphonamides; many were not.[32]

Septic Abortion and Social Factors

Figure 15.1 shows that the trend in deaths from septic abortion fell into three distinct phases between 1935 and 1950. The first phase was a steep fall from 1935 to 1940. This was followed by a rise and a plateau of mortality from 1941 to 1944; and finally, from 1945 to 1950, mortality fell more steeply than ever before. It is difficult to explain the initial fall in deaths from septic abortion in terms of social and economic factors although one could speculate that improved conditions following the depression led to better maternal health and greater resistance to infection, and also removed some of the desperation at the prospect of another mouth to feed.

What is striking, however, is the way that deaths from septic abortion rose

[30] A. Davis, '2,665 Cases of Abortion: A Clinical Survey', *British Medical Journal* (1950), ii. 123–30.

[31] Ibid. 124.

[32] Ibid. 152 (tables V and VI).

during the war. A rise in deaths suggests a rise in the incidence of induced abortion, and immediately raises the possibility of changes in social behaviour. For instance, it was widely believed that the war increased the likelihood of casual sexual encounters. Millions of young men and women left home, escaping from the watchful eyes of families and neighbours. With the wartime tendency for restraints to be removed and caution thrown to the winds, an increase in unwanted pregnancies was probably inevitable.

War mentality is a mixture of violent contrasts . . . There is much loneliness but also much social activity . . . there is comradeship and there is love . . . As millions of men and women are taken out of their usual surroundings, new associations are formed . . . Meanwhile in the ports, in the amusement centres of the cities and in the public houses of country towns and villages, British, Dominion, and Allied soldiers, sailors and airmen with money in their pockets and time on their hands seek entertainment and companionship.[33]

If there was an increase in unwanted pregnancies, it is likely that some were conceived by married women during their husbands' absence in the armed services or elsewhere. In these, the motives for terminating the pregnancy before their husbands returned home were obviously powerful. The number of such abortions is, of course, unknown, but it may have been large enough to play a significant part in the rise in deaths from septic abortion. The next and more difficult question is that of unwanted pregnancies conceived out of wedlock.

Septic Abortion and Illegitimacy

The majority of cases of, and deaths due to, septic abortion between 1935 and 1950 occurred amongst married women. Did the war produce a rise in septic abortion amongst single women? We may well think so, because of the very considerable rise in the percentage of illegitimate births from 1940 to 1945, followed by a fall in 1946 and 1947. This can be seen in column 3 of Table 15.5. There was also a marked fall in the percentage of premarital conceptions in which the parents married before the baby was born, as shown in column 4 of the same table. Taken together, these statistics suggest that the war led to a rise in premarital conceptions from casual sexual encounters with the possibility of a corresponding rise in induced abortion.

This was widely believed during the war. It was regarded as axiomatic that changed attitudes had led to moral laxity and a large increase in casual sex. It was often said that premarital conceptions in which the father was over the hills and far away long before the baby was born, were a wartime feature. If that was true, unmarried mothers left high and dry and in danger of losing their jobs and their wartime billets, would have had strong motives for an induced abortion. But was there, in fact, a rise in premarital conceptions?

---

[33] Ferguson and Fitzgerald, *History of the Second World War*, 88–99.

TABLE 15.5 *Maternal Deaths from Abortion and Illegitimate Maternities, England and Wales, 1938–1948*

Year	Rate of deaths due to septic abortion[a]	Rate of deaths due to non-septic abortion[b]	Illegitimate maternities as a percentage of all maternities[c]	Irregular conceptions regularized by marriage (percentage)[d]	Maternities conceived out of wedlock (percentage of all maternities)[e]
1938	3.5	2.0	4.30	70.2	14.6
	100	100	100	100	100
1939	3.9	1.8	4.20	69.4	13.8
	111	90	98	99	94
1940	2.6	1.7	4.39	68.1	13.7
	74	85	102	97	94
1941	3.3	1.9	5.43	57.4	12.7
	94	95	126	82	87
1942	3.5	1.1	5.64	52.0	11.8
	100	55	131	74	81
1943	3.5	1.2	6.44	45.4	11.8
	100	60	149	65	81
1944	3.2	0.9	7.39	40.1	12.3
	91	45	172	57	84
1945	2.5	1.0	9.36	37.1	14.9
	71	50	217	53	102
1946	1.3	0.6	6.61	44.1	11.8
	37	30	154	63	81
1947	1.0	0.5	5.32	55.7	12.0
	28	25	124	79	82
1948	1.1	0.5	5.41		
	31	25	126		

Note: For each year, the upper row of figures is the rate of percentage, and the lower row gives values indexed to 100 in 1938.

   [a] Rate of deaths per 10,000 total births.
   [b] Rate of deaths per 10,000 total births.
   [c] Illegitimate maternities expressed as a percentage of all maternities.
   [d] Maternities conceived out of wedlock (irregular maternities) but regularized by marriage of the parents before birth, expressed as a percentage of all irregular maternities.
   [e] Total maternities conceived out of wedlock, consisting of all illegitimate maternities and all maternities conceived out of wedlock but regularized by marriage, expressed as a percentage of all maternities, legitimate and illegitimate.

Source: Registrar General's Statistical Reviews; A. Macfarlane and M. Mugford, *Birth Counts: Statistics of Pregnancy and Childbirth* (London, 1984); S. Ferguson and H. Fitzgerald, *Studies in Social Services* (London, 1954), 91.

Premarital conceptions were common before the war. In 1938 the Population (Statistics) Act showed that a large proportion of first births to married women were conceived before marriage; approximately one-seventh of all children born 1938–9 were products of premarital conceptions. The surprising fact, however, is that during the war the proportion of premarital conceptions which ended in childbirth not only failed to rise; it actually fell compared with 1938 and 1939 (see column 5 of Table 15.5).

The explanation is simple. Total premarital conceptions are calculated by adding together the two categories, illegitimate births and births conceived out of wedlock but occurring within wedlock. Although there was a sharp rise during the war in the first category, there was a marked fall in the second. About 37,000 legitimate births were conceived out of wedlock in 1943 and 1944 compared with 66,000 in 1938 and 60,000 in 1939.[34] As Ferguson and Fitzgerald explain, 'It can only be concluded that war factors prevented or hindered the regularisation of maternities conceived out of wedlock.' Apart from unmarried fathers being killed on active service or taken prisoner, there was the 'transfer of men to war stations. This made immediate marriage increasingly difficult and, in many cases, quite impossible.'[35]

The popular notion that the war produced a huge increase in premarital conceptions in young girls is a myth.[36] When premaritally conceived maternities were calculated in terms of maternal age, it was found that during the war they were more common in women aged 25–9, and even more in women aged 30–4 than they were in women under the age of 25.[37]

If, then, we are tempted to argue that a wartime increase in premaritally conceived maternities was probably accompanied by a corresponding rise in premarital conceptions which were aborted, since there was no increase in births conceived out of wedlock there is no reason to postulate an increase in induced abortion in unmarried women. There is, however, a weakness in this argument. There is no necessary connection between premarital conceptions on the one hand, and unwanted pregnancies and induced abortions on the other. It is, for instance, highly likely that a majority of premarital conceptions before the war occurred not as a result of casual sex between strangers, but amongst young men and women who had often known each other for some time and had every intention of getting married sooner or later. They would simply marry and produce a 'premature' baby. It was much the same during the war except that wartime separation often prevented marriage until after the child was born. During the war, however, there may have been a much higher incidence of premarital conceptions from casual sexual encounters in which there was no likelihood of marriage, and consequently stronger motives

---

[34] Ibid. 91 (Table 2).
[35] Ibid. 92.
[36] Ibid. 95.
[37] Ibid. 93–96 (Table 3).

for an induced abortion. This, of course, is speculation, for the data do not distinguish between illegitimate births resulting from casual sex, and those resulting from what one might call delayed marriage.

Thus, if there is a social explanation for the wartime rise in deaths from septic abortion, it may have been the result of a rise in the incidence of induced abortion in three categories of women. First, married women who were pregnant by another man while their husbands were away; second, pregnancies in single women as a result of casual sexual encounters; third, married women with several children who became pregnant by their husbands, and in the atmosphere of sexual liberation during the war were more ready to seek the services of an abortionist than they would have been before the war.

Septic Abortion and Clinical Factors

The role of social factors in the trend in septic abortion is inevitably uncertain. When we come to clinical factors we are on slightly firmer ground. The initial fall from 1935 to 1940 in deaths from septic abortion may well have been due to the treatment of cases in which the infection was due to an organism which responded to the sulphonamides.[38] The levelling out of the death rate during the war may have reflected the residual mortality due to infections by organisms which did not respond to the sulphonamides. By the end of the war, however, penicillin became available and proved to be an effective treatment for many of the cases of septic abortion in which the sulphonamides were ineffective. The introduction of the sulphonamides was the major advance in post-partum sepsis; penicillin was the major advance in the treatment of septic abortion. And this is shown by the steepness of the post-war decline in septic abortion deaths which brought the mortality rate down to a level in 1950 which was 17 per cent of the rate in 1935 (Table 15.1). It seems most likely that antibiotics were largely responsible for the decline in septic abortion deaths before and after the war, while the plateau of deaths during the war may have been due to a combination of social and clinical factors.

Non-Septic Abortion

From 1935 to 1941 the mortality trend in non-septic abortion followed a similar pathway to septic cases. From 1941 until 1944, however, the trends for septic and non-septic abortion followed different paths. Deaths from non-septic abortion fell while those from septic abortion remained high. Haemorrhage was much the most common cause of death in non-septic abortion.[39] It

---

[38] Davis, '2,665 Cases of Abortion'. In this review of 2,665 cases, gross infection occurred in 124 cases. There were 373 cases in the years before penicillin which were treated by sulphonamides, showing that this antibiotic was in fact used in septic abortion before penicillin became available.

[39] Ibid. In this review of 2,665 cases, 'gross haemorrhage requiring transfusion' occurred in 68 cases.

is probable that the wider availability of blood transfusion was the reason for the decline in deaths from non-septic abortion during the war. This suggestion is strengthened by the finding that the most conspicuous fall occurred between 1941 and 1942 when the rate was reduced from 1.9 to 1.1, and that this coincided with the fall in deaths due to post-partum haemorrhage.

We can summarize these findings as follows:

- It is possible that the fall in mortality due to septic abortion between 1935 and 1940 was mainly due to the sulphonamides, but improved social and economic circumstances may have played a part as well.
- It is probable that the plateau of deaths from septic abortion during the war was largely due to an increased incidence of illegal abortion associated with unwanted pregnancies; but an additional factor may have been that mortality levelled out as a result of a substantial number of deaths due to organisms insensitive to the sulphonamides.
- Almost certainly the steep fall in septic abortion deaths from 1944 to 1945 was due to penicillin, for it was also seen in other countries from the time when penicillin became available.
- The fall in non-septic deaths during the war was probably due most of all to increased blood transfusion.

CONCLUSIONS

We hear much criticism of maternity services today. Childbirth, it is said, has become too technological and impersonal, too much dominated by male obstetricians and divorced from the family. Obstetricians, it is said, are prone to resort too readily to induction, instrumental delivery, or Caesarean section, and too little attention is paid to maternal satisfaction. A minority of women would like to see the reintroduction of home delivery, placing childbirth back in the heart of the family. At the same time mothers today expect a satisfying delivery and a perfect baby. It is a trace ironic that women and their families rarely sued a doctor for malpractice before the Second World War when cases of negligence were often gross and not uncommon, yet today, when such malpractice is rare, obstetrics is the speciality most plagued by actions for malpractice.

Whatever the merits of current criticisms and legal actions, there can be no doubt of the dramatic reduction in maternal and perinatal mortality. The years 1935–50 saw the beginning of a trend which has transformed the process of childbirth. Women still die in childbirth, but only one dies today where fifty died less than sixty years ago and a similar reduction in perinatal mortality has been achieved.

At the beginning of this study I asked two questions. First, why was there a plateau of maternal mortality? Second, what factors were responsible for the steep decline in maternal deaths? We can now see that the answer to the second question was a wide range of factors which came into effect not simultaneously but one after the other in sequence. There can be no doubt of the paramount importance of clinical factors such as the sulphonamides, penicillin, blood transfusion, and ergometrine; and obstetricians would point to other important advances: greatly improved obstetric anaesthesia and the expectant treatment of placenta praevia are two examples. Equally there is little doubt that obstetric education has improved. Likewise, ever since the 1930s there have been marked improvements in the provision of maternal care with co-operation to a degree that was rare during the inter-war period between general practitioners, midwives, and obstetricians. Without close co-operation antenatal care and prevention is almost inevitably ineffective. There has also been a steady improvement in the availability of maternal care at all levels, and mothers are in general more healthy than they used to be. It would be difficult to exaggerate the contribution of the National Health Service to all these changes.

Knowing what has happened since, how should we view maternal care in Britain between 1900 and the beginning of the decline in maternal mortality just before the Second World War? A charitable view would be that this was a period in which the foundations were laid without which all the improvements listed above could not have occurred. Changes did occur, and if they were slow and incomplete such processes often are. They take time. They cannot be hurried. If you want evidence of change and appreciation of the need for change you can find it in the reports on maternal mortality. The authorities and the committees—the obstetric 'establishment'—were aware of the dangers of childbirth, were not afraid to criticize doctors and midwives where criticism was deserved, and were capable of producing sensible recommendations. In short, people concerned with maternal care did the best they could in difficult circumstances. In the light of the political and social and economic circumstances of the time, and in the absence of any effective treatment for puerperal fever, little more could have been done than was done. If maternal mortality was high it was the best that could be achieved.

That might be one view, but it would be hard to defend. It would be nearer the truth to say that maternal care in the inter-war period was characterized by apathy, patchiness, parsimony in the provision of funds, national and local government, a tendency in medical schools to treat obstetrics as 'midder'—an unimportant part of the medical curriculum, not to be taken too seriously, which the student got out of the way as quickly as possible—and by standards of obstetric care which were clearly deficient if not negligent by the standards and knowledge of the time. It is true that it would not have been possible to reduce maternal mortality in the inter-war period to the level achieved in 1950 of less than 10 per 10,000 births, but it should have been possible to reduce it well below 30. The work of a few people such as Dr Andrew Topping in

Rochdale and Dr Oxley in the East End of London, as well as the record of the Queen's Institute rural nurse-midwives, demonstrates the enormous gap that existed between what could be achieved and what was achieved; and the maternity services of the Second World War showed that the provision of maternal care could be transformed in a very short time, given the will.

Here then I have presented two views of maternal care and maternal mortality in the period from 1900 to 1935. Perhaps the truth lies somewhere in the middle. But I think we will be in a much better position to pass judgement when we have looked at the provision of maternal care in other countries and compare them with Britain. And I would stress that by maternal care I mean not only the actions of governments, institutions, bodies, and committees, with their headed notepaper, but everything that bears on child-birth from deliveries by neighbours in remote areas to deliveries in large and prestigious maternity hospitals in the cities. This brings us to the chapters on childbirth in the United States of America.

16

The Geography and Politics of Maternal Care in the USA: Introduction

In the analysis of maternal mortality one of the factors which is often over-looked is the geographical features of a region or country. To some extent they are the key to understanding the differences between the USA and European countries. Europeans often forget the sheer size and variety of the USA. Many states are larger than European countries. Texas could accommodate the whole of France and the whole of England and Wales except for Devon and Cornwall. England and Wales, which are almost exactly the same size as Georgia, could be fitted with room to spare into some twenty states, while the area of Belgium and the Netherlands combined is actually smaller than that of forty states in the USA.

Differences in size were accompanied by differences in density of population. In 1900 the population density of Montana (a state more than twice the size of England and Wales) was about 2 persons per square mile. Arizona, when it was incorporated in the Union in 1912, had only 1.1 persons per square mile. Even the more heavily populated states had population densities which were lower than the countries of Europe. In 1900, Pennsylvania and New York State had population densities of 140 and 150 respectively compared with 588 for Belgium, 558 for England and Wales, 448 for the Netherlands, 290 for Germany, and 189 for uncrowded France (Appendix Table 24). Apart from size and density of population, the extraordinary range of physical, social, and racial factors in the USA could scarcely fail to affect the nature and provision of medical care in general, and maternal and infant care in particular.

In the first half of this century there was a much wider variety in maternal care in the various states of the USA than there was in the whole of Western Europe. In England it was rare, even in the nineteenth century, for country patients to live more than seven or eight miles from a medical practitioner or twenty miles from a hospital. In the USA it was not uncommon in the 1920s to find that the only birth-attendant within fifty miles was a neighbour, an amateur with a smattering of self-taught midwifery. It was not that medical practitioners were rare; just that the population was so often scattered. In 1910 there was one doctor for every 609 members of the population—more than in any country in Europe. 'Even the most adventurous medical graduates, travelling to the settlements in the West, often found other doctors there before them.[1] Size and distance meant isolation, not only for patients but also for practitioners living in isolated areas, cut off from hospitals, colleagues, and all knowledge of medical advances unless they were assiduous readers of medical journals.[2]

Isolation also allowed the perpetuation within immigrant communities of childbirth customs imported from Europe. In rural communities of Polish origin it was still common in the 1920s to find home deliveries attended solely by a midwife and an attendant group of women, with men rigidly excluded from the delivery room. Physicians were rarely summoned, and only for the most dire emergencies. This could occur when, in nearby communities of native-born Americans in the same state who were living under similar conditions, following the same occupations, and enjoying the same standards of living, mothers were invariably delivered by physicians (often in small hospitals) and midwives were unknown. A much larger proportion of the American population than the European lived in remote rural areas. In the general migration of the rural population to towns which took place in all Western countries, the urban population in England had reached the 50 per cent mark *c.*1850. In 1935, 54 per cent of the population of the USA were still living in areas designated as rural and in 1940 one-third of the population lived in areas designated as 'isolated' (Table 16.1).

There was, then, a great deal of rural midwifery, and much of it was rough and ready. It is true that when hospital delivery was thoroughly fashionable in the 1940s, hospitals were often found even in small remote towns. Some were well equipped, but others were little more than a back room with two beds behind a physician's office, masquerading under the title of 'clinic' or 'maternity home'.[3]

There was almost as much variety in cities where recent immigrants often employed fellow-countrywomen as midwives for home deliveries when a few blocks away their native-born American counterparts would invariably employ a physician and choose delivery in a hospital. The variety of maternal care, rural and urban, was associated (but not by any means in a straightforward fashion) with a wide range of maternal mortality rates. With such a large and scattered population the statistics of maternal mortality in the 1920s were alarming:

---

[1] Rosemary Stevens. *In Sickness and in Wealth: American Hospitals in the Twentieth Century* (New York, 1989), 53. In the USA there were 164 physicians per 100,000 population in 1910 compared with 55 in England and fewer than 50 in Austria and the German Empire.

[2] In 1906 the average distance between places having physicians in the USA was 12 miles. In New England states it was 6.9 miles. In the central states it ranged from about 8 to 12 miles. In the mountain states it was 38.7 miles. By 1923 these figures had hardly altered. *Final Report of the Commission on Medical Education* (New York, 1932), table 65.

[3] F. E. Whitacre and E. W. Jones, *Maternity Care in Two Counties, Gibson County, Tennessee and Pike County, Mississippi, 1940–41, 1943–44* (New York, 1950).

TABLE 16.1 *Characteristics of County Groups in the States of the USA Based on the 1940 Census*

County Group	Number of counties	Number of States having counties of given kind	Proportion of US births 1944–8 (percentage)
Metropolitan	240	—	52
Greater[a]	63	14	26
Lesser[b]	177	39	26
Adjacent[c]	668	44	15
Isolated	2,168		33
Semi-rural[d]	1,116	45	25
Rural[e]	1,052	43	8
All counties USA	3,076	—	100

[a] Counties including cities of 1 million inhabitants or more.
[b] Counties including cities of 0.5–1 million inhabitants.
[c] Counties bordering on or having ready access to a greater or lesser metropolitan county.
[d] Counties not so bordering and having 2,500 or more population.
[e] All other counties.

Source: Children's Bureau, Statistical Series No. 12. *Infant and Maternal Mortality in Metropolitan and Outlying Counties, 1944–1948*, Federal Security Agency, Social Security Administration, Children's Bureau (Washington, DC, 1950).

Statistics compiled by the Children's Bureau . . . indicate that of the more than two million full-term pregnancies occurring in this country annually, nearly twenty-five thousand of the mothers succumb . . . For every patient who succumbs, it does not seem too much to claim that ten are seriously ill, or in other words, that the annual puerperal morbidity in this country totals not less than two hundred and fifty thousand . . . [It is] a catastrophe that does not find a parallel in our social or economic life.[4]

THE POLITICS OF MATERNAL CARE IN THE USA

In most Western European countries, maternal care was subject to some degree of control and regulation by the state, local government, medical institutions such as medical colleges and academies, or a combination of all three. Although the degree of control varied, policies on maternal care were generally supported by the public and the medical and nursing professions. Legislation on maternal and child health was seen as a proper activity for governments from the nineteenth century onwards. This was not the case to anything like the same extent in the USA.[5]

[4] P. Brooke Bland, 'Puerperal Morbidity and Mortality', *Medical Journal and Record*, 129 (1929), 83.
[5] In this brief account of the maternal and child programmes in the USA I am especially indebted to the work of R. W. Wertz and D. C. Wertz, *Lying-in: A History of Childbirth in America*

When Lemuel Shattock (1793–1859), storekeeper, bookseller, and publisher (but not physician) moved to Boston in the mid-1830s he undertook the work which led to the publication of his *Report of the Sanitary Commission* in 1850. It has been described as the most significant document on public health ever published in the USA, and he observed that governments in the USA had 'legislated for property, but not for life. They have cared for the lands, the cattle, the money of their constitutents, but not for their health and longevity.'[6] The explanations are commonplace. America was a young country. It had taken centuries in Europe with its stable populations to establish systems of medical care from which maternal and child welfare evolved. Numerous isolated communities and highly mobile populations made legislation difficult to enforce. Most of all, perhaps, it was the tradition of rugged individualism and the frontier mentality which provoked hostility to 'unnecessary interference' in social and medical matters.

Nevertheless, if the population demanded action for mothers and children politicians ignored them at their peril. American motherhood was a sacred concept. For this reason, a small but powerful group of educated middle-class women in the nineteenth century, who were involved in such philanthropic schemes as Hull House in Chicago and the Henry Street Settlement in New York, were able to play an important part in improving the treatment of mothers and children in deprived areas.[7] Two of them, Lillian Wald and Florence Kelly, persuaded President Theodore Roosevelt in 1909 to convene the first of a decennial series of White House Conferences on the health of children. The idea of the Children's Bureau emerged from this conference. It was an immensely influential institution, staffed mostly by a series of able, energetic, and remarkable women. The Bureau produced a long series of reports on all aspects of maternal and child health and welfare from maternal and infant mortality to juvenile delinquency. For the historian of maternal and child health these reports are the single most important source from 1912 to the 1940s. The Bureau was also instrumental in the establishment of the birth registration area in 1915, and in a series of measures which led to the Maternal and Infancy Act (the Shepperd–Towner Act) of 1922.

(New York, 1977), chap. 7. Other main sources include W. M. Schmidt, 'The Development of Health Services for Mothers and Children in the United States', *American Journal of Public Health*, 63 (1973), 419–27; A. J. Lesser, 'The Origin and Development of Maternal and Child Health Programs in the United States', *American Journal of Public Health*, 75 (1985), 590–8; and J. C. Snyder 'Public Health in the USA', in J. Walton, P. B. Beeson, and R. B. Scott, *The Oxford Companion to Medicine* (Oxford, 1986), ii. 1173.

[6] J. H. Cassedy, *American Medicine and Statistical Thinking, 1800–1860* (Cambridge, Mass., 1984); Snyder 'Public Health in the USA'.

[7] Wertz and Wertz, *Lying-in*, chap. 7. Four women in particular were founders of national systems of maternal and infant care: Florence Kelly, a factory inspector in Illinois, Grace Abbott and Julia Lathrop, who were to become members of the Children's Bureau (Julia Lathrop became head of the Bureau), and Lillian Wald, a professional nurse and founder of the Henry Street Settlement in New York.

The Shepperd–Towner Act (named after the two senators who sponsored it) allowed federal funds to be provided for advice to expectant mothers, but not for clinical care. The Act was passed on the condition that for every dollar provided by central government a dollar had to be provided by each state. Even so, it had a difficult passage, and two states rejected the offer. The women who ran the Children's Bureau were ridiculed and subjected to cheap invective. They were called: 'Female celibates too refined to have a husband.' It would be better, said the opponents of the bill, to set up a committee of married women to teach 'old maids' to get married and have children of their own. The *Illinois Medical Journal* reached the lowest depths when it described the Act as being sponsored by 'endocrine perverts [and] derailed menopausics'.[8]

Faced with such hostility, the Bureau was always conscious of how much it would like to do, and how little it was allowed to. It was not until the Second World War that it became politically acceptable to provide federal support for the 'wives of our boys' in the army and navy. An emergency programme for servicemen's wives was established which provided care for $1\frac{1}{4}$ million mothers and 230,000 infants by the time it was terminated in 1948. It was the largest public health programme the country had ever known, but it was strictly a wartime measure, not the foundation of a peacetime reform of maternal and child health.[9]

Laws passed by states on aspects of maternal care were often neglected or ineffective. Physicians were free to practise obstetrics as they wished regardless of standards of training or evidence of experience. Laws to license, control, or outlaw midwives, were enforced in a desultory fashion if at all. Draconian laws to suppress abortion were seldom enforced, at least when the abortionist was a doctor. Several consequences flowed from all this. In the absence of uniformity imposed by regulation, maternal care in the USA was dictated by local circumstances. Schemes to reform maternal care tended to be isolated and patchy. Because medical care in the USA was primarily a commercialized, competitive, free-enterprise system, most women were expected to pay for maternity care. Some charitable organizations and some state-funded systems existed here and there, but for many women cost prohibited the employment of a trained birth-attendant. Farm women in isolated areas complained bitterly that the government provided free veterinary care for sick hogs and cattle, but it wouldn't lift a finger for a sick mother or child.[10]

But the well-to-do who could afford a physician were not necessarily better

---

[8] Wertz and Wertz, *Lying-in*, 207–8.

[9] Schmidt, 'The Development of Health Services for Mothers and Children in the United States', 419–27.

[10] *Domestic Needs of Farm-Women*, US Department of Agriculture, Report No. 104 (Washington, DC, 1915).

off. Competition often fostered bad obstetrics when physicians courted the well-to-do with promises of 'modern' and 'scientific' techniques of pain relief and delivery which carried a high risk. As in Britain, a high risk of maternal mortality could be due to untrained birth-attendants or to over-zealous interference by medical practitioners. Low risk lay between these extremes, consisting of careful and conservative management of pregnancy and labour by a trained birth-attendant. During the late nineteenth and early twentieth century one gains the impression this was a rarer commodity in the USA than it was in Britain.

MATERNAL MORTALITY AND THE PUBLIC HEALTH

The recognition in the USA that maternal mortality was appallingly high and associated with many unnecessary maternal deaths cannot be dated precisely. It was a slow process, starting in the nineteenth century but coming to a head in 1917 with the publication of a seminal report by Grace Meigs of the Children's Bureau.[11] This was also the year in which the Committee on Public Health Relations of the New York Academy of Medicine began to interest itself in maternal mortality as a national problem. George Kosmak, an influential New York obstetrician who was later to become the editor of the *American Journal of Obstetrics and Gynaecology*, told the committee that 'while the death rates [in the USA] from other preventable causes had been steadily declining, the deaths from puerperal causes had remained stationary'. This was a new and startling observation in 1917, but it had become a commonplace by 1920 when the National Committee on Maternal Welfare was established.

Thereafter, conferences on maternal mortality were held and state maternal mortality committees were established, the first in Pennsylvania in 1934.[12] In addition, numerous reports on maternal care and maternal mortality were published. Collectively, they exceed in quality and quantity anything produced by other countries, especially the reports published by the Children's Bureau. Most of the other reports (with the notable exception of the White House Conference Report of 1933) were the products of state health departments, state medical associations, medical academies, and medical societies. A few were the product of individuals, and there were numerous papers published in a wide range of medical periodicals.

Two reports, both published by the Children's Bureau, stand head

[11] Grace Meigs, *Maternal Mortality from all Conditions Connected with Childbirth in the United States and Certain other Countries*, Children's Bureau Publication, No. 19 (Washington, DC, 1917).
[12] J. G. Marmol, A. L. Scriggins, and R. F. Vollman, 'History of the Maternal Mortality Committees in the United States', *Obstetrics and Gynaecology*, 34 (1969), 123–38. This is an excellent source on the growth of official and semi-official bodies concerned with maternal mortality from 1917 to the 1960s.

and shoulders above the rest. The first, already mentioned, was Grace Meigs's 1917 report on maternal mortality. The second was Robert Morse Woodbury's *Maternal Mortality: The Risk of Death in Childbirth and from all Diseases Caused by Pregnancy and Confinement* (1926), the 152nd report published by the Bureau, which extended the analysis with much greater statistical sophistication. Both had the rare virtue of being international in outlook. Through these reports, Americans learnt of their unenviable position at the top of the list of countries ranked according to their levels of maternal mortality. Many physicians found this hard to accept, and tried, unsuccessfully, to dismiss it as a statistical artefact. The volume of publications on maternal mortality, the thoroughness of many of the investigations, and the ruthless criticism of individuals and institutions, reflects the anger and concern of the medical profession which liked to believe that it led the world in all aspects of medical care, including obstetrics.

17

Home Deliveries and the General Practitioner

In the nineteenth century, the American general practitioner, just like his British counterpart, saw midwifery as a central feature of his practice. In 1885 a Massachusetts general practitioner, echoing his British contemporaries, stressed the importance and difficulties of practising midwifery in the context of general practice when he wrote, 'There is no branch of medicine which demands more skill, presence of mind, or justifiable daring than midwifery. It needs a man who can neither be overwhelmed by disaster nor unduly elated by success . . .'.[1]

Dr Ward of New York, writing in 1926, was explicit:

Obstetrics is the general practitioner's specialty, and, with the possible exception of pediatrics, there is no one of the special departments of our profession which concerns him so greatly and which touches so vitally the welfare of the community.[2]

By the 1920s, however, one finds growing opposition to the general practitioner from specialist obstetricians intent on obtaining a monopoly of obstetric care. Many British and American obstetricians of this period shared the same scorn for general practitioners. The American obstetricians were brutally blunt and accused the general practitioner of being to blame for the high maternal mortality:

The middle class medical man, or general practitioner, so-called, is the greatest danger in obstetrics. A midwife under strict control does comparatively little harm, but the doctor who does obstetric work to get the medical practice of the family, giving as little time and attention as possible because it pays but little, is the one responsible for many obstetric disasters.[3]

In these respects there were close analogies between the two countries. But there were striking contrasts. One was the relative absence of midwife deliveries in American towns. In Philadelphia between 1821 and 1830, twenty-two midwives delivered one-seventh of the babies, and 134 physicians delivered the remaining six-sevenths. Within another decade the midwives

[1] W. Symington Brown, 'Forty years of Experience in Midwifery', *Boston Medical and Surgical Journal*, 112 (1885), 241–3.

[2] G. G. Ward, 'Our Obstetric and Gynaecologic Responsibilities', *Journal of the American Medical Association*, 87 (1926), 1–3.

[3] G. C. Mosher, 'Maternal Morbidity and Mortality in the United States', *American Journal of Obstetrics and Gynaecology*, 7 (1924), 294–8, 326–30.

had dwindled to six. Thus the physicians had the monopoly of practice in towns, but the work was unevenly divided: 'some [physicians] possess a very limited portion of the practice, whilst others have a very great monopoly'.[4]

By the mid-nineteenth century a few lying-in hospitals and maternity beds had been established in the USA. As in Britain, they catered for a very small proportion of total deliveries, and those who entered these hospitals were almost always the very poor and the 'abandoned'.[5] For everyone else, home deliveries were the rule, and almost all were undertaken by physicians. Those who had the lion's share of deliveries and delivered the most affluent patients formed the nucleus for the future development of the speciality of obstetrics.

Charles Meigs (1792–1869) who opposed Oliver Wendell Holmes so bitterly on the contagiousness of puerperal fever (Chapter 4) was one of the lions. He graduated from the University of Pennsylvania in 1817 and practised briefly in Georgia before returning to Philadelphia where he began to lecture on midwifery at what was called the 'School of Medicine' in 1830. He published his textbook *The Philadelphia Practice of Midwifery* in 1838, and was elected professor of obstetrics and diseases of women in the Jefferson Medical College in 1841. He had a huge private practice.[6] His contemporary, John Wiltbank, who held the post of professor of midwifery and the diseases of women and children at the University of Pennsylvania, published *A Plea for Obstetrics* in 1848 in which he said that although midwifery was not so *publicly* despised as it was in England, it was still regarded in America as the lowest form of medical care, partly because women were regarded as an inferior species, partly because most labours are normal and not a medical concern, and partly because physicians tended to see midwifery an art, not a science; which was just what his British contemporaries were saying a little more diplomatically.

If we jump forward some eighty years from the mid-nineteenth century to 1930, we find that the provision of obstetric care had altered much more dramatically in America than in Britain. In Britain, home deliveries by mid-wives and general practitioners formed what the authorities referred to as the 'backbone of the maternity service', the status of the midwife was increasing, and midwife deliveries accounted for rather more than 50 per cent of the total. Hospital deliveries overall were still a long way from 50 per cent, and were only approaching that proportion in a few places like Manchester and London.

To Americans this was very old fashioned. By 1930 about 70 per cent of urban deliveries in the USA took place in hospitals and it was very uncommon

[4] G. Emerson, 'Medical Statistics', *American Journal of Medical Sciences*, 9 (1831–2), 21–5. James H. Cassedy, *Medicine and American Growth, 1800–1860* (Madison, Wis., 1986).
[5] C. E. Rosenberg, *The Care of Strangers: The Rise of America's Hospital System* (New York, 1987), 269.
[6] *American Dictionary of National Biography*.

for an urban, native-born, American mother from the middle or affluent classes, to be delivered at home by a midwife or a general practitioner. They employed a specialist, although that term covered a wide range of practitioners in terms of skill (see the section entitled 'What Michigan demonstrates' in Chapter 21). Urban home deliveries, and midwife deliveries in general, whether urban or rural, were largely confined to the poorest classes and the black population.

By 1940 this tendency was even more marked, and was accompanied by a clear difference between northern and southern states. This can be seen in Table 17.1 which shows that if the southern states are excluded some 90 per cent of all deliveries of white women, both urban and rural, took place in hospital and midwife deliveries had almost totally disappeared. The tide had been flowing strongly in this direction for several decades, but it was accelerated by the introduction during the Second World War of the Emergency Maternity and Infant Care Program.[7] In 1945 an advisory committee of the Children's Bureau recomended that the national goal should be 'the delivery of all women in good hospitals under the care of competent physicians'.[8] By 1950 the goal had to all intents been achieved except in isolated areas. Home deliveries by midwives and by general practitioners had become as obsolete as the apocryphal stories of kitchen-table appendicectomy.

By 1950 maternal mortality was falling rapidly in the USA and Britain. Obstetricians in the USA often saw this as a simple cause and effect. They took the credit. Maternal mortality had fallen because home deliveries had disappeared and deliveries by midwives and general practitioners had been abolished. Whatever one feels about this hypothesis—and it is far too simple to command respect—it does raise some of the questions I will try to answer in this chapter. What was the standard of general practitioner obstetrics? What was the nature of their practice? Were American general practitioners responsible for the high maternal mortality in the USA before the Second World War? The disappearance of the GP from the obstetric scene was an international tendency which progressed at a different rate in various countries. Some applaud the tendency, others deplore it. How much was gained or lost by the disappearance of the GP obstetrician in the USA?

Obstetricians did not hesitate to say that his disappearance was inevitable and essential, but some mothers were ambivalent. On the one hand they demanded the best medical care and equated this with hospitals and specialists; on the other there was a certain nostalgia at the disappearance of the home delivery. Delivery by a specialist obstetrician in hospital might be safer, but it was less satisfying than the comforting sympathy of that familiar

[7] A. J. Lesser, 'The Origin and Development of Maternal and Child Health Programs in the United States', *American Journal of Public Health*, 75 (1985), 590–8.

[8] 'Next Steps in Maternal and Child Health' (editorial), *American Journal of Public Health*, 35 (1945), 122.

TABLE 17.1 Hospital and Home Deliveries in Selected American States, Showing the Percentage of Hospital and Home Deliveries by Physicians, and Home deliveries by Midwives, 1945–1946

	White			Non-white			Maternal mortality rate
	Physician		Midwife	Physician		Midwife	
	Hospital Delivery %	Home Delivery %	Home Delivery %	Hospital Delivery %	Home Delivery %	Home Delivery %	
USA	87.1	11.2	1.7	45.2	20.0	34.8	15.7
Connecticut	99.0	1.0	0.0	96.2	3.6	0.2	9.2
Oregon	98.0	1.5	0.5	92.1	2.6	5.3	10.3
Maryland	86.6	11.9	1.5	54.5	28.0	17.5	11.1
New York	97.1	2.7	0.2	94.4	4.6	1.0	12.0
Indiana	88.2	11.7	0.1	64.5	35.1	0.4	13.1
Pennsylvania	88.3	11.6	0.1	84.0	15.7	0.3	15.2
Texas	75.8	14.7	9.5	45.5	22.6	31.9	16.2
South Carolina	76.2	21.3	2.5	13.8	20.2	66.0	27.4
Florida	87.8	9.9	2.3	30.8	15.1	54.1	30.0
Mississippi	69.3	27.7	3.0	9.6	21.4	69.0	31.4

Note: The maternal mortality rate (deaths per 10,000 births) is shown in the last column for the combined white and non-white population. The various states are ranked in order of ascending maternal mortality rates.

Source: Further Progress in Reducing Maternal and Infant Mortality, Children's Bureau Statistical Series No. 4, Federal Security Agency, Social Security Administration, Children's Bureau (Washington, DC, 1948). In the original source the term used for deliveries not undertaken by physicians was 'non-medical personnel'. Since 'non-medical personnel' consisted in practice of a few trained midwives, untrained midwives, and neighbours, 'midwife' has been substituted for the purposes of this table.

figure, the old-style family doctor who had known you for most of your life, addressed you by your Christian name, and delivered you in your own bedroom. Did all that really have to go?

THE OLD STYLE OF FAMILY DOCTOR

The special qualities of 'Doc', the old-style American family doctor, were captured by Norman Rockwell's inimitable illustrations for the *Saturday Evening Post* of the 1940s. 'Doc' was always late middle-aged, stout, bluff, reassuring and easy-going, never in a white coat but always in a crumpled suit with a bottle of medicine sticking out of one pocket and a stethoscope dangling from the other. With decades of experience behind him, he knew his flock and was proud to have brought so many of them into the world. 'Doc Mellhorn', said one of Rockwell's captions, 'was just a good doctor who knew us inside out'. Ideally, you found him in small towns where he made 'house-calls' in his battered car. He knew your family, delivered your baby, cared for your adolescent acne, and when you left school and got married he delivered the next generation of babies.[9] Stereotypes can become models. In Britain, and doubtless in America, family doctors sometimes fashioned their behaviour and appearance to resemble their public image.[10] 'Doc Melhorn' was real, but what was the reality of his practice?

If we turn from the *Saturday Evening Post* to medical journals, many of the papers published by general practitioners give an impression of obstetric practice not as a series of cosy home deliveries in the bosom of the family, but rather as a series of hair-raising emergencies. Some of the numerous papers by general practitioners on their midwifery practice are very slight in content; and some have extraordinary stories to tell.[11] Abnormal cases, of course, form the centrepiece of reports in medical journals because there is little to say about a normal labour. Reading these papers it is easy to forget the 95 per cent or more of straightforward deliveries which were easy but time-

[9] Dr Russell who was the subject of one of the most vivid illustrations was Rockwell's own physician who did his house calls in a battered Ford coupé. For an authentic series of illustrations of medicine during this period see J. D. Stoeckle and G. A. White, *Plain Pictures of Plain Doctoring: Vernacular Expression in New Deal Medicine and Photography* (Cambridge, Mass., 1985).

[10] The evolution of the role of the family doctor in Britain is discussed in I. Loudon, 'The Concept of the Family Doctor', *Bulletin of the History of Medicine*, 58 (1984), 347–62.

[11] M. Reece, 'The Use of Antiseptics in Puerperal Cases', *Journal of the American Medical Association*, 3 (1884), 120–1. This, for example, is an extraordinary paper about a woman who developed puerperal sepsis and was desperately ill with an abdomen distended to the size of full-term. The author washed out her uterus with half a gallon of water in which was dissolved potassium permanganate and the odour of the discharge was 'like that one acquires in the dissection of bodies'. The next day she was much better—'in short the effect was simply magical'—although they had told the husband there was no chance of recovery. The husband was instructed to administer the intra-uterine injections with a rubber tube every three hours. He did and she recovered.

consuming and often tedious. We have seen the British tendency to intervene in normal labours to 'hurry things up'. Was the same tendency found in the USA?

The answer depends on the period to which the question refers. The ledger of Dr John Metcalf of Massachusetts shows that between 1826 and 1831 he delivered 107 women, passing many hours waiting patiently at the bedside. It appears he never used forceps and his only major intervention was the manual removal of the placenta from a patient who was 'flooding'.[12] But John Metcalf was practising in what we could call the conservative phase of obstetrics.

THE CONSERVATIVE PHASE OF OBSTETRIC PRACTICE

In the first half of the nineteenth century, practitioners on both sides of the Atlantic had great faith in the powers of nature. A conservative, patient, and watchful approach to obstetric care, with minimal surgical interference was customary. It was advised by all the textbooks of the period. Samuel Bard in his *Compendium on the Theory and Practice of Midwifery* (New York, 1807), said that forceps were needed in no more than four or five cases out of every 2,000, not even in England 'where great numbers employed in unhealthy manufacture ... must increase in a tenfold degree, the number of crooked and distorted women'.

There are numerous accounts of such conservative practice emphasizing the dangers of interference. In 1847 Dr Bliss of New York reported 850 deliveries and used the forceps only three times; in one case only after labour had continued for eighty-one hours.[13] In contrast, when Dr Brown of Stoneham, Massachusetts published an account of his obstetric practice in 1885, fashions had changed dramatically. There was a much greater tendency for surgical intervention. Brown used chloroform frequently if sparingly to produce a state just short of unconsciousness and used forceps very frequently, remarking that 'in 1842 forceps were rarely used' because it was a period when 'many physicians entertained a strong prejudice against their employment except in extreme cases'.[14]

---

[12] John George Metcalf, ledger containing his dissertation, record of obstetric cases and his family history. MSS Boston, Countway Medical Library. Similar manuscript records of obstetric practice in the 19th cent. included in the collection of the Countway library include the records of William Workman (1797–1850) for the year 1846–7. Benjamin Cushing (1822–95) wrote a valuable account of the obstetric practice between 1801 and 1852 of his uncle Robert Thatcher who delivered 2,600 women, encountered difficulty in only 191 cases, used the forceps 4 times, undertook craniotomy 4 times and may have had as few as 4 or 5 maternal deaths. See also the notebook of Austin Flint with its account of women he delivered between 1785 and 1834.

[13] J. C. Bliss, 'Statistics of Private Obstetric Practice', *New York Journal of Medicine*, 8 (1847), 88–94.

[14] W. S. Brown, 'Forty Years of Experience in Midwifery', *Boston Medical and Surgical Journal*, 112 (1885), 241–3.

In 1889 James Eldredge of Greenwich, Rhode Island, published an account of his father's midwifery practice between 1811 and 1838, noting that labours in those days were always conducted on a temporary bed or couch. After delivery 'the woman was placed in her bed by the arms of the attendant, and this was what was in common phrase called "putting to bed". To do this a strong arm was sometimes required, but it was the custom and was always expected.' His father had delivered 1,243 women 'among all sorts and conditions of men and women; but then as now, the greater number of children were born among the poor and middling classes...'. The results are summarized in Table 17.2 and show a 1.1 per cent forceps rate. It is interesting that this conservative manner of practising midwifery was regarded as very old-fashioned by the audience of general practitioners who heard this paper in 1895. One of them remarked that 'It is certain that they [forceps] are used much oftener now, both in private practice and in the public institutions, than they were during the period of this record.'[15]

INCREASED INTERVENTION IN HOME DELIVERIES

The change in obstetric practice from excessive conservatism to excessive intervention which often reached astonishing proportions by the 1920s, is attested by numerous reports.[16] Interestingly it occurred at almost exactly the same time in the USA as in Britain, and sometimes went a good deal further. Caesarean sections in home deliveries may not have been common, but they were not unknown. Dr Janvier recalled in 1922 how, as a young physician, he had given an anaesthetic 'for a very clever and daring operator'. The patient was a young black woman in labour in a third-storey servant's room. The 'clever operator' diagnosed a simultaneous intra- and extra-uterine pregnancy and immediately performed a Caesarean section. The diagnosis was confirmed when the abdomen was opened, but 'the victim, only lightly anaesthetised, suddenly clawed at her intestines and breathed her last; the infants lived twenty four hours'.[17]

Such terrible stories suggest that an excess of obstetric intervention led to a rise in maternal mortality; but was there such a rise? The answer is by no means clear, partly because the phase of intervention (which might have been

---

[15] J. H. Eldredge, 'A Record of 1243 Cases of Confinement in the Care of a General Practitioner, 1811–1838', *Transactions of the Rhode Island Medical Society*, 4 (1890–2), 164–9. Records of his father's practice.

[16] C. B. Brown, 'Obstetrical Work by the Country Doctor', *Illinois Medical Journal*, 14 (1908), 552–66; M. D. Westley, 'Obstetrics in a Rural Community', *Journal-Lancet*, 37 (1917), 181–5; J. Ross, 'Analysis of 6,677 Cases of Midwifery Attended by James Ross MD, Toronto, between the Years 1852 and 1892', *American Journal of Obstetrics of New York*, 32 (1895), 380–7; and J. E. Stetson, 'Statistical Record of 1,000 Consecutive Cases in Private Practice', *Yale Medical Journal*, 8 (1901–2), 102–17.

[17] G. V. Janvier, 'The More Important Obstetrical Emergencies Met by the General Practitioner', *Pennsylvania Medical Journal*, 26 (1922–3), 284–8.

TABLE 17.2 *A Series of Deliveries in the Private Practice of an American General Practitioner between 1811 and 1838*

	Number	%
Total deliveries	1,243	100.0
Cases recorded without remark and assumed to be uneventful deliveries	1,069	86.0
Remaining cases amongst whom some of the complications which were recorded were as follows:	174	14.0
Complications of labour		
Breech	30	2.4
Deliveries of twins	18	1.4
Face to pubes	20	1.6
Arm or shoulder presentation	3	0.2
Retained placenta	5	0.4
Forceps deliveries	14	1.1
Craniotomy	3	0.2
Stillbirths	30	2.4
Maternal deaths	11	0.9
Puerperal fever	6	
Haemorrhage (placenta praevia)	2	
Convulsions	1	
Sudden death	1	
Phthisis	1	
(Maternal mortality rate per 10,000 births	88.4)	

Source: J. H. Eldredge, 'Twelve Hundred and Forty-Three Cases of Confinement in the Care of a General Practitioner from March 23 1811 to June 23 1838, a Period of Twenty-Seven Years', *Transactions of the Rhode Island Medical Society*, 4 (1889–93), 164–9. The cases were recorded by his father, Charles Eldredge of East Greenwich, RI.

expected to produce a rise in deaths from puerperal fever) more or less coincided with the introduction of antisepsis.[18] There is little evidence that increased intervention led to increased deaths from puerperal fever. The rates reported from general practice after 1880 seem to be much the same as they were before, although it could be argued they should have been much lower. That was certainly the official view when the reduction in puerperal fever deaths in hospitals was contrasted with the rise in private practice and general

---

[18] In fact, most cases of puerperal fever occurred in the USA as elsewhere after normal deliveries, and puerperal fever in the 19th cent. was often an epidemic disease. In 1887 Dr Whitcomb of Norristown in Pennsylvania reported 32 cases in quick succession (none died) and 'the epidemic ceased as suddenly as it had commenced, and I have not had a case since'. This epidemic occurred although Dr Whitcomb claimed to be most careful in the use of antisepsis. H. H. Whitcomb. 'A Report of 616 Cases on Labor in Private Practice', *Medical and Surgical Reporter*, 56 (1887), 201–3.

practitioners were warned: 'Every physician should enter upon the task of delivery . . . with as much caution . . . as in entering the abdominal cavity.'[19]

Evidence concerning the use of antiseptics in private practice is rare: but Dr Warren of Portland, Maine published a revealing paper in 1905. Before 1870, he wrote, most students said, even when they came straight from the post-mortem room, 'What is the use of washing one's hands before making a vaginal examination? Will they not be just as dirty after it?' When these students graduated, most made no attempt to practise antisepsis, 'looking with apathy on new-fangled theories'. Those who graduated between 1870 and 1880 were mostly conscientious about antisepsis, but those who graduated after 1890 and became obstetricians were invariably enthusiasts and 'avowedly antiseptists'. Some midwives practised antisepsis, but most did not and were, in his opinion, responsible for sepsis 'running riot'.[20]

There are many records of general practitioners who were scrupulous in the use of antisepsis and seldom had a patient with puerperal fever,[21] but they were probably exceptional. The poor standard of antisepsis in home deliveries was considered to be a feature of the majority of general practitioner obstetricians whose numerical dominance in the early twentieth century, in towns as well as rural areas, is suggested by the following statistics. In 1919 the American Medical Association registered 516 surgeons but only 24 obstetricians, in New York, Philadelphia, Boston, and Chicago—an average of only six obstetricians in each major city.[22]

THE GENERAL PRACTITIONER AND MATERNAL MORTALITY

The records of nineteenth-century general practice in the USA provide a fairly consistent picture of a MMR in the region of about 60 per 10,000

---

[19] 'Puerperal Infection in Private Practice' (leading article), *Journal of the American Medical Association*, 33 (1902), 1008–9. See also J. W. Byers, 'An Address', *American Journal of Obstetrics*, 44 (1901), 433–41, in which the author said: 'It is a terrible blot on our obstetric art that while within the memory of many of us puerperal fever has been banished from maternities in which formerly it was so prevalent, the same good results have not followed in general practice.'

[20] S. P. Warren, 'The Prevalence of Puerperal Septicaemia in Private Practice at the Present Time Contrasted with that of a Generation ago', *American Journal of Obstetrics*, 51 (1905), 301–31.

[21] J. S. Templeton, 'Obstetrics in Country Practice', *Illinois Medical Journal*, 39 (1918), 90–3; W. Wormely, '1,000 Obstetrical Cases Occurring in General Practice', *Medical Times of New York*, 30 (1902), 231–4. Dr Wormley presented Dr Rosenthal's cases. Rosenthal had a most varied practice. Only 122 of his cases were American born. The rest were immigrants, including 644 Russians. He noted that 'the Scandinavians seemed to suffer most pain, and the Russian were the most noisy. They seemed to have the idea that the louder the cries the easier the confinement. Next in order came the Irish, while the Americans were the quietest.' See also C. B. Brown, 'Obstetrical Work by the Country Doctor'; Westley, 'Obstetrics in a Rural Community'.

[22] H. P. Newman, 'The Specialty of Obstetrics', *American Journal of Obstetrics*, 80 (1919), 464–71.

births, including associated deaths. With the exclusion of associated deaths this is not very much higher than the level in nineteenth-century England. But the same provisos apply here as they did when this subject came up in connection with British general practitioners. In these reports the number of births was usually too low for statistical confidence, and the general practitioners who kept careful records and published papers were a self-selected literate minority. We cannot assume their records were representative, but if they were, it seems that the mid-nineteenth-century American general practitioner delivering his patients at home did no worse, and possibly a little better, than his successors who delivered their patients in hospitals in the 1920s and 1930s.

How can this be explained? In 1920, Dr R. W. Holmes of Chicago, in a paper aptly named 'The Fads and Fancies of Obstetrics' pointed out that 'the death rate most for women in hospitals is as great today as it was a hundred years ago'. He believed that 'the rise and fall of the efficiency in judgement of the general practitioners in their obstetric work are reflections of the attitude and efficiency of the obstetric teachers' who were chiefly to blame because they emphasized surgical obstetrics and showed 'the modern trend of obstetric practice has been to apply surgical manipulation to normality to a degree which is not in consonance with refinement of judgement'.[23]

Similarly, Dr Brumbaugh, a Pennsylvania obstetrician, read a paper in 1922 on 'The Present Standard of Obstetrical Practice in Rural Pennsylvania' and noted that:

During the last two decades the standards of obstetrical practice have lagged far behind in the general advance common to other branches of medicine ... It is a reproach to our civilisation that approximately 20,000 mothers perish annually in these United States as a consequence of childbearing ... The increasing use of forceps and unwarranted use of pituitrin to shorten labor and relieve pain cannot be too severely condemned ... Our undergraduate teaching institutions are not entirely blameless ... Nor are our rural hospitals doing their full duty to the communities they serve. Many of our large city hospitals are open to the same criticism. Outside of the teaching hospitals an obstetrical service worthy of the name is a rarity. Common usage permits any man who has hospital privileges, regardless of his surgical training, to do any major operation short of cesarean section ... Can we doubt that maternal mortality and fetal mortality are unnecessarily high?[24]

Notice the penultimate sentence: 'Any man who has hospital privileges, regardless of his surgical training ...'. This reminds us of the difficulties in comparing American deliveries with British. In Britain during the 1920s and

---

[23] R. W. Holmes, 'The Fads and Fancies of Obstetrics: A Comment on the Pseudo-Scientific Trend of Modern Obstetrics', *American Journal of Obstetrics and Gynaecology*, 2 (1920), 225–37.

[24] C. G. Brumbaugh, 'The Present Standard of Obstetrical Practice in Rural Pennsylvania', *Pennsylvania Medical Journal*, 26 (1922–3), 283–4. Brumbaugh estimated that 20,000 mothers a year were dying in childbirth and the rate was rising.

1930s it is safe to make the broad assumption (provided cottage hospitals are excluded) that, apart from midwife deliveries, home deliveries were undertaken by general practitioners and hospital deliveries by practitioners who were generally specialist obstetricians, albeit in a limited sense in provincial hospitals. An appointment to a voluntary hospital was something of a distinction, possessed by a small minority of medical practitioners.

In the USA, however, when the rapid growth in hospitals began (we come to this later) every medical practitioner had access to hospital beds if there was a hospital in his area and if he satisfied the local committee which allocated hospital privileges. He did not need to provide evidence of postgraduate training, special skills, or special qualifications. The dividing-line between general-practitioner obstetricians and obstetric specialists was very blurred indeed. We cannot compare the mortality of home and hospital deliveries and assume we are comparing the general practitioners and specialists. Not surprisingly, Kosmak noted in 1927 that the high maternal mortality 'is pretty evenly distributed . . . hospital confinements are perhaps as culpable as those conducted in the homes . . .'.[25]

One of the very few reports to attempt an analysis of the relative mortalities of midwife, general practitioner, and specialist deliveries, was based on a survey carried out in Cleveland, Ohio, in 1931. It is an interesting paper because it shows wide differences in type of birth-attendant according to the economic status of the patients (the American equivalent of divisions by social class) as well as showing that the maternal mortality rate in general-practitioner deliveries was significantly higher than it was in obstetrician deliveries, but lower than the rate in midwife deliveries (Tables 17.3 and 17.4). Although the number of births is low (especially for midwife deliveries) the differences are statistically significant. But it is difficult to know how much economic status affected outcome and it is by no means certain that Cleveland was representative of the USA as a whole.

RURAL AND URBAN MATERNAL MORTALITY

One of the important differentials in the study of maternal mortality is town versus country. Rural areas were the stamping-ground of the general practitioner. With the invention of the telephone, better roads, and motor cars, the range of obstetric care was extended and the number of physician (general practitioner) deliveries increased. In 1917 a report on maternity and infant care in a rural county in Kansas showed that 273 out of a total of 332 births in the study were attended by doctors and distance presented few problems.

[25] G. W. Kosmak, 'Results of Supervised Midwife Practice in Certain European Countries', *Journal of the American Medical Association*, 89 (1927), 2010.

TABLE 17.3 *Place of Delivery and Birth Attendant at Delivery according to Economic Status, Cleveland, Ohio, 1931*

| | Economic area groups[a] (per cent) | | |
	$10–15	$35–40	$75–100
Delivery in hospitals	28.0	51.0	99.5
Delivery at home			
by physicians	41.5	48.0	0.3
by midwives	30.5	1.0	0.2

[a] Cleveland was divided up into fourteen groups called economic area groups depending on equivalent monthly rentals, rising in increments of $5 from the $10–15 group to the $75–100 group.

Source: R. A. Bolt, 'Maternal Mortality Study for Cleveland, Ohio', *American Journal of Obstetrics and Gynaecology*, 27 (1934), 309–13.

TABLE 17.4 *Maternal Mortality according to Type of Birth-Attendant, Cleveland, Ohio, 1931*

Birth attendant	Number of births	Number of maternal deaths	Maternal mortality rate (per 10,000 births)
All deliveries	16,279	151	92.7
Physicians (all)	16,014[a]	142	88.6
Obstetricians	c.7,500	55	73.4[a]
General practitioners	c.8,000	87	109.0[a]
Midwives	175	9	514.2
Maternity hospitals	—	—	59.0
General hospitals with a maternity licence	—	—	144.0

Note: The survey was based on 16,279 live births and 592 stillbirths in Cleveland in 1931, but the births shown above and the calculation of the MMR was based on live births only.

[a] The shortfall of c.500 is composed of partial specialists.

The differences in maternal mortality rates between deliveries by obstetricians, general practitioners, and midwives are significant at the 95% level.

Source: R. A. Bolt, 'Maternal Mortality Study for Cleveland, Ohio', *American Journal of Obstetrics and Gynaecology*, 27 (1934), 309–13.

Even 20 miles is not a prohibitive distance in this country of smooth level roads where, under normal circumstances, the doctor's automobile can cover that distance within an hour of receiving a call . . . Some chance, such as a flood in the river, a winter storm, the doctor's 'being out on a case', a delayed summons, or a brief labor is more likely to be the cause of the doctor's failure to arrive on time than is distance.[26]

By comparing urban and rural areas we obtain a rough-and-ready comparison between general-practitioner deliveries and obstetrician deliveries. Rural deliveries were undertaken by general practitioners and midwives, with the latter predominating in the southern states. A large majority of urban deliveries were undertaken by physicians: a mixture of general practitioners and partial and complete specialists. Tables 17.5 and 17.6 show the results of two investigations into urban and rural maternal mortality. Table 17.5 is based on what appears to have been a careful and reliable study, and it shows a marked urban–rural differential. Unfortunately, Table 17.6 is based not on maternal mortality rates but on the unsatisfactory denominator of total population; but it also suggests that rural maternal mortality was lower than urban, and that the urban death rate for sepsis was often two to three times higher than it was in rural areas.[27] There may of course have been many reasons why the risk of maternal deaths was lower in rural areas apart from differences in the type of birth-attendant. Rural areas may have provided a healthier environment, less septic abortion, and less likelihood of being exposed to the streptococcus.

An important confounding factor, however, is that in some states women from rural areas were coming to cities in the 1930s in increasing numbers in order to be delivered in hospitals. Many of these were 'high-risk' mothers selected for hospital delivery. Since the statistics of rural and urban deliveries were based on place of delivery rather than place of residence, there may well have been an excess of high-risk mothers from the surrounding countryside shown in the statistics as urban deliveries.[28] It was found, for example, that the MMR in Baltimore in 1935 was reduced from 68 per 10,000 births or to 59 if non-resident deaths were excluded.[29] This and other investigations suggest that by the mid-1930s in certain northern states there was probably no significant difference between rural and urban maternal mortality and by the 1940s the picture was reversed. Maternal mortality had fallen faster in towns and overtaken the level in rural areas. This is shown in Table 17.6 where it

[26] Elizabeth Moore, *Maternity and Infant Care in a Rural County in Kansas*, Children's Bureau Publications, No. 26 (Washington, DC, 1917).

[27] W. A. Piper, 'Rural Obstetrics and a Comparative Study of its Relation to Puerperal Mortality Statistics', *Minnesota Medicine*, 9 (1926), 489–99.

[28] A careful county-by-county analysis of urban–rural differences in mortality, and the complexity of such studies is shown in the admirable report: J. V. DePorte, *Maternal Mortality and Stillbirths in New York State: 1915–1925* (New York, 1928).

[29] J. H. Mason Knox, 'Reduction of Maternal and Infant Mortality in Rural Areas', *American Journal of Public Health*, 25 (1935), 68–75.

TABLE 17.5 *Maternal Mortality Rate (Deaths per 10,000 Births) in Rural and Urban Areas of Kentucky, 1936–1939*

Year	Rural	Urban	Total
1936	49	67	53
1937	36	75	44
1938	36	67	42
1939	38	57	41

Source: C. B. Crittenden and Lois Skaggs, *Maternal Mortality in Kentucky: A Study of Puerperal Deaths, 1932–1939*, Kentucky State Department of Health (1940).

TABLE 17.6 *Death Rates from Puerperal Causes per 100,000 Population in Cities and Rural Districts of the USA and of Certain Selected States, 1926*

	The puerperal state		Puerperal sepsis	
	Cities	Rural areas	Cities	Rural areas
All states	17.3	13.5	7.0	4.4
California	14.1	11.8	4.8	3.9
Illinois	14.3	9.2	6.2	4.0
Indiana	15.4	11.1	7.4	4.9
Maine	31.0	14.7	8.7	3.1
Massachusetts	16.4	6.2	5.5	1.9
Minnesota	14.0	9.3	6.9	3.3
New York	13.9	7.4	5.2	2.7
Virginia				
white population	16.2	11.9	8.8	3.7
black population	33.7	25.4	9.8	8.1
South Carolina				
white population	38.5	18.1	17.0	5.8
black population	61.3	35.1	12.2	4.6
Mississippi				
white population	34.2	14.8	9.4	4.2
black population	51.4	27.5	14.9	8.9

Source: W. A. Piper, 'Rural Obstetrics and a Comparative Study of its Relation to Puerperal Mortality Statistics', *Minnesota Medicine*, 9 (1926), 489–99.

TABLE 17.7 *Maternal Mortality Rates (Deaths per 10,000 Births) in County Groups of the USA, 1941–1945 and 1944–1948*

County Group[a]	Average rate 1941–5	Average rate 1944–8	Percentage reduction
All counties	25.0	16.4	34.4
Metropolitan	21.5	13.8	35.8
Greater	20.2	12.8	36.6
Lesser	22.7	14.7	35.2
Adjacent	25.5	16.8	34.1
Isolated	30.1	20.4	32.2
Semi-rural	29.8	19.9	33.2
Rural	31.0	22.0	29.0

[a] For definitions of county groups see Table 16.1, above.

Source: Children's Bureau, Statistical Series No. 12, *Infant and Maternal Mortality in Metropolitan and Outlying Counties 1944–1948*, Federal Security Agency, Social Security Administration, Children's Bureau (Washington, DC, 1950).

can be seen that the highest MMR in the 1940s was found in isolated rural and semi-rural areas, and the lowest in greater metropolitan areas.

In the end we have a collection of not very satisfactory statistics. So, what is the verdict? If the American general practitioner of the inter-war period had been charged in a court of law with responsibility for the high national rate of maternal mortality, he would have been acquitted; not because his innocence was proved beyond doubt, but because the case against him would have been weak and unproven. If the standard of obstetric care was low, it was low all round and the primary fault was education, which we consider next.

MEDICAL EDUCATION AND OBSTETRICS IN THE USA

Echoing what I said about Britain before the Second World War, if I was forced to identify one factor above all others as the determinant of high maternal mortality in the USA, I would unhesitatingly choose the standard of obstetric training in the medical schools; not only the content but also the attitudes instilled by these schools. These were the features which underlay the many faults so clearly identified by surveys of maternal mortality: the carelessness, the impatience, the scorn of proper standards of antisepsis, and the numerous instances of clumsy, dangerous, and unnecessary interference in the birth process. Obstetric training in Britain was bad enough, but on the evidence of American observers it was even worse in the USA.

In the nineteenth and early twentieth centuries most practitioners graduated with little or no instruction, let alone practical experience, in delivering babies. In large cities the inexperienced practitioner, if sufficiently motivated, could call in experienced colleagues, attend meetings, borrow books from libraries, and arrange for himself a kind of postgraduate education. In rural areas the isolated general practitioner learnt what he could in the rough school of experience at the expense of his patients. Sometimes an anecdote speaks volumes, and the following is an example.

In 1894 Dr Fulton of Kansas City, Kansas, recalled his early experiences of obstetrics in general practice. In 1870 he arrived as a young newly graduated physician in Fort Scott, Kansas, the proud possessor of a pair of shiny new forceps in his midwifery bag. He had absolutely no experience of delivering babies and he had never been taught how to apply obstetric forceps. Indeed, he had neither applied them himself nor had he seen them applied by anyone else. No sooner had he arrived than he was called to an obstetric case by three other medical men who all possessed forceps but had not the slightest idea how to use them. As the newcomer, Fulton was persuaded by the others to try his luck. 'To my utter astonishment, and theirs as well, I introduced the forceps at once and delivered the child in a few minutes. *I thereupon became an expert.*'[30]

That this was not an unusual state of affairs was shown by various investigations into the state of medical education in the USA. The low standard of obstetric education was recognized in 1910 by Abraham Flexner in his famous report on medical education in the USA and Canada. Medical education as a whole was deplorable, but 'the very worst showing is made in the matter of obstetrics'. In virtually every medical school, practical experience for students ranged from the absurdly inadequate to the non-existent.[31]

The most devastating attack was published in 1912 by J. Whitridge Williams of Baltimore (1866–1931), professor of obstetrics at the Johns Hopkins medical school, and possibly the most distinguished obstetrician in the USA in the early twentieth century. His account of the state of obstetric education was based on a questionnaire to professors of obstetrics all over the country. He found that medical schools were inadequately equipped. Many had no connection with a lying-in hospital. Professors of obstetrics were for the most part incompetent. Over a third were general practitioners and 'several accepted the professorship merely because it was offered to them but had no special training or liking for it ... Many of them admit that their students are not prepared to practice obstetrics on graduation, *nor do they learn to do so later*' [my italics]. With disarming frankness he wrote:

---

[30] A. L. Fulton, 'An Experience of 25 Years in Midwifery Practice', *Kansas City Medical Record*, 11 (1894), 325–9.
[31] A. Flexner, *Medical Education in the United States and Canada: A Report for the Carnegie Foundation for the Advancement of Teaching*, Bulletin No. 4 (New York, 1910), 117–18.

After eighteen years' experience in teaching what is probably the best body of medical students ever collected in this country—the student body at Johns Hopkins Medical School . . .—I would unhesitatingly state that my own students are unfit on graduation to practise obstetrics in its broad sense, and are scarcely prepared to handle normal cases.

If this was true of Johns Hopkins, one trembles to think what it was like elsewhere. Williams had no doubt about the connection between poor education and maternal mortality:

One half of the answers [to his questionnaire] state that ordinary practitioners lose proportionately as many women from puerperal infection as do midwives, and over three-quarters that more deaths occur each year from operations improperly performed by practitioners than from infection in the hands of midwives.[32]

Thirteen years later, in 1925, Austin Flint of New York conceded that slight improvement had occurred but obstetric education was still grossly inadequate, especially in the management of normal cases. Responsible teachers agreed there were two major defects in obstetric education. First, the poor instruction on the management of normal labours; secondly, the emphasis on operative obstetrics, which was too little for the education of the specialist obstetrician but too much for the general practitioner as it encouraged him to undertake procedures beyond his abilities.[33] Many teachers of obstetrics intervened whenever they could and their students watched, noted, and imitated. Obstetric education often consisted of observing highly complex (and often unnecessary) obstetric procedures but little theoretical or practical instruction in the management of normal labours. It was a system which might have been designed to maximize maternal mortality.

I am wary of dogmatic statements, but there is to my mind little doubt that had obstetrics been given pride of place over internal medicine and surgery in the student curriculum, maternal mortality would have been substantially lower. The extent to which obstetrics was neglected and scorned by the teachers, examiners, and boards of governors of medical schools is without question one of the greatest blots on medical education in nineteenth- and early twentieth-century America and Britain. It was a blot for which the leaders of the medical profession were wholly to blame.

[32] J. Whitridge Williams, 'Medical Education and the Midwife Problem in the United States', *Journal of the American Medical Association*, 58 (1912), 1–76. This paper was frequently quoted. As the title suggests it had a greater part (the awful state of obstetric education) and a lesser part (the problem of untrained midwives). Alexander Gordon's treatise in 1795 also had a greater part (the proof that puerperal fever was contagious) and a lesser (that heavy bleeding was curative in puerperal fever). Just as Gordon's was quoted as an authoritative source on the efficacy of bleeding while his views on contagion were ignored, so Williams was quoted frequently by those who wished to abolish the midwife and less frequently for his revelations on medical education.

[33] Austin Flint, 'Responsibility of the Medical Profession in Further Reducing Maternal Mortality', *American Journal of Obstetrics and Gynaecology*, 9 (June 1925), 864–6 and discussion, 704–8.

18

The American Midwife

Compared with the physicians who formed a more or less coherent group of middle-class professionals, sharing a similar sort of background and education, American midwives were so diverse, socially and professionally, that they are elusive, shadowy figures, difficult to define and impossible to quantify for the country as a whole. At one end of the scale the American midwife was literate and competent. Many had received formal training in Europe, some in the United States. At the other end of the scale, the midwife was neither more nor less than a neighbour with a reputation for delivering babies. She played the part of midwife as occasion demanded out of sheer neighbourliness. Some of these, when their reputation was established, accepted a small fee or a gift in lieu of money; but few of the 'neighborhood midwives' who were typical of rural America made a living by the practice of midwifery. They delivered babies because there was no one else to do so.

Between these extremes was a host of women of widely different origins who earned some sort of a living (sometimes substantial) by delivering babies and often by carrying out illegal abortions. As Woodbury observed in 1926, 'Midwives who have been trained in recognised schools either in this country or abroad are in an entirely different class from those who, often without even a common-school education and with no special training in their profession, are sometimes found in attendance upon negro mothers in the Southern States.'[1]

Understanding the history of the American midwife is complicated not only by this diversity, but by rapid changes in their number and regional distribution. It is certain that the number of midwives was declining through the first half of this century, rapidly in towns but much more slowly in rural areas. In the USA as a whole midwife deliveries declined from about 50 per cent of total deliveries in 1900 to 12.5 per cent in 1935. But there were still some 50,000 midwives in the USA in 1930 compared with 200,000 trained nurses, 150,000 practical nurses, and 156,000 physicians. The decline in midwives was most marked in the north and west. By 1930, over 80 per cent of the midwives were confined to the southern states.[2]

[1] R. M. Woodbury, *Maternal Mortality*, Children's Bureau Publications, No. 152 (Washington, DC, 1926).
[2] *Final Report of the Commission on Medical Education*, Office of the director of the study (New York, 1932), app. (Table 2). A term used in this and many American publications for

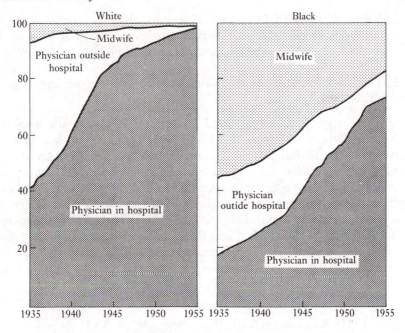

Fig. 18.1 USA, 1935–1954. Live births by attendant
Source: *Perinatal, Infant, and Childhood Mortality, 1954*, Children's Bureau Publications, No. 42 (Washington, DC, 1957).

Figure 18.1 shows live births in the USA by attendant and place of delivery between 1935 and 1954. It shows not only the decline of the midwife, but also the very large difference between white and non-white mothers in the choice of birth-attendant. In 1935 very few white women were being delivered at home by midwives; but a large number—roughly one half—were still being delivered by physicians. These, in the large majority of cases, were deliveries by general practitioners in rural areas and small towns far from large urban centres. Only twenty years later, however, virtually all white women were delivered by physicians in hospitals. But nearly a quarter of non-white women were still delivered at home, mostly by midwives. This, then, was the rapidly changing situation at the end of the period covered by this study.

If we go back from the 1930s to the late nineteenth and early twentieth centuries we can recognize four main groups of American midwives:

1. The immigrant midwives, found mainly in the cities.
2. The rural 'neighbour-midwives'. Some were recent immigrants; most were not.

the deliveries by midwives and neighbours was deliveries by 'non-medical personnel'. I have preferred the term 'midwife' and use it here to avoid confusion.

3. A small number of fully trained midwives, such as those employed by the Kentucky Frontier Nursing Service (which we come to later in this chapter) or the Maternity Center Association of New York City from 1930.
4. The black midwives of the southern states, by far the largest group numerically.

As a rough generalization one could say that the heyday of the *domiciliary* midwife in Britain was from the 1920s until the rapid decline in home deliveries in the 1960s. In the USA, if the midwives had a heyday at all, it lasted from the final decade of the nineteenth century through to the 1930s. The British midwife continues today to play a central role in maternal care, partly in the provision of ante- and postnatal care in the community, but largely by undertaking normal deliveries in hospital. The status of the midwife in Britain has never been higher, and there is absolutely no doubt that without midwives the maternity services of Britain would collapse. In the USA, on the other hand, although she still has a few fervent supporters, the midwife was all but abolished by the end of the Second World War.

THE REGISTRATION AND EDUCATION OF AMERICAN MIDWIVES

In contrast to most European countries, there was no federal system for the education, licensing, or supervision of midwives in the United States. It was left to individual states to make their own arrangements. Some, such as Massachusetts, passed laws outlawing the practice of midwives, but it was rare for them to be implemented.[3] Instead, most states required, but few enforced, the licensing of midwives. Even when licences were issued, all that was usually required was a fee and they could be bought over the counter, as they were in New York in 1907 where

In reality [registration] does not guarantee that the midwife so registered is in the possession of even a modicum of intelligence, let alone any fitness, professional or otherwise, beyond what is shown by the recommendation of two physicians or a certificate from a school of midwifery.[4]

Most of the diplomas had been obtained from:

so-called schools of midwifery in this country—with two exceptions, schools conducted here in New York city—or they were certificates from physicians who, for considerations best known to themselves, have in many instances seen fit to certify to

---

[3] J. L. Huntington, 'Midwives in Massachusetts' in J. B. Litoff, *The American Midwife Debate: A Sourcebook on its Modern Origins* (New York, 1986).
[4] F. E. Crowell, 'The Midwives of New York', *Charities and the Commons* (17 Jan. 1907), 557–677 reprinted in Litoff, *The American Midwife Debate*.

the proficiency of ignorant, incompetent women desiring to practice midwifery. I am convinced that this collusion between the physician and midwife points to an agreement that he is to be called upon for assistance for all difficult cases ... The diplomas of the New York schools are utterly worthless ... In some cases I found they had been granted to women who were unable to read or write, but who had the price—$66.[5]

Nevertheless, many midwives felt it was safer, and possibly more profitable, to hold a licence, certificate, or diploma of some kind. Many did so in New York and Chicago and other cities. Most of these bits of paper were worthless, although there were exceptions. New York, for instance, began to establish proper training programmes, beginning in 1911 with the Bellevue School for midwives which, according to Van Blarcom in 1914, was the only school for midwives of undoubted high standards in the whole of the USA until it was followed by the Maternity Center Association of New York City.[6] It was said of the midwives' diplomas in Chicago that they were no more than the products of 'diploma mills' and so-called 'schools of midwifery' held in a back office in the house of an unscrupulous physician for the purpose of charging as much as possible for the bare minimum of instruction. When the physician moved house the 'school' ceased to exist.[7]

To find out the situation throughout the country at the beginning of this century, Josephine Baker sent enquiries about midwives in 1912 to the boards of health in every state. Thirty-five sets of answers were received. Thirteen states had laws regulating the practice of midwives. Only six knew the number of midwives in the state. Only one could state the number of births reported by them. In answer to the question concerning schools for midwives, all except two replied either that they had none or that they knew of none. The exceptions were Ohio which claimed one school, and Utah which claimed to have two.[8] In most states the only requirement for registration was evidence that the midwife was not, as far as any one knew, a drug addict or an alcoholic. Literacy and competence were irrelevant.

The attempts by states to regulate their midwives could hardly have been more desultory. Laws relating to health, unless they were initiated and

---

[5] Ibid.

[6] Carolyn von Blarcom was a central figure in the history of American midwifery. She wrote a text on obstetrics for nurses and was influenced by the work of Mary Breckinridge (described later in this chapter). The Maternity Center Association in New York, established in 1918, began to train nurse-midwives in 1930. See Litoff, *American Midwives: 1860 to the Present* (Westport, Conn., 1978), and R. H. Bremner (ed.), *Children and Youth in America* (Cambridge, Mass., 1971).

[7] R. W. Holmes, *et al.*, 'The Midwives of Chicago', *Journal of the American Medical Association*, 50 (1908), 1346–50.

[8] Josephine Baker, 'Schools for Midwives', *American Journal of Obstetrics*, 65 (1912), 256–70, reprinted in Litoff, *The American Midwife Debate*. Baker's table (ibid. 160–1) shows that three states, Alabama, District of Columbia, and Montana, reported the number of midwife-registered births, but she may well have discounted the small numbers reported by the last two. Alabama reported 25,000, which sounds realistic.

TABLE 18.1 *Authorized and Unlicensed Midwives in Certain States in the USA in 1923*

State	Number Authorized to practise	Number Unlicensed (estimated)	Percentage of births attended
Alabama	1,862	n.a.	32
California	104	n.a.	8
District of Columbia	33	n.a.	4
Georgia	1,800	n.a.	n.a.
Kentucky	1,500	n.a.	18
Maine	n.a.	65	n.a.
Maryland	339	346	22
Massachusetts	none	117	n.a.
Mississippi	3,218	991	48
New Hampshire	7	none	n.a.
New York	1,976	n.a.	11
North Carolina	2,500	4,000	35
North Dakota	n.a.	2	n.a.
South Dakota	n.a.	133	3
Oklahoma	none	16	n.a.
Virginia	6,036	n.a.	35
Wisconsin	361	n.a.	10

n.a. = data not available

Source: Based on R. M. Woodbury, *Maternal Mortality: The Risk of Death in Childbirth and from all the Diseases Caused by Pregnancy and Confinement*, Children's Bureau Publications, No. 152 (Washington, DC, 1926), 81 (Table 53).

supported by the medical profession, received a very low rating, especially when those who employed midwives, the poor, the blacks, and the recent immigrants, were people with very little influence. State boards of health which knew (or claimed to know) precisely how many women had been delivered in hospitals or at home by physicians, were hopelessly vague about the number of midwife deliveries that took place every year within their boundaries. Table 18.1 shows this state of affairs in 1923.

THE IMMIGRANT MIDWIVES

As successive waves of immigrants arrived from Europe in the late nineteenth and early twentieth centuries, midwives, mostly trained in Europe, brought their skills to America. 'Wherever the immigrant settled,' said Brickman, 'midwives flourished',[9] practising within their own tight-knit communities and

[9] Janet P. Brickman, 'Public Health, Midwives and Nurses, 1880–1930', in E. C. Lagermann (ed.), *Nursing History: New perspectives, New Possibilities* (New York, 1983).

separated by language-barriers from native-born Americans. As these women grew old the communities they served became Americanized and the babies they delivered grew up and adopted the American custom of employing a physician. Midwifery was therefore one of the few occupations that was brought over from Europe which failed to take root in the USA. The striking feature of most immigrant midwives was their advanced age, which played a crucial role in their elimination.

In New York the percentage of deliveries by midwives fell from over 40 per cent in 1909 to 26 per cent in 1920, 21 per cent in 1923, and 8.5 per cent in 1933.[10] In Baltimore in 1909, 47 per cent of the midwives were foreign-born, 30 per cent were black native-born, and 87 per cent of these were over the age of 40. In Minnesota in 1923, 87 per cent of midwives were foreign-born and predominantly Scandinavian; 80 per cent were 50 or over. In New Jersey in 1926 we find the same pattern: 80 per cent of midwives were foreign-born and 63 per cent between the ages of 40 and 65.[11] By the 1930s the midwives in the cities were a dying race.[12]

What sort of people were these midwives, and what was the standard of their practice? An answer is provided by a report on the midwives of New York, published in 1907 (see Table 18.2).[13] It provides such a dreadful picture that it is important to understand it was not a polemic by an anti-midwife obstetrician but the work of an intelligent and perceptive graduate nurse. The midwives of New York came from a wide variety of nationalities. Only 9 per cent were born in the USA. The homes, personal appearance, and clothing of these women was classed as 'absolutely filthy' in 136 out of the total of 500. Of the remainder, two-thirds were classed as fair and one-third as excellent. Out of 500, 30 per cent were unable to speak English, and 51 were unable to read or write, although most had lived in the USA for many years.

Typically, midwives were married to carpenters, street cleaners, stonemasons, bartenders, tailors, peddlers, cooks, drivers, and so on. Amongst the Italians there were husbands who were musicians and artists and in one case an architect. Among the Jewish midwives there were several real-estate agents and one politician. One American-born midwife was married to a policeman. One educated and competent Russian midwife was married to a physician, and her son was a physician as well: 'Speaking of her son's obstetrical practice she said, "That little tad, I taught him all he knows", and nodding to her husband she added, "and I taught him all *he* knows". The husband smilingly

---

[10] Ibid.
[11] Neal Deavitt, 'The Statistical Case for the Elimination of the Midwife', *Women and Health*, 4 (1979), 81–96, 169–86. In the 1920s, 77% of Italian women in New York were delivered by midwives. Austin Flint, 'Responsibility of the Medical Profession in Further Reducing Maternal Mortality', *American Journal of Obstetrics and Gynaecology*, 9 (1925), 864–6.
[12] Deavitt, 'The Statistical Case'.
[13] Crowell, 'The Midwives of New York'.

TABLE 18.2 *Certain characteristics of the midwives of New York and Chicago at the beginning of the twentieth century*

	New York (1907)	Chicago (1908)
Nationality		
USA	123	4
Italian	355	8
German	311	84
Austrian	278	5
Russian	206 (Jewish)	5
Norwegian ⎫		4
Swedish ⎭	18	13
British	18	2
French	13	2
Swiss	9	
Finnish	4	
Turkish	3	
Greek	2	
Dutch	2	
Polish		36
Bohemian		31
Hungarian		4
Danish		2
Belgian		1
Unclassified	2	22
Total	1344	223
Diplomas held		
US diploma	573	111
Foreign diploma	512	67
None	259	6
Age		
Under 35	25	14.5
35–50	50	47.0
Over 50	25	38.5

Source: New York: Josephine Baker, 'Schools for Midwives', *American Journal of Obstetrics*, 65 (1912), 256–70, except for ages of midwives for which the source was F. E. Crowell, 'The Midwives of New York', *Charities and the Commons* (17 Jan. 1907), 557–677 (reprinted in J. B. Litoff, *The American Midwife Debate: A Sourcebook on its Modern Origins* (New York, 1986); Chicago: R. W. Holmes, *et al.*, 'The Midwives of Chicago', *Journal of the American Medical Association*, 50 (1908), 1346–50.

confirmed the wife's statement.'[14] If this successful and upwardly mobile woman had a daughter it is unlikely she would have persuaded her to take up midwifery. In Europe it was common for midwives to keep their practice in the family. In the USA the most successful midwives put their sons through medical or law school and hoped their daughters would make a 'good' marriage. American was a country that welcomed lawyers and doctors, but not midwives.

As Table 18.2 shows, many New York midwives held a foreign diploma. Only 10 per cent of these, however, were judged as efficient. Immigrant midwives arrived in the USA only to find that their work was despised by the medical profession and neither supervised nor supported by professional colleagues. No one, or at least no one in authority, cared what the midwife did or how she did it. It was a degraded occupation. What is remarkable is the extent to which immigrant midwives forgot their training and neglected not only the principles of antisepsis and good obstetric care, but even standards of ordinary cleanliness. In a telling comment, Crowell remarked on the efficient portable sterilizers these women had brought from Europe which were stowed, rusting and unused, on the top of a wardrobe or under the bed. When asked why sterilizers and antiseptics were not used Crowell was told, 'It is not necessary, nobody cares what we use; the bag is handier and everyone uses it here.'[15]

The midwife's bag was usually filthy. The contents, said Crowell, which usually consisted of dirty rags, rusty scissors, dirty string, and a bit of cotton and vaseline, beggar description. Some midwives went out to a delivery with nothing more than scissors on their belt and a bit of string in their pocket, hoping to find all they needed in the patient's home. Many carried quite openly in their bags, dilators and curettes, or more commonly a gum-elastic catheter with a piece of wire to stiffen it, which was used repeatedly and without benefit of sterilization to procure abortions.

Crowell classed 176 out of a total of 500 midwives as definitely undertaking criminal abortions, and 119 as suspicious.[16] Some midwives who carried out abortions, boarded patients in their homes and advertised their services in foreign-language newspapers. It was a well-paid and recognized part of their

---

[14] Ibid.

[15] A physician remarked in 1916 that foreign-born women often felt that the wearing of rubber gloves reminded them of an autopsy, while 'cleansing the field of operation makes them angry, as they feel it implies uncleanliness on their part . . . I have seen and had many cases where, through no fault of mine, the asepsis was as bad as it could be.' J. M. Leavitt, 'The Growth of Medical Authority: Technology and Morals in Turn-of-Century Obstetrics', *Medical Anthropology Quarterly*, 1/3 (1987), 232. This provides an added explanation not only for the preference for midwives by foreign women, but also for those midwives to abandon the aseptic practices they may had been taught abroad.

[16] Crowell, 'The Midwives of New York', reported that a conservative estimate of the number of abortions in New York in the first decade of this century was 100,000. There was no firm evidence to support this extraordinary piece of guesswork which must be regarded with suspicion.

work. Others sold drugs and claimed to cure infertility. If a complication occurred in their midwifery practice they often tried to deal with it themselves, even when it was a serious condition. From the evidence she uncovered of this gloomy obstetric and gynaecological underworld, Crowell concluded that the number of competent, well-trained, and reliable midwives in New York was negligible. Chicago was similar.

In 1907 the Council of the Chicago Medical Society appointed a committee to investigate the city's midwives. Because of her New York report, Elizabeth Crowell was engaged to supervise the Chicago survey and write the report, which was as excellent as her previous one. A nurse interviewed 233 midwives from all districts of Chicago. Later the same midwives were visited by a specially trained female agent, acting incognito 'for the purpose of obtaining information regarding their criminal practice'.[17]

In Chicago (see Table 18.2) there was an even larger proportion of immigrant midwives, but they were on the whole younger, cleaner, and more literate than those of New York. The small number of Russian Jewish midwives reflected the success of the Chicago Lying-in Hospital and Dispensary which were patronized by this group of women. The Italians had the highest proportion of midwife deliveries because 'the repugnance of the Italian mother to the presence of the physician in the lying-in chamber is well-nigh insuperable'. Italians would only allow a physician to be called when they were at death's door, but they were happy to employ foreign-born midwives from a wide range of nationalities.[18]

The Chicago midwives were terrifyingly confident of their ability to 'deliver a breech or a transverse presentation, remove an adherent placenta, or treat a post-partum haemorrhage'. With the same bland confidence they carried out abortions using stiffened catheters, dilators, curettes, and forceps, which they carried unsterilized in their bags. At least one-third were definitely classed as abortionists but many more were suspected. One of the tasks of the special agent was to pretend to be a woman requesting an abortion. Forty-nine said without hesitation that they would carry one out. Four offered to sell her abortifacient drugs rather than use instruments. One, married to a physician, refused but her husband promptly offered to sell her an abortifacient drug for $3.

In Chicago, as in New York, midwives often admitted women to their homes which they called 'boarding-houses' because lying-in hospitals had to be licensed by the city authorities. There were few full-term deliveries in

---

[17] Holmes, *et al.*, 'The Midwives of Chicago'. The exact number of midwives in Chicago at the time was unknown, but was estimated at between 500 and 600.

[18] Crowell, 'The Midwives of New York', reported that, because of the reluctance of Italian women to employ a physician, some midwives after a longish labour, pretended that an emergency had arisen. By pre-arrangement a physician was called, put on the forceps, delivered the baby, and said he had been called in the nick of time to save mother and baby.

these places. They were 'abortion shops, pure and simple'. The danger that a death due to illegal abortion would be discovered was often averted by collusion with a physician who was able to certify an abortion death as a death due to pneumonia or heart failure. On at least one occasion the physician was the son of the midwife. Sometimes collusion operated in the opposite direction with the physician referring patients to an abortionist midwife and splitting the fee with her. The frequency of abortions must be understood in the context of the times. In the USA, as in other countries, it was often the only means of limiting family size that was available to the poor:

Contrary to the general opinion, applications for this sort of service [instrumental abortion] came not alone from unfortunate or immoral women, but in the majority of instances from otherwise respectable married women...because the pressure of economic conditions is so great that the possibility of another mouth to feed becomes a tragedy to be avoided at any cost.[19]

A similar picture of city midwifery was given in the 1920s by Dr Julius Levy of Newark, New Jersey, one of the greatest supporters of midwife deliveries, whose work is considered later. In Newark there was the same appalling level of cleanliness and care and the same dreary tale of abortions carried out by elderly immigrant midwives. Everywhere in urban America it seems that the competent and conscientious midwife was a rarity in the early decades of this century. There is no reason to believe the accounts of the extremely low standard of urban midwifery were exaggerated, or to doubt that these mid-wives must have been responsible for many unnecessary maternal deaths due to abortion or complications in full-term deliveries.

RURAL MIDWIFERY IN THE EARLY TWENTIETH CENTURY

Setting aside for the time being the black midwives of the southern states, the rural midwives were both more diverse and more wholesome than their counterparts in the cities. Probably there were rural midwives who were unwashed, careless, and willing to carry out abortions, but they do not dominate the picture.

In rural areas, midwives who were fully employed and delivering a hundred or more women a year were rare for the obvious reason that most rural populations were small and scattered. Most of the midwives of the north and west were white, native-born Americans who came into the category of 'neighbour-midwives'. There were also pockets of immigrant midwives living in rural immigrant communities. In a small Polish township in Wisconsin in 1919, only five out of fifty-nine confinements were attended by a physician.

[19] Ibid.

Amongst the Polish women: 'the opinion was not uncommon that a mother should be practically able to deliver herself, and that a physician is not only superfluous but even undesirable. The midwives here had no formal training, but some delivered 30 cases a year.'[20] In a neighbouring township of native-born Americans, however, only 9 out of 151 confinements were attended by midwives; 139 were physicians' cases and 3 had no regular attendant.

In the mountainous country in Georgia, an area of countless valleys, ravines, and gaps which form a labyrith of intricate passageways, it was found in 1923 that one woman had never travelled beyond the nearest village, and had not gone even there for nine years of her married life. Another had not been to the nearest settlement, 6 miles away, in twenty years. Childbearing amongst the mountain women started early. Three-fifths were married before their twentieth birthday, many were married by the age of 16, some by 14, and families of ten or more children were common. When they went into labour two-thirds called a physician, but in a large number of cases he either refused to answer the call, or arrived long after the baby was born. A physician could spend all day travelling for a visit only 8 miles distant and charged $10–15. 'One mother, suffering from childbed fever, endured with Spartan fortitude a wagon ride over 15 miles of rough road to the nearest physician.' In this investigation it was found that 139 deliveries (one-third of the total in the survey) were attended by forty-three local midwives, known as 'granny women', whose ages ranged from 50 to 80 and who charged $2–5. Often a midwife was preferred because she charged less, stayed longer, and because of the dislike of being attended by a man.[21] Frequently, local neighbourhood midwives were old women, each delivering only a few cases a year, charging little, earning little, and gaining little experience.

That the choice of birth-attendant was influenced by immigrant status, by cost, and above all by geographic location, was shown in a memorable study by Grace Meigs. She described two rural German communities, the first a progressive and prosperous community in a 'northern central state' in 1916. It was a dairy-farming area with a fertile soil. The farmers were well off. With a population of mainly German descent it would not have been surprising to find a high proportion of deliveries by immigrant midwives. In fact there was none. All deliveries were attended by physicians.

But in the other community of German descent, the people lived in wild country under 'practically pioneer conditions', scarcely making enough to live. Most families never saw a doctor, and many of the farmsteads were so remote that almost all births were attended by local women, 'neighbourhood mid-wives'. Few had any training, but one who had supervised the delivery of all

[20] Elizabeth Moore, *Maternity and Infant Care in Two Rural Counties in Wisconsin*, Children's Bureau Publications, No. 46 (Washington, DC, 1919).
[21] Glenn Steele, *Maternity and Infant Care in a Mountain County in Georgia*, Children's Bureau Publications, No. 120 (Washington, DC, 1923).

her neighbours as well as her numerous grandchildren, had received training abroad. She had delivered all her own twelve children and lost little time from work on the farm.

A massive weather-beaten woman, she still, though old, works in the field with the men, and can lift a huge kettle full of potatoes to the stove as though it were a feather. The neighbourhood midwife develops quite naturally . . . A woman may be called in once to a neighbour in an emergency. The case is normal, all goes well; the doctor when he comes may compliment the neighbour woman on what she has done, and possibly give her a few words of advice about care at childbirth. Later the patient gratefully gives her a present of a few dollars. . . . Gradually she acquires a reputation in the immediate neighbourhood; her neighbours get in the habit of calling her and she takes care of them from kindness, often quite aside from a desire for the present of $2 to $3 which she may receive for her help. . . . [These women are] the wives of farmers and do not depend on their practice . . . many of them undoubtedly are unaware that they need to have a licence.[22]

Viola Paradise from the Children's Bureau, described the problems in a vast rural area of Montana in 1919 where it was climatic and geographic factors that dominated the provision of obstetric care and the MMR for the five years covered in the survey was 110 per 10,000 births—twice the level for white mothers in the USA as a whole. The population was almost entirely American-born, but there were so few doctors that over a fifth of mothers left the area to have their babies:

One mother who was feeling very ill drove into the nearest city—a five-day trip by wagon—about a month before her confinement. It snowed every day on the journey . . . When she and her husband reached their destination they moved into a shack 1½ miles from town . . . She was unable to do housework and had to engage help. She did not have hospital care but a physician attended her. When the baby was 10 days old they started back on their five-day trip.

Of those who remained at home half were delivered by neighbouring women 'in a very few instances trained nurses, in a considerable number of cases practical nurses, but for the most part women quite untrained in obstetrics'; a third were attended by physicians; many were delivered by their husbands; and three women delivered themselves.

Bad weather, swollen rivers and creeks and impassable roads frequently defeated plans to employ a physician or travel elsewhere for the confinement . . . [One] mother was all alone when her first baby was born. Her husband left at noon to go for a physician, but was lost in a storm and did not get back until 6 o'clock next morning. It was March. The baby was born at nine in the evening. The mother cut and tied the cord herself. She was alone through the night, the fire went out, and she had no food . . . This was

[22] G. L. Meigs, 'Rural Obstetrics', *Transactions of the American Association for the Study and Prevention of Infant Mortality*, 7 (1916), 46–61. Grace Meigs was a prominent member of the Children's Bureau.

her first child and she was badly torn . . . Nearly every neighbourhood had known of a death or a narrow escape from death on account of childbirth . . . There are no licensed midwives in the area. When a doctor cannot be secured, a neighbour is usually called in to care for the mother through her confinement . . . She seldom charges for her services. 'One neighbour does it for another out here', one mother remarked. Gradually some of the more self-reliant women acquire a reputation for skill in such cases and are called upon so often that they become the main reliance of a neighbourhood and decide to consider their services as at least professional nursing and to charge a fee of $1.50 or $2 a day.[23]

In another case:

the mother was confined in midwinter. No physician had been engaged . . . the night before birth the family and a neighbour sat up late reading a 'doctor book' . . . Half an hour after delivery the mother began to feel ill . . . the nearest physician lived fifteen miles away. The snow was deep and it took two teams of two horses each to get the doctor and bring him to the home. But six hours before the father returned with the physician the mother had died.[24]

The desperate fears of farm women facing childbirth alone in remote farms were expressed in a series of pathetic and moving letters to the Children's Bureau and to the Department of Agriculture. The poverty of rural life was a constant theme. Often these women pleaded for help from the Children's Bureau, when all the bureau could do was provide advice. One mother wrote from Wyoming in 1916:

I live sixty five miles from a Dr. and my other babies (two) were very large at birth . . . I have been *very* badly torn each time, through the rectum last time . . . I am 37 years old and I am so worried and filled with perfect horror at the prospects ahead. So many of my neighbours die at giving birth to their children. I have a baby 11 months old in my keeping whose mother died—when I reached their cabin last Nov it was 22 below zero and I had to ride 7 miles horse back. She was nearly dead when I got there and died after giving birth to a 14 lb. boy . . . I am far from a Dr. and we have no means, only what we get from this rented ranch . . . If there is a[n]ything what I can do to escape being torn again wont you let me know.[25]

The absence of anything more than the most primitive forms of obstetric care was a feature of rural poverty well into the 1930s, and it was not confined to the vast farming areas of the mid- and far-west. There are similar stories from up-state New York in 1937 of women delivered at home by neighbourhood midwives because they were so poor and because they lived so far from the nearest physician.[26]

[23] Viola Paradise, *Maternity Care and the Welfare of Young Children in a Homestead County in Montana*, Children's Bureau Publications, No. 34 (Washington, DC, 1919).
[24] Ibid.
[25] Molly Ladd-Taylor, *Raising a Baby the Government Way: Mothers' Letters to the Children's Bureau, 1915–1932* (New Brunswick, NJ, 1986).
[26] Helen A. Bigelow, 'Maternity Care in Rural Areas by Public Health Nurses', *American Journal of Public Health*, 27 (1937), 975–90.

Many more examples of the difficulties of providing maternal and infant care in rural America can be found in the reports of the Children's Bureau. The hazards of midwifery in remote rural areas are obvious enough. And yet, as we have seen, before the 1940s, maternal mortality was usually significantly lower than it was in towns. It seems that the hazards of delivery by 'neighbour-midwives' may have been cancelled out by the hazards of delivery by poorly educated physicians and unsavoury midwives in urban areas. So far we have for the most part dealt with the delivery of white women by white midwives. A far greater number of midwife births occurred amongst the black population in the south and played a large part in determining the level of maternal mortality in the USA as a whole.

THE BLACK MIDWIVES OF THE SOUTHERN STATES[27]

In 1937, 1 child out of every 8 born alive in the USA was black, but there were large regional variations. The proportion was 1 in 4 in the southern states, 1 in 27 in the northern states, and 1 in 115 in the western.[28] In the northern states where most black women lived in cities, 97 per cent of the deliveries in 1937 were attended by physicians and 62 per cent took place in hospitals. In the southern states, most black births were home deliveries and 79 per cent were attended by midwives. White women in the southern states, however, were mostly delivered in hospitals by physicians. This can be seen in the tables for rural Mississippi in 1920, Alabama in 1935, and South Carolina in 1934–5, Tables 18.3, 18.4, and 18.5. It was only in the southern states that the percentage of midwife deliveries approached the levels seen in European countries (Table 18.6).

Two features are beyond doubt. The enormous difference in type of birth-attendant and place of delivery according to colour, mentioned above; and the much higher maternal mortality of black mothers, shown in Tables 18.4 and 18.5. Table 18.5 also shows that maternal mortality amongst white

[27] American reports on maternal and infant mortality frequently refer to differentials in terms of 'race' or 'color'. I have no wish to cause offence by using terms which would be regarded as unacceptable today. At the same time it is, for historical reasons, important to preserve in quotations the terms which were used in the past. They are part of the historical record, and the changes in terminology are in themselves interesting. Thus 'negro' tended to be replaced by 'black' in the 1930s, and then by 'colored' or 'non-white', but without distinction between 'blacks' and 'hispanics'. Apart from direct quotations in the text and the tables, I have tended to use 'black' in preference to the imprecise terms 'colored' or 'non-white'.

[28] Some of the main sources for this section are Helen M. Dart, *Maternity and Child Care in Selected Rural Areas of Mississippi*, Children's Bureau Publications, No. 88 (Washington, DC, 1921); E. Tandy, *Infant and Maternal Mortality among Negroes*, ibid. No. 243 (Washington, DC, 1937); B. M. Haines and E. T. Marsh, 'Four Years of the Federal Maternal and Infancy Act', *Nation's Health*, 8 (1926), 729–32; R. H. Bremner (ed.), *Children and Youth in America* (Cambridge, Mass., 1971); Litoff, *American Midwives*; *The American Midwife Debate*; and G. Erickson, 'Southern Initiative in Public Health Nursing', *Journal of Nursing History*, 3 (1987), 17–29.

TABLE 18.3 *The Birth-Attendants in a Series of Deliveries in Rural Mississippi in 1920*

	White mothers	Black mothers
Total confinements included in survey	296	380
Confinements attended by:		
Physician	234	32
Midwife	48	334
Other woman	12	12
Father	2	1
No one	0	1

Source: Helen M. Dart, *Maternity and Child Care in Selected Rural Areas of Mississippi*, Children's Bureau Publications, No. 88 (Washington, DC, Government 1921).

TABLE 18.4 *Care by Different Types of Birth-Attendant and the Outcome of Deliveries, Alabama, 1935*

	Number of live births	Percentage black	Percentage hospital deliveries	Maternal mortality rate	Stillbirths per 1,000
3 Obstetricians	1,718	1	85	6	26.2
3 white GPs	833	28	62	36	21.6
3 black GPs	1,431	100	4	28	57.3
All midwives	1,372	82	0	44	61.2

Source: J. D. Dowling, 'Points of Interest in a Survey of Maternal Mortality', *American Journal of Public Health*, 27 (1937), 803–8.

mothers was higher in southern states than in the USA as a whole, a finding which was consistent throughout the southern states. Can the higher mortality of black mothers be attributed to any specific cause or causes of maternal mortality? Table 18.7 suggests some differences. There was a larger proportion of deaths due to puerperal sepsis and toxaemia amongst white women in Kentucky, and of deaths due to abortion, embolus, and 'other causes' (which would include some associated or indirect maternal deaths) amongst black women. But the differences are slight and not supported by other reports (see Table 18.5) except that a small excess of toxaemia deaths amongst white women is a more or less consistent finding in several reports. However, the similarities between black and white mothers in this respect are much more impressive than the differences.

Elizabeth Tandy made a special study of this aspect of maternal mortality in

TABLE 18.5 *Maternal Deaths by Cause and by Race, South Carolina, 1934–1935*

	White population	Non-white population
Deliveries by		
Doctors	16,937	3,115
Midwives	2,291	17,593
Others	92	79
Maternal deaths (associated deaths not included)	128[a]	215[a]
Deaths as a percentage of total maternal deaths		
Septic abortion	8.3	8.6
Full term sepsis	14.8	19.5
Total sepsis	23.1	28.1
Albuminuria and eclampsia	43.0	36.2
Haemorrhage	10.0	19.5
Maternal Mortality Rate (deaths per 10,000 births) South Carolina, 1934	66.2	103.4
USA as a whole, 1930–4 (USA death registration area)	57.5	108.1

[a] The difference in mortality rates is highly significant: $P < .001$.

Source: South Carolina Medical Association, Committee on Maternal Welfare, *Maternal Mortality in South Carolina, 1934–5* (1936), Supplement for 1940–1 (1941).

her investigation of infant and maternal mortality amongst blacks in 1937.[29] She concluded that more black women than white died in childbirth, not from any single specific cause, but from all maternal causes, suggesting they received a lower standard of obstetric care all round. It is interesting to see in Table 18.8 that in recent years (specifically 1968–75) the differential between white and black maternal mortality has not only persisted, but has widened with a higher rate of deaths due to abortion and toxaemia amongst black mothers.

Probably the single most important factor during the 1920s and 1930s which caused the high maternal mortality in the USA was excessive mortality in the southern states; and the primary reason for this was the maternal mortality of black women delivered at home by black midwives. What, then, is known about the black midwives of the south in the 1920s and 1930s?

In 1921 Helen Dart of the Children's Bureau visited certain rural areas of Mississippi where there were about 100 women recognized as midwives. The nearest hospital was about 100 miles away, the equivalent in England to living in rural Gloucestershire when the nearest hospital was in London. A few of the midwives were white and literate. Most were black, and two-thirds of

[29] Tandy, *Infant and Maternal Mortality among Negroes*.

TABLE 18.6 *The Proportion of Births Attended by Midwives in Various Countries and Various States in the USA*

Country	Year	Midwife-attended births expressed as percentage of total
Australia	1922	24.0
Scotland	1923	37.0
England and Wales	1923	53.6
The Netherlands	1916	58.9
Sweden	1921	84.3
Norway	1918	85.0
USA		
Mississippi	1923	48.0
North Carolina	1923	35.0
Alabama	1923	32.0
Kentucky	1923	18.0
New York State exclusive of New York City	1918	16.0
New York City	1921	26.0
Wisconsin	1923	10.0
Michigan	1923	7.0
Indiana	1923	5.0
Iowa	1923	0.1

Source: R. M. Woodbury, *Maternal Mortality: The Risk of Death in Childbirth and from all the Diseases Caused by Pregnancy and Confinement*, Children's Bureau Publications, No. 152 (Washington, DC, 1926), 88.

TABLE 18.7 *Maternal Deaths by Cause, Kentucky, 1932–1936*

Cause	White	Black	Total
Puerperal septicaemia	24.0	19.0	24.0
Abortion	12.0	15.0	12.0
Toxaemia	13.0	10.0	13.0
Haemorrhage	9.0	7.0	8.0
'Other conditions of pregnancy'	12.0	9.0	12.0
'Other accidents of childbirth'	24.0	25.0	24.0
Ectopic gestation	2.0	5.0	3.0
Embolus and sudden death	0.3	1.2	0.4
Other causes	c.4.0	c.7.0	c.4.0

Source: C. B. Crittenden and Lois Skaggs, *Maternal Mortality in Kentucky: A Study of Puerperal Deaths, 1932–1939*, Kentucky State Department of Health (1939).

TABLE 18.8 *Maternal Mortality Rates per 10,000 births in the USA, 1968–1975*

	Total	White	Black	Ratio:black/white
Approximate maternal mortality rates in 1930–5 for comparison		60.00	110.00	1.8
Total maternal mortality rate	1.87	1.31	4.8	3.7
Pregnancy with abortive outcome	0.42	0.24	1.37	5.7
Legally induced abortion	0.02	0.01	0.05	5.0
Illegally induced abortion	0.09	0.05	0.29	5.8
Complications of pregnancy	0.51	0.34	1.34	3.9
Eclampsia/toxaemia	0.30	0.18	0.87	4.8
Complications of delivery	0.47	0.34	1.14	3.3
Placenta praevia	0.03	0.02	0.06	3.0
PPH/retained placenta	0.09	0.06	0.24	4.0
Complications of puerperium	0.46	0.37	0.94	2.5
Sepsis	0.06	0.05	1.29	25.8

Source: R. W. Rochat, 'Maternal Mortality in the USA', *World Health Statistics Quarterly*, 34 (1984), 1–13.

these were illiterate. Not only were most of them old, but many were worn out and continued in practice only because black mothers distrusted young midwives. This preference for the older 'granny midwife' and distrust of young black midwives who, through training and association with white doctors had ceased to be regarded as traditional, persisted in rural areas of the southern states at least until the 1960s and made the improvements in obstetric care a difficult process.[30]

When Helen Dart undertook her survey in 1921 neither the black nor the white midwives were adequately trained. Some had 'taken to' the job and received some instruction from physicians. Many followed in the steps of their mothers and grandmothers. Some said they had been 'called by God'. As far as they and their patients were concerned, training by professional white folk was not a necessary qualification; it was often a positive disadvantage.[31] Many of these midwives dealt with major complications with no appreciation of the danger of their methods.

[30] B. Mongeau, H. Smith, and A. Maney, 'The "granny" Midwife: Changing Roles and Functions of a Folk Tradition', *American Journal of Sociology*, 66 (1961), 497–505, reprinted (in part) in R. Dingwall and J. McIntosh (eds.), *Readings in the Sociology of Nursing* (Edinburgh, 1978), 135–49. I am grateful to Dr R. Dingwall for drawing my attention to this paper.
[31] The importance of custom in the choice of birth-attendant was shown by a black mother who, although she lived in a town close to a doctor and could have afforded to employ him, preferred to send 3 miles out into the country for a midwife to deliver her. Dart, *Maternal and Child Care in Mississippi*.

Some of their methods were primitive. Over nine tenths used no antiseptics whatever ... One said 'No washing is necessary if grease is used plentifully'. Various
questionable expedients were used to bring away the afterbirth; some of the midwives
used a method of warming the patient suddenly by putting her over a bucket of hot
ashes or burning feathers, while two advocated putting an umbrella or black hat over
her face.[32]

Black women often married early and had large families. Out of 675 deliveries
in Helen Dart's study 3 mothers died of maternal causes—2 from puerperal
septicaemia, and 1 from haemorrhage—leaving 13 motherless children
between them. One death on the fourth postnatal day, attributed to malaria,
was probably due to puerperal septicaemia. In addition, 10 mothers died
within eight months of their confinement of diseases such as pellagra,
tuberculosis, and nephritis.[33]

Similar findings were published in a report on midwife deliveries in the
region of Austin, Texas in 1924.[34] Here the majority of midwives were
Mexican or black and some of the descriptions were bizarre. The Director of
the Bureau of Child Hygiene who wrote this report said:

I wish it were possible to picture to the reader of this report the usual class of women
practising as midwives ... Illiterate, usually dirty and in rags, gesticulating, oftentimes
not able to talk or understand the English language, superstitious and suspicious,
often with the only knowledge of obstetrics and nursing as handed down to them by
their mothers ... [their] practice is seldom if ever in accord with modern science.

The Mexican midwife was often 'difficult to manage ... highstrung and
suspicious of the Americans'. Fearing prosecution or some kind of interference from authority, 'a very common occurence on a second visit to a
Mexican midwife is to find both midwife and house gone—nothing left to tell
the tale except a vacant lot'.[35]

Two of the midwives who were interviewed were completely blind. They
managed, they said, because they had been endowed 'with divine power'. In
one county a midwife was found with three-quarters of her face sloughed
away, leaving a discharging open cavity. She had been treated in a hospital
and advised to discontinue her practice, but 'she is still merrily going on'.
This report describes many of the traditional measures taken by midwives
such as stuffing the birth canal with a mixture of sugar and soot in cases of
post-partum haemorrhage. It was obvious that amongst the clientele of these
midwives many births were unregistered and many stillbirths and infant
deaths not reported. It is highly probable that a number of maternal deaths in

---

[32] Ibid.
[33] Ibid.
[34] M. Duggan, *Report on the Midwife Survey in Texas, January 2nd, 1925*, in Litoff, *The American
Midwife Debate*, 67–81.
[35] Ibid.

the 1920s never reached the official statistics. The MMR amongst the black population delivered by black women was not exaggerated; almost certainly it was larger than the records suggest.

American health authorities were, as one would guess, shocked by these reports. During the 1930s a number of southern states began to establish training programmes for midwives, and there is evidence that younger midwives were eager to learn. The South Carolina Medical Association remarked in 1936 that there had been a considerable improvement in the practice of midwives. But they also noted that it was still customary for the midwife to be paid at best with a few dollars, and more often with the gift of a chicken, some eggs, or a few vegetables. As a result, the more intelligent and better-educated midwives found occupation amongst the middle classes where, 'while they fill a very useful purpose, the money and time spent on them by the Board of Health has not been justified in so far as increasing [trained] midwife care to those who need it'.[36]

The higher mortality rate in childbirth of black mothers compared with white was, and remains, a difficult problem. There was no doubt in the minds of southern health authorities in the 1920s and 1930s that the answer to the problem was provision of orthodox care by training midwives and providing black physicians. Some of these authorities, failing to appreciate the power of tradition, became impatient when the black population rejected young well-trained midwives and preferred the old 'grannies'. It could be argued that this was naïve (some have called it 'racist') and the right approach would have been to respect and support the traditions and the choices of southern black mothers at a time when orthodox obstetric care in the USA was not necessarily an attractive alternative.

It is also true that the health of black women was worse in all respects than the health of white women, and that this, rather than the conduct of black midwives, may have been an important factor in the high level of black maternal mortality. Poor health was certainly a factor, but it would be foolish to deny that many of the childbirth practices of the black midwives were extremely dangerous and must have caused many unnecessary maternal deaths. When trained midwives were established in a predominantly black community, although the morbidity and mortality of women of childbearing age seldom altered significantly, their risk of dying in childbirth was reduced substantially. In rural Kentucky the introduction of a trained midwife service in the 1930s not only lowered maternal mortality but led to the interesting observation that 'the districts in which the maternal death rates are lowest are those in which there are fewest physicians'.[37] The ability of trained midwives

---

[36] South Carolina Medical Association, *Maternal Mortality in South Carolina, 1934–5* (1936).
[37] C. B. Crittenden and Lois Skaggs, *Maternal Mortality in Kentucky: A Study of Puerperal Deaths, 1932–1939*, Kentucky State Department of Health (1940).

to lower maternal mortality is a very important feature of the history of maternal mortality, as we see in the next section of this chapter.

THE KENTUCKY FRONTIER NURSING SERVICE

I regard this as one of the most remarkable episodes in the history of maternal and child care in the United States. There are only a few occasions when an individual established a technique or a service which had a profoundly beneficial effect on maternal care. Gordon of Aberdeen and Semmelweis are obvious and famous examples. At the level of small communities, Dr Andrew Topping, the Medical Officer of Health at Rochdale in the early 1930s (the 'Rochdale experiment') is known to most historians of maternal care in Britain. Probably the least well known is Mary Breckinridge and the service she established in 1925: the Kentucky Frontier Nursing Service.[38]

Born in 1881, Mary Breckinridge came from the upper levels of southern society where her family was politically as well as socially prominent. Following the sudden death of her first husband shortly after marriage she decided to devote her life to the cause of children and trained as a nurse at St Lukes Hospital in New York, entering at the age of 25 and graduating in 1910. She then remarried, postponed her nursing career, and bore two children; the first was stillborn and the second, a son, died at the age of 4. It was a devastating blow, but she was a woman of remarkable strength. The death of her adored son, followed by the divorce of her husband, made her determined to undertake nursing and remain free of family ties. She worked briefly for the Children's Bureau until she left for France in 1918 as a volunteer in the American Committee for Devastated France, and she organized an extensive scheme of child welfare in the Aisne region. While there, she acquired an extensive knowledge of French hospitals and of French and British nursing; and she noticed that:

In France midwives were not nurses. In America nurses were not midwives. In England trained women were both nurses and midwives. After I had met British nurse-midwives, first in France and then on my visits to London, it grew upon me that nurse-midwifery was the logical response to the needs of the young child in rural America ... Work for children should begin before they are born, should carry them through their greatest hazard which is childbirth and should be most intensive during their first six years of life.[39]

---

[38] The main sources on the Frontier Nursing Service are the autobiography of Mary Breckinridge, *Wide Neighbourhoods: A Story of the Frontier Nursing Service* (New York, 1952) and her short paper 'The Nurse-Midwife, a Pioneer', *American Journal of Public Health*, 17 (1927), 1141–51. See also N. S. Dye, 'Mary Breckinridge, the Frontier Nursing Service and the Introduction of Nurse-Midwifery in the United States', *Bulletin of the History of Medicine*, 57 (1983), 485–507; K. E. Wilkie and E. R. Moseley, *Frontier Nurse: Mary Breckinridge* (New York, 1969). An account of recent work by this Service can be found in H. E. Browne and G. Isaccs, 'The Frontier Nursing Service: The Primary Care Nurse in the Community Hospital', *American Journal of Obstetrics and Gynaecology*, 121 (1976), 14–17.

[39] Breckinridge, *Wide Neighbourhoods*, 111.

She decided to establish a service for children in her home territory, Leslie County, Kentucky, with a population of 10,000. It was a remote mountainous area with numerous valleys and ravines. Journeys were only possible on foot or horseback and a visit to the nearest town a few miles away took all day. The people, scattered through the valleys, were mostly white and of British origin 'with a sprinkling of Huguenot and Dutch Pennsylvanians'. They were poor, with no access to medical care, and they suffered high rates of maternal and infant mortality, and a very high level of chronic ill-health from disorders such as anaemia, tuberculosis, and worm infestation.[40] Almost all deliveries were by midwives, and all except one of the fifty-three midwives that she interviewed and stayed with were white. Their average age was 60. They were typical of the neighbour-midwives of rural America. Two were illiterate, about fifteen were conspicuously dirty, but most were 'intelligent women whose homes were tidy and gay with flowers'. None, however, was trained, and there were harrowing stories of preventable maternal deaths.

She saw that she needed obstetric training. In 1923, at the age of 42, she enrolled as a pupil-midwife at the Woolwich British Hospital for Mothers and Babies (previously the British Lying-in Hospital), put on the cap, uniform, and apron of the pupil and 'stepped back' into the work of a student nurse. It was a remarkable step for a woman, no longer young, who had already made a name for herself nationally with her public health work in America and France. She qualified as a midwife in 1924 and with the help and encouragement of a London obstetrician, Dr J. S. Fairbairn, and Sir Leslie Mackenzie—who was instrumental in establishing the Highlands and Islands Medical and Nursing Service—she toured Scotland to see how the service worked. She was so deeply impressed that in 1925 she returned to Kentucky and established the Frontier Nursing Service on the model of the Highlands and Islands Service.

In the Kentucky service the nurse-midwives were either recruited from England or sent from America to England to be trained. All were required to hold the certificate of the English Midwives' Board. By 1930 there were more than thirty nurses, most of whom lived in pairs in outpost nursing centres. Each nurse covered about 75 square miles of the total of 700 square miles of territory, travelling on horseback with two pairs of saddle-bags, one for general nursing, the other for midwifery, and also a lantern because 'very few of our homes have a light other than the open fire'.[41]

By 1928–9 the new service had been adopted by the population for almost all deliveries. A family could register for general health care for $1 a year. The midwifery service cost $5. Fees were paid in cash or, more commonly, in kind. For every patient the same nurse-midwife carried out antenatal care,

---

[40] Ibid. 169.
[41] Details of the work of the service can be found in Breckinridge, 'A Frontier Nursing Service', *American Journal of Obstetrics and Gynaecology*, 15 (1928), 867–72.

TABLE 18.9 *Maternal Mortality Rate of Deliveries Undertaken by the Kentucky Frontier Nursing Service*

	Maternal mortality rate (per 10,000 births)
Frontier nursing service, 1925–1965[a]	
Direct and indirect deaths	9.2
Direct deaths only	7.5
USA, 1939–41	36.3
Frontier nursing service, 1925–37[b]	6.6
Kentucky state (white population only), 1925–1937	44–53
White women delivered in hospitals by physicians in the city of Lexington, Kentucky, 1925–37	80–90
USA, 1925–37	
Total population	56–70
White population	51–63
Non-white population	90–120

[a] Over 12,000 deliveries: 2 indirect deaths and 9 direct deaths.
[b] Approx. 3,000 deliveries: 2 maternal deaths.

Source: N. S. Dye, 'Mary Breckinridge, The Frontier Nursing Service and the Introduction of Nurse-Midwifery in the United States', *Bulletin of the History of Medicine*, 5 (1983), 501; H. E. Browne and G. Isaccs, 'The Frontier Nursing Service: The Primary Case Nurse in the Community Hospital', *American Journal of Obstetrics and Gynaecology*, 121 (1976), 14–17.

delivered the baby, and looked after the mother and child thereafter. Intervention was kept at a very low level. In the period 1925–37, the period of the first 3,000 deliveries, physicians were called in to perform Caesarean section on six occasions, and forceps were used fourteen times—a forceps rate of less than 1 per cent.

The results in terms of maternal mortality, which were astonishing, can be seen in Table 18.9. Between 1925 and 1937, the MMR achieved by this service was about one-seventh of the rate for women in the state of Kentucky, one-tenth of the rate for the USA as a whole, and one-twelfth of the mortality of white women delivered by physicians in hospital in the nearby city of Lexington. During the depression, which occurred in this period, thousands of men from the mountains who had sought better opportunities for their families outside the area, lost their jobs and poured back into the mountains without cows, pigs, or chickens in a county where the margin of living was never far from bare subsistence.[42] Infant mortality rose, but maternal mortality did not, in line with the general principle that infant mortality is sensitive to social and economic change to a much greater extent than maternal mortality.

[42] Dye, 'Mary Breckinridge', 503–5.

For the general public, the Frontier Nursing Service was an appealingly romantic story of wild country, horseback riding, and dedicated nurses battling with the elements. An article 'Nurses on horseback', published in *Good Housekeeping* in the early 1930s, was one of a series to appear in magazines.[43] But the image was that of a service for remote areas, which allowed urban obstetricians to praise her work while stressing its irrelevance to mainstream American obstetrics and the trend throughout the USA to hospital rather than home deliveries. Breckinridge had no illusions. She knew this, and repeatedly stressed that the service was designed for the 'remotely rural areas' where she could achieve the independence on which her plans had depended.[44]

Very few appreciated the momentous implications of the Frontier Nursing Service. Louis Dublin, a statistician with a special interest in maternal welfare, saw the Frontier Service as the 'new midwifery' with 'national implications with reference to the health and welfare of mothers and children within our frontiers'.[45] George Kosmak, the influential editor of the *American Journal of Obstetrics and Gynaecology*, was influenced favourably towards midwives both by the Kentucky service and by a visit to Scandinavia.[46] But that was the extent of support for what was one of the most remarkably efficient and safe maternity services anywhere in the USA at this time. Such was the prejudice against midwives that Breckinridge even met opposition in her own state. The staff of the Frontier Nursing Service established a Kentucky State Association of Midwives, but it received no support, and a plan to introduce a system for the certification of midwives along the lines of the English system was unsuccessful. We see next just how powerful was the opposition to the midwife in the USA.

OBSTETRICIANS AGAINST MIDWIVES

In the USA during the inter-war period, midwives received no support from hospital nurses. Even the public health nurses, who were more supportive, opposed the concept of the independent midwife. So strong was the prejudice against the word 'midwife', that nurse-midwives who followed a career in nursing found it wise when applying for posts to suppress their midwifery training. American obstetricians would accept an obstetric nurse who worked alongside a physician. What they would not accept was a competitor in the form of an independent midwife working largely on her own.[47]

[43] Ibid. 503.
[44] Ibid. 505.
[45] Ibid. 504.
[46] G. W. Kosmak, 'Result of Supervised Midwife Practice in Certain European Countries', *Journal of the American Medical Association*, 89 (1927), 2009–12.
[47] Dye, 'Mary Breckinridge', 506.

The opposition of the medical profession in the USA to the midwife was expressed in a series of unrelenting attacks so vitriolic they take your breath away. The typical midwife was, in the words of physicians, 'filthy and ignorant and not far removed from the jungles of Africa'; 'typically old, gin-fingering, guzzling . . . with her pockets full of snuff, her fingers full of dirt and her brains full of arrogance and superstition'; 'pestiferous' and 'vicious', and not least 'un-American'.[48]

J. B. DeLee of Chicago and Williams of Baltimore, usually at odds with each other, were united in the belief that the midwife should be abolished. DeLee's view was that:

The midwife is a relic of barbarism. In civilized countries the midwife is wrong, has always been wrong. The greatest bar to human progress has been compromise, and the midwife demands compromise between right and wrong. All admit that the midwife is wrong; it has been proven time and again that it impossible to make her right . . .

In ignorance or defiance of evidence to the contrary he also held that: 'European countries for centuries have been trying to bring the midwife up to a tolerable standard, and, measured even by their low standards, have failed miserably.'[49] To provide further examples from the long list of the abusive descriptions would be tedious and repetitive when so much of it was based on anecdote and sheer prejudice. More to the point is to ask why midwives were attacked with such savagery and why America chose the option of abolishing the midwife instead of the European plan of educating her and regulating her practice?

The simple answer is crude self-interest in the competitive world of American medical practice where too many doctors and midwives were chasing too few deliveries. Money, in other words. But it was more than that. If obstetricians were to establish their speciality on the same level as internal medicine and surgery, the abolition of the general practitioner obstetrician and the midwife was seen as an essential part of that strategy. Obstetricians had to prove their worth. As DeLee observed: 'The public reasons correctly. If an uneducated woman of the lowest classes may practice obstetrics, is instructed by doctors and licensed by the state, it surely must require little knowledge and skill—surely it cannot belong to the science and art of medicine.'[50] In addition, if the midwife was trained, regulated, and accepted, 'she would come under public supervision, often as a salaried employee in a public clinic. Her survival would necessarily strengthen the public sector of

---

[48] Neal Deavitt, 'The Statistical Case for the Elimination of the Midwife', *Women and Health*, 4 (1979), 89.

[49] J. B. DeLee, 'Progress toward Ideal Obstetrics', *American Journal of Obstetrics*, 73 (1916), 407–15.

[50] Quoted by Deavitt, 'The Statistical Case', 91.

medicine . . . in a privately controlled and unregulated market.'[51] This ruled out the possibility of close co-operation between midwives and obstetricians.

Yet, amongst the very poorest parts of the population, competition did not come into it. Few physicians relished the prospect of delivering a woman and being paid with a chicken or a few eggs. The physicians of Texas in the 1920s deplored the ignorance and incompetence of the black and Mexican midwives, but admitted they were a necessary evil.

Midwifery persisted throughout the South as an explicitly second-class health care delivery system for blacks. Provided that midwives knew, and kept, their place, the white doctors allowed them to continue to practice unhindered among clients whom the doctors had no desire to take on. In return, the doctors passed on advances in their knowledge and allowed black midwives to use their assistant's role at white deliveries as a source of learning about improved practice.[52]

The stories of the immigrant midwives of the cities, and the black midwives of the southern states, provided the obstetricians with plenty of ammunition. The most ferocious attacks on the midwives date from around the time of the First World War when it was realized that maternal mortality in the USA was not falling but rising. In the eyes of the obstetricians the midwife was a hazard to the public health, which was a better reason for attacking her than mere self-interest. Yet the belief that the scourge of maternal mortality could be laid at the door of the midwives was not always supported by the evidence. There are in fact two questions about midwives in the USA which need to be answered. First, were midwives responsible for the high level of maternal mortality? Secondly, were midwife deliveries necessarily more dangerous than deliveries by physicians?

The answer to the first question is 'sometimes'. There seems little doubt that in the southern states, or at least some parts of those states, high maternal mortality was associated with the dangerous practices of untrained midwives. And the same is probably true of some immigrant areas of New York and Chicago in the early years of this century. We have reviewed the evidence for this, but the evidence did not apply to the USA as a whole.

As for the second question, there is no doubt that the properly trained midwife produced results as good if not better than the physician. One can find no more eloquent evidence of the value of the trained nurse-midwife than the Kentucky Frontier Nursing Service. It could be argued that remote areas are special, but there is important evidence from the work of Julius Levy, the Director of the Division of Child Health in the Board of Health in Newark.

[51] See the perceptive chapter by Janet P. Brickman, 'Public Health, Midwives and Nurses, 1880–1930', in Ellen C. Lagermann (ed.), *Nursing History: New Perspectives, New Possibilities* (New York, 1983).
[52] R. Dingwall and J. McIntosh, *Readings in the Sociology of Nursing* (Edinburgh, 1978), 137.

TABLE 18.10 *Maternal Mortality by Birth-Attendant in Various States in the USA, 1914–1928*

Attendant	Live births	Maternal deaths	Maternal mortality rate
Newark, 1916–21			
Physician	38,706	267	69[a]
Midwife	30,945	47	15[a]
Total	69,651	314	45
Philadelphia, 1914–30			
Physician	593,861	4,428	74.6[a]
Midwife	90,926	77	8.5[a]
Total	684,787	4,505	65.8
Alabama, Kentucky, and Virginia, 1927–8[b] (White births)			
Physician	192,760 (90%)	787	41[c]
Midwife	22,336 (10%)	98	44[c]
Total	215,096	885	41
(Black births)			
Physician	34,741 (38%)	386	111[a]
Midwife	57,336 (62%)	295	51[a]
Total	92,077	681	74

[a] The difference is significant: $P < 0.001$.
[b] Maternal mortality after seven months' gestation.
[c] The difference is not significant.

Source: N. Devitt, 'The Statistical Case for the Elimination of the Midwife', *Women and Health*, 4 (1979), 173–4.

Newark, like New York and Chicago, had many immigrant midwives. When Levy began his investigations into the midwives of Newark in 1914, he found the same deplorable state of affairs that existed across the river in New York, the same dirtiness, the same procuring of abortions, the same neglect of elementary principles of good obstetric practice, and the same low morale. He established a programme of reform through education and persuasion and found that the midwife with low standards was often an apt pupil.

In three years Julius Levy had transformed the standards and the sense of professional pride of the midwives to such an extent that it was safer to be delivered by a midwife than by a physician in Newark in the 1920s. The evidence can be seen in Table 18.10. Can we accept the Newark evidence at face value? It was often argued that midwives achieved better results than physicians by off-loading their complicated cases and retaining the straightforward ones. But in Newark, as Levy explained, the evidence was obtained in spite of the scales being loaded against the midwife: 'every puerperal death where it appears that a midwife was in attendance *at any time* is charged to the midwife ... even when it appears that the result was due to unnecessary interference or negligence on the part of the doctor' [*original italics*].[53] Several other reports from public health departments and various associations—the South Carolina Medical Association, for example—show a great improvement in midwife morale and standards of care as a result of midwife training programmes.[54]

Inevitably, this account of the midwives of the USA is incomplete. A great deal about their practice remains unknown, although excellent studies have been published by American scholars such as Litoff, Leavitt, and Kobrin. The American midwife remains a fruitful subject for further research. A recent paper by Charlotte Borst provides new data which suggests there were exceptions to some of the generalizations made in this chapter.

Her study of the midwives of Wisconsin shows there were two schools of midwifery in Milwaukee founded by German immigrant women (the first in 1879, the second in 1885). She distinguishes between three classes of midwives: the neighbour-women, the apprenticed-trained midwives, and the school-educated midwives. Between 1870 and 1920 there was a steady evolution from the first to the third. There was often quite close co-operation between physicians and midwives not only in the country where it might be expected, but in towns such as Milwaukee. Where most researchers have described the midwife as a victim of the crisis in the professionalization of obstetricians, she sees the crisis of professionalization as one between trained ('schooled') midwives on the one hand and untrained midwives on the other.[55]

In view of the evidence of the low maternal mortality achieved by midwives when they were trained and imbued with professional pride, there is little support for the belief of the obstetricians of the 1920s and 1930s that the midwife was necessarily dangerous or that she was to blame for the high level of maternal deaths in the USA as a whole. Nation-wide programmes of midwife recruitment and training could have done more than anything else

---

[53] J. Levy, 'The Maternal and Infant Mortality in Midwifery Practice in Newark, N.J.', *American Journal of Obstetrics*, 77 (1918), 41–53. Other lines of enquiry showed similar results. Table 18.10, for instance, shows that, in the states of Alabama, Virginia, and Kentucky in the late 1920s, midwives did no better (but equally no worse) than physicians in the delivery of white women. But midwives did much better than physicians in the delivery of black women. On the whole it seems that the existence of training and supervisory programmes was the key to a low maternal mortality. As Janet Brickman remarked of midwives in general in the early years of this century: 'When city departments regulated her, the midwife often established effective mutuality with health officials. Regulations seemed to inspire midwives' professional pride.' Brickman, 'Public Health, Midwives and Nurses, 1880–1930'.

[54] South Carolina Medical Association, *Maternal Mortality in South Carolina*.

[55] C. G. Borst, 'The Training and Practice of Midwives: A Wisconsin Study', *Bulletin of the History of Medicine*, 62 (1988), 606–27.

to reduce deaths in childbirth in the critical period of the 1920s. The intemperate attacks on midwives by obstetricians were ill-considered, unjust, and had a lasting effect. They laid the foundations of the deep and unjustified prejudice against midwives in the USA which persists to the present day.

19

The American Lying-in Hospital, 1850–1910

Although there were certain differences between British and American lying-in (maternity) hospitals—for instance many British lying-in hospitals had been founded in the eighteenth century, the obstetricians were unpaid honorary consultants, and they always employed midwives to undertake the majority of deliveries—the similarities tended to outweigh the differences.[1] In both countries lying-in hospitals were small institutions delivering only a few hundred women a year when certain European state maternities were delivering several thousand. None the less, in Britain and the USA, although they contributed little to the totality of maternal care, these hospitals were potent symbols of civic pride, medical progress, and the philanthropic impulse tempered with morality. Their patients were the 'deserving poor'. It was common to refuse admission to prostitutes and those judged guilty of blatant immorality. The Minnesota Maternity in Minneapolis was founded in the 1880s specifically for 'the confinement of married women who are without means or suitable abode and care at the time of childbirth and may also admit girls who under the promise of marriage have been led astray'.[2] Similar rules could be found in some British lying-in hospitals. Another feature which they shared with every other Western country was the dreadful nineteenth-century rate of maternal mortality.

In 1887 Hirst published a paper which showed that the maternal mortality of American lying-in hospitals was even higher than those of Europe (Table 19.1), confirming what Garrigues had already found a decade earlier (Table 19.2). Hirst concluded that: 'No hospital, whether supported by the community or by private charity, has the right to subject its inmates to a danger of death much greater than if they had remained in their own homes no matter how squalid they might be.'[3] When maternal mortality rates of over 200 per

---

[1] The most comprehensive contemporary account of 19th-cent. lying-in hospitals in the USA is the classic paper by Henry J. Garrigues, 'On Lying-in Institutions, especially those of New York', *Transactions of the American Gynaecological Society*, 2 (1878), 593–649. Two outstanding histories of the American hospital, to which I am indebted, have been published recently: C. E. Rosenberg, *The Care of Strangers: The Rise of America's Hospital System* (New York, 1987), and R. Stevens, *In Sickness and in Wealth: American Hospitals in the Twentieth Century* (New York, 1989).

[2] Quoted in Rosenberg, *The Care of Strangers*, 270.

[3] B. C. Hirst, 'The Death Rate of Lying-in Hospitals in the United States', *Medical News of Philadelphia*, 50 (1887), 253–6. Hirst was obstetrician to the Maternity Hospital in Philadelphia and obstetrical registrar to the Philadelphia Hospital.

TABLE 19.1 *The Maternal Mortality Rates of Lying-in Hospitals in Different Countries and of American Lying-in Hospitals in the 1880s*

Country	Number of deliveries	Maternal mortality rate (per 10,000 deliveries)
Germany		
47 hospitals, 1874–83	104,328	137
England		
10 hospitals, 1870–5	18,369	105
Vienna I, 1880–5	15,070	70
Vienna II, 1882–5	8,355	52
Paris		
Maternité, 1876–82	1,223	49
Selected USA hospitals, 1880–5		
New York Infirmary for Women and Children	613	48
Philadelphia Maternity	503	79
Chicago Lying-in	515	135
Minneapolis Hospital	45	222
New York Blackwell's Island	2,842	292
Boston Lying-in	1,599	310
Philadelphia Almshouse Hospital	1,099	434
Detroit Women's Hospital	295	474
Indianapolis City Hospital	323	526
New Orleans Charity Hospital	1,808	532
Chicago Women's Refuge	60	666
USA 34 Hospitals, 1880–5	19,902	259

Source: B. C. Hirst, 'The Death Rate of Lying-in Hospitals in the United States', *Medical News of Philadelphia*, 50 (1887), 253–6.

10,000 deliveries were commonplace in hospitals, Hirst suggested—rather surprisingly in view of his statement quoted above—that an acceptable level of maternal mortality in a lying-in hospital would be a rate which did not exceed 1.5 per cent or 150 deaths per 10,000 births. Although this mortality rate was about three times the rate for home deliveries in England and Wales or the Eastern States of the USA, Hirst could accept it because many lying-in hospitals were situated in or close to working-class ghettos and slums where they represented islands of humanity and public concern in seas of deprivation. Not that the internal economy of hospitals was ideal. Far from it. Apart from the more spectacular stories of neglect, bad food, and rats in the wards, lying-in women were often exploited and singled out for harshly moralistic

TABLE 19.2 *Maternal Mortality Rate in New York's Lying-in Hospitals between 1856 and 1876 and the Estimated Rate for Home Deliveries in New York in 1870*

	Women confined	Deaths	Maternal mortality rate (per 10,000 births)
Private lying-in hospitals			
Lying-in Asylum, 1856–76	1,923	21	109
Infant Asylum, 1872–6	418	5	120
Infirmary for Women and Children	995	12	121
Nursery and Child's Hospital			
City, 1867–76	1,479	60	405
Country, 1872 and 1874–7	365	11	301
Public lying-in hospitals			
Charity Hospital, 1874–6 (2½ years)	1,381	36	260
Emigrant Hospital, 1868–76	3,766	99	262
Home deliveries, New York, 1870	273,428	2,922	107

Source: Henry J. Garrigues, 'On Lying-in Institutions, especially those of New York', *Transactions of the American Gynaecological Society*, 2 (1878), 593–649.

treatment.[4] At the Sloane Hospital for Women in New York there was a tradition of employing what they called 'waiting women' who, in return for hospital care, spent their pregnancy working as cleaners. Most were homeless and many spent months in the hospital before disappearing from sight. It was 1920 before this was abolished and cleaners were employed on a regular basis.[5]

Why did women apply for admission to lying-in hospitals when they were subjected to harsh treatment and a high risk of dying of puerperal fever? It was likely they knew how they would be treated by the staff through ordinary gossip, but they would not necessarily appreciate the extent of the danger (after all, an MMR as disastrous as 500 per 10,000 births is a 95 per cent survival rate). Even if they knew of the danger, however, most of the women were homeless or came from homes where warmth, care, regular meals, and fees for medical care were scarce or non-existent. For them, the ordered environment of the hospital and the provision of warmth and shelter at the

---

[4] The two illustrations opposite p. 182 in Rosenberg, *The Care of Strangers*, neatly illustrate both sides of the picture. On the one hand impressive architecture and civic pride; on the other a rat-infested ward. See also Rosenberg's descriptions of 'Ladies of charity and their erring sisters', ibid. 267.

[5] W. E. Studdiford, 'The Relation of Obstetrics to Preventitive Medicine', *Boston Medical and Surgical Journal*, 191 (1924), 617–30.

time of childbirth outweighed the disadvantages. The mothers of remote areas of Montana, mentioned in the last chapter, faced with the problems of childbirth in the depths of winter, would have given their eye-teeth for the warmth of a hospital bed and the comfort of a physician on hand.

Therefore, in spite of the high mortality, and for a variety of reasons—some humanitarian, some self-serving—the retention of the lying-in hospitals was supported by the medical profession and civic authorities. Faced with the statistics of mortality, they argued that comparisons between home and hospital were unfair. It was the same problem we met in comparing home with hospital mortality in Britain; where a maternity hospital admitted a selected population of high-risk cases and emergency admissions (and in fact few did before the late nineteenth century) this argument had some force. A paper on the first 5,000 obstetrical cases at the Johns Hopkins Hospital was published in 1908. Although it does not specify the number of emergency admissions, it makes an important point. Johns Hopkins ran both in-patient and out-patient maternity services. The former had delivered 2,250 cases, the latter 2,750. 'Wherever possible, abnormal or complicated cases occurring in the outside service are brought into hospital. This explains the preponderance of fatalities among the hospital cases, among whom 48 out of the 55 deaths occurred.'[6]

The analysis of mortality in institutional deliveries is seldom straight-forward. That selection of high-risk cases and the admission of emergencies was partly responsible for high hospital mortality is probable. That it was the whole or even a large part of the reason for high hospital mortality is unlikely. But the question became largely academic with the introduction of by far the most important measure in the history of the maternity hospital: the techniques first of antisepsis and then of asepsis. Antisepsis was in-troduced in the leading American hospitals around 1884.

ANTISEPSIS AND HOSPITAL DELIVERIES

Table 19.3 shows the MMR of patients in the Boston Lying-in Hospital in successive decades from 1873 to 1944. It can be seen that the sudden fall from an MMR of 329 to 85 was largely due to a fall in deaths from sepsis.[7] Total maternal mortality fell in the decade 1885–94 to a quarter of its value in the previous decade; deaths from sepsis to less than a tenth. The number of births is small, rising from about 300 a year to 600 by the end of the

---

[6] F. C. Goldsborough, 'Maternal Mortality in the First 5,000 Obstetrical Cases at the Johns Hopkins Hospital', *Johns Hopkins Hospital Bulletin*, 19 (1908), 12–19. Goldsborough was Instructor in Obstetrics at the Johns Hopkins Hospital, Baltimore.

[7] Hirst said that the introduction of antisepsis and 'the sudden decrease in the mortality of the Boston Lying-in Hospital, in 1884, was the result of a letter calling the attention of the managers to the really murderous death-rate of former years in that institution.' Hirst, 'The Death Rate of Lying-in Hospitals', 254.

TABLE 19.3 *Boston Lying-In Hospital: The Outcome of In-Patient and Out-Patient Deliveries, 1873–1944*

	Deliveries	Total maternal deaths	Deaths from puerperal sepsis	Maternal mortality rate (per 10,000 births)	Puerperal sepsis deaths as a percentage of total deaths
In-patient deliveries					
1873–84	2,921	96	64	329	66
1885–94	4,368	37	6	85	16
1895–1904	6,260	91	13	145	14
1904–14	8,151	176	37	215	21
1915–24	9,899	175	29	176	17
1925–34	22,555	172	43	76	25
1935–44	26,612	66	9	25	14
Boston Lying-in Hospital out-patient department					
1881–1940	74,093	82	—	11	—
Boston Lying-in Hospital in-patient deliveries					
1885–1944	77,845	717	—	92	—

Source: The data were abstracted from the records of the Boston Lying-in Hospital, in the Rare books division, Countway Medical Library, Boston.

century. With such small numbers, the results shown in this table are only convincing in the context of the generality of the post-1884 decline in other lying-in hospitals. This was the subject of a leading article in the *Journal of the American Medical Association* in 1902 which pointed out that maternity hospitals had for the first time achieved a lower mortality from sepsis than that observed in private practice.[8]

In 1902, George Englemann, President of the Obstetrical Society of Boston, read a paper in which he discussed maternal mortality in the 'post-antiseptic era'.[9] 'This era', he said, 'was earlier in the [nineteenth] century in one country than it is in another; earlier in the hospital than in the community at large.' In Austrian hospitals it began in 1879; in Parisian hospitals in 1882. In Germany throughout the community in 1883 and in the USA in 1884. As a result of antisepsis, maternal mortality had fallen in the New York Maternity from 417 maternal deaths per 10,000 births to 18, in the Boston Lying-in

---

[8] 'Puerperal Infection in Private Practice' (leading article), *Journal of the American Medical Association*, 38 (1902), 541–2.

[9] G. J. Englemann, 'Birth and Death Rate as Influenced by Obstetric and Gynecic progress', *Boston Medical and Surgical Journal*, 146 (1902), 505–8, 541–4.

Hospital from 600 to 80, in the City of New York from 110 to 42, in the state of Michigan from 170 to 140 and in the state of Rhode Island from 67 to 51.

Against the background of the previous appalling levels, the fall in hospital mortality was striking. In Europe and the USA maternal mortality in lying-in hospitals had sometimes reached 10 per cent or 1,000 per 10,000 deliveries, especially in the 1870s when hospital mortality had been high everywhere. This, Englemann explained, was because hospitals 'had become saturated with the deadly germ, never free from its ravages'. Now, however, he felt there was every reason for great optimism: 'We know that hospital mortality has been reduced to almost *nil*... in view of the splendid results which hospital statistics prove attainable, deaths should be few indeed in the community.'[10] It was true that lying-in hospital mortality in the USA had not reached the low levels that were reported from certain European countries, and it was worrying that as early as 1902 the initial fall due to antisepsis was being followed in some hospitals by a rise in mortality. Englemann, however, ended his paper on an optimistic note. The problem of maternal mortality, it seemed, was coming to an end. Neither he nor anyone else would have guessed what was to happen in the following decades, or that maternal mortality in 1930 would be considerably higher than it was in 1900.

MATERNAL CARE AND THE HOSPITAL, 1900–1935

The salient features of maternal care in America in the twentieth century were the increasing number of hospital deliveries which now included all classes of mothers instead of just the deserving poor, and a corresponding increase in the status and prominence of the obstetrician. There was also a marked increase in the tendency to surgical intervention in labour. What were the forces which brought this about? The central role of the hospital in American medicine may, perhaps, be traced back to the 1870s when hospitals no longer treated only the poorest of the poor and began to admit an increasing number of white-collar workers. At the Massachusetts General Hospital, for instance, 16.9 per cent of the patients were 'white-collar workers' in 1870, 18.1 per cent in 1880, and the upward trend continued.[11]

A similar trend occurred in the lying-in hospitals. Much earlier in the USA than in Britain, private lying-in hospitals were established and voluntary hospitals admitted a mix of charity and private patients. In New York during the 1870s, you could be delivered in a private lying-in hospital for a fee as high as $100. At the same time voluntary maternity hospitals began to admit a mixture of private and charitable patients, commonly charging about $25 for those who could afford to pay, but treating most of their patients gratuitously.

[10] Ibid.
[11] M. J. Vogel, 'Patrons, practitioners and patients', in J. W. Leavitt and R. Numbers, *Sickness and Health in America* (Madison, Wis., 1978), 173–84.

This was the new system of private and charity cases delivered in a voluntary hospital supported by voluntary contributions.[12] As early as the beginning of this century

the American hospital was already a hybrid combining a tradition of voluntary charitable care with fee-paying patients and government aid ... The doctor's quid pro quo for hospital access was donating services to the hospital where needed. A doctor thus received a double benefit: fees from paying patients and a reputation for charity.[13]

What Rosenberg has called the private-patient revolution came around the time of the First World War when established hospitals began not only to accept, but to become dependent upon the fees of paying patients. They smartened themselves up and new private hospitals sprang up all over the country, freed from the stigma of poverty and charity that stuck to some of the older institutions. Many appeared in small towns and semi-rural areas where no hospital had existed before.[14] Very little of this sort of thing occurred in Britain before the 1920s. The voluntary hospitals were—and their successors still are—the territory of consultants, specialists who gave their services free in the voluntary hospitals. Direct access to hospital care by general practitioners was confined to the cottage hospitals which were established specifically as general practitioner territory. In Britain direct access to specialist care at hospitals was and is restricted to some out-patient departments and accident and emergency departments. Otherwise, patients needing hospital care are referred to the hospital by their general practitioner. The general practitioner in Britain became the gateway to hospital care.

This peculiarly British principle of referral, which has been described by some as one of the strengths and by others as one of the weaknesses of British medicine, was gradually accepted by the profession in the second half of the nineteenth century. It arose when general practitioners rebelled against the flourishing out-patient departments of hospitals for the possession of patients in the mid- to late-nineteenth century. The principle is now enshrined as a system designed to operate in the best interest of the patient. This may well be true, but it was not the original motive. The practical consequence of this principle was summarized by Rosemary Stevens when she wrote: 'The physician and surgeon retained the hospital but the general practitioner retained the patient.'[15]

In Britain the principle of referral acted as an effective brake on hospital deliveries. As long as general practitioners undertook a substantial part of obstetric care, apart from the minority with access to private nursing homes or cottage hospitals, they were tied to home deliveries. In America, however,

[12] Garrigues, 'On Lying-in Institutions'.
[13] Stevens, *In Sickness and in Wealth*, 21–2.
[14] Rosenberg, *The Care of Strangers*.
[15] Stevens, *Medical Practice in Modern England* (New Haven, Conn., 1966).

hospitals were open to general practitioners and specialists alike, and there were few incentives for either to continue with home deliveries which were seen as unscientific and old-fashioned if a hospital was available. Hospitals became attractive places for the treatment of illness and the delivery of babies for the wealthy as well as the poor:

The twentieth century hospital was virtually a new institution—technological and interventionist. The best hospitals were models of cleanliness, efficiency, and expertise. Where, only twenty or thirty years before, there had been noise, dirt and disarray, there was now control and organisation . . . Henry James, returning from Europe in 1905, described the Presbyterian Hospital in New York and Johns Hopkins Hospital in Baltimore as symbols of stillness, whiteness, poetry, manners and tone—necessary values, he considered, amidst the violence, vulgar materialism, and hurly-burly of America.[16]

In 1913, according to *Popular Science Monthly*, the public approached the hospital, 'with confidence instead of apprehension, with alacrity instead of reluctance, and with hope of life rather than the fear of death'.[17]

Stevens has also described the way in which the First World War strengthened the position of hospital specialists. Before the war they had tended to work in isolation. During the war groups of medical and surgical specialists were thrown together in the military hospitals of the Western Front where they learned the value of teamwork, and developed an awareness of 'the advantages of co-operative multispecialist groups'. American doctors found themselves, as one of them expressed it, in a situation where they 'were working without rivalry, without a spirit of gain, for noble ends'. It was a process of bonding which lasted into the post-war years.[18]

There was no obstetrics at the Western front, of course, but many obstetricians served as surgeons. When they returned to obstetrics and gynaecology, they returned as members of a corp of medical and surgical specialists, in the new community of hospitals. To prove their worth in the hospital setting—technological and interventionist—they practised obstetrics as a branch of surgery.

The persuasive image of the hospital presented to the public was one of a clean, safe, germ-free environment, where their babies could be safely delivered by the latest scientific methods. By 1930 the obstetrician-gynaecologists had managed to obtain a very large slice of the hospital cake. The most common reason for admission to hospital in 1929–31 was that easy, highly profitable, and almost entirely unnecessary operation, tonsillectomy and adenoidectomy which accounted for 27.5 per cent of all admissions. Next came deliveries, abortions, pregnancy complications, and female genital

---

[16] Ead., *In Sickness and in Wealth*, 18.
[17] Ibid. 30.
[18] Ibid. 93.

diseases which amounted to 21.6 per cent of all admissions. Next on the list were accidents (9.0 per cent) followed by appendicectomy (8.3 per cent) and digestive diseases (5.9 per cent).[19]

After the First World War the hospitals became the stage on which the American obstetrician would claim his right to a monopoly of urban midwifery amongst all classes of patient. Rural areas would remain for a considerable time in the hands of general practitioners and midwives. From the late nineteenth century there were no serious financial problems in providing hospital care for paying patients. For charitable care, however, hospitals were always expensive to build and maintain, and invariably they were dogged by the worry that voluntary contributions would fall short of expenditure. Moreover, even in the most charitable communities, the lying-in hospitals and the maternity departments of general hospitals could only deliver a tiny fraction of those who needed help. How could maternal care for the poor be provided by trained obstetricians at low cost? The answer was the provision of maternal care in the homes of the poor. Of the institutions which were established for this purpose, some were separate lying-in charities initiated by philanthropic individuals, but most were out-patient divisions of lying-in hospitals. They were rarely found on the Continent of Europe, but they were a well-known feature of maternal care in Britain from the eighteenth century and the United States from the late nineteenth century. What was their contribution to maternal care in the United States?

OUT-PATIENT MATERNITY SERVICES

In fact, the provision of maternal welfare in the United States took many forms. The Shepperd–Towner Act of 1922, discussed in Chapter 16, was one example of a federal initiative, and the programme for maternal and infant welfare in the Second World War was another. In addition there were numerous local initiatives. Antenatal clinics were provided on a large scale, sometimes by charitable organizations, but often by state authorities. Advice and assistance were also available for low-income mothers from mothers' health clubs, county fairs for rural mothers, rural advice centres, and so on.[20]

Here, however, we are concerned solely with the provision of the out-patient antenatal and delivery services which were provided for the poor, mostly in large cities and in association with hospitals. Some provided a highly organized maternity service and achieved an astonishingly low rate of maternal mortality in populations which, by every indicator of social and economic

---

[19] Ibid. 106 (Table 5.1). The table shows admissions to hospital, excluding mental and tuberculosis hospitals, by major diagnosis as reported in a household survey of 8,758 white families, 1929–31.

[20] See e.g. Florence McKay, 'What New York State is Doing to Reduce Maternal Mortality', *American Journal of Obstetrics and Gynaecology*, 9 (1925), 704–8.

status, were grossly deprived. Like their sister institutions in Britain, what they showed was most revealing. When trained personnel were provided, home delivery under the worst of conditions was actually safer—not just a little safer, but much safer—than delivery in the majority of hospitals, at least before the late 1930s. When Dr Davis described the out-patient service of the Brooklyn Maternity Hospital in 1924, he wrote that patients were delivered:

in surroundings so bad that none worse can be found, and yet with results, as to complications, morbidity, and mortality, so good, that they rival those of the best equipped maternity hospitals. In effect this sort of work in the tenements is private practice under the most adverse conditions . . . Not long since we completed four and a half years showing *over ten thousand deliveries without a maternal death, in the tenements.* [my italics][21]

Johns Hopkins Hospital ran a service in the late nineteenth century in which 2,250 of the first 5,000 deliveries were delivered as in-patients and 2,750 by the out-patient service.[22] The Boston Lying-in Hospital provided an out-patient lying-in service from 1883 through to the 1940s. In the first fourteen years of the service only 11 per cent of maternal deaths were due to puerperal sepsis. During the same period 66 per cent of maternal deaths in the hospital were due to sepsis. Table 19.4 shows the difference in the mortality of in- and out-patients.[23] Cornell University ran a clinic affiliated with the medical school. Out-patient services provided a useful way of teaching students and providing interns with experience of home deliveries. The Cornell service was run from a special building which housed twelve nurses and four residents. By the 1920s, however, it was difficult to keep the scheme going because most women opted for in-patient delivery.[24]

In New York a Maternity Center was founded in 1918 to draw the attention of the public to the need for better obstetric care. At first it confined itself to providing antenatal care. When it was shown, however, that some New York Hospitals recorded an MMR of 110 per 10,000 deliveries (twice the national average) a full delivery and postnatal service was provided as well. Dublin (a medical statistician who was closely associated with the Center) believed that the low level of maternal mortality achieved by the Center would, if extrapolated to the country as a whole, prevent some 10,000 maternal deaths per year. If such low mortality was possible in the worst slums of New York it should have been possible everywhere in the USA.[25]

[21] Asa B. Davis, *American Journal of Obstetrics and Gynaecology*, (1924) 7, 327–8.
[22] Goldsborough, 'Maternal Mortality'.
[23] Records of the Boston Lying-in Hospital, Rare books division, Countway Medical Library, Boston.
[24] H. Bailey, 'Maternal and Infant Mortality in 4488 Cases in an Out-door Clinic, 1922–25', *American Journal of Obstetrics and Gynaecology*, 12 (1926), 817–24.
[25] L. I. Dublin, 'The Problem of Maternity: A Survey and a Forecast', *American Journal of Public Health*, 29 (1939), 1025–313. See also the most informative paper by J. Antler and D. M. Fox, 'The Movement Toward a Safe Maternity: Physician Accountability in New York City, 1915–1940', *Bulletin of the History of Medicine*, 50 (1976), 569–95.

TABLE 19.4 *The Outcome of Out-Patient Obstetric Services in the USA at Various Periods*

	Period	Number of cases	Maternal mortality rate (per 10,000 births)	Transferred cases included?[a]
USA as a whole	1915–35		60–70	
Boston Lying-in Hospital				
Out-patient service	1881–1940	74,093	11	uncertain
Out-patient service	1884–95	7,844	23	—
(In-patient service)	(1873–85)	(5,147)	(328)	—
Johns Hopkins Hospital, Baltimore				
Out-patient service	pre-1908	2,750	25	No[b]
(In-patient service)	(pre-1908)	(2,250)	(213)	—
Cornell Medical School				
Outdoor clinic	1922–5	4,488	15	No
Outdoor clinic	1922–5	4,488	27	Yes
Chicago Maternity Center				
Outdoor service	1932–6	over 12,000	—	Yes
Direct and indirect (associated) deaths			14	Yes
Direct maternal deaths only			9	Yes

[a] This column shows whether cases booked for delivery at home, but transferred to hospital because of some complication, were included in the statistics (see text).
[b] Out of the 48 deaths which occurred amongst the in-patients it was recorded that a substantial (but unspecified) number came from the outdoor clinic.
Source: See text.

Perhaps the most famous of all out-patient obstetric services was the Chicago Maternity Center established in 1895 by Joseph B. DeLee (see Chapter 21). This Center was run on strict lines in which every detail of care from the beginning of the antenatal period to the end of the postnatal was laid down and strictly observed. Births were attended by a physician, a student, and usually by an obstetric nurse. None of the patients was delivered by unsupervised students. DeLee insisted on a strict non-interventionist technique in this service and complicated cases were admitted to the Chicago Lying-in hospital. From the beginning the results were excellent. DeLee was able to claim in 1906 that 1,500 cases a year were treated in the heart of the poorest district of Chicago at the Dispensary 'with a mortality and morbidity that challenge the work of the best maternities in the world'.

From 1932 to 1936, in a series of over 12,000 consecutive deliveries, 18 women died—an MMR of 14 per 10,000 deliveries when the rate for the USA as a whole was around 60. These figures included all cases referred by the Maternity Center service to hospital, whether in pregnancy, labour, or the postnatal period. Of the 18 women who died, 4 died from sepsis, 4 from toxaemia, 2 from post-partum haemorrhage, and 8 from associated diseases (tuberculosis, pneumonia, and meningitis). If the associated deaths are excluded, the mortality rate for direct maternal deaths was only 9.

By the 1930s quite complicated procedures were carried out by this Center in patients' homes, including forceps deliveries, craniotomy, and version and extraction. Most were carried out under local anaesthesia. But the operative rate, 6 per cent of all deliveries, was exceptionally low compared with rates amongst hospital in-patients. A strict but simple antiseptic regime, a trained obstetrician present at all deliveries, the availability of blood transfusion much earlier than was general, and the avoidance of unnecessary interference, were the main factors to which the Center's success was attributed.[26]

Usually, the only data recorded by these out-patient services were mortality rates. But an interesting attempt to measure puerperal morbidity and compare morbidity rates in hospital and out-patient deliveries for the period 1906 to 1921 was carried out in Iowa in 1923. Morbidity was defined as a fever of 100 °F or more for three successive postnatal days. Morbidity was 8.6 per cent in hospital cases with 10 deaths per 10,000 births from sepsis. Amongst the home deliveries the morbidity rate was 2 per cent and there were no deaths from sepsis. The primary reason why home deliveries were safer was the lower risk of puerperal sepsis.[27]

The remarkably low MMRs, which are summarized in Table 19.4, were often achieved even when cases transferred to hospital were included in the statistical returns. They are a vivid indication of the inherent danger of hospital delivery in the 1920s and 1930s. Eno explained the anomaly succinctly: 'In the homes of the very poor dirt is dirt, but in hospital dirt is germs.' Almost certainly he was right.[28]

With hindsight, the logic of these findings is clear. If urban maternity services had been run on the lines of the Chicago Maternity Center, with a large majority of deliveries at home and in-patient care reserved for the most

[26] The most important sources on the Chicago Maternity Center are: J. B. DeLee, 'The Technique of the Chicago Lying-in Hospital and Dispensary', *Surgery, Gynaecology and Obstetrics*, 3 (1906), 805–15, which gives a complete account of the techniques used by the Center; B. E. Tucker and H. B. Benaron, 'Maternal Mortality of the Chicago Maternity Center', *American Journal of Public Health*, 27 (1937), 33–6, which shows it was still a thriving institution maintaining the same high standard in the 1930s; and the really excellent recent account by J. W. Leavitt, 'Joseph B. DeLee and the Practice of Preventive Obstetrics', *American Journal of Public Health*, 78 (1988), 1953–9.

[27] E. Eno, 'A Study in Puerperal Morbidity', *Surgery, Gynaecology, and Obstetrics*, 36 (1923), 797–801.

[28] Ibid.

complicated cases and emergency admissions, and if rural maternity services had been modelled on the Kentucky service devised by Mary Breckinridge, with the bulk of deliveries undertaken at home by trained nurse-midwives, the lives of tens of thousands of mothers might have been saved in the 1920s and 1930s, and tens of thousands of children might not have been orphaned. But there was never the slightest chance of reversing the tide of hospital care. Patient demand and the ambitions of obstetricians went hand in hand. Hospital delivery was the modern way. Home delivery was old-fashioned. In the hospital the obstetrician could justify his fees, demonstrate his skill by intervention, and distance himself from the midwife; and he could justify the American way of childbirth by pointing to three factors which seemed to demand hospital and specialist delivery as the only possible way for a civilized country: the new methods of pain relief, a firm belief that women and indeed the very nature of childbirth had altered as a result of 'civilization', and the high rate of maternal mortality which obstetricians, without a moment's hesitation, attributed to the general practitioner, the midwife, and unsanitary deliveries at home. Changing attitudes to childbirth and methods of pain relief come next.

20
Attitudes to Childbirth and the Problem of Pain

PRIMITIVE AND CIVILIZED WOMEN

To the men-midwives or accoucheurs of the eighteenth and first half of the nineteenth centuries it was self-evident that childbirth was a physiological process. Nature managed very well on her own in the large majority (variously estimated as between 95 per cent and 99 per cent) of deliveries. Interference in normal labours was to be deplored. It was only in the small minority that medical assistance was needed; and even then the type of assistance was often slight.[1] The duty of the birth-attendant was therefore to watch, wait, and be patient. In the eyes of those who opposed the involvement of medical men in routine midwifery, it was a powerful argument for leaving childbirth to midwives. But it was also the accepted wisdom of the established accoucheurs or obstetricians of this period. They taught their students to be very conservative in their approach to labour. Wait, they said, wait and do not intervene unless you are certain it is essential.

In the second half of the nineteenth century this view was challenged. It was said that modern ways of living had led to an alteration in women. Civilized women were no longer capable of withstanding the pain and stress of labour. To deny them the benefits of modern aids such as anaesthesia and instrumental delivery would not only be inhumane, it might be fatal. It was therefore the duty of the birth-attendant routinely to administer pain relief and intervene if not in every labour, at any rate in a large majority. This startling new attitude to childbirth was never held by all obstetricians. There were always some who regarded it as nonsense; but it was held by a very large number of American obstetricians—probably a majority—from around the 1880s until the 1930s. These dates are not of course precise. Fundamental changes in attitude rarely appear or disappear overnight. They grow and fade away gradually. But it was between these dates that the practical consequences of this view can be seen most clearly. It was a feature of obstetrics noted by the White House conference on child health protection in 1933:

[1] S. Merriman, *A Synopsis of the Various Kinds of Difficult Parturition* (London, 1814), and Fleetwood Churchill, *On the Theory and Practice of Midwifery* (London, 1850), who quoted estimates of normal labours according to past authorities as varying from 914 in 1,000 to 990 in 1,000.

Until comparatively recently forceps were used very infrequently and then only when the mother was unable to deliver herself, fetal indications not being recognised. The old doctor knew how to sit and wait, and the number of spontaneous deliveries was astounding. One elderly physician, who had always practised in rural communities, boasted that he had used instruments only four times in more than three thousand deliveries during a practice extending over more than fifty years. By contrast, there are now a few clinics in this country in which the application of forceps is routine, except when a precipitate delivery interferes with a physician's plans. In the former instance, obvious indications must have been overlooked, whereas in the latter, much absolutely needless interference is being practised.[2]

One can see this change in people's perceptions of childbirth as part of a widespread notion of the corrupting effects of modern civilization; ideas that might be traced back at least to the eighteenth century and Rousseau's picture of the 'noble savage' consisting of primitive men and women free, happy, and unencumbered by civilization. It was also a notion which owed something to the reaction against the enlightenment view of the inevitable progress of civilized life. From the end of the eighteenth century observers could see at one end of the scale the poverty and overcrowding due to the progress of civilization and industry, and at the other the accentuation of the maladies of self-indulgence and luxury. Both could generate ill-health. Indeed, the notion that there were specific diseases of the rich which arose from a self-indulgent life-style was prevalent in the writings of medical practitioners in the eighteenth and early nineteenth centuries.[3] The rich (and their servants) got diseases such as gout, chlorosis, nervous complaints, and so on, as a consequence of their life of idle luxury.[4] But no one, as far as I can discover, extended this notion to childbirth and labour until the mid-nineteenth century when there were hints from commentators who believed that American women were turning into a race of invalids, with the danger that 'America's traditionally bountiful human fertility, and with it the country's rapid growth, might well be nearly at an end if matters were not improved.'[5]

By far the clearest exposition of the idea that the process of childbirth was no longer a 'natural' physiological process was put forward by George J.

---

[2] White House Conference on Child Health Protection, *Fetal, Newborn and Maternal Morbidity and Mortality* (New York, 1933).

[3] See Roy Porter and Dorothy Watkins, *In Sickness and Health* (London, 1988), 181–2. 'All this luxury chorused the critics, was bad for morals, bad for political liberty, and, not least, bad for health . . . .'

[4] In 1781 Robert Bland attributed the high incidence of puerperal fever amongst the rich to their hot stuffy rooms and life of luxury. But this was a specific reference to puerperal fever, not to childbirth itself. Bland, 'Midwifery Reports of the Westminster General Dispensary', *Philosophical Transactions*, 71 (1781), 355–71.

[5] J. H. Cassedy, *Medicine and American Growth, 1800–1860* (Madison, Wis., 1986), 174–5. Although in this instance the fear was based on the extent of chronic illness and hypochondria rather than the explicit effects of luxury *per se*, it implied that women had become 'delicate', and so unable to produce children without medical help.

Englemann in the 1880s when he held the post of Professor of obstetrics at Missouri Medical College. His book, *Labor among Primitive Peoples*, published in 1882, is an explicit description of the deleterious effect of civilization on labour and its complications. In effect, Englemann crystallized and brought together notions that had been held widely but vaguely, and showed their relevance to the management of childbirth. His book was profoundly influential. It became, in Garrison's words, an 'anthropological classic' frequently cited by medical practitioners on both sides of the Atlantic.[6]

Englemann's thesis is simply stated:

Among primitive people, still natural in their habits and living under conditions which favour the healthy development of their physical organisation, labour may be characterised as short and easy, accompanied by few accidents and followed by little or no prostration . . . The squaws of the Madoc Indians—a tribe which has been but little affected by the advance of civilisation—suffers but an hour or even less in the agony of childbirth . . . two hours being the average time for North American Indians.[7]

He quoted examples of Indian women going for a 'pack of wood', giving birth *en route*, and returning calmly with the wood and the child. Wherever there were primitive people, he said, there were easy births; and the closer primitive people came to civilization the longer their labours and the more their complications. He supported this view by reference to various North American Indian tribes and primitive peoples in other countries. Primitive people, he wrote, had far fewer complications than white women because of their lifestyle and racial purity. 'How different', he wrote, 'from those which we find in our centers of luxury where people intermarry regardless of differences in race or frame of body.'[8] It was partly intermarriage (as when a large Swedish man married a small Mediterranean woman) which led to difficult and long labours, but also the modern tendency to the 'idle life, abuses of civilisation, its dissipations and follies of fashion' which produced malpositions and a 'languid neurasthenic condition'. Modern, civilized, American white women were no longer capable of standing the pain and stress of labour.

It is tempting to suggest that Englemann's study initiated the change in

---

[6] G. J. Englemann, *Labor among Primitive Peoples* (1st edn., St Louis, Ind., 1882). Englemann's obstetric qualification was Master of Obstetrics in the University of Vienna. His book went into several editions. If it is a classic, it is one that is highly suspect. There is no evidence that Englemann really knew how many complications of labour or how many maternal deaths occurred amongst the tribes he describes. He gives no sources for the evidence on which his ideas were based, a fault noted with some scorn when it was reviewed in the (British) *Lancet*. Englemann's thesis would only command respect if it was based on a careful survey of a long series of deliveries amongst the tribes he mentions. It is not surprising that no such survey, to the best of my knowledge, had been carried out. The book was based on rumour and assertion. Nevertheless the notion that the more primitive the woman the more easily she gives birth is still prevalent today.

[7] Ibid. (2nd edn., 1883), 7.

[8] Ibid. 9–10.

obstetric fashion from the conservative management of labour to large-scale intervention, which we have described for Britain and the USA. But the timing is wrong. The change in fashion was well under way in Britain and the USA at least a decade before Englemann's book was published. Nevertheless, Englemann's ideas were seen as the justification for intervention and the use of anaesthesia and analgesia in normal labour. If civilized women were no longer able to withstand the pain of labour, new methods of pain-relief were needed. The methods themselves as well as the change in attitudes to childbirth, increased the tendency to intervene in normal labours, and thus—or so it was argued—made hospital delivery essential. These three features of twentieth-century childbirth—new methods of pain relief, massive intervention in normal labours, and admission to hospital for as many cases as possible—were linked together. Although they were introduced in the belief that they were in the best interests of the patient, all three heightened the risk of maternal mortality. As far as I can discover, this pervasive belief that women had been weakened by civilization to such an extent that pain relief and intervention on a massive scale had become essential, was not found in all Western countries; but it was a commonly held view in the English-speaking ones. Thus we find frequent references to it in the USA, in Britain, and in Australia. But I have not found that the view had any prominence on the continent of Europe. We come back to this subject briefly in Chapter 26 in connection with a visit to Denmark in 1930 by Dorothy Mendenhall, a member of the Children's Bureau in Washington.

PAIN RELIEF IN CHILDBIRTH

Before 1847 the use of the only effective analgesic, opium and its derivatives, was probably much more widespread in Britain and the United States than one would guess from the rarity with which it is mentioned in obstetric texts.[9] By the 1840s morphine, the active alkaloid of opium, was being administered in Britain by 'an instrument made for the purpose', the hypodermic syringe, which was introduced in America in 1856. It was thought to be safer, less addictive, and more pleasant than oral opium which produced nausea, constipation, and other side-effects. In fact gross over-use of morphine and widespread addiction were the consequence.[10] Morphine was far from ideal

---

[9] Siebold, reviewing obstetric practice in Europe between the late 18th cent. and 1845, said that the English differed from the French not only in the rejection of Caesarean section and the free use of forceps, which was well recognized, but in the use of 'huge quantities of opium' in prolonged labours. E. G. J. de Siebold, *Essai d'une histoire de l'obstétrice*, trans. from German by F. J. Herrgot (Paris, 1891).

[10] See David T. Courtwright, *Dark Paradise* (Cambridge, Mass., 1982) for the use of opium and morphine in the USA, and Virginia Berridge and Griffith Edwards, *Opium and the People: Opiate Use in Nineteenth-Century England* (London, 1981). According to Courtwright, morphine was isolated in 1817. Berridge and Edwards, however (pp. 135–6), show that the isolation of

in childbirth. If given in sufficient dosage to abolish pain it was liable to cause foetal asphyxia, to abolish or weaken contractions, and to increase the risk of haemorrhage. The introduction of inhalation anaesthesia was therefore hailed, and rightly so, as a great advance.

The beginning of anaesthesia in midwifery followed the discovery of the anaesthetic properties of ether by the American dentist, Morton, in 1846. By 1847 ether was being used in childbirth by James Young Simpson in Britain and by Augustus K. Gardener of New York and Walter Channing in Boston in the United States.[11] The news of this new advance spread with surprising rapidity through Europe. Simpson first used ether on 19 January 1847, and reported its use to the Obstetrical Society of Edinburgh on 10 February. It was used in France by Deschamps only eight days later. By the end of February it had been used in six cases of labour by Professor Dubois of the French Academy of Medicine. In March it was used by Stoltz in Strasburg and by Delmas in Montpellier and its use soon spread to Germany. Subsequently, the French used anaesthetics less frequently than the British. The difference, said Cazeaux, was that in normal labours 'French women chatter to each other and this is better than a state akin to concussion.'[12] As far as Simpson and many of his Scottish colleagues were concerned, anaesthesia was a total success. It was safe and it was highly effective; but its use was opposed by some on religious grounds, and by others who feared clinical complications.[13] The clinical opposition, however, was more formidable than the religious.

In November 1847, Simpson abandoned the use of ether in favour of chloroform. Ether is a safe anaesthetic. It is very difficult, if not impossible, to kill a patient by overdosage with ether in the method by which it was given in the nineteenth century. But ether is much more difficult to administer and much more unpleasant for the patient than chloroform. Chloroform is given in

morphine was the work of three men beginning with Derosne, a French manufacturing chemist, in 1803, followed by Sertürner of Hanover who investigated the new substance more accurately than anyone before and named it after Morpheus, the God of sleep. But the significance of his work which began in 1805 was not recognized until 1816.

[11] A. K. Gardener, *A History of the Art of Midwifery . . . Showing the Past Inefficiency and Present Natural Incapacity of Females in the Practice of Obstetrics* (New York, 1852); J. W. Leavitt, *Brought to Bed* (Oxford, 1986).

[12] P. Cazeaux, *A Theoretical and Practical Treatise on Midwifery, including the Diseases of Pregnancy and Parturition*, revised and annotated by S. Tarnier (5th American edn. from the 7th French edn. of 1868; Philadelphia, Pa., 1873).

[13] At the root of the religious objection was the biblical sentence 'In sorrow shalt thou bring forth children.' The story that Simpson dealt with this in a public debate by quoting 'And God put Adam into a deep sleep' is probably apocryphal. What he did, however, was to dispute the translation from the Hebrew that produced the word 'sorrow' in the above sentence. He suggested that 'travail' or 'labour' was more correct and refused to believe that 'in sorrow' should be interpreted as an expression of God's will, inflicting everlasting pain on labouring women. See James Young Simpson, *Answer to Religious Objections Advanced against the Employment of Anaesthetic Agents in Midwifery and Surgery* (Edinburgh, 1848), and Protheroe Smith, *Scriptural Authority for the Mitigation of the Pains of Labour by Chloroform and other Anaesthetic Agents* (London, 1848).

small quantities, is rapid, and pleasant to inhale. But the risk of overdosage is high. The gap between the dose required for anaesthesia and the dose which causes cardiac arrest is wide for ether but narrow for chloroform. Simpson knew this, and he gave chloroform with great care and safety. Certain leading London obstetricians, however, objected to ether and chloroform not on the grounds of the danger of death through overdosage, but on the grounds that they might cause long-term complications, like paralysis. This was the basis of a bitter dispute between Simpson and his close friend Francis Henry Ramsbotham in London, a steadfast opponent of the use of chloroform. The two friends argued furiously from 1847 to 1852 and it nearly destroyed their friendship.[14] By 1850, chloroform was used all over Scotland, even in remote villages, while London obstetricians were reluctant to use it at all. It was said that women travelled from London to Edinburgh to be delivered under chloroform. Simpson told Ramsbotham, 'There is no doubt whatever your grandchildren and mine will . . . wonder at us dreaming of *not* relieving human agony when we had the power and the means of doing it. As to bad results, I have see none.'[15] Ramsbotham was unconvinced and infuriated Simpson in 1852 by publishing an account of paralysis which occurred many months after childbirth and attributing the paralysis to chloroform. Simpson said this was complete nonsense, adding once more that future generations would condemn anyone who had failed to use anaesthetics in midwifery.[16]

The reluctance of London obstetricians seems to have disappeared when Queen Victoria was delivered under light chloroform anaesthesia in 1853. As an experienced mother she knew about labour pains and thoroughly approved of the method which became known as *chloroform à la reine*.[17] If it was good enough for a queen it was certainly good enough for her subjects, and chloroform in childbirth was firmly established in Britain by 1853. Ether was still used to a considerable extent in the USA.[18] To what extent did anaesthesia alter the management of labour?

Anaesthesia did not lead to the increased use of Caesarean section in Britain or America, because the high death rate for the operation was not due to the agony and shock of operation without anaesthesia, but to the inability to control bleeding from the uterus. Nor, surprisingly, did it lead to an immediate increase in forceps delivery. The reason was that the 1840s and 1850s still lay in the period of conservative obstetric practice when forceps were used (by most obstetricians) very sparingly on clinical grounds, and the

[14] The dispute was conducted by a series of letters which can be found in the manuscript collection of the National Library of Medicine, Bethesda. Correspondence between Francis Henry Ramsbotham and James Young Simpson. MC 22.

[15] Ibid. Sept. 1847.

[16] Ibid. 25 Apr. 1852.

[17] The anaesthetic was administered to the Queen by Dr John Snow.

[18] As late as 1899, Lusk of New York was advising ether rather than chloroform, at any rate for 'lengthy operations'. W. T. Lusk, *The Science and Art of Midwifery* (2nd edn., London, 1899).

question of pain relief was irrelevant. By the end of the century however, many general practitioners in Britain were using the combination of chloroform and forceps almost as a routine in all except quick and easy labours, and continued to do so until the mid-twentieth century.

Anaesthesia was, of course, an enormous benefit for women who had to undergo surgical procedures in labour—forceps or craniotomy, for instance— and without anaesthesia the development of a safe technique for Caesarean section at the end of the nineteenth century would not have been possible. But chloroform was used far more often in normal or slightly prolonged labours than complicated ones. It was cheap, easy to use, and portable. It would be carried in the bag in a small dropper bottle. It was administered by placing a few drops on a clean linen handkerchief rolled up in the shape of a cone which could be placed over the patient's nose and mouth. That was how Simpson used it. Used correctly and with care it was a safe procedure and highly popular with patients. For some fifty years, chloroform in Britain and ether and chloroform in the USA, were unchallenged. But the complications, though relatively slight, led to a hunt for a safer method. Twilight Sleep appeared to be the answer.

TWILIGHT SLEEP

Twilight Sleep was introduced in Germany in 1902 by Steinbüchel of Graz. His purpose was to devise a completely safe form of pain relief which did not interfere with contractions, caused no harm to the baby, and did not preclude the additional use of anaesthesia if that became necessary. The basis of the method was the use of two drugs: morphine and scopolamine. The usual method was to give an initial injection of both drugs early in labour. Further injections (usually of scopolamine alone) were given as indicated. The aim of Twilight Sleep was not to produce anaesthesia but amnesia. In theory the patient would be fully conscious throughout labour, but she would remember nothing about it afterwards.[19]

Initially Twilight Sleep was a great success which became fashionable in America just before the First World War. It was introduced largely because of a group of women who accused the medical profession of a 'medical expropriation of knowledge' and demanded the technique for themselves. Their demands, supported by some physicians, were effective. 'Although it neither originated from scientific investigations nor utilised scientific

---

[19] The name 'Twilight Sleep' was actually invented in 1906 by Gauss of Freiburg who published an account of 500 cases so treated. For a full account of the method see A. M. Claye and W. Stanley Sykes, *The Evolution of Obstetric Analgesia* (Oxford, 1939). For a general and excellent review of methods of pain relief in the USA, see M. Sandelowski, *Pain and Pleasure in American Childbirth: From Twilight Sleep to the Read Method, 1914–1960* (Westport, Conn., 1984), to which I am indebted.

methodology, the Twilight Sleep was promoted as the scientific solution to the greater problem of childbirth itself.'[20]

Soon, however, it became clear that it was not a simple procedure. It was difficult to judge the dose of drugs. Too little and there was no pain relief, too much and the patient was unconscious with all the disadvantages of anaesthesia. More commonly, the combination of drugs produced an intoxicated and uncontrollable patient, thrashing round the delivery bed, unable to co-operate, difficult to manage, and requiring continuous supervision by someone trained in the technique and able to give injections.

One of the greatest advocates of Twilight Sleep was William Knipe, Professor of Obstetrics at the New York Post-Graduate Medical School, who went to Freiburg to learn the technique. He insisted it could only be used in hospital.[21] Bertha van Hoosen, the Attending Gynaecologist at Cook County Hospital, Chicago, was another enthusiast who published a paper in 1915 which went far beyond the idea that Twilight Sleep should be accepted just because it was a modern scientific invention. She drew a parallel between Twilight Sleep and birth among primitive people. Twilight Sleep, she said, 'renders the process of childbirth one of reflex action which resembles the delivery of primitive woman'. Pain in childbirth was a result of civilization which had made the sexual organs primarily organs for pleasure rather than reproduction.

Centuries of use of the reproductive organs for other purposes than that of reproduction may have rendered the organs so hypersensitive that the real function, so relatively seldom performed, has become universally and persistently painful [for which] it is our duty to advise corrective measures.[22]

Carried away by enthusiasm, she suggested that Twilight Sleep would, 'strike at the evils of our civilisation' such as abortion, divorce, sexual excesses in married life, and inability to perform lactation. With the restoration of painless labour many of these evils would disappear and 'that most beautiful of relations between men and women—the relation of lovers—would be restored'.

In the United States, Twilight Sleep, like so many innovations in childbirth, aroused strong feelings. Some physicians congratulated the women who brought the technique to the public's notice. Others denounced it as a form of German quackery or said it was unnecessary because the pains of labour 'strengthened a woman's character', inciting the wrath of Bertha van Hoosen who likened this argument to those against women's suffrage.[23]

---

[20] Sandelowski, *Pain and Pleasure in American Childbirth*, 12–15.

[21] W. H. W. Knipe, ' "Twilight Sleep" from the Hospital Viewpoint', *Modern Hospital*, 3 (1914), 250–1.

[22] Bertha van Hoosen (attending gynaecologist at Cook County Hospital, Chicago), 'The New Movement in Obstetrics', *Woman's Medical Journal*, 25 (1915), 121–3.

[23] Ibid.

In Britain Twilight Sleep was a less emotive issue. It was time-consuming, and so it was employed, but not very widely, for middle-class deliveries at home or in nursing homes. It was well into the 1920s before it faded away.[24] In the United States, however, no sooner had the battle for Twilight Sleep been won than it went out of fashion. It arrived around 1912 and was dead by 1920. R. W. Holmes, in a paper on 'The Fads and Fancies of Obstetrics', wrote in 1920: 'we all recall the fiasco of the Twilight Sleep Furor.'[25] 'Twilight Sleep has come and fortunately gone', wrote another in 1921,[26] and 'Twilight Sleep has fortunately died out', said a third in 1922.[27] Although Twilight Sleep was little more than a passing craze, it has been credited with influencing the development of American obstetrics in several ways. Sandelowski believes it was the first occasion when 'the whole body of patients had risen to dictate to the doctors' and revealed the power of popular demand.[28] Twilight Sleep has also been credited with creating the demand for hospital delivery, which is true only to a marginal extent because the tide was already flowing strongly in that direction. It was, however, a technique which encouraged the use of a 'cocktail' of drugs, given by injection and repeated as necessary. It strengthened the position of the male doctor in the delivery room, it fortified the idea that advances in the management of childbirth were dependent on science, and it underlined the notion that in modern times childbirth should take place in hospital and not at home. In these ways it played a small but significant part in the development of maternal care in the United States.

PAIN RELIEF AFTER TWILIGHT SLEEP

When Twilight Sleep was abandoned, pain relief was achieved by the 'cocktail' of drugs, usually a combination of morphine or heroin with an injectable barbiturate, followed at delivery on many occasions by full anaesthesia. This became more or less routine in American hospital practice. The perceived ideal was for the patient to go to sleep early in labour and stay asleep until the baby was in its cot. There was no thought in the 1920s of active participation by women in their labour, or of having the husbands present so that husband and wife could experience the birth of their baby together. Still less was there

---

[24] See e.g. Claye and Sykes, *The Evolution of Obstetric Analgesia* (London, 1939), chap. 2; H. M. Gerson, 'Twilight Sleep', *Lancet* (1922), i. 428–9; and 'Twilight Sleep' (leading article), *Nursing Times* (4 Oct. 1919), 1041–2.

[25] R. W. Holmes, 'The Fads and Fancies of Obstetrics: A Comment on the Pseudo-Scientific Trend of Modern Obstetrics', *American Journal of Obstetrics and Gynaecology*, 2 (1920), 225–37.

[26] B. M. Anspach, 'The Drudgery of Obstetrics', *American Journal of Obstetrics and Gynaecology*, 2 (1921), 245–8.

[27] C. G. Brumbaugh, 'The Present Standard of Obstetrical Practice in Rural Pennsylvania', *Pennsylvania Medical Journal*, 26 (1922–3), 283–4.

[28] Sandelowski, *Pain and Pleasure in American Childbirth*, 13.

any idea that childbirth was a matter of 'negotiation between physicians, birthing women, and family members'.[29] In the pursuit of the ideal whereby no effort and no suffering—indeed, no consciousness of the process of birth—was demanded of the mother, childbirth became a surgical procedure to be undertaken in a surgical theatre. It had taken a century for the fashion to swing from the extreme conservatism of the 1820s and 1830s to the apogee of intervention in the 1920s and 1930s. A reaction was inevitable. When it came it was a complete swing to the other extreme, but in a new and different way.

What came to be known rather self-consciously as 'natural childbirth' was first associated with the ideas of the obstetrician Grantley Dick-Read. He developed his ideas in the 1930s and published his book *Natural Childbirth* in Britain in 1933 and his second book *Childbirth without Fear* in 1942. His ideas were known in the USA in the 1930s, but *Childbirth without Fear* was not published in the USA until 1944, where his ideas only became fashionable after the end of the war.[30] Read introduced the idea of what was later called psychoprophylaxis in childbirth; others, notably Lamaze, took up the notion and extended it much further in the 1950s. Read's basic tenets were quite simple. Fear of childbirth caused tension, tension caused pain, and pain reinforced fear. To break the vicious circle, tension must be abolished by relaxation. Then pain would disappear and analgesic drugs would be unnecessary. The technique of relaxation was taught by intensive training during pregnancy and was constantly reinforced during labour. By relaxation alone, said Read, normal and *enjoyable* childbirth was within the reach of every woman, with the added bonus of the sense of achievement which natural childbirth could offer.

Read had many devoted followers and many scornful opponents. Natural childbirth was criticized on several grounds. The technique required so much time before and during labour that only a few could hope to afford it. The success of the technique depended on the persuasiveness of the doctor or midwife who used the technique. Not everyone could inspire self-confidence in frightened women. In Read's hands the technique was very effective. He was a dominant and persuasive man, almost hypnotic in his influence on women. Some of his disciples were less successful, and it was the disciples rather than Read himself who were often unable to see that women differed in their response to pain and the ability to relax, and slow to admit that in some labours natural childbirth was not possible. When instrumental assistance under anaesthesia became necessary for a woman who had been promised an easy normal delivery, the need for intervention was often recognized only

[29] J. W. Leavitt, *Brought to Bed: Childbearing in America, 1750–1950* (New York and Oxford, 1986), 215.
[30] Sandelowski, *Pain and Pleasure in American Childbirth*, 85–97.

after a prolonged and unnecessary suffering; for example, after prolonged and painful labour due to a persistent occipito-posterior presentation in a primiparous patient. Women who required surgical intervention were often made to feel guilty and inadequate at their own failure, so that natural childbirth had its cruel side. Finally, Read's method was criticized because it was authoritarian. The patient was told exactly what to do. Any deviation from instruction would carry the penalties of pain in labour and guilt for the failure to relax.

Lamaze's method was in part a reaction against this aspect of natural childbirth. It was an explicitly non-authoritarian method in which women were invited to control their own labours. The trained obstetrician was there in the background to help if necessary. Its popularity in the USA 'indicated women's desire to regain control over major aspects of their labors'.[31] There was substance in the criticisms of Grantley Dick-Read and his followers, but they must not overshadow the importance of natural childbirth in this respect. It brought to an end the silly and dangerous belief that civilization had rendered women incapable of unassisted normal delivery. And thus it lessened, but by no means abolished, the unnecessary level of drug administration and intervention. To this extent, the concept of natural childbirth was one of many factors in the reduction of maternal mortality in the 1940s and thereafter.

[31] Ibid. 129.

21
The Orgy of Interference

The title of this chapter comes from a paper given by the British obstetrician James Young when he was invited, in 1935, to address the American Association of Obstetricians, Gynaecologists, and Abdominal Surgeons.[1] 'A study of the British and American reports', he said, 'conveys the impression that one of the most sinister features of Anglo-Saxon midwifery is to be found in the extent to which interference with the course of labour is practised.'[2] In Holland, he said, the rate of interference was under 1 per cent. In Sweden it was 3.2 per cent, and in Denmark, 4.5 per cent. In New York it was 20 per cent, and the death rate due to sepsis was 40 per 10,000 births for cases in which interference had taken place compared with 4 per 10,000 in spontaneous deliveries. In Britain, although there were few reliable statistics, 'it is well known that in some industrial areas with a poorly organised maternity service...more than 50 per cent of the deliveries are admitted to be instrumental.' In both countries 'the necessity for interference was often not apparent', and the penalty for interference was high maternal mortality. James Young had no doubt that Holland and Scandinavia had low rates of maternal mortality because they had succeeded in 'protecting their midwifery from being swept along by the surgical stream that within recent decades has increasingly tended to overwhelm the American and British systems'.[3]

We have already discussed the problem of interference in labour in several parts of this study. There was one important difference between Britain and the United States. In Britain unnecessary interference was mainly a problem of general practice. It was not a feature of the larger hospitals with trained obstetricians in charge. In the United States, however, interference on a grand scale was found in home and hospital obstetrics. Some of the worst examples occurred in the large teaching hospitals which set an example that influenced the country as a whole. Thus the problem of obstetric interference in the United States, especially during the inter-war period, was so striking, and so

---

[1] J. Young, 'Maternal Mortality and Maternal Mortality rates', *American Journal of Obstetrics and Gynaecology*, 31 (1936), 198–212. The lecture he gave was the Joseph Price lecture for 1935.
[2] The reports he referred to were: New York City Public Health Committee and New York Academy of Medicine, *Maternal Mortality in New York, 1930, 1931, 1932* (New York, 1933); Ministry of Health, *Final Report of Departmental Committee on Maternal Mortality and Morbidity* (London, 1932).
[3] Young, 'Maternal Mortality', 204–7.

much worse than it was in Europe, that we must try to discover why it occurred.

Some obvious reasons come to mind. Crude self-interest, for example. By surgical flamboyance the obstetrician set himself apart from the midwife and justified his fees. It was also a way in which the obstetrician could earn his spurs in the increasingly technological world of hospital medicine, and surgical interference was, as we have seen, closely tied to changed attitudes about childbirth in civilized women and new methods of pain relief. The absence of institutional or governmental control or restraints in a free-enterprise system allowed excesses to continue unchecked. Another and often neglected factor was the personality of the leading obstetricians—a factor which had nothing to do with a cool and rational scientific approach (although irrational decisions were often clothed in apparently rational scientific terms) but a great deal to do with the background and temperament of the obstetrician.

We must remember that obstetrics stood apart from other medical disciplines in one important respect. In the medical schools there was a general consensus on how the mainstream subjects—the management of medical and surgical disorders—should be taught. There were, of course, differences of opinion on this and that which were often hotly debated, but they were usually concerned with points of detail. In obstetrics the management of normal and abnormal labours was taught in different medical schools in ways so diverse as to leave one gasping. There was no general consensus on basic procedures in normal labours amongst the élite obstetricians in the United States, whose views were frequently separated by unbridgeable gaps. It is not surprising that obstetrics was often derided by other specialists as an emotional and unscientific subject. Nor is it surprising that some students left medical school to spend their lives delivering women in ways which were, to say the least, peculiar.

These basic features of American obstetrics are shown most vividly by two obstetricians who dominated the field from the 1890s to the 1930s: Joseph Bolivar DeLee (1869–1942) of Chicago and John Whitridge Williams (1866–1931) of Baltimore. Equally famous for their teaching and practice, DeLee championed intervention in labour on every possible occasion, while Williams, no less devoted to his speciality, no less skilful or confident, intervened only rarely and advocated a careful conservative approach to childbirth. Both men studied medicine in Europe, and both wrote textbooks which went into many editions. Both were convinced that obstetrics was a scientific discipline whose future lay in the hands of hospital specialists, and both strenuously opposed the midwife, Williams in firm but temperate language, DeLee with venom. They were almost exact contemporaries. Yet, in professional attitudes, background, and character, the two could hardly have been more different; and they failed to agree on the essentials, not just the details, of obstetric practice.[4]

DeLee came from a Jewish immigrant family in New York where, in his youth, he sold doorbells to supplement the family income. His father was in the dry-goods business and hoped his son would become a rabbi; but his mother, the dominant member of the family, encouraged him to become a physician and he graduated from the North Western University Medical School in 1891.

While he was a student, DeLee paid his way by working at a 'baby farm' in Chicago where he was shocked by the high death rate and the large number of mentally subnormal children who were, he believed, brain-damaged at birth—a belief that had a profound influence on his practice as an obstetrician. When he returned to Chicago from his period of study in Europe, he founded the Chicago Lying-in Dispensary in 1895 which led to the establishment of the famous Chicago Lying-in Hospital. The dispensary was retained as the Chicago Maternity Center. At both institutions, his word was law. DeLee was chairman of the department of obstetrics and gynaecology first at North Western University Medical School and then, from 1929, in Chicago University. Throughout his life he showed the touchiness, aggression, and the mixture of tight-fistedness and generosity that is the mark of a man who had achieved fame and financial success but who never forgot the poverty of his youth.

Whitridge Williams's background was totally different. He came from an old-established east-coast family. His father was a prominent physician and there was a continuous line of practising physicians on his mother's side for more than 160 years (Whitridge was his mother's maiden name). Educated at the Baltimore City College and Johns Hopkins University, Williams graduated from the University of Maryland in 1888. After two visits to Europe to study bacteriology and obstetrics, he was appointed assistant professor of obstetrics and gynaecology in Johns Hopkins medical school in 1896 and professor of obstetrics when the chair was divided in 1899.

There can be no doubt that both men were highly skilled and experienced obstetricians. They were extremely influential and both were widely read in the discipline to which they were devoted. Each in his own way was highly compassionate, with great and genuine concern for the poor. Williams's reputation is untarnished. If DeLee was remembered solely for his services to the poor and his Chicago Maternity Center his reputation would be golden: but he is remembered and often reviled for 'the prophylactic forceps oper-

---

[4] For biographical accounts, see *American Dictionary of National Biography*; J. W. Leavitt, 'Joseph B. DeLee and the Practice of Preventive Obstetrics', *American Journal of Public Health*, 78 (1988), 1353–9; D. D. Danforth, 'Contemporary Titans: Joseph Bolivar DeLee and John Whitridge Williams', *American Journal of Obstetrics and Gynaecology*, 120 (1974), 577–88.

ation', based on the principle of maximum surgical intervention in labour, and the exact reverse of everything conveyed by the term 'natural childbirth'.

DELEE AND THE PROPHYLACTIC FORCEPS OPERATION

DeLee's paper on the prophylactic forceps operation, published in 1921, is probably the paper most frequently quoted by historians of American obstetrics in the inter-war period.[5] The paper laid down his method of delivery for all labours, not just for prolonged or complicated ones. What he advocated was astonishing. 'It is not', he wrote of his operation, 'a complete reversal of watchful expectancy... but I cannot deny that it interferes much with Nature's process. *Were not the results I have achieved so gratifying, I myself would call it meddlesome midwifery. For unskilled hands it is unjustifiable*' [my italics].[6]

In brief, the operation consisted of administering morphine and scopolamine (harking back to Twilight Sleep) when the cervix was opened 2–3 centimetres. This was followed by more drugs in the first stage of labour including chloral and sodium bromide. In the second stage of labour the patient was anaesthetized with ether, a wide lateral episotomy was performed, and she was delivered by forceps. If the third stage was not completed rapidly and spontaneously he employed a form of manual removal of the placenta which he termed the 'shoehorn maneuver'. More morphine and scopolamine was given for repair of the episotomy and tears in the cervix. He justified his method, which turned normal childbirth into a major surgical operation, by claiming:

> The results of the operation are all that one could wish. As yet no mother or baby has died; there has been no case of infection or cerebral haemorrhage. The babies have thrived, the mothers have not shown the exhaustion and anaemia of former days. The restoration of the parturient canal has been always perfect...

Anticipating his critics he stressed that the prophylactic forceps operation should not be undertaken by unskilled operators in unsuitable surroundings. 'I have always felt', he said, 'that we must not bring the ideals of obstetrics down to the level of the general and occasional practitioner—we must bring the general practice of obstetrics up to the level of that of the specialist.'

What reasons were given for such extreme interference in normal labours? First, DeLee maintained it was the only way to reduce maternal mortality and morbidity. Quoting Englemann in support, DeLee insisted that childbirth was

[5] J. B. DeLee, 'The Prophylactic Forceps Operation', *American Journal of Obstetrics and Gynaecology*, 1 (1920–1), 34–44; discussion, 77–84. The paper was read by DeLee on 24 May 1920 at the 45th meeting of the American Gynaecological Society, which was held in Chicago.

[6] The final sentence explains an apparent paradox. In the Chicago Maternity Center, treating patients in their own homes, DeLee insisted on conservative and non-interventionist obstetrics. For this he has been accused of inconsistency or hypocrisy. Not so. The staff of the Maternity Center were junior obstetricians in training and students.

no longer a physiological process but a pathological one. Indeed, he went further in a famous sentence: 'I have often wondered whether Nature did not deliberately intend women should be used up in the process of reproduction, in a manner analogous to that of the salmon, which dies after spawning.'[7]

His second reason was based on his memories as a student in the baby farm, where he saw many mentally defective children. DeLee believed that brain injury was not the result of clumsy instrumental deliveries; it was due to compression of the foetal head against the perineum in normal labours. He went on to make the extravagant claim that this explained why 'not the first-born, but the children of subsequent labours, were the people who moved the world. Benjamin Franklin was the seventeenth child.' He claimed that the number of infants seriously and permanently damaged in the course of normal labours was 'legion . . . numerous accoucheurs and neurologists of scientific standing . . . support this view'.[8] The routine use of forceps protected the baby's head from compression. Thus, he claimed, the prophylaxis forceps operation reduced, at one fell swoop, maternal mortality, maternal morbidity, and mental subnormality.

DeLee was a vain man who needed to demonstrate his perfectionism and surgical skill. His passionate and unbalanced attacks on midwives showed his obsession with the status of obstetrics. He made films on the prophylactic forceps operation in which he was the star performer. He was one of those doctors who are desperate to do everything possible for their patients, with the emphasis on 'doing': often a dangerous tendency, but especially so in obstetrics. The prophylactic forceps operation with its aggressive intrusive qualities reflected the character of its inventor.

DeLee devoted his life to obstetrics. He never married and avoided making close friends. He could be arrogant, autocratic, stubborn, and even fanatical. In his later years he mellowed and regretted the operation for which he was once famous and later infamous.[9] In his prime, however, he saw himself as a crusader, unwilling to compromise when maternal mortality and brain-damaged infants were at stake. Within Chicago he may have done more good than harm. Nationally his teachings were pernicious. It would be easy, but superficial, to dismiss DeLee as a man motivated solely by surgical arrogance and self-seeking showmanship. But he was no charlatan. He was a complex man and an interesting example of the extent to which new medical procedures reflect the personal qualities of those who introduce them.

---

[7] DeLee, 'The Prophylactic Forceps Operation'.

[8] Ibid. The 'numerous supporters' for this extraordinary theory on the cause of mental subnormality turned out to be just one: Arthur Stein of New York, and whether he really held such a view I have been unable to discover.

[9] It is significant (and surprising) that in 1936 DeLee wrote to Grantley Dick-Read to congratulate him on his book *Natural Childbirth*. He promised to include an account of Dick-Read's work in the next edition of his textbook on obstetrics. See M. Sandelowski, *Pain and Pleasure in American Childbirth* (Westport, Conn., 1984), 87.

Williams was in the audience when DeLee presented his paper and spoke in the discussion. There were, he said, just two things in the paper with which he agreed: the need to allow spontaneous dilatation of the cervix, and the correctness of certain anatomical features described by DeLee. 'With the rest of it I do not agree . . . if his practice were to become general and widely adopted women would be worse off . . . .' On DeLee's management of the third stage of labour, Williams said, 'I do not hesitate to state that I think it has been perniciously active.' Williams was not alone. It is important to recognize that of those who took part in the discussion the majority opposed DeLee's prophylactic forceps operation.[10]

In April 1922, a year after DeLee's famous lecture, Williams read a wide-ranging paper on obstetric practice in the USA at the annual meeting of the Medical Society of the State of New York. He took the opportunity to launch a scathing attack on those who interfere in normal labours.[11] In doing so he recognized the danger of being labelled as old-fashioned and conservative. 'I do not come before you', he said, 'as an obstructionist, nor as one who opposes progress . . . some may say I am too conservative and tend to react unfavourably to innovations of any sort. I do not believe so.' And he listed the five sins of American obstetrics:

- DeLee's so-called prophylactic forceps operation.
- The employment of version as a routine method of delivery.
- Routine episotomy ('cutting and reconstructing the perineum in every primipara').
- The induction of labour at a fixed date.
- The abuse of Caesarean section.

Williams had a difficult task. In a country that admired progress and innovation at a time when surgery was forging ahead with new operations, a paper which preached conservatism in obstetric practice was neither exciting nor sensational. But Williams's approach was always cool and reasonable, reflecting the character of a man who had no need to prove himself to anyone. Socially secure, broadly educated, and a lover of old books, he was un-aggressive, straightforward, sociable, conservative in outlook, and not in the least complex. He was known as a loyal friend and a devoted family man. He was twice married, with three daughters by his first wife who died in 1929.

---

[10] Amongst those whose contributions to the discussion were published were Williams; Thomas Watts Eden of London, who was visiting and politely opposed the whole principle of the operation; John Polak of Brooklyn, New York, who agreed with some of the techniques described by DeLee but not with others; Henry Byford of Chicago, who opposed the method as a routine, but felt it applicable to a minority of cases; and Edward Davis of Philadelphia, who opposed the operation and its underlying principles.

[11] J. Whitridge Williams, 'Criticism of Certain Tendencies in American Obstetrics', *New York State Journal of Medicine*, 22 (1922), 493–9.

Williams was greatly admired by British obstetricians; they saw eye to eye. DeLee was not.[12]

THE EXTENT OF INTERFERENCE

By presenting the two extremes of obstetric practice, I have left open the question of the middle. Which of the two was the more representative of American obstetrics? Was the practice of the average American obstetrician skewed towards the extremism of DeLee or the conservatism of Williams?

If DeLee had been alone in his extremist approach his influence might have been slight. But there were others whose maverick behaviour put DeLee in the shade. Dr Potter of Buffalo was a notorious example. His method, which he said was developed to spare the woman the pain of the second stage of labour, was based on his 'extraordinary facility in the performance of version and extraction'. He taught that in every normal case, when the cervix was fully dilated, version should be performed: that is, the baby should be turned round inside the uterus so that it could be grasped by the legs and hauled out.[13] In 1920, Potter personally delivered 1,113 patients. Twelve lucky women delivered spontaneously before his arrival. Of the remainder, all were delivered by operative means including 920 by version and extraction and 80 by Caesarean section.[14] There was also Dr Pomeroy of Brooklyn who advised routine episotomy, cutting straight down through the anal sphincter as soon as the head began to crown and repairing it accurately as soon as the child was born. By doing so, Pomeroy claimed, he could restore the patient's genitalia 'to the state of a "virgo intacta"'.[15]

One could argue that Potter belonged to the lunatic fringe of American obstetrics. Unnecessary interference usually came in more ordinary forms such as promising delivery on a certain day by induction on the grounds of convenience, using intra-uterine bags or bougies—methods in which the risk of infection was high—and most of all in the form of unnecessary forceps deliveries, version, and Caesarean section. Such failings, said Williams, were

a result of, as well as an arraignment of, our present system of obstetrical education . . . What is needed in this country are not so much men who are keen to operate

[12] The British obstetrician, Mr Gibberd of Guy's Hospital, referred to Williams in 1931 as 'The greatest of American Obstetricians'. G. F. Gibberd, 'Streptococcal Puerperal Sepsis', *Guy's Hospital Reports*, 81 (1931), 32. Williams was the first person to be elected to an honorary fellowship of the British College of Obstetricians and Gynaecologists although, as it happened, his election was confirmed on the day he was buried.

[13] This procedure, which is extremely difficult in the unanaesthetized patient, was made possible only by deep chloroform anaesthesia which causes relaxation of the uterine muscle.

[14] Williams, 'A Criticism of Certain Tendencies in American Obstetrics', *New York State Journal of Medicine*, 22 (1922), 493–9. Potter delivered 1 in every 14 patients by Caesarean section. If Williams had done the same he would have performed 1,600 sections instead of the 213 he actually performed.

[15] Ibid.

whenever possible, as those who are so intimately acquainted with the capabilities of Nature that they can assure their patients that they are as well prepared for child-bearing as were their mothers and grandmothers...[16]

Williams was not the only critic of the surgical approach to normal childbirth. Many shared his views. One condemned the growth of Caesarean section in memorable terms:

Belly-ripping has become a mania and its maniacal ravages have invaded the realm of obstetrics to the extent of threatening to supplant many well tried and altogether reliable manual means of delivery thru the natural passages...I have sometimes suspicioned that [the obstetrician] views the natural passages as a makeshift exit to be used only when [he] is otherwise engaged.[17]

In more measured but wide-ranging terms, the author of the 1933 White House conference on child health protection, protested at the 'operative furor' and believed it was responsible for the rise in maternal mortality. The reasons for unnecessary intervention were:

- The often false sense of security engendered by the use of modern antiseptics.
- The almost universal employment of anaesthetics.
- An exaggerated idea of the value of the infant's life as compared to the life and health of its mother.
- The demand on the part of obstetric patients for shorter and more comfortable labours.
- Extension of the indications for operative induction or termination of labour to include the convenience of the patient, husband, doctor, or other person.
- The education of the laity to a higher scale of fees for operative procedures, although often the value of services in non-operative deliveries is much greater.[18]

That there was a connection between unnecessary intervention and maternal (and neonatal) mortality in the 1920s was suggested by the following. In the USA as a whole between 1915 and 1929 there was a rise in the MMR of 14.3 per cent accompanied by a rise in neonatal deaths attributed to birth injury of 41 per cent. Significantly, infant mortality and neonatal mortality from all other causes was falling throughout this period. This seems to pinpoint an excess of unnecessary operative deliveries as the underlying cause.[19]

To take this a stage further we need more detailed reports on obstetric

---

[16] Ibid.

[17] P. Findley, 'The Lost Art of Obstetrics', *Northwest Medicine*, 17 (1918), 67–70.

[18] White House Conference on Child Health Protection, *Fetal, Newborn and Maternal Morbidity and Mortality* (New York, 1933), 217.

[19] Ibid.

TABLE 21.1 *Analysis of 91,000 Deliveries in Iowa for the Years 1930–1932*

	Type of delivery		
	Spontaneous	Operative	Total
State-wide (percentage)	80,920	10,818	91,738
	(88.2)	(11.8)	(100)
Communities over 10,000 people all	25,115	5,136	30,251
deliveries (percentage)	(83.0)	(17.0)	(100)
Communities under 10,000 people all	55,805	5,682	61,487
deliveries (percentage)	(90.7)	(9.3)	(100)
Communities over 10,000 people percentage			
of hospital deliveries			61.14
Hospital deliveries (number)	14,416	4,247	18,663
Hospital deliveries (percentage)	(77.2)	(22.7)	(100)
Home deliveries (number)	10,969	889	11,858
Home deliveries (percentage)	(92.5)	(7.5)	(100)
Communities under 10,000 people			
percentage of hospital deliveries			19.3
Hospital deliveries (number)	10,273	1,672	11,945
Hospital deliveries (percentage)	(86.0)	(14.0)	(100)
Home deliveries (number)	45,805	4,010	49,815
Home deliveries (percentage)	(91.9)	(8.1)	(100)

Source: E. D. Plass and H. J. Alvis, 'A Statistical Study of 129,539 Births in Iowa with Special Reference to the Method of Delivery and the Stillbirth Rate', *American Journal of Obstetrics and Gynaecology*, 28 (1934), 297–305.

practice as a whole in large populations, such as a state or a series of states. Several were published, and two in particular are valuable. The first was based on an investigation in Iowa in 1930–2.[20] The main results, which are summarized in Table 21.1, fall into three parts. First it can be seen that the percentage of hospital deliveries was much higher (60.8 per cent) in large communities than small ones (19.5 per cent), as one would expect. Secondly, although the state-wide rate of surgical intervention of 11.8 per cent was not particularly high, the percentage of operative as opposed to spontaneous deliveries was higher in large communities than small ones; and the important finding is that the difference was due to hospital methods of practice. Operative measures were used to the same extent (approximately 8 per cent) in home deliveries whether they took place in large or small communities, and operative measures were used more often in hospitals in large communities

[20] E. D. Plass and H. J. Alvis, 'A Statistical Study of 129,539 Births in Iowa with Special Reference to the Method of Delivery and the Stillbirth Rate', *American Journal of Obstetrics and Gynaecology*, 28 (1934), 297–305.

than small ones—the difference being 23.1 per cent in the former and 14 per cent in the latter. This confirms that a high rate of intervention was associated with hospital delivery in large towns. On this point, the authors of the report (who were themselves practising obstetricians from Iowa) stated that 'a large number of unnecessary and ill-advised operations' occurred in the largest hospitals.

The final feature of this table is the quantification of various types of surgical procedure, which speaks for itself; but it should be noted that although forceps deliveries topped the list, the pernicious method of version and extraction was practised over 1,000 times, and was more common than Caesarean section.

MICHIGAN: A TYPICAL STATE?

The other state for which data are available is Michigan for the period 1935–6.[21] The first of two reports in the 1930s provides a demographic picture of maternal care in Michigan in 1936. Michigan was neither a poor nor a rich state. The population was overwhelmingly white. Only 3 per cent of total births were to black mothers (almost all in Detroit) and there were very few midwives. In terms of maternal mortality, Michigan came somewhere near the middle. When the MMR for the USA as a whole was 74 per 10,000 births, with a range of 62–112, Michigan recorded a rate of 77.

If any state can be said to be a typical northern state in terms of maternal care and maternal mortality, it might be Michigan. The state possessed a number of hospitals of varying size, but none with a national reputation. There was still a substantial proportion of home deliveries in 1936: 76 per cent in rural areas, and between 30 per cent and 40 per cent in the towns. There were two medical schools: one at Ann Arbor, and another in Detroit, compared with ten in New York state in 1930 and six in Pennsylvania.[22] In 1936 there were 5,900 physicians in Michigan of whom 2,800 were judged to be those 'practising obstetrics'. Few of these, however, carried out a substantial number of deliveries and only 2 per cent could be regarded as trained obstetricians. The latter, together with so-called partial specialists (approximately half of the total number of physicians practising obstetrics) had the lion's share of practice, undertaking 85 per cent of all deliveries. Younger

[21] My sources here are two unusually comprehensive reports. The first, which dealt with Michigan state, was carried out by the United States Public Health Service, and was based on a report of 21,000 births which took place in Michigan in the first quarter of 1936: *Maternal Care in Michigan: A Study of Obstetric Practices*, National Institute of Health, United States Public Health Service (Washington, DC, 1938). This was bulletin no. 8 of the series *Preliminary Reports of the National Health Survey, Sickness and Medical Care*. The second was a study of maternal mortality in Pontiac. It was undertaken by the Bureau of Maternal and Child Health of the Michigan Department of Health, *Maternal Mortality Survey, 1935–1939* (Pontiac, Mich., 1940).

[22] *Final Report of the Commission on Medical Education* (New York, 1932).

TABLE 21.2 *Type of Operation Employed in 10,818 Operative Deliveries in Iowa for the Years 1930–1932*

Type of operation	Number	Percentage of all deliveries	Percentage of all operations
Forceps	6,474	7.1	59.8
Version and extraction	1,236	1.4	11.4
CS	955	1.0	8.8
Breech extraction	711	0.8	6.6
Craniotomy	4	0.004	0.04
Operative not specified[a]	1,438	1.6	13.3

[a] It was thought nearly all of these were forceps deliveries.

Source: E. D. Plass and H. J. Alvis, 'A Statistical Study of 129,539 Births in Iowa with Special Reference to the Method of Delivery and the Stillbirth Rate', *American Journal of Obstetrics and Gynaecology*, 28 (1934), 297–305.

physicians were most likely to shun obstetrics. Those who practised obstetrics extensively were older than those working in other specialities, and the older they were the more prone to surgical interference and lax antiseptic procedures.

Many general practitioners who undertook occasional deliveries in home and hospital carried out a wide range of surgical procedures including difficult forceps deliveries, manual removal of placenta, version and extraction, and the occasional Caesarean section. This group, the inexperienced, occasional obstetricians (especially the older ones) rarely wore gloves or masks and always delivered their patients while wearing their 'ordinary street clothes'. The white sterile gown, cap, and mask, were used mostly by the specialists in obstetrics. Specialist obstetricians carried out a slightly higher proportion of forceps deliveries than general practitioners (18 per cent against 14 per cent) and more Caesarean sections (3.5 per cent against 1.3 per cent). General practitioners were much more likely than specialists to undertake the potentially dangerous procedure of induction of labour (21 per cent against 11 per cent), and more likely to resort to the dangerous use of pituitrin for the purpose (15 per cent against 7 per cent). All patients who were delivered in hospital, whether they were rich or poor and regardless of the status and expertise of the birth-attendant, were much more likely to be delivered with forceps (24 per cent in hospital against 9 per cent in home deliveries) and very much more likely to undergo an episotomy and other surgical procedures (44 per cent against 8 per cent). The difference was not explicable in terms of selected high risk or emergency patients in hospital. It was the environment of the hospital with its emphasis on surgical prowess which encouraged intervention in normal cases.

TABLE 21.3 *Allocation of Maternal Deaths by Place of Delivery, Pontiac, Michigan,*
1935–1939

Institution	Number of deliveries	Number of maternal deaths	Maternal mortality rate (per 10,000 live births)	Percentage of deliveries in the city	Percentage of maternal deaths in the city
Hospital A	2,023	42	208	22.2	53.2
Hospital B	3,730	35	94	40.9	43.0
Both Hospitals	5,753	77	134	63.1	96.2
Home Deliveries	3,065	4	13	33.6	3.8
Maternity Homes	216	0	0	2.4	0
Osteopaths	90	0	0	0.9	0
Midwives	1	0	—	—	—

Note: One death in Hospital A and one in the home deliveries were due to 'incidental disease' and were not included in the determination of mortality of percentage rates. The significance of the differences between the mortality rates in Hospital A and B and between Hospital B and home deliveries was as follows: Hospital A compared with hospital B: $\chi^2 = 12.3$. $P < 0.001$, Home deliveries compared with hospital B: $\chi^2 = 31.3$. $P < 0.001$.

Source: Michigan, Bureau of Maternal and Child Health, *Maternal Mortality Survey, 1935–1939* (Pontiac, Mich., 1940).

The second report, on maternal mortality in Pontiac (population 66,000), provides a bleak picture of maternal care in a medium-sized American town in the 1930s. In 1936–9, when the MMR for the state as a whole had fallen to 34.9 per 10,000 deliveries, it was officially recorded in Pontiac as 55.8. When all suspect deaths of women of childbearing age were investigated, however, the true rate was found to be 89.5, well above the average for the white population of the USA at the time the survey was carried out.

Two large hospitals undertook 63 per cent of the deliveries, 34 per cent took place at home, and about 3 per cent in maternity homes.[23] Out of the total of 9,125 deliveries, just one was undertaken by a midwife. Out of the ninety-one doctors in Pontiac, eight were listed in the American Medical Association Directory as obstetricians and gynaecologists, but most delivered only a few cases, devoting the greater part of their time to other specialities. Only two were certified by the American Board of Obstetricians and Gynaecologists; each of these delivered over 100 women a month. Physicians who delivered very few babies showed a high MMR. Doctors who delivered

[23] There were two maternity homes of a notoriously low standard which advertised themselves as 'maternity hospitals' in spite of protests from the public health department. Neither had proper facilities by the standards of the time and one was presided over by a large tabby cat who had the full run of the institution.

fewer than ten babies a month (less than a quarter of all who undertook obstetric practice) were responsible for half the maternal deaths. Forty-three of the eighty-one deaths in Pontiac were associated with operative procedures which were judged to be unnecessary. Out of eight deaths following Caesarean section, seven were the work of one man. It was often asserted that dangerous obstetric practice was not the work of full-time obstetricians, but of the part-time specialists and general practitioners who undertook difficult and dangerous procedures not only unnecessarily, but only occasionally so that they lacked experience and judgement. The data from Pontiac tend to confirm the assertion. They show that half the maternal deaths were due to infection and that the rate of septic deaths was highest in the patients of the physicians who did fewest deliveries and were most prone to unnecessary interference. Consultations in cases with a fatal termination were infrequent and generally much too late (a consultation was sought in only twenty-six out of the eighty-one mothers who died).

The authors of the report came to the conclusion that out of eleven Michigan cities, 'Pontiac was the most hazardous and dangerous locale for any mother...'.[24] The mortality rates in Pontiac are shown in Table 21.3. It should be noted that the higher mortality rate of hospital A appeared to be associated with a high rate of surgical procedures and not to the admission of a larger number of complicated and difficult cases than hospital B.

WHAT MICHIGAN DEMONSTRATES

In round figures, at least 300 women in Michigan died annually from maternal causes in the mid-1930s. There is no shadow of a doubt that many of the deaths were due to unnecessary interference. Nor is there any doubt that for this and other reasons many of the deaths were preventable by the application of standards of practice well recognized at the time. If my assumption that Michigan was a typical northern state is correct, we have a fairly comprehensive picture of maternal care in the United States in the 1930s. Obstetrics was a branch of medical practice which, it was believed, every graduated doctor was competent to undertake. Half of those in Michigan decided to do so. Many delivered so few babies that they combined inexperience with carelessness and over-ambition. It was more dangerous to be delivered by general practitioners and partial specialists than specialist obstetricians, but the latter were very few. Unexpectedly it was generally safer to be delivered by younger practitioners in spite of their lesser experience than by many of the older ones who seem to have clung to the bad habits of the past. It was still

---

[24] The other Michigan cities and their official MMRs for 1935–9 were as follows: Bay City 2.66; Grand Rapids 3.09; Lansing 3.60; Kalamazoo 3.71; Muskegon 3.79; Saginaw 3.80; Jackson 4.11; Detroit 4.25; Battle Creek 4.55; Flint 5.18.

much safer in the mid-1930s to have a normal delivery at home rather than in hospital (any physician with hospital privileges could admit his patient to hospital regardless of expertise or qualifications) partly because of increased risk of cross-infection, but mainly because the very fact a patient was delivered in a hospital encouraged unnecessary intervention.

American obstetrics was a highly competitive system which allowed every physician the freedom to practise obstetrics at all levels, regardless of experience or expertise. There was little if any control or guidance by city, state, or federal authorities and no formal post graduate education. When a dangerous situation arose, consultation was often absent or too late. Competition encouraged practice in relative isolation. Investigations carried out by professional bodies and public health departments often revealed gross errors and usually said so fearlessly; but there was no way of enforcing their recommendations. Broadly speaking this unflattering picture of obstetrics in Michigan in the 1930s was confirmed by other surveys in other states which are listed in Appendix 3.

22

Maternal Mortality in the USA

In previous chapters we have seen the wide variety of maternity care in the USA and noted the rapidity with which changes took place in the place of birth and type of birth-attendant. What general conclusions, if any, can be drawn about the quality of maternal care in the country as a whole? At the simplest level, was it good, bad, or indifferent compared with other countries, and did it improve or worsen in the period with which we are concerned?

Since the 1950s, when maternal deaths became increasingly rare, quality of maternal care has usually been measured by perinatal rather than maternal mortality. Until the middle of this century, however, maternal mortality was virtually the only statistical yardstick for the measurement of the efficiency of maternal services, maternal morbidity being inherently unmeasurable. And by that yardstick, the USA did particularly badly. Josephine Baker remarked in the 1920s that 'The United States comes perilously near to being the most unsafe country in the world for the pregnant woman, as far as her chance of living through childbirth is concerned.'[1] It was a humiliating, indeed a frightening statement by a well-known authority on maternal care. But was it true? Did the statistics provide an accurate measure of the trend in maternal mortality? Woodbury remarked in 1926:

The maternal mortality rate is increasing if the statistics can be accepted. Apart from the question of the reliability of the figures, such a conclusion is surprising in view of the increased attention paid to medical education and to public health adminis- tration ... Before the conclusion can be accepted, therefore, the evidence for the increase in the rate of maternal mortality should be examined critically.[2]

What were the factors which needed critical examination?

Judged by the statistics, the general trend in the first thirty years of this century was upward, suggesting a worsening in the standard of maternal care (Figure 22.1). The sharp peak in 1918, was, of course, due to the influenza pandemic, and can be ignored in the arguments which follow. It is convenient to divide this period into three phases: 1900–20, 1920–9, and 1929–35 and examine them separately.

[1] S. J. Baker, 'Maternal Mortality in the United States', *Journal of the American Medical Association*, 89 (1927), 2016–17. Dr Josephine Baker served in the New York City Department of Health for some 25 years.

[2] R. M. Woodbury, *Infant Mortality and its Causes* (Baltimore, Md., 1926), app.: 'The Trend of Maternal Mortality Rates in the United States Death Registration Area, 1900–1921', 181.

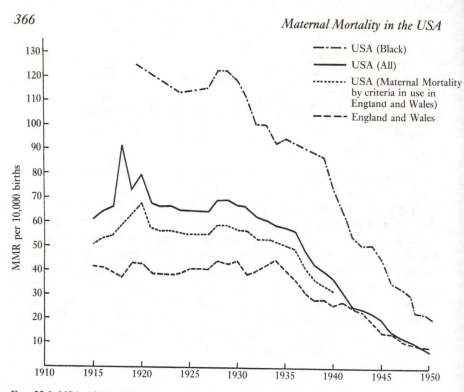

FIG. 22.1 USA, 1915–1960. Trend in Maternal Mortality. Annual rates
Source: Appendix Tables 5 and 6.

During the first phase, 1900–20, there were two main problems. The first was the expanding death-registration area which was mentioned in Chapter 2. If you look at Figure 22.2 (and Appendix Table 23 on which Figure 22.2 is based) you will see the dates when various states were included in the death-registration area. In 1900, maternal mortality in the USA was based on data derived from a small area of the north-east of the country which contained 40.5 per cent of the population. Thereafter, other states were added one by one until 82.2 per cent of the population was included in the death-registration area by 1920, and the whole population by 1933.[3] Figure 22.3 shows the states of the USA shaded according to their levels of maternal mortality.[4] If Figure 22.2 is compared with Figure 22.3 it is clear that the states with the highest rates of maternal mortality were by and large those in the south which were the latest to be added to the death-registration area. The inference is obvious. Statistics based on the expanding death-registration area would inevitably show an increase due to the incremental addition to the

[3] Ibid. 182.
[4] This figure is based on mortality rates for 1940, but the distribution of states according to the relative levels of maternal mortality in the 1930s was closely similar.

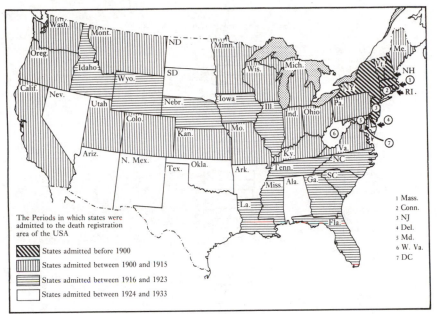

FIG. 22.2 The periods in which States were admitted to the United States Death Registration Area
Source: Appendix Table 23.

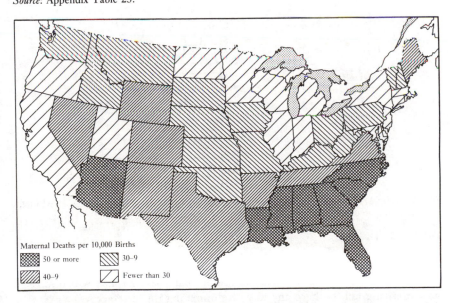

FIG. 22.3 USA 1938–1940. Interstate variations in Maternal Mortality Rates in terms of four categories of Maternal Mortality
Source: *Births, Infant Mortality, and Maternal Mortality*, Children's Bureau Publication, No. 288 (Washington, DC, 1945).

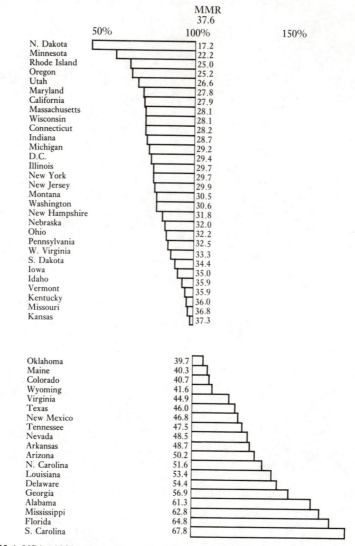

FIG. 22.4 USA, 1938–1940. States ranked according to their level of Maternal Mortality expressed as a percentage above or below the national average
Source: *Births, Infant Mortality, and Maternal Mortality*, Children's Bureau Publication, No. 288 (Washington, DC, 1945).

death-registration area of states with the highest mortality. Such a process could, in theory, produce an *apparent* rise in maternal mortality which masked an underlying fall. Is there any way of eliminating this artefact?

One way which was often used was to bypass the problem. This was done by confining the data used for the construction of the national trend to the

1900 death-registration area. By using the same states and ignoring data from the states which joined the death-registration area after 1900, consistency was obtained at the cost of comprehensiveness. This was clearly unsatisfactory, and Woodbury preferred the bolder step of attempting to estimate the direction and extent of distortion that resulted from the addition of each new state to the expanding death-registration area. He concluded that between 1900 and 1920 'the result of the additions of new states to the [1900 death-registration] area was to increase slightly the mortality rates from all puerperal causes in 1906, 1911, 1913, 1916, 1917, and 1919, and to decrease them slightly in 1908, 1909, 1910, 1914, 1918, and 1920'.[5] Because the increases were largely cancelled out by the decreases (but only up to 1920) the problem of the expanding death-registration area had only a slight distorting effect on the trend in maternal mortality. But this does not mean the statistics for this period (1900–20) were accurate. There was another problem, the problem of 'hidden maternal deaths' (see Appendix 1) which was a much more important distorting factor.

This was discussed in Chapter 2 where we saw that in 1900 the General Register Office in England and Wales had been persuading doctors to follow the official nosology and getting them used to the process of death certification for over fifty years. In the United States the amassing of vital statistics at the national level was only a recent discipline in 1900 and it was much more difficult in a country where the population tended to be scattered and highly mobile. Most physicians were not aware of, or instructed in, the use of a standard nosology and the need for consistent and accurate death certification. Not surprisingly, then, a large number of maternal deaths were hidden in vague or inaccurate death certificates. This led to a campaign for better death registration. Woodbury, the Director of Statistical Research at the Children's Bureau in Washington, conducted an investigation of doubtful death certificates and sent letters to physicians, seeking clarification of vague or suspect certificates. He estimated that the 'proportion of [maternal] deaths classified as due to ill-defined and unknown causes in the death-registration states was 3.8 per cent in 1900, whereas in 1920 in the same area it was only 0.2 per cent'.[6]

In other words, 1900–20 was a period of great improvement in the quality of vital statistics. The results of Woodbury's calculations for the period 1900–20 can be seen in Table 22.1. The wide gap between the crude and the estimated rate of mortality in 1900 had virtually disappeared by 1920. The crude data, in which no allowance is made for hidden maternal deaths, show that maternal mortality rose from 1900 to 1920. The corrected data—that is,

---

[5] Woodbury, *Infant Mortality*, 182.

[6] Woodbury explains his method in his two publications *Maternal Mortality*, Children's Bureau Publications, No. 152 (Washington, DC, 1926), and *Infant Mortality* (1926), the account in the latter coming in the appendix at the end of his book.

TABLE 22.1 *Maternal Mortality by Cause of Death in the USA in Five-Year Periods from 1900 to 1920*

Maternal mortality rate	Year				
	1900	1905	1910	1915	1920
Crude data[a]					
All puerperal causes	52	60	63	62	76
Trend (1900 = 100)	100	115	121	119	146
Puerperal septicaemia	22	26	28	25	26
Trend (1900 = 100)	100	118	127	114	118
All other causes	30	34	35	37	50
Trend (1900 = 100)	100	113	117	123	167
Estimated data[b]					
All puerperal causes	85	80	69	69	78
Trend (1900 = 100)	100	94	81	81	92
Puerperal septicaemia	43	38	31	26	27
Trend (1900 = 100)	100	88	72	60	63
All other causes	42	42	38	43	51
Trend (1900 = 100)	100	100	90	102	121

[a] Based on the states included in the 1900 death-registration area. Maternal mortality rates per 10,000 live births for crude data and for estimated 'correct' data. All values to nearest whole number.
[b] The estimated trend in maternal mortality by cause of death made allowance for the steady improvement in certification of causes of death.

Source: R. M. Woodbury, *Maternal Mortality*, Children's Bureau Publications No. 152 (Washington, DC, 1926), 140; id., Woodbury, *Infant Mortality and its Causes* (Baltimore, Md., 1926), 191.

the estimated data after allowing for improvement in death certification— show a very different trend. Maternal mortality as a whole fell slightly from 1900 to 1920, and this fall was due to a reduction in deaths due to septicaemia, which had been under-reported in the early years of this period. Deaths from other causes rose, but only at the very end of the twenty-year period.

Therefore, from 1900 to 1920, improving standards of death-certification led to an apparent rise in maternal deaths, masking an underlying fall in deaths due to sepsis.[7] From 1920 to 1929, however, when there was also a

---

[7] Woodbury found that not only had vague diagnoses of death become much less common, but that there had been 'marked decreases in mortality from "septicaemia", "peritonitis", and "convulsions (unqualified)" ... during the twenty year period 1900–1920. ... The figures therefore raise a strong presumption that the mortality from puerperal septicaemia actually decreased from 1900 to 1920, while that from other puerperal causes remained approximately the same.' *Infant Mortality*, 191 (Table 48).

rise in the MMR, the degree of inaccurate certification had become trivial. Now the main problem was the addition to the death-registration area of the residue of states almost all of which (North and South Dakota were the notable exceptions) showed high levels of maternal mortality. Nevertheless this alone did not account for the rising rate of maternal mortality, because the upward trend was still present from 1920 to 1929 if data were confined to the states of the 1918 death-registration area and data from other states were excluded. Almost certainly a rise in deaths due to abortion (which was seen in most if not all Western countries during the 1920s) and the 'orgy of interference' were more important factors.

During the early 1930s, however, the trend in maternal mortality in the USA took a sudden downward turn, no longer keeping company with the trends in European countries where maternal mortality was still rising. This fall in mortality in the USA occurred in both the white and the black populations, as shown in Table 22.3. Two points should be mentioned. First, this fall in maternal mortality coincided with the economic depression; secondly, (see Table 22.3) infant and neonatal mortality did not follow the same trend, but rose during 1933–4. If economic circumstances had been an important determinant in the level of maternal mortality, 1929–35 is just the period when a rise in maternal mortality should have occurred; a point to which we return in Chapter 28.

Why did maternal mortality begin to decline in the USA in the period from about 1929 to 1935? One factor was the completion of the death-registration area: no longer was there an annual increment due to the inclusion of high maternal mortality states. A second possibility is a decline in streptococcal virulence; but in so far as there is evidence on this point, it points in the other direction of increasing virulence.

The third possibility, for which there is some evidence, albeit somewhat scattered and only partially conclusive, is an improvement in the quality of maternal care. This probably occurred in two ways. First, when the excesses of surgical intervention in the 1920s had been exposed they were to some extent diminished. Second, and more importantly, there was better provision of maternal care for the poor, notably in the southern states. State-financed and voluntary systems of medical care began to be introduced in the late 1920s and early 1930s. It is difficult to assess the extent to which this took place throughout the USA, but in some states (in Virginia, for example, to which we come later) the evidence is quite substantial.

REGIONAL DIFFERENCES IN MATERNAL MORTALITY

We have considered the trend in maternal mortality in the USA as a whole. With a country as large as the USA, however, combining the mortality rates of all the states is not unlike combining the rates of all European countries from Sweden and Finland down to Spain and Portugal. One could argue that systems of maternal care, climatic conditions, and geographical features, as well as rates of maternal mortality, varied as widely between the northern and the southern states as they did between the countries of northern and southern Europe. In the 1930s there were states such as Connecticut and Minnesota with MMRs as low as 25–30 when others such as South Carolina and Nevada recorded levels as high as 70–90. And since I have stressed how much higher maternal mortality was in the USA than Britain it is important to note that in 1937 there were twenty-five states in which maternal mortality was lower than it was in Scotland and three in which the rate was lower than it was in England and Wales.

Figure 22.3 shows that the states with the highest rates were largely confined to the south, stretching from Virginia and North Carolina in the east, down through Alabama, Mississippi, Louisiana and Texas, and out to Arizona and Nevada in the west. The states with the lowest mortality were mainly those on the Pacific coast, the northern central areas, and New England. Figure 22.4 shows the rank order of all the states in 1938–40. For each state, the MMR is expressed as a percentage above or below the national average. The rank order in terms of maternal mortality was on the whole remarkably stable throughout the inter-war period[8] (Appendix Table 25).

Were regional differences linked to any particular aspect of maternal care? Figure 22.5 provides an answer. It shows the number of non-white births and midwife deliveries by state during the same period, 1938–40. For statistical reasons, all states with fewer than 500 non-white births in 1940 were excluded. In each state a pair of values is shown. The upper value is the number of non-white births expressed as a percentage of total births; the lower value (in parentheses) shows the percentage of non-white births attended by 'non-medical persons'. In short it shows interstate variation in the proportion of black mothers and amongst those black mothers the proportion delivered by midwives.

It is clear that there was a fairly close association between high maternal mortality on the one hand, and on the other a high proportion of births to black mothers as well as a high percentage of black mothers being delivered by midwives. For example, in Mississippi, the state with the third highest MMR (62.8), black births formed 55 per cent of total births and 83 per cent of black mothers were delivered by midwives. In states like Kansas, Illinois, Indiana, and Ohio, where rates of maternal mortality ranged from 28.7 to 37.3, black births amounted to between 4 per cent and 6 per cent of total births and 2 per cent or less of black mothers were attended by midwives.

---

[8] Examples of the rank order of states by maternal mortality in the early 1920s (when of course many were still excluded from the death-registration area) can be found in Woodbury, *Maternal Mortality*.

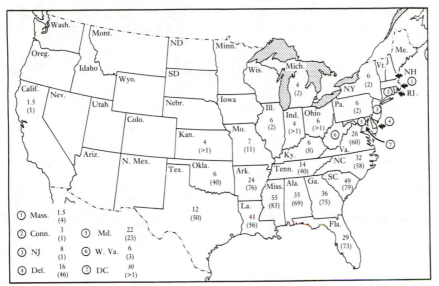

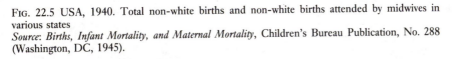

Fig. 22.5 USA, 1940. Total non-white births and non-white births attended by midwives in various states
Source: *Births, Infant Mortality, and Maternal Mortality*, Children's Bureau Publication, No. 288 (Washington, DC, 1945).

Two notable exceptions to the general rule that the highest rates of MMRs were found in the southern states and were associated with a high proportion of births to black women and a high proportion of deliveries of black women by midwives, were Arizona in the south and Maine in the north. Why was maternal mortality so much higher in the non-white population? Was it simply the place of delivery and the type of birth-attendant?

MATERNAL MORTALITY AND RACE IN THE USA

Let us look more closely at the difference in maternal mortality between black and white mothers on the one hand, and three variables on the other: geographical location (south versus north), place of delivery (home versus hospital), and type of birth-attendant (midwife versus physician).

Table 22.2, which shows MMRs according to colour in eight northern and eight southern states in 1938–40, is revealing. It shows, as all studies from the beginning of this century to the present have shown, that black women were at much greater risk of dying in childbirth than white. But it also shows that for all women, white as well as black, the risk was higher in the southern than the northern states by virtually the same amount. Mathematically the risk of delivery in the south compared with the north was 1.196 times greater for white women and 1.23 for black. When the relative risks of black and white

TABLE 22.2 *Maternal Mortality Rates according to Colour in States with Few Births[a] and with Many Births to Black Women, 1938–1940*

State	Maternal deaths (per 10,000 live births)		Ratio
	White	Black	Black:white
States with few black births			
California	29.5	81.9	2.77
New Jersey	30.8	57.6	1.87
New York	30.8	79.9	2.59
Michigan	31.4	57.3	1.82
Indiana	32.3	79.1	2.45
Massachusetts	33.3	67.8	2.04
Pennsylvania	34.8	62.7	1.80
DC	35.5	66.1	1.86
Average	32.3	69.0	2.15
States with many black births			
Kentucky	37.9	87.5	2.31
North Carolina	39.4	75.2	1.91
Louisiana	41.9	81.0	1.93
Mississippi	44.3	73.3	1.65
Georgia	46.6	80.3	1.72
Alabama	47.2	87.7	1.85
South Carolina	47.4	89.2	1.88
Florida	52.0	106.4	2.05
Average	44.6	85.0	1.9

[a] Births to black women in the first group amounted to 1% or less of total births.

Source: Children's Bureau Publications, US Department of Labor, Washington, DC, Government Printing Office, No. 288, *Births, Infant Mortality and Maternal Mortality* (1945), Graphic presentation.

women were compared for the north and the south, we find, surprisingly, that this differential was actually larger in the northern states than the southern, the factors being 2.14 in the north and 1.9 in the south. In other words, black mothers who moved from the south to the north would on average reduce their *absolute* risk of dying in childbirth from eighty-five to sixty-nine (in round numbers) but they would *increase* their *relative* risk—relative to white women, that is—by a small amount.

This effectively rules out the black midwives of the southern states as the one and only explanation for the higher mortality of black mothers in the USA. The probable explanation of this curious finding is that most of the

TABLE 22.3 *Maternal and Infant Mortality Rates in the USA, 1930–1938*

	1930	1931	1932	1933	1934	1935	1936	1937	1938
Maternal mortality rate (per 10,000 live births)									
Total	67.3	66.1	63.3	61.9	59.3	58.2	56.8	48.9	43.5
White Women	60.8	60.1	58.1	56.4	54.4	53.1	51.2	43.6	37.7
Black Women	118.9	112.5	100.5	100.0	93.1	95.5	98.1	86.2	86.1
Infant mortality rate (per 10,000 live births)									
First year[a]	64.6	61.6	57.6	58.1	60.1	55.7	57.1	54.4	51.0
First day[b]	15.0	15.0	15.0	15.1	15.4	15.0	15.1	14.7	14.1
First month[b]	35.7	34.6	33.5	34.0	34.1	32.4	32.6	31.3	29.6
Second to twelfth month[c]	30.0	28.0	24.9	25.0	26.9	24.1	25.4	23.9	22.1

[a] Infant mortality.
[b] Neonatal mortality.
[c] Post-neonatal mortality.

Source: Children's Bureau Publications, US Department of Labor, Washington, DC, Government Printing Office, No. 288, *Births, Infant Mortality and Maternal Mortality* (1945), Graphic presentation.

TABLE 22.4 *Maternal Mortality Rate, Percentage Delivered in Hospital, and Percentage Delivered by Physicians in the USA, 1937*

	Maternal mortality rate (per 10,000 live births)	Percentage delivered in hospitals	Percentage delivered by physicians
USA as a whole			
Total	49	44.8	89.4
White women	44	48.2	95.5
Black women	86	13.7	39.2
Massachusetts			
Total	46	76.6	99.6
White women	46	76.8	99.6
Black women	84	66.6	96.6
Minnesota			
Total	31	56.9	97.3
White women	30	56.8	97.4
Black women	115	68.5	87.9
Alabama			
Total	63	12.7	64.8
White women	55	17.0	88.6
Black women	76	5.7	26.0
Florida			
Total	68	32.3	70.2
White women	53	42.7	90.2
Black women	103	8.4	24.2

Source: L. I. Dublin, 'The Problem of Maternity: A Survey and a Forecast', *American Journal of Public Health*, 29 (1939), 1212.

black population in the north was urban, while in the south it was mostly rural. Many surveys showed that high maternal mortality (and infant mortality) was a consistent finding in the poorest sections of urban areas and black ghettos.[9]

If we now look at the white–black differential in maternal mortality in terms of place of birth and type of birth-attendant, Table 22.4 shows that for the USA as a whole fewer black women than white were delivered in hospital and delivered by a physician. In Massachusetts and Minnesota, however, the percentage of black and white women delivered in hospital, and the percentage delivered by physicians was virtually the same. (In fact a higher percentage of black than white women in Minnesota were delivered in hospital.) Yet this similarity in place of delivery and type of birth-attendant

[9] See C. B. Crittenden and Lois Skaggs, *Maternal Mortality in Kentucky: A Study of Puerperal Deaths, 1932–1939*, Kentucky State Department of Health (1940).

did nothing to eliminate the difference in maternal mortality. The mortality differential was even larger in Minnesota than it was in Alabama and Florida.[10]

This shows that the mortality differential appears to have been to a large extent unaffected by the place of delivery or type of birth-attendant. It is possible, however, that the hospitals and physicians available to black women were different in kind from those available to white women. There is some supporting evidence for this to which we shall return. First, however, we must deal with the question of whether this mortality differential was rooted in the greater degree of poverty and deprivation amongst the black population of the USA.

POVERTY AND MATERNAL MORTALITY AMONGST NON-WHITE WOMEN

In Chapter 3 we discussed in general terms the relative importance of socio-economic status and standards of maternal care as determinants of maternal mortality. In subsequent chapters we noted some specific examples such as the 'Rochdale experiment' in England and the Frontier Nursing Service in Kentucky. Here, where we are faced with the problem of explaining the high maternal mortality of black women in the USA, it is appropriate to consider the question of poverty in more depth.

It is well known that the black population of the USA suffered a much lower standard of living than the white population and was subjected to a much greater degree of medical and social neglect. There is historical evidence of malnutrition and high levels of morbidity and mortality amongst the black population of the southern states and to a lesser degree amongst the poor whites. Recent work by Beardsley has revealed the extent and causes of medical neglect of the blacks and the poor-white mill workers in the twentieth-century south.[11] He has shown there was little improvement in the provision of care, even as late as the 1950s, in spite of a patchy provision of health centres manned by physicians as 'the only way to head off large-scale government intrusion into medicine'.[12] The greater poverty of the black population of the USA compared with the white seems an obvious explanation for their high maternal mortality. But what do we mean by poverty, and in what way could poverty have led to higher maternal mortality?

Sen has explored the wide variety of meanings which have been attached to poverty in the context of famines.[13] Instead of the orthodox view that famines are always caused by a major decline in the food supply, Sen has put forward

---

[10] For brevity, only four states are shown in Table 22.3, but they were representative in this respect. Comparison between other northern and southern states revealed the same features.

[11] E. H. Beardsley, *A History of Neglect: Health Care for Blacks and Mill Workers in the Twentieth-Century South* (Knoxville, Tenn., 1987).

[12] Ibid. 276.

[13] A. Sen, *Poverty and Famines* (Oxford, 1981), 9–23.

The entitlement approach to starvation and famines [which] concentrates on the ability of people to command food through the legal means available to society . . . A person starves *either* because he does not have the ability to command enough food, *or* because he does not use this ability to avoid starvation.[14]

Thus famines may occur not through FAD ('food availability decline') but through lack of entitlement in one form or another. Some of these ideas may be useful in understanding the concept of poverty in relation to maternal mortality.

As far as maternal mortality is concerned, the classical explanation of the effects of poverty points to the association with malnutrition. Malnutrition, it is said, increases the risk of dying in childbirth in various ways: through rickets which can cause pelvic deformity, through anaemia which increases the risk of death from haemorrhage, and through a sort of general effect in the sense that a malnourished woman has less resistance (or greater susceptibility) to death from all obstetric complications.

Sen has shown that deaths due to famine are generally mediated through an increase in normal causes of death ('famine mortality as magnified normal mortality') and increased mortality persists, often for years after the famine has ended.[15] We can extend this idea to malnutrition and maternal mortality and propose that the risk of maternal mortality from all causes is increased by malnutrition. This, however, is to make a basic assumption that famine is malnutrition writ large; that the difference between the two is simply a difference of degree. In famines, death rates are raised to dramatic levels with the dead lying in the streets, and I have not the slightest doubt that gross starvation under conditions of famine greatly increases the risk of maternal mortality. In lesser degrees and more chronic forms of food deprivation—in malnutrition in the sense of too little of one or more foodstuffs essential for good health (lack of protein, iron, vitamins, and so on)—increased mortality may be less visible but its effects might be revealed by statistical studies. If we are happy to accept the idea that famine and malnutrition differ only in degree, we will expect to find raised maternal mortality wherever we encounter malnutrition. This means that in theory at least, the abolition of poverty by social or welfare services (and above all by an adequate food supply), could have reduced the maternal mortality of black women to the level of white.

There are, however, difficulties. There is evidence that poverty which causes deprivation rather than destitution (although of course they are vague terms and one can argue about where you draw the boundary between the two) tends to raise the level of morbidity rather than the level of mortality for some groupings. This seems to be true, at least to some extent, for both infant

---

[14] Ibid. 45.
[15] Ibid. 210–16.

and maternal mortality (see Chapter 28). Table 22.3 suggests that the depression in the 1930s had no effect on maternal mortality in the USA and only a slight effect (in 1933/4) on infant and neonatal mortality. These, however, are aggregate statistics which may hide much larger changes in certain areas.

Here I would stress that I believe malnutrition associated with poverty does indeed increase the risk of dying in childbirth: but the point at issue is not whether it does but how important it was in the past compared with other factors. If there was an association between poverty and high maternal mortality in the USA—and there is little doubt that there was—it may be explicable in terms of Sen's theory of 'entitlement'. Thus poverty may increase maternal mortality either because a mother does not have the ability to command the resources of maternal care, or because she chooses not to employ adequate maternal care. We saw earlier that many black women in the south showed a preference for older untrained midwives even when delivery by a physician or by younger trained midwives was available; and we come to the striking example of the Faith Assembly at the end of this chapter.

These are examples of the rejection of available care. There is also evidence of the other element of the entitlement approach: that black women in general were unable to 'command' maternal care of the kind available to white women. If this is more important than malnutrition *per se* there is an important corollary with relevance to maternal care in the third world today. Many more maternal deaths in a deprived as opposed to a destitute or starving population may be saved by the provision of trained maternal care, either free or at very low cost, rather than by improvement in diet, sanitation, and housing. The reader may remember the exasperated Medical Officer of Health in Wales who said what was needed to reduce maternal mortality was 'a herd of cows, not a herd of specialists' (see Chapter 3). For all that he had the lovely Welsh gift of the gab, he was probably wrong.

Historically, several lines of evidence appear to support this view. Black women in the USA often had large families and were unable to meet the repeated expense of employing a physician or even an untrained midwife for all their deliveries. This was shown by a survey in Gibson County, Tennessee, in the 1940s:

Economic distress has influenced the trend of obstetric practice to a considerable extent, because patients attempt to do without medical care in order to decrease the expense of having children, often to the point of imperilling the lives of both mothers and infants. Actually, fifty-five per cent of the maternal deaths in Gibson County during the period studied [the early 1930s] were among women who had never consulted a doctor until labor had begun or until the terminal complication had developed.[16]

[16] M. E. Lapham, 'Study of Maternity Care in Gibson County', *Journal of the Tennessee Medical Association*, 28 (1945), 223–38.

In Kentucky, maternal mortality amongst the black population was exceptionally high until 1933 (see Figure 22.9). This led to the provision in ten counties of a state-funded nursing and maternity service which was followed by a remarkable fall in the MMR amongst black mothers in the space of a few years from a level of over 140 deaths per 10,000 births to about 40.[17] The importance of the quality of maternal care emerged from a survey of maternal mortality in Jefferson County, Alabama during the years 1931–5. The author, Dr Dowling, found that maternal mortality from all causes was 78 per cent higher in black mothers compared with white. Although 'the general education and mental ability of midwives are so low as to constitute a grave hazard for the patients they attend', Dowling found that the progressive elimination of midwives and the increasing number of deliveries of black women by physicians had failed to produce the expected reduction in the difference between white and black maternal mortality. 'Even with the extension of the medical service to the vast majority of colored women at the time of delivery, the problem of maternal mortality among Negroes has in no way been solved.' In this survey there were approximately equal numbers of white and black patients and the total number of cases was 5,354 (see Table 18.4). Ninety-one per cent of the black mothers were delivered by midwives or black general practitioners, and 92 per cent of white mothers were delivered by the obstetricians or by the white general practitioners. No white women were delivered by black general practitioners. The racial separation was almost complete.

In Dowling's opinion the excess mortality amongst black women was due to the low standard of care they received. 'Errors in judgement and technic, and neglect on the part of the attending physician, were 50% more frequent among the colored mothers.' Black mothers who escaped the dangers of delivery by untrained midwives fell into the hands of physicians who were more likely to subject them to unnecessary Caesarean section, unskilled operative delivery, poor surgical judgement, and neglect throughout pregnancy, labour, and the postnatal period.[18] Dowling's conclusion—that poor obstetric care by midwives and by physicians attending black women was the reason for the high MMR amongst the black population—was shared by Elizabeth Tandy of the Children's Bureau in her special study of this problem.[19]

Confirmation of this thesis comes from certain features which did *not* occur but which would have been expected to occur if poverty had operated directly through malnutrition rather than indirectly through the medium of the birth-

[17] Crittenden and Skaggs, *Maternal Mortality in Kentucky*. The nursing and maternity service was influenced by the success of the Frontier Nursing Service.

[18] J. D. Dowling, 'Points of Interest in a Survey of Maternal Mortality', *American Journal of Public Health*, 27 (1937), 803–8. Dr Dowling worked in the health department in Birmingham, Alabama.

[19] E. Tandy, *Infant and Maternal Mortality amongst Negroes*, Children's Bureau Publications, No. 243 (Washington, DC, 1937).

attendant. Where state schemes were introduced to provide a high standard of maternal care for non-white mothers (as in Kentucky), maternal mortality fell steeply although economic and social circumstances did not alter. During the depression, when poverty increased, maternal mortality was falling as rapidly amongst non-white mothers as white, and sometimes (as in Mississippi and Oklahoma) even more rapidly. Deaths due to haemorrhage complicated by anaemia and deaths due to associated diseases (both of which reflect ill health) were higher in absolute terms in black than white mothers, but when they were expressed as a percentage of maternal deaths from all causes, they were no higher. Thus deaths associated with malnutrition do not account for the differential between the MMRs according to colour.[20]

One detail remains to be considered which was only connected marginally if at all with poverty. Abortion was a very important element in maternal mortality during the inter-war period, and it was often said that deaths from abortion were exceptionally high amongst black women. This appears to have been true in certain surveys, including those in Alabama and Kentucky, quoted above. Table 22.5, however, shows that although the mortality rate from abortion was higher in absolute terms in black women compared with white, abortion deaths as a percentage of all maternal deaths were slightly lower in black women than white. Once more we find that maternal mortality was higher in black women for all causes, but the frequency of the causes relative to each other was broadly the same in the black and white populations in the USA as a whole.

SECULAR TRENDS IN MATERNAL MORTALITY IN VARIOUS STATES

Broadly speaking the trends in various states fall into two distinct patterns: the northern and the southern. In the northern states the trends corresponded more or less closely to the trends seen in Europe, showing a plateau or rising slope up to the 1930s, and the distinctive downturn in mortality between 1935 and 1940 which coincided with (and was probably due to) the sulphonamides. Two northern states are shown in Figures 22.6 (Massachusetts) and 22.7 (Minnesota). The southern pattern differs mainly in showing a more or less steady decline from 1929/30, with only slight evidence of an abrupt change in direction in the period 1935–40. Three southern states are shown in Figures 22.8 (Mississippi), 22.9 (Kentucky), and 22.10 (Virginia).

The data for Massachusetts are, as far as I could discover, unique in starting around 1850. Figure 22.6 shows the high level in this state during the nineteenth century with the characteristic peak in the mid-1870s, a well-

---

[20] *Maternal Mortality in Fifteen States*, Children's Bureau Publications, No. 223 (Washington, DC, 1934).

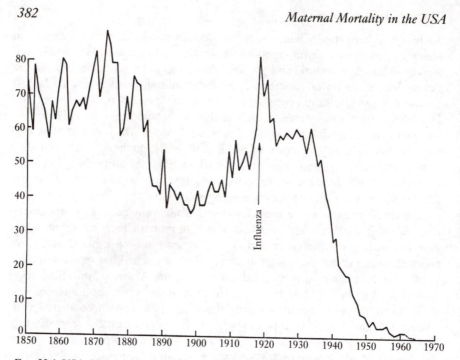

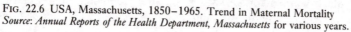

FIG. 22.6 USA, Massachusetts, 1850–1965. Trend in Maternal Mortality
Source: *Annual Reports of the Health Department, Massachusetts* for various years.

FIG. 22.7 USA, Minnesota, 1915–1947. Trend in Maternal Mortality
Source: Data kindly supplied by Dr L. G. Wilson.

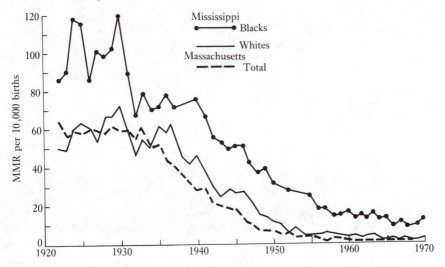

FIG. 22.8 USA, Mississippi, 1920–1970. Trend in Maternal Mortality
Source: National Library of Medicine, Bethesda, Md., *State Health Reports for the State of Mississippi*.

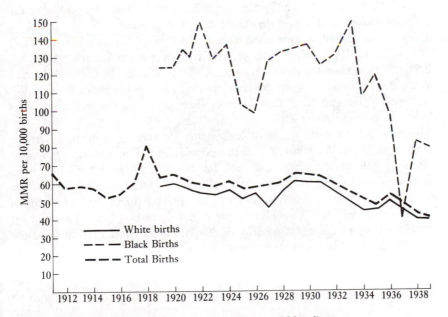

FIG. 22.9 USA, Kentucky, 1911–1939. Trend in Maternal Mortality
Source: Kentucky Health Dept., *State Health Reports of the State of Kentucky*.

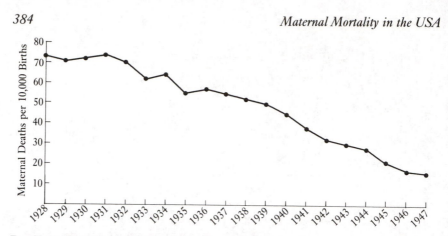

FIG. 22.10 USA, Virginia, 1928–1947. Trend in Maternal Mortality
Source: Virginia State Board of Health, *Annual Report of the Virginia State Board of Health for 1947* (Richmond, 1948).

marked fall between 1880 and 1900, and a rise from 1900 to the late 1920s. Then there is a brief plateau until the mid-1930s followed by a downturn in maternal mortality which was steep and continuous except for a few trivial interruptions. The trend in Massachusetts is remarkably similar to that in Scotland from 1910 (Figure 13.1), and even more so to that in Sweden (Figure 24.2). Compared with Sweden and Scotland, however, the level in Massachusetts was consistently higher until the mid-1930s: the shape of the graph is similar but it was, so to speak, displaced upwards.

There is a similar resemblance in the trend for Minnesota (Figure 22.7) from 1915 to 1935, where the general rate of maternal deaths was only slightly higher than the rates that prevailed in Britain. As in England and Wales, the first year in which maternal mortality fell to a significantly new low level was 1937, and from that year on there was a steep and continuous decline in maternal mortality.

In the southern states the most conspicuous feature is the wide difference in the trends for the white and black populations. This can be seen most vividly in Mississippi where the rate for black mothers, which had been running at the level of ninety to 120 deaths per 10,000 births (almost double the level in the worst periods of nineteenth-century Britain) showed a sudden decline from 1930 to 1932, followed by a plateau until 1940. The trend for Kentucky (Figure 22.9) was broadly similar, although from 1920 to 1933 the mortality for the black population was even higher, reaching levels of 120 to 150 maternal deaths per 10,000 births. But once again there is a sudden and very striking fall in black maternal mortality from about 1933. By 1948 maternal mortality in Kentucky had fallen to 11 compared with the level of 53 in 1933.[21]

[21] F. G. Dickinson and E. L. Welker, 'Maternal Mortality in the United States in 1949', *Journal of the American Medical Association*, 114 (1950), 1395–400.

The state which shows the 'southern pattern' most vividly is Virginia (Figure 22.10) where the analysis of maternal mortality by cause provides some clues to the 'southern' trend in maternal mortality.[22] It might be argued that the trend reflected changes in the demographic structure of the population from 1930 to 1950 when the population of Virginia was increasing. But there was little change in the crude birth rate, which was only slightly higher for black women than white being 22.6 and 18.9 respectively in 1940, and the relative proportions of the white and black population hardly altered, with the white population constituting around three-quarters of the total. There was also little alteration in the urban and rural proportions of the population; throughout the period 1930–50 two-thirds of the population was classified as rural, one-third as urban. There were, however, changes in place of birth and type of birth-attendant. In 1936 only 20 per cent of all deliveries took place in hospitals; by 1947 this had increased to 64 per cent. Deliveries by physicians (of both black and white mothers together) rose from 75 per cent in 1936 to 90 per cent in 1947. Thus, while the main demographic structure of the population altered relatively little between 1932 and 1952, the provision of maternal care altered significantly.

For instance, in 1925 midwife registration and a midwife-training programme was started with the stated purpose of ultimately eliminating the midwife, but until that occurred, of ensuring that those who practised were trained. In 1925 it was estimated that 6,500 midwives were practising. By 1929 the number had been reduced to 3,000 of which about one-third were trained. In 1941 Virginia introduced an 'MCH hospitalisation plan for the hospitalisation of medically indigent mothers and infants', claiming it was the only state to have undertaken such a plan. This allowed for free hospital delivery of over 1,000 women a year. From 1942 there was also the wartime Emergency Maternity and Infant Care Program, a national programme which provided medical and hospital care for wives and infants of enlisted men in the four lowest pay grades. Under this programme over 23,000 maternity cases in Virginia were treated between 1942 and 1948. Thus free hospital care for poor mothers, both black and white, was available on a considerable scale from the early 1940s. Figure 22.10 and Table 22.6 should be seen against this background.

The striking 'southern' feature of Figure 22.10 is the steady decline in mortality from 1932 with very little to suggest a sudden change in direction in the late 1930s. If we take Virginia as a typical southern state, there are some clues to understanding why these states showed a steady decline in maternal mortality from around 1930, and why that decline was most marked in the black population. The decline was of course too early for the sulphonamides,

[22] The data for this section on Virginia and for Table 22.6 and Figure 22.10, come from the reports of the Virginia State Health Department (Richmond, Va.) for various years.

TABLE 22.5 *Maternal Mortality Rates in Fifteen States in the USA in 1934 due to Various Types of Abortion*

Cause of death	Total urban and rural	Maternal mortality rates (per 10,000 live births)			
		Urban only	Rural only	White	Black
All puerperal causes	63	75	55	57	107
Abortion deaths					
Induced	7	11	4	7	5
Spontaneous	5	6	4	4	10
Therapeutic	2	2	1	2	1
Unspecified	2	3	2	2	5
Total abortion	16	22	11	15	21
All abortion deaths as percentage of all maternal deaths in each group	25.4	29.3	20.0	26.3	19.6

Source: Children's Bureau Publications, US Department of Labor, Washington, DC, Government Printing Office, No. 223, *Maternal Mortality in Fifteen States* (1934); F. J. Taussig, *Abortion, Spontaneous and Induced: Medical and Social Aspects* (London 1936), 378.

and if it had been due to economic change, one would have expected to see a rise associated with the depression not a fall. So, why did it occur?

Table 22.6 which shows maternal mortality according to colour and for various causes in 1932 (before the sulphonamides were introduced), in 1940 (when one would have expected them to have had an effect), and in 1952. The most obvious features of this table are first that maternal mortality was consistently higher for all causes in black mothers compared with white, and second that there was a profound fall in mortality from all causes, separately and combined. These are features we have met already. But there are other features to which I want to draw the reader's attention. First of all, the single most common cause of death in 1932 was not puerperal sepsis as it was almost everywhere else, but toxaemia. Indeed, the mortality rate attributed to toxaemia in black mothers (42.1) exceeded the mortality from all causes together in England and Wales in 1932. In Virginia toxaemia accounted for 38 per cent of puerperal deaths in black women and the mortality rate was three times as high as it was for white mothers.

Why the rate for toxaemia deaths should have been so high for black mothers is hard to understand. One obvious answer is that black mothers received no prenatal care, but in England and Wales in the five years 1872–6

TABLE 22.6 *Maternal Mortality in Virginia in 1932, 1940, and 1952 by Cause and according to Colour*

Cause and year	White population			Black population		
	Number of deaths	Maternal mortality rate (per 10,000 live births)	Percentage of total	Number of deaths	Maternal mortality rate (per 10,000 live births)	Percentage of total
Total puerperal deaths						
1932	217	56.2	100.0	179	110.8	100.0
1940	146	38.6	100.0	125	83.3	100.0
1952	29	4.3	100.0	44	19.3	100.0
Puerperal sepsis (non-abortive)						
1932	50	12.9	23.0	40	24.8	22.3
1940	25	6.7	17.1	29	19.3	23.2
1952	2	0.3	6.9	5	2.2	11.4
Toxaemia (puerperal albuminuria and convulsions)						
1932	55	14.2	25.3	68	42.1	38.0
1940	29	7.7	19.9	38	28.3	30.4
1952	10	1.5	34.5	9	3.9	20.4
Haemorrhage						
1932	18	4.6	8.3	19	11.7	10.6
1940	17	4.5	11.6	11	7.3	8.8
1952	10	1.5	34.5	9	3.9	20.4

TABLE 22.6 (*Continued*)

Cause and year	White population			Black population		
	Number of deaths	Maternal mortality rate (per 10,000 live births)	Percentage of total	Number of deaths	Maternal mortality rate (per 10,000 live births)	Percentage of total
Septic abortion						
1932	24	6.2	11.0	17	10.5	9.5
1940	23	6.1	15.7	13	8.6	10.4
1952	0	0	0	8	3.5	18.2
Non-septic abortion						
1932	11	2.8	5.1	5	3.1	2.8
1940	7	1.85	4.8	6	4.0	4.8
1952	1	0.1	3.4	2	0.9	4.5
Total live births						
1932	38,613			16,154		
1940	37,780			15,005		
1952	67,178			22,839		

Source: Alderman Library, University of Virginina, Charlottesville, Va., Annual reports of the Virginia State Department of Health.

when there was no prenatal care, the rate for deaths from toxaemia was only 6.5 per 10,000 births, approximately one-sixth of the rate in Virginia in 1932. It should also be noted that the mortality rate from toxaemia in white mothers in Virginia in 1932 (it was 14.2 per 10,000 births) was also high, being more than double the rate in England and Wales in the 1870s. Whether the Virginian data reflect climatic or racial effects is uncertain because so little is known of the cause of the condition. Deaths from toxaemia, obstetric hae-morrhage, and abortion were decisive in shaping the graph of maternal mortality; all were declining in a steady fashion from 1929 to 1947. Although the sharp downturn in sepsis deaths which was so obvious elsewhere did occur in the late 1930s, and in Virginia was probably due to better antisepsis and the use of the sulphonamides, it was lost against the background of the steady decline in deaths from other causes. Hence the absence of the usual sharp downturn in the second half of the 1930s.

Why, then, did deaths from causes other than sepsis fall from the early 1930s? The confident answer of the state health authorities was better maternal care for all classes, and in the absence of any other explanation we must assume this was correct. Indeed, there is corroborative evidence from other southern states in which a simultaneous steep downturn in the maternal mortality of black mothers was associated with the introduction of a variety of systems of nursing and maternity care. We have described such a system in Kentucky. Studies carried out in Tennessee and Mississippi also suggest that state-funded programmes led to a profound fall in maternal mortality in the black population.[23] But this is at best a tentative explanation. To my mind the high rate of deaths from toxaemia in Virginia, and the general downward trend in the MMR in southern states from 1930 is an unsolved problem, and a fruitful area for further research. Few problems in the history of maternal mortality are as difficult and challenging as the high mortality in the black population of the southern states of the USA from the 1920s (when in general statistics first became available) to the 1950s. In this book I have put forward some tentative hypotheses, but I would emphasize that I am conscious of having done no more than touch on the surface of the many and diverse problems that surround this subject. Records are available, especially the records of state health departments. I hope that what I have written will stimulate further research, and I expect that such research will overturn some of my tentative ideas.

Taking the USA as a whole, and the southern states in particular, maternal mortality was much higher than it was in most other western countries. Once it had begun to decline, however, how did the USA and various states within

---

[23] Lapham, 'Study of Maternity Care in Gibson County'; F. E. Whitacre and E. W. Jones, *Maternity Care in Two Counties, Gibson County, Tennessee and Pike County, Mississippi, 1940–41, 1943–44* (New York, 1950).

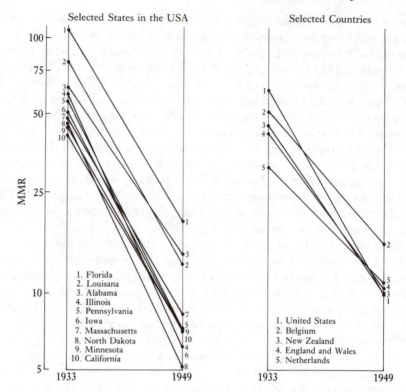

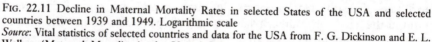

FIG. 22.11 Decline in Maternal Mortality Rates in selected States of the USA and selected countries between 1939 and 1949. Logarithmic scale
Source: Vital statistics of selected countries and data for the USA from F. G. Dickinson and E. L. Walker, 'Maternal Mortality in the United States in 1949', *Journal of the American Medical Association*, 144 (1950), 1395–400.

the USA compare in performance with European countries? We discussed this in Chapter 9 (see Table 9.2). Figure 22.11 is an addition to that discussion, underlining one of the most remarkable features in the history of maternal care. Here, the MMRs of various states in the USA and in various countries are shown for 1933 and 1949, and are joined by a straight line. The scale is logarithmic, so that the slope of the line represents the rate of fall between these two points. North Dakota, Iowa, and Massachusetts showed the steepest rate of fall with Louisiana close behind. Although the starting-points of these states were widely different, the rates of fall in each state was so similar that by and large they kept their rank order. In fact America made up lost ground. The rate of fall in the USA was slightly greater than it was in other Western countries.

That the rate of fall in the MMR was so similar in populations and places

TABLE 22.7 *Maternal Mortality in the Philadelpha Lying-in Hospital, 1929–37, 1938–45, and 1946–53*

	1929–37	1938–45	1946–53
Number of live births	17,916.0	18,128.0	23,360.0
Number of maternal deaths	100.0	33.0	17.0
Maternal deaths (per 10,000 live births)	55.8	18.2	7.3
Maternal deaths by cause			
Infection			
Number	40.0	4.0	0.0
Rate per 10,000 live births	22.3	2.2	0.0
Haemorrhage			
Number	23.0	8.0	0.0
Rate per 10,000 live births	12.8	4.4	0.0
Toxaemia			
Number	17.0	4.0	3.0
Rate per 10,000 live births	9.5	2.2	1.3
Heart disease			
Number	9.0	7.0	4.0
Rate per 10,000 live births	5.0	3.9	1.7
Caesarean sections[a]			
Number of live births	18,443.0	18,528.0	23,784.0
Caesarean sections			
Number	990.0	1,213.0	1,638.0
Incidence (%)	5.4	6.5	6.9
Caesarean deaths	24.0	6.0	3.0[b]
Mortality rate (%)	2.42	0.49	0.18

[a] A slightly different time period was used for the analysis of Caesarean sections: hence the different birth totals.

[b] Post-mortem Caesarean sections excluded.

Source: R. McNair Mitchell, 'Maternal Mortality in Pennsylvania Hospital: Tabular Review of Maternal Deaths, 1929–1953', *Obstetrics and Gynaecology*, 5 (1955), 123–36.

as dissimilar as England and Wales, New Zealand, Florida, Alabama, and North Dakota can only be regarded as remarkable, suggesting that common factors were in operation. This notion receives some support from the analysis of the decline in terms of specific causes. The findings in the USA and in various states is so similar to those already described for Britain, there is no need to consider them further in detail except in the form of a table and a figure. Table 22.7 traces the decline in maternal mortality in the Philadelphia Lying-in Hospital 1929–37 and 1946–53. Figure 22.12 is a graphic representation of the fall in maternal mortality for the USA as a whole from 1939 to 1948.

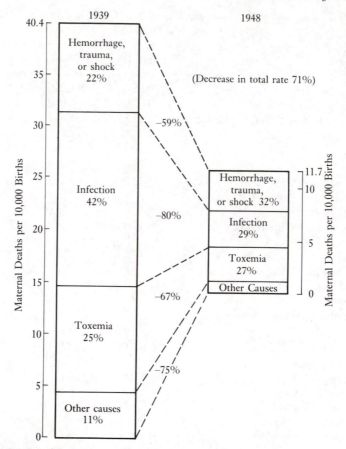

FIG. 22.12 United States, 1939–1948. The proportionate reduction in Maternal Mortality by various causes
Source: *Changes in Infant, Childhood, and Maternal Mortality over the Decade 1939–1948*, Children's Bureau Publication No. 6 (Washington, DC, 1950).

CONCLUSIONS

In the period with which we are concerned, medical care in the United States was dominated by the belief in the virtues of competitive free enterprise combined with an intense distrust of government interference. From 1900 increasing emphasis was placed on specialization and hospital care. Hospital privileges were granted, as of right, to a majority of practitioners instead of a few. Compared with European countries there was little control over the standard of medical education and even less over specialist training. Except in rural areas the general practitioner began to decline after the First World

War. The partial obstetrician-gynaecologist (in effect a general practitioner who claimed a special interest and expertise in surgery and obstetrics) was a common feature of obstetric practice, often combining inadequate training and experience with enormous confidence in his ability to undertake every aspect of surgical obstetrics. Michigan, as we have seen, had them in abundance.

Believing that hospital delivery by a physician was the only proper way, the midwife was driven out for all but the very poor, and stigmatized as a 'relic of barbarism'. As a form of private practice, obstetrics paid well and provided a regular, predictable succession of patients. In terms of annual admissions and bed occupancy, obstetrics came high on the list in many general hospitals where proximity to surgical wards brought the continual danger of cross-infection and added to the toll of maternal mortality.[24]

The American way of childbirth during the inter-war period was typically a hospital delivery by version, forceps, or Caesarean section under anaesthesia or deep sedation. Whatever we may feel about this kind of maternal care, to most Americans it was a system taken for granted or praised for its modernity. The Chairman of the North Dakota Committee on Maternal and Child Welfare reviewed maternal mortality in North Dakota in 1941, liked what he saw, and concluded:

The significant decline in maternal mortality in North Dakota justifies the conclusion that private medical practice, by its insistence on the personal relationship which must exist between patient and physician, has made another valuable contribution to the safety of American democracy.[25]

Others were less complacent. In the practice of unnecessary interference the USA was not alone; it occurred in many countries, but rarely if ever on the lavish scale that moved George Kosmak (in the context of the New York City survey) to say:

It is appalling to think that any man, a graduate of a hospital, would do some of the things we hear about. For example, a man does a version, tears the body away from the head, and the head is left in utero. Then he promptly does a Caesarean section, with the assistance of his brother, and gets the head out. That is not an isolated instance but an example of many.[26]

One of the virtues of American obstetricians was that so many had the capacity for open self-criticism almost to the point of self-flagellation, of

[24] J. B. DeLee and H. Siedentopf, 'The Maternity Ward of the General Hospital', *Journal of the American Medical Association*, 100 (1933), 6–14.

[25] J. H. Moore, 'Maternal Mortality in North Dakota', *Journal of the American Medical Association*, 116 (1941), 1887–9.

[26] R. F. Porges, 'The Response of the New York Obstetrical Society to the Report by the New York Academy of Medicine on Maternal Mortality, 1933–34', *Obstetrics and Gynaecology*, 152 (1985), 642–9.

which the above is an example. The series of reports on maternal mortality listed in Appendix 3, are ferocious and hard-hitting condemnations of poor obstetric practice. In none is there the slightest suggestion of a cover-up or a lame excuse. On the other hand one of the least-attractive aspects of American obstetrics was the way that profit and the perceived need to validate obstetrics as a surgical speciality were used so blatantly as an indication for obstetric interference when the risks involved were, or should have been, well known. A report by the United States Public Health Service noted in 1941 that:

The relation between receipt of maternal services and economic status is strikingly apparent with respect to obstetric techniques employed during delivery. For each of the techniques studied (caesarean section, episiotomy, and forceps) a sharp rise with income is found in the proportion of cases in which the technique was employed.[27]

The United States was no place for a rich woman who wanted a normal labour by the unhindered forces of nature. In a very real sense the more she paid the more she got.

And yet, one of the oddest features is that very rarely did the obstetricians who lacerated themselves and their colleagues for the high maternal mortality of the USA, pay attention to regional differences. Those who practised in the New England, Middle Atlantic, North Central, and Pacific regions could have pointed out that very often their states recorded lower rates of maternal mortality than those found in European countries, including France, Scotland, and sometimes England and Wales. They could have dismissed the dozen or so states in the South Atlantic and South Central regions as backward and atypical, and they should have seen that it is genuinely very difficult to provide maternity care in remote mountainous regions or huge under-populated states. Providing maternal care in England or the Netherlands was a very different task from providing it in Montana or Kentucky or Texas. But it seems that patriotic pride was seen only in national terms. Obstetricians seem to have been concerned more with the American than the Massachusetts, the Vermont, the Illinois, or the North Dakota way of obstetrics. Moreover, they showed almost total preoccupation with clinical factors. The social and political aspects of maternal mortality were largely ignored by practising physicians. This was not a charge which could be laid at the door of the Children's Bureau whose reports were remarkable for their analysis of the multiple factors underlying maternal and infant mortality. They were as rich in clinical detail as any, but they placed clinical matters firmly in the context of locality and a wide range of social, economic, and cultural factors.

In this account of maternal care in the USA I may have over-emphasized the tendency to interfere unnecessarily and laid too much stress on the

---

[27] Anon., 'Medical and Nursing Services for the Maternal Cases of the National Health Survey', *Public Health Reports*, 56 (1941), 855–6.

motives of greed and self-advancement. To redress the balance I should stress that the record of charitable care is better than often recognized by those familiar with the history of British hospitals, partly because it is so difficult for outsiders to unravel the intricate mixture of private and voluntary hospital care in the USA.[28]

In spite of its faults, the American system of maternal care produced some truly remarkable schemes which might not have flourished in a country less devoted to the encouragement of free enterprise and individual initiative. Examples we have quoted are the Chicago and New York Maternity Centers, the Kentucky Frontier Nursing Service, Julius Levy's introduction of a highly effective system of care by midwives in New Jersey, and the systems of nurse-midwife care in Mississippi and Tenessee. Most arose from the enterprise of one person with the determination to swim against the tide. In terms of total number of deliveries they may have been slight. For the student of maternal care, however, they possess an importance out of all proportion to their size. Almost all pointed in the same direction. Home delivery by trained midwives, backed up by a system of physician care in hospitals for a selected minority of abnormal cases, was capable of achieving a rate of maternal mortality that was not just a little lower, but staggeringly lower than the general level of maternal mortality in the USA. Unfortunately, however, these initiatives pointed in exactly the opposite direction to that taken by American medicine with its emphasis on hospitals, surgery, and technology. Thus they were doomed, and the chance was lost to introduce a nation-wide service of nurse-midwives in the very country above all others in which such a service could have been comprehensive, relatively inexpensive, and highly effective.

MATERNAL CARE AND MORTALITY IN TWO NORTH AMERICAN RELIGIOUS GROUPS

I end with an account of childbirth in two religious groups in the 1970s and early 1980s, even though the story lies outside the chronological limits of this study. The first of the two groups—in the language of experimental science, 'the controls'—is the Hutterites of the Western and Great Plains areas of Canada and the United States. The second is the Faith Assembly group of Indiana.[29]

---

[28] The best account of this aspect of hospital care is R. Stevens, *In Sickness and in Wealth: American Hospitals in the Twentieth Century* (New York, 1989).

[29] My sources on the Hutterites are T. A. Converse, R. S. Buker, and R. V. Lee, 'Hutterite Midwifery', *American Journal of Obstetrics and Gynaecology*, 116 (1973), 719–25, and a seminar given by and personal communication from, Mary Renfrew of the National Perinatal Epidemiology Unit, the Radcliffe Infirmary, Oxford, who visited one of the Hutterite communities recently. For the Faith Assembly, see A. M. Kaunitz, *et al.*, 'Perinatal and Maternal Mortality in a Religious Group Avoiding Obstetric Care', *American Journal of Obstetrics and Gynaecology*, 150 (1984), 826–32.

The Hutterites live in self-sufficient colonies. They are efficient and prosperous farmers. Within the communities they practise communal living, own little or no personal property, and their religious beliefs dominate every aspect of their lives. They have no social contact with their non-Hutterite neighbours and do not adopt any part of the life-style of the average North American population, having no radio, television, or newspapers, and no pictures, music, or books except for those of a religious nature. Hutterites always marry Hutterites. Any Hutterite who marries 'outside', excommunicates himself or herself from all members of the group, including family. Birth-control is forbidden and the Hutterites have been described as the population with the highest fertility ever recorded. Their diet is excellent, consisting of home-produced foods, and they buy and use the best of American farming (and cooking) equipment, and are astute in the world of business. Most important for our purposes, they find their medical services outside the community, using orthodox American medical care. As far as childbirth is concerned, up to about the 1970s most deliveries were conducted within the colonies by trained midwives; now, most take place in hospitals alongside non-Hutterite mothers. Not surprisingly, their infant and maternal morbidity and mortality rates do not differ significantly from those of non-Hutterite Caucasian groups in the United States.

The Faith Assembly religious group has been active in Indiana since 1973. 'Nearly all members are white; they represent diverse socio-economic strata.' Unlike the Hutterites it appears they do not live in colonies and do not cut themselves off from the local population. But they come together when they attend weekly religious services.

Faith Assembly tenets hold that members should not receive medical care for any health problems. Pregnant women therefore receive no prenatal care and give birth at home without obstetric assistance. Although it has been reported that 'lay midwives' have attended some Faith Assembly births, these attendants are unlicensed and have no formal training in obstetrics.[30]

Women belonging to the Faith Assembly were less likely than other women in Indiana to have certain demographic characteristics which are risk factors for maternal and perinantal mortality—being black, for instance, or adolescent, unmarried, or of low educational attainment. In short, they are a healthy normal population marked off by their religious beliefs and refusal to employ any form of orthodox medical or nursing care.

From 1975 to 1982, the number of maternal deaths in Indiana was sixty-four and the number of live births was 675,072. Within the Faith Assembly there were three maternal deaths and 344 live births. The MMR for Indiana as a whole was 9 per 100,000 live births; for the Faith Assembly it was 872

---

[30] Kauniz, *et al.*, 'Perinatal and Maternal Mortality in a Religious Group', 827.

per 100,000 live births. 'Hence the maternal mortality rate for Faith Assembly members . . . was 92 times higher (95 per cent confidence limits 19–280) than for the remainder of the state of Indiana.' The perinatal mortality rates, neonatal, and foetal mortality rates were all significantly higher in the Faith Assembly, although they were 'probably substantial underestimates . . . Faith Assembly members may have hidden perinatal deaths from local health authorities.' One unreported foetal death was only discovered when it was exhumed from the garden.

The risk of a Faith Assembly mother dying in childbirth, relative to other mothers in Indiana, was at least 19 times higher, and at most 280 times higher. It might be argued (although I can think of no conceivable reason why it should be) that membership of a religious group is in itself a risk factor in childbirth, and that this, rather than the absence of clinical care, explains the high mortality in the Faith Assembly. The Hutterites (the 'controls') show this to be untrue, for they accepted orthodox maternal care, and their maternal, neonatal, and infant mortality rates were not significantly different from their non-Hutterite neighbours.

The Faith Assembly are of special interest. From time to time one meets people who assert that childbirth is a normal process which has been un-necessarily 'medicalized'. Some appear to believe that for modern healthy women, natural childbirth without any medical assistance whatsoever would, with very rare exceptions, be perfectly safe. The experience of the Faith Assembly shows the probable consequence of acting on such a belief: a level of maternal mortality of 872 per 100,000 births, which is close to the rate in England during the second half of the eighteenth century.

23
Europe: Introduction

The following chapters which deal with maternal care and mortality in Europe do not pretend for one moment to be comprehensive; indeed, they are highly selective. To write a complete account of European maternal care would be an admirable ambition, but a long and difficult task. Here, I have confined myself to comparing certain aspects of childbirth in some parts of Europe with those in Britain and the United States. And I use the term 'Europe' for brevity to mean the continent of Europe including Scandinavia but excluding Britain. Most of my sources have been drawn from the Netherlands, Denmark, Sweden, France, and Belgium, with only a passing glance at a few other countries. The general outline of many of the issues surrounding maternal care and maternal mortality—the problems of measuring maternal mortality, for example—have already been considered in previous chapters and need not be repeated here except for the occasions when European evidence adds to our understanding of such matters.

SOME GENERAL DIFFERENCES

When childbirth in Europe is compared with Britain and the United States, certain differences stand out. With a much longer tradition behind them, European midwives were on the whole better trained, more closely regulated, more highly regarded by the public and the medical profession, and probably better paid than their British and American counterparts. Likewise, obstetrics as a branch of medical practice was more highly regarded within the European medical profession than the British or American. In the nineteenth century European obstetricians did not face the sneering attitudes of their physician and surgical colleagues in the way they did in Britain, and it is rare to find the British or American accoucheur discussing the need to preserve their image with their midwifery patients. Not so the French. Surgeons who practise midwifery, said Dionis in 1718, ought to be well bred. 'Clownishness is somewhat pardonable in army, town or hospital surgeons; but 'tis intolerable in one who has to do with ladies.' The accoucheur 'must be virtuous, of a sweet temper, affable, full of compassion and always contented with any handsome or moderate fee'.[1] According to Witkowski, in the eighteenth

---

[1] Pierre Dionis, *Treatise on Midwifery* (London, 1719).

and early nineteenth centuries, when the fashion for men was shaving and powdering, accoucheurs would sometimes grow beards to 'make themselves ugly' and deflect accusations of impropriety from their patients or jealous husbands.[2]

In the conduct of labour, Dutch and Scandinavian (but not the French or German) obstetricians were less prone to unnecessary interference than American or British; and the French, partly for religious reasons, seemed to have faith in the ability to carry out Caesarean section long before the operation became acceptable in Britain and elsewhere at the end of the nineteenth century. Lying-in hospitals in Europe tended to be older, larger, more prestigious, and more numerous. Most were state-funded, unlike the voluntary hospitals of Britain and the United States. Indeed, state control of maternal care began earlier and was generally more comprehensive than it was in the English-speaking countries. All these differences were conspicuous in the eighteenth and nineteenth centuries and perhaps a little less so in the early twentieth.

These are sweeping generalizations. It may well be that we find so many exceptions when we look more closely that some will have to be modified or discarded, but they can serve as a starting-point. And there is no doubt about one feature: Europe had a head-start on Britain. Man-midwifery was well established in Europe by the end of the seventeenth century. If we date the birth of man-midwifery from the time when substantial numbers of women began to engage medical men to attend them in their confinements, normal and abnormal, then the starting-point in Britain was 1740 or thereabouts.

In England before 1740, if you wanted to learn about midwifery you had to go to Europe. When Sir Richard Manningham established his Lying-in Infirmary in or about 1740, he stressed that men had been admitted to the practice of midwifery so recently in England that 'knowledge of the practice of Midwifery could not easily be obtained without going into foreign countries'. His aim was to establish an institution in London where midwifery could be taught to midwives and man-midwives.[3] By 1769 a man-midwife noted, 'now that midwifery is so well taught in London' there was no need to go abroad.[4]

---

[2] G.-J. Witkowski, *Histoire des accouchements chez tous les peuples* (Paris, 1887). Witkowski quotes Girouard who, in his *Défenseur des accoucheurs* (Paris, 1804), was angry at the damage done to the image of respectable accoucheurs by the fashionable and snobbish accoucheur who boasted that all his patients lived in the best areas of the town and came from only the highest classes of society. All his deliveries were complicated and needing instruments and he was apt to say how lucky it was that he had arrived just in time to save mother and baby by his exceptional skill. On arriving at the house he affected exhaustion and told of sleepless nights spent in the relief of the sufferings of women. He moved the mother and her husband to cry out in admiration, 'Quel talent! quelle peine! quelle obligations on doit vous avoir, pour vous sacrificier ainsi au soulagement de l'humanité souffrante! Monsieur, voudriez-vous accepter un consommé?' He happily accepted not only the consommé but also the high fee he demanded.

[3] *Charitable Infirmary for the Relief of Poor Women Labouring of Child and During their Lying-in; Next Door to Sir Richard Manninghams in Jermyn Street* (London, n.d., *c*.1740).

[4] R. W. Johnson, *A New System of Midwifery* (London, 1769).

Nevertheless, many still crossed the channel to spend a year or more at old and well-established centres of instruction, and continued to do so until the twentieth century.

The early dominance of Europe can be seen most clearly in the authorship of midwifery texts. Until the 1730s, those that circulated in Britain were almost entirely translations of European texts. Maubray complained in 1725, 'What books have we ever had in England but bare translations?'[5] There was a profitable business in translating and publishing the works of foreigners such as Mauriceau, Portal, Peu, Deventer, Roleau, Amand, and Mauquest de la Motte—all French except for Deventer who was Dutch. The French obstetrician, François Mauriceau (1637–1709), was regarded as the greatest authority. His *Traité des maladies des femmes grosses et accouchées* published in 1668 and translated by Hugh Chamberlen in 1672, was the standby of the English some seventy years after it was first published. After 1730, however, we find a steady increase in midwifery texts by English authors. It has been said that the centre for publications on midwifery moved from Paris to London in the mid-eighteenth century, and this may be one of the few of my generalizations that can survive close scrutiny. Certainly there was a flood of publications from the 1740s onwards.

When David Spence published his *System of Midwifery* in Edinburgh in 1784 he apologized for yet another text on the subject. There were already so many they 'might seem to render the present one unnecessary'. He listed what he believed were the most important texts in chronological order, beginning with Mauriceau in 1668 and ending with Dr Butter in 1775. There were thirty-nine works in his list. Of the first thirteen, all published before 1737, eight were by French authors, one (Deventer) by a Dutch author, and there were four slight works by the English authors, Maubray, Giffard, Chapman, and Dawkes. From 1737 to 1775, however, of the twenty-six texts listed by Spence, twenty-one were by British authors, two by German authors, and three by French. And this was before the major British publications of the eighteenth century by William Hunter, Thomas Denman, Charles White, and Alexander Gordon of Aberdeen. Thus we can understand why British authors constantly quoted European authorities in the first half of the eighteenth century, but British authors were being quoted in Europe by the end of the century.[6]

Nevertheless, in some respects Europe was still the mecca for the aspiring accoucheur. Take, for example, Augustus Bozzi Granville who became Physician-Accoucheur to the Westminster General Dispensary in 1818 and was the founder of the Obstetrical Society of London in its first incarnation.

---

[5] J. Maubray, *Midwifery Brought to Perfection by Manual Operation* (London, 1725), p. xii.

[6] A more comprehensive list of midwifery texts, published between 1660 and 1760, can be found in J. Glaister, *Dr. William Smellie and his Contemporaries: A Contribution to the History of Midwifery in the Eighteenth Century* (Glasgow, 1894).

He was born in Milan. Deciding on a career as a London accoucheur, he took advice from the leading accoucheurs of the capital who advised him to go back to Europe to get a proper grounding. Granville therefore spent 1816 and 1817 at maternity hospitals in Paris before returning to London.[7] The two famous American obstetricians—Joseph Bolivar DeLee and J. Whitridge Williams—both started their careers by studying in Germany at the end of the nineteenth century. Germany was especially favoured by young doctors from the English-speaking world for its pre-eminence in pathology with France as well as Germany for bacteriology and obstetrics.

By the twentieth century, however, the European connection was beginning to weaken. In Britain and the United States the young obstetrician was content to find his postgraduate education at home. It was a pity in a way. From the late eighteenth to the early twentieth century (and once again this is a tentative generalization) British and American obstetricians knew a great deal more about European obstetrics, profited much more often from travel abroad, and were less parochial than they were thereafter. It was of course to a great extent force of circumstance, the circumstance being the deplorable level of nineteenth-century obstetric education in Britain and the USA.

When the educational links with Europe began to weaken, British and American obstetricians tended to strengthen connections between their two countries by exchanges of letters and visits, and quite frequent references to each other's work in medical journals. Their interest in European obstetrics, however, continued at a much lower level until the inter-war period, when British and American obstetricians and health authorities were becoming alarmed at the high level of maternal mortality. Then they turned to Europe, and specifically to north-west Europe, not because they thought they could learn from European advances in obstetric technology, but for one specific reason: maternal mortality. When they saw that the Netherlands and the Scandinavian countries appeared to be achieving much greater success in maternal care than Britain and the United States, a number of well-known British and American authorities visited Scandinavia and the Netherlands. Most of them travelled to seek answers to four questions: were the low levels of maternal mortality in certain European countries due to racial differences? Were they due to different systems of maternal care? Were they due to different social and economic conditions? Or were they artefacts, due to different ways of measuring maternal mortality? We come to their reports later, for they are important sources on the differences between British and American systems of maternal care and those in Europe, especially in regard to the midwives with whom we begin the European comparison.

[7] A. B. Granville. *Autobiography* (London, 1874).

24

European Midwives

THE FRENCH MIDWIVES

To put my cards on the table, I will be arguing that for most of the period covered in this study, certain European countries were safer places to have a baby than Britain or the United States not so much because of what European doctors did or did not do and still less because European lying-in hospitals were safer, but largely because their system of maternal care placed great importance on home deliveries by trained midwives. I will suggest they chose this course because of their long-standing tradition of training and regulating midwives, and thus that until the mid-1930s historical tradition was at least as important as technical innovations in determining the comparative effectiveness of national systems of maternal care.

Until 1902 English midwives were not regulated by local authorities or the state. They had no system of formal training. A few in the eighteenth century had certificates in the form of an episcopal licence, and a few in the nineteenth had certificates from the Obstetrical Society of London or a hospital where they had been taught. But these were a tiny minority. For the most part they relied entirely on local reputation. In these respects, Britain lagged far behind Europe.

In France there was also licensing by the church but there is little to suggest it was effective or important.[1] In England, episcopal licensing faded out in the eighteenth century, and when it had ceased there was nothing to replace it. In Europe, however, regulation of midwives by the church (such as it was) was accompanied and later supplanted by regulations imposed by municipalities and the state. It was lay rather than church authorities in Europe which had the power to regulate midwives. By so doing, the state and lay municipal authorities underlined the importance and the relatively high status of the European midwife. Regulation was important, not only to ensure that midwives were properly trained and knew their job, but also to ensure that the respectable women became midwives. The ignorant, the illiterate, the dishonest, the disreputable, the maimed, and the diseased, should not be

---

[1] In France in the 18th cent. the bishop's duty in the course of his pastoral trips was confined to enquiring of the curate if there was a midwife in the parish, and if she did her work properly. See R. L. Petrelli, 'The Regulation of French Midwifery during the *ancien régime*', *Journal of the History of Medicine and Allied Sciences*, 26 (1971), 291, an excellent source on French midwifery.

allowed entry to what was universally acknowledged to be an important occupation and a position of trust.

In the Netherlands, for example, Deventer insisted in 1719 that the women who should *not* be allowed to become midwives were those who were too old, were virgins, were young and unmarried, were diseased and consumptive, were so gross and fat and whose hands and arms so thick and fleshy that they 'cannot long sit incommodiously', and those who were maimed with crooked fingers, were stupid and dull of sense, and last but not least, those who were not handy. Mrs Gamp would not have passed the test.[2] Deventer would have preferred midwives who were the wives or daughters of surgeons, 'but unfortunately so many are necessitous widows who accept low fees that husbands will not allow wives to take up the art'. He was right. Midwives were often necessitous widows.[3]

Similar views on the need for respectable midwives can be found in many sources. In France in the sixteenth century, the midwife had to be a woman of honour, worthy of the title *matrone et sage-femme*, someone who would not provoke insult or work in poor company.[4] The midwife had to be honest, conscientious, and above all discreet, for her duties were not confined to delivering babies; she was also the arbiter in delicate questions of virginity, legitimacy, and paternity. Careful selection, training, and regulation were essential. Training in sixteenth-century France consisted of an apprenticeship to a senior midwife followed by the presentation of a certificate of good conduct to a barber-surgeon and the priest of the parish. Midwives were required to call either a surgeon or a senior *matrone jureé* in abnormal cases. In the seventeenth century the midwives of Paris obtained their licences either by apprenticeship to a *Matrone de la ville*, or by association with the maternity department of the Hôtel Dieu where student midwives appear to have been accepted for the first time in 1630. Midwives trained at the Hôtel Dieu were the most prestigious. Admission to the school was a great honour and confined to those who were French, married, and Catholic, and able to afford the high tuition fees. Elsewhere in France a woman became a midwife by studying for three years with a *sage femme jurée* at the end of which time she took an oath. Provincial towns such as Lille and Bordeaux had their own rules about the regulation and training of midwives which were often complex and firmly enforced. In Lille midwives were required to attend the poor as well as the rich.

In the eighteenth century many provincial towns established lying-in hospitals which served for training midwives. There was little training or

---

[2] Henry à Deventer, *The Art of Midwifery Improved* (London, 1716), probably translated by Maubray.
[3] Ibid. See also J. Gélis, *A History of Childbirth: Fertility, Pregnancy and Birth in Early Modern Europe*, trans. Rosemary Morris (Cambridge, 1991), 104–6.
[4] Petrelli, 'The Regulation of French Midwifery', 281.

regulation in the countryside, but a famous itinerant Paris-trained midwife, Madame du Coudray, led a nomadic life travelling throughout France in the second half of the eighteenth century, armed with a Royal patent, to teach midwifery in rural areas. In 1730 a statute was introduced with the intention of regulating midwifery throughout France. Thus, during the last years of the *ancien régime* a system had evolved by which midwives were subject to regulation at three levels: the state, the church, and local government. Even if regulation was incomplete and the quality of care and training variable, the existence of such a system demonstrates the long tradition of midwifery in France.[5]

Unfortunately there is as yet little information about relative numbers of deliveries by midwives and surgeons. According to Bardet, however, in Rouen, the capital of Normandy, there were twenty midwives and thirty surgeons in 1720, and eighteen midwives and thirty-seven surgeons in 1790. Most deliveries took place at home, and less than 10 per cent in the city's Hôtel Dieu. From the records of 38,228 deliveries in Rouen in the eighteenth century Bardet estimated an MMR of about 109 per 10,000 deliveries, compared with 90 in Sweden between 1776 and 1800.[6]

By the early years of the nineteenth century training had become more comprehensive and organized. French midwives dominated the lying-in hospitals. In 1770, they expelled medical students from the Hôtel Dieu in Paris, for their 'levity and indecent behaviour',[7] and according to Siebold, the doors of the larger Maternités in Paris remained closed to medical students in the early years of the nineteenth century who had to obtain instruction in private clinics and from midwives.[8] During the early nineteenth century there were two notable Parisian midwives, Mme La Chapelle (1769–1821) and Mme Bovin (1773–1841). Mme La Chapelle published a treatise on midwifery, was conversant with current obstetrical literature, and made original observations on the nature of various malpresentations and how they should be managed. Her book was based on statistical deductions from 40,000 cases.[9]

Midwives of the nineteenth century were clearly demarcated in two groups. The first and better trained, the *première classe* who dominated the lying-in hospitals in Paris and the provinces, were trained by residence in the Maternité for one to two years. They were able to charge 130 fr. for a delivery (the equivalent at the time of about 6 guineas in England, and therefore a

[5] Ibid.

[6] J.-P. Bardet, *et al.*, 'La Mortalité maternelle autrefois: Une étude comparée (de la France de l'ouest à l'Utah)', *Annales de démographie historique* (1981), 89–104.

[7] A. Tolver, *The Present State of Midwifery in France* (London, 1770).

[8] E. G. J. de Siebold, *Essai d'une histoire de l'obstétrice*, trans. from German by F. J. Herrgot (Paris, 1891).

[9] L. Devraigne, *L'Obstétrique à travers les âges* (Paris, 1939); F. H. Garrison, *An Introduction to the History of Medicine* (4th edn., Philadelphia, Pa., 1929).

considerable fee). The *deuxième classe* attended a theoretical course for six months spending a day and a night each week at the Clinique des accouchements. They could only charge 25 fr. for a delivery, were not allowed to practise outside the area in which they were licensed and were closely supervised. The *deuxième classe* was intended primarily for small towns and rural areas, where it was said that such was the general ignorance of midwives their only skill was the ability to swaddle a baby ('emmailloter un enfant').[10] In England the two classes of French midwife were well known to Miss Rosalind Paget, one of the founders of the Midwives Institute. In her evidence to the Select Committee on Midwives Registration in 1892 she remarked that 'Ours is the only European country which does not legislate for its midwives . . .'. In France, the *sage femme première classe* is 'a very superior article to anything we have in England . . . but the *sage femme seconde classe* is more like our ordinary midwife'. She added that in France, 'most women are delivered by women; the doctors have very little practice unless it is upon an emergency . . . the men have not got the possession of midwifery practice in France as they have in England'.[11]

Miss Paget may have understated the part played by French doctors. During the late nineteenth century midwives came under increasing competition from medical practitioners for home deliveries and there was little love lost between them.[12] By a statute of 1892 midwives were restricted to births free from all complications, at the same time as similar restrictions on other European countries to which we shall come. But there was another side to midwives which we touched on in Chapter 7; namely, that French midwives sometimes earned more by performing abortions than delivering babies.[13] The underlying reason may have been that during the mid- to late nineteenth century, hospital births were rapidly increasing. In Paris in the 1890s there were approximately 60,000 births a year and at least half took place in publicly assisted institutions. This meant that 30,000 home births had to be shared amongst 1,000 midwives and close to 4,000 doctors. With a shortage of maternity cases, midwives turned to abortion in order to survive. According to McLaren they sometimes did so on such an astonishing scale that however tolerant the public's attitudes to abortion (and attitudes were surprisingly tolerant) the reputation of French midwives as a whole must have suffered.[14] Whether this tendency of midwives to act as abortionists was an important feature throughout the nineteenth century, and whether it played a significant part in the low French fertility rate is a question of interest. At all events, in

---

[10] G.-J. Witkowski, *Histoire des accouchements chez tous les peuples* (Paris, 1887).

[11] *Report of the Select Committee on Midwives' Registration*, PP 1892, xiv, Q. 115–28.

[12] Witkowski, *Histoire des accouchements*.

[13] A. McLaren, 'Abortion in France: Women and the Regulation of Family Size', *French Historical Studies*, 10 (1978), 461–85.

[14] Ibid. 472–3.

terms of status and power, the heyday of the French midwife was probably the end of the eighteenth and the beginning of the nineteenth centuries, but she has continued to play a large part in French maternal care in this century. The present position of the midwife in France is similar to that in Britain. The proportion of deliveries in France in recent years was 41 per cent by obstetricians, 39 per cent by midwives, and 20 per cent by doctors other than obstetricians.[15]

THE SWEDISH MIDWIVES

Outside observers in Britain and the United States during the inter-war period saw the Swedish midwife as the most highly trained and efficient in the world. In 1926, the American obstetrician, George Kosmak (the obstetrician who edited the *American Journal of Obstetrics and Gynaecology*) visited Sweden and wrote in lyrical terms of the 'Bright, healthy looking, intelligent young women from whom our best class of trained nurses would be recruited in this country'. He noted with approval they were trained 'to perform certain obstetric operations including manual removal of placenta, external, internal and combined version, extraction in breech presentation, and even the use of low forceps'. Not surprisingly, his suggestion that there were lessons from Sweden for the United States received little support from his anti-midwife colleagues in the USA.[16] The training in obstetric operations, frequently mentioned by observers from other countries, was largely a reflection of the fact that Sweden was a large country with a small population and many remote and inaccessible rural areas where medical care was unavailable. In fact instrumental delivery was of minor significance compared with the Swedish tradition of thorough training and close regulation.

The regulation of midwives by doctors and lay authorities was established in 1663 by the Swedish Collegium Medicum. It created a formal relationship between doctors and midwives which to a large extent reduced conflicts between the two of the kind that occurred in Britain and the United States. Midwives knew they were held in high regard, but they also knew their place.[17] Formal training began, albeit on a limited scale, in 1711 and included instruction on the use of instruments.[18] In 1777 a new regulation allowed

[15] B. Blondell, *et al.*, 'Some characteristics of Antenatal Care in 13 European Countries', in J. M. L. Phaff (ed.), *Perinatal Health Services in Europe* (London, 1986), 5

[16] G. W. Kosmak, 'Results of Supervised Midwife Practice in Certain European Countries. Can we Draw a Lesson from this for the United States?', *Journal of the American Medical Association*, 89 (1927), 2009–12.

[17] Brändström, *De kärlekslösa mödrana* (1984), quoted in Christina Romlid, 'The Swedish Maternal Mortality Rate in the 19th Century' (*c.*1989). I am most grateful for permission to cite this valuable unpublished paper.

[18] Ulf Högberg, *Maternal Mortality in Sweden*, Uneå University Medical Dissertations, NS 156, (Umeå, 1985), 54.

midwives to use instruments only when distance prevented them from sending for a doctor in time. Another regulation in 1819 stated that parishes were only allowed to employ trained midwives, and another regulation in 1829 laid down the conditions for the use of instruments by midwives. Only those who had completed a three-month course were allowed to use instruments, and even then only when it was impossible to summon a doctor, and only in the presence of a witness. If a midwife undertook an instrumental delivery she was required to write a report which had to be signed by the local medical officer of health.[19]

In the second half of the nineteenth century there never was any question of midwives using forceps with the excessive frequency of a late nineteenth-century British general practitioner. Högberg found that the average annual number of deliveries undertaken by rural midwives in the second half of the nineteenth century was thirty-seven. Forceps were used by rural midwives in 1 in every 133 to 180 deliveries with an annual case fatality rate of 27–39 deaths per 1,000 operations. This means that a rural midwife would on average use forceps only once every three to five years, or about ten times in thirty years of practice.[20] In 1894 there were approximately 105,000 deliveries by midwives in the whole of Sweden with only 612 forceps deliveries. Their rate of instrumental delivery of 0.58 per cent must be compared with a rate of 3 per cent and 5 per cent for the most conservative of British general practitioners. During the twentieth century that rate declined sharply because of better communications with doctors by telephone, the building of hospitals in country districts, and an increasing proportion of the population moving to towns. In 1927, only thirty-six forceps deliveries were performed by midwives.[21]

Thus the feature most quoted about Swedish midwives, the use of instruments in complicated labours, was uncommon in the nineteenth century, and rare in the twentieth. Figure 24.1 shows that the number of Swedish midwives examined each year increased through the second half of the nineteenth century from about 60 to about 120 and the number authorized to use instruments rose even more steeply. From about 1908, however, this trend was reversed. Fewer midwives were being examined each year, but nearly all were authorized to use instruments.

A side of Swedish midwifery which has only recently begun to attract

[19] Romlid, 'The Swedish Maternal Mortality Rate'.

[20] U. Högberg and G. Brostrom, 'The Impact of Early Medical Technology on Maternal Mortality Rate in Late 19th Century Sweden', *International Journal of Obstetrics and Gynaecology*, 24 (1986), 251–61.

[21] Ministry of Health, *Final Report of Departmental Committee on Maternal Mortality and Morbidity* (London, 1932), 49–89 ('The Maternity Services of the Netherlands, Denmark and Sweden'). The authors of this chapter who visited the Netherlands, Denmark, and Sweden were Dr Oxley of the East London Maternity Hospital, Prof. Miles Phillips, and Dr James Young of Edinburgh.

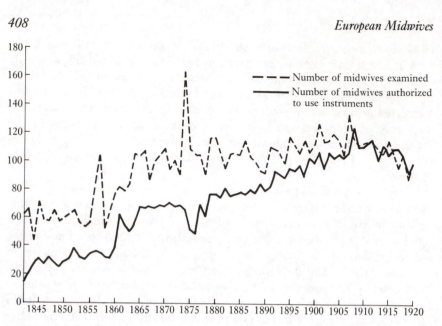

FIG. 24.1 Sweden, 1842–1920. Annual number of midwives examined and authorized to undertake instrumental deliveries
Source: Unpublished data, Christina Romlid, Uppsala University, by kind permission.

attention is the contribution of the traditional midwife or *jordgumma*. Although the laws regulating midwives were generally enforced, until the mid-nineteenth century more deliveries were undertaken by traditional midwives than by trained midwives and doctors put together.[22] There is recent evidence that as late as 1908 certain parishes in Sweden were flouting the law and refusing to abandon and replace her with a trained one.[23] The rejection in rural Swedish communities of the trained midwife has echoes of a similar refusal by many non-white mothers in the southern states of the USA. It will be interesting to see if other examples of a preference for the traditional midwife when trained midwife care was available can be found in the history of European midwifery, and whether this still occurs to a significant extent in developing countries today.

This leads us to an important question concerning nineteenth-century European midwifery. Great importance was attached in all countries to the regulation and training of midwives. The purpose was to ensure that midwives were strong, healthy, and respectable women who, because of selection and training, were safer birth-attendants than the untrained traditional midwives. In the end, the main purpose of regulation and training was to save lives.

[22] Högberg, *Maternal Mortality in Sweden* (fig. 3).
[23] Personal communication, Christina Romlid, Mar. 1991.

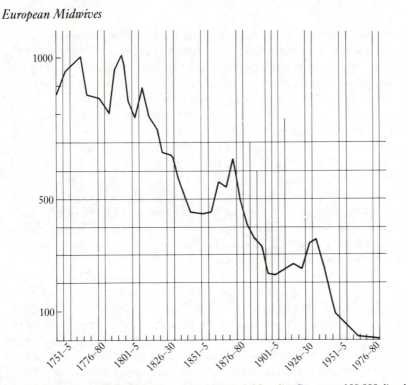

FIG. 24.2 Sweden, 1751–1980. Trend in Maternal Mortality Rate per 100,000 live births. Annual mean, five-year periods
Source: Ulf Högberg, *Maternal Mortality in Sweden*, Umeå University Medical Dissertations, NS 156 (Umeå, 1985). Reproduced by kind permission.

That this aim was achieved might be regarded as self-evident but proof is notoriously difficult. It is rare to find simultaneous records of deliveries by trained and untrained midwives from which a statistical comparison can be made. There is some evidence from Sweden and Norway that trained midwives reduced maternal mortality, even though it is indirect and rather complex.

We must begin by examining the trend in maternal mortality in Sweden from 1750 to 1900, shown in Figure 24.2. Maternal mortality fell from about 100 maternal deaths per 10,000 births in 1750, to between 45 and 50 by 1850 and 23 by 1900.[24] How much of the decline was due to better care and the training of midwives? For the period from 1750 to 1850, when maternal mortality fell to half of its original value, there is too little evidence to answer this question. In Chapter 10 it was noted from the limited data available that

---

[24] Högberg, *Maternal Mortality in Sweden*, 30. See also Appendix Tables.

there was probably a fall of the same order in England from the second half of the seventeenth to the second half of the eighteenth century. I suggested, very tentatively, that the fall might have been due to improving standards of care by midwives (albeit untrained and unregulated midwives), and I did so from being unable to think of a convincing alternative.

In Sweden, however, where there is the advantage of reliable national data from the eighteenth century, the fall in maternal mortality from 1750 to 1850 might have been due to an increased number of trained midwives. But it is a bit too early for that explanation to be convincing. If I interpret his views correctly, Högberg believes that during the century from 1750 to 1850 improving social and economic factors were almost wholly responsible for the decline in maternal mortality. He came to this conclusion by finding a similar rate of decline in female mortality from all causes, which led him to suggest that maternal mortality fell not because of improved maternal care, but because mothers became more healthy.[25]

From 1850, however, two other factors became dominant. First there was a rapid increase in the proportion of deliveries by trained midwives; secondly, the introduction of antisepsis after 1880.[26] The evidence that training of midwives had an impact on maternal mortality comes from examination of the trend during the second half of the nineteenth century. Looking at the broad features of Figure 24.2, there were two major interruptions in the general decline from the late eighteenth century to the late twentieth. The smaller of the two interruptions occurred between 1900 and 1935. There was a larger upturn in maternal mortality 1850 and 1875. Why did it occur, and how can this be reconciled with the undoubted increase in trained midwives during this period?

As Figure 24.1 shows, there was a steady increase in the output of trained midwives. In Sweden as a whole from 1861 to 1894, home deliveries by trained midwives increased from 37 per cent to 78 per cent (1861 was the date after which birthbooks had a separate column in which the clergy were required to enter whether a woman was attended by a trained or untrained midwife). There were very few institutional deliveries in this period to confuse the picture: they increased from only 3 per cent to 5 per cent of all deliveries between 1860 and 1900.[27]

Högberg carried out a study of rural maternal mortality from 1861 to the end of the century. If an increase in deliveries by trained midwives reduced

[25] Ibid. 49.

[26] Ibid. 30. See also id., 'The Decline in Maternal Mortality in Sweden 1750–1980: A Comparative Study', paper presented at the International Conference on Medical Education in the field of Primary Maternal Child Health Care, Egypt, December 1983. Antiseptic technique was introduced at the Public Maternity Hospital in Stockholm in 1878. Personal communication, Christina Romlid, 1991.

[27] Högberg, *Maternal Mortality in Sweden*, 51, and Romlid, 'The Swedish Maternal Mortality Rate'.

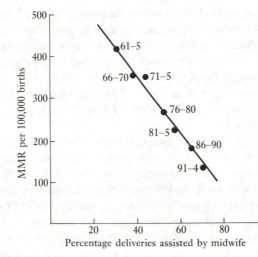

FIG. 24.3 Sweden rural areas, quinquennial periods, 1861–1894. Trend in Maternal Mortality Rates due to causes other than sepsis, and percentage of deliveries by trained midwives
Source: Ulf Högberg, *Maternal Mortality in Sweden*, Umeå University Medical Dissertations, NS 156 (Umeå, 1985). Reproduced by kind permission.

maternal mortality it should have been obvious during this period. Figure 24.3 suggests that it was, for it shows a close correlation between the rapid increase in deliveries by trained midwives and the falling rate of maternal mortality.[28] A causal connection may seem obvious, but two points should be noted. First, this graph is based on a few rural parishes. Secondly, deaths from sepsis were excluded. This last feature is most important. It explains the apparent contradiction between the downward trend shown in Figure 24.3 and the upward trend for maternal deaths from all causes in Sweden between 1860 and 1874 which is shown in Figure 24.2. Figure 24.4, which is based on data from rural areas of Sweden, provides the means for resolving this contradiction.[29]

The top line in Figure 24.4 is the trend in maternal mortality from all causes. Below are the trends in deaths from puerperal sepsis and from all other (non-septic) causes which are shown separately for 1861–5 and to the beginning of the twentieth century. From 1861 Romlid has found that deaths from causes other than puerperal sepsis were declining. The line showing this is closely similar to the findings of Högberg in Figure 24.3. Deaths from puerperal sepsis, on the other hand, were increasing rapidly from 1861 to 1874/5. In fact they nearly trebled during this period. From about 1875 to the end of the century, however, deaths from sepsis and from other causes were falling in unison.

[28] Högberg, *Maternal Mortality in Sweden*, 51 (fig. 3).
[29] Romlid, 'The Swedish Maternal Mortality Rate'.

The crucial observation is that a rise in maternal mortality between 1850 and the peak of 1874 occurred elsewhere, notably in Britain (see Chapter 14) and also in Norway which we will come to soon. It was almost certainly due to an unprecedented increase in the virulence of the streptococcus. Recent evidence from the work of Romlid has shown that a high peak of cases and deaths due to puerperal fever deaths in 1874 was widespread throughout Sweden. It was most conspicuous in the city of Stockholm but was found in a majority of counties as well.[30]

The 1874 peak in deaths due to puerperal sepsis was in effect a widespread epidemic streptococcal outbreak of exceptional virulence, seen in many countries. As such it was a factor beyond the control of the birth-attendant. Before antisepsis in 1880, there was nothing trained midwives could do that would stem the rising rate of deaths due to puerperal sepsis. On the other hand, trained midwives might have been able to deal more effectively with non-septic complications (especially haemorrhage). It is therefore suggestive that Figure 24.4 shows quite a steep decline in maternal deaths due to non-septic causes at the very time when the number of trained midwives was increasing. A direct relationship is far from certain, but it is suggestive. This notion is reinforced by findings from Norway.[31]

In Norway there was a marked increase in the number of trained midwives in parallel with Sweden. The number in practice increased annually from about 480 in 1860 to about 1,200 in 1900. The graph of maternal mortality in Norway from 1860 to 1900 is also shown in Figure 24.4 and there is a remarkable resemblance to the graph in Sweden. In both there is the rise in total mortality from all causes from 1860 to a peak in 1874, and then a decline. In Norway, too, the 1860–74 rise was due to deaths from puerperal fever. Deaths due to non-septic causes were decreasing, possibly because of the increasing number of trained midwives. Maternal mortality *as a whole* rose between 1861 and 1874 in Sweden and Norway because the rise in deaths from sepsis was steeper than the fall in deaths from non-septic causes. From 1875 to the end of the century, the decline in maternal mortality (which incidentally was much more conspicuous in Sweden than in Britain) was probably due to three factors:

- The improvement in the standard of maternal care associated with the increase in trained midwives: a factor which was absent in Britain but probably important in Sweden and Norway.

[30] For instance, Uppsala county, Södermanlands county, Malmöhus county, and Västerbottens county. But it was absent in certain other counties. The significance of this is as yet uncertain. Christina Romlid, personal communication, 1991.

[31] The data on Norway were most kindly sent to me by Dr Kristina Kjærheim who has undertaken research on maternal mortality and midwives in 19th-cent. Norway. I am most grateful to her.

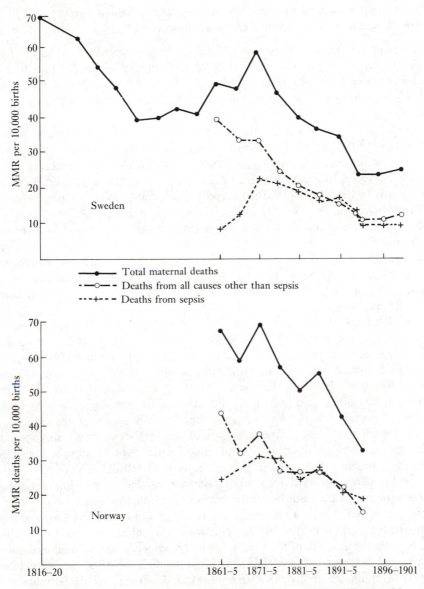

FIG. 24.4 Sweden and Norway. Quinquennial periods, 1861–5 to 1900–5. Trend in Maternal Mortality shown as maternal deaths from all causes (in the case of Sweden from 1816–21 to 1901–5), maternal deaths due to puerperal fever, and maternal deaths due to causes other than puerperal fever
Source: Sweden: Christina Romlid, 'Maternal Mortality in Sweden', unpub. paper; data reproduced with kind permission; Norway: graph constructed from data kindly supplied by Kristina Kjærheim of Oslo.

- The introduction of antisepsis and asepsis from about 1880.[32]
- A decline in the virulence of the streptococcus.

Generally speaking it is extremely difficult to find statistical evidence that trained midwives lowered the MMR of any country or any region in the nineteenth century. The evidence from Sweden and Norway is only tentative; but it is as far as I am aware the only available at this time. Further research is needed on this most interesting question.

When we come to the twentieth century, there can be little doubt of the beneficial influence of the trained midwife in Sweden. Some of the most important evidence comes from British and American obstetricians who visited Sweden in the 1920s and 1930s and were deeply impressed by what they saw. In 1926 George Kosmak reported favourably on the training schools for midwives in Stockholm and Gothenburg, noting that 84.3 per cent of deliveries were attended by midwives in Sweden and 85 per cent in Norway. He also noted the low rate of forceps deliveries and Caesarean section. In Sweden the operative incidence in hospitals was 4 per cent while in American hospitals it varied from 10 per cent to 30 per cent; and the maternal mortality rate in home, hospital, and total deliveries was much lower in Sweden than the United States.[33]

A delegation from England was also impressed, but they placed more emphasis on social and environmental factors, noting that Sweden was unlike Britain in many ways. It was a thousand miles in length and half as large again as Great Britain and Ireland, with a population of a little over 6 million in 1930 which was less than the population of greater London. There was little poverty, few slums, and little heavy industry and atmospheric pollution. They spoke favourably of the healthy appearance and life-style of the Swedish. 'Temperamentally the women are placid and self-controlled, and appear mentally as well as physically fit for child-bearing.' In childbirth, they felt Sweden 'has an easier problem to face than has the British Isles'.[34]

In Sweden, doctors did not undertake normal deliveries. They were the sole province of the midwife whose course of instruction lasted for two years and far exceeded in breadth, detail, and time spent in theoretical and practical instruction, anything available to midwives or medical students in Britain. Under the supervision of the head midwife or trained sister, student midwives delivered between 100 and 125 cases during their training and were then given a month on trial before final approval. Until the age of 50 midwives were required to undertake regular review courses. The delegation watched and described a delivery at the Gothenburg Maternity Hospital by a midwife and found the standard of care and aseptic technique was meticulous.

---

[32] Högberg and Brostrom, 'The Impact of Early Medical Technology'.
[33] Kosmak, 'Result of Supervised Midwife Practice in Certain European Countries'.
[34] Ministry of Health, *Final Report of Departmental Committee on Maternal Mortality and Morbidity*.

In 1936, in the course of a lecture delivered in the United States, James Young remarked, 'By contrast with the course followed in Great Britain, in the Netherlands and in Scandinavia the midwife succeeded from the beginning in maintaining her primary position in the obstetric hegemony.' He believed 'There are several strong advantages inherent in a maternity service which is based on the well-trained midwife.' It formed the 'stable foundation' of a maternity service, it got rid of the handywoman, it was an economical method for dealing with the more than 90 per cent of normal deliveries, and it allowed the normal deliveries to be undertaken by a person who was expert in that part of midwifery, taking it out of the hands of doctors whose training 'has tended to a preoccupation with the abnormal and the morbid'.[35]

If British and American systems of maternal care had been created *de novo* in the 1930s, the Swedish or Dutch model would have had much to commend it. But in every country systems of maternal care are the product of an evolutionary process. The extent and direction of reforms in health services are always to a large extent constrained by historical developments and vested interests. The strength of the Swedish system stemmed from the length of its tradition and the fact it seems to have suited the Swedish population. For the midwife it had been from the beginning of the eighteenth century a highly authoritarian system firmly under the control of the state and medical profession. The strict regulation, however, came at the beginning of her career. Once she was trained and had satisfied the examiners, the Swedish midwife was allowed a wide measure of independence. She was able to undertake a large proportion of deliveries on her own and resort to instrumental delivery when a doctor was not available, because she was respected and sanctioned by statute. It seems to have been a system which worked remarkably well.

THE DUTCH MIDWIVES

The Netherlands is well known today as the only European country to have persisted with a large proportion of home deliveries attended and supervised entirely by midwives who possess a large degree of autonomy. Critics who believe that the only safe policy in the late twentieth century is hospital delivery for all parturient women under the supervision of obstetricians, find themselves disarmed by the fact that the Netherlands has one of the lowest rates of maternal and perinatal mortality of any country in the world. It is a distinction it has held throughout this century.

For this reason the visiting obstetricians from the USA and Britain whose reports we have just discussed in the previous section on Sweden were especially interested in examining the maternity services of the Netherlands. Their evidence comes later. First we consider some recent historical research

[35] J. Young, 'Maternal Mortality and Maternal Mortality Rates', *American Journal of Obstetrics and Gynaecology*, 31 (1936), 208–9.

which has emphasized the complexity of the history of Dutch midwifery. 'The story of the Dutch midwives', say van Lieburg and Marland, 'is one of pluses and minuses'; and they point to features which make comparisons with other countries difficult:

Holland differed enormously from other countries, not only in its institution of regulation, formal educational arrangements and licensing, but also in its arrangements for childbirth (the sketchiness of the institutional facilities for lying-in women . . .), and in the way legislation was achieved (that is, it was initiated chiefly by the government, not the midwives, medical profession or other concerned pressure groups).[36]

A kind of training for midwives seems to have been available in the seventeenth century in the form of municipal courses on anatomy and obstetrics, given by medical practitioners in the larger Dutch towns. There is a particularly interesting account of a Dutch midwife in the late seventeenth and early eighteenth centuries which suggests a high standard of practice for such an early period.[37] The midwife, Catharina Schrader (1656–1746), was born in Germany, the daughter of a court tailor. She married a barber-surgeon in 1683. Two years after her husband died in 1691, Schrader began to practise as a midwife (with some surgical practice as well), confirming Deventer's contention that midwives were often necessitous widows. She delivered, on average, over a hundred cases a year until 1713. Then she married Thomas Higt, who played a leading role in local government in Dokkum, a town to which she had moved in 1695 so that her children by her first marriage would be able to attend the local grammar school. Until the death of her second husband in 1721, she delivered very few cases, but when she entered her second period of widowhood she once more became active as a midwife and remained so for a period of over twenty years until, as she approached her eightieth year, she deliberately restricted her practice to some twenty cases a year.

Her extensive memoirs show her as a capable and highly literate midwife, but was she typical? Van Lieburg believes she was unusual in her education (which she may have obtained in part from her first husband) and also in her

---

[36] M. J. van Lieburg and H. Marland, 'Midwife Regulation, Education, and Practice in the Netherlands during the Nineteenth Century', *Medical History*, 33 (1989), 296–317. I am indebted to Mart van Lieburg and Hilary Marland in many ways and this section owes much to their work. See also Floor van Gelder, 'The Case of the Midwives: A Forgotten Profession. Social Consciousness of Working Women in the Dutch Public Health c. 1900', paper given at the third Anglo-Dutch Labour History Conference, Maastricht, 1982. For contemporary British opinions of midwifery in the Netherlands, see especially Ministry of Health, *Final Report of Departmental Committee on Maternal Mortality and Morbidity*, 49–89. See also 'Childbirth in Holland' (leading article), *Lancet* (1934), ii. 713–14, and 'The Maternity Services in Holland' (leading article), ibid. (1936), i. 736–7.

[37] H. Marland, *Mother and Child were Saved: The Memoirs (1693–1740) of the Frisian Midwife, Catharina Schrader* with introductory essays by M. J. van Lieburg and G. J. Kloosterman (Amsterdam, 1987).

social position.[38] Certainly it was common for men-midwives to complain of the ignorance and low class of women who were midwives, although in Holland, as elsewhere, male practitioners were apt to puff themselves up by denigrating the midwife. But Schrader herself was critical of her colleagues labelling some of them as 'incompetent' or 'dreadful know-nothings' or 'messy-bunglers'. She had a sharp tongue and was a woman of wit, given to inventing nicknames for her patients and their husbands such as 'bungler', 'lopsided neck', 'dirty', 'ram's nose', 'clod-farmer', 'skirt-chaser'.

Her records are interesting in the way they confirm the seventeenth-century custom of having other women present at a birth. This was especially true with respect to Dokkum, where the so-called 'duty to one's neighbours' was officially enforced, suggesting perhaps that it was the duty of friends and neighbours not just to provide comfort for the patient, but also to monitor the activities of the midwife, in much the same way that the Swedish midwife who applied forceps was required to have a witness present. In her long lifetime it seems likely that Catharina Schrader delivered over 3,000 cases and perhaps as many as 4,000. There are records of twenty deaths in these memoirs, giving a maternal mortality rate of 50 to 70 per 10,000 births. This is rather lower than the figure for the same period in England (see Chapter 10). Because of her skill, however, Schrader was often called in by other midwives to difficult cases. If the cases in which she acted as the equivalent of a consultant were excluded, the maternal mortality rate of her own cases may have been considerably lower. If so, it is evidence that even in the seventeenth century midwives such as Catharina Schrader were capable of providing maternal care that was safe and effective by the prevailing standards of the time and as safe as the general standard of maternal care available in the nineteenth century.

Regulation of midwives, however, did not begin until the nineteenth century when new laws were enacted in 1818 which affected doctors and midwives. Midwives were examined after spending a year studying the theory of midwifery followed by apprenticeship to a midwife. But there was another pathway from 1823 when schools for training midwives in hospitals were set up in Amsterdam, Rotterdam, and in four other towns. Admission to these schools was confined to women between the ages of 20 and 30 who were healthy, literate, and of irreproachable character, but their output was very slight; only about eight midwives graduated annually from these schools between 1824 and 1867. The majority followed the old-style apprenticeship system. Both pathways led to examination and certification by provincial medical committees.[39] Although there are echoes here of the French system, there is no evidence in the Netherlands of an officially recognized division between a

---

[38] Ibid. 18–19.
[39] van Lieburg and Marland, 'Midwife Regulation', 300 (Table 1).

first-class midwife trained in the clinical schools and a second-class midwife trained by apprenticeship. Whichever pathway was followed it was possible for a midwife to become a very important figure in her community. There is an example of just such a midwife whose casebook has survived.

Vrouw Waltman, who practised as a midwife in Dodrecht, just south of Rotterdam, was born in 1802, the daughter of a millwright. She married a painter in 1823 who died nine years later. Some years later she joined the ranks of the 'necessitous widows' who became midwives, taking her midwifery examination before the local provincial medical committee in 1841. Within a few years she was delivering over 200 women a year. What is interesting is that Dodrecht had one doctor of obstetrics, twelve men-midwives, and ten midwives. There was no lack of competition. But when she was at her most active, Vrouw Waltman succeeded in capturing about a quarter of all the maternity cases in the town, and in 1860 she was appointed the town midwife. As was so often the case, the most successful midwives were much in demand, and data on the average number of midwife deliveries often hide a wide variation around the mean. In this example, while other midwives had ten or fewer cases a year, Vrouw Waltman undertook some 5,000 deliveries in thirty years and only had to call in a man-midwife or another midwife for 1 per cent of these deliveries.

Vrouw Waltman and her predecessor Catharina Schrader provide an impressive if unrepresentative picture of the Dutch midwife. Nevertheless, it could be argued that even if they were exceptional, they owed their success to a strong underlying tradition in the Netherlands. The activity of the midwife became more restricted with the Medical Act of 1865. In effect, this act produced an overstocked medical profession and a sudden increase in the number of doctors practising obstetrics in the Netherlands. The act restated what had always been the case—that the midwife was only allowed to attend normal cases. In several countries—France, Sweden, Denmark, for example, as well as the Netherlands—as the practice of obstetrics by doctors increased, so they tended to insist that they alone were fit to deal with abnormalities of pregnancy and labour. In the restrictions imposed on midwives, competition with doctors for cases was certainly an important motive. There was no reason why the highly trained Dutch midwife should not have been taught to deal with minor abnormalities including low forceps delivery. With this reassertion of restrictions, in the second half of the nineteenth century, midwives, unlike doctors, did not increase in proportion to the increase in the population, and they continued to be drawn predominantly from the lower middle classes. Most were the daughters of farmers, shopkeepers, carpenters, tailors, clerks, or minor civil servants. Many were the daughters of midwives. Very few came from the middle or professional classes.[40]

On the other hand, there were moves to improve midwife training. In 1865

[40] Ibid. 309.

examination by provincial medical committees was replaced by state licensing. New schools were opened at Rotterdam and Amsterdam, and although the failure rate in these schools was high, they trained far more midwives than the earlier schools. Certainly there was hostility towards midwives from some medical practioners, but equally there was support from others. A survey of the opinions of doctors concerning the practice of midwives was carried out in 1911. On the whole, the midwives scored well. Questioned on what they thought of the midwifery skills of midwives, 197 doctors said 'good', 199 'satisfactory', 17 'moderate', and 23 'bad'. These were much more favourable answers than would have been obtained in Britain or the United States.[41]

One of the consequences of state licensing was tight control on the number of midwives. In 1895 there were 830 midwives, in 1910 there were 924, and twenty years later in 1930 the number was still only just over 900, and it was not for lack of applicants to the training schools. Table 24.1 shows that the number of midwives per million population was much lower in the Netherlands than in Scandinavian countries. This was probably because Norway and Sweden possessed many remote areas where a local midwife would have few cases, a situation that altered as communications improved allowing greater access to medical care. In Norway, for instance, Table 24.2 shows that the number of midwives and medical practitioners per million population increased from 1860 to 1930, but the rate of increase was greater for medical practitioners than midwives. Since 1930, medical practitioners have continued to increase, but the number of midwives has fallen. When Sweden and the Netherlands are compared, it is worth noting that the population per square mile in Sweden in 1930 was 35 compared with 627 in the Netherlands. The Dutch midwives were able to make up for their small numbers by delivering over 100 cases a year on average, a large case-load and much higher than in other countries.[42] We will see why in a moment.

When the British obstetricians visited the Netherlands in 1930 and found 'the maternity service in the Netherlands is exceptionally efficient', there were three training schools for midwives, one each in Amsterdam, Rotterdam, and Haarlem. There was stiff competition. Only a quarter of applicants were successful, allowing selection of candidates with high standards. The training schools were for midwives only. This avoided the competition between pupil midwives and medical students for an insufficient number of cases which was the bugbear of British teaching hospitals. Training took three years and was extremely thorough. Pupils saw on average 1,800 deliveries and spent their third year on home deliveries under the supervision of a midwife. The standard of antenatal care and antisepsis was very high.[43]

---

[41] Ibid. 313.
[42] Ibid. 315.
[43] Ministry of Health, *Final Report of Departmental Committee on Maternal Mortality and Morbidity*, 49–89, on which this account is largely based, together with leading articles, 'Childbirth in Holland', 'The Maternity Services in Holland'.

TABLE 24.1 *Population, Total Number of Midwives, and Midwives per Million Population in the Netherlands, Denmark, Norway, and Sweden, 1929–1930*

Country	Population	Number of midwives	Midwives per million population
The Netherlands (1929)	7,832,000	919	117
Denmark (1929)	3,518,000	1,063	302
Sweden (1930)	6,130,826	2,754	449
Norway (1930)	2,812,710	1,590	565

Source: Ministry of Health, *Final Report of Departmental Committee on Maternal Mortality and Morbidity* (London, 1932), 49–89; *Norges Officielle Statistik: Historik Statistikk*, Statistisk Sentralbyrå (Oslo, 1968), 54.

TABLE 24.2 *The Number of Midwives and Doctors, and the Proportion of each to Total Population, Norway, 1860–1960*[a]

Year	Number of physicians	Number of midwives	Physicians per million population	Midwives per million population
1860	334	484	196	284
1870	415	551	241	320
1880	565	720	297	379
1890	696	887	348	444
1900	890	1,144	397	510
1910	1,266	1,364	527	568
1920	1,346	1,466	508	553
1930	1,826	1,590	652	567
1940	2,472	1,496	797	482
1950	3,397	1,397	1,029	423
1960	4,260	1,104	1,183	306

[a] The population of Norway rose from approximately 1.7 million in 1860 to 3.6 million in 1960.

Source: *Norges Officielle Statistik: Historik Statistikk*, Statistisk Sentralbyrå (Oslo, 1968), 54.

Once the patient was delivered, however, the role of the midwife was only supervisory. All nursing of the lying-in mother and the newborn was delegated to a nursing assistant, either a *Baker* or a *Kraamverzorgster*. The *Baker* (translated as 'maternity nurse') received training for six months in a midwifery school and eighteen months 'on the district'. The *Kraamverzorgster* (literal translation: 'someone who takes care of women') was a registered nurse who took the same training as the *Baker*. Neither was allowed to undertake deliveries. The *Kraamverzorgster* was generally employed by the well-to-do while the *Baker* worked mostly amongst the poor. In the Netherlands the state ensured that the poor were adequately cared for. Every commune had by statute to provide the services of a trained midwife. Thus the Dutch midwife was freed from the British system of daily postnatal visits and time spent in simple basic nursing duties, allowing her to carry a heavier caseload of deliveries without becoming exhausted. It was a system which allowed the midwife in the Netherlands to be seen as a 'state servant with a high status', midway perhaps between the nurse and the doctor.[44]

Although, or perhaps because the midwife in the Netherlands has been regulated since the late seventeenth century, she practised like the Swedish midwife with a great deal of independence until the mid-nineteenth century. Her independence was threatened following the 1865 medical act when she faced increasing competition from doctors, but it cannot be said that she lost her central position in the Dutch maternity services. Strong competition for entry to training schools, where training was far advanced beyond anything available in Britain or the United States, ensured that she retained her high reputation in this century. Today 'the midwife [in the Netherlands] is entitled by law to supervise a normal pregnancy and spontaneous birth on her own responsibility, without any assistance from a doctor. The midwife is not a nurse-midwife; she completes a three-year course that fully entitles her to independent practice.'[45] Such independence would have been unlikely without the unusually strong Dutch tradition going back to women like Catharina Schrader in the eighteenth century and Vrouw Waltman in the nineteenth.

THE DANISH MIDWIVES

When Dorothy Mendenhall from the Children's Bureau in Washington visited Denmark in 1926 to investigate the maternity services, she confirmed her impression of a visit thirty years earlier. It was country which was 'spotless and orderly'.[46] The maternity services reflected the same qualities. They too were spotless, orderly, neat, and efficient. 'System and simplicity', she wrote,

---

[44] Ministry of Health, *Final Report of Departmental Committee on Maternal Mortality and Morbidity*, 55; 'The Maternity Services in Holland'.

[45] J. M. L. Phaff, 'The Organisation and Administration of Perinatal Services in the Netherlands', in Phaff, *Perinatal Health Services in Europe* (London, 1986).

[46] This description of midwives in Denmark is based largely on two very thorough accounts by visiting obstetricians: Dorothy Reed Mendenhall, *Midwifery in Denmark*, US Dept. of Labor, Children's Bureau (Washington, DC, 1929), and Ministry of Health, *Final Report of Departmental Committee on Maternal Mortality and Morbidity*. Some slight additional material can be found in G.-J. Witkowski, *Histoire des accouchements chez tous les peuples* (Paris, 1887); E. G. J. de Siebold, *Essai d'une histoire de l'obstétrice*; Kosmak, 'Result of Supervised Midwife Practice in Certain European Countries'.

'seemed to be the keynote of governmental activities, including the health program of the Government.' It was not in the least like England or the United States. It was characteristic of Denmark that quackery was unknown. Regulations against irregular practice, strictly enforced, were introduced in 1672.

Mendenhall was deeply impressed by the status of the Danish midwife. 'The difficult thing for us [Americans] to realize', she said, 'is the position of trust and respect in which the midwife is held in Denmark . . . and especially the cordial relations existing between the physicians and midwives. Conducting a normal labour is not considered part of a physician's duty; it is really a little "infra dig."'. Danish general practitioners did not undertake normal home confinements. They attended only when called by a midwife: 'The doctor would never hesitate to consult with the midwife or help her out in emergencies beyond her training, for in many instances he has referred her to the family and expects in future cases to be called in by her in consultation.'

Apart from the poor who occupied the beds of the teaching hospitals, all social classes in the 1920s were delivered by a midwife, nearly always at home but occasionally in a nursing home. 'One university professor's wife described the midwife she had had with each of her four children and said the midwife always stayed two days and when she left sent in a nurse to take charge of the mother and baby.'[47]

In Denmark, a state service of midwives had existed since 1714. Before that, midwives were licensed by the church. From 1787 their training was centralized in Copenhagen, first at the Royal Maternity Hospital and then at the Rigs-Hospital which (in a manner reminiscent of Vienna in the time of Semmelweis) was divided into two parts: one for the training of medical students and the other for the training of midwives.

Midwives were usually the daughters of the small farmer class, but a few came from the professional classes. Entry was highly competitive. Only one in four was accepted in the 1920s. The period of training was one year until 1925 when, at the insistence of the midwives themselves, it was increased to two years. After examination and licensing, the midwife might go into private practice but most were employed by local health authorities. Each county employed one or more midwives, and each midwife was provided free of charge with a house (always described as neat and tidy), transport, and midwifery equipment. She was required to keep a record of every case, and her casebook was inspected and discussed in detail by the medical officer for the county once a year.

The Danish midwife in the 1920s was paid a retaining fee equivalent to between £37 and £55 a year. She was also allowed to charge a fee which was calculated in an orderly Danish manner as 1 per cent of the husband's income

[47] Mendenhall, *Midwifery in Denmark*, 8–9.

within a range from a minimum equivalent to 17s. 6d. in England and a maximum of £8. Midwives could quite easily earn a steady annual income equivalent to £400–£500 a year, much more than an English midwife and close to the average income of a British general practitioner. A midwife's fee had a preferential claim on the estate of a deceased: a mark of status if ever there was one.

Midwives were strictly confined to normal cases. They were noted for their high standard of hygiene, patience, and non-intervention in normal deliveries. They had their own journal from 1890 and to protect their professional and economic interests they formed their own union in 1891. In contrast to England where the status of the midwife was no higher, if as high, as that of the nurse, in Denmark nurses were not even licensed, on the grounds that licensing would lead to a demand for higher wages. The Danish midwife was quite definitiely a cut above the nurse.

Mendenhall described the Danish midwives in these rather idyllic terms. The British observers whose report appeared in the 1932 report on maternal mortality were more guarded.[48] They confirmed in essence all the historical, educational, administrative, and clinical details outlined above as described by Mendenhall, and they gave the Danish midwives high marks for cleanliness and antisepsis. But they thought their antenatal care was imperfect. Midwives were not taught to take the blood pressure of their patients, and some patients were delivered without having had any antenatal care at all. Postnatal care was perfunctory, lasting only two or three days. Thereafter the patient was left to her own devices. There appears to have been no Danish equivalent to the Dutch maternity nurse. The British observers concluded the standards of the Danish midwife were no higher than those of the British. That, however, was in 1930. Without question the Danish midwife was superior in the nineteenth century and at least the first two decades of the twentieth. Perhaps the greatest strength of the Danish system was the close and cordial relationship between midwives and doctors concerned with maternity work. The insistence that a doctor must be called even to slight abnormalities of pregnancy or labour, and the readiness with which those calls were met must have provided an effective means of treating complications of labour. In this respect there really was a large difference in the inter-war period between Denmark on the one hand, and Britain and the United States on the other.

THE EUROPEAN MIDWIFE

If we put ourselves in the position of a perceptive traveller with an interest in midwifery who toured through north-west Europe and Britain in the 1820s,

---

[48] Ministry of Health, *Final Report of Departmental Committee on Maternal Mortality and Morbidity*, 64–75.

we would have found that everywhere there were medical practitioners, whether they called themselves men-midwives, accoucheurs, or obstetricians, who regularly attended normal as well as abnormal deliveries. Obstetrics was still a relatively new medical discipline which was awarded an honourable position by the medical profession in some countries and denigrated in others. We would also have found lying-in hospitals, some as separate institutions, others as departments of general hospitals. In England, but probably nowhere else, we would have noted a number of thriving out-patient lying-in charities.[49] But the most striking difference would have been that between British and the Continental midwives.

Almost everywhere on the Continent we would have noted that midwives were licensed by the state or local government. Licensing was still concerned with recruiting the 'right' sort of woman. But there was greater emphasis on training and regulation than there had been in the eighteenth century. Midwifery in the limited sense of the practice of midwives had become a profession, or at the very least a skilled and respected craft or trade.

Nevertheless, the traditional untrained midwife—the *Jordgumma* of Sweden and the handywoman of England—still existed. As far as I know, no European country had succeeded in outlawing the traditional midwife who was often preferred because she was cheaper, or more familiar (she might be one of a long line of mothers and daughters well known for delivering babies), or because she was not too grand to help with menial tasks and the housework after the baby was born (which in most normal home confinements was always the prime consideration for lying-in women), and sometimes simply because women disliked being 'bossed-about' in their own home by someone in a position of authority. All of these were important practical points.

Nevertheless, over a long period of time the traditional midwife on the Continent was replaced by the trained midwife. Because it was a prolonged process, I suspect—but do not really know—that it was a relatively painless one. It is not too fanciful to say that on the Continent the licensed midwife and licensed obstetrician grew up together from infancy to adulthood. In the 1820s there were still many traditional midwives in rural areas, working beside and competing with, the trained and licensed midwives. But in large cities there would have been a larger proportion of trained midwives—the *sage femmes première classe* of Paris for instance—who were influential, powerful, responsible, and formidable women.

Touring through England we would have found a very different state of affairs. Normal deliveries had to a large extent become the province of medical practitioners, especially the surgeon-apothecaries who were now

---

[49] Léon le Fort undertook such a tour in the mid-19th cent. in order to write his memorable work *Des maternités* (Paris, 1866), and remarked that out-patient maternity charities were a peculiarity of British maternal care.

becoming known as the general practitioners.[50] The midwives of England had no formal training and no licensing, not even by the church, let alone the state or local government.[51] Almost to a man, English medical practitioners would have told us that the majority of midwives were dirty, ignorant, and incompetent and confined in their practice to patients too poor to pay a doctor's fee. The minority of better-class midwives were either employed by doctors as maternity nurses when they were strictly confined to nursing care, or they found employment in the hospitals or lying-in charities where they usually received some sort of training.

Why did Britain in the early nineteenth century fail to license and regulate midwives along the lines of the Continent? Were there any opportunities for doing so? There were, and the most important was in 1812 when the Association of Apothecaries and Surgeon-Apothecaries drew up a plan to regulate the medical profession which became a Parliamentary bill. At the insistence of the Colleges of Physicians and Surgeons, the bill was subjected to radical revision and finally reached the statute book as the Apothecaries Act of 1815.[52]

One of the items in the original bill was the licensing of midwives. Here, however, the motive was self-interest. The emphasis was not on training but on the outlawing and prosecution of untrained midwives so that there would be a small number of licensed midwives firmly under the thumbs of the doctors. This plan, which was linked to a proposal to outlaw the quacks or irregular practitioners with whom the midwives were bracketed, was dropped at an early stage. It was impossible to outlaw quacks, and impossible to outlaw midwives at a time when they were delivering at least half the mothers in the kingdom.

In Britain, the absence of any plans to train and license midwives until the late nineteenth century was due to the indifference of the medical establishment and the opposition of general practitioners. The control of medical practice in Britain was mediated through bodies such as the General Medical Council. The Council was dominated by the medical corporations, and the corporations were dominated by physicians and surgeons who were for the most part indifferent or hostile to obstetrics, and much more concerned with the quality of nurses than midwives. The main opposition came from the general practitioners who, with a contrariness which has marked the politics of general practitioners to the present day, had changed their ground between 1812 and the end of the century. Once the licensing of midwives became a genuine possibility, they took fright and opposed the plans on the grounds that

---

[50] I. Loudon, *Medical Care and the General Practitioner: 1750–1850* (Oxford, 1986).
[51] Except in the very limited sense that some midwives and nurses were employed by the poor law authorities and their being chosen was a sort of official recognition.
[52] Loudon, *Medical Care and the General Practitioner*, 152–70.

the trained midwife would be a much more dangerous form of opposition than the untrained; as indeed proved to be the case.

When, after a long uphill struggle, the Midwives Act of 1902 was introduced, it was unable to produce overnight a system such as that which had developed in the Netherlands, Sweden, and Denmark over a period of many years. For pragmatic reasons England was forced to license untrained women already in practice, the 'bona fides' (see Chapter 13). Moreover, midwifery was seen as a branch of nursing rather than a profession *sui generis*. Many who sat for the certificate of midwifery did so to further their careers as nurses and never practised as midwives.[53]

It might be argued that the nurse-midwife was a better article than the plain midwife. Mary Breckinridge (see Chapter 18) believed as much and it was probably true in rural areas. On the other hand, the subordination of midwifery to nursing (the exact opposite to the Netherlands and Denmark), the lateness of introducing state licensing, and the millstone round the neck in the form of the bona fides from 1902 to the late 1920s, prevented the British from developing a profession of midwives comparable in quality to that seen on the Continent until the 1930s; and by that time in most Western countries the move from home to hospital deliveries was already well under way.

I think my argument that there were much greater differences between Britain and the United States on the one hand and European countries on the other in the development of midwives than there were in the development of care provided by medical practitioners and lying-in hospitals is probably true. If it is, the crucial question is whether trained midwives made for better and safer childbirth. It may seem silly to ask such a question for which an affirmative answer seems self-evident. After all, systems of training and licensing midwives were introduced to provide a better system of maternal care. But that was not their only purpose. To many practitioners licensing was a means of keeping the midwife in a subordinate position and limiting her activities. The Swedish midwife was allowed to use instruments: but when she did she had to write a report justifying their use: Swedish doctors did not. Relationships between doctors and midwives in countries like Denmark may have been cordial, but it was a relationship which was based on medical dominance.

To return to the question of the effectiveness, or if you like, the safety of the trained midwife. We have already seen favourable evidence in this chapter in the case of Swedish midwives in the mid-nineteenth century. And in previous chapters there was the further evidence such as the Kentucky Frontier Nursing Service, the Queen's Institute nurse-midwives in Britain, and the out-patient lying-in charities which depended largely on the midwives trained by those institutions. In fact, throughout the years I have spent on this

---

[53] R. Dingwall, A. M. Rafferty, and C. Webster, *An Introduction to the Social History of Nursing* (London, 1988), 169.

study, I have found—and it was not a finding I had expected—that wherever a city, a county, a region, or a nation, had developed a system of maternal care which was firmly based on a body of trained, licensed, regulated, and respected midwives (especially when the midwives worked in close and cordial co-operation with doctors and lying-in hospitals) the standard of maternal care was at its highest and maternal mortality was at its lowest. I cannot think of an exception to that rule. Whether as a consequence the record of maternal care on the Continent of Europe was better than it was in Britain or America is a conclustion which must follow consideration of deliveries by European doctors and European lying-in hospitals.

25
European Lying-in Hospitals and Obstetricians

During the nineteenth century the continental maternity hospitals were larger, more numerous, and more prestigious than they were in Britian. Le Fort confessed he was surprised to find how small and few were the London maternities, for he had a very high regard for the state of obstetrics in Britain.[1]

Total deliveries by all the London maternity hospitals 1860–4 was a little over 1,000, accounting for only 0.7 per cent of total births in London. In the same period the Parisian maternity hospitals (there were ten in Paris compared with four in London) delivered over 7,000 women a year, which came to 12 per cent of all births in Paris. Lyons came next with two maternity hospitals in which, on average, 1,335 women were delivered annually in the 1860s: rather more than the annual total of all the London lying-in hospitals. Elsewhere in France, however, although there were many provinical maternity hospitals they were small. In Lille the maternity hospital in the 1860s delivered on average 170 women a year, in Bordeaux about 130, in Toulouse about 120, in Marseilles and Chateauroux about 100, in Amiens about 90, in Nancy and Nantes about 80, and in Orléans about 70.[2]

Apart from Paris and Lyons, the average number of deliveries in French maternity hospitals in the 1860s was between one and three a week—a level of deliveries found in many English cottage hospitals situated in market towns from the 1920s to the 1960s. Although maternity hospitals played a larger part in maternal care in France than Britain, it is important to remember that Paris apart, in the mid-nineteenth century only a small proportion (less than 1 per cent in all probability) of deliveries in France took place in maternity hospitals.

Nevertheless, maternity hospitals played a larger part in the world of continental obstetrics than the number of deliveries would suggest. The majority were financed by the state, the province, or *département*, or by the town in which they were situated. They derived much of their status

---

[1] See Léon Le Fort, *Des maternités: Études sur les maternités et les institutions charitables d'accouchement à domicile dans les principaux États de l'Europe* (Paris, 1866), a massive work of great detail in which, judging by his descriptions of the situation in Britain, he was remarkably thorough and accurate.

[2] Ibid. 22–31.

from the fact they were institutions of national or local government. Some European maternities were separate hospitals (Munich, Dresden, the 'Maison d'Accouchement' in Paris, Berlin, Leipzig, Frankfurt). Others were departments of general hospitals (the 'Clinique' in Paris, Vienna, Brussels, Stuttgart, Zurich) and a few were joined to orphanages or 'hospices des enfants-trouvés' (Prague, Moscow, and St Petersburg).[3]

The directors of these hospitals, known in France as the 'médicins en chef', were always doctors, not laymen. Next in line were the medical assistants who undertook most of the care of the abnormal cases. The director and the assistants were salaried servants of the financing bodies, not unpaid honoraries as in Britain.[4] Subordinate to these was the *sage-femme en chef* (the equivalent of the matron in a British hospital) whose duties in addition to delivering patients consisted of training pupil midwives and looking after the housekeeping. She was assisted by a number of *aides-sage-femmes* under her command. The Liège maternity in Belgium was not large by Parisian standards, but in 1906 the personnel consisted of the Surgeon-Director, the chief midwife (*Maîtresse sage-femme économe*), a medical assistant (unpaid), two or three nurses, three cooks, two servants, a commisionnaire, two clerks, and a variable number of student midwives.[5]

Some maternity hospitals trained only midwives, others only medical students. Many trained both, sometimes with a Box-and-Cox system, with medical students during the winter months and the pupil midwives during the summer; or, as in Vienna, with separate clinics for medical and midwife students.[6] Although the women admitted to European maternity hospitals were nearly always from the poorest sections of society, a few maternity hospitals had private clinics. There was one at the Vienna maternity hospital. They seem to have been surrounded to some extent by a discrete silence, possibly because of the existence of what Le Fort calls 'divisions des accouchements secrets'. There was one at the Prague maternity hospital where women were not obliged to give their name, or say where they came from or where they were going to after the baby was born. Similar arrangements existed at St Petersburg, Moscow, and Budapest. At the maternity hospital in Brussels the patient's name had to be given to the director but to no one else, and the director was sworn to secrecy.[7]

---

[3] Ibid. 138.

[4] Sometimes there was a lay administrator, but he does not seem to have been a person with the power of some of the British equivalents such as the treasurer of Guy's Hospital in the time of Thomas Hodgkin. See A. M. E. Kass and E. H. Kass, *Perfecting the World: The Life and Times of Thomas Hodgkin, 1798–1866* (Boston, 1988).

[5] Jean-Louis Louche, 'La Maternité de Liège ou cent ans de l'évolution d'un hospice', *Annales de la société belge d'histoire des hôpitaux et de la santé publique*, 22 (1984), 5–25. These details refer to the personnel at the Maternité de la rue des Carnes.

[6] Ibid. 141.

[7] Ibid. 144.

It seems that unmarried mothers were admitted more readily to continental maternities than they were to some of the English and Amerian lying-in hospitals. Voluntary hospitals always had to be careful not to offend the moral sensibilities of subscribers who would object to their donations being used for the relief of unmarried women and prostitutes. There also seems to have been a recognition in some continental maternity hospitals that infanticide was a major problem which might be avoided by providing 'divisions des accouchements secrets' linked to arrangements whereby unwanted babies could be transferred to orphanages with which the maternity hospitals were connected. There was, as far as I am aware, no parallel in the British or American voluntary lying-in hospitals.

THE PROBLEM OF PUERPERAL FEVER

The continental maternity hospitals may have been more prestigious than the British and American, but they were dogged by the same terrible problem—the dreadful rate of maternal mortality. Table 25.1 shows that an extremely high rate of mortality was found throughout Europe with the highest rates in Paris. Those who ran these hospitals knew, for they had the statistics before them, that the mortality in home deliveries in the town in which they were situated was very much lower than it was in the hospital wards. This can be seen in Tables 25.2 and 25.3. There is no doubt that the high hospital mortality was due to puerperal fever, and not to the selection of complicated high-risk cases for hospital delivery.

The chance of a woman contracting puerperal fever, even after a normal delivery let alone a complicated one, was around seven times as high if she was delivered in a Parisian maternity hospital in the mid-nineteenth century than it would have been if she had been delivered at home. In the Parisian maternity hospitals in 1862, 83 per cent of maternal deaths were due to puerperal fever. At the 'Clinique' puerperal fever accounted for 86 per cent of all maternal deaths, at the Maternité for 85 per cent, at the Hôtel Dieu 81 per cent, at the Charité 71 per cent, and at the Pitié 67 per cent.[8]

The totals on which these percentages are based included all deaths, including those attributed to intercurrent disease such as chest diseases (including phthisis) which accounted for 18 out of the grand total of 481 deaths in all the Parisian maternities in 1862, typhoid (4 deaths), erysipelas (4 deaths), and smallpox (3 deaths). If these indirect deaths are excluded, deaths due to puerperal fever amounted to 89 per cent of direct maternal mortality. The true figure may have been even higher for various reasons, including the habit in some maternity hospitals of moving some of their

---

[8] Le Fort, *Des maternités*, 35. These percentages were based on a single year, 1862, and the differences between the first four are not significant, falling within the range of random variation.

TABLE 25.1 *Maternal Mortality in Certain European Lying-in Hospitals in the Nineteenth Century*

	Number of deliveries	Deaths per 10,000 deliveries
Paris Maternité (1802–62)	160,704	560
Paris, Clinique de la Faculté (1835–64)	24,295	470
Paris, Hôtel Dieu (1802–64)	25,314	320
Paris, Saint Antoine (1811–64)	5,204	670
Paris, Saint-Louis (1807–64)	19,038	400
Rouen, Hôpital Généraux (1860–3)	1,275	70
Lyon, Charité (1860–3)	3,325	170
Lyon, Hôtel Dieu (1860–3)	2,016	160
Bordeaux Maternité (1860–3)	714	420
Vienna, 1st Clinic (1834–63)	104,492	432
Vienna, 2nd Clinic (1834–63)	88,008	348
Berlin, Clinique de l'Université (1864)	401	270
Leipzig, Ancien Maternité (1810–55)	5,137	170
Leipzig, Nouvelle Maternité (1856–8)	594	330
Dresden Maternité (1814–60)	15,536	270
Munich Maternité (1859–62)	4,064	210
Gratz Maternité (1859–61)	3,089	310
Prague Maternité (1848–62)	41,477	333
Stockholm Maternité (1861)	650	560
St Petersbourg Maternity (1845–59)	16,011	515
Moscow, Maternité de la maison des enfants trouvés, 1832–1857	27,759	280
Total deliveries and average maternal mortality of all hospital deliveries investigated by Le Fort	883,312	340

Source: Léon Le Fort, *Des maternités* (Paris, 1866), 14–31.

feverish patients to an infirmary where they disappeared from the lying-in hospital's statistics, and the universal tendency not to certify a death as puerperal fever if it could be slipped into any other category. In the worst years at the Maternité about one woman in ten died in childbirth, compared with an average of 1 in 200 to 250 in England and Wales during the same period.[9]

Le Fort examined at length the reasons for the high rate of maternal mortality and considered three possible explanations. First, that the cause was direct transmission from one patient to another in the manner of contagious diseases such as smallpox. Secondly, that the cause lay in the walls, bedding,

[9] Ibid.

TABLE 25.2 *Home Deliveries and Maternal Mortality in Various European Towns*

	Number of deliveries	Deaths per 10,000 deliveries
City of Paris (1861–2)	87,277	51
Paris, 12th Arrondissement (1856)	3,222	31
Paris, Bureau de bienfaisance (1861–2)	12,634	55
Leipzig Polyclinique (1849–59)	1,203	108
Berlin Polyclinique (1864)	500	140
Munich Polyclinique (1859–63)	1,911	84
City of St Petersburg (1845–52)	209,612	67
London, all home deliveries (1860–4)	562,623	39
Edinburgh, all home deliveries (1858)	5,486	50
Total deliveries and average maternal mortality of all home deliveries investigated by Le Fort	934,781	47

Source: Léon Le Fort, *Des maternités* (Pairs, 1866), 32–3.

TABLE 25.3 *Deliveries, Maternal Deaths, and Maternal Mortality per 10,000 Deliveries in Hospital, Home, and Total Deliveries, Paris, 1862*

	Number of deliveries	Number of maternal deaths	Maternal mortality rate
Hospital deliveries	6,971	481	690
Home deliveries	49,218	265	54
Total deliveries in Paris	56,189	746	133

Source: Léon Le Fort, *Des maternités* (Pairs, 1866).

and furniture, of the hospitals which were staturated with the noxious influence which caused puerperal fever. In support of this theory (and with no reference to the lengthy section of Semmelweis's treatise which effectively ruled out this possibility) he pointed to the high mortality in old dilapidated hospitals, the apparent benefits of repainting and fumigating such hospitals after an epidemic, and the fact that when a new maternity hospital was built it usually escaped outbreaks of puerperal fever for a number of years, but when an outbreak did occur it was followed by a series of epidemics. The third possibility was both the most important and the most controversial explanation: the transmission of the disease by midwives, students, and doctors from one maternity case to the next. He recognized that this was supported by a mass of evidence which he reviewed, going over much of the ground covered by Oliver Wendell Holmes, without acknowledging or apparently being aware of Holmes's essay, and paying what now seems scant attention to Semmelweis's work.

One of the features which troubled Le Fort and everyone else in the mid-nineteenth century, was the problem of finding a unitary explanation for the cause of puerperal fever which was consistent with the mountain of evidence concerning home and hospital deliveries. Why was puerperal fever relatively rare in ordinary domiciliary practice? And why, when it did appear, was it so often confined to the cases of one midwife or medical practitioner, while their colleagues in the same town at the same time had none? We discussed this in Chapter 4 where we mentioned the cases of Dr Rutter of Philadelphia, Dr West of Abingdon, and several others. Yet Fort told of another example, so striking that it is worth recounting.

On 2 December 1842, a Belgian doctor, M. Grisar, attended a case of prolonged labour. The woman was delivered of a dead baby by forceps, and two days later she died of puerperal fever. Between 2 December and 19 March, M. Grisar delivered 64 women of whom 16 developed puerperal fever and 11 died. Since none of his colleagues in the same town had a single case of the disease, M. Grisar concluded that he was responsible for transmitting the disease. He took all the usual precautions such as changing all his clothes and repeatedly washing himself because this was thought to be the right procedure, although none could say precisely how it worked (in 1842 Semmelweis had not yet graduated). At all events, the outbreak ceased.

From March 1842 until the end of 1862, a period of nearly twenty years, Grisar continued to deliver a large number of patients and had not one single case of puerperal fever. Then, on 5 December 1862, one of his cases died of the disease, once more after a forceps delivery. From 5 December 1862 to 26 January 1863, out of 9 deliveries, 8 developed the disease and 4 died. M. Grisar ceased all obstetric practice for a period of one month. Thereafter he had no more cases of puerperal fever.[10]

In this example, it appeared that the precautions taken by M. Grisar were effective. What was disturbing, however, were the numerous recorded instances in home and hospital practice when practitioners who had attended a case of puerperal fever (or erysipelas) and took all the accepted measures to prevent contagion, changing all their clothes and washing assiduously, and yet, as Holmes put it, 'this rare disease followed their footsteps like a beagle through the streets . . .'.[11]

If all cases of puerperal fever were iatrogenic, why were some doctors

---

[10] Le Fort, *Des maternités*, 113.
[11] Oliver Wendell Holmes: see Chap. 4.

singled out when others, no more careful or knowledgeable than their unfortunate colleagues, were spared? And if there was an outbreak what was the
cause of the first case? In ordinary private practice puerperal fever was
uncommon. Many fortunate practitioners never saw a case, or only one or two
in their lifetime. It was clear that in the community when puerperal fever
appeared it had the habit of suddenly erupting and then disappearing for
years or even decades. In maternity hospitals, however, it was endemic. There
were always some cases, every year, forming the background to the explosive
epidemics that took place in certain years, particularly 1873–5. If it was
endemic, where was it lurking? The only logical explanation seemed to be
within the fabric of the hospital itself. On the evidence available most of us
would have been forced to that conclusion, and for this reason Le Fort
concluded that although Semmelweis was correct in saying the disease could
be transmitted from the post-mortem room to the labour ward by the unwashed hands of the birth-attendant, this explained only a proportion of cases.
There was, in other words, no unitary hypothesis. Puerperal fever, he said,
had many causes, and in the 1860s this view was shared by almost everyone in
Europe.

TARNIER AND PUERPERAL FEVER IN PARIS

In the mid-nineteenth century the surgeons of the Paris Maternité were close
to despair. There is a legend to the effect that one of them, meeting on the
Boulevard Port Royal a poor woman on her way to the hospital, cried out 'Do
not come in here unless you wish to die.'[12] In 1862, a Paris obstetrician,
M. Billet, resurrected the idea which had been discussed for some years of
closing all the maternity hospitals in Paris and returning to home deliveries.
Instead, a policy of isolation was introduced by the leading French authority
on puerperal fever, Tarnier.[13]

Étienne Stéphane Tarnier (1828–97) was the son of a country doctor who
received his medical education at Paris. He developed a burning desire to
solve the problem of puerperal fever in the maternity hospitals, choosing this
as the subject of his inaugural thesis in 1856. In this thesis he maintained that
puerperal fever was a contagious disorder and compared hospital mortality
with the mortality of home deliveries in a way that was an implicit (and wholly
justified) condemnation of hospital practice. His thesis caused offence. Far
from being acclaimed, Tarnier was forced to accept a menial post in the
Bureau de Bienfaisance and almost abandoned medicine. But in 1858 the
Académie de Médicine held a discussion on the nature of puerperal fever

[12] C. J. Cullingworth, 'Biographical Note on Étienne Stéphane Tarnier', *Transactions of the Obstetrical Society of London*, 40 (1898), 78–89.
[13] Gabriel-Paul Ancelet, *Essai historique et critique sur le création et la transformation des maternités à Paris* (Paris, 1896).

which extended over four months. Tarnier's thesis was so frequently quoted that Dubois, one of the leading obstetricians of the time, sought out Tarnier and promised him a post as *chef de clinique* at the Maternité. Tarnier promptly wrote a fresh monograph which was published in 1858.[14]

In 1861, Tarnier was appointed *chef de clinique* and in 1867 as the director of the Maternité. From 1867 to 1870, in spite of his protests, Tarnier was unable to alter the ways of the hospital. Tarnier called the period to the end of 1869 the period of inaction. From 1870 he introduced a policy of isolation by which the healthy were kept apart from the sick. Women who showed even slight signs of illness were promptly removed to the infirmary and the two institutions were rigidly separated. The staff of the infirmary were forbidden to enter the lying-in hospital and vice versa. The idea of isolation was extended to the provision of a special isolation pavilion, built in 1876 and named the 'Pavilion Tarnier'. The period from 1870 to 1881 was called by Tarnier the period of the 'struggle against contagion'. From 1881 isolation was combined with antisepsis, and this third period was called the period of antisepsis.[15]

In the first period, the period of inaction from 1858 to 1869, the MMR in the Maternité was 931 per 10,000 deliveries. In the second period, from 1870 to 1880, the period when isolation alone was used, the MMR fell to 232, and in the period of antisepsis, from 1881 to 1889, when isolation was combined with antisepsis, the MMR fell to 105. In publishing these figures Tarnier made sure they were beyond criticism. Aware of the danger of deception, he insisted that every death which took place in the Maternité, regardless of cause, should be included in the published statistics. An MMR of 105 deaths per 10,000 deliveries in 1889 (Tarnier's third period) was not remarkable by international standards, but it was a remarkable improvement for Paris.

Tarnier's chief claim to fame was the invention of axis traction forceps, considered the most important improvement to forceps delivery since the introduction of the pelvic curve. 'Let who will', said Professor Alexander Simpson of Edinburgh, 'continue to use oridinary curved forceps; an obstetrician who has used the Tarnier forceps in a few test cases will no more think of reverting to the other than a man who can afford to keep a carriage will continue to practise as a peripatetic.' When he died Tarnier was in the process of revising the proofs of the third volume of his monumental *Traité de l'art des accouchements*.[16]

Tarnier was one of the most famous obstetricians of his day. In France he

---

[14] When Tarnier took his manuscript to the famous Parisian medical publisher, M. J. B. Baillière, the latter said 'I know of only one man in Paris who is competent to deal with such a subject... Dr Tarnier', to which Tarnier was able to reply, no doubt with immense pleasure, 'I am Dr Tarnier.' C. J. Cullingworth, 'Biographical Note on Tarnier'.
[15] Ibid.
[16] Ibid.

was regarded as the leading authority on puerperal fever. From 1880, like his colleagues throughout Europe, he recognized the importance of Listerian antisepsis and saw that it was introduced into hospital practice; but his policy before 1880—the policy of isolation with no mention of antiseptic practice— suggests that before the work of Pasteur and Lister, Semmelweis's treatise had very little influence. Was this because Semmelweis was unknown, or because he was not believed?

MATERNAL MORTALITY AND ANTISEPSIS ON THE CONTINENT

It is often believed that Semmelweis's discoveries were totally ignored in Europe. It is true that many authorities initially rejected his ideas, but many others simply felt, as was pointed out in Chapter 4, that he had gone too far in his insistence on a unitary hypothesis. Nevertheless, his work was more influential than is generally conceded.

Hebra published Semmelweis's discoveries in flattering terms. Haller and Skoda also praised and supported his work. Virchow (in 1846–7) studied the nature of puerperal fever and agreed it was a contagious condition as did Tarnier in his treatise of 1858. In 1864 Hirsch published a memoir on puerperal fever which denied a miasmatic origin and insisted on contagion. He agreed with Semmelweis's views and emphasized the connection with erysipelas, which had previously been emphasized most of all by English writers. In the 1860s, many obstetricians in Germany still held to the old beliefs that puerperal fever was due to a mixture of causes including sup- pression of the lochia, lacteal metatases, accumulation of bile, inflammation of the intestines, erysipelatous inflammation, and general feebleness. But when Boehr addressed the Obstetrical Society of Berlin in 1868 he not only emphasized the contagious nature of puerperal fever but insisted on rigorous hand-washing in the manner prescribed by Semmelweis as a means of preventing the disease. Spiegelberg took the same view and stated that puerperal fever was a 'true inoculation . . . the ordinary vehicle is the finger or instrument'.

Semmelweis's discoveries began to make sense when Pasteur identified the streptococcus from the lochial discharge of infected women. Pasteur's work inspired Coze and Feltz in Strasbourg in 1867 and 1869 to examine the blood in cases of puerperal fever. They found 'la présence de nombreux points mobiles isolés ou disposés en chainettes infusoires' and found this also in cases of septicaemia and typhoid. This was the first report of bacteria in the blood of cases of puerperal fever which was published in *La Gazette médicale de Strasbourg*. Little attention was paid to the paper at the time. Widal was the first to state in 1888 that the organism which caused erysipelas and puerperal fever was one and the same.[17]

By the 1880s, most accepted that contagion was the central feature of puerperal fever. Few authorities were left who still rejected the combined discoveries of Semmelweis, Pasteur, and Lister. Antisepsis, now given a sound theoretical basis, had come to stay and there was a mounting volume of evidence that it was in some circumstances quite dramatically effective. Take, for instance, the maternity hospital in Liège which was established in 1804 as a teaching hospital for midwives. Soon it became the main teaching hospital for medical students, and in 1908 the professor of obstetrics at the university clinic became the director of the Maternité.[18]

Between 1833 and 1881, when this hospital in common with most others was plagued by recurrent epidemics of puerperal fever, the MMR was on average between 200 to 300 deaths per 10,000 births with wide annual variations. This can be seen in Figure 25.1 which serves as an illustration of the pattern of maternal mortality in a typical European maternity hospital. Note that the highest recorded level of maternal mortality occurred in 1873, the year before it peaked in Britain, Sweden, and other countries, providing just a hint that a virulent strain of the streptococcus may have started in or near Belgium and spread outwards the following year. But that is pure speculation.[19]

All kinds of measures were taken to combat the high mortality, including the fumigation of clothes, beds, furniture, syringes used to irrigate the uterus and other instruments, lime-washing of the walls of the hospital, and even the isolation of infected patients. None was effective, and it was not until the early 1880s, when antisepsis was introduced, that mortality began to decline, especially when phenol was replaced by sublimate of mercury as a disinfectant in 1884. Thereafter the epidemics with very high rates of mortality suddenly ceased and, as Figure 25.1 shows, were not seen again.[20] Just before mercury sublimate was introduced in Liège in May 1884, the septic morbidity rate was 8.87 per cent and the mortality rate 3.22 per cent. Afterwards, the rates were 3.54 per cent and 0 per cent respectively. In 1885 there were only three cases of puerperal fever and all three survived. In addition, infant ophthalmia (ophthalmia neonatorum) was greatly diminished.

In 1891 the Director tried the experiment of replacing antisepsis by asepsis

[17] This section is largely based on L. Devraigne, *L'Obstétrique à travers les âges* (Paris, 1939).

[18] Louche, 'La Maternité de Liège'.

[19] As in many maternity hospitals the published figures of maternal deaths in the Liège maternity are an underestimate. Some of the patients with puerperal fever (it is not known how many) were transferred to other hospitals, and patients who died after transfer to the infirmary did not appear in the Maternité's books. Ibid.

[20] It should be noted that during the 1880s phenol was replaced by sublimate of mercury in most maternity hospitals in France and Belgium.

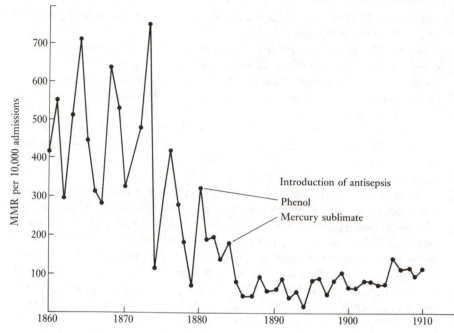

FIG. 25.1 Liège Maternity Hospital, 1860–1910. Maternal Mortality and the introduction of antisepsis
Source: Jean-Louis Louche, 'La Maternité de Liège ou cent ans de l'évolution d'un hospice', *Annales de la société Belge d'histoire des hôpitaux et de la santé publique*, 22 (1984), 5–25.
MMR per 10,000 admissions. Data on the number of deliveries are not available, and it is known that the records of admissions were imperfect in the nineteenth century. Moreover, the number of admissions before 1900 (around 200–300 a year) and the number of maternal deaths were small. For both reasons this graph is not an accurate presentation of the exact rate of maternal mortality, but rather a broad picture which indicates the effect of antisepsis.

alone, but septic morbidity and mortality both rose promptly and he abandoned the experiment. What is striking is that once the fall in mortality had taken place, the number of patients admitted rose steeply. From 1830 to 1880, admissions ran at a level of 200 to 300 a year. By 1903 they had risen to 1,000 and by 1938 to 1,569. The mortality rate rose slowly after 1884 and continued to rise until the 1930s. This was probably due to a selective increase in complicated cases and an increase in cases of septic abortion.[21] There is a wealth of evidence concerning what has been called the antiseptic revolution in the large and well-known maternity hospitals. But there is very little analysis of the extent of the revolution in a country as a whole. For this reason a treatise on the development of antisepsis in the practice of midwifery in the Netherlands, published in 1911, is of considerable historical interest.[22]

[21] Louche, 'La Maternité de Liège'.
[22] Catharine van Tuessenbrooek, *De Ontwikkeling der Aseptische Verloskunde in Nederland [The*

The author, Catharine van Tuessenbrooek, was the second woman to qualify in medicine (in 1887) in the Netherlands. She specialized in obstetrics and gynaecology, working at the clinic of Mendes de Leon in Amsterdam. She was also on the editorial board of the journal of the Dutch Gynaeco-logical Association. As a student she must have seen the tail-end of the appalling phase of maternal mortality in the Amsterdam hospital, and must have watched many women die in agony from puerperal peritonitis. When she qualified and became a member of staff she would have witnessed the truly remarkable fall in mortality and she investigated the extent to which the use of antisepsis extended beyond the hospital and Amsterdam itself. What, she asked, was happening in the rest of the country? To answer this question she undertook a statistical investigation of maternal deaths in other towns, comparing home with hospital deliveries, and deliveries by doctors with deliveries by midwives. The main findings of her work are presented here in Tables 25.4 to 25.8. When we look at these it is important to remember the usual proviso that in some of the cells in some of the tables the number of maternal deaths was small and the range of random variation correspondingly large.

The first of these, Table 25.4, shows maternal mortality in Amsterdam in the last third of the nineteenth century. The top group of figures shows the number of deliveries in the town and in the hospital. The second group shows maternal deaths from all causes and the bottom line of this group shows the sharp fall in maternal mortality in the hospital, which began in 1885. There was a similar fall in maternal mortality in the town which consisted of all home deliveries by doctors and midwives, but it began rather later, first becoming evident in 1895. If the fall in maternal mortality in the hospital and the town was due to antisepsis it should show up in the maternal deaths due to sepsis rather than the deaths due to other causes. The third and fourth groups of figures show that this was in fact what occurred. The fall in maternal mortality due to causes other than sepsis was very slight by comparison.[23]

What was happening elsewhere? Table 25.5 shows the mortality rates for the four large towns in the Netherlands and for thirteen secondary towns. All show a decline in maternal mortality between 1865 and 1900, but not to the

Development of Aseptic Midwifery in the Netherlands] (Haarlem, 1911). For finding this important source and for translations of the relevant sections and for biographical details of the author, I am greatly indebted to Dr Hilary Marland.

[23] It is worth noting in this table and in the preceding table (25.3), that even where hospital deliveries amounted to only a small proportion of the deliveries in the town in which the maternity hospital was situated, the maternal mortality of the town as a whole was significantly raised by the hospital mortality. Thus in Paris in 1862, the MMR in the town excluding the maternity hospitals was 54, but when the deaths in the maternity hospitals were included it was raised to 133. In Amsterdam, where hospital deliveries accounted for only about 5% of all deliveries in the town, the hospital mortality in 1865 raised the maternal mortality from 81 for the town alone to 98 when town and hospital deaths were included together. It is an important point when mortality rates in a series of towns are compared, some of which possessed a maternity hospital but others did not.

TABLE 25.4 *Deliveries and Maternal Deaths in the Town and the Maternity Hospital, Amsterdam, 1865–1900*

	1865	1875	1885	1895	1900
Number of deliveries					
Town and maternity hospital	9,413	10,521	14,315	14,615	15,507
Town alone	8,963	10,208	13,898	14,118	15,093
Maternity hospital alone	450	313	417	497	414
Maternal deaths from all causes					
Town and hospital, Number	92	84	101	63	50
Maternal mortality rate	98	80	71	43	32
Town alone, Number	73	67	93	56	47
Maternal mortality rate	81	66	67	40	31
Hospital alone, Number	19	17	8	7	3
Maternal mortality rate	422	543	192	141	72
Maternal deaths from puerperal sepsis					
Town alone, Number	38	35	51	26	22
Maternal mortality rate	42	34	37	18	15
Hospital alone, Number	13	11	3	1	0
Maternal mortality rate	288	351	72	20	0
Maternal deaths from all causes other than sepsis					
Town alone, Number	35	32	42	30	25
Maternal mortality rate	39	32	30	22	16
Hospital alone, Number	6	6	5	6	3
Maternal mortality rate	134	192	120	121	72

Source: Catharine van Tuessenbrooek, *De Ontwikkeling der Aseptische Verloskunde in Nederland [The Development of Aseptic Midwifery in the Netherlands]* (Haarlem, 1911).

same extent as Amsterdam. The fall was least impressive in the thirteen secondary towns. This is not surprising. When antisepsis was introduced it was first used in the largest teaching centres from which it spread out slowly into other towns with smaller hospitals or no hospitals at all, and then into the practice of general practitioners and midwives. Indeed, there was initially a tendency amongst those whose practice was confined to home deliveries to believe that antisepsis was a technique which was only relevant to the specific problem of hospital mortality. Since midwives were controlled, however, it was possible for the authorities to insist that they used antisepsis in everyday practice and there is evidence that Dutch midwives were using antisepsis routinely in the final years of the nineteenth century. Table 25.6 is therefore of interest in so far as it shows that maternal mortality was significantly higher in deliveries carried out by doctors than by midwives in the period 1865–95. It is possible that the higher rate in doctors' deliveries was due to an excess of

TABLE 25.5 *Various Towns in the Netherlands: Deliveries and Maternal Deaths from all Causes*

	1865	1875	1885	1895	1900
Total deliveries					
Amsterdam	9,413	10,521	14,315	14,615	15,507
Rotterdam	4,635	5,695	6,264	9,667	11,892
The Hague	3,272	3,880	5,227	5,553	6,093
Utrecht	2,245	2,536	3,013	3,269	3,332
13 secondary towns	10,989	12,689	14,556	15,793	16,294
Total maternal deaths from all causes					
Amsterdam	92	84	101	63	50
Rotterdam	33	28	35	51	54
The Hague	14	26	20	32	28
Utrecht	18	27	27	15	14
13 secondary towns	96	104	102	69	81
Maternal mortality rates					
Amsterdam	98	80	71	43	32
Rotterdam	71	49	56	53	46
The Hague	43	67	38	58	46
Utrecht	81	107	90	46	42
13 secondary towns	87	82	70	44	50

Source: Catharine van Tuessenbrooek, *De Ontwikkeling der Aseptische Verloskunde in Nederland* (Haarlem, 1911).

TABLE 25.6 *Total Deliveries, Maternal Deaths, and Maternal Mortality in Two Groups of Towns, the Netherlands, 1865–1895*

	Group A (Doctors)[a]	Group B (Midwives)[b]
Number of deliveries	33,757	18,736
Number of maternal deaths	209	81[c]
Maternal mortality rate	62	43

[a] Towns in which all deliveries were undertaken by doctors.
[b] Towns in which very nearly all deliveries were undertaken by midwives.
[c] Chi-square = 7.89 (significant at 0.01 and 0.005 level).

Source: Catharine van Tuessenbrooek, *De Ontwikkeling der Aseptische Verloskunde in Nederland* (Haarlem, 1911).

complicated cases, but the data as presented do not support this as the explanation.

It is worth noting that the levels of maternal mortality in Amsterdam, Rotterdam, the other large towns, and in the secondary towns were higher,

TABLE 25.7 *Total Maternal Deaths and Deaths from Abortion in the Four Largest Towns in the Netherlands, 1865–1900*

	1865	1875	1885	1895	1900
Amsterdam					
Total maternal deaths	92.0	84.0	101.0	63.0	50.0
Deaths from abortion	4.0	6.0	5.0	8.0	10.0
Abortion deaths as a percentage of					
total maternal deaths	4.3	7.1	4.9	12.7	20.0
Rotterdam					
Total maternal deaths	—	—	35.0	51.0	54.0
Deaths from abortion	—	—	0	2.0	4.0
Utrecht					
Total maternal deaths	—	27.0	27.0	15.0	14.0
Deaths from abortion	—	2.0	0	1.0	0
The Hague					
Total maternal deaths	19.0	26.0	20.0	32.0	28.0
Deaths from abortion	0	1.0	0	3.0	4.0
Total of all four towns					
Total maternal deaths	111.0	137.0	183.0	161.0	146.0
Deaths from abortion	4.0	9.0	5.0	14.0	18.0
Abortion deaths as a percentage of					
total maternal deaths	3.6	6.6	2.7	8.7	12.3

Source: Catharine van Tuessenbrooek, *De Ontwikkeling der Aseptische Verloskunde in Nederland* (Haarlem, 1911).

and often substantially higher, than the mortality in London and in England and Wales as a whole during this period. A possible explanation is that Dutch doctors and midwives were more efficient and more honest than the English in the certification of maternal deaths and that as a consequence there were fewer hidden maternal deaths in the Netherlands. This is not the case. Catharine van Tuessenbrooek investigated the death certificates and showed that the problem of hidden maternal deaths—especially deaths due to sepsis—was at least as great in the Netherlands during this period as it was in England and Wales. Until 1895, maternal mortality was at least as high in the Netherlands and probably higher than it was in England and Wales.[24]

[24] In the 1920s, when the MMR in the Netherlands was lower than it was in England and Wales, Dame Janet Campbell ascribed the difference to the Netherlands being a country which had little heavy industry and no remote rural areas. See J. Campbell, 'Maternal Mortality', *Reports of Public Health and Medical Subjects*, 25, Ministry of Health (London, 1924); J. Campbell, I. D. Cameron, and D. M. Jones, 'High Maternal Mortality in Certain Areas', *Reports on Public Health and Medical Subjects*, 68, Ministry of Health (London, 1932); and J. Campbell, *Maternity Services* (London, 1935). The evidence from the 1890s tends to refute this theory.

There was, however, another problem: the problem of abortion. Table 25.7 shows that there were early signs of the rising tide of deaths due to abortion which would continue to rise into and through the interwar period. The number of deaths is small, but I think that the trend is convincing and it looks as if the problem was greatest in Amsterdam. The obvious explanation is a rising incidence of instrumental abortion, but other possible causes must not be forgotten; for instance, a greater readiness to consult doctors in cases of abortion which did badly, a greater tendency to admit cases of abortion to hospital, and the more remote possibility that deaths due to abortion had been hidden under other headings in the early part of the period. I have been unable to verify if any such factors were able to account for the rising number of deaths due to abortion, which in 1900 had risen to the high level of 20 per cent of total maternal mortality in Amsterdam.

Van Tuessenbrooek's treatise shows beyond reasonable doubt that anti-sepsis led to a profound fall in maternal mortality in the Netherlands, which, between 1880 and 1900, was greatest in Amsterdam but occurred throughout the Netherlands. It is true that mortality from all causes of deaths in women aged 20–50 was falling during the last quarter of the nineteenth century; but maternal mortality fell more steeply.[25]

A similar fall in maternal mortality occurred in Sweden where the national level of maternal mortality declined from 42 per 10,000 births in 1875–80 to 23 in 1900–4. There is little doubt the fall occurred as a consequence of antisepsis.[26]

In England and Wales from 1880 to 1910 it was widely held that antisepsis had been very effective in hospital practice but ineffective in the practice of general practitioners and midwives. In 1880 hospital mortality far exceeded mortality in home deliveries. By 1900 this had been reversed. Maternal mortality in home deliveries had to all intents and purposes stayed still, while hospital maternal mortality had fallen to a level substantially below the level of home deliveries. It was in this most important respect that the Netherlands differed from England and Wales. Table 25.8 suggests that by 1900 in the Netherlands maternal mortality in home deliveries in the four major towns had fallen to a lower level than that which obtained in the Amsterdam maternity hospitals. Although the difference is not statistically significant, the important point is that an overall fall in maternal mortality, albeit to a different extent, had taken place in home and hospital deliveries, in large towns and

---

[25] The mortality rate per 1,000 women living aged 20–50 was 8.9 in 1875, 7.3 in 1885, 5.4 in 1895, and 5.6 in 1900. Maternal deaths as a percentage of total deaths in this age group fell between 1875 and 1900 from 12.3% to 9.7%. Van Tuessenbrooek, *De Ontwikkeling der Aseptische Verloskunde in Nederland*.

[26] U. Högberg, and G. Brostrom, 'The Impact of Early Medical Technology on Maternal Mortality Rate in late 19th Century Sweden', *International Journal of Obstetrics and Gynaecology*, 24 (1986), 251–61.

TABLE 25.8 *Maternal Mortality in Two Groups of Deliveries, the Netherlands,*
1900

	Group A Hospital deliveries[a]	Group B Home deliveries[b]
Total deliveries	1,104	61,726
Maternal deaths (all maternal causes)	8	258[c]
Maternal mortality rate	72	42
Deaths from sepsis	3	91
Maternal mortality rate from sepsis	27	17

[a] Deliveries in maternity hospitals and schools of midwifery.
[b] Home deliveries in the four major towns, 13 secondary towns, and 46 small towns.
[c] Chi-square = 2.3 (not significant).

Source: Catharine van Tuessenbrooek, *De Ontwikkeling der Aseptische Verloskunde in Nederland* (Haarlem, 1911).

small towns, in every province of the Netherlands, and in deliveries by doctors as well as midwives.

There may have been other factors in operation, but it would be perverse to reject van Tuessenbrooek's conclusion, based as it was on a most careful study and rigorous analysis by someone who was a witness to the event, that at least the largest part of the decline in maternal mortality was due to antisepsis. Why was this the case in the Netherlands and not in England and Wales? The probable explanation is the high standard of trained midwives, and the better standard of obstetric education for doctors in the Netherlands. Beyond that, however, there may be a more fundamental reason. Schama has shown the long tradition—even obsession—of the Dutch with cleanliness, characterized by the endless scrubbing of house and home, of pavement and street.[27] With such a tradition it is likely that Dutch midwives would have taken more readily and applied in a more determined fashion than the English midwife new measures such as antisepsis in the war against sepsis with its connotations of dirt and disease; and the expectations of Dutch mothers may have reinforced that determination.

[27] S. Schama, *The Embarrassment of Riches: An Interpretation of Dutch Culture in the Golden Age* (New York, 1987).

26

Maternal Care and Maternal Mortality in Selected European Countries

The purpose of this chapter is to examine in some detail the levels and the trends in maternal mortality in certain European countries, and see if it is possible to explain the differences between them. We can start by looking at Table 2.5 (Chapter 2) which shows the range of maternal mortality in various countries during the inter-war period. If the MMR for England and Wales in 1920 is allotted the value of 100, then the rate for the USA was 177, but the rate for Norway was 79, for Sweden 59, and for the Netherlands and Denmark only 54. Only a small part of these differences could be attributed to differences in methodology. Thus America on the one hand and the Netherlands and Scandinavia on the other, lay at opposite ends of the spectrum of maternal mortality in the developed world, with England and Wales sitting somewhere in the middle. Why was it apparently so much safer to have a baby in north-west Europe than North America?

As we have seen, these countries not only recorded wide differences in maternal mortality, they developed very different systems of maternal care in the sense of the training and regulation of midwives, medical education, the development of obstetrics both as a branch of general practice and as a speciality, the provision of lying-in institutions and antenatal clinics, the publication of data on maternal health (without which sensible policies cannot be framed), and the extent to which maternal and child health departments within local and national government allocated resources of money, time, and energy to improve the lot of childbearing women. Thus the spectrum of mortality rates was accompanied by quite radically different systems of maternal care. Do the two mesh neatly together? Can we conclude that the mortality rates were a direct expression of the different systems of maternal care? It is an explanation of seductive simplicity, but is it the whole story?

GENETIC, SOCIO-ECONOMIC, AND CULTURAL DIFFERENCES AS THE EXPLANATION OF MATERNAL MORTALITY RATES

In 1926 a professor of midwifery in Denmark gave a simple answer to what he saw as a simple problem. It was all a question of the approach to the management of labour. 'It is easy to see what is the cause of the high maternal mortality in the United States', he said to Dorothy Mendenhall during her visit to Denmark, 'You interfere—operate too much. We give nature a chance.'[1] Mendenhall was inclined to agree. 'Hurry has become part of our [American] national temperament', she wrote, 'and has even affected the medical profession. When hurry in the confinement attendant meets fear in the mother the combination certainly militates against safe and sane obstetrics.'[2]

She illustrated her point by a description of a delivery in a Danish hospital:

It was a marvel to an American doctor to see a long and difficult delivery of a primipara by a pupil midwife without the use of any anaesthetic, the woman making absolutely no outcry until the actual expulsion of the head. The child was skillfully brought into the world vigorous and uninjured. No exhaustion, apparently, followed the delivery, for a few seconds after the birth of the baby the mother inquired in a loud voice, 'Is it a boy?' I wondered if the Scandinavian woman has more fortitude or less sensibility than her American descendant—or have we developed a fear complex in our mothers?[3]

Many, however, thought it was more than the question of non-interference in normal labours and the restrained use of anaesthesia. They spoke instead of 'racial' factors, which were in fact a hotchpotch of speculations on possible genetic, environmental, social, economic, and cultural differences. It was said that Dutch and Scandinavian women were members of a race which was genetically more suited to childbearing than the British or Americans. It was also said that Dutch and Scandinavian women were unusually healthy, partly because they lived in a clean non-industrial environment, and partly because there was less (or less obvious) poverty. British observers wrote in lyrical terms of the fresh complexions, the healthy build, and the sprightly step of Scandinavian women, the open air and the cleanliness of their towns. As a result, or so it was suggested, there was less rickets and less pelvic deformity than was found in Britain and the USA. They also emphasized the difference in temperament. Whether this was genetic, social, or cultural was a matter of indifference. Dutch and Scandinavian women were said to react quite differently to the pains of labour when compared with the British and American.[4]

Thus it was widely believed that Dutch and Scandinavian women were unusually healthy, stolid, sturdy, uncomplaining, and gifted with broad hips and a large pelvis through which their babies could slip with comparative ease. Here then were the reasons for the very low rates of intervention and the low

[1] D. Mendenhall, *Midwifery in Denmark*, Dept. of Labor, Children's Bureau (Washington, DC, 1929), 11.

[2] Ibid. 13.

[3] Ibid. 12.

[4] Ministry of Health, *Final Report of Departmental Committee on Maternal Mortality and Morbidity* (London, 1932), 48–89 ('The Maternity Services of the Netherlands, Denmark and Sweden').

maternal mortality of these countries. Mendenhall believed that 'Rickets is not prevalent in Scandinavia, and rachitic deformities of the pelvis are relatively uncommon.'[5] Young, Oxley, and Miles Phillips quoted the low rates of craniotomy and Caesarean section as evidence of a low incidence of contracted pelvis.[6]

All this is superficially persuasive. Rickets and pelvic deformity were probably less common in Oslo, Stockholm, Amsterdam, and Copenhagen than they were in Glasgow, Manchester, and Pittsburgh. It is unlikely, however, that this was an important factor in the difference in rates of maternal mortality. Where pelvic deformity was so gross that there was no possibility of a vaginal delivery, the only answer (apart from very early induction of labour) was craniotomy or Caesarean section. In lesser degrees of pelvic contraction, however, an optimistic or conservative Danish obstetrician might be prepared to wait, while a pessimistic and interventionist American one might intervene and perform craniotomy or Caesarean section at an early stage. In other words, the incidence of these operations is both a measure of the incidence of certain complications and a measure of the tendency to intervene or to wait.

Contracted pelvis, however, was not a major factor in international differences: if maternal deaths which may have been due to pelvic deformity—deaths following craniotomy, and deaths associated with Caesarean section, obstructed labour, or ruptured uterus (except where these deaths were linked to some other complication)—are removed from the lists of mortality, the international differences remain. But there is another more subtle argument which was discussed in Chapter 8: that minor degrees of pelvic contraction, too slight to prevent vaginal delivery and too slight to be detected or recorded as cases of pelvic deformity, may have been enough to cause long difficult labours with an increased risk of mortality. This is a hypothesis which seeks to implicate rickets and contracted pelvis in a much wider range of complications than the gross and obvious cases. There is evidence which suggests that this was not an important factor.

High maternal mortality could occur in communities where the incidence of rickets had always been extremely low. The classic example is New Zealand, the country, during the inter-war period, with the lowest recorded infant mortality rate in the world, yet the rate of maternal mortality in New Zealand was one of the highest. New Zealand, however, may have been a special and atypical case. But there is persuasive evidence which is based on people from Norway, Sweden, and Denmark who emigrated to the USA. The relevant data are shown in Table 26.1. When these people emigrated they took with them their genetic constitution, their broad pelvises, and their stoicism, but

[5] Mendenhall, *Midwifery in Denmark*, 13.
[6] *Ministry of Health, Final Report of Departmental Committee on Maternal Mortality and Morbidity*, 60–1.

TABLE 26.1 *Maternal Mortality Rates in Scandinavia and in Native White and Scandinavian-Born Immigrants in the USA in 1921*

Country	Puerperal causes		
	All puerperal causes	Puerperal septicaemia	Other puerperal causes
Denmark	20	13	7
Norway	23	8	15
Sweden	27	13	14
USA birth-registration area (1921)	68	27	41
Native white	66	26	39
Foreign-born Scandinavians	64	23	42

Source: R. M. Woodbury, quoted in Children's Bureau Publications, US Department of Labor, Washington, DC, Government Printing Office, D. R. Mendenhall, *Midwifery in Denmark* (1929), 4.

not of course their native country's systems of maternal care. When they gave birth in the USA, their MMRs were as high as their native white neighbours'. It was also shown that certain states such as Minnesota 'in which a larger proportion of the population is of Scandinavian stock' did not exhibit low levels of maternal mortality. 'All such comparisons tend to indicate a higher mortality in the United States than in the other countries with similar racial stocks.'[7]

This suggests that the predominant factor in determining the level of maternal mortality was the type and standard of maternal care. Explanations based on supposed 'racial factors' and differences in 'racial stocks', which were much in favour in some quarters in the eugenic 1920s, cannot explain either the whole or even a large part of the international range of MMRs.[8]

TRENDS IN EUROPEAN MATERNAL MORTALITY

So far we have considered international differences in the early decades of the twentieth century. In the nineteenth century the rank order of Western

---

[7] R. M. Woodbury, *Maternal Mortality* (Children's Bureau Publications, No. 152, Washington, DC, 1926), 57–63.

[8] It is not easy to obtain 19th-cent. time series of maternal mortality rates from many European countries, either from primary or secondary sources. When vital statistics were published in the mid- or late nineteenth century, maternal deaths were often excluded altogether or presented in an incomplete manner. As far as I can discover there are few secondary sources although some recent research has been carried out for earlier periods, e.g.: J.-P. Bardet, *et al.*, 'La Mortalité maternelle autrefois: Une étude comparé (de la France de l'ouest à l'Utah), *Annales de démographie historique* (1981), 31–48, and A. Bideau, 'Accouchement naturelle et accouchement à haut risque', *Annales de démographie historique* (1981), 49–66.

TABLE 26.2 *Maternal Mortality in Various Countries and Cities in 1875–1879 and in 1900–1904*

Country	Maternal mortality rates		
	1875–9	1900–4	1990–4 rates as a percentage of the 1875–9 rates
England and Wales	44	44	100
Scotland	47	48	102
Eire	66	58	88
Belgium	74	57	77
Denmark	50	38	76
The Netherlands	41	24	58
Sweden	89	23	26
Paris	74	35	47
Amsterdam	51	19	37

Source: R. M. Woodbury, *Maternal Mortality*, Children's Bureau Publications, No. 152 (Washington, DC, 1926); A. Macfarlane and M. Mugford, *Birth Counts: Statistics of Pregnancy and Childbirth*, 2 vols. (London, 1984); *Sveriges Officiella statistik* (Stockholm, 1911–50); U. Högberg, *Maternal Mortality in Sweden*, Umeå University Medical Dissertations, NS 156 (Umeå, 1985); *Statisteik van de sterfte naar den leeftid en de oorzaken van den dood*, Central bureau voor de statisteik (1911–38); *Summary of Causes of Death in the Kingdom of Denmark*, National Health Services of Denmark, (1949); *Annuaire statistique de la Belgique et du Congo Belgique*, Office central de statistique (Brussels, 1851–1951); *Official Statistics, Commonwealth of Australia*, Commonwealth Bureau of Censuses and Statistics: Population and Vital Statistics (Melbourne, 1907–50); *Infant, Fetal and Maternal Mortality*, National Center for Health Statistics, series 20 no. 3, US Department of Health Education and Welfare (Washington, DC, 1966).

countries was quite different. The rates of maternal mortality in the Scandinavian countries were at or above the level of Britain. During 1875 to 1879 the MMR in England and Wales (in round figures) was about 44, in Scotland 47, and in the Netherlands about 41; but in Sweden it was in the high 80s. Clearly some dramatic changes took place between the 1870s and 1910 and the separation of the sheep from the goats, so to speak, took place in the short period from 1880 to 1900, the period when antisepsis was introduced. This is shown in Table 26.2 which measures the change in maternal mortality between the five-year period just before antisepsis, 1875–9, and the five-year period 1900–4, when the importance of antisepsis and asepsis was fully established.

Table 26.2 speaks for itself and suggests Britain was less successful after 1880 in the application of the techniques of antisepsis and asepsis than continental countries. This was certainly believed at the time and the blame was laid fairly and squarely on the untrained midwives of Britain and the

TABLE 26.3 *Deaths Due to Puerperal Fever as a Percentage of Total Maternal Mortality in Various Countries, 1920–1924*

Country	Maternal mortality rate	Percentage of deaths due to puerperal sepsis	Percentage of deaths due to accidents of childbirth
The Netherlands	24.0	33	67
Sweden	24.6	46	54
Denmark	27.1	37	63
England and Wales	39.0	36	64
Australia	49.6	34	66
New Zealand	53.4	35	65
Belgium	57.6	46	54
USA	68.9	37	63

Source: R. M. Woodbury, *Maternal Mortality*, Children's Bureau Publications, No. 152 (Washington, DC, 1926); A. Macfarlane and M. Mugford, *Birth Counts: Statistics of Pregnancy and Childbirth*, 2 vols. (London, 1984); *Sveriges Officiella statistik* (Stockholm, 1911–50); U. Högberg, *Maternal Mortality in Sweden*, Umeå University Medical Dissertations, NS 156 (Umeå, 1985); *Statisteik van de sterfte naar den leeftid en de oorzaken van den dood*, Central bureau voor de statisteik (1911–38); *Summary of Causes of Death in the Kingdom of Denmark*, National Health Services of Denmark, (1949); *Annuaire statistique de la Belgique et du Congo Belgique*, Office central de statistique (Brussels, 1851–1951); *Official Statistics, Commonwealth of Australia*, Commonwealth Bureau of Censuses and Statistics: Population and Vital Statistics (Melbourne, 1907–50); *Infant, Fetal and Maternal Mortality*, National Center for Health Statistics, series 20 no. 3, US Department of Health Education and Welfare (Washington, DC, 1966).

general practitioners whose reprehensible indifference to antisepsis in the period from 1880 to the early 1900s was described in Chapter 13.[9] Table 26.2 suggests that countries like Sweden, which showed the greatest fall in maternal mortality after 1880, would have done so by reducing their rates of death due to puerperal sepsis while deaths from other causes remained relatively unaffected. Therefore, deaths from sepsis expressed as a percentage of all maternal deaths should have been lower after 1900 in Scandinavia than in countries such as England and Wales, Scotland, and Australia which failed to reduce their maternal mortality.

There is some supporting evidence for this assumption. In Amsterdam, for example, 43 per cent of the deaths during 1875 to 1879 were due to puerperal septicaemia, but in 1900–4 only 19 per cent (see Appendix Table 15). When it comes to countries as a whole, however, our expectations are not confirmed. Countries with low rates of maternal mortality from all causes did not show a consistent low percentage of deaths from sepsis. This can be seen in Table 26.3 and Appendix Table 29. There was an *absolute* fall in the MMR from

[9] W. Williams, *Deaths in Childbed* (London, 1904).

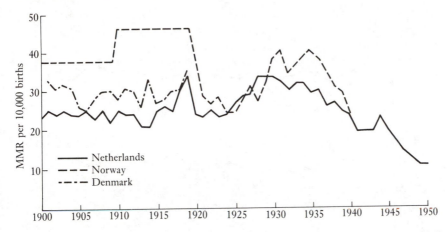

FIG. 26.1 The Netherlands 1900–1950, Norway 1900–1920, and Denmark 1900–1940.
Trends in annual rates of Maternal Mortality
Source: Appendix Tables 8 and 9. For Norway, R. M. Woodbury, *Maternal Mortality*, Children's
Bureau Publications, No. 152 (Washington, DC, 1926), 153.
Denmark, data for towns only 1900–9; data for whole country 1910–19 and annual rates for the
whole country thereafter.

puerperal sepsis in countries such as Sweden, but no fall in septic deaths as a
proportion of maternal deaths from all causes. This was an unexpected
finding. The probable explanation (for want of a better one) is that where
there was a marked decline in deaths from sepsis due to antisepsis, there was
an accompanying decline in deaths from non-septic causes, due to better
training and better care.

Before the First World War, then, the picture is fairly clear. In the nineteenth century the trend in maternal mortality in European countries (including Britain in this instance) was, as far as we know, uniformly high and
'spikey'. There were wide annual variations in the number of maternal deaths,
almost certainly because of alterations in the virulence and/or prevalence of
the streptococcus. By 1910 that 'spikeyness' had been lost. Various countries
had responded in a widely different manner to the introduction of antisepsis,
rearranging themselves in a rank order which remained much the same, with
their trends running more or less on parallel lines until the mid-1930s. This is
most clearly seen in Figure 9.1 (Chapter 9). But the curious feature is the
upward turn in the slope after 1910 (Figure 26.1). Why did it occur during a
period when everyone expected maternal mortality to decline?

To answer this question it is helpful to examine the trends in maternal
deaths according to cause by dividing them into three categories: non-septic
deaths, and deaths due to sepsis divided into abortion and post-partum sepsis.
Figure 26.2 shows the trend in the first of these three—deaths from causes
other than sepsis. In Sweden, Scotland, and England and Wales, the trend is

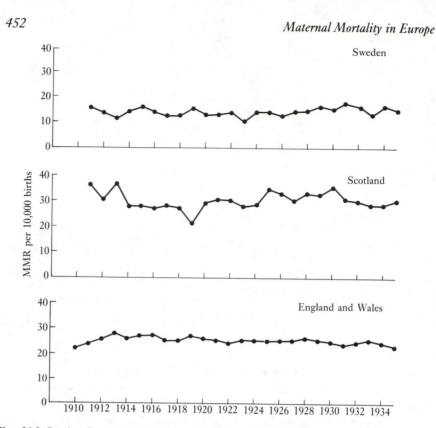

FIG. 26.2 Sweden, England and Wales, and Scotland, 1910–1934. The trend in direct maternal deaths per 10,000 births due to causes other than puerperal sepsis and abortion
Source: Sweden: *Sveriges Officiella Statistik* (Stockholm, various years); Scotland: P. L. McKinlay, *Maternal Mortality in Scotland, 1911–1945* (HMSO, Edinburgh, 1947); England and Wales: Appendix Table 1.

close to a straight line and there is no evidence of either a rise or a fall between 1910 and 1934. This in itself is interesting. Deaths in this category included deaths from toxaemia and haemorrhage. Many such deaths were considered at the time to be preventable by better antenatal care and better care at the delivery.

In Britain the first antenatal clinics provided by local authorities were started in London in 1915. By 1918 there were 120 clinics in England and Wales and by 1938 there were 1,795. This development was accompanied by an increase in the number of maternity hospital beds.[10] There was a large investment in maternal services between the First and the Second World Wars. What elements of maternal mortality could this investment have been expected to reduce? Clearly, there was little if anything that public health

[10] R. M. Titmuss, *Birth, Poverty and Wealth: A Study of Infant Mortality* (London, 1943), 33–4.

TABLE 26.4 *Maternal Mortality Rates after the Exclusion of Deaths from Abortion in Various Countries during the Inter-War Period*

	Total maternal mortality rate including deaths due to abortion	Maternal mortality rate due to abortion	Maternal mortality rate excluding deaths due to abortion
Sweden (1931–5)	32.6	7.5[a]	25.1
Netherlands (1925–9)	29.7	2.2[b]	27.5
	29.7	5.5[c]	24.2
England and Wales (1930)	42.2	6.3[d]	35.9
Scotland (1931–5)	61.3	5.1[d]	56.2
Eire (1938)	41.1	3.3[d]	37.8

[a] Septic abortion only
[b] Non-septic abortion only
[c] Estimate of total abortion based on indirect evidence that at least one third of deaths due to sepsis were due to septic abortion.
[d] Total abortion—septic and non-septic.

Source: See text.

departments, doctors, or midwives, could do to stem the rising tide of abortion.[11] Equally, there was nothing they could do to affect the virulence of the streptococcus, even if they had recognized it was increasing.[12] It is therefore not surprising that the inter-war rise in maternal mortality was associated with septic causes.

There is no doubt about the rise in abortion; we discussed this in previous chapters, and the extent of abortion as a cause of maternal mortality in certain countries during the inter-war period can be seen in Table 26.4. Equally, there is little doubt that in most Western countries the death rate from full-term sepsis also rose. It was seen most clearly in Scotland (see Chapter 15) where deaths from post-partum and post-abortive sepsis were shown separately from the beginning of this century. It is most unlikely that a rise in deaths from post-partum sepsis can be attributed to worsening standards of care and a falling standard of antisepsis. All the evidence points in the other direction. In Britain, older doctors whose student days preceded antisepsis, were dying off; and untrained midwives were continually being replaced by trained and supervised ones. It is difficult to suggest any other reason for the rise in deaths from full-term sepsis than increasing streptococcal virulence.

[11] Except of course to make birth-control methods widely available and the resistance to this measure during this period is well known.
[12] In fact, the downward trend in deaths from scarlet fever suggested streptococcal virulence was decreasing: a red herring that is discussed in Appendix 5.

Thus the rising trend in maternal mortality from 1910 to the mid-1930s, which was seen in Britain and on the Continent, was due first of all to a rise in deaths from septic abortion and next to a rise in deaths post-partum sepsis which was probably associated with an increase in streptococcal virulence. The absence of a fall in maternal deaths from non-septic causes, in spite of the growth of maternal welfare in the 1920s and 1930s, is surprising. It shows, perhaps, that in the absence of certain factors which only became available after 1935—in particular antibiotics, widely available blood transfusion, and better systems of integrated maternal care and obstetric education—the problem of maternal mortality in the inter-war period was greater and more resistant to the measures which were introduced than anyone realized at the time.

Once the great decline in maternal mortality had begun in the mid-1930s, the trends in maternal mortality would probably have converged rapidly—as indeed they had by 1960. But the Second World War intervened. The effect of the war on maternal (and infant) mortality is instructive; it forms the last section of this chapter.

THE EFFECTS OF THE SECOND WORLD WAR

As far as mothers and children are concerned, war can lead to deprivation, danger, and distress, sometimes slight, sometimes overwhelming. The question I want to consider is the effect of the Second World War on mothers and infants in the European countries directly involved in the war.[13]

During the war, food supplies in the countries occupied by the German forces were often sparse but generally they were nutritionally adequate. The dreadful hunger-winter of certain parts of the Netherlands to which we return later was a conspicuous exception. Medical services were often impaired by the imprisonment or execution of doctors, and certain medical supplies and drugs (including the sulphonamides) were in short supply, partly through their being commandeered by the Germans. Some hospitals and houses were destroyed and some mothers were delivered in prison camps, while in hiding, or in war-damaged surroundings while suffering the continual stress and anxiety of occupation. The extent to which these and other deprivations occurred in different parts of Europe at different periods of the war is difficult to ascertain; but there is no doubt that for women, infants, children, and indeed the whole population of the occupied countries, the war provided a special form of physical and psychological stress and deprivation.

In Britain, although there was a shortage of food, rationing and special supplements for expectant mothers not only prevented dietary deficiency in

---

[13] In this section I have included data on infant as well as maternal mortality because the contrast between the two is important. The general question of the relationship between maternal and infant mortality is discussed in Chapter 28.

mothers and infants, but may well have improved the quality of the diet as well as providing an adequate quantity. It has often been said that rationing combined with full employment increased the entitlement of the poor to adequate quantities of food as well as providing a balanced diet (see the last section of Chapter 15). It is true that in Britain as in occupied Europe there was a shortage of doctors through military service. Likewise many houses and some hospitals (mostly in London) were damaged or destroyed. On the other hand the war led to huge improvements in maternal welfare which more than compensated for the loss of doctors to the armed services; and morale in wartime Britain was high. It is therefore not surprising that maternal and child health was not adversely affected. The downward trend in maternal and infant mortality continued through the war; indeed, from an inspection of the trends shown in Figure 26.3 one would never guess a war had taken place.[14]

In the occupied countries, however, there was a very different pattern. Infant mortality rose and maternal mortality, which until 1939/40 had been falling, levelled out until the end of the war (Figure 26.4). The latter process can also be seen in Figure 26.5 where deaths from puerperal sepsis in France and England and Wales between 1925 and 1950 are contrasted. They fell in unison from 1935 to 1939; thereafter the fall continued in England and Wales while deaths in France levelled out until the end of the war showing a return to a rapid decline after 1945. There is some evidence that supplies of the sulphonamides were drastically restricted in France during the war.[15] A similar levelling out of maternal mortality through the war years in Belgium can be seen in Appendix Table 10, but the most striking demonstration of the effects of the war on maternal and infant mortality is found in the Netherlands.

From 1939 to the middle of 1944, infant mortality in the Netherlands had

---

[14] The only exception was a slight rise in infant mortality in 1940 and 1941, but the rate had fallen back to the 1939 levels by 1942 in England and Wales and by 1943 in Scotland. During the Second World War, however, there was a steep decline in stillbirths. The reasons for this are not clear. J. M. Winter, in his chapter 'Public Health and the Extension of Life Expectancy in England and Wales, 1901–1960', in M. Keynes, D. Coleman, and N. Dimsdale (eds.), *The Political Economy of Health and Welfare* (London, 1988), proposes an explanation based on a thesis put forward by Sir Dugald Baird that periods of social and economic deprivation produce female babies who, a generation later, give birth and suffer a high perinatal and neonatal loss. Conversely, women who were born in periods of relative prosperity might show a low rate of perinatal loss. Thus Winter seems to imply that the decline in stillbirths in the 1940s had its roots in the favourable conditions for mothers and infants in and after the First World War. For Baird's thesis see his 'Environment and Reproduction', *British Journal of Obstetrics and Gynaecology*, 87 (1980), 1057–67. An early example of this concept in terms of general death rates as well as infant mortality can be found in W. O. Kermack, A. G. McKendrick, and P. L. McKinlay, 'Death Rates in Great Britain and Sweden', *Lancet* (1934), ii. 698–703.

[15] Personal communication, Roussel Laboratories Ltd., 1986. In France, Roussel produced the sulphonamide 'Rubiazol'. Successful clinical trials of this drug were published in 1935, the year before the corresponding trials in England. During the war supplies of this drug which had been used extensively between 1935 and 1939 were curtailed.

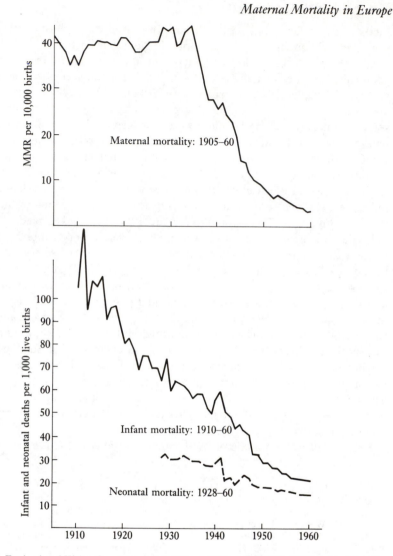

FIG. 26.3 England and Wales. Secular trends in Maternal Mortality 1905–1960; Infant Mortality 1910–1960 and Neonatal Mortality 1928–1960
Source: A. Macfarlane and M. Mugford, *Birth Counts*, ii.

risen, and maternal mortality had levelled out. At the time of the battle of Arnhem, railway men in the Western Netherlands, stung by accusations of collaboration, demonstrated their willingness to resist by going on strike. They did so in anticipation of an early allied victory. When the battle of Arnhem failed, the plan to liberate the Netherlands was delayed. In the early autumn of 1944, the Germans, in revenge, imposed a total blockade on the area that

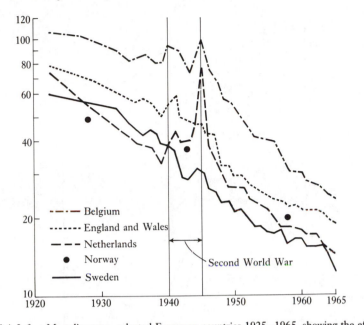

FIG. 26.4 Infant Mortality rates, selected European countries 1925–1965, showing the effects of
the Second World War
Source: *Infant Loss in the Netherlands*, Vital and Health Statistics, ser. 3, no. 11, US Department of
Health, Education and Welfare (Washington, DC, 1968).

took part in the strike. This led to the 'hunger-winter' of 1944/5, marked by
intense cold, lack of fuel, and a fall in food supplies to starvation levels.
People were reduced to cooking with engine oil, eating tulip bulbs, and
burning any wood they could get their hands on, including furniture. Many
died of starvation and there were numerous cases of famine oedema. The
period of starvation came to an abrupt end with the dropping of food supplies
by the Royal Air Force in the spring of 1945.

During this period, infant mortality rose to a very high level, neonatal
mortality rose slightly, early-neonatal mortality was scarcely affected, and
maternal mortality, which had been falling from 1935 to 1940, levelled out
and did not decline again until the end of the war (Figure 26.6).[16] The Dutch
hunger-winter was a unique famine in that exact records were kept of the
timing and extent of deprivation of various types of nutrient and of the effects
on the population both short- and long-term. The records suggest that in
severe progressive famine post-neonatal mortality is a very sensitive indicator

[16] *Infant Loss in the Netherlands*, US Dept. of Health, Education and Welfare, National Center
for Health Statistics, ser. 3, no. 11 (Washington, DC, 1968).

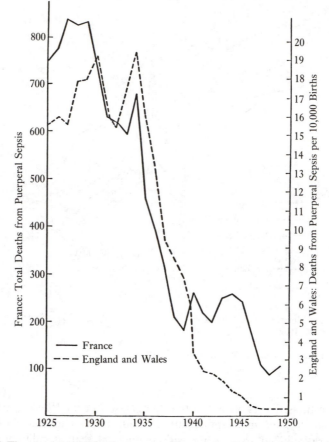

FIG. 26.5 The trend in deaths from puerperal sepsis in France and England and Wales, 1925–1950, showing the effects of the Second World War
Source: Registrar General for England and Wales, *Annual Statistical Reviews*; France: J. Varlin and F. Meslé, *Les Causes des décès en France de 1925–1949* (Institut national d'études démographiques, 1950).

of nutritional deprivation, while neonatal and maternal mortality are relatively insensitive. This episode showed the extraordinary resilience of pregnancy and childbirth under conditions of severe starvation; it also showed, against expectations, that the children who survived the famine showed few if any long-term signs of physical or psychological damage. Recent work, however, has uncovered a long-term effect on reproductive efficiency.

When female babies who were *in utero* during the famine grew up, married, and became mothers, their infants were found to have been affected by the famine; their birth weights were lower than average and so were certain other measurements such as crown–heel length and the Quetelet index, and the

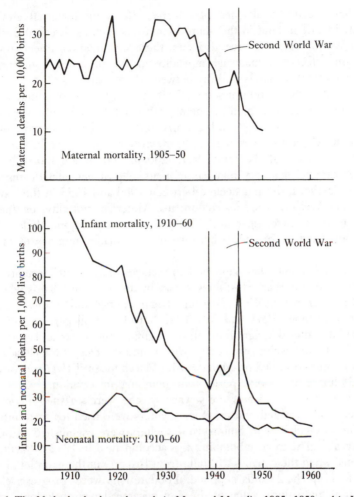

FIG. 26.6 The Netherlands. Annual trends in Maternal Mortality 1905–1950 and in Infant and Neonatal Mortality 1910–1960, showing the effects of the Second World War
Source: Appendix Table 9 and *1899–1979 tachtig jaren statistiek in tijdreeksen*, Centraal bureau voor de statistiek (The Hague, 1979).

placental weights were lower. The careful and detailed investigation which demonstrated these features, together with the previous work of Baird, shows that the effects of nutritional deprivation can stretch twenty years or more to the next generation.[17]

[17] Quetelet's index is height to weight. The work referred to here is L. H. Lumey, 'Obstetric Performance of Women after *in Utero* Exposure to the Dutch Famine', Ph.D. thesis (Columbia University, 1988). For a more extensive discussion of these points, see I. Loudon, 'On Maternal and Infant Mortality', *Social History of Medicine*, 4 (1991), 44–5.

We have seen the absence of adverse effects on maternal and infant mortality in Britain (and in the neutral countries such as Sweden) during the Second World War. We have also seen there were marked effects on infant and slight effects on maternal mortality in the occupied countries. The experience of Malta stands midway between these extremes.[18]

Malta, with a population of some 270,000 in 1941, was of course a British colony. It was never occupied by enemy forces but it came under siege during the war. From the late nineteenth century to the mid-1930s the level of infant mortality in Malta was extremely high, the average rate being 260 deaths per 1,000 live births, and the range from 200 to 300. Infant mortality, which consisted largely of a very high component of post-neonatal deaths due to infantile diarrhoea, did not decline between 1900 and 1935 in the way it did in all other Western European countries. Maternal mortality, on the other hand, was, on average, close to the level seen in England and Wales. Annual values fluctuated more widely because of the smaller number of births in Malta.

Figure 26.7 shows what happened to maternal and infant mortality during the Second World War. Hostilities began in the Maltese Islands when Italy entered the war in June 1940. Bombing began at once and rapidly intensified. Between December 1941 and July 1942 'attacks on all parts of the Island continued day after day right through the nights; while on some days the alerts persisted without respite very nearly twice round the face of the clock'.[19] The weight of bombs dropped on Malta during March to April 1942 was twice that dropped during the worst periods of bombing in London.[20] Towns and villages were destroyed, water and sewage systems were smashed. People lived in shelters and damaged houses. Rock-shelters were used for maternity cases and 'maternity cubicles in bomb-proof shelters were established in many of the villages'.[21] The intense bombing was accompanied in 1942 by 'acute siege conditions' when the convoys to Malta from Britain ran the gauntlet of enemy attacks to keep the Islands supplied. Food rations were 'progressively curtailed' until 'the calorie value of the diet became dangerously low . . .'. The siege, which lasted some 900 days, brought the population to the very edge of starvation. It ended abruptly in December 1942 with the retreat of Rommel in North Africa.[22]

During the war, Malta's emergency medical services seem to have worked

[18] The main sources for this account of Malta are the *Annual Report of the Maltese Islands*, annually, 1890–1972 (Malta, Government Printing Office); Paul Cassar, *Medical History of Malta* (London, 1964); C. Savona-Ventura, 'Reproductive Performance on the Maltese Islands during the Second World War', *Medical History*, 34/2 (1990), 164–77. I am grateful to Dr Savona-Ventura for providing me with additional details on maternal mortality in Malta.
[19] Savona-Ventura, 'Reproductive Performance'.
[20] *Annual Report of the Maltese Islands for 1941* (Malta, Government Printing Office, 1942), p. i.
[21] *Annual Report of the Maltese Islands for 1942* (Malta, Government Printing Office, 1943), p. i.
[22] Ibid.

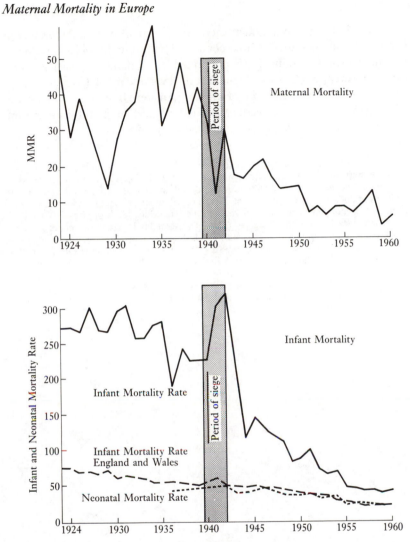

FIG. 26.7 The Maltese Islands. Maternal, Infant, and Neonatal Mortality, 1924–1960. Showing the effects of the siege during the Second World War. Infant Mortality for England and Wales shown for comparison.
Source: *Annual Reports of the Maltese Islands* (Malta, Government Printing Office, for various years).

well. Figure 9.1 shows that although there was a peak of maternal mortality in 1942 of twenty-one maternal deaths compared with nine in 1941, the downward trend which began in 1935 continued throughout the siege. Infant mortality, however, rose to the highest level ever recorded (345 per 1,000 births) in 1942.[23] After the end of the war, maternal mortality in all the occupied countries we have considered fell steeply, catching up by about 1960 with the more fortunate countries which had escaped invasion.

[23] The analysis of infant mortality by month is especially striking. Like all countries with high post-neonatal mortality due to infantile diarrhoea, there had always been summer peaks of mortality. Before the war, infant mortality in Malta during the months of June, July, and August reached levels of 300–400 falling to levels of about 120–30 in January and February. During the siege years, infant mortality in the summer reached the astonishing levels of 600–700. By 1943, however, monthly levels began to fall steeply. The infant mortality rate in the spring of 1944 was around 70, rising in the summer to between 140 and 180; high enough, but well below pre-war levels. *Annual Report of the Maltese Islands for 1943* (Malta, Government Printing Office, 1944), p. vi (table). By 1943, when the siege was lifted but two years before the war had ended, infant mortality fell steeply. The fall is attributed to the rebuilding of water and sewage systems and new housing. By 1949 the annual rate of infant mortality had fallen below 100 for the first time, a level reached in England and Wales around 1912, and the decline continued.

27
Australia and New Zealand

AUSTRALIA

The first major survey of health in Australia, carried out by the 'Committee concerning causes of death and invalidity in the Commonwealth', was published in 1916.[1] It identified a number of important health problems. At the head of the list, however, came the three items which had the most worrying implications for an underpopulated country: the high rate of infant mortality, the falling birth rate, and the high rate of 'puerperal mortalities'.

The lowest infant mortality rate recorded in Australia by 1916 was 68.5. Although this compared favourably with England and Wales where it was 91, it compared unfavourably with their nearest neighbour, New Zealand, where infant mortality in 1914 was only 51.4. The committee, while deploring high infant mortality and the low birth rate, saw no easy answers to either problem. With maternal mortality, however, they saw at once that it was a scandal and said so in no uncertain terms. 'Puerperal septicaemia', they said, 'is probably the gravest reproach which any civilised nation can by its own negligence offer to itself.'[2] Note the word negligence, for they went even further when they said:

The principal causes of death are five in number: 1. Accidents of pregnancy. 2. Puerperal haemorrhage. 3. Other accidents of labour. 4. Puerperal septicaemia. 5. Puerperal albuminuria and convulsions. The results obtained in hospitals or where skilled attention is available show that these last four causes of death can be *almost entirely eliminated* [my italicsl]. Had this result been obtained in the Commonwealth in 1915, instead of 576 deaths during labour there would have been only 154 deaths.[3]

There were and still are close links between medicine in Australia and Britain so that the extent to which maternal care and the problems of maternal

---

[1] Parliament of the Commonwealth of Australia, Department of Trades and Customs, *Committee concerning causes of death and invalidity in the Commonwealth*, *Preliminary Report*, Government Printer for the State of Victoria (1916), No. 295. F5541; *Report on Maternal Mortality in Childbirth* (Melbourne, 1917), C. 7867. The chairman of the committee was an MP, James Mathews. The other members were three doctors: H. B. Allen, J. H. L. Cumpston, and A. Jeffreys.

[2] *Report on Maternal Mortality*, 9.

[3] Ibid. 10. 'Accidents of pregnancy' included abortion.

mortality in Australia resembled Britain is not surprising. For instance, in the early days of settlement a benevolent association established a lying-in ward in Sydney. The consequent mortality was just as horrific as it was in Britain and the Governor in the 1870s immediately sent to England for a 'lady trained in nursing by Florence Nightingale. Accordingly the first matron, Miss Osburn, arrived with five sisters.' The mortality rate was diminished but it still would have been better 'if the poor mothers had been left alone to bear their children under the gum trees or by the banks of the Tank Stream'.[4]

One of the earliest reports on maternal mortality in Australia in 1887 showed that the death rate was higher in Australia than England and Wales. In common with so many British doctors the author placed the blame at the door of the 'midwives or nurses, often possessed of little or no training or knowledge'. He also believed that the under-reporting of maternal deaths was even worse (and thus the gap in mortality rates even larger) than it was in England and Wales.[5]

Plans to regulate and train midwives were modelled on the English Midwives Act of 1902, but varied from state to state. The Midwives Act of Victoria, introduced in 1915, was 'practically identical' to the English Act and included a concession to untrained midwives who had been in practice for two years prior to the Act; they were allowed to register up to the end of 1917. Western Australia had similar regulations, closely modelled on the English Act. In New South Wales, midwives who had been trained in a hospital for a year could register, but there was no obligation for midwives to be registered, and a similar system operated in Queensland. In Tasmania, midwives only had to attend a course of lectures to be registered; practical instruction was not compulsory. In South Australia there was (in 1916) no Act governing the registration or practice of midwives.[6] In short, because midwife training and regulation was devolved to states, the system was a bit more of a mess than it was even in England and Wales, and a very long way from the orderly systems of the Netherlands and Scandinavia.

The trend in maternal mortality followed the English trend remarkably closely. Between the late nineteenth century and the early twentieth maternal mortality declined slightly, reaching the lowest level of 48.3 per 10,000 births in 1912. Then it climbed steadily to 59.8 per 10,000 births by 1936. From 1937 maternal mortality fell steeply in common with other Western countries. This can be seen in Figure 27.1

The organization of maternal care as a whole was close to the English model. General practitioners and midwives competed for cases. Midwives

---

[4] Constance D'Arcy, 'The Problem of Maternal Welfare' (The Anne Machenzie oration), *Medical Journal of Australia* (1935), i. 390.

[5] James Jamieson, 'Childbirth Mortality in the Australian Colonies'. *Australian Medical Journal*, NS 9 (1887), 842–8.

[6] *Report on Maternal Mortality in Childbirth*, 12–13.

FIG. 27.1 Australia and New Zealand. 1905–1950, Annual trends in Maternal Mortality
Source: Official Statistics, Commonwealth of Australia and Government of New Zealand.

tended to deliver more of the poor and general practitioners more of the middle classes. Untrained midwives persisted alongside trained ones through the first thirty years of this century. The main differences were that in Australia a larger proportion of deliveries were carried out by doctors than midwives in the inter-war period (see Table 27.2), and there was a larger

TABLE 27.1 *Cause of Death of Females Aged 15–49*
in Australia in 1923

Cause	Number
Tuberculosis all forms	1,138
Puerperal state	691
Cancer: all forms	526
Diseases of heart and blood vessels	473
Cerebral haemorrhage, thrombosis, and embolism	158
Total deaths from all causes	5,839

Source: E. S. Morris, 'An Essay on the Causes and Prevention of Maternal Morbidity and Mortality', *Medical Journal of Australia* (1925), ii. 301–39.

proportion of hospital deliveries. Maternity hospitals and nursing homes were concentrated in the most highly populated areas and staffed by a mixture of consultant obstetricians and general practitioners.

An inquiry in Victoria in 1925 found that 67 per cent of the patients in the state were delivered in hospital, 33 per cent at home. 194 practitioners said they preferred attending patients in hospital. Only eight preferred home confinements. In answer to a question concerning the proportion of women delivered by midwives in their practices, twelve general practitioners said nil, forty-three said less than 5 per cent, twenty-five said between 5 per cent and 10 per cent, and twenty-five said between 10 per cent and 30 per cent. This was a much lower level of midwife deliveries than England and Wales in the same period.[7]

The high proportion of hospital and nursing home deliveries was largely the result of a rapid increase following the introduction of the Maternity Allowance Act in 1913. This allowed a flat-rate payment of £5 on evidence of childbirth, with no prior contributions by the patient. By 1920 £4.3 million had been paid in maternity bonuses 'to tempt the wives of Australia to become mothers'. The medical profession thought it was money wasted. Some, with a logic which escapes me, said it perpetuated the untrained midwife; others that the money would have been better spent on antenatal and hospital provision to reduce maternal mortality.[8]

Although there were differences between England and Australia in the organization of maternal care, a general practitioner from a provincial town in England could emigrate to Victoria or New South Wales in the 1920s and notice very little difference in medical practice. He would still need to undertake midwifery if he was going to succeed but he would find there was rather less competition from midwives, and rather greater opportunities for delivering his patient in a small hospital or nursing home. He would, however, find the manner and the standard of midwifery practice was very much what he had become accustomed to in 'the mother country'.

AUSTRALIA: STANDARDS OF MATERNAL CARE IN THE INTER-WAR PERIOD

In 1925 E. Sydney Morris, the Senior Medical Officer of the Department of Public Health, New South Wales, published a notable report on maternal

[7] 'Report of the Obstetric Inquiry Committee of the Victorian Branch of the British Medical Association', *Medical Journal of Australia* (1925), 295–7. There was, however, some regional variation. In Melbourne and its suburbs, hospital deliveries varied from 20 per cent to 80 per cent depending on the district. The largest maternity hospital, 'The Women's Hospital' (a teaching hospital with high standards) had 132 beds and delivered over 2,500 women a year. Most hospitals were much smaller. R. Marshall Allen, 'Interim Report on Maternal Mortality and Morbidity in Victoria', ibid. (1927), i. 1–10.

[8] Leading articles: 'The Maternity Bonus', *Medical Journal of Australia* (1919), ii. 554–5, and 'The Five-Pound Bonus', ibid. (1920), i. 509–10.

TABLE 27.2 *Maternal Mortality Rates, Deliveries and Population Density in Australia in 1923*

	Maternal mortality rate			Percentage delivered by doctors	Density of population (persons per square mile)
	1908–15	1916–23	percentage change		
New South Wales	51.8	51.2	− 1.1	73	6.75
Victoria	44.6	44.7	+ 0.2	87	17.36
Queensland	51.9	53.8	+ 3.6	67	1.12
South Australia	48.5	49.9	+ 2.9	90	1.29
Western Australia	45.7	47.7	+ 4.4	71	0.34
Tasmania	45.8	43.8	− 4.4	71	8.13
Commonwealth	47.9	49.3	+ 2.9	77	1.82

Source: E. S. Morris, 'An Essay on the Causes and Prevention of Maternal Morbidity and Mortality', *Medical Journal of Australia* (1925), ii. 301–39.

mortality in Australia in which many of his findings and recommendations were remarkably close to those which appeared in the Ministry of Health's reports for England and Wales during the inter-war period.[9]

In Australia in the 1920s, some 700 mothers died annually from maternal causes, leaving nearly 2,000 children motherless. The distribution of maternal deaths by cause was similar to that in Britain and the USA, and he noted that amongst women aged 15–49, maternal deaths ranked second only to deaths from tuberculosis (Tables 27.1, 27.2 and 27.3).[10]

There was relatively little regional variation. Maternal mortality rates in the states varied from 43.8 in Tasmania to 53.8 in Queensland, rates which were significantly higher than in England and Wales but similar to the levels in Scotland. In the states there was no correlation between mortality rates and density of population, and no evidence that states with the highest proportion of deliveries by doctors had a significantly lower (or for that matter higher) rate of maternal mortality (Table 27.2).

As in Britain and the USA the most disturbing finding was that maternal mortality was rising. Morris was clear that this could not be attributed to worsening social and economic circumstances, or to increasing primiparity. In

[9] E. Sydney Morris, 'An Essay on the Causes and Prevention of Maternal Morbidity and Mortality', *Medical Journal of Australia* (1925), ii. 301–45. This essay won the prize of the Melbourne Committee for Postgraduate Work.

[10] Ibid. 301.

TABLE 27.3 *Distribution of Maternal Deaths by Cause, Total Births, and Maternal Mortality Rate from All Causes, Commonwealth of Australia, 1920–1923 and New South Wales, 1928–1933*

Cause of death	Number of deaths	Percentage of total
Australia, 1921–3		
All causes	2,638[a]	100
Puerperal septicaemia	887	33.6
Puerperal albuminuria and eclampsia	502	19.0
Accidents of pregnancy (mostly abortion)	383	14.5
Puerperal haemorrhage	353	13.4
Other accidents of childbirth	289	11.0
Phlegmasia alba dolens and sudden death	213	8.0
Total births	545,322	
New South Wales, 1928–33		
All causes	1,719[b]	100.0
Post-partum sepsis	255	14.8
Post-abortive sepsis	213	12.4
Illegal operations	238	13.8
Total sepsis and illegal operations	(706)	(41.0)
Puerperal albuminuria and eclampsia	345	20.1
Accidents of pregnancy (mostly abortion)	144	8.4
Puerperal haemorrhage	222	12.9
Other casualties of childbirth	172	10.0
Phlegmasia alba dolens and sudden death	130	7.6

[a] Maternal mortality per 10,000 births from all causes = 48.3.
[b] Maternal mortality rate from all causes including illegal operations = 55.7.

Source: E. S. Morris, 'An Essay on the Causes and Prevention of Maternal Morbidity and Mortality', *Medical Journal of Australia* (1925), ii. 301–45; Constance D'Arcy, 'The Problem of Maternal Welfare', *Medical Journal of Australia* (1935), i. 385–99.

1912 the proportion of primiparae was 27.9 per cent, in 1923, 29 per cent—too small an increase to have a significant effect.[11]

For many years, it had been the habit of doctors in Australia to blame the midwives for the high rate of maternal mortality. Morris showed the evidence pointed, if anything, in the opposite direction.[12] He attributed the high

[11] Ibid. 305
[12] Ibid. 310, 314.

mortality in deliveries by doctors to a poor standard of practice in which the desultory application of antiseptic principles was combined with widespread and unnecessary interference and a willingness by the inexperienced to undertake difficult operative procedures. Morris complained:

In the practice of midwifery there seems to be an unwritten law that every medical man who considers himself competent, should be prepared to manage successfully [and] generally single handed each and every serious obstetric operation, compared with which from the point of view of danger the majority of surgical operations dwindle into insignificance.[13]

Although the large maternity hospitals tended to deal with a selected population of high-risk cases and emergency admissions, their forceps rates ranged between 3 per cent and 6 per cent. The forceps rate in home deliveries by general practitioners, on the other hand, varied between 10 per cent and an astonishing 80 per cent. General practitioners justified such gross interference by the excuse of 'pressure of work', or pressure from relatives to 'do something' and end the sufferings of the woman in labour. Or they fell back on that explanation we met in previous chapters: that modern women were weakened by civilization and could not be expected to deliver themselves unaided.[14]

Unnecessary interference was certainly a factor in the incidence of puerperal fever, but the incidence is impossible to estimate because of the same problem encountered in Britain: notifications of puerperal sepsis were so inaccurate as to be useless. It was common to find that deaths either exceeded notifications or were virtually the same, giving impossible fatality rates close to or over 100 per cent. Thus in Victoria from 1921 to 1925 there were 237 notifications of puerperal sepsis and 213 deaths.[15] Rates of infection were usually low in the large hospitals, but here too disasters could occur when nurses were sent for duty on obstetric wards straight from gynaecological or surgical wards. An explosive and disastrous outbreak of puerperal sepsis was traced to just such a

[13] Ibid. 319. See also Ralph Worrall, 'Some Common Faults in Midwifery Practice', *Medical Journal of Australia* (1918), ii. 386–8, who listed as common faults in general practice the application of forceps with an undilated cervix, bad management of occipito-posterior presentations (with the memorable statement by one general practitioner that he knew when he had to deal with an occipito-posterior because 'the nippers slip'), bad management of the third stage of labour, incompetent repair of perineal tears, and the frequent use of pituitrin to hasten labour.

[14] Allen, 'Interim Report'. See also H. Jacobs, 'The Causes and Prevention of Maternal Mortality', *Medical Journal of Australia* (1926), i. 607; Allen, 'Avenues of Progress in Maternal Welfare', ibid. (1936), i. 251–8; Kenneth Wilson, 'Notes on Maternal Mortality', ibid. (1935), ii. 287, recommended group practice. If a general practitioner was detained for a long time by a midwifery case his partners could look after his other patients.

[15] Allen, 'Interim Report'. In the same period in New Zealand there were 1,260 notifications and 246 deaths giving a realistic fatality rate of 19.5%.

cause in the 1920s.[16] The high death rate from eclampsia was a scandal because the histories of those who died from eclampsia nearly always showed there had been classic warning signs which were unnoticed or ignored by family doctors. Eclampsia is most common in first pregnancies and 70 per cent of eclamptic deaths occurred in primiparae in Australia in the 1920s, causing at least 100 such deaths in young mothers each year.[17]

It was agreed by most Australian obstetricians that poor standards of practice were the direct result of poor obstetric education.[18]

In 1935 the problem of maternal care and maternal welfare was reviewed again by Constance D'Arcy who began by saying 'The position in Australia is alarming ... amongst women confined of full-term babies, one woman in every two hundred dies, or, including those who die after illegal operations, one in every 180.'[19] The situation was bad in the 1920s and worse, if anything, in the 1930s, mainly because of the combination of a continuing high rate of deaths due to post-partum sepsis and eclampsia, and an ominous rise in deaths from abortion (Table 27.3).

In 1925 Morris had advised the routine use of sterilized rubber gloves but he never mentioned wearing masks. By 1935, Constance D'Arcy, who knew of Colebrook's work (she described an outbreak of puerperal sepsis traced to a nurse carrying the haemolytic streptococcus in her throat), appreciated the danger of droplet infection and recommended wearing masks in all deliveries.[20] It was often said in Australia, as it was in Britain and the USA, that after the First World War no sane doctor would have dreamt of performing an abdominal operation without the full paraphernalia of antisepsis including sterile gowns, sterilized gloves, and surgical masks, unless the doctor was working under primitive conditions in a remote area where such facilities were not available. Such standards were seldom applied in the practice of midwifery in spite of the known dangers of infection.[21]

When the danger of droplet infection was recognized, it seemed likely that a high proportion of doctors and nurses could be carriers because of their frequent contacts with streptococcal disease. It is surprising how few investigations were carried out in any country to see if this was the case and to identify those at risk of infecting their patients. There was, however, a very

---

[16] Morris, 'An Essay', 318.

[17] Ibid. 324.

[18] H. W. Webster, 'The Teaching of Obstetrics', *Medical Journal of Australia* (1921), ii. 231–2; G. Hill, 'The Teaching of Obstetrics', ibid. (1922), i. 610–12.

[19] D'Arcy, 'The Problem of Maternal Welfare', 385–99.

[20] Four years later, however, in 1939, a report of a meeting of the Obstetrics and Gynaecology section of the Australian Medical Association was told that the importance of using masks of proper design (four layers of fine dental gauze as recommended by Dr Paine of Sheffield in England) routinely in midwifery was only just beginning to be recognized in Australia; much the same, however, was true of Britain. *Medical Journal of Australia* (1937), ii. 698–702.

[21] See A. Halford, 'Maternal Mortality', *Medical Journal of Australia* (1935), i. 34, and J. W. Barrett, 'Maternal Mortality', ibid. 193.

interesting investigation in Australia in 1936. Out of thirty-six medical practitioners and nurses who had been in contact with cases of puerperal pyrexia, one-third were found to be carrying the streptococcus in their throats. A similar investigation was carried out on student nurses who had just begun their hospital training. Amongst these nurses a carrier rate of 18 per cent was found in May and June; by August and September the carrier rate had risen to 38 per cent. The peak period for streptococcal infections in Britain was in the winter, December to February. In Australia, as one would expect, it was in August and September.[22]

Against the background of this evidence we can attempt to answer the question why did the maternal mortality rate fail to decline in Australia in the first thirty-five years of this century? The reader may notice the similarity between the answers for Australia and those we discussed in connection with Britain and the USA. There was the probable rise in the virulence of the streptococcus (see Appendix 5). There is evidence that some of the antiseptics in vogue were ineffective.[23] Before the recognition of the streptococcal carrier and droplet infection, the strategies used to prevent infection (dipping hands and instruments in a bowl of antiseptic, and worse still douching the vagina with an antiseptic solution) were at best partially effective and at worst harmful.

These factors could explain the high rate of deaths due to post-partum sepsis. But what about other causes of maternal mortality? Here the underlying cause was the poor standard of obstetric education in Australia compared with—and these countries were instanced—the excellent training in Scandinavia and the Netherlands.[24] Poor training meant the inculcation of habits and attitudes which not only led to poor antiseptic practice, but also to excessive intervention in normal labours combined with lack of skill and training in the use of forceps, the misuse of pituitrin as a way of hastening labour, the mismanagement of the third stage of labour, and the unfortunate belief that it was acceptable to carry out difficult and dangerous obstetric operations in general practitioner home deliveries.

This raises a point which is I think an important one because it applied not just to Australia but to all the English-speaking world. The point is this. If such dangerous practices were commonplace—while allowing that there were probably many safe and cautious general practitioners—we may well ask why practitioners failed to learn from experience and to alter their ways. Were they all hopelessly stupid, uncaring, and arrogant? I think not. Self-interest

---

[22] Dr Lucy Bryce. Report of the Australian Branch of the British Medical Association, *Medical Journal of Australia* (1936), ii. 798–803.
[23] 'A critical analysis of the bactericidal power of common antiseptics shows that many have a deodorant effect only and do not destroy bacteria.' D'Arcy, 'The Problem of Maternal Welfare', 393.
[24] Ibid. 397–8.

alone—the penalty of a damaged reputation following poor obstetric practice—should have been enough incentive anyway. The simple answer is that a
doctor could practice midwifery for years in a careless and hurried manner,
'get away with it' and congratulate himself on his speed and his skill. He
would see no reason to change his ways if he never 'lost' a patient, or believed
that those who died, died from unavoidable causes.

In domiciliary confinements, a careless and unskilled practitioner, judged
by the standards of the 1920s would, on average, produce an MMR somewhere in the region of 50 maternal deaths per 10,000 deliveries, or 1 death in
200. A practitioner who had been well trained and practised with great care by
the standards of his time would, on the other hand, expect an MMR of about
20 maternal deaths per 10,000 deliveries, or 1 in 500.

If we assume that ordinary general practitioners delivered on average fifty
patients a year, after ten years of continuous practice the unskilled practitioner
could expect to have two or three maternal deaths in his practice whereas the
skilled doctor would only have had one. That is a very small difference.
Random variation could easily have reversed the difference so that the skilled
and careful practitioner suffered more maternal deaths in his practice than the
unskilled. In the practice of midwifery, personal experience was always a poor
indicator of the standard of care, yet the phrase 'in my experience' rang from
the lips of doctors and especially the teachers in teaching hospitals with a
degree of confidence that made it sound like incontrovertible evidence.
Statistics rarely played a part in medical education. Most doctors in this
period were scornful of statistics and utter strangers to the notions of random
variation or statistical significance. The lack of such training could be disastrous in all sorts of ways. Moreover, even when the cause of death in each
case was recorded it was often difficult to draw a sharp line between the
avoidable and the unavoidable maternal death. It was only too easy for a
practitioner, swayed by wishful thinking, to convince the relatives as well as
himself that the death of a mother was very sad, but nothing could have been
done to prevent it.[25]

Thus for a busy general practitioner working in isolation who seldom
attended medical meetings and never read medical journals, there was often
no incentive from his own experience to improve his standard of care. With

---

[25] An example is provided by an investigation of 3,218 home deliveries by medical practitioners
in the state of Queensland, which was not noted for a high standard of obstetric care. It revealed
10 maternal deaths (a rate of 31 per 10,000 births). Four were due to puerperal fever and of these
one followed a normal delivery with no interference. Two followed the manual removal of the
placenta and the fourth followed the replacement of the cord and a forceps delivery. In all four it
could be argued that bad luck rather than bad management was the cause of death. Two women
died of eclampsia and their deaths might have been avoided by care. Three died of haemorrhage,
but two of these died after an accidental haemorrhage, an unpredictable high-risk complication
not easily managed at the time even by a skilled obstetrician in hospital, especially as one of these
was a 'debilitated woman'. K. Wilson, 'Notes on Maternal Mortality', *Medical Journal of Australia*
(1935), ii. 281–5.

luck on his side it was easy for him to become complacent and acquire a local reputation as a safe family doctor, even if he broke the most elementary rules of good obstetric practice. It was only by careful statistical enquiries into the outcome of a large number of deliveries that the importance of bad midwifery was revealed.

In this and previous chapters we have discussed the numerous reports by departments of health and medical associations and the even more numerous papers and leading articles in medical journals. Most of them identified very clearly the nature and extent of bad obstetric practice and avoidable maternal deaths which were virtually the same throughout the English-speaking world. Yet these reports and papers were often unknown to and unread by the very people who were undertaking the majority of the deliveries in countries such as Britain, Australia, and the United States. In the long run, however, investigations of maternal mortality produced such a mountain of evidence that reform of maternal care was inevitable; but it was a slow process. And there was one aspect of maternal mortality in the inter-war period which had nothing to do with obstetric education or the standard of care provided by birth-attendants. This was the problem of deaths following abortion.

ABORTION IN AUSTRALIA

Although the exact extent of maternal mortality due to abortion in the inter-war period is uncertain in every Western country, and although the Australian statistics of maternal mortality (at least before 1930) leave much to be desired, there can be no doubt that abortion was a major cause of death in Australia. The statistics can be seen in Tables 27.3 and 27.4.

For the historian, the way maternal statistics were presented in the 1920s can be very confusing. The first part of Table 27.3, which covers the years 1920–3, is hard to interpret. Deaths from non-septic abortion were buried with other causes in 'accidents of pregnancy' while the more numerous deaths due to post-abortive sepsis were included with deaths from post-partum sepsis in the single category 'puerperal septicaemia'. In short it is impossible to disentangle abortion deaths as a whole from other causes.

The second part of Table 27.3, which covers the years 1928–33, is more explicit, but oddly constructed. The category 'illegal operations' is vague and not a proper category of death. But it seems from the text that these were abortion deaths in which it was *known* an illegal operation had been performed, while the other category—post-abortive sepsis—consisted of deaths in which it was *suspected* an illegal operation had been carried out. Adding these two categories together provides an estimate of the total number of deaths due to post-abortive sepsis in New South Wales, 1928–33. The total is 451 compared with 255 attributed to post-partum sepsis. Even then, as D'Arcy stated, 'This is probably far short of the real number, deaths being

TABLE 27.4 *Maternal Mortality Rates from Post-partum Puerperal Sepsis and Septic abortion, Australia, New Zealand, and England and Wales, 1931–1950*

Year	England and Wales		Australia		New Zealand	
	full term sepsis	septic abortion	full term sepsis	septic abortion	full term sepsis	septic abortion
1931	—	—	8.6	12.4	6.8	10.9
1932	—	—	7.5	14.3	5.2	10.4
1933	—	—	8.2	12.5	5.2	10.4
1934	—	—	8.9	14.5	7.0	17.3
1935	10.4	4.2	8.6	14.0	3.3	9.6
1936	8.9	3.8	10.7	18.3	3.6	5.6
1937	5.5	2.8	5.2	10.0	5.4	9.2
1938	4.3	2.7	5.2	11.9	7.7	11.0
1939	3.9	2.6	3.9	9.3	5.5	6.9
1940	3.2	1.9	4.2	11.2	4.0	4.3
1941	2.4	2.4	3.1	7.8	4.8	6.8
1942	2.2	2.6	3.9	7.2	4.4	8.0
1943	1.9	2.4	3.6	7.6	2.6	5.0
1944	1.4	2.2	1.7	5.2	2.4	5.7
1945	1.2	1.6	1.0	3.2	1.1	3.0
1946	0.6	0.8	1.5	2.3	1.2	2.9
1947	0.4	0.6	0.4	3.0	0.7	2.2
1948	0.4	0.7	0.5	1.2	—	2.0
1949	0.4	0.8	0.2	1.4	—	0.7
1950	0.4	0.5	0.1	1.2	—	—

Source: *Registrar General's Statistical Reviews*, England and Wales; Government statistics of Australia and New Zealand.

concealed under other headings.' If one adds the estimated deaths from non-septic abortion to the known deaths from post-abortive sepsis, even if no allowance is made for deaths deliberately concealed by incorrect certification so that the estimate is if anything an underestimate, it seems certain that by the early 1930s there were, in round figures, at least two deaths from abortion to every death from post-partum sepsis.

This astonishing level was not confined to one area or one state. It was general throughout the Commonwealth of Australia. At the national level, deaths from post-partum and post-abortive sepsis were not shown separately until 1930. From 1921 to 1930, the annual number of deaths from the two forms of sepsis was consistently over 200 a year, reaching a peak of 242 in 1930. When deaths from post-abortive sepsis were removed and 'puerperal septicaemia' consisted solely of deaths due to post-partum sepsis, the total had fallen to 85 in 1932. Thus a rate of abortion deaths which was about double the rate of deaths from post-partum sepsis was general throughout Australia and, as Table 27.4 shows, continued from 1931 to 1950. This table shows the contrast in this respect between Australia and England and Wales.

With such a high rate of abortion, one of the obvious questions is whether the rising trend in maternal mortality in Australia from the end of the First World War to 1936 was simply due to a rising incidence of abortion? The answer may well be 'yes', but in the absence of accurate statistics there can be no certainty. The best we can say is that if it was possible to remove deaths due to abortion, the trend from other causes might have been level, but it would not have declined.

Illegal abortion was such a serious problem it is not surprising that Constance D'Arcy described it as 'a menace which must be eradicated'. At one point in her paper she appeared to toy with the idea that induced abortion had become so common it should be legalized: but she discussed this only to dismiss it. 'Abortion in this continent', she said, 'is a crime and should be stamped out as other crime is.'[26] The statistics of abortion deaths by age show that they occurred in all age groups, 15–19 to 40–4, with the highest death rate in women over 30. This corresponds to the findings of other countries and confirms the view, now generally accepted, that during the 1920s and 1930s abortion was primarily a method of birth-control utilized by married women with children who did not desire or could not afford any more children. Logic dictated that if illegal abortion was a crime like any other crime, respectable mothers with young families who resorted to abortion because they wanted no more children were criminals like other criminals who should be locked up in gaol. Faced with the implications of such a conclusion it is not surprising that prosecutions were few and a discreet uncomfortable silence was maintained about the subject. The obvious remedy—widespread advice in birth-control—was opposed by many people in and outside the medical profession, either on moral grounds or for eugenic reasons in a country wishing to expand its population and worried already by the fall in the birth rate. The result was a terrible toll of dead mothers and orphaned children.

THE DECLINE IN MATERNAL MORTALITY IN AUSTRALIA

While we have noted certain differences between Britain and Australia in the organization of maternal services, the general pattern of maternal care and maternal mortality was closely similar in the two countries, the only major difference being Australia's huge problem with abortion.

[26] D'Arcy, 'The Problem of Maternal Welfare'.

From the mid-1930s the similarity between the two countries was just as striking. Maternal mortality began its steep and uninterrupted descent in 1937, but the lowest level ever recorded was not reached until 1939. Although sulphonamides were used in midwifery in Australia soon after they were introduced in Britain, initial worries about their toxicity may have prevented their widespread use.[27] A year later, in 1940, it was conceded that the sulphonamides were effective in post-partum sepsis, but stressed that they were of limited value in post-abortive sepsis.[28] Penicillin (highly effective against a wide range of organisms including those most usually implicated in septic abortion) came into general use in Australia in 1945 (possibly in limited quantities in 1944). Thereafter deaths from puerperal sepsis as a whole fell rapidly to very low levels. Mobile blood transfusion units were introduced in Australia in 1939[29] and there was a conscious effort to improve obstetric education as there had been in Britain. Once again a combination of factors ended the long period of high and unacceptable maternal mortality which had been just as much a feature of maternal care in Australia as it had been of maternal care in Britain and the USA.

NEW ZEALAND

Maternal care in New Zealand, like Australia, was based on the British rather than the American or European models, with a mixture of home and hospital deliveries in which home deliveries were shared between midwives and general practitioners. But the proportion of midwife deliveries (like Australia) was low compared with Britain.[30] In New Zealand, however, the provision and co-ordination of maternal care in a small country with a small population, was much easier than it was in Australia or the USA. Thus the number of births in New Zealand in 1930 was 26,797 compared with 128,399 in Australia and over 2 million in the United States. Even more striking is the comparison with a city such as Paris where, in 1930, there were 45,322 births.

With maternity on such a small scale, policies could be implemented by a few determined and strong-minded individuals who were able to mould the

[27] J. Chesterman, 'Puerperal Infections due to Haemolytic Streptococcis', *Medical Journal of Australia* (1938), i. 237–42. In a leading article in 1939 'Maternal Welfare: A Notable Advance', ibid. (1939), i. 197–8, much prominence was given to streptoccocal infections but astonishingly the sulphonamides were never mentioned.

[28] G. Lowe, 'Puerperal and Post-Abortional Sepsis', *Medical Journal of Australia* (1940), ii. 550–1.

[29] Leading article, 'Maternal Welfare'.

[30] There was a Midwives Act in 1904 closely similar to the 1902 Act in England and Wales which also recognized the New Zealand equivalent of the bona fide midwives—the 'handywomen and Gamps'. P. M. Smith, *Maternity in Dispute: New Zealand. 1920–1939*, Wellington, New Zealand, Dept. of Internal Affairs, Historical Publications Branch (1986), 16–18. Smith's book cannot be recommended too highly. I have used it extensively in writing this section.

pattern of maternal care in the fashion they thought best: and New Zealand had more than its fair share of such people. One of their policies was moving childbirth to hospital very rapidly in the 1920s and 1930s. In 1920, about 26 per cent of births took place in private hospitals, 5 per cent in Hospital Board and Salvation Army hospitals, and 4 per cent in the state St Helen's hospitals, making 35 per cent in all. By 1935, 78 per cent of all deliveries took place in hospitals, mainly through the growth of the public maternity hospitals which had lost their taint of charity. No other country had such a high proportion of hospital deliveries in 1935.[31]

In 1901 the population of New Zealand was 772,719 whites with 43,143 Maoris (by 1981 the population had risen to 3.175 million). The key to understanding the evolution of maternal care in New Zealand was the small population and the falling birth rate from the early years of this century, with fears of being overtaken at some time in the future by the Maoris. New Zealand's first priority was to increase their white population, and child welfare was at the top of the agenda in government policies. Here they could claim some success. The New Zealand climate was good and the country had none of the urban and industrial problems of Europe. Largely for these reasons New Zealand was able to achieve one of the lowest levels of infant mortality in the world. Maternal mortality, however, was not recognized as a matter for concern until 1921 when Parr, the Minister of Health, came across Grace Meigs's report on maternal mortality in the USA and other countries.[32] As soon as he saw that the level of maternal mortality in New Zealand was only just below that of the USA, which was the highest in the world, 'Parr reacted impetuously to his discovery and in doing so set in motion a panic about maternal death rates which "snowballed" once it hit the press.'[33]

The unnecessary loss of mothers in childbirth which, apart from the human misery entailed, meant loss of reproductive capacity on top of the falling birth rate, led to an immediate campaign to reduce maternal mortality. Initially Truby King was appointed to head the campaign, but he was neither an obstetrician nor a general practitioner and he was not a success. He aroused the anger of the general practitioners by accusing them of the high maternal mortality through the excessive use of forceps delivery, without gaining their respect. There were two other leading figures in the campaign against maternal mortality who were much more influential.[34]

The first was Dr Paget (one of the famous medical dynasty of that name)

---

[31] Ibid. 1. See also T. F. Corkhill, 'The Trend of Obstetric Practice in New Zealand', *New Zealand Medical Journal*, 32 (1933), 41–52.

[32] Grace Meigs, *Maternal Mortality from all Conditions Connected with Childbirth in the United States and Certain other Countries*, Children's Bureau Publications, No. 19 (Washington, DC, 1917).

[33] Smith, *Maternity in Dispute*, 7.

[34] Ibid. 9.

who had been a well-known general practitioner for thirty years. He once endeared himself to his patients by swimming naked across a flooded river to attend a case, dragging a rope behind him to haul across his clothes and black bag. New Zealand doctors seem to have been that kind of people. Both the men and the women involved in the reform of maternity can be seen in their photographs as large, square-jawed, determined individuals who seem to be cast in the same mould as the gigantic and formidable All Blacks rugby teams.

The second and most important leading figure was Dr Jellet. He was an obstetrician with an international reputation and author of a widely used text on midwifery. Before the First World War he was Master of the Rotunda (the lying-in hospital in Dublin) when that post was still the top of the obstetrics tree in the United Kingdom. From his knowledge of the Queen's Institute nurse-midwives in England he was a firm supporter of the midwife, which went a bit against the grain in New Zealand.[35] During the 1914–18 war, Jellet served with the Royal Army Medical Corps in Flanders. The reason for his appearance in New Zealand was that when he returned from the war he found that as a Protestant he was *persona non grata* with Sinn Fein. So he emigrated to New Zealand where the fishing was better anyway.[36] Jellet could be abrasive and arrogant, but his vast experience commanded respect and he was not a man easily deflected in his role as the power behind (or more usually at the very front of) the campaign against maternal mortality.

Certainly New Zealand had serious obstetric problems. It had unusually high mortality rates from toxaemia and post-partum sepsis. Jellet blamed poor antenatal care and unnecessary intervention by general practitioners. New Zealand general practitioners protested that the attacks on them were unfair. Mein Smith shows us that many of the arguments we have already discussed raged in New Zealand as elsewhere. A group of general practitioners, headed by the formidable Doris Gordon,[37] held tenaciously to the endogenous theory of puerperal infection, refusing to accept that high rates of puerperal sepsis could be due to poor antisepsis and high intervention rates by general practitioners. Jellet responded by marshalling evidence of the high rates of puerperal sepsis in mixed hospitals and the low mortality achieved by the non-interventionist deliveries by midwives.[38]

The opposition may have been vociferous but in the end it was no match for the solid conviction of Paget and Jellet that the only way to reduce maternal mortality was to foster the training of midwives and get as many

[35] In this he was supported by J. B. Dawson, 'Doctor and Midwife, Colleagues or Rivals?' *New Zealand Medical Journal*, 32 (1933), 20–3, but attacked by Corkhill, 'The Trend of Obstetric Practice in New Zealand', who believed midwives did not have the extensive experience needed to spot the abnormal.

[36] Smith, *Maternity in Dispute*, 12–13.

[37] Author of two well-known books: *Backblocks Baby-Doctor* (London, 1955), and *Doctor Down Under* (London, 1958).

[38] Smith, *Maternity in Dispute*, 60–2.

women as possible into hospital—separate maternity hospitals rather than mixed hospitals—where cross-infection would cease to be a problem and where methods of delivery, and above all the use of antisepsis, could be closely supervised. In these aims it appears that the campaign for hospital delivery was successful. New Zealand was alone in the extent to which maternal mortality in general and deaths from post-partum sepsis in particular began to decline rapidly in the late 1920s.[39]

It does not follow, of course, that because this decline in mortality occurred at the same time as the increase in hospital deliveries the two were causally connected. A similar if somewhat later turn towards hospital delivery in the USA was not accompanied by a similar fall in deaths from sepsis. But New Zealand was different. In the hospitals the majority of deliveries were by midwives, and a non-interventionist policy prevailed. It seems likely that hospital care and the reduction of home deliveries by general practitioners was the cause of the decline in mortality.

Once the fall in deaths from post-partum sepsis had begun, the enormous problem of deaths from septic abortion came to the fore. It is just like Australia all over again, and once more the dominant influence was the falling birth rate. The government and the medical profession had always actively discouraged contraception. Dr Elliott wrote in 1922:

If countries suitable for the white races, are not to be fully populated and developed by the white races, it means one of two results, either these countries will be over-run by coloured races, or there will be the most bloody and horrible wars for racial supremacy. The mind shrinks from either alternative...[40]

The Indecent Publications Act of 1910 was used to prevent the entry of books on contraception including Marie Stopes's *Married Love* (1924). The Director-General of Health had no time for birth-control, saying in 1930 that is was 'much better for a married woman to hold a baby in her arms than a pet poodle...'.[41]

Doctors would not supply contraceptives or provide contraceptive advice. The married women of New Zealand, especially in the depression when money was short, rebelled. Strong healthy out-of-doors New Zealanders were not the kind of people to look favourably on sexual abstinence to limit the size of their families, so women turned to abortion as the only means of birth-control open to them. Some aborted themselves, others employed midwives, nurses, or other women to carry out the operation. The result was havoc. Between 1931 and 1935, 109 married women died of septic abortion leaving 338 motherless children of whom 261 were under the age of 16. That may

[39] Corkhill claimed no other country had achieved such a fall in deaths from sepsis. 'The Trend of Obstetric Practice in New Zealand'.
[40] Quoted in Smith, *Maternity in Dispute*, 110.
[41] Ibid. 112.

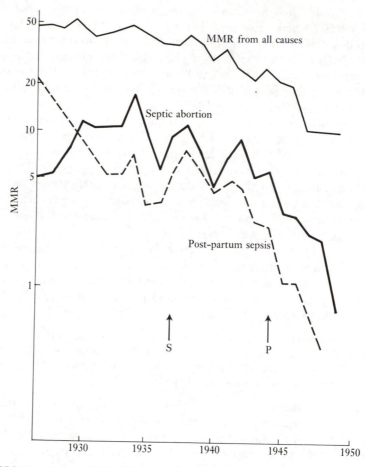

Fig. 27.2 New Zealand, 1927–1950. Annual rates of Maternal Mortality from all causes, from post-partum sepsis, and from septic abortion. Logarithmic scale
Source: *Reports on the Vital Statistics* (Census and Statistics Office, Wellington, New Zealand).

not seem very many until one remembers that it occurred in a population smaller than that of many European cities.[42]

The effect on maternal mortality in New Zealand can be seen in Fig. 27.2. From 1927, deaths from post-partum sepsis (represented in the Figure by the line with dashes) were falling steeply; at the same time deaths from septic abortion (the heavy continuous line) were rising steeply to reach a peak in 1934. Deaths from septic abortion actually exceeded deaths from post-partum

---

[42] Ibid. 107. If the same death rate from septic abortion had occurred in England and Wales, the number of deaths from septic abortion amongst married women 1931–5 would have been close to 2,900, which was over twice the actual recorded number.

sepsis from 1930. I believe Australia and New Zealand may have been the only countries in which this occurred in the 1930s, or at least by such a wide margin. It was not until 1936 that a New Zealand doctor published a paper saying that the situation was so serious that contraception was 'the only way to reduce the slaughter of illegal abortion'.[43]

We can now begin to understand the trend in maternal mortality in New Zealand from the late 1920s to the late 1940s. Figure 27.2, in which the letter 'S' represents the time when sulphonamides became available and the letter 'P', penicillin, is especially revealing. The thin continuous line at the top shows the trend in maternal mortality from all causes from 1927 to 1950. What is conspicuous for its absence is the sudden steep downturn in maternal mortality seen in Britain and elsewhere following the introduction of the sulphonamides; and the post-1937 decline in deaths from post-partum sepsis in New Zealand is also unimpressive. The reason seems to be that the sulphonamides were little used in New Zealand. A careful search of the *New Zealand Medical Journal*, which published many reports on maternity and maternal mortality, revealed no more than one or two occasions when the sulphonamides were mentioned. Apart from these there was no recognition of their importance until 1943 when there was a medical meeting in Auckland at which two American doctors referred to the sulphonamides as 'a new therapy of bacterial infections which has been little short of miraculous'.[44]

Negative evidence is always difficult, but it seems that before 1943 the sulphonamides were used much less frequently in New Zealand compared with Britain. Part of the reason may be that New Zealand obstetricians were obsessed at the time by the high death rate due to toxaemia, on which many articles were written. New Zealand had already achieved a reduction in deaths from post-partum sepsis over some eight years before the sulphonamides became available; so they may have felt that problem had already been solved.

The use of penicillin, however, was quite different and illustrates the importance of chance encounters. In the North African campaign in the Second World War, a New Zealand army doctor, Lt.-Col. Eardley Button, met Sir Hugh Cairns and Professor Florey who had flown out from Oxford to North Africa with some precious penicillin. Button was deeply impressed and determined that penicillin would be obtainable in New Zealand as soon as possible. It was in fact introduced in 1944, when 50 million units a week were

---

[43] W. H. B. Bull, 'Abortion and Contraception', *New Zealand Medical Journal*, 35 (1936), 39–44.

[44] Report of postgraduate meeting in Auckland in a supplementary issue of the *New Zealand Medical Journal*, 42 (1943). The use of sulphonamides in a case of pelvic sepsis is mentioned in J. B. Dawson, 'Treatment of Pelvic Sepsis with sulphonamides', *New Zealand Medical Journal*, 36 (1937), 56–8. There is a note ibid. 39 (1940), to the effect that sulphonamides are dangerous and should be conserved for certain conditions such as erysipelas but not puerperal fever. There were no reports of the use of the sulphonamides in series of cases in hospitals.

flown in. Initially its use was closely controlled by four hospital pathologists, but this control was removed as early as March 1945 and doctors were then free to prescribe penicillin.[45]

Penicillin was a very effective treatment for both kinds of puerperal sepsis —post-abortive and post-partum. Figure 27.2 shows the downturn in deaths from post-partum sepsis beginning around 1943 when the importance of the sulphonamides was realized rather late in the day, and then it shows the steep fall in both forms of puerperal sepsis from 1944.

What happened in New Zealand is important confirmatory evidence in this respect. At first sight the trend in maternal mortality in New Zealand from the mid-1930s to 1943 appears to contradict the idea that the sulphonamides were responsible for the rapid decline in maternal mortality during this period in other countries. If it had occurred in Britain, a similar rapid decline should also have occurred in countries with close ties to Britain such as New Zealand. In fact the absence of a sudden post-1937 fall in maternal mortality in New Zealand can be traced to the lack of use (probably partial rather than complete) of the sulphonamides. And thus New Zealand strengthens the case for believing that the steep post-1937 fall in maternal mortality in Britain can indeed be attributed mainly to the sulphonamides.

[45] *New Zealand Medical Journal*, 43 (1944), 225–6, and ibid. 44 (1945), 201.

28

Maternal and Infant Mortality

Although this has been a study of maternal care and maternal mortality, it is obvious that two individuals are at risk in childbirth, the mother and the infant. In every pregnancy there are four possible outcomes: the mother and infant both survive, the mother survives but the infant dies, the infant survives but the mother dies, or both die. The survival or death of both individuals must be linked. What, then, is the relationship between maternal and infant mortality? The attempt to answer that question may appear at first sight to be little more than a rather abstruse exercise in statistical analysis; a sort of mathematical game. But, as I hope to be able to show, the relationship between maternal and infant mortality is not only an important question for historians; it is a question which concerns the authorities whose work is concerned with health in developing countries today.

In previous chapters infant mortality has only been mentioned in passing; for example, in the different response of maternal and infant mortality to the Second World War. This is not for lack of historical sources. Compared with maternal mortality there is an enormous literature on infant mortality. Secular trends and comparative levels have been described and analysed in great detail. Causes of death and associations between death rates and a wide range of factors have been and still are debated, for it is a highly complex field which has justly been described as a methodological minefield.[1] Nevertheless, the one aspect of infant and maternal mortality which has largely been ignored is the relationship of the two to each other.

So powerful are the pervasive images, secular and sacred, of mother and child, and so familiar are terms such as 'maternal and child health' or 'maternal and infant welfare', that a close connection between the two mortalities seems to be a matter of common sense. Case histories of major obstetric complications leading directly to the death of both mother and child suggest that the same factors probably determined the levels of infant and maternal mortality, a view which seems to be supported by certain statistics. Robert Morse Woodbury, whose knowledge of maternal and infant mortality in the 1920s was unsurpassed, remarked that 'the trend in maternal mortality . . . is of great interest in connection with the trend of the infant mortality

---

[1] R. H. Gray, 'Maternal Reproduction and Child Survival', *American Journal of Public Health*, 74 (1984), 1080–1.

TABLE 28.1 *Neonatal and Stillbirth Rates according to whether the Mother Survived or Died, New York State (exclusive of New York City), 1936–1938*

	Deliveries in which the:		Total deliveries
	Mother survived	Mother died	
Infant survived	243,385	413	243,798
Infant died (total)	14,431	296	14,727
Stillbirths	6,964	213	7,177
Neonatal deaths	7,467	83	7,550
Stillbirth and neonatal mortality rates			
Stillbirth rate[a]	27.0	300.4	27.8
Neonatal mortality rate[b]	29.8	167.3	30.0

[a] Per 1,000 total births (including stillbirths).
[b] Per 1,000 total live births.

Source: J. Yerushalmy, M. Kramer, and E. M. Gardiner, 'Studies in Childbirth Mortality: Puerperal Fatality and Loss of Offspring', *Public Health Reports*, 55 (1940), 1020.

rate'. To illustrate the point he presented the compelling evidence of the effect of maternal mortality on infants:

Infants whose mothers died within one year following the confinement appeared to be subject to a considerable handicap, for their mortality rate, 450.0 per 1,000, was over 4 times as high as that for other infants, 109.2. In those cases in which the mother died within one month of confinement the mortality was even higher. Six in every ten of these babies died before the end of the first year.[2]

These findings were confirmed in 1940 by Yerushalmy and his colleagues. His findings are summarized in Table 28.1. They show that when the mother died in childbirth, the risk of the infant dying in the first month of life was five and a half times as high as it was when the mother survived. Both of these authors were distinguished scholars and statisticians. Yet, as far as I am aware, neither, having raised the question, undertook a systematic study of the links between maternal and infant mortality.[3]

What, in fact, do we mean by 'links' in this context? I suggest that a close link implies that infant and maternal mortality rates responded in very much the same way to a number of well-recognized determinants of mortality such as income levels, social class, the quality of the environment (housing, water-

[2] R. M. Woodbury, *Infant Mortality and its Causes* (Baltimore, Md., 1926), 43.
[3] Robert Morse Woodbury was Director of Statistical Research at the Children's Bureau in Washington. Jacob Yerushalmy, whose work on maternal and infant mortality was mostly published in the 1940s, was a statistician with the United States Public Health Service.

supplies, sanitation, population density, the climate), the effects of living in urban or rural areas, nutrition, parity, sibship size, maternal age, and, of course, the quality of medical care. To talk of 'close links' also implies that we should expect to find similar secular trends, and similar levels when the rates in different countries and regions are compared. If, as we have shown, certain countries suffered a high (or low) rate of maternal mortality in the 1920s, we should expect infant mortality rates in those countries to follow suit. In short, each mortality rate would have predictive power. If we knew the rate of one mortality we could predict the level of the other, not with complete certainty of course for there would be exceptions; but at least with reasonable confidence on most occasions. That seems to be the common assumption, but is it correct?

DEFINITIONS OF MORTALITY RATES

In previous chapters we have dealt with the definition of maternal mortality rates. Infant mortality is defined as the number of deaths of infants under the age of one year, per 1,000 live births. Thus infant mortality, like maternal, uses births as the denominator, but infant mortality is split into several components.[4] The components are shown in Figures 28.1 and 28.2. Those with which I am specially concerned are the infant mortality rate (IMR), the neonatal mortality rate (NMR), and the post-neonatal mortality rate.

THE DETERMINANTS OF INFANT MORTALITY

The importance of separating infant deaths into those occurring in the first month of life (neonatal mortality), and those occurring between the end of the first month and the end of the first year (post-neonatal mortality) lies in the fact that each has its separate list of causes and determinants. Neonatal mortality was, and is, for the most part associated with events during pregnancy or childbirth, factors which are often referred to as the 'natal' or 'endogenous' causes of infant mortality. The three most common causes in the past were prematurity (pre-term labour), congenital malformations, and birth injury.

Post-neonatal mortality on the other hand was largely due to respiratory and gastro-intestinal infections which were associated with adverse environmental conditions such as poor sanitation, contaminated water supplies, overcrowding and exposure to infection, and the vagaries of the climate. Such causes were often called 'environmental' or 'exogenous'. The importance of

---

[4] In England and Wales the process of splitting infant mortality into neonatal and post-neonatal mortality was a consequence of the report of the Inter-Departmental Committee on Physical Deterioration in 1904 which showed the poor standards of health amongst the recruits for the Boer War.

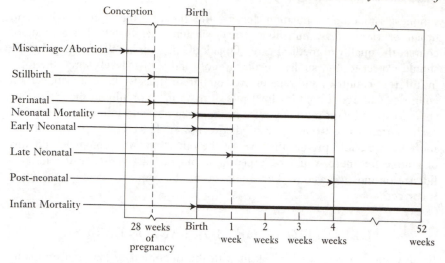

FIG. 28.1 Diagram showing the definitions of mortality rates as they apply to the foetus, the neonate, and the infant
Source: Based on A. Macfarlane and M. Mugford, *Birth Counts*, with kind permission.

breastfeeding as a determinant of infant mortality (breastfeeding protects infants from infection) cannot be exaggerated. The high levels of infant mortality in the past associated with artificial feeding (especially in the summer months) are well known. Much research has been devoted to this aspect of infant mortality and to the complex links between infant feeding, fertility, parity, sibship size, and birth interval.[5] Of course, as Table 28.2 shows, a baby could die of a congenital malformation after the end of the first

[5] See e.g. J. E. Knodel and A. J. Hermalin, 'Effects of Birth Rank, Maternal Age, Birth Interval and Sibshipsize on Infant and Child Mortality: Evidence from 18th and 19th Century Reproductive Histories', *American Journal of Public Health*, 74 (1984), 1098–106. Knodel, *Demographic Behaviour in the Past: A Study of Fourteen German Village Populations in the Eighteenth and Nineteenth Centuries* (Cambridge, 1988); R. I. Woods, P. A. Watterson, and J. H. Woodward, 'The Causes of the Rapid Infant Mortality Decline in England and Wales, 1862–1921', *Population Studies*, 42 (1988), 343–66; ibid. 43 (1989), 113–32; and Shyam Thapa, R. Short, and M. Potts, 'Breast Feeding, Birth Spacing and their Effects on Child Survival', *Nature* 335 (20 Oct. 1988), 679–82. R. I. Woods and his colleagues have argued cogently that the rise in infant mortality in England and Wales at the end of the nineteenth century was due to a succession of hot summers leading to an excess of diarrhoeal deaths. These masked an underlying fall in infant mortality from non-diarrhoeal causes in the late nineteenth century, such as was seen for total infant mortality in Sweden. They also describe a number of models to demonstrate the way breast-feeding reduces infant mortality by reducing the risk of infective infant deaths and (if prolonged) by reducing fertility which also reduces the rate of infant mortality by lowering the risks associated with high parity and short birth interval. High infant mortality may stimulate fertility (the need to replace the loss of an infant) leading to added infant deaths from high parity—a point to which we return later—while low infant mortality can be an incentive to the greater use of birth-control and thus to the reduction of parity and birth-interval risks.

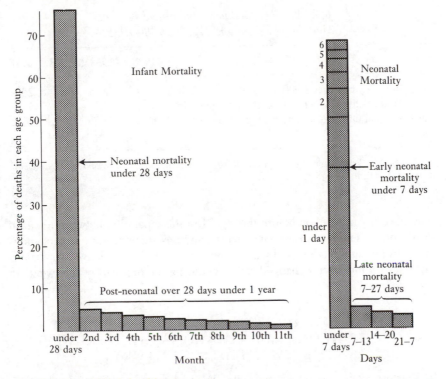

FIG. 28.2 USA, 1954. Infant Mortality by age
Source: E. P. Hunt and R. R. Moore, *Perinatal Infant and Maternal Mortality, 1954*, US Dept. of Health, Education, and Welfare, Social Security Administration, Children's Bureau (Washington, DC, 1957).

TABLE 28.2 *Causes of Neonatal and Post-Neonatal Deaths, USA 1939.*
(Percentages to nearest whole number)

Neonatal mortality (percentage)		Post-neonatal mortality (percentage)	
Premature birth	48	Chest infections	33
Birth injury	15	Gastro-intestinal infections	18
Congenital malformations	10	Congenital malformations	6
Asphyxia & atelectasis	4	Other specified causes	39
Chest infections	4	Ill-defined and unknown	4
Other specified causes	17		
Ill-defined and unknown	2		

Source: Based on Charts I-A and I-B in 'Changes in Infant, Childhood and Maternal Mortality over the Decade 1939–1948'. Children's Bureau Statistical Series, No. 6, Federal Security Agency, Social Security Administration, Washington, DC (1950).

TABLE 28.3 *The Decline in Infant and Neonatal
Mortality, England and Wales, 1928–1958*

Year	1928	1938	1948	1958
Infant mortality rate (per 1,000 live births)	65.1	52.7	34.5	22.5
Neonatal mortality as a percentage of infant mortality	47.7	53.7	57.3	72.0
Early neonatal mortality as a percentage of neonatal mortality	69.4	74.5	79.2	85.2

Source: A. Macfarlane and M. Mugford, *Birth Counts: Statistics of Pregnancy and Childbirth* (London, 1984), ii.

month, or of an infection before that age. But the separation between neonatal deaths due to endogenous or natal factors, and post-neonatal due to exogenous or environmental factors held true in most cases; and the relative proportions of these two mortalities changed radically during the first half of the twentieth century.[6]

THE SHIFT OF INFANT MORTALITY FROM POST-NEONATAL TO NEONATAL DURING THE TWENTIETH CENTURY

In Western countries infant mortality declined more or less steadily either from the late nineteenth century (Sweden and the Netherlands) or the early twentieth (Britain). Most of the decline took place in post-neonatal mortality. Few believe that clinical medicine—what doctors and nurses did (or did not do) at the bedside—was a significant factor in this decline before the 1930s. Some argue that the decline was wholly due to rising standards of living and nutrition. Others place more emphasis on public health measures in the broad sense of better water, housing, sanitation and so on—environmental reform in other words. I confess I find it hard to discern an essential difference between these points of view when it is likely both played a part and the two were interconnected.

At all events, post-neonatal mortality declined steeply and neonatal mortality much less steeply; and if neonatal deaths were split into early and late, the early neonatal death rates fell more slowly than the late (see Table 28.3,

[6] The most common cause of post-neonatal deaths in Britain and the USA today is sudden infant death syndrome (SIDS) or 'cot deaths', the cause or causes of which are still debated. In the USA 36% of post-neonatal deaths were due to SIDS in 1987, followed by 18% due to congenital anomalies and 18% due to infections. J. H. Johnson, 'U.S. Differentials in Infant Mortality: Why do they Persist?', *Family Planning Perspectives*, 19 (1987), 227–32. In England and Wales in 1989, over half of all post-neonatal deaths were cot deaths. It is impossible to know how many cases of SIDS occurred in the past and were attributed to other causes. But it seems more likely that the syndrome is recently recognized rather than a new disorder.

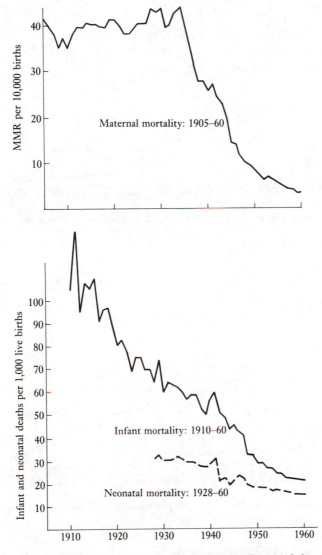

Fig. 28.3 England and Wales, 1905–1960. Secular trends in Maternal, Infant, and Neonatal Mortality
Source: A. Macfarlane and M. Mugford, *Birth Counts*, ii.

and Figures 28.3, 28.4, and 28.5). As a result of these different gradients, the proportion of the neonatal component of infant mortality, and of the early neonatal component of neonatal mortality, steadily increased. By the 1950s a large majority of infant deaths were clustered together close to the time of birth. This can be seen for the United States in 1954 in Figure 28.2.

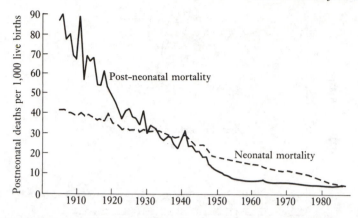

FIG. 28.4 England and Wales 1905–1985. Secular trends in Post-Neonatal and Neonatal Mortality
Source: OPCS mortality statistics, ser. DH3.

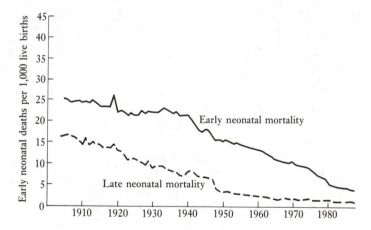

FIG. 28.5 England and Wales 1905–1985. Secular trends in Early and Late Neonatal Mortality.
Source: OPCS mortality statistics, ser. DH3.

Thus the two major features of the graphs of infant mortality in the first half of the twentieth century were the decline in total infant mortality and the different gradients of the graphs of neonatal and post-neonatal mortality (Table 28.3 and Figure 28.6). Since neonatal mortality was largely due to natal factors, logic suggests that if there are close links between maternal and infant mortality, they will be found in the neonatal component. It therefore follows that the continual proportionate increase in neonatal mortality should have led to continually closer links between maternal mortality and infant mortality. This is not in fact the case, for reasons which will appear.

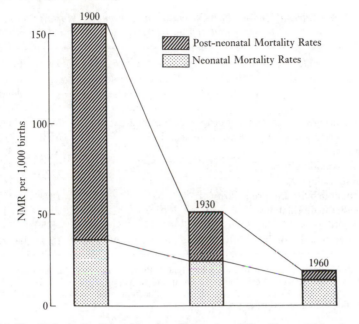

Fig. 28.6 The Netherlands. Infant Mortality, Neonatal, and Post-Neonatal Mortality in 1900, 1930, and 1960
Source: *1899–1979 tachtig jaren statisteik in tijdreeksen*, Centraal bureau voor de statisteik (The Hague, 1979).

SECULAR TRENDS IN INFANT AND MATERNAL MORTALITY

Figure 28.3 shows the secular trends in maternal, infant, and neonatal mortality in England and Wales. In a previous chapter, Figure 26.6 showed the corresponding trends in the Netherlands. Table 28.4, which shows the percentage change in maternal, infant, and neonatal mortality in the USA over the short period of fifteen years between 1915 and 1929, could serve as a model for what was happening in most Western countries during the 1920s. Maternal mortality was level or rising, post-neonatal mortality was declining rapidly, neonatal mortality was declining more slowly.

These figures and tables make it absolutely clear that the trends in maternal mortality on the one hand, and neonatal, post-neonatal, and infant mortality on the other, were quite different. The trend in maternal mortality was characterized by its two phases—the plateau from 1900 to the mid-1930s and the subsequent steep fall—while infant mortality and its components showed a steady decline from the beginning of this century with no discontinuity in the mid-1930s. It is important to emphasize that this difference was not

TABLE 28.4 *Maternal, Infant, Post-Neonatal, and Neonatal Mortality in the USA in 1915 and 1929*

	1915	1929	Percentage increase or decrease
Maternal mortality rate: expanding birth-registration area	60.8	69.5	+14.3
Maternal mortality rate: birth-registration area 1915	60.8	65.0	+ 6.9
Infant mortality rate	99.9	67.6	−32.3
Post-neonatal mortality rate	55.5	30.7	−44.7
Neonatal mortality rate	44.4	36.9	−16.9
Congenital debility and prematurity	27.2	18.9	−30.5
Congenital malformations	5.6	5.7	+ 1.8
Birth injuries	3.9	5.5	+41.0
Death rate in first day of life	15.0	15.3	+ 2.0

Source: White House Conference on Child Health Protection, *Fetal, Newborn and Maternal Morbidity and Mortality* (New York, 1933); E. Hunt and R. Moore, *Perinatal, Infant, and Maternal Mortality, 1954*, US Department of Health, Education and Welfare, Social Security Administration, Children's Bureau (1957).

confined just to one or a few countries: it was universal throughout the Western world, and the implication is clear. Where secular trends were so markedly different, it is likely the determinants were different. In short, the trends do not support the notion of a close link between maternal and infant mortality. This was one major difference between maternal and infant mortality; the next is the relationship to social class.

THE EFFECTS OF SOCIAL AND ECONOMIC DEPRIVATION ON MATERNAL AND INFANT MORTALITY

The social-class gradient of infant mortality has been established beyond all doubt; and one of its outstanding features is its resistance to change. Hence the remark of Sir Arthur Newsholme that 'Infant mortality is the most sensitive index we possess of social welfare and of sanitary administration, especially under urban conditions.'[7] In 1943 Titmuss showed that the wide social inequality demonstrated by the Registrar General's figures for 1911 persisted through 1921–3 to 1930–2 in spite of a fall in the absolute levels in each class.[8] This can be seen in Table 28.5 where the social class difference

[7] Supplement to the *39th Annual Report of the Local Government Board, 1909–1910*.
[8] R. M. Titmuss, *Birth, Poverty and Wealth: A Study of Infant Mortality* (London, 1943): a marvellously perceptive and beautifully written short study.

TABLE 28.5 *Infant and Neonatal Mortality Rates*
according to Social Class, England and Wales,
1911–1932

Social class	1911	1921–3	1930–2
Infant mortality			
All classes	125	79	62
Class I	76	38	33
Class II	106	55	45
Class III	113	77	58
Class IV	122	89	67
Class V	153	99	77
Neonatal mortality			
All classes	39.1	33.9	30.2
Class I	30.2	23.4	21.7
Class II	36.5	28.3	27.2
Class III	36.8	33.7	29.4
Class IV	38.6	36.7	31.9
Class V	42.5	36.9	32.5

Source: R. Titmuss, *Birth, Poverty and Wealth: A Study of Infant Mortality* (London, 1943), 26, 37.

is obvious. In 1911 the rate was 76 in class I, but 153 in class V. Even then the extent of social inequality was partly hidden by the process of grouping together certain occupations. For example, the infant mortality rate in 1911 was just over 40 for the children of army and naval officers and 48 for those of Church of England clergymen, when, at the other end of the scale, it was over 160 for the infants of miners.[9]

A social-class gradient also occurred in neonatal mortality, as shown in this table; but it was less steep than the gradient for infant mortality. In other words, most of the social inequality was found in post-neonatal mortality and probably, therefore, in deaths due to environmental causes as opposed to natal causes. Titmuss demonstrated this in a most interesting table, reproduced in part as Table 28.6. It shows the infant mortality rate in 1921–3 and 1930–2 for two groups of causes: first, two of the major causes of neonatal deaths, congenital malformations and injury at birth; secondly, some typical causes of post-neonatal deaths, namely tuberculous diseases, bronchitis and pneumonia, and diarrhoea and enteritis.

The huge differential by social class in the second group of causes is obvious. But in the first group of causes, congenital malformation and injury

[9] Ibid. 23.

TABLE 28.6 *Infant Mortality by Certain Causes in Social Classes I and V, England and Wales, 1921–1932*

Social class	1921–3		1930–2	
	Congenital malformations and injury at birth	Tuberculous diseases, bronchitis and pneumonia and diarrhoea and enteritis	Congenital malformations and injury at birth	Tuberculous diseases, bronchitis and pneumonia and diarrhoea and enteritis
Class I	5.7	8.1	7.3	5.1
Class V	5.1	39.1	7.4	28.0

Source: R. Titmuss, *Birth, Poverty and Wealth: A Study of Infant Mortality* (London, 1943), 50.

at birth, there was no significant difference in the rates in class I and class V. There is no reason to believe the incidence of congenital malformations was class-related, and it might be argued (although there are some minor difficulties to be discussed later) that birth injury is a measure of obstetric efficiency. It is a fair assumption that during this period a majority of women in social class I were delivered by doctors, and a majority of class V by midwives. At the time it was generally believed that the advantage of a doctor delivery was greater safety for mother and infant. We have seen, however, that there are good reasons for believing this was not true in the inter-war period because of the increasing tendency of doctors to intervene unnecessarily in normal labours. Table 28.6 certainly seems to suggest that as far as the infant was concerned deliveries by doctors were no safer than deliveries by midwives. Indeed, what is surprising is the rise in the rate of mortality in this group (congenital malformations and birth injury) between 1921–3 and 1930–2. That this was not an isolated anomaly is suggested by a similar rise in the USA around the same time. Table 28.4 shows a 41 per cent rise in the death rate due to birth injuries between 1915 and 1929 which certainly suggests that this was the price paid by infants for what I described in Chapter 21 as the 'orgy of interference'.

On the broad question of the social-class gradient in infant mortality, the United States resembled Britain. Woodbury found clear evidence of links between economic status and infant mortality in seven American cities between 1912 and 1915. Infant mortality rates ranged from 210.9 per 1,000 births in the lowest income-groups to 59.1 in the highest. The neonatal mortality rate showed a similar but slighter gradient, ranging from 60.7 for those with the lowest incomes to 38.2 for those with the highest. These differences were independent of parity and maternal age.[10]

In view of the strong social-class gradient and the implied link between poverty and high infant mortality, we would expect to find evidence of a rise in infant mortality during the depression of the 1930s in Britain and the USA. In the USA there was in fact a rise in infant mortality from 1933 to 1936, mostly due to a rise in post-neonatal mortality. Maternal mortality, however, declined through the depression years, falling between 1930 and 1935 by 19.7 per cent for black mothers and by 12.6 per cent for white mothers. Between 1930 and 1938 the maternal mortality for both black and white mothers had fallen by 27 per cent.[11] Several investigators have examined the links between unemployment and infant mortality.[12] The results have been equivocal. When unemployment tended to be patchy as it was in Britain and the USA, aggregate national statistics can smother the evidence of associations between infant mortality and unemployment which were limited to certain deprived areas. Local studies are therefore more valuable. We have seen an example in the Kentucky Frontier Nursing Service, described in Chapter 18. The area where this service operated was hard hit by the depression which reduced a previously poor population to severe levels of nutritional deprivation. Infant mortality rose sharply but maternal mortality was unaffected.[13] By concentrating on deprived areas, Webster has shown convincingly that the thirties were both hungry and unhealthy in many parts of Britain. There were dire effects on the health of certain age-groups; school children, for instance. He also demonstrated the tendency of authorities to cover up evidence of the inadequacies of welfare, and the 'paradox that services were frequently least developed where most needed'.[14] Winter, who also argued from local studies,

[10] Woodbury, *Infant Mortality*, 123–52.

[11] In the USA the MMR was, and still is, much higher in the black than the white population: in the period 1938–40 the MMRs were 35 per 10,000 births for the white population and 80.4 for the black.

[12] For instance, Brenner, who used data on unemployment as an index of economic deprivation, took a longer view and claimed to show that a close correlation existed between levels of infant mortality and periods of unemployment in the USA from 1915 to 1965. M. H. Brenner, 'Fetal, Infant and Maternal Mortality during Periods of Economic Instability', *International Journal of Health Services*, 2 (1973), 145–59. His work, however, has been criticized by several authors, notably by Winter, on the grounds that the correlations between unemployment and infant mortality was based (most oddly) on first-day neonatal deaths and not post-neonatal mortality where an association would be logical. Brenner's statistical methodology has also been severely criticized. J. M. Winter, 'Unemployment, Nutrition and Infant Mortality in Britain, 1920–1950' in id. (ed.), *The Working Class and Modern British History* (Cambridge, 1983).

[13] Mary Breckinridge, *Wide Neighbourhoods: A Story of the Frontier Nursing Service* (New York, 1952); N. S. Dye, 'Mary Breckinridge, the Frontier Nursing Service and the Introduction of Nurse-Midwifery in the United States', *Bulletin of the History of Medicine*, 5 (1983), 485–507; K. E. Wilkie and E. R. Moseley, *Frontier Nurse: Mary Breckinridge* (New York, 1959). See chap. 18.

[14] C. Webster, 'Health, Welfare and Unemployment during the Depression', *Past and Present*, 109 (1985), 204–29, and id., 'Healthy or Hungry Thirties?', *History Workshop Journal*, 13 (1982), 110–29.

is sceptical of a link between unemployment and infant mortality during the depression in Britain. He suggests that unemployment insurance, however miserly and demeaning, was sufficient to provide 'a buffer for the unemployed which helped to separate deprivation from destitution' and prevent a rise in infant mortality. Mortality is a much cruder index of deprivation in times such as the depression than morbidity; but reliable and comprehensive statistics of morbidity are extremely hard to find.[15]

In spite of these equivocal results, however, the main conclusion—that in terms of social class gradients, infant mortality and maternal mortality were quite different—stands on firm foundations. The absence of a link between social class and maternal mortality, or a gradient which was the reverse of infant mortality (higher maternal mortality in class I than class V as shown in Table 14.3), has been emphasized in previous chapters, especially Chapter 14. The account of the effects of the Second World War on infant and maternal mortality in Chapter 26 supports the view that the responses of maternal and infant mortality to social and economic adversity were different. The difference might be summarized by saying that the well-to-do were able to purchase good health for their infants by providing a good diet and a favourable environment, but they could not be sure of 'buying' a safe delivery by paying a high fee; it depended on the doctor they chose.

In passing it is interesting to note that the social-class gradient of infant mortality has persisted in both the United States and Britain; but the 'reverse' social class relationship in maternal mortality disappeared in Britain after the Second World War; since then, maternal mortality has resembled infant mortality, being highest in manual occupations, lowest in non-manual.[16]

INTERNATIONAL AND REGIONAL COMPARISONS OF INFANT AND MATERNAL MORTALITY

Another approach to infant and maternal mortality was mentioned at the beginning of this chapter. It consists of testing the proposition that if maternal mortality was high (or low) in a certain country or a state or region within a country, infant mortality would follow suit. Each mortality rate would have predictive power with regard to the other.

Table 28.7 is designed to test this proposition. It shows the maternal, infant, and neonatal mortality rates for ten countries in 1920, arranged in rank

[15] Winter, 'Unemployment, Nutrition and Infant Mortality'. These points are discussed at greater length in the paper on which this chapter is based, published in *Social History of Medicine*, 4/1 (1991), 29–73.

[16] For a discussion of the persistence and interpretation of social gradients in England and Wales, see I. Chalmers, 'Short, Black, Baird, Himsworth and Social Class Differences in Fetal and Neonatal Mortality Rates', *British Medical Journal*, 291 (1985), ii. 231–3. For the same phenomenon in the USA, see J. H. Johnson, 'U.S. Differentials in Infant Mortality: Why do they Persist?', *Family Planning Perspectives*, 19 (1987), 227–32.

TABLE 28.7 *Maternal Mortality, 1921–1924, and Infant and Neonatal Mortality, 1924 in Certain Countries*

	Maternal deaths per 10,000 births 1921–4		Infant deaths per 1,000 births 1924		Neonatal deaths per 1,000 births 1924
Netherlands	25	New Zealand	40.2	Netherlands	18.6
Japan	33	Australia	57.1	New Zealand	24.0
Uruguay	33	Netherlands	67.3	Ireland	26.6
England and Wales	39	Ireland	68.9	Australia	29.8
Australia	45	USA	70.8	England and Wales	33.1
Scotland	46	England and Wales	75.1	Uruguay	38.4
Ireland (1917)	49	Scotland	97.7	Scotland	38.4
New Zealand	51	Canada (1926)	102.0	USA	38.6
Canada (1926)	56	Uruguay	103.6	Canada (1926)	48.1
USA	68	Japan	166.4	Japan	67.5

Note: Rank correlation coefficients (Kendall).
Maternal mortality rate—Infant mortality rate
    τ = −0.15 standard error, 0.102
Maternal mortality rate—Neonatal mortality rate
    τ = 0.08 standard error, 0.08
Infant mortality rate—Neonatal mortality rate
    τ = 0.64 standard error, 2.50
(The standard error needs to exceed 1.96 to achieve the 95% level of confidence)

Source: Children's Bureau Publications, US Department of Labor, Washington, DC, Government Printing Office, No. 142, R. M. Woodbury, *Maternal Mortality* (1926); *Birth, Stillbirth and Infant Mortality Statistics for the Birth Registration Area of the United States*, 10th Annual Report, Department of Commerce, US Bureau of the Census (Washington, DC, 1926); S. A. Cudmore and J. T. Marshall, *A Study in Maternal, Infant and Neonatal Mortality in Canada*, Dominion Bureau of Statistics (Ottawa, 1942).

order for each mortality rate.[17] There was, as expected, a highly significant correlation between the infant and neonatal mortality rates of different countries. But there was no correlation between maternal mortality on the one hand and infant or neonatal mortality on the other. The USA and New Zealand both had high rates of maternal mortality. Infant mortality in New Zealand, however, was the lowest in the world while the USA ranked fifth out of ten for infant mortality and eighth for neonatal. Japan had a low rate of maternal mortality and a high rate of infant and neonatal, while England and Wales occupied a more or less mid-position ranking fourth, sixth, and fifth respectively for maternal, infant, and neonatal mortality. The table illustrates how easily a false conclusion could be reached by taking the values for England and Wales (or the Netherlands) in isolation.

Regional comparisons are more complex, as illustrated by the United States. By the 1940s there was a steadily growing volume of vital statistics from each of the states showing a very wide range of maternal and infant mortality rates. The range of maternal mortality is shown in Chapter 22 as Figures 22.3 and 22.4, and of maternal and infant mortality in Appendix Table 26.

In the states with the highest rates of maternal mortality—those which lie in a belt across the south stretching from Virginia and the Carolinas in the east down through Georgia, Florida, and Alabama and across to Nevada in the west—there was a highly significant correlation between their rates of maternal and infant mortality. In the remaining states, however, where the rates of maternal mortality were below the national average, there was no significant correlation between maternal and infant mortality.[18]

The closest correlation was seen in the ten states with the highest rates of maternal mortality: Florida, Kentucky, Louisiana, Arkansas, North Carolina, New Mexico, Georgia, South Carolina, Alabama, and Mississippi, states which shared the common features of a high level of rural poverty, a low standard of general health, and for the most part a poor standard of medical care, a conjunction of factors which one would expect to produce high maternal and high infant mortality.

In the states of the north and the west, however, the level of infant mortality could not be predicted from the level of maternal mortality. In 1955, for

---

[17] The rank orders shown here were substantially the same from 1920 to 1940, even though the absolute values for each country were changing. See J. Yerushalmy, 'Infant and Maternal Mortality in the Modern World', *Annals of the Academy of Political and Social Sciences*, 237 (1945), 135 (Table 1).

[18] Using Spearman's rank correlation coefficent for the correlations between maternal and infant mortality in the first group (the states with above-average maternal mortality), $\tau = 0.96$; $P > 0.1$. In the second group (the state with below-average maternal mortality) $\tau = 3.04$ and $P < 0.01, > 0.001$. Pearson's product moment correlation gave closely similar results. The data employed for this calculation were for the year 1955. I am grateful to Dr Richard Smith for carrying out these calculations.

example, Arizona ranked twenty-seventh out of forty-eight states in terms of its MMR, but forty-sixth out of the forty-eight in terms of infant mortality. Wyoming, which was seventh for maternal mortality was thirty-second for infant mortality. Idaho, which was twenty-ninth for maternal mortality was second for infant mortality, and so on.[19]

Turning to England and Wales, we find from the nineteenth century to the late 1930s, that the country was divided in two in terms of maternal mortality by a line from the Severn to the Wash. Most counties above that line showed a higher than average rate of maternal mortality, while most below the line showed a below average rate.[20]

Infant mortality rates showed a rather different pattern. In the late nineteenth century when all parts of Wales suffered a high rate of maternal mortality, only Glamorgan returned a corresponding high rate of infant mortality. The rural counties of mid- and west Wales showed average or below average rates of infant mortality.

In England, generally speaking, high maternal and high infant mortality was typical of counties dominated by industry (Lancashire, some of the Midlands, the West Riding of Yorkshire, and the industrial north-east). It seems that areas of heavy industry, mining, iron and steel production, and the mill and potteries towns, fostered an adverse environment for infants and a poor standard of maternal care with a high rate of streptococcal infection.[21] Rural counties with scattered populations and remote areas such as Cumberland often showed high maternal mortality but low infant mortality, probably because infants gained from the non-industrial environment and absence of overcrowding, but mothers suffered from the absence of easily available maternal care. In the mostly rural, well-populated, and relatively prosperous counties with good communications, stretching from East Anglia across the south of England to Cornwall, the usual pattern was relatively low rates of maternal and infant mortality. Nevertheless, a significant number—Warwickshire, Leicestershire, Essex, and Wiltshire—showed either a high-rate maternal mortality alongside low infant mortality, or the reverse; so also did Westmorland and the East Riding of Yorkshire.

In short, there was not a close correlation between rates of maternal and infant mortality analysed by administrative county whether the data came from

---

[19] E. P. Hunt and R. R. Moore, *Perinatal, infant, childhood and maternal mortality, 1955*, US Dept. of Health, Education and Welfare, Social Security Administration, Children's Bureau (Washington, DC, 1958). The rank order of states was almost exactly the same 1938–40. The 1955 data were used, however, because they were more complete.

[20] See Chap. 14 and Appendix Table 18. See also A. Macfarlane and M. Mugford, *Birth Counts: Statistics of Pregnancy and Childbirth*, 2 vols. (London, 1984), i. 55 and 204, and W. Williams, 'Puerperal Mortality', *Transactions of the Epidemiological Society of London*, 15 (1895–6), 100–33.

[21] This hypothesis of a close link between rates of puerperal fever and rates of industrial accidents and infected wounds was argued cogently by G. Geddes in his *Statistics of Puerperal Sepsis and Allied Infectious Diseases* (Bristol, 1912).

the late nineteenth century or the inter-war period. Once again, this suggests that the rates of the two mortalities were governed by different sets of determinants.

MATERNAL MORTALITY AND MATERNAL AGE AND PARITY

One of the most complex issues in the study of maternal mortality on the one hand, and infant and neonatal mortality on the other, is the association between these mortality rates and maternal age and parity. A number of

TABLE 28.8 *Maternal Mortality Rate per 10,000 Deliveries by Order of Birth (Parity) for Mothers of All Ages, New York State (exclusive of New York City), 1936–1938*

Order of birth	Total deliveries (including stillbirths)	Maternal mortality rate (per 10,000 deliveries)
1	96,954	28.2
2	63,974	19.8
3	35,794	18.5
4 and 5	22,594	29.5
6 and 7	14,892	37.9
8 and over	12,258	55.1

Source: J. Yerushalmy, C. Palmer, and M. Kramer, 'Studies in Childbirth Mortality. II. Age and Parity as Factors in Puerperal Fatality', *Public Health Reports*, 55 (1940), 1195–220.

TABLE 28.9 *Maternal Mortality Rate per 10,000 Deliveries by Maternal Age for Mothers of All Parities, New York State (exclusive of New York City), 1936–1938*

Age of mother	Total deliveries (including stillbirths)	Maternal mortality rate (per 10,000 deliveries)
Under 20	22,264	15.5
20–4	77,920	16.7
25–9	72,545	23.4
30–4	47,750	32.9
35–9	25,597	50.0
40 and over	9,237	74.7

Source: J. Yerushalmy, C. Palmer, and M. Kramer, 'Studies in Childbirth Mortality. II. Age and Parity as Factors in Puerperal Fatality', *Public Health Reports*, 55 (1940), 1195–220.

TABLE 28.10 *Neonatal Mortality Rates per 1,000 Live Births by Parity and by Age of Mother, New York State (exclusive of New York City), 1936–1938*

By order of birth		By age of mother	
Order	Rate	Age	Rate
1	30.6	Under 20	37.9
2	25.9	20–4	28.3
3	26.7	25–9	25.8
4	30.4	30–4	29.8
5	35.1	35–9	35.8
6 and 7	37.6	40 and over	44.3
8 and 9	37.2		
10 and over	48.3		

Source: B. Yerushalmy, C. Palmer, and M. Kramer, 'Studies in Childbirth Mortality. II. Age and Parity as Factors in Puerperal Fatality', *Public Health Reports*, 55 (1940), 1195–220.

people have studied this association.[22] We can begin by referring to the work of Yerushalmy and his colleagues who undertook a study based on births in New York State (exclusive of New York City) in 1936, 1937, and 1938.[23] Tables 28.8, 28.9, 28.10, and 28.11 and Figures 28.7, 28.8, 28.9, and 28.10 are based on the results of this study.

If maternal mortality and neonatal mortality for mothers of all age-groups are plotted against parity, the graphs are broadly similar (Figure 28.7). They conform to a shape usually described as 'J'-shaped or 'U'-shaped although the shape is more like a tick. Mortality is high in first births, descends to the lowest levels in second and third births, and then climbs steadily, increasing with each subsequent birth.

[22] According to Yerushalmy, the first important investigation into the effects of age and parity were carried out in Australia in 1899: T. A. Coghlan, *Childbirth in New South Wales: A Study in Statistics*, Government Printer (Sydney, 1899). Coghlan's findings were confirmed by several authors but not extended significantly until Woodbury's study of infant mortality in 1926 referred to above and Yerushalmy's important work in 1940: J. Yerushalmy, C. E. Palmer, and M. Kramer, 'II. Age and Parity as Factors in Puerperal Fatality', *Public Health Reports*, 55 (1940), 1195–220. Woodbury analysed the effects of age and parity on infant mortality separately and showed that age *per se* had a significant effect in raising infant mortality in very young mothers, but it had relatively little effect after the age of 20. The increased risk in parities of five and over was almost entirely a parity effect with age playing little part. See also E. S. MacPhail, 'A Statistical Study in Maternal Mortality', *American Journal of Public Health*, 22 (1932), 612–26. For recent studies of earlier periods see J. E. Knodel and A. Hermalin, 'Effects of Birth Rank, Maternal Age, Birth Interval and Sibship size, on Infant and Child Mortality: Evidence from 18th and 19th Century Reproductive Histories', *American Journal of Public Health*, 74 (1984), 1098–106, and Knodel, *Demographic Behaviour in the Past* (Cambridge, 1988), 111 (Fig. 5.1).

[23] Yerushalmy, *et al.*, 'Age and Parity as Factors'.

TABLE 28.11 *The Associations between Age and Maternal Mortality and between Parity and Maternal Mortality, showing that Maternal Age and Parity are Independent Factors in the Determination of the Level of Maternal Mortality, New York State (exclusive of New York City), 1936–1938*

Order	Age of mother					
	under 20	20–4	25–9	30–4	35–9	40 and over
1	16.8	21.4	27.2	57.1	95.3	174.3
	(18,341)[a]	(41.561)	(24.588)	(9,282)	(2,621)	(459)
2	11.0	12.0	20.1	31.1	36.3	31.3
	(3,725)	(22,583)	(21,179)	(11,684)	(3,884)	(644)
3	—	5.5	23.3	20.7	24.8	44.8
	(522)	(9,231)	(12,228)	(8,823)	(4,090)	(898)
4 and 5	—	18.4	15.6)	22.7	51.4	96.8
	(67)	(4,495)	(11,149)	(10,385)	(6,511)	(1,982)
6 and 7	—	—	33.7	24.1	43.8	78.4
	(4)	(408)	(3,351)	(5,101)	(4,208)	(1,819)
8 and over	—	—	48.1	42.5	59.3	62.9
	—	(37)	(854)	(3,139)	(4,669)	(3,556)

[a] Maternal mortality rates per 10,000 deliveries. In brackets are the number of births on which each of these maternal mortality rates is based.

Note that births and deliveries are not the same. There were in this series 258,525 births. It is likely that of these 1 in 80 (3,231) would be twin births, and 1 in 6,400 (40) would be births of triplets. The number of deliveries would therefore be approximately 258,525 − (3,231 + 80) = 225,214.

Source: B. Yerushalmy, C. Palmer, and M. Kramer, 'Studies in Childbirth Mortality. II. Age and Parity as Factors in Puerperal Fatality', *Public Health Reports*, 55 (1940), 1195–220.

Figure 28.7 also shows that when maternal and neonatal mortality rates are plotted against maternal age for all parities, neonatal mortality conforms to the same type of curve: high in first births, low in second and third, but climbing again in higher parities. Figure 28.7 shows a continuous and steep rise in maternal mortality with increasing maternal age. Unfortunately the data on which this figure is based did not show as a separate category the maternal mortality for very young mothers under the age of 17, a category which is shown consistently in other studies to have suffered a high rate of maternal mortality. Had these been shown the tick-shaped curve would have been evident.[24] Note that the MMR in mothers aged 40 or over was about five times as high as that for mothers under the age of 20.

[24] In Yerushalmy's study, the youngest age-group is 'under 20'. Thus it gives no data on maternal mortality in very young mothers which other studies have shown to be very high. In a study of 287,163 births in Kentucky covering the years 1932 to 1936, the MMR for mothers

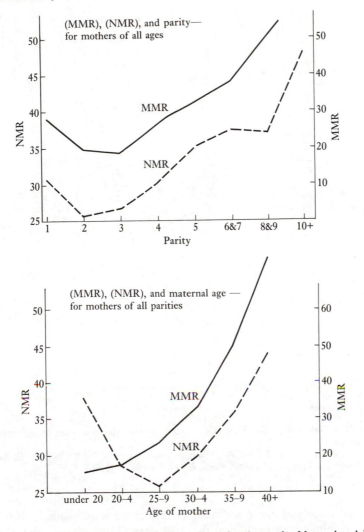

Fig. 28.7 New York State, 1936–1938. The effect of parity on the Maternal and Neonatal Mortality Rates for mothers of all ages
Source: J. Yerushalmy, C. E. Palmer, M. Kramer, 'Studies in Childbirth Mortality. II. Age and Parity as Factors in Puerperal Fatality', *Public Health Reports*, 55 (1940), 1195–220.

aged 10–14 was 140 per 10,000 births, for mothers aged 15–19 it was 42, and for mothers aged 20–4 it was 37. For older age groups the MMR increased steadily to 147 in the group aged 45 and over showing the 'J-' or tick-shaped curve was present in the graph of maternal age and maternal mortality as well as parity and maternal mortality. C. B. Crittenden and L. Skaggs, *Maternal Mortality in Kentucky: A Study of Puerperal Deaths, 1932–1939*, Kentucky State Board of Health (1939).

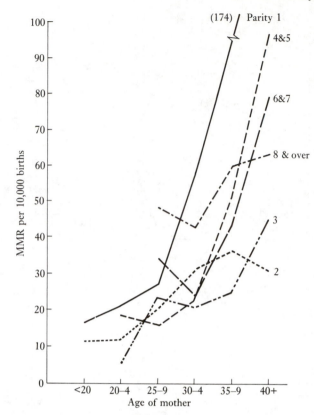

FIG. 28.8 New York State, 1936–1938. The effect of age on Maternal Mortality for mothers of various parities
Source: J. Yerushalmy, C. E. Palmer, M. Kramer, 'Studies in Childbirth Mortality. II. Age and Parity as Factors in Puerperal Fatality', *Public Health Reports*, 55 (1940), 1195–220.

Obviously, age and parity are connected because most mothers with large families are older than mothers with small ones. The question, therefore, is whether we are looking at one determinant in two different ways, or whether age and parity are in fact two separate and independent determinants. The answer is provided by Table 28.11, and Figures. 28.8 and 28.9; but a word of warning is necessary when these are examined in detail.

Maternal deaths are much less common in relation to births than neonatal deaths. The ratio in this series of cases was 1:7. Most reports of maternal mortality which include data on maternal age and parity for periods before the Second World War were based on small numbers of births, too small to stand up to detailed analysis. Conversely, data on maternal mortality in large populations seldom included information on age and parity. The data from

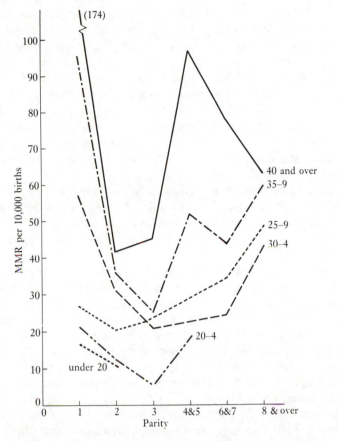

FIG. 28.9 New York State, 1936–1938. The effect of parity on Maternal Mortality Rates for
mothers of various ages
Source: J. Yerushalmy, C. E. Palmer, M. Kramer, 'Studies in Childbirth Mortality. II. Age and
Parity as Factors in Puerperal Fatality', *Public Health Reports*, 55 (1940), 1195–220.

New York State for 1936–8 are exceptional. They were based on 258,525
deliveries, 1,122 maternal deaths, and 7,550 neonatal deaths. In only 59
deliveries were data on maternal age and parity not available. Even here,
however, the MMR in some of the cells in Table 28.11 was based on such
small numbers of births that the range of probable error was large. The
maternal mortality in mothers aged 40 or over having their first baby, for
example, was based on only eight maternal deaths, and that for mothers aged
40 and over having their second babies on only two maternal deaths. In
contrast, the MMR for first births in women aged 20 (the cell with the largest
number of births) was based on 89 maternal deaths. We can feel much more
confident about the latter rates than the former. With these provisos in mind,
we can examine Figures. 28.8 and 28.9.

Figure. 28.8 shows that for all parities, maternal mortality increases with age, but the effect of increasing age is most striking in first births and fourth and over births. In second and third births, although maternal mortality rises with age the extent of the rise is small. Figure. 28.9 shows that at all ages there is a higher maternal risk in first births than second or third. Thereafter, regardless of maternal age, increasing parity usually led to an increased risk of maternal mortality. (The downturns in the graphs in parities 4 and over in women aged 35 and aged 40 and over, are probably artefacts.) Overall, however, we can be confident that age and parity were independent determinants of maternal mortality. This conclusion was confirmed, albeit in less detail, by other studies.[25]

What clinical factors were associated with these patterns of maternal mortality? First pregnancies have the highest incidence of toxaemia. First labours tend to be more prolonged, more difficult, and more liable to surgical intervention. Before 1935, primiparity was associated with high death rates from sepsis, toxaemia, shock, and trauma; but the risk of haemorrhage was usually lower in first than in any other births. With increasing multiparity, especially when it was linked to age over 30, labours tended to be quick, deaths due to sepsis were relatively uncommon, but deaths due to haemorrhage were frequent partly because of a higher incidence of placenta praevia in older women and women of high parity, but more often because of postpartum haemorrhage due to the poor ability of the 'tired and worn-out' multiparous uterus to contract firmly.

Today, deaths from puerperal sepsis and haemorrhage have become rare in the West because of better general health, better obstetric care, antibiotics, and blood transfusion. As a consequence the distribution of the direct causes of maternal mortality in recent years is very different from that which obtained in and before the mid-1930s. One might expect that the associations between maternal mortality and age and parity would have altered or disappeared altogether. In fact, as Figure 28.10 shows, they have not.

The latest of the series *Reports on Confidential Enquiries into Maternal Deaths in England and Wales*[26] includes an analysis of maternal mortality in terms of age and parity for England and Wales from 1976 to 1984. In spite of the profound fall in the overall MMR, the associations between maternal mortality, and maternal age and parity, correspond remarkably closely to those shown in Table 28.11. There has been a world-wide reduction in maternal mortality.[27] What is surprising is how little impact this has had on the relative risks for women of different ages and different parities. Mortality differentials for mothers and infants are not immutable, but they are remarkably stable.

---

[25] See n. 22, above.

[26] Department of Health, *Report on Confidential Enquiries into Maternal Deaths in England and Wales, 1982–84*, Report on Health and Social Subjects, No. 34 (London, 1989), 7 (Table 1.10).

[27] The MMRs (per 10,000 live births), recorded in recent years, were 1.6 in France (1981),

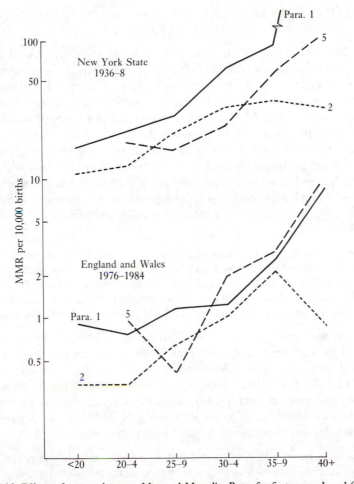

Fig. 28.10 Effects of maternal age on Maternal Mortality Rates for first, second, and fifth births in New York State, 1936–1938 and England and Wales, 1976–1984
Source: J. Yerushalmy, C. E. Palmer, M. Kramer, 'Studies in Childbirth Mortality. II. Age and Parity as Factors in Puerperal Fatality', *Public Health Reports*, 55 (1940), 1195–220, and England and Wales, Department of Health, *Reports on Confidential Enquiries into Maternal Death in England and Wales, 1982–84*, Reports on Health and Social Subjects, No. 34 (London, HMSO, 1989), 7.

1.0 in the USA (1979), Belgium (1981), and England and Wales (1981), 0.8 in the Netherlands (1981), 0.7 in Switzerland (1981), 0.6 in Canada (1978), and 0.4 in Denmark and Sweden (1981). *Maternal Mortality Rates*, World Health Organisation, Division of Family Health (1985).

NEONATAL MORTALITY AND MATERNAL AGE AND PARITY

Figure 28.7 and Table 28.10 show that neonatal mortality plotted against age or parity follows the similar J-shaped or tick-shaped curve as that for maternal mortality and parity. The high rates of maternal and neonatal mortality associated with first deliveries may well reflect common causes on some occasions, such as high rates of toxaemia and of prolonged and difficult births leading to a high rate of intervention. But the high rates of neonatal and infant mortality associated with high multiparity and increasing maternal age cannot be explained by common underlying causes. It was with these problems in mind that Gray described the investigation of infant mortality as 'a methodological minefield'.[28] The complexity of the precise relationships between maternal reproductive patterns and infant mortality is due to the way in which:

The reproductive variables of maternal age, parity, and birth interval are highly interrelated . . . Short birth intervals may be either a cause or consequence of child death . . . The death of a child may lead to a short birth interval because the cessation of lactational amenorrhea results in an early resumption of fertility, or because mothers of dead children tend to replace the lost child and go on to further pregnancies.[29]

Here, Gray was writing about the work of Knodel and his study of German villages in the eighteenth and nineteenth centuries. As far as maternal age is concerned, Knodel's study showed that neonatal mortality rose with increasing maternal age. It rose less, however, than the rise in maternal mortality with increasing maternal age; and 'post-neonatal mortality . . . displays essentially a pattern of a modest direct increase with mother's age'.[30] As far as parity and infant mortality were concerned, Knodel found there was

little association between birth order and [infant] mortality risk. In contrast, the total number of children born to a mother *is* related to infant mortality, regardless of the child's birth rank. For large sibships, infant mortality is high for children of all birth orders, while for smaller sibships, infant mortality is lower regardless of birth rank.[31]

This is an important observation for it seems to show that whereas parity is closely related to maternal mortality, it is sibship size and not parity that is related to infant mortality.

Common explanations for high infant mortality in large families include too little food to go round, increased exposure of infants to infections from siblings, and neglect of later-born infants by mothers worn out by age and

---

[28] R. H. Gray, 'Maternal Reproduction and Child Survival', *American Journal of Public Health* (1984).
[29] Ibid.
[30] Knodel, *Demographic Behaviour in the Past*.
[31] Ibid.

having to cope with a large family on a low income. This, however, would usually be true only for large families with short birth intervals. If birth intervals were long, the older children would either have left home before the younger ones were born, or remained at home to become providers, thereby increasing family income.

For large sibships with short birth intervals it has been suggested by Gray that breastfeeding habits were critical. A short duration of lactation would be associated with short birth intervals, higher infant mortality, and large completed families. Further, the 'replacement of loss' factor could also explain why high infant mortality occurred selectively in large sibships, especially in modern periods when birth-control had become widespread. 'Women who lose children selectively progress to further pregnancies, but women without child loss selectively stop reproduction.' Gray stresses the importance of Knodel's methodology:

It is clear that the association between high birth order or parity and increased mortality observed in previous retrospective or cross-sectional studies is, in part, an artifact due to the inappropriate comparison of families at different stages of formation, since lower birth ranks may arise from either small or incomplete large families, but higher birth ranks can only occur in larger families.[32]

This glimpse of modern work on the associations between maternal reproductive patterns and infant mortality is enough to show the complexity of a subject in which there are still unsolved problems. As far as the effects of maternal age and parity are concerned, there appear to be close similarities in the tick-shaped graphs of maternal and neonatal mortality. On the one hand, the high rates of maternal and neonatal mortality in first births and young mothers, shown by the short left-hand segment of the tick-shaped curve, probably represents the effects of the same or similar determinants; for example, high rates of toxaemia and difficult labours. On the other hand, the increasingly high rates of both maternal and neonatal mortality associated with increasing parity and older mothers almost certainly reflects the effects of two quite different sets of determinants in maternal mortality and neonatal mortality respectively. There cannot be many occasions when one finds two closely similar graphs in which similarity of the first part of each graph represents common underlying causation, while the similarity of the second part is coincidental in the sense of being due to quite different underlying causes. The relationship between maternal and neonatal mortality is indeed complex.

THE DIRECT CAUSES OF MATERNAL AND INFANT MORTALITY

In 1968, it was argued on slender grounds by Shapiro and his colleagues that 'the same forces, economic, social and medical that influence the level of

[32] Gray, 'Maternal Reproduction and Child Survival'.

infant and perinatal mortality affect the rate of maternal mortality'.[33] The
evidence we have reviewed suggests this conclusion was wrong. The forces (or
determinants) were not the same. The evidence, however, has been based on
the study of mortality rates within large populations. We have dealt with the
deaths of mothers and babies *en masse*. Moving from the general to the
particular, can we link our findings to individual instances—in other words to
the direct causes of maternal, neonatal, and post-neonatal mortality to see if
they 'make sense'? If they do not, we would do well to suspect that our
conclusions are wrong.

There is no problem with post-neonatal deaths. They occurred at least a
month after delivery. The large majority were caused by infections associated
with environmental causes. Apart from uncommon cases such as late deaths
due to congenital malformations, there is no logical reason to suspect a
necessary connection between deaths after the age of a month and events
occurring at or before birth. The problems come with neonatal deaths. They
are the ones which should show close links with maternal deaths, through the
shared experience of events during intrauterine life and the process of birth.
Yet, as I said earlier, in spite of the increasing demographic shift from the
beginning of this century whereby the component of infant mortality due
to neonatal deaths has steadily increased while post-neonatal deaths have
decreased, there is no evidence at all that this process led to closer links
between maternal and neonatal mortality. That really is surprising, especially
with the compelling evidence of Woodbury and Yerushalmy, quoted at the
opening of this chapter. To discover why maternal and neonatal mortality
were not, as common sense would suggest, closely linked, we must start by
examining the three most important causes of neonatal mortality: prematurity,
congenital malformations, and birth injury. All three sound like straightforward causes, but they are not quite as simple as they appear.

PREMATURITY AND PRE-TERM DELIVERY

Prematurity was originally described rather than defined as babies which were
born too early and were therefore small. When a precise definition was
needed, prematurity was defined in terms of birth weight, estimates of gesta-
tional age being considered too unreliable. Any baby weighing less than 5 lbs.
was by definition premature. The metric value of 2,500 gms. instead of 5 lbs.
was suggested by the Ministry of Health in Britain in 1936 and adopted by
the World Health Organization in 1950. This definition, however, was unsatisfactory. It failed to distinguish between babies which were small because
they were born too early ('premature babies' in the ordinary sense), and babies

[33] S. Shapiro, E. R. Schlesinger, and R. E. L. Nesbitt, *Infant, Perinatal, Maternal, and
Childhood Mortality in the United States* (Cambridge, Mass., 1968).

which were born at or near term but were small because they were unable to grow to their proper size as a result of placental insufficiency ('small for dates' babies). The prognosis of the two groups is different.[34] Since 1969 prematurity has been called pre-term delivery. It is now defined as deliveries which take place at less than thirty-seven weeks' (259 days') gestation, regardless of birthweight. Pre-term deliveries, then, are not a single homogeneous group but a number of different groups differing in outcome, cause, and in their links with foetal and maternal pathology.[35]

At the present about 12 per cent of pre-term babies have either died *in utero* (stillbirths), or have lethal congenital malformations incompatible with life (neonatal deaths). Congenital malformations can themselves be the direct cause of pre-term delivery so that a neonatal death may occur from the coexistence of these two factors.[36] Today a relatively large number of babies are pre-term because of elective delivery by induction or Caesarean section. In these, the reason for elective delivery is often a maternal complication such as toxaemia (hypertensive disease of pregnancy) or placenta praevia. Others are spontaneous pre-term deliveries, but about half of these are associated with maternal or foetal pathology.[37] Gross immaturity is more common in spontaneous than elective pre-term delivery.

In a recent (1976) review of pre-term deliveries 28 per cent were elective, 10 per cent were associated with multiple pregnancy, 24 per cent were spontaneous but associated with maternal or foetal complications, and 38 per cent were of unknown cause, occurring in apparently healthy mothers.[38] Although some pre-term (premature) deliveries are, and were in the past, associated with maternal pathology a substantial proportion were of unknown cause and not associated in any way with maternal risk factors. Even when pre-term deliveries were associated with maternal pathology, the pathology was not always a risk factor for the mother (this is discussed below). That being the case, there is no reason to expect in the majority of cases that there should be a link between maternal deaths and the most common neonatal deaths, those due to prematurity.

[34] Common sense might suggest that 'small for dates' babies would be more likely to die than premature (in the ordinary sense of the word) babies of the same weight, because the former were starved and sickly with retarded growth. In fact the opposite is true. The genuinely premature are not only small, they are immature, not having had time to develop properly. The 'small for dates', although small for their age, are not immature and have had time to develop. In addition, having been exposed to deprivation they may have adapted to adversity enabling them to cope better with independent life. Such are the kind of hypotheses put forward to explain the better prognosis of the 'small for dates' babies. Personal communication: Dr Iain Chalmers.

[35] M. J. N. C. Keirse, 'Preterm Delivery', in I. Chalmers, M. Enkin, and M. J. N. C. Keirse, *Effective Care in Pregnancy and Childbirth*, 2 vols. (Oxford, 1989), 1270–92.

[36] Ibid.

[37] Ibid.

[38] R. W. Rush, *et al.*, 'Contribution of Preterm Delivery to Perinatal Mortality', *British Medical Journal* (1976), ii. 965–8.

BIRTH INJURY

The term birth injury carries the implication that somebody, presumably the birth-attendant, was responsible for inflicting or failing to prevent injury to the baby during labour. It is only a short step to suppose that those who so injured the baby would probably have injured the mother providing a logical link between maternal amd neonatal mortality in cases of neonatal deaths ascribed to birth injury. As we have seen there is little doubt that sometimes this was true. Recent research, however, has questioned the implications of the emotive terms 'birth injury' and 'brain damage'. The research has been concerned mainly with the supposed close link between birth injury and cerebral palsy, a link which forms the basis of many legal actions today. Illingworth published a paper in 1985 entitled 'A paediatrician asks—why is it called birth injury?' in which he drew attention to the lack of any clear association between so-called 'brain damage' and difficult labours, and the frequent occurrence of cerebral palsy in babies after easy straightforward labours.[39] The aetiology of cerebral palsy is still poorly understood. Cerebral palsy and birth injury are not the same. These observations, however, warn us that implications of negligence, of roughness, of injury in the ordinary sense are not always justified. Thus it follows that in some cases where birth injury was the certified cause of death of the infant, there was no necessary abnormality in the labour as far as the mother was concerned.

CAUSES IN INDIVIDUALS AND POPULATIONS

With these provisos in mind we can consider individual cases. Although the following case histories of maternal and neonatal deaths are hypothetical, they were all commonplace events in childbirth in the past.

A. Because of cervical incompetence in a healthy mother, rupture of membranes occurred and a baby was born at thirty weeks after a quick easy labour. The baby died of immaturity associated with pre-term delivery. The mother's health was not in jeopardy.[40]

B. A mother contracted rubella during pregnancy. She had an easy delivery but the baby died within the first month from multiple congenital abnormalities.

C. A mother developed severe toxaemia of pregnancy and died shortly after delivery during an eclamptic fit. The baby was small because of retarded

[39] R. S. Illingworth, 'A Paediatrician Asks: Why is it Called Birth Injury?', *British Journal of Obstetrics and Gynaecology*, 92 (1985), 122–30. See especially a recent review of this subject by D. M. B. Hall, 'Birth Asphyxia and Cerebral Palsy', *British Medical Journal* (1989), ii. 279–82.

[40] In normal pregnancies, the internal os of the cervix remains tightly closed until the onset of labour. In some instances, the os opens slightly during pregnancy allowing the membranes to bulge into the cervical canal with a high risk of premature rupture in late pregnancy. This is cervical incompetence.

intrauterine growth associated with toxaemia, and died soon after birth, the cause being registered as prematurity.

D. During her first delivery a mother had a prolonged and difficult labour with an occipito-posterior presentation. After six hours in the second stage at home, she was admitted to hospital by her doctor as a case of 'failed forceps'. She was delivered on admission but died of shock. The baby died soon after delivery and death was attributed to birth injury.

E. After a quick easy labour, a mother developed puerperal fever on the fifth postnatal day and died a few days later. The baby survived and was healthy.

F. After an uneventful pregnancy and labour a mother developed a deep vein thrombosis and died of a pulmonary embolus on the tenth postnatal day. The baby remained healthy.

In cases A and B, the babies died of causes associated with forms of maternal pathology (cervical incompetence and rubella in pregnancy) which carried no maternal risk. In cases C and D a common underlying cause (toxaemia/eclampsia and a 'failed forceps in a difficult labour') provided a clear and obvious link between the deaths of the mothers and the infants. In cases E and F (puerperal fever and pulmonary embolus) the causes of the mothers' deaths were not risk factors as far as the infant was concerned.

By taking case histories such as these, one can see that the answer to the question: 'Does analysis of the immediate causes of maternal amd neonatal deaths demonstrate a clear link between the two?' is 'sometimes yes, sometimes no'. When we turn from individual cases to populations, the closeness of the link between maternal and neonatal mortality clearly depends on the proportion of the cases which come into the 'yes' and the 'no' categories respectively. This is not very difficult to determine.

Table 28.12 shows maternal deaths by cause for England and Wales in 1934. It is divided into two groups. The first group consists of causes of maternal mortality in which the maternal risk factors were also neonatal risk factors. This group accounted for 28.2 per cent of all maternal deaths. The second group consists of categories of maternal mortality in which there was no association between maternal and neonatal deaths. This group is dominated by sepsis and abortion which accounted for almost half the total maternal deaths. The whole group accounted for 71.8 per cent of total maternal deaths. Therefore, causal links between neonatal and maternal mortality can be postulated in just over a quarter of all maternal deaths in 1934. In countries which included associated (indirect) maternal deaths in their calculation of maternal mortality (for instance the USA and Australia) the percentage of maternal deaths in which maternal and neonatal factors coexisted (the first group of Table 28.12) would be even smaller in relation to the total, probably in the region of 20 per cent.

TABLE 28.12 *Causes of Maternal Mortality and their Relationship to Neonatal Mortality, England and Wales, 1934*

	Number of Deaths	Percentage
Total deaths from all causes	2,768	100
Causes of maternal death in which an associated neonatal death was likely to occur		
Toxaemia of pregnancy plus puerperal albuminuria and convulsions	494	(17.8)
Placenta praevia	109	(3.9)
Accidental haemorrhage	16	
Certain accidents of childbirth, namely		
Contracted pelvis	54	
Instrumental delivery	8	
Version	1	
Difficult or prolonged labour	89	
Caesarean section	9	
Total	780	28.2
Causes of maternal death in which an associated neonatal death was impossible or unlikely		
Non-septic abortion	99	(3.6)
Post-abortive sepsis	295	(10.6)
Non-abortive puerperal sepsis	917	(33.1)
Ectopic gestation	88	
Other accidents of pregnancy	28	
Post-partum haemorrhage	83	
Retained or adherent placenta	57	
Other toxaemias of pregnancy, namely		
Chorea	2	
Uncontrolled vomiting	44	
Other accidents of childbirth apart from those specified above	132	
Other or unspecified causes	85	
Total	1,988	71.8

Source: Registrar General's Statistical Review for the Year 1934 (New Annual Series, no. 14), 118–20.

Do these calculations help us to understand what we have found about maternal and neonatal mortality in demographic terms? Do they make sense of those findings? The answer is emphatically that they do. For instance, many of the causes of maternal mortality in the first group in Table 28.7 (toxaemia, accidental haemorrhage, and those included under the heading 'certain accidents of childbirth') were more common in first than subsequent pregnancies. They provide a basis for understanding why maternal and neonatal mortality were both substantially higher in first deliveries than later ones (Figure. 28.7). We have also seen that the steep and sustained fall in maternal mortality which began in the mid-1930s was not accompanied by a similar fall in neonatal mortality. The explanation is that the steep fall in maternal mortality was initially due to a reduction in deaths which belong to the second group in Table 28.7, the group in which the causes of maternal mortality were not linked to neonatal deaths; notably puerperal sepsis, abortion, and post-partum haemorrhage. The cause of maternal death which showed the least fall in the period following the mid-1930s was toxaemia; and toxaemia was the only one of the *major* causes of maternal deaths which was closely linked to neonatal deaths.

Thus the links between neonatal and maternal mortality were tenuous. They certainly existed, but only in a minority of cases. They were swamped by the majority in which such links did not occur. To refer to the non-environmental factors of neonatal mortality as 'natal factors' is both permissible and useful as a way of distinguishing them from the environmental factors of post-neonatal mortality. But it is clear that 'natal should not be taken to imply that maternal risk factors and neonatal risk factors were closely linked, and still less that they were identical. If we accept the absence of close links between post-neonatal and maternal mortality because post-neonatal deaths are due to environmental causes, we can also accept the absence of close links between neonatal and maternal deaths. The study of immediate causes provides a logical explanation. It shows that the 'natal' causes of maternal mortality were generally quite separate from the 'natal' causes of neonatal mortality.

How, then, can we reconcile this with the evidence of Woodbury and Yerushalmy, quoted at the beginning of this chapter, that babies whose mothers have died suffer a 'considerable handicap' which makes them four to six times more likely to die before their first birthday than those whose mothers survived when this seems to be such convincing evidence of a close link between maternal and infant mortality? The brief answer is that in spite of the increased risk, only a small minority of infant deaths were associated with a maternal death. The consequence can be demonstrated by the following calculations.

Let us suppose we have a population in which the MMR is on average 5 per 1,000 births and the IMR 100 per 1,000 births. Mortality rates of this order were common in Western countries near the beginning of this century.

First let us suppose that the death of a mother did *not* increase the risk of the infant dying. For every 1,000 deliveries there were on average one-tenth of that number of infant deaths; that is 100 infant deaths but only 5 maternal deaths. For the 995 deliveries in which the mother survived, there would have been on average 99.5 infant deaths. For the 5 mothers who died there would have been on average 0.5 infant deaths. Total infant deaths would then of course have been 100.

Now we can repeat the calculation; but this time we allow for the extra handicap imposed on those infants whose mothers died. For these infants the chances of them dying in the first year were increased by a factor of six compared with the cases in which the mother survived. What difference would that make to the overall infant mortality rate of the population?

For the 995 mothers who survived, the number of infant deaths would have been the same as above, 99.5. But in the case of the mothers who died, the number of infants dying would have been multiplied by 6. So the expected number of deaths associated with the 5 maternal deaths would not have been 0.5, as above, but $0.5 \times 6 = 3.0$. This means that the total number of infant deaths would have been $99.5 + 3.0 = 102.5$. We can see that the effect of the 'considerable handicap' on the IMR of the total population was only slight. Therefore, wide differences in maternal mortality between populations, or in the same population at different periods, would not produce differences of the same order in infant mortality.

We can take this a stage further by repeating the above calculation for a population in which the MMR was twice as high; namely 10 maternal deaths per 1,000 deliveries rather than 5. Then the IMR would have been 99.0 amongst the infants of the 990 mothers who survived, and $6.0(1.0 \times 6)$ in the infants whose mothers died. The IMR of the population would have been raised only to $99.0 + 6.0 = 105$. Thus the effect of the handicap was so slight in demographic terms that a 100 per cent increase in MMR would have produced an increase in infant mortality of no more than about 2 per cent.

CONCLUSIONS

1. Broadly speaking, the predominant form of infant mortality in the West was post-neonatal mortality in the nineteenth century, neonatal in the twentieth. As the twentieth century progressed, the proportion of neonatal deaths in infant mortality increased steadily, and the proportion of early neonatal deaths in neonatal mortality likewise increased. In most Western countries by the 1960s, early neonatal deaths formed by far the largest part of infant mortality.

2. That there were not in general close links between maternal and infant mortality rates was shown by comparing secular trends, by comparing the levels of each in different countries and different regions, and by comparing the associations of each mortality rate with a number of determinants of mortality such as social class, maternal age and parity, urban and rural differences, and so forth. It should be added that the associations between maternal reproductive patterns and infant survival is perhaps the most complex problem and one that is still most debated.

3. The lack of association between maternal and post-neonatal mortality is

logical because most post-neonatal deaths were due to environmental factors rather than natal ones.

4. The lack of close links between neonatal and maternal mortality was unexpected but can be explained by the finding that most maternal deaths were due to causes which did not put the neonate's life at hazard. Conversely, many neonatal deaths (especially those due to congenital deformities and most due to prematurity) were due to maternal or foetal pathology which did not put the mother's life at hazard.

5. If the *determinants* of mortality as opposed to the *immediate causes* are considered in relation to maternal, post-neonatal, and neonatal mortality, the following generalizations are, I believe, true in most cases. Levels of maternal mortality were determined most of all by standards of care provided by birth-attendants. Poor obstetric care could either consist of ignorance of basic procedures (judged by the standards of the time), or it could consist of dangerous and unwarranted interference by trained personnel. Maternal mortality was relatively insensitive to social and economic determinants except in so far as these determined the type and quality of birth-attendant. High maternal risk could be associated with cheap untrained midwives or expensive over-zealous and unskilled doctors. Sound obstetric practice by well-trained midwives could produce low levels of maternal mortality even in populations which were socially and economically deprived.

Levels of post-neonatal mortality were determined mostly by breastfeeding customs and environmental circumstances. Post-neonatal mortality was sensitive to social and economic deprivation, especially in countries subjected in war to siege or occupation. Sanitary measures were very important determinants of post-neonatal mortality, but treatment by nurses or doctors at the bedside was seldom important in determining the level of post-neonatal mortality before the second half of this century.

Levels of neonatal mortality were determined to a great extent by factors we do not understand. The quality of maternal care probably played a minor, but certainly not a large part.

6. Mortality rates are a fairly insensitive measure of the effects of economic deprivation. Morbidity rates would be a more sensitive index, but the necessary data are seldom available. Quite severe degrees of maternal, infant, and child morbidity can exist without obvious changes in mortality rates, although there is a growing body of evidence which suggests that long-term effects from *in utero* or neonatal deprivation can occur.

7. If these suggestions are correct, it is clear that measures designed to reduce maternal and infant mortality required quite different approaches. This has some relevance to certain third world countries today in which levels of maternal and infant mortality are similar to and sometimes exceed those seen in the West in the early years of the twentieth century.[41]

[41] A. Rosenfield and D. Maine, 'Maternal Mortality: A Neglected Tragedy. Where is the M in MCH?', *Lancet* (1985), ii. 83–5.

Appendix 1
Hidden Maternal Deaths

In the *Forty-Fourth Annual Report of the Registrar General* (Abstracts of 1881), the Registrar General wrote:

> Not rarely, the real cause of death is purposely disguised in order to spare the susceptibilities of friends, or, it may be, to conceal the existence of infectious disease . . . More frequently, however, the deficiencies in the certificates are not intentional but due to carelessness . . . An effort was made this year to remedy this evil, and to get greater precision in the statement of causes. With this object, letters of inquiry were sent out to medical men who had given certificates in which the causes of death were imperfectly stated, asking for further particulars. The exigencies of office work did not allow of this being done to more than a very limited extent. Still, a beginning was made . . . In all some 1,200 letters of inquiry were sent out . . .

These enquiries, although they dealt with only a sample of unsatisfactory certificates, revealed that out of 183 deaths certified as 'blood poisoning, pyaemia, septicaemia' a puerperal cause was found in 89. Out of 321 inquiries concerning deaths due to 'peritonitis', a puerperal cause was found in 136. Altogether, a total of 330 'hidden' maternal deaths were discovered, of which 80 per cent were deaths due to puerperal fever. All these deaths which, had there been no enquiry would have been assigned to non-puerperal causes, were allocated to puerperal sepsis. The 330 deaths represented an addition of 8 per cent to total maternal mortality and 12 per cent of deaths due to puerperal fever. It is probable therefore that before 1880 maternal deaths as a whole, and puerperal sepsis deaths were under-recorded to at least the same extent.

Farr's successor at the General Register Office, Dr Ogle, carried out a similar exercise on a larger scale. He instituted a confidential enquiry between the General Register Office and the certifying medical practitioners of England and Wales. The results were published in the Decennial Supplement for the years 1881–90.[1]

More than 20,000 letters were sent out. About 4,000 related to deaths certified as being due to 'peritonitis' occurring in women of childbearing age. Of these, more than 1,000 were eventually transferred to puerperal fever. Of 3,000 deaths certified as 'pyaemia, septicaemia' 700 were found to have been due to puerperal causes. Of 272 deaths certified as 'haemorrhage', 69 were connected with childbirth, and of 244 attributed to 'metritis' (a term which means inflammation of the uterus) more than half were found to have been connected with the puerperal state. In all, nearly 3,000 deaths in the decennium, in which the certifying practitioners had written a vague cause of death, were found to be deaths in childbirth. After the corrections had been made the

---

[1] *Supplement to the 55th Annual Report of the Registrar General* (1895).

total childbirth deaths for the decade amounted to 42,092. 'Hidden' deaths therefore amounted to a *minimum* of 7 per cent of the total, and the large majority of these were deaths due to puerperal fever.

It was clear that in the 1890s as well as the 1880s, many deaths due to childbirth were, deliberately or accidentally, certified in such a way that they appeared to be deaths from non-puerperal causes. Medical practitioners continued to be resistant to exhortations to improve the accuracy of certification. Ogle told the Select Committee on Death Registration in 1893 that practitioners often replied to his inquiries with abuse, and complained of the absence of a fee for death certification, and, like their successors today, of 'interfering bureaucracy', and the tedium of filling up forms.

By 1898, the level of accuracy was still deplorable. 'The causes of 23,039, or 4.2 per cent of the total deaths, were so unsatisfactorily stated in the registers as to be useless for purposes of classification.' The largest number of these were deaths under the age of 1, of which 17.9 per cent were unsatisfactory—a point to be remembered by historians of infant mortality. But it was also found that out of 454 deaths returned as 'peritonitis, pelvic cellulitis, metritis', and 291 certified as 'pyaemia and septicaemia', 101 and 30 respectively were deaths due to puerperal fever. Once again, some 10 per cent of hidden maternal deaths were discovered in the Registrar General's Office and reallocated to puerperal causes.[2]

By 1923, the accuracy of certification had greatly improved. A total of 8,788 inquiries were sent to medical practitioners and replies were received from 7,905. Because of expense and the considerable amount of work involved, this was, as before, only a sample of imperfect certificates. Out of 182 inquiries concerning deaths certified as 'pyaemia and septicaemia' only 8 were due to puerperal sepsis. Out of 183 inquiries concerning deaths certified as 'peritonitis' only 5 were due to childbirth causes.[3] The results of continuing enquiries during the years 1927–32 can be seen in Table A1.1. The Registrar General managed to restore a certain proportion of maternal deaths to their rightful place by carefully searching deaths attributed to septicaemia and peritonitis. But this was not the only way that maternal deaths were hidden.

We saw in Chapter 2 that deaths due to puerperal fever were sometimes attributed to a non-septic puerperal cause such as 'haemorrhage' to avoid the accusation of a poor standard of antisepsis. Hospitals and obstetricians tended to be sensitive to such an accusation and sometimes yielded to the temptation to transfer a death from a septic to a non-septic category to improve the look of the annual report. While the total mortality from childbirth would be unaltered, the mortality from sepsis would be reduced. If 'haemorrhage' was chosen, however, the deceit could be exposed by the time of the death. Deaths due to puerperal fever usually occur between the seventh to fourteenth postnatal day, deaths due to haemorrhage in the first few hours or days at the most (Appendix Table 27). However, around the fourteenth day is the period in which most deaths from deep vein thrombosis and pulmonary embolism occur, deaths which used to be classified as 'phlegmasia alba dolens, embolism and sudden death'. This provided a much safer classification to anyone who wanted to hide a death due to puerperal fever.

---

[2] *61st Annual Report of the Registrar General for 1898.*
[3] *Registrar General's Statistical Review for 1925* (1927).

TABLE A1.1 *England and Wales, 1927–1932. Showing the Reallocation of Certain Causes of Death as a Result of Enquiries into Death Certificates in which the Recorded Cause of Death was Indefinite in the Two Categories in which 'Hidden' Deaths from Puerperal Sepsis were Found, Namely 'Pyaemia and Septicaemia' and 'Peritonitis'*

Causes of death	1927	1928	1929	1930	1931	1932
Pyaemia/Septicaemia						
Replies received	170	168	202	181	216	197
Cause of death reallocated as:						
Diseases teeth and gums	7	14	5	11	13	10
Tonsillitis	6	8	6	7	19	22
Diseases of skin	18	15	20	21	32	29
Disease of umbilicus	—	—	5	—	—	—
Puerperal sepsis	9	9	3	6	5	6
Peritonitis						
Replies received	177	122	100	85	78	83
Cause of death reallocated as:						
TB of peritoneum	3	4	5	3	3	—
Syphilis	1	—	1	—	—	—
Cancer	6	2	4	2	3	1
Gastric and duodenal ulcer	9	5	6	7	10	1
Appendicitis	21	21	11	12	5	15
Intestinal obstruction	3	8	6	8	4	6
Disease of the female generative organs:	6	7	7	15	5	—
Bacilliary dysentry	—	—	—	—	1	—
Puerperal sepsis	4	10	5	4	3	3
Total recorded deaths from puerperal sepsis for each year:	1,026	1,184	1,157	1,243	1,050	1,596
Deaths reallocated to puerperal sepsis (totals):	13	19	8	10	8	9
Deaths reallocated to puerperal fever as a percentage of total deaths from puerperal fever (percentage):	1.3	1.6	0.7	0.8	0.8	0.6

Source: Registrar General's Statistical Reviews for the appropriate years.

In 1923, the Registrar General investigated this possibility, revealing a Scotland Yard capacity for detective work. He knew there was a seasonal fluctuation in the death rate from puerperal fever, with a winter maximum and a summer minimum. It was a consistent pattern in all countries from which records could be obtained. He showed that a slight but similar fluctuation in deaths from non-septic puerperal causes also occurred which turned out to be confined to a well-marked seasonal fluctuation in deaths assigned to the group of deaths assigned to 'puerperal phlegmasia alba dolens, embolism and sudden death'. Death from this cause is not seasonal, so there was every reason to believe it was due to a substantial number of 'hidden' deaths due to puerperal fever, falsely certified as sudden death and embolism.[4] Table A1.1 shows that by the early 1930s the number of hidden deaths due to puerperal sepsis which were discovered and reallocated by the Registrar General's Office had fallen to no more than about 1 per cent of total deaths in that category.

Since the Registrar General's office had always stressed it was impossible to inquire into more than a small proportion of unsatisfactory certificates, it is virtually certain that a certain number of maternal deaths allocated to other causes remain hidden in the lists of the Registrar General to this day. I doubt if it is possible to estimate the number hidden by placement in the wrong category of maternal mortality—in other words the number transferred from one puerperal category to another as described above. At least these did no harm to the estimation of total maternal mortality. But it seemed to me that it should be possible to discover at least some of the maternal deaths hidden in the non-puerperal categories of 'septicaemia' and 'peritonitis', and that it was worth trying because these would give an estimate of the extent to which the MMR as a whole was distorted. (Incidentally, the enquiries of successive Registrars General suggest that when maternal deaths were hidden, a large majority found a home in 'septicaemia' and 'peritonitis', and not elsewhere.) The hunt for these hidden deaths was conducted by the following method.

The method is based on searching for an excess of deaths amongst women of childbearing age in the two categories, 'peritonitis' and 'septicaemia', and it was carried out by searching the Registrar General's Decennial Reviews from the 1880s to 1950. In both categories, if there were no 'hidden' maternal deaths one would expect to find either equal death rates for both sexes, or an excess of male deaths. In particular, there should have been an excess of male deaths due to septicaemia because of greater exposure to accidents and injuries which turned septic. There was in fact a considerable excess of male over female deaths due to septicaemia at all ages and in every decennium. In the 1920s, for example, the number of female deaths in this category expressed as a percentage of male deaths was 52 per cent in ages 5–14, 59 per cent in ages 15–44, and 50 per cent in ages 45–64. I drew a blank in this part of the hunt, and I concluded there was no evidence to suggest that a substantial number of puerperal sepsis deaths remained hidden in the columns allocated to this category.

When the distribution of deaths in the category 'peritonitis of unstated origin' was examined, the result was quite different and much more complex. First, however, it is necessary to note that the total deaths allocated to this category fell very steeply in the early part of this century, as Table A1.2 shows. There is a simple explanation for the enormous fall in deaths allocated to this category. The three most common conditions which could lead to death from peritonitis were appendicitis, gastric ulcer, and duodenal ulcer. Appendicitis and gastric ulcer were only described and recognized as common diseases at the end of the nineteenth century; duodenal ulcer not until the early twentieth. Appendicitis and gastric ulcer were first tabulated as a separate cause of death in 1901, duodenal ulcer in 1911. Previously, deaths due to these diseases which were accompanied by signs of peritonitis (as many were) were certified simply as

---

[4] *Registrar General's Statistical Review for 1923* (1925), 90–6.

TABLE A1.2 *Total Deaths in the Category 'Peritonitis of unstated Origin' from 1881–90 to 1950 Showing the Fall in the Number of Deaths in this Category as a Result of the Recognition of Appendicitis and of Gastric and Duodenal Ulcer as Disease Categories in the Early Years of the Twentieth Century*

Decennium	Total deaths
1881–90	23,123
1891–1900	22,247
1901–10	8,884
1911–20	4,807
1921–30	3,851
1931–40	3,265
1941–50	1,592

Source: Registrar General's Reports, *Decennial Supplements*.

deaths due to 'peritonitis'. This fall was therefore a reflection of the change in nomenclature, not a change in the prevalence of diseases which caused peritonitis.[5] Before 1901, buried in this huge category of deaths labelled as 'peritonitis', was a small number of deaths due to puerperal sepsis. They might be more numerous then than later; but they would be less obvious because they were obscured by the size of this category. After 1911—and gradually rather than suddenly because it takes time for new diagnostic categories to be accepted—deaths due to puerperal sepsis would be more obvious as an excess. This can be seen in Table A1.3 which shows an excess of deaths amongst women of childbearing age in the category 'peritonitis of unstated origin'. The column for the age-group 15–44 shows a steep fall in the total number of deaths (here expressed as total deaths per million living in that age-group) but a rise in the excess of female deaths over male. In the older age-groups, there is a constant excess of male deaths except for ages 45–64 in the 1890s which was probably due to the well-known excess of gastric ulcer in women in this group; when gastric ulcer became a certifiable cause of death, that excess disappeared.

In the decade 1901–10, the excess of female deaths per million population was forty-seven. Because the category as a whole was so large, however, the excess expressed as a ratio of female deaths divided by male was only 1.34. By the decade 1921–30, the excess had fallen to twenty per million, but total deaths in this category had become so small that the ratio had increased to 1.47.

How do we know that this excess was due to hidden deaths from puerperal sepsis and not some other cause? We can never, of course, be certain. But the hypothesis is supported by an analysis of the age-distribution of the excess of female deaths over male within the age-group 15–44 which showed that the excess was greatest between the ages of 20 and 35, the ages in which most births occurred.

[5] *Registrar General's Statistical Review for 1926* (1928).

TABLE A1.3 *Deaths from 'Peritonitis of Unstated Origin'. Death Rates per Million Living in each Sex and Certain Age Groups, and the Ratio of Female Deaths to Male. Decennial Periods 1891–1900 to 1931–40. England and Wales*

	Age groups		
	15–44	45–64	65 +
1891–1900			
Total deaths per million living			
Males	502	1,168	2,530
Females	511	1,193	1,995
Ratio, female deaths/male deaths	1.02	1.02	0.79
1901–10			
Total deaths per million living			
Males	139	379	989
Females	186	326	759
Ratio, female deaths/male deaths	1.34	0.86	0.77
1911–20			
Total deaths per million living			
Males	63	204	387
Females	94	158	269
Ratio, female deaths/male deaths	1.49	0.77	0.69
1921–30			
Total deaths per million living			
Males	44	115	219
Females	64	86	143
Ratio, female deaths/male deaths	1.45	0.75	0.65
1931–40			
Total deaths per million living			
Males	37	104	174
Females	46	67	94
Ratio, female deaths/male deaths	1.24	0.64	0.54

Source: *Registrar General's Decennial Supplements.*

Assuming that the total excess of female deaths over male in the category 'peritonitis' consisted of hidden puerperal sepsis deaths, how many were there in comparison to total deaths from puerperal sepsis? The answer is given in Table A1.4. This suggests that hidden deaths due to puerperal sepsis—that is, deaths due to puerperal sepsis hidden and not discovered by the Registrar General in the category 'peritonitis'—may have been no more than 3 per cent at the end of the nineteenth century, falling to 2 per cent by the 1930s. By 1950, there were very few hidden in this manner. The excess of female deaths in the category 'peritonitis' during the quinquennium 1946–50 was only fifteen and fell to nil soon afterwards.

It is unlikely that the tables to this appendix show the whole number of hidden

TABLE A1.4 *Total Deaths from Puerperal Sepsis (including Septic Abortion), and the Excess Deaths of Females over Males in Age Groups 15–44 in the Category 'Peritonitis of Unstated Origin'. England and Wales, for all decades from 1891–1900 to 1931–40*

Decade	Total deaths from puerperal sepsis	Excess deaths in females aged 15–44 from 'Peritonitis of unstated origin'[a]	2nd Column as a percentage of 1st Column
1891–1900	21,605	639	2.9
1901–10	16,270	595	3.6
1911–20	12,460	406	3.2
1921–30	11,612	290	2.5
1931–40	7,722	158	2.0

[a] Expressed as total deaths and as a percentage of registered total deaths from puerperal sepsis.
Source: Registrar General's Decennial Supplements.

maternal deaths. At best one can guess that the total number of 'hidden' puerperal sepsis deaths in the twentieth century seldom exceeded 5 per cent of the correctly certified number. Since deaths from puerperal sepsis amounted, in round figures, to about half of total maternal mortality, the extent to which the MMR was understated because of hidden maternal deaths was probably around 2.5 per cent by the 1920s, but may have been higher—possibly nearer to 5 per cent in the late nineteenth century. There is therefore no reason to believe that deception and carelessness by certifying doctors led to a gross distortion of the MMR as a whole. Up to the mid-1930s, puerperal fever was usually the most common cause of maternal deaths (possible exceptions include certain southern States of the USA such as Virginia). Usually the published records show puerperal fever as the cause of about 40 per cent (or a little less) of total maternal deaths. Because of the phenomenon of hidden puerperal fever deaths I am inclined to suspect that 50 per cent would be nearer the truth.

Appendix 2
England and Wales: The Classification of Maternal Deaths

It was not until the seventh annual report of the Registrar General for 1843–4 that deaths in childbirth were included in the published lists of causes of death. It was in that report that Farr published his nosology and childbirth deaths were split into two. Deaths from metria or puerperal fever were number 18 in the list of zymotic (i.e. infective) diseases, while deaths from 'childbirth' appeared separately and were numbered as 104a. Number 104b was 'abortus'. A footnote distinguished between miscarriages and abortions. The former, it was said, were abortions which occurred up to six weeks of pregnancy; the latter between six weeks and six months. In fact, abortion deaths were not shown separately until 1881, and this odd distinction between miscarriages and abortions was a passing anomaly which served no useful purpose and can be forgotten.

In the Report for 1847 essentially the same classification was used. 'Metria' was placed in Class 1, the zymotic diseases, where it was numbered 16, and 'childbirth' in Class 9—the developmental diseases—where it was now number 80. There were some further alterations in the Report for 1858 but the same separation of deaths remained. 'Metria' was now number 10 in Class 1, Order 1 and deaths from 'childbirth' in Class 4, Order 2; the latter category was not split up into its components. This separation of puerperal fever deaths from all other childbirth deaths was a system followed in some other European countries, such as Belgium, at the same time. It also appears in the early reports of deaths in Massachusetts.

In the texts of the reports there were paragraphs devoted to childbirth deaths in which the two were brought together and shown in special tables in the two categories: 'metria' and deaths from other causes. The last were now entitled 'accidents of childbirth'. This was common usage in the nineteenth and early twentieth centuries. Different authors, however, later began to treat the term 'accidents of childbirth' in different ways. By the 1920s, some were using 'accidents of childbirth' as a term for all maternal causes of death *except* the three most common—puerperal sepsis, haemorrhage, and toxaemia. They would include, for example, causes such as ruptured uterus and 'embolism and sudden death'. In short, the reader should be aware that the term 'accidents of childbirth', and another term 'accidents of pregnancy', were not used consistently in spite of attempts by various authorities to define them precisely. It is well to bear this in mind when examining the statistics.

In 1881, following the retirement of William Farr and his replacement by William Ogle, a new nosology, influenced by the Royal College of Physicians' *Nomenclature of Disease* but by no means identical, was introduced. One of the changes was that the group of diseases formerly known as the 'zymotic diseases' was renamed 'specific, febrile and zymotic diseases' and split into a number of sub-groups. The sixth subgroup was the 'septic diseases' and it was here that deaths from puerperal fever were placed, continuing the rather surprising and muddling separation of these from other childbirth deaths. Deaths from 'childbirth' were now replaced by a separate group called the 'diseases of parturition'; and the groups were subdivided as follows:

Abortion, miscarriage;
Puerperal mania;
Puerperal convulsions;
Placenta praevia, flooding;
Phlegmasia dolens;
Other accidents of childbirth.

This classification of childbirth deaths remained essentially the same until 1911 when major alterations were introduced as a result of the adoption by Great Britain of the nomenclature of the International Classification of Diseases (ICD). The fourth revision of the *Manual of the International Classification of Diseases* (1929) listed the large number of synonyms for puerperal sepsis. Disease number 140 was 'Post-abortive sepsis', 145 was 'Puerperal sepsis', and 145*a* 'Puerperal septicaemia and pyaemia', which included the following synonyms used at various times by certifying practitioners:

Post-partum pyaemia
Post-partum sepsis
Post-partum septicaemia
Puerperal abscess of broad ligament
Puerperal bacillus coli infection
Puerperal cellulitis
Puerperal endometritis
Puerperal erysipelas
Puerperal fever
Puerperal infection
Puerperal inflammation of the uterus
Puerperal lymphangitis
Puerperal metritis
Puerperal metroperitonitis
Puerperal metrosalpingitis
Puerperal parametritis
Puerperal para-uterine abscess
Pelvic abscess
Puerperal pelvic cellulitis
Puerperal pelvic peritonitis
Puerperal pelvic peri-uterine cellulitis
Puerperal pelvic pyrexia
Puerperal pelvic salpingitis
Puerperal pelvic sapraemia
Puerperal pelvic sepsis
Puerperal pelvic septic phlebitis

However, in spite of this list of synonyms, the ICD system led to a more or less uniform system of nomenclature of maternal deaths. For the historian, the main problems occur in the nineteeth century where countries followed their own systems of disease classification and the various causes of death in childbirth might be scattered in different groups of diseases.

This account may give the false impression that tracing the statistics for maternal mortality is a very difficult exercise. In fact it is not. It is only necessary to bear in mind that maternal deaths were split in the various ways mentioned above, and that classifications changed.[1] Then it is simply a matter of time to search each annual report thoroughly and make sure no maternal deaths have been missed.

---

[1] A somewhat complex but comprehensive chart showing the changing classification of maternal deaths after 1911 can be found in Ministry of Health, *Report of an Investigation into Maternal Mortality* (London, 1937). Cmd. 5422, PP 1936/37, XI, app. 6, p. 302.

Appendix 3
Reports on Maternal Mortality in the USA

The following is a selection of the most important reports on maternal mortality in chronological order by date of publication. There were many others, most of which were carried out by state authorities and were concerned with local rather than national problems of maternity.

Grace Meigs, *Maternal Mortality from all Conditions Connected with Childbirth in the United States and Certain other Countries*, Children's Bureau Publications, No. 19 (Washington, DC, 1917).

This was the first major report on maternal mortality in the USA as a whole. Through international comparisons it alerted medical authorities to America's unenviable position in the international league table of maternal mortality. It was the first of a series of remarkable reports published by the Children's Bureau to deal with maternal mortality, and it was followed by reports on maternal and child welfare based on the reports by field workers sent by the Bureau to various parts of the country. Some are listed in the American bibliography under 'Children's Bureau'.

R. M. Woodbury, *Maternal Mortality: The Risk of Death in Childbirth and from all the Diseases Caused by Pregnancy and Confinement*, Children's Bureau Publications, No. 152 (Washington, DC, 1926).

This outstanding report extended the work started by Grace Meigs, and is notable for its greater detail, its emphasis on international comparisons, and for the depth of its statistical analysis. Few if any reports on maternal mortality came up to the standard of this one, except perhaps the 1937 report on maternal mortality in England and Wales published by the Ministry of Health (see British bibliography under 'Ministry of Health'). There is also a very useful appendix on maternal mortality in Woodbury's *Infant Mortality and its Causes* (Baltimore, Md., 1926).

J. V. DePorte (Director, Division of Vital Statistics, New York State Department of Health), *Maternal mortality and stillbirths in New York State: 1915–1925* (New York State Department of Health, 1928).

This study was based on deaths in New York State exclusive of New York City (although data on New York City were included in some of the sections). The total number of maternal deaths was 15,876. The MMR for the whole period of ten years was 58.5. It was the same in the first and second five-year periods, showing that no improvement had occurred. Although there was a fall in deaths from sepsis during the ten years it was accompanied by a rise in deaths from haemorrhage. The maternal death rate was lower in rural than urban areas because 'the country physician usually lacks the convenient facilities for operation and, therefore, there is less interference with the course of labor than in cities'. Amongst deaths from all causes in women of childbearing age tuberculosis came first with 26.3 per cent, all puerperal causes came second with 11.4 per cent, and diseases of the heart third with 9.8 per cent. But puerperal causes accounted for 26 per cent of all deaths in the age group 20 to 24. Needless obstetrical interference was identified as the major cause of preventable maternal deaths. Puerperal septicaemia was much the most common cause of death accounting (in round numbers) for 21 deaths per 10,000 births, compared with 16 due to toxaemia and 7 for haemorrhage.

New York City Public Health Committee and New York Academy of Medicine, *Maternal Mortality in New York City, 1930, 1931, 1932* (New York, 1933). Director of study, R. S. Hooker.[1]

This was the most famous and influential of all the reports and almost the only one to be reported in detail in Britain. It was also the report which aroused most controversy. It originated in 1928 when the Public Health Relations Committee of New York deputed Dr George Kosmak to submit plans for a study of obstetrics in New York City. The New York Obstetrical Society granted a loan for initial expenses and the investigation also received a grant from the Commonwealth Fund. The study embraced the years 1930, 1931, and 1932 in which there were 2,041 puerperal deaths. The most striking conclusion was that 65.8 per cent of the deaths would have been preventable 'if the care of the woman had been proper in all respects'—a startling condemnation of the practice of obstetrics in New York City. Operative procedures were carried out in 24.3 per cent of all deliveries when it was estimated they were necessary in not more than 5 per cent of deliveries. Deaths were five times more frequent in operative cases than in those with no intervention. Caesarean section accounted for 2.2 per cent of deliveries but 19.8 per cent of total deaths. Most preventable deaths were due to incompetence, unnecessary anaesthesia, and un-necessary intervention. The report recommended more home deliveries and also that 'the medical profession must accept the midwife as one of its adjuncts . . . they must regard her as an ally in the effort to reduce the mortality and morbidity associated with childbearing . . . a different type of woman must be brought into the field.' The report as a whole, and especially the recommendations on midwives, was the cause of an intense and acrimonious debate amongst New York obstetricians.[2]

White House Conference on Child Health Protection, *Fetal, Newborn and Maternal Morbidity and Mortality* (New York, 1933).

This is outstanding for its clarity, with the additional virtue of providing a good short account of the history of puerperal sepsis. It stressed the dangers of the 'operative

[1] A useful abstract of this report can be found in the *Journal of the American Medical Association*, 101 (1933), 1826–8.
[2] Excellent accounts of the controversies which surrounded the New York Report can be found in J. Antler and D. M. Fox, 'The Movement toward a Safe Maternity: Physician Account-ability in New York City, 1915–1940', *Bulletin of the History of Medicine*, 50 (1976), 569–95, and R. F. Porges, 'The Response of the New York Obstetrical Society to the Report by the New York Academy of Medicine on Maternal Mortality, 1933–34', *Obstetrics and Gynaecology*, 152 (1985), 642–9. In the latter it is reported that Iago Galdston ('now 88 years old') who published *Maternal Deaths: The Way to Prevention* in 1937, firmly believed that the New York report led to the decline in maternal mortality in the USA. In fact the decline began in 1930 and was well established by 1933 when the New York Study was published; but the report may well have been an important contributory factor to the general decline in maternal mortality during and after 1933.

furore' and demonstrated the extraordinary range of operative deliveries between different obstetricians and different institutions which clearly had little to do with clinical indications but a great deal to do with different fashions. It was almost alone in stressing the importance of the asymptomatic carrier in spreading puerperal fever, cutting the ground from under the feet of those who still favoured the theory of endogenous puerperal infection. The report sternly denounced the poor standard of aseptic practice. 'Masks should always be worn . . . There can be no doubt that many of the serious infections originate in chronic carriers of pathogenic bacteria.' There is an exceptionally comprehensive analysis of Caesarean and forceps rates, showing beyond doubt the link between unnecessary operative intervention and high mortality. It was suggested that the elimination of unnecessary Caesarean sections alone would reduce the maternal mortality by 10 per cent. The report deplored the excess of hospital deliveries. 'The increased hospitalistion of patients has not decreased, but rather has increased, the total morbidity and mortality.' In the end, the root cause of high maternal mortality was identified as poor obstetric education.

Maternal Deaths: A Brief Report of a Study Made in Fifteen States, Children's Bureau Publications, No. 221 (Washington, DC, 1933).

The states included in this study were Alabama, Kentucky, Maryland, Michigan, Minnesota, Nebraska, New Hampshire, North Dakota, Oregon, Rhode Island, Virginia, Washington, and Wisconsin for the two years 1927 and 1928, and California and Oklahoma for 1928 only. It is a detailed report, not easy to read, but essential for any serious study of maternal mortality in the USA, not least because the history of every one of the over 7,000 maternal deaths was examined individually. The overall MMR in the fifteen states in 1927/8 was 63 per 10,000 births, ranging from 57.5 for white mothers to 108.5 for black mothers. In urban areas the MMR was 75 and in rural areas 55. Amongst the features which this report uncovered was that 9 per cent of the women who died had no medical attention whatsoever or only attention when they were already dying. Inaccessibility due to distance and bad roads was only part, but still an important part of the explanation. The report also stressed that many hospitalized cases were emergencies, especially amongst black women, and few hospital admissions were planned early in pregnancy. The lack of adequate pre-natal care was stressed. Unfortunately, no data were collected which would allow a comparison of mortalities in home and hospital deliveries. This may have been a deliberate avoidance of contentious ground. More than half the women in the study had been subjected to an operative procedure before death. Of these operative procedures, forceps, version, and Caesarean section were employed in roughly equal proportions. Aseptic techniques were unsatisfactory, operative procedures often unnecessary, and manual dilatation of the cervix was frequently employed. Out of the total of 7,211 deaths, 7 per cent followed Caesarean section in the fifteen states as a whole, but the range was extremely wide: from 2 per cent of all deaths in North Dakota to 24 per cent in California. By far the most frequent reason given for Caesarean section was eclampsia and pre-eclampsia although the risk attached to Caesarean section for toxaemia was widely recognized. Of all the deaths attributed to 'puerperal septicaemia' (a total of 2,948) 45 per cent were due to abortion. Many of these followed curettage although it was widely recognized that curettage in septic cases is extremely dangerous. This report laid much more emphasis than others on mortality from septic abortion. Ninety per cent of the women whose deaths followed abortion were married suggesting that abortion was used as a way of limiting the size of families. In all, 1,825 women died following an abortion, and in 73 per cent of these the cause of deaths was put down as 'puerperal septicaemia'. Many deaths followed a therapeutic abortion for which the principal given reason was 'pernicious vomiting of pregnancy'. This is not a very common disorder, still less a common indication for a therapeutic abortion. Although the report refrained from comment, it seems likely that 'pernicious vomiting' was a convenient euphemism. Deaths from abortion were more common amongst black than white women, and more common in urban than rural areas. The loss of life from sepsis was described as 'enormous' and 'nothing short of appalling'. Like the other reports, this one stressed the poor quality of obstetric education in the medical curriculum.

Philadelphia County Medical Society, Committee on Maternal Welfare, *Maternal Mortality in Philadelphia, 1931–33* (Philadelphia, 1934).

The text of this report has all the appearances of being written by a committee. It was mainly concerned with deliveries in fifty-five hospitals. Overall, the most common cause of deaths was septic abortion which accounted for 22.6 per cent of deaths followed by post-partum sepsis which accounted for 16.6 per cent. The chief interest of this report was its demonstration of the extremely wide range in the percentage of operative deliveries in different hospitals—from 63.5 per cent to 8.3 per cent—a range for which no logical or clinical explanation could be discovered. There was a remarkable *absence* of any correlation between the size of the hospitals and the proportion of operative deliveries, and also between the percentage of operative deliveries and MMR of individual hospitals, possibly because the number of maternal deaths in many hospitals was so small that a wide range of mortality rates from random variation was to be expected.

Appendix 4
Numbers of Births and Statistical Significance

An important question, sometimes overlooked in studies of maternal mortality, is the size of the population and the number of births. Although in the past maternal deaths were common in relation to other causes of death amongst women of childbearing age, maternal deaths seen in the context of total deliveries were uncommon events. Even a level of maternal mortality as high as 100 per 10,000 births can be turned round and expressed as a survival rate of 99 per cent. In the comparison of MMRs a large number of births is needed to achieve statistical confidence. This is shown in the table accompanying this appendix which assumes an MMR of 50 deaths per 10,000 births.

If there was no such thing as random variation the figures in the third column under the heading 'critical range of variation' would all be 50. What, then, is the range of random variation? Common sense would tell us that if we had data from two towns, A and B, which showed that in a certain year there were two maternal deaths in town A and three in town B, it is unlikely that such a small difference had any validity. If on the other hand we had data from two large countries and found that in country A there were 20,000 maternal deaths a year while in country B there were 30,000 maternal deaths a year, it would be highly probable that the risk of dying in childbirth in country B was genuinely higher than it was in country A. We would feel that such a large difference was unlikely to be due to chance; in other words it could not be attributed to random variation.

Table A4.1 shows the extent of random variation in MMRs in a selection of places in which the annual number of births varied from as few as 1,000 to as many as 100,000. It is assumed that in all of them the average rate of maternal mortality was 50 per 10,000 births. Supposing for the sake of argument that we could identify a large

TABLE A4.1 *Showing the Range of Random Variation (Critical Range of Variation) in Maternal Mortality Rates in Relation to the Number of Births, assuming a Rate of Maternal Mortality of 50 Maternal Deaths per 10,000 births*

Annual births	Maternal deaths	Critical range of variation	Regions with birth rates close to these values during the 1930s
1,000	5	5–95	Doncaster, Darlington
5,000	25	30–70	Bristol, Newcastle upon Tyne
10,000	50	35–65	Manchester, Amsterdam
25,000	125	40–60	Lancashire, Middlesex, New Zealand
50,000	250	43–57	Paris
100,000	500	45–55	Sweden, Belgium, Australia

series of towns which, like Manchester and Amsterdam, had 10,000 births a year, and from which we had accurate vital statistics. Let us also suppose that through some form of God-like omniscience we *knew* that the true MMRs in all these towns was *exactly* the same: 50 per 10,000 births. It would be very odd if, in practice, the actual number of maternal deaths was exactly 50 for every 10,000 births. Random variation would be certain to destroy such neatness, and mortality rates would vary. But by how much? Here the answer is 35–65. This means that there is a 95 per cent likelihood that although the rates would vary, they would not stray outside that range.

Putting it another way, if one town (Manchester, for instance) recorded a rate of 64, while another (Amsterdam) recorded a rate of 36, although at first sight it would look as if Amsterdam was a much safer town to have a baby in, the difference is not statistically significant at the 95 per cent level. We could say Amsterdam was *probably safer*, but no more. Of course the degree of statistical certainty (and thus the range of critical variation) depends on the degree of statistical significance that we choose. It may be 90 per cent, 95 per cent, 99 per cent, or 99.9 per cent; there never is or can be absolute certainty. Here, in this table, we have chosen 95 per cent certainty and the calculation for that degree of certainty ('statistical confidence') is based on twice the standard error.

The practical lesson is that generally speaking comparisons of annual values of maternal mortality are only useful if populations and the number of births are very large. Differences revealed by local studies based on counties and small towns generally achieve significance only when they show consistent trends over a period of several years in order to accumulate enough births for differences in mortality rates to be significant. Comparisons have been made and false conclusions drawn by ignoring the factor of statistical significance. It also means that a time-series of rates of maternal mortality will, other things being equal, show wider swings on either side of the average rate if the number of maternal deaths is small than if the number is large. This can often be seen in the nineteenth century when graphs of annual rates of maternal mortality in lying-in institutions are compared with graphs of maternal mortality in whole countries.

Appendix 5
The Problem of Streptococcal Virulence

This appendix is concerned with the problem of streptococcal virulence and its relevance to the history of puerperal fever. I shall put forward three propositions. First, that fluctuations in streptococcal virulence played a very important and largely unrecognized part in determining trends in maternal mortality. Secondly, that different strains of *Streptococcus pyogenes* caused puerperal fever and erysipelas on the one hand and scarlet fever on the other. Thirdly, that changes in virulence may have resulted from changes in the *prevalence* of certain varieties, strains, or in modern terminology certain streptococcal serotypes. Because these propositions are relevant to several chapters, and because some of what I will say is speculative, it seemed sensible to relegate this section to an appendix rather than the main text.

What is not speculative but established beyond reasonable doubt, is the following.

1. Until the late 1930s, puerperal fever was the most common cause of maternal mortality.

2. A large majority of puerperal fever deaths (as opposed to cases) were due to infection with the β-haemolytic streptococcus Lancefield group A (hereafter referred to as 'the streptococcus'). When epidemics of puerperal fever occurred they appear to have been purely streptococcal in origin.

3. The shorter the time between childbirth and the onset of puerperal fever, the higher the mortality. Rapid onset and high mortality were common if not invariable features of epidemics.

4. Epidemics of puerperal fever could occur in towns and villages as well as in lying-in hospitals. When this happened such epidemics were frequently associated with concomitant outbreaks of erysipelas. Gordon of Aberdeen in 1795 and West of Abingdon in 1815 were two of many examples quoted in Chapter 4. Both described the simultaneous arrival, peak periods, and departure of epidemics of puerperal fever and erysipelas. No authors describing these outbreaks mentioned simultaneous outbreaks of scarlet fever or sore throats although both were well-recognized conditions. Epidemics of puerperal fever were common in the eighteenth and nineteenth centuries but they had become rare by the beginning of the twentieth century.

5. Wide fluctuations in annual mortality rates of both puerperal fever and erysipelas were a feature of the nineteenth century. In contrast, fluctuations were comparatively slight in the period 1900–35 when epidemics of puerperal fever and erysipelas had become rare. See Figures 13.1, 13.2, and 13.3.

6. Secular trends in deaths due to erysipelas and puerperal fever followed each other very closely, while the trends in deaths due to scarlet fever bore only a loose relationship to those of puerperal fever and erysipelas. This can be seen in Figure 4.3 and its significance is discussed below.

7. Studies carried out in the inter-war period showed that when streptococcal

illness was prevalent the asymptomatic carrier rate (that is, the proportion of the population who were not ill but carried streptococci in their noses or throats, often for long periods) usually rose significantly.

8. Not all asymptomatic carriers were liable to act as a source of streptococcal infection. Some authors have drawn a useful distinction between carriers and 'dispersers', the latter being those carriers who were infectious and thus the unwitting source of streptococcal cases and epidemics. Most dispersers were nasal carriers rather than throat carriers.[1]

There are numerous strains of *Streptococcus pyogenes*, differentiated by varying possession of two sets of antigens, the M and T antigens. These provide a means of identifying individuals as the source of epidemics. The identification of strains, however, has not provided any consistent correlation between particular strains and specific types of streptococcal disease. The complexity of the streptococcus, as studied in the laboratory, prompted Christie to comment that 'it is unlikely that a simple epidemiological pattern for streptococcal infections could emerge and, in practice, this has been the case'.[2]

In spite of the absence of supporting laboratory evidence, clinical and epidemiological evidence suggests that at least two distinct groups of strains exist, or at least existed in the past. One group was associated with scarlet fever, streptococcal sore throat and tonsillitis, and mastoiditis. Scarlet fever is due to a particular strain which produces erythrogenic toxins; if the patient has no protective antibodies against these toxins they produce the characteristic skin rash.[3] The other group of streptococcal strains was the causative agent in erysipelas, most cases of severe puerperal fever, and probably of streptococcal wound and skin infections. The evidence for separating streptococcal infections into two groups is as follows.

Clinically, the two groups of diseases are distinct. Scarlet fever and streptococcal tonsillitis and sore throats are predominantly diseases of children. Scarlet fever is associated with a rash and confers immunity. Until the second half of this century this group was associated with the serious complications of acute rheumatic fever and acute nephritis. Both complications are now rare in affluent Western countries, but they are still quite common in developing countries.

In the nineteenth century erysipelas was a disease of infancy and old age. During the twentieth century, cases in infancy gradually disappeared and it is now a disease of later life. Neither puerperal fever nor erysipelas are associated with a rash. Neither disease confers immunity. Indeed, erysipelas is well known for its tendency to recur. It was uncommon for erysipelas to act as the precursor of rheumatic fever or acute nehpritis, and as far as I can discover there are no records of these complications following puerperal fever. The response to the sulphonamides was different. In the late

---

[1] J. M. Boissard and R. M. Fry, 'Streptococcal School Outbreaks: A Method of Investigation and Control', *Journal of Hygiene of Cambridge*, 64 (1966), 221–30.

[2] A. B. Christie, *Infectious Diseases: Epidemiology and Clinical Practice*, 2nd edn. (London, 1974), 1010–15.

[3] D. C. Turk, I. A. Porter, B. I. Duerden, and T. M. S. Reid, *A Short Textbook of Medical Bacteriology*, 5th edn. (London, 1983), 42. A vivid account of childhood deaths from mastoiditis during an epidemic of scarlet fever in Glasgow in 1935, which underlines how recently the streptococcus pyogenes was still a deadly organism in Britain, can be found in S. C. McEwan, 'Personal View', *British Medical Journal* (27 Oct. 1990), 993.

1930s and early 1940s before penicillin became available, the sulphonamides were highly successful in the treatment of puerperal fever and erysipelas, but they were described as 'disappointing' in the treatment of scarlet fever. These are the clinical differences which suggest that the strains of the streptococcus which cause scarlet fever may not be the same as those which cause erysipelas and puerperal fever.

The epidemiological evidence comes from several sources. Deaths from streptococcal diseases show a marked seasonality. During the late nineteenth century the peak of deaths from scarlet fever, erysipelas, and puerperal fever always occurred during the winter. By the 1920s, the peak for scarlet fever had moved to the spring while the peak for deaths from erysipelas and puerperal fever remained in the winter.[4] The existence of two groups of strains is also suggested by the similarity between the secular trends for puerperal fever and erysipelas and the rather separate pathway followed by scarlet fever. This can be seen in Figures 4.2 and 4.3.

In 1935 Hektoen wrote a paper entitled 'The Specificness of Certain Haemolytic Streptococci' in which he quotes the evidence of Ruth Tunnicliff who, in 1931, suggested 'the streptococci of scarlet fever and of erysipelas form distinct groups'. Hektoen pointed out that in contrast to the frequent coexistence of epidemics of erysipelas and puerperal fever, he found no records of epidemics in which some patients suffered from scarlet fever and some from erysipelas. He instanced the Faroe Islands where, in 1873, scarlet fever was introduced. There had been no cases of the disease in the previous fifty-seven years. During the epidemic which followed 38.3 per cent of the population had scarlet fever but there were no cases of erysipelas.[5]

Although I have been unable to find any historical accounts of simultaneous outbreaks of scarlet fever and puerperal fever, it is true that following the discovery of the streptococcus it was thought to be as unwise to attend a lying-in woman after attending a case of scarlet fever as it was after attending a case of erysipelas. That seemed, on common-sense grounds, to be sound practice because of the a priori assumption that there would be a high risk of cross-infection; but there is no evidence the assumption was correct.

One of the most persuasive lines of evidence for the existence of two different groups of streptococcal illness comes from the study of their fatality rates. This can be seen in Table A5.1 and Figure A5.1. It will be recalled that the fatality rates for puerperal fever are meaningless before the end of the 1920s (and still flawed in the 1930s). For notification purposes the disease was defined as puerperal septicaemia which was widely interpreted as meaning the end-stage of the disease. Mild cases were seldom notified and puerperal fever as a whole was under-notified to such an extent that calculations of fatality rates are totally unreliable. The apparent fall in the fatality of puerperal fever shown in Table A5.1 between 1918 and 1925 simply reflects increasing rates of notification.

The important comparison is therefore between the fatality rates of erysipelas and scarlet fever. The table and the figure show that between 1918 and 1934, the former

[4] W. T. Russell, 'The Statistics of Erysipelas in England and Wales', *Journal of Hygiene*, 33 (1933), 426.

[5] L. Hektoen, 'The Specificness of Certain Haemolytic Streptococci', *Journal of the American Medical Association*, 105 (1935), 1–2.

TABLE A5.1 *Deaths as a Percentage of Notifications:*
Scarlet Fever, Erysipelas, and Puerperal Pyrexia.
England and Wales, 1918–1945

Year	Scarlet fever	Erysipelas	Puerperal pyrexia
1918	2.1	4.8	70.0
1919	1.5	4.2	57.3
1920	1.1	5.2	59.7
1921	0.9	5.5	52.9
1922	1.3	5.3	50.5
1923	1.2	5.0	50.5
1924	1.0	5.2	46.6
1925	1.1	5.7	46.3
1926	0.8	5.8	25.0[a]
1927	0.7	5.5	13.6
1928	0.5	5.4	15.0
1929	0.6	5.8	14.5
1930	0.6	5.6	15.1
1931	0.6	6.6	13.0
1932	0.6	6.8	13.0
1933	0.5	6.6	13.4
1934	0.6	7.1	14.3
1935	0.5	6.2	12.3
1936	0.5	6.0	10.2
1937	0.4	3.8	6.7
1938	0.4	2.5	6.0
1939	0.3	1.7	6.0
1940	0.2	1.6	4.4
1941	0.2	1.5	3.9
1942	0.1	1.2	3.3
1943	0.1	1.0	3.3
1944	0.1	1.1	2.7
1945	0.1	1.2	

[a] The apparent abrupt fall in fatality rates for puerperal fever
in 1926–7 is an artefact due to the introduction of a new
definition of puerperal fever.

Source: Annual reports of the Registrar General and Registrar
General's Statistical Reviews.

rose and the latter declined. They went, in other words, in opposite directions. Note
also that from 1937, when sulphonamides first became available, there is a pronounced
fall in the fatality of erysipelas and puerperal pyrexia, but only a slight downward step
in the already declining fatality of scarlet fever. This confirms contemporary clinical

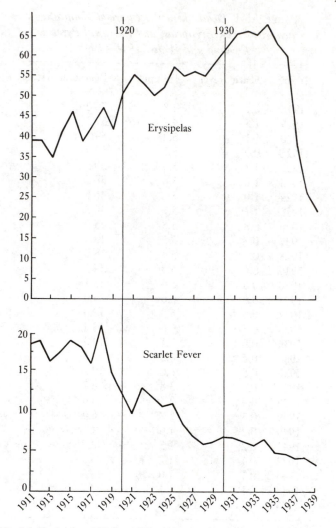

FIG. Appendix 5.1 England and Wales, 1911–1939. Fatality rates of scarlet fever and erysipelas
Source: Registrar General for England and Wales, *Decennial Supplements*.

opinion that the sulphonamides were 'disappointing' in the treatment of scarlet fever.[6] It is important to note in passing that confident statements during the inter-war period that streptococcal virulence was declining were based on the trend in the case fatality rate of scarlet fever. Few, if any, undertook comparative studies of the different pathway followed by erysipelas.[7]

This brings us to the vexed question of virulence on which Turk has observed:

> The term virulence is often used in an attempt to quantitate pathogenicity, but caution is needed here. It is sometimes convenient to be able to describe a strain as highly virulent, or of reduced virulence or avirulent; but we can give mathematical expression to virulence only if we define carefully the conditions under which it is measured.[8]

The 'conditions' in this context are the health and resistance to infection of the population. If we think of virulence as one side of a coin, susceptibility (or its reciprocal, 'resistance') is the other. An unusually serious outbreak of an infectious disease may be due to a highly virulent strain, or to a population weakened by malnutrition and poor health, or both. Thus it is sometimes said that the pandemic of influenza in 1918–19 killed so many people because of a low state of health following four years of war and deprivation—an unlikely hypothesis if only because the death rate was as high in non-combatant as combatant countries. A simple analogy would be the risk of death from a bite by a venomous snake. The chance of dying would be determined in part by whether the victim was large, strong, and healthy, or small, weak, and frail; and in part by the variety of snake (corresponding to the type of streptococcus) and also by the amount of venom injected (corresponding to the prevalence or 'dose' of infection, discussed below).

Historians, noting changes in fatality rates, usually turn to the health and nutrition of the population and search for correlations with periods of affluence or deprivation. They do so because of the implicit assumption that the toxicity or virulence of the infective organism is a constant. Yet a moment's reflection shows that in the nineteenth century it is unlikely that the susceptibility (or resistance) of the population could have varied so widely and rapidly that it accounted for the rapid swings in mortality due to puerperal fever. Still less is it possible to correlate peaks of deaths from streptococcal disease with periods of economic decline. It therefore seems likely that observed changes in fatality were due to changes in bacterial virulence rather than changes in

---

[6] Notifications of scarlet fever between 1911 and 1944 showed annual fluctuations with peaks in 1921 and 1934; but the general trend between these dates was level. In other words, the incidence (the number of new cases a year) of scarlet fever did not alter appreciably. Deaths from scarlet fever, however, fell sharply from the late 19th cent. In the 1870s the annual rate was about 14 deaths from scarlet fever per 100,000 total population. The number had fallen to 7.7 in 1914 and continued downwards to 1.2 by 1936. In the case of erysipelas, annual rates of notifications and deaths both rose from the beginning of the century to 1934. But the death rate increased more sharply than the rate of notifications so that the fatality rate rose from 3.9 per cent in 1911 to nearly 7 per cent by 1934.

[7] The link between erysipelas and puerperal fever was explored by Russell in 'The Statistics of erysipelas'. He made the fatal error of using cases of puerperal fever rather than deaths without apparently realizing that the bacteriology of cases differed significantly from that of deaths, or that the case-notifications before 1927 were unreliable. This undermines his conclusions.

[8] Turk, Porter, Duerden, and Reid, *A Short Textbook of Medical Bacteriology*, 42.

host susceptibility or resistance. If we assume from the evidence above that the same streptococcal strains were implicated in erysipelas and puerperal fever, we can take the fatality rates of erysipelas as proxy for the fatality rates of puerperal fever. This would lead to the conclusion that the strains responsible for causing puerperal fever were increasing in virulence between 1910 and 1934, accounting in part for the rise in maternal mortality which was a feature common to most Western countries.[9]

What mechanisms may be involved in an increase in virulence in this particular context? 'Virulence' seems to imply some kind of change in the character of the streptococcus making it especially toxic in some years, irrespective of any change in the susceptibility or resistance of the population at risk, and relatively non-toxic in other years. We have seen that there are numerous strains, differing in their M and T antigens. These antigens are thought to be related to pathogenicity. Increased virulence might appear to occur as a result of a *relative increase in the proportion of highly virulent strains* and a corresponding decrease in less-virulent strains. Higher mortality would follow as a result of what has been called the 'dosage effect' of toxic organisms. As Turk explains:

> The number ('dose') of organisms taking part in an infection has an important influence on its outcome. In an epidemic, or in an outbreak of common-source illness such as food-poisoning after a party, it is often found that some of those exposed have symptomless infections, some are mildly ill and some are more severely affected. In general such variations are likely to be determined, in part at least, by differences in the dose of pathogens reaching individuals, though other factors such as host immunity can also be important.[10]

What is suggested is that changes in the prevalence of the streptococcus within a given population can occur at two levels. First, changes in the prevalence of all strains of the streptococcus; secondly, changes in the relative proportions of virulent and less-virulent strains, independently of changes in total prevalence. This provides an attractive model for the wide and rapidly fluctuating variations in the incidence and death rate of streptococcal diseases which were such a feature of the nineteenth century.

To take a specific instance, deaths from puerperal fever and erysipelas swung from a low level in 1872 to a very high level in 1874, and back down to an even lower level in 1878 (the mortality rates of puerperal fever in these years were 17.0, 36.3, and 15.9 respectively). This huge swing up to a peak and down again could have been due to a rapid upsurge in the prevalence of a highly virulent strain, followed by its (temporary) diminution or disappearance.

Evidence on these points comes from modern work.[11] It has been shown that

---

[9] There is one possible objection, however, which must be mentioned to be dismissed. We have seen that the age-incidence of cases of erysipelas changed through the early decades of the 20th cent. The *proportion* of cases in infancy dwindled relative to those in late-middle and old age. This raises the question of whether the increasing fatality of erysipelas between 1911 and 1934 was an artefact associated with this change in age-incidence. That this was not the case is shown by calculating the age-specific fatality rates for erysipelas. They show that the fatality rate of erysipelas rose separately and similarly in the old and the young.

[10] Turk, Porter, Duerden, and Reid, *A Short Textbook of Medical Bacteriology*, 42.

[11] E. Gaworzewska and G. Colman, 'Changes in the Pattern of Infection Caused by *Streptococcus Pyogenes*', *Epidemiology and Infection*, 100 (1988), 257–69, and Colman, A. Efstratiou, and E. T. Gaworzewska, 'The Pyogenic Streptococci', *PHLS Microbiology Digest* 5/1 (1988), 5–7.

changes in the prevalence of different streptococcal strains or 'serotypes' do in fact occur independently of each other over periods of a few years. It is also clear that the links between serotypes and specific disorders are highly complex. For example, in one study cases of erysipelas were strongly associated with M-type 1, scarlet fever with types 3 and 4, and the predominant strain in cases of puerperal fever was type 28. It was usual, however, to find many serotypes rather than one were associated with each particular streptococcal disorder. Finally, it is likely that variations in the virulence of certain serotypes can occur. Thus the authors of one study in 1987 wrote: 'It seems clear that the strain, or strains, of M-type 1 that is currently being isolated is particularly virulent.'[12]

Modern methods of typing the streptococcus were not of course available in the pre-sulphonamide era. We will never know what serotypes predominated in the past. But it is reasonable to postulate that the trends and fluctuations in deaths from puerperal fever, erysipelas, and scarlet fever were associated with fluctuations in the prevalence of certain serotypes which varied widely in their toxicity or virulence; and some of them may now have become extinct.

There are still many unexplained features of streptococcal disease in the past. For example, the tendency for severe epidemics of erysipelas and puerperal fever to sweep through towns and villages in the eighteenth and nineteenth centuries, and the rarity of such epidemics by the early years of this century; the increasing mildness of scarlet fever in Western countries since the Second World War; the virtual disappearance of rheumatic fever and acute nephritis in Western countries. Whatever explanations are put forward to explain these phenomena or to elucidate the nature of bacterial virulence, it seems certain that before the introduction of specific therapy in the mid-1930s, levels of puerperal fever in any given period—and thus levels of maternal mortality—were to a large extent determined by the bacterial changes we have discussed.

[11] Gaworzewska and Colman, 'Changes in the Pattern of Infection', 267.

Appendix 6

TABLE 1. *England and Wales. Annual Rates of Maternal Mortality, 1847–1945, 1946–1981. Maternal Deaths per 10,000 Births*

Year	Puerperal sepsis	Other causes	Total
1847	14.5	45.2	59.7
1848	24.2	37.0	61.2
1849	20.2	37.6	57.8
1850	18.8	36.0	54.8
1851	16.4	37.0	53.4
1852	15.6	36.4	52.0
1853	13.0	37.0	50.0
1854	15.0	32.4	47.4
1855	17.0	29.9	46.9
1856	16.2	27.7	43.9
1857	12.6	29.4	42.0
1858	16.3	31.5	47.8
1859	17.9	32.8	50.7
1860	14.4	32.0	46.4
1861	12.7	30.3	43.0
1862	13.2	30.0	43.2
1863	15.9	33.4	49.3
1864	20.0	34.3	54.3
1865	17.8	33.3	51.1
1866	15.9	32.9	48.8
1867	13.9	30.5	44.4
1868	15.2	29.1	44.5
1869	15.3	27.1	42.4
1870	18.8	30.1	48.9
1871	18.1	30.9	49.8
1872	17.0	29.0	46.0
1873	21.0	28.6	49.6
1874	36.3	33.0	69.3
1875	29.4	30.1	59.5
1876	19.7	26.9	46.6
1877	16.3	22.5	38.8
1878	15.9	21.1	37.0
1879	16.6	21.3	37.9

TABLE 1. (*cont.*)

Year	Puerperal sepsis	Other causes	Total
1880	18.8	20.8	39.4
1881	25.8	22.0	47.8
1882	28.9	22.0	50.9
1883	29.4	21.2	50.6
1884	27.2	20.7	47.9
1885	27.1	22.7	49.8
1886	23.9	19.9	47.2
1887	28.0	18.9	46.9
1888	24.9	20.1	47.3
1889	20.9	19.5	40.5
1890	22.4	26.2	48.9
1891	21.5	30.6	52.4
1892	26.2	31.6	57.8
1893	33.0	31.9	65.1
1894	24.3	29.2	53.6
1895	20.0	25.6	45.7
1896	22.4	27.4	49.8
1897	19.9	26.2	46.1
1898	18.4	25.6	44.1
1899	20.5	26.3	46.6
1900	20.9	27.1	48.1
1901	22.4	24.9	47.3
1902	20.3	24.4	44.7
1903	16.7	24.0	40.7
1904	16.5	22.3	38.8
1905	17.5	24.5	42.0
1906	16.5	23.7	40.2
1907	15.0	23.3	38.3
1908	13.9	21.8	35.7
1909	14.8	22.1	36.9
1910	13.6	21.9	35.5
1911	14.3	24.4	38.7
1912	13.9	25.9	39.8
1913	12.6	27.0	39.6
1914	15.5	26.2	41.7
1915	14.7	27.1	41.8
1916	13.8	27.4	41.2
1917	13.1	25.8	38.9
1918	12.8	25.1	37.9
1919	16.7	27.0	43.7
1920	18.1	25.2	43.3
1921	13.8	25.3	39.1
1922	13.8	24.3	38.1

TABLE 1. (*cont.*)

Year	Puerperal sepsis	Other causes	Total
1923	13.0	25.1	38.1
1924	13.9	25.1	39.0
1925	15.6	25.2	40.8
1926	16.0	25.2	41.2
1927	15.7	25.4	41.1
1928	17.9	26.3	44.2
1929	18.0	25.3	43.3
1930	19.2	24.8	44.0
1931	15.9	23.5	39.5
1932	15.5	24.9	40.4
1933	17.5	25.7	43.2
1934	19.5	24.7	44.1
1935	16.1	23.2	39.4
1936	13.4	23.1	36.5
1937	9.4	21.7	31.1
1938	8.6	21.1	28.2
1939	7.4	20.8	28.2

Year	Post-Abortive Infection	Infection in Childbirth and Puerperium	Abortion Without Sepsis	Other Maternal Causes	Total
1940	2.5	5.4	1.8	16.4	26.1
1941	3.5	4.7	1.9	17.5	27.6
1942	3.5	4.2	1.1	15.9	24.7
1943	3.4	3.9	1.1	14.5	23.0
1944	3.2	2.8	0.9	12.4	19.5
1945		2.4		12.3	14.7
1946					14.3
1947					11.7
1948					10.2
1949					9.7
1950					8.7
1951					7.6
1952					6.7
1953					7.1
1954					6.5
1955					5.9
1956					5.2
1957					4.5
1958					4.3

TABLE 1. (*cont.*)

Year	Post-Abortive Infection	Infection in Childbirth and Puerperium	Abortion Without Sepsis	Other Maternal Causes	Total
1959					3.8
1960					3.9
1961					3.3
1962					3.5
1963					2.8
1964					2.5
1965					2.5
1966					2.6
1967					2.0
1968					2.4[a]
1969					1.9
1970					1.8
1971					1.7
1972					1.5
1973					1.3
1974					1.3
1975					1.3
1976					1.3
1977					1.3
1978					1.1
1979					1.2
1980					1.2
1981					1.0

[a] Revision of the ICD

Note: Data up to 1939 are based on the revised statistical method introduced in 1926 which incorporated the international classification of maternal causes of death introduced in 1911. This means that the data from 1911 to 1939 are comparable in the sense that they were all based on the same method of classification. In 1939 the new method of classifying maternal deaths which involved showing abortion deaths separately and dividing them into 'post-abortive sepsis' and 'abortion without mention of sepsis' was introduced.

Source: *Registrar General's Annual Reports*; *Registrar General's Annual Statistical Reviews*; A. Macfarlane and M. Mugford, *Birth Counts: Statistics of Pregnancy and Childbirth*, 2 vols. (London, 1984).

TABLE 2. *The Number of Births, the Number of Maternal Deaths, and the Maternal Mortality Rates for England and Wales for the Years 1872–1878 inclusive, in order to Demonstrate the Extent of the Registration Effect of the Births and Deaths Registration Act of 1874*

	1872	1873	1874	1875	1876	1877	1878
A. Births × 1,000	825.9	829.8	855.0	850.6	888.0	888.1	892.0
Maternal deaths	3,803	4,115	5,927	5,064	4,142	2,413	3,300
Maternal mortality rate	46.0	49.6	69.3	59.5	46.6	38.4	37.0
B. Births × 1,000	825.9	829.8	855.0	869.0	880.0	887.0	892.0
Maternal deaths	3,803	4,115	5,927	5,064	4,142	2,413	3,300
Maternal mortality rate	46.0	49.6	69.3	58.2	46.6	38.4	37.0

Note: In this table the upper part, A, is based on the published number of births. In the lower section, B, the births in 1875, 1876, and 1877 represent the probable number of births which actually occurred on the assumption that the trend in annual births was smooth. Section B is therefore an attempt to iron out the anomaly due to the introduction of the 1874 Act.

Source: Text, chap. 2.

TABLE 3. *Scotland. Annual Rates of Maternal Mortality, 1856–1950. Maternal Deaths per 10,000 Births*

Year	Maternal mortality rate	
	all causes	puerperal sepsis
1856	48.5	14.0
1857	43.4	14.0
1858	43.6	14.6
1859	48.8	16.4
1860	53.4	22.3
1861	47.7	19.0
1862	40.6	12.1
1863	52.2	17.8
1864	55.9	22.6
1865	56.1	18.7
1866	38.4	15.9

TABLE 3. (*cont.*)

Year	Maternal mortality rate	
	all causes	puerperal sepsis
1867	42.4	14.3
1868	42.8	12.1
1869	49.7	13.5
1870	50.5	17.5
1871	55.5	19.4
1872	51.3	18.4
1873	48.1	21.0
1874	66.3	30.6
1875	53.4	31.5
1876	47.8	18.2
1877	43.9	12.8
1878	42.9	12.9
1879	46.2	14.6
1880	49.7	14.8
1881	56.6	18.6
1882	53.6	21.1
1883	63.4	29.1
1884	54.7	26.0
1885	61.7	29.6
1886	46.9	21.1
1887	49.2	22.1
1888	53.5	25.1
1889	50.7	22.6
1890	56.5	26.7
1891	57.0	30.0
1892	55.0	25.2
1893	46.2	19.8
1894	50.4	22.9
1895	48.0	20.0
1896	44.7	17.0
1897	44.7	17.1
1898	40.9	15.7
1899	45.7	16.4
1900	43.1	17.1
1901	47.4	21.7
1902	51.5	2.1
1903	53.0	22.7
1904	46.4	18.5
1905	54.6	20.4

TABLE 3. (*cont.*)

Year	Maternal mortality rate	
	all causes	puerperal sepsis
1906	54.3	20.8
1907	53.2	18.2
1908	51.4	18.3
1909	54.4	17.0
1910	57.2	18.4
1911	57.4	14.2
1912	55.0	15.7
1913	58.8	13.3
1914	60.2	18.5
1915	61.1	19.4
1916	56.9	16.8
1917	58.9	16.9
1918	69.8	11.5
1919	62.2	14.1
1920	61.5	17.7
1921	63.8	20.3
1922	65.0	19.8
1923	64.2	19.5
1924	58.2	17.2
1925	61.6	16.4
1926	64.0	16.9
1927	64.3	19.0
1928	69.8	24.2
1929	68.7	23.8
1930	69.5	23.4
1931	59.1	19.8
1932	63.3	23.1
1933	59.2	21.5
1934	62.0	23.0
1935	63.0	20.2
1936	55.5	18.2
1937	48.3	13.9
1938	48.7	11.5
1939	44.9	7.7
1940	43.9	8.3
1941	48.7	9.9
1942	41.7	9.3
1943	37.6	6.7
1944	29.4	5.6

TABLE 3. (*cont.*)

Year	Maternal mortality rate	
	all causes	puerperal sepsis
1945	28.0	3.8
1946	22.0	5.4
1947	20.0	3.0
1948	16.0	3.0
1949	13.0	2.0
1950	11.0	2.0

Note: The data under the heading 'Puerperal sepsis' include deaths from septic abortion from 1946, but not in any previous years.

Source: 1856–1910: *Detailed Reports of the Registrar General for Scotland*; 1911–45: P. L. McKinlay, *Maternal Mortality in Scotland, 1911–1945* (Edinburgh, 1947), 12; 1945–50: *Reports of the Scottish Health Department*.

TABLE 4. *Ireland/Eire. Annual Rates of Maternal Mortality, 1870–1950. Maternal Deaths per 10,000 Births*

	Puerperal sepsis	Other causes	Total
1871–80	25.0	41.0	66.0
1881–90	28.0	43.0	71.0
1891–1900	26.0	40.0	66.0
1901	22.8	39.0	61.8
1902	21.6	40.7	62.3
1903	22.9	33.4	56.3
1904	20.8	35.4	56.2
1905	22.1	33.6	55.7
1906	22.6	36.0	58.6
1907	16.0	33.6	49.6
1908	18.6	33.4	52.0
1909	21.6	33.0	54.6
1910	18.7	34.4	53.1
1911	18.3	32.2	50.5

TABLE 4. (*cont.*)

	Puerperal sepsis	Other causes	Total
1912	21.3	33.1	54.3
1913	19.3	33.3	53.6
1914	23.7	28.4	52.1
1915	20.6	32.4	53.0
1916	24.5	32.9	57.4
1917	20.0	28.5	48.5
1918	17.2	31.1	48.3
1919	18.0	29.1	47.1
1920	20.3	28.4	48.7
1921	20.2	29.3	49.5
1922	23.6	33.0	56.6
1923	19.0	29.2	48.2
1924	16.1	31.7	47.8
1925	16.9	30.0	46.9
1926	18.8	30.0	48.9
1927	12.8	32.3	45.1
1928	17.4	31.9	49.3
1929	13.7	27.3	41.0
1930	13.9	33.8	47.7
1931	11.6	31.5	43.1
1932	13.9	31.6	45.5
1933	13.9	30.5	44.4
1934	18.0	28.8	46.8
1935	15.3	31.4	46.7
1936	17.9	29.1	47.0
1937	9.0	27.1	36.1
1938	8.1	33.0	41.1
1939	6.8	27.1	33.9
1940	9.7	27.0	36.7
1941	7.6	24.5	32.1
1942	6.5	18.2	24.7
1943	5.6	16.9	22.5
1944	4.9	18.9	23.8
1945	5.2	18.5	23.7
1946	2.9	17.2	20.1
1947	4.5	14.4	18.8
1948	2.7	13.1	15.8
1949	2.8	15.3	18.1
1950	2.2	13.4	15.6

Source: *Annual Reports of the Registrar General*, Ireland and Eire.

TABLE 5. *USA. Maternal Mortality in the USA from 1900 to 1920, Based on Data from those States which Comprised the Death Registration Area in 1900*

Year	All puerperal causes	Puerperal sepsis	Other puerperal causes
1900	8.5	4.3	4.2
1901	8.0	3.7	4.3
1902	7.4	3.6	3.8
1903	7.0	3.3	3.6
1904	7.9	3.9	4.0
1905	8.0	3.8	4.2
1906	7.1	3.2	3.9
1907	7.2	3.3	3.9
1908	6.7	3.0	3.7
1909	7.0	2.9	4.1
1910	6.9	3.1	3.8
1911	7.0	3.2	3.8
1912	6.5	2.7	3.8
1913	6.8	2.9	3.9
1914	7.1	2.9	4.2
1915	6.9	2.6	4.3
1916	6.7	2.7	4.0
1917	6.6	2.8	3.9
1918	9.3	2.5	6.8[a]
1919	7.5	2.4	5.0
1920	7.8	2.7	5.1

[a] Increase due to influenza.

Source: Children's Bureau Publications, US Department of Labor, Washington, DC, Government Printing Office, No. 152, R. M. Woodbury, Maternal Mortality: The Risk of Death in Childbirth and from all the Diseases Caused by Pregnancy and Confinement (1926).

TABLE 6. *USA. 1915–1953. Annual Rates of Maternal Mortality by Race*

Year	Rate per 10,000 live births		
	Total	White	Non-white
1915	60.8	60.1	105.6
1916	62.2	60.8	117.9
1917	66.2	63.2	117.7
1918	91.6	88.9	139.3
1919	73.7	69.6	124.4

TABLE 6. (*cont.*)

Year	Rate per 10,000 live births		
	Total	White	Non-white
1920	79.9	76.0	128.1
1921	68.2	64.4	107.7
1922	66.4	62.8	106.8
1923	66.5	62.6	109.5
1924	65.6	60.7	117.9
1925	64.7	60.3	116.2
1926	65.6	61.9	107.1
1927	64.7	59.4	113.3
1928	69.2	62.7	121.0
1929	69.5	63.1	119.9
1930	67.3	60.9	117.4
1931	66.1	60.1	111.4
1932	63.3	58.1	97.6
1933	61.9	56.4	96.7
1934	59.3	54.4	89.7
1935	58.2	53.1	94.6
1936	56.8	51.2	97.2
1937	48.9	43.6	85.8
1938	43.5	37.7	84.9
1939	40.4	35.3	76.2
1940	37.6	32.0	77.3
1941	31.7	26.6	67.8
1942	25.9	22.2	54.5
1943	24.5	21.1	51.0
1944	22.8	18.9	50.6
1945	20.7	17.2	45.5
1946	15.7	13.1	35.9
1947	13.5	10.9	33.5
1948	11.7	8.9	30.1
1949	9.0	6.8	23.5
1950	8.3	6.1	22.2
1951	7.5	5.5	20.1
1952	6.8	4.9	18.8
1953	6.1	4.4	16.6

Source: Elizabeth P. Hunt and Ruth R. Moore, *Perinatal, Infant and Maternal Mortality, 1954*, Children's Bureau, US Department of Health, Education and Welfare, Social Security Administration (1957).

TABLE 7. *Sweden. 1756–1950. Maternal Mortality from All Causes: Maternal Deaths per 10,000 Births*

Data	Maternal Mortality rate
1756–60	109.0
1761–5	109.0
1766–70	87.0
1771–5	n.a.
1776–80	89.0
1781–5	83.0
1786–90	93.0
1791–5	101.0
1796–1800	85.0
1801–5	78.0
1806–10	89.0
1811–15	79.0
1816–20	74.0
1821–5	67.0
1826–30	66.0
1831–5	57.0
1836–40	51.0
1841–5	44.0
1846–50	45.0
1851–5	44.0
1856–60	45.0
1860–70	c.58.0
1870–4	63.0
1875–80	42.0
1880–4	39.0
1885–9	35.0
1890–5	23.0
1900–4	23.0
1905–9	25.0
1911	26.6
1912	23.2
1913	22.7
1914	26.0
1915	29.0
1916	26.6
1917	24.5
1918	25.1
1919	31.1
1920	25.9
1921	26.2
1922	24.5

TABLE 7. (*cont.*)

Data	Maternal Mortality rate
1923	22.6
1924	23.8
1925	26.3
1926	29.4
1927	25.1
1928	32.1
1929	36.9
1930	33.8
1931	35.7
1932	33.4
1933	29.8
1934	32.3
1935	30.0
1936	30.6
1937	30.1
1938	23.2
1939	22.0
1940	20.9
1941	19.9
1942	15.3
1943	15.1
1944	15.4
1945	13.1
1946	10.8
1947	8.5
1948	7.3
1949	6.5
1950	6.0

Source: 1756–1860: R. Schofield, 'Did the Mothers Really Die? Three Centuries of Maternal Mortality in "The World we have Lost"', in L. Bonfield, R. Smith, and K. Wrightson (eds.), *The World we have Gained: Histories of Population and Social Structure* (Oxford, 1986); 1860–1910: U. Högberg, *Maternal Mortality in Sweden*, Umeå University Medical Dissertations, NS 156 (Umeå, 1985); 1911–50: *Sveriges officiella Statistik*, Stockholm.

TABLE 8. *Denmark. Maternal Mortality, 1890–1940.*
Maternal Deaths per 1,000 Births

Year	Puerperal fever	Other causes	Total
1890–9 (towns only)	2.21	2.45	4.66
1900–9 (towns only)	1.48	2.31	3.79
1910–9 (towns only)	1.17	3.45	4.62
Whole country			
1921	1.28	1.59	2.87
1922	0.94	1.60	2.63
1923	0.95	1.94	2.89
1924	0.87	1.57	2.44
1925	0.90	1.54	2.44
1926	1.05	1.70	2.75
1927	1.04	2.06	3.09
1928	1.17	1.53	2.71
1929	0.99	2.16	3.15
1930	1.17	2.64	3.80
1931	1.25	2.76	4.01
1932	1.06	2.41	3.47
1933	1.29	2.32	3.61
1934	1.49	2.34	3.83
1935	1.37	2.60	3.97
1936	1.26	2.56	3.82
1937	1.06	2.42	3.48
1938	0.92	2.17	3.09
1939	0.74	2.21	2.95
1940	0.64	1.75	2.39

Source: Summary of causes of death in the Kingdom of Denmark published by the National Health Service of Denmark, 1949.

TABLE 9. *The Netherlands, 1900–1950. Maternal Mortality Expressed as Maternal Deaths per 10,000 Births*

Date	Total maternal mortality	Puerperal sepsis[a]
1876–80	41.0	13.0
1881–5	40.0	12.0
1886–90	36.0	12.0
1891–5	30.0	11.0

TABLE 9. (*cont.*)

Date	Total maternal mortality	Puerperal sepsis[a]
1896–1900	25.0	7.0
1901–5	24.0	7.0
1905	24.0	7.0
1906	25.0	8.0
1907	23.0	8.0
1908	25.0	7.0
1909	22.0	7.0
1910	25.0	7.0
1911	24.0	7.0
1912	24.0	7.0
1913	21.0	6.0
1914	21.0	6.0
1915	25.0	8.0
1916	26.0	10.0
1917	25.0	8.0
1918	30.0	10.0
1919	34.0	12.0
1920	24.0	8.0
1921	23.1	n.a.
1922	24.9	n.a.
1923	23.2	n.a.
1924	23.9	n.a.
1925	26.4	n.a.
1926	28.5	n.a.
1927	29.0	n.a.
1928	33.4	n.a.
1929	33.3	n.a.
1930	33.3	n.a.
1931	32.0	n.a.
1932	30.0	n.a.
1933	31.7	5.7
1934	31.8	7.2
1935	29.3	6.7
1936	30.2	6.3
1937	25.7	4.5
1938	26.8	4.5
1939	24.7	n.a.
1940	23.5	n.a.
1941	19.2	n.a.
1942	19.5	n.a.
1943	19.5	n.a.
1944	22.9	n.a.

TABLE 9. (*cont.*)

Date	Total maternal mortality	Puerperal sepsis[a]
1945	19.4	n.a.
1946	14.9	n.a.
1947	14.0	n.a.
1948	12.2	n.a.
1949	10.9	n.a.
1950	10.5	n.a.

[a] Sepsis includes deaths from septic abortion.

Source: 1876–1920: Children's Bureau Publications, US Department of Labor, Washington, DC, Goverment Printing Office, NO. 152, R. M. Woodbury, *Maternal Mortality: The Risk of Death in Childbirth and from all the Diseases Caused by Pregnancy and Confinement* (1926); 1933–1938: *Statisteik van de sterfie naar den leeftid en de oorzaken van den dood*, Central bureau voor de statistiek (various years); 1921–1950: *1899–1979 tachtig jaren statisteik in tijdreeksen*, Centraal bureau voor de statistiek (The Hague, 1979).

TABLE 10. *Belgium, 1851–1950. Maternal Mortality from All Causes. Maternal Deaths per 10,000 Births to Nearest Whole Number*

Year	Maternal mortality rate
1851	66
1855	55
1856–60	44
1865	77
1866	64
1867	35
1868	54
1869	104
1870	78
1871	95
1872	83
1874	130

Table 10. (*cont.*)

Year	Maternal mortality rate
1875	84
1876	77
1877	72
1878	70
1879	68
1880	90
1881	75
1882	72
1883	78
1884	79
1885	85
1886	77
1887	77
1888	67
1889	65
1890	55
1891–7	57
1898	51
1900	54
1901	53
1902	55
1903	63
1904	61
1905	53
1906	55
1907	57
1908	61
1909	59
1911	58
1912	65
1913	55
1914–19	80
1920	61
1921	51
1922	61
1923	57
1924	58
1925	50
1926	55
1927	57
1928	60
1929	62
1930	52

TABLE 10. (*cont.*)

Year	Maternal mortality rate
1931	50
1932	48
1933	52
1934	54
1935	42
1936	46
1937	38
1938	40
1939	38
1940	38
1941	40
1942	38
1943	39
1944	40
1945	35
1946	29
1947	25
1948	21
1949	16
1950	15

Source: *Annuaire statistique de la Belgique et du Congo Belgique*, Office central de statistique (Brussels).

TABLE 11. *Iceland. 1911–1960. Maternal Mortality Rate per 10,000 Births*

Period	Number of maternal deaths	Maternal mortality rate	
		Puerperal sepsis	All causes
1911–15	43	13.4	36.0
1916–20	39	12.2	32.0
1921–5	43	17.4	32.6
1926–30	47	9.5	34.4
1931–5	42	9.1	31.8
1936–40	30	8.2	24.6
1941–5	50	7.5	31.6
1946–50	30	3.1	15.7
1951–60	26	0.0	12.1

Source: Official mortality statistics of Iceland.

TABLE 12. *Maternal Mortality in the Commonwealth of Australia and Certain States from 1871 to 1950. Maternal Mortality Rate Expressed as Maternal Deaths per 10,000 Births*

Year	Accidents of childbirth	Puerperal fever	Total maternal mortality rate
State of Victoria			
1871–80	47.2	17.1	64.3
1881–90	38.7	20.5	59.2
1891–1900	35.8	20.2	56.0
1901–5	41.3	19.6	60.9
1906	37.3	16.5	53.8
State of New South Wales			
1893–6	41.8	23.9	65.7
1897–1900	51.8	24.6	76.4
1901–4	44.9	25.5	70.4
1905–8	50.1	17.9	68.0
Commonwealth of Australia, 1907–30			
1907	39.4	16.0	55.6
1908	36.2	18.0	54.2
1909	33.0	17.6	50.6
1910	32.0	18.6	50.6
1911	29.4	17.1	50.5
1912	31.0	17.3	48.3
1913	31.5	17.3	48.8
1914	30.4	15.5	45.9
1915	29.2	13.5	42.7
1916	31.3	21.4	52.7
1917	37.1	19.2	56.3
1918	32.6	14.5	47.1
1919	33.1	13.5	46.6
1920	31.8	18.3	50.1
1921	32.0	15.2	47.2
1922	31.0	14.2	45.2
1923	33.8	17.2	51.1
1924	35.0	19.6	54.6
1925	39.0	17.3	56.3
1926	36.6	16.3	52.9
1927	37.6	21.5	59.1
1928	39.3	20.5	59.8
1929	33.6	17.1	50.7
1930	34.1	18.8	52.9

Source: Official Statistics, Commonwealth of Australia, Commonwealth Bureau of Census and Statistics, Melbourne. Populations and Vital Statistics, 1907–50; *Report on Maternal Mortality in Childbirth*, Committee concerning causes of death and invalidity in the Commonwealth, Commonwealth of Australia, Department of Trades and Customs (Melbourne, 1917), for pre-1907 data.

TABLE 13. *Maternal Mortality in the Commonwealth of Australia, 1931–1950*

Year	Total maternal mortality rate	Total deaths from sepsis	Deaths from full-term sepsis	Deaths from septic abortion
Commonwealth of Australia, 1931–50				
1931	54.7	19.0	8.6	12.4
1932	55.6	21.8	7.5	14.3
1933	51.1	20.7	8.2	12.5
1934	57.8	23.4	8.9	14.5
1935	52.9	22.0	8.0	14.0
1936	59.8	19.0	10.7	18.3
1937	46.1	15.2	5.2	10.0
1938	46.5	17.1	5.2	11.9
1939	40.8	13.2	3.9	9.3
1940	40.6	15.4	4.2	11.2
1941	36.3	10.9	3.1	7.8
1942	35.0	11.1	3.9	7.2
1943	33.2	11.2	3.6	7.6
1944	28.4	6.9	1.7	5.2
1945	21.4	4.2	1.0	3.2
1946	18.4	3.8	1.5	2.3
1947	18.5	3.4	0.4	3.0
1948	13.9	1.7	0.5	1.2
1949	12.0	1.6	0.2	1.4
1950	12.2	1.2	0.1	1.2

Source: Official Statistics, Commonwealth of Australia, Commonwealth Bureau of Census and Statistics, Melbourne. Populations and Vital Statistics, 1907–50; *Report on Maternal Mortality in Childbirth*, Committee concerning causes of death and invalidity in the Commonwealth, Commonwealth of Australia, Department of Trades and Customs (Melbourne, 1917), for pre-1907 data.

TABLE 14. *New Zealand, 1872–1950. Maternal Mortality Rates. Maternal Deaths per 10,000 Births to Nearest Whole Number*

Year	Mortality rate
1872–6	51
1873–7	52
1874–8	62
1875–9	49
1876–80	44

TABLE 14. (*cont.*)

Year	Mortality rate
1877–81	45
1878–82	47
1879–83	47
1880–4	52
1881–5	59
1882–6	60
1883–7	60
1884–8	62
1885–9	56
1886–90	59
1887–91	51
1888–92	50
1889–93	47
1890–4	51
1891–5	51
1892–6	50
1893–7	50
1894–8	51
1896–1900	44
1897–01	44
1989–02	46
1899–03	48
1900–4	48
1901–5	49
1902–6	48
1903–7	46
1904–8	44
1906–9	45
1906–10	45
1907–11	46
1912	36
1913	36
1914	41
1915	47
1916	58
1917	60
1918	52
1919	50
1920	64
1921	51
1922	51
1923	51
1924	50

TABLE 14. (*cont.*)

Year	Mortality rate
1925	46
1926	42
1927	49
1928	49
1929	48
1930	51
1931	48
1932	40
1933	44
1934	48
1935	42
1936	37
1937	36
1938	41
1939	36
1940	29
1941	34
1942	25
1943	22
1944	27
1945	22
1946	20
1947	10
1948	10
1949	10
1950	9

Source: 1872–1911: *Appendices to the Journals of the House of Representatives* (1921–2). H-31B (Report of a special committee set up by the Board of Health to consider the deaths of mothers in childbirth), 2, and also (1924), H-31A, 21. I am most grateful to Dr Linda Bryder of the University of Auckland for providing me with these data. From 1911: *Reports on the Vital Statistics*, Census and Statistics Office, Wellington, New Zealand.

TABLE 15. *Amsterdam, 1875–1949. Maternal Mortality Rate for Puerperal Fever and all Puerperal Causes. Maternal Deaths per 10,000 Births*

Year	Puerperal fever	All causes
1875	36.0	55.0
1876	25.0	57.0
1877	23.0	54.0
1878	15.0	55.0
1879	12.0	33.0
1880	26.0	42.0
1881	26.0	49.0
1882	28.0	44.0
1883	29.0	59.0
1884	23.0	38.0
1885	28.0	52.0
1886	19.0	39.0
1887	28.0	46.0
1888	17.0	36.0
1889	18.0	37.0
1890	12.0	26.0
1891	18.0	27.0
1892	19.0	28.0
1893	18.0	38.0
1894	9.0	24.0
1895	8.0	23.0
1896	9.0	20.0
1897	10.0	31.0
1898	5.0	19.0
1899	1.0	18.0
1900	4.7	18.0
1901	4.5	18.0
1902	3.9	17.0
1903	1.3	20.0
1904	4.0	22.0
1905	1.3	14.0
1906	6.2	25.0
1907	5.5	16.0
1908	10.8	34.0
1909	8.1	26.0
1910	2.9	23.0
1911	6.1	26.0
1912	7.3	32.0
1913	4.3	27.0
1914	3.4	22.0
1915	7.5	36.0

TABLE 15. (*cont.*)

Year	Puerperal fever	All causes
1916	7.5	29.0
1917	9.2	28.0
1918	9.4	32.0
1919	7.1	27.0
1920	8.0	26.0
1921	11.0	27.0
1922	7.8	25.0
1923	4.2	20.0
1924	9.2	29.0
1925	10.2	33.0
1926	14.8	38.0
1927	7.2	37.0
1928	12.6	43.0
1929	16.0	44.0
1930	19.8	45.0
1931	13.4	27.0
1932	18.0	49.0
1933	13.4	39.0
1934	10.4	41.0
1935	15.3	42.0
1936	8.5	35.0
1937	17.5	38.0
1938	11.4	31.0
1939	8.1	22.0
1940	8.3	33.0
1941	11.2	22.0
1942	13.3	27.0
1943	15.7	29.0
1944	21.3	33.0
1945	12.3	23.0
1946	8.8	15.8
1947	8.3	16.7
1948	4.3	12.9
1949	3.4	10.1

Note: The total annual number of maternal deaths was not large. Before 1945 it was on average 30 and 45 maternal deaths a year, ranging from 20 to just over 70.

Source: *Amsterdam Statistical Bulletin* (Amsterdam Bureau of Statistics).

TABLE 16. *Paris. 1880–1950. Maternal Mortality Rates. Maternal Deaths per 10,000 Births*

Year	Maternal mortality rate
1880	74.0
1885	55.7
1890	60.4
1895	42.1
1900	32.7
1901	36.0
1902	37.6
1903	36.8
1904	33.4
1905	38.5
1906	46.2
1907	58.5
1908	56.3
1909	56.8
1910	50.5
1911	66.5
1912	60.3
1913	52.1
1914	58.0
1915	39.3
1916	48.6
1917	42.4
1918	51.3
1919	50.4
1920	59.9
1921	51.4
1922	37.2
1923	37.6
1924	36.2
1925	32.2
1926	37.4
1927	34.8
1928	36.9
1929	33.2
1930	33.5
1931	31.4
1932	29.1
1933	27.8
1934	23.3
1935	31.3
1936	33.4

TABLE 16. (*cont.*)

Year	Maternal mortality rate
1940	20.8
1941	24.7
1942	24.7
1943	17.5
1944	23.0
1945	20.5
1946	10.7
1947	7.9
1948	6.2
1949	7.0
1950	7.4

Source: *Annuaire statistique de la ville de Paris* (various years).

TABLE 17. *Maternal Mortality in Rural Bangladesh, 1982–1983. Maternal Mortality Rate per 10,000 Live Births. (Total number of births = 9,317)*

Maternal deaths by cause	(percentages)	Maternal mortality rates
Direct maternal deaths		
Sepsis	31.0	
Post-abortive	(20.6)	
Puerperal fever	(10.4)	
Eclampsia	20.7	
Difficult labour	17.2	
Haemorrhage	10.3	
Tetanus	6.9	
Total direct maternal deaths	(86.1)	
Indirect maternal deaths		
Cardiovascular disease	8.6	
Suicide	1.7	
Not diagnosed	3.5	
Total indirect maternal deaths	(13.8)	
All live births		62.3
According to age of mother:		
Under 20		57.3
20–4		26.6
25–9		47.1
30–4		73.7
35–9		178.3
40 and over		250.0

Source: A. R. Khan, F. A. Jahan, and S. F. Begum, 'Maternal Mortality in Rural Bangladesh: The Jamalpur District', *Studies in Family Planning*, 17/1 (1986), 7–12.

TABLE 18. *The Administrative Counties of England and Wales Ranked in Order of their Maternal Mortality Rates per 10,000 Births during the Decennium 1924–1933*

Group I. Areas in which the mortality rate was higher than that of England and Wales by an amount which may be regarded as definitely significant:

Anglesey	67.9
Denbigh	65.6
Cardigan	63.9
Carmarthen	63.4
Glamorgan	58.5
Pembroke	57.0
Flint	56.3
Lancashire	54.1
West Riding	53.7
Cumberland	52.0
Monmouth	51.8
Durham	47.2

Group II. Areas in which the mortality rate was higher than that of England and Wales by an amount which may be regarded as very probably significant:

Merioneth	58.4
Westmorland	53.6
Caernarfon	50.5

Group III. Areas in which the mortality rate did not differ significantly from that of England and Wales:

Radnor	52.7
Isle of Wight	50.9
Montgomery	47.6
North Riding	45.5
Cornwall	45.2
Worcester	45.0
Hunts.	44.9
Brecon	44.8
Northumberland	44.5
Cambridge	43.6
Gloucester	43.6
Cheshire	43.2
Derby	43.0
Hereford	42.8
Soke of Peterborough	42.5
Warwick	42.3
Shropshire	42.2
Devon	40.9
Somerset	40.7
East Riding	40.6
Rutland	40.5
Lincs. Lindsey	40.1

Table 18. (*cont.*)

Dorset	39.6
Notts.	39.5
Northants.	39.2
Berks.	39.1
Leicester	39.1
Bedford	38.6
Isle of Ely	38.5
West Sussex	38.4

Group IV. Areas in which the mortality rate was lower than that of England and Wales by an amount which may be regarded as very probably significant:

East Sussex	36.4
Bucks.	36.2
East Suffolk	35.8
West Suffolk	33.9

Group V. Areas in which the mortality rate was lower than that of England and Wales by an amount which may be regarded as definitely significant:

Southants.	37.3
Essex	36.1
Norfolk	34.7
Kent	34.3
Herts.	36.1
Staffs.	35.9
Surrey	35.7
Wilts.	35.2
Middlesex	35.1
Lincs. Kesteven	33.4
London	33.4
Oxford	32.6
Lincs. Holland	30.2

Statistical note: 'Definitely significant' indicates a difference equal to at least twice the standard error. 'Very probably significant' indicates a difference at least 1.35 times the standard error, but less than twice the standard error. 'Not significantly different' indicates a difference equal to less than 1.35 times the standard error.

Source: Ministry of Health, *Report of an Investigation into Maternal Mortality* (London, 1937), Cmd. 5422, Appendices.

TABLE 19. *England and Wales. 1921. Causes of Death amongst Women Aged 15–44*

ICD Number	Cause of death	Number of deaths
3	Respiratory tuberculosis	11,087
87/96	Circulatory diseases	3,701
143/150	Puerperal state	3,272
97/107	Other respiratory diseases[a]	2,905
43/49	Total cancer	2,785
46	Cancer female generative organs	924
47	Cancer of the breast	641
108/127	Diseases of digestion	1,944
57	Diabetes	481
51	Rheumatic fever	442
1	Enteric fever	198
38	Syphilis	100
41	Purulent infections	71

[a] i.e. respiratory infections other than tuberculosis.

Source: *Registrar General's Statistical Review.*

TABLE 20. *England and Wales. 1872–1876. Maternal Deaths by Cause. (Percentages to the Nearest Whole Number)*

Causes of death	Total number of deaths	Percentage of total
Total deaths	23,051	100.0
Puerperal fever	12,865	55.8
Accidents of childbirth		
Flooding (post-partum haemorrhage)	3,524	15.3
Puerperal convulsions	2,692	11.7
Placenta praevia	1,308	5.7
Puerperal mania	573	2.5
Abortion	568	2.5
Miscarriage	356	1.5
Phlegmasia dolens	456	2.0
Retention of placenta	354	1.5
Ruptured uterus	181	0.8
Deformed pelvis	112	0.5
Extrauterine foetation	54	0.2
Breast abscess	51	0.2
Caesarean operation	16	0.1
Ruptured perineum	1	—

Source: Registrar General, *Annual Report for the Year 1876*, 244.

TABLE 21. *England and Wales. 1872–1876, 1930, and 1979–1981. Total Number of Maternal Deaths, Maternal Mortality Rate, and the Percentage of Deaths Due to Certain Causes*

	Number of deaths	Percentage of total deaths	Maternal mortality rate (per 10,000 births)
1872–6			
Total	23,051	100	54.2
Average *annual* number of deaths	4,610		
Deaths due to:			
Puerperal fever	12,805	55.5	
Haemorrhage	4,832	21.0	
Puerperal convulsions	2,692	11.7	
Phlegmasia dolens	456	2.0	
1930			
Total	2,854	100	44.0
Deaths due to:			
Puerperal sepsis	1,243	43.5	
Toxaemia of pregnancy	467	16.3	
Puerperal haemorrhage	348	12.2	
Embolism and sudden death	167	5.8	
1979–81			
Total	176	100	1.1
Average *annual* number of deaths	58		
Deaths due to			
Hypertensive disease of pregnancy	36	20.4	
Pulmonary embolism	23	13.1	
Haemorrhage	14	8.0	
Sepsis	8	4.5	

Source: Registrar General's Report for 1876; Registrar General's Statistical Summary for 1930; Department of Health, Report on Confidential Enquiries into Maternal Deaths in England and Wales, 1979–81 (London, 1986), Report on Health and Social Subjects, No. 29.

TABLE 22. *Maternal Mortality at the Dublin Lying-in Hospital under Successive Masterships[a] from 1745 to 1940.*

Date	Maternal mortality rate (per 10,000 births)
1745–59	110
1759–66	128
1766–73	137
1773–80	106
1780–6	76
1786–93	117
1793–1800	79
1800–7	110
1807–14	110
1814–21	140
1821–6	150
1826–33	96
1833–40	170
1840–7	130
1847–54	120
1854–61	240
1861–8	340
1868–75	220
1875–82	205
1882–9	108
1889–96	77
1896–1903	37
1903–10	35
1910–19	51
1919–26	61
1926–33	62
1933–40	50

[a] The Director of the Dublin Lying-in Hospital (the 'Rotunda') was and is known as the 'Master of the Rotunda'. It was customary to publish the statistics of the hospital's deliveries at the termination of each mastership.

Source: O'Donel T. D. Browne, *The Rotunda Hospital 1745–1945* (Edinburgh, 1947).

TABLE 23. *The Dates at which the Various States of the USA were Admitted to the USA Death-Registration Area*

States admitted before 1900
Connecticut
Delaware
District of Columbia
Massachusetts
New Hampshire
New Jersey
New York
Rhode Island
Vermont

States admitted between 1900 and 1915
California
Colorado
Indiana
Kansas
Kentucky
Maine
Maryland
Michigan
Minnesota
Missouri
Montana
Ohio
Oregon
Pennsylvania
Utah
Virginia
Washington
Wisconsin

States admitted between 1916 and 1923
Florida
Georgia
Idaho
Illinois
Iowa
Louisiana
Mississippi
Nebraska
North Carolina
South Carolina
Tennessee
Wyoming

TABLE 23. (*cont.*)

States admitted between 1924 and 1933
Alabama
Arizona
Arkansas
Nevada
New Mexico
Oklahoma
North Dakota
South Dakota
Texas
West Virginia

TABLE 24. *Land Areas and Population Densities in 1900 and 1980 of Certain Countries and Selected States of the USA*

Country or state	Area	Population density	
		1900	1980
United Kingdom	160	343	599
England and Wales	100	558	847
Scotland	51	150	172
Sweden	299	31	48
Norway	258	15	27
Denmark	29	167	300
Netherlands	23	448	1,071
Belgium	20	588	837
France	367	189	257
Switzerland	27	217	404
USA	6,102	21	64
Texas	452	12	54
California	269	10	151
Montana	250	2	5
Arizona	195	1	24
Kansas	141	18	29
Minnesota	137	22	51
Georgia	100	37	94
Michigan	98	42	162
Wisconsin	94	38	86
Alabama	87	35	77
North Carolina	84	39	120

TABLE 24. (*cont.*)

Country or state	Area	Population density	
		1900	1980
New York State	82	151	370
Mississippi	81	33	47
Pennsylvania	77	140	264
Maine	53	23	36
Vermont	16	38	55
New Hampshire	15	46	102
Massachusetts	13	358	733
Rhode Island	2	406	898
Canada	6,138	2	15
Australia	5,117	1	5
New Zealand	179	7	31

Note: The land area of England and Wales (58,050 square miles or 149,640 square kilometres) has been alloted the value of 100 as the basis for comparison. Population densities: persons per square mile, expressed to the nearest whole number.

TABLE 25. *Maternal Mortality in the USA by State. 1940 and 1960*

	1940		1960		
	A	B	C	D	E
	Maternal mortality rate[a]	Percentage	Maternal mortality rate	Percentage	C as percentage of A
USA	37.6	100.0	3.59	100.0	9.5
States with below average maternal mortality rates in 1940					
North Dakota	17.2	45.7	2.73	76.0	15.8
Minnesota	22.2	59.0	1.12	31.0	5.0
Rhode Island	25.0	66.4	1.27	35.3	5.1
Oregon	25.2	67.0	1.92	53.5	7.6
Utah	26.6	70.7	2.45	68.2	14.7
Maryland	27.8	73.9	3.11	86.6	11.2
California	27.9	74.2	2.84	79.2	10.2
Massachusetts	28.1	74.7	1.94	54.0	6.9
Wisconsin	28.1	74.7	2.60	72.4	9.3
Connecticut	28.2	74.7	2.36	65.7	8.4

TABLE 25. (*cont.*)

	1940		1960		
	A	B	C	D	E
	Maternal mortality rate[a]	Percentage	Maternal mortality rate	Percentage	C as percentage of A
Indiana	28.7	76.3	3.17	88.3	11.0
Michigan	29.2	77.6	3.62	100.8	12.4
District of Columbia	29.4	6.43	78.2	179.1	21.9
Illinois	29.7	2.80	79.0	78.0	9.4
New York	29.7	4.63	79.0	117.2	15.6
New Jersey	29.9	79.5	3.48	96.9	11.6
Montana	30.5	81.1	2.00	55.7	6.5
Washington	30.6	81.4	1.83	51.0	6.0
New Hampshire	31.8	84.6	3.34	84.6	10.5
Nebraska	32.0	85.1	2.07	57.6	6.4
Ohio	32.2	85.6	2.45	68.2	7.6
Pennsylvania	32.5	86.4	2.82	78.5	8.7
West Virginia	33.3	88.5	5.0	139.2	15.0
South Dakota	34.4	91.5	2.52	70.1	7.3
Iowa	35.0	93.1	1.70	47.3	4.9
Idaho	35.9	95.5	3.11	86.6	8.6
Vermont	35.9	95.5	1.46	40.6	4.1
Kentucky	36.0	95.7	4.49	125.1	12.4
Missouri	36.8	97.9	2.73	76.0	7.4
Kansas	37.3	99.2	2.70	75.2	7.2
Average					9.6
Standard deviation					4.02

States with above average maternal mortality in 1940

	A	B	C	D	E
Oklahoma	39.7	105.6	3.35	93.3	8.4
Maine	40.3	107.1	2.19	61.0	5.4
Colorado	40.7	108.2	2.60	72.4	6.4
Wyoming	41.6	110.6	2.48	69.1	6.0
Virginia	44.9	119.4	4.47	124.5	10.2
Texas	46.0	122.0	4.56	127.0	10.2
New Mexico	46.8	124.0	5.18	144.2	11.2
Tennessee	47.5	126.3	4.48	125.0	9.5
Nevada	48.5	129.0	2.29	63.7	4.7
Arkansas	48.7	129.5	4.91	136.8	10.1
Arizona	50.2	133.5	3.84	107.0	7.6

TABLE 25. (*cont.*)

	1940		1960		
	A	B	C	D	E
	Maternal mortality rate[a]	Percentage	Maternal mortality rate	Percentage	C as percentage of A
North Carolina	51.6	137.2	5.05	140.6	9.8
Louisiana	53.4	142.0	4.19	116.7	7.8
Delaware	54.4	144.7	3.17	88.3	5.8
Georgia	56.9	151.3	4.98	138.7	8.7
Alabama	61.3	163.0	7.48	208.4	12.2
Mississippi	62.8	167.0	8.41	234.2	13.4
Florida	64.8	172.3	4.27	108.1	6.6
South Carolina	67.8	180.3	6.52	181.6	9.6
Average					8.6
Standard deviation					2.37

[a] The maternal mortality rate is shown for each state as a total and as a percentage of the maternal mortality rate for the USA as a whole for 1940 (columns A and B) and for 1960 (columns C and D). The rate in each state in 1960 is shown as a percentage of the rate in 1940 in column E. Direct maternal deaths only; that is, indirect (=associated) deaths are not included. Maternal mortality rates expressed per 10,000 births.

Source: *Changes in Infant, Childhood and Maternal Mortality over the Decade 1939–1948: A Graphic Analysis*, Children's Bureau Statistical Series No. 6, Federal Security Agency, Social Security Administration, Children's Bureau, Washington, DC; *Infant, Fetal and Maternal Mortality, United States, 1963*, National Center for Health Statistics, Series 20, No. 3, US Department of Health, Education and Welfare (Washington, DC, 1966).

TABLE 26. *USA. 1955. Maternal Mortality, Perinatal Mortality, and Infant Mortality by State*

State	Maternal mortality		Perinatal mortality		Infant mortality	
	rate[a]	Percentage	rate[b]	Percentage	rate[c]	Percentage
USA	5.0	100.0	35.6	100.0	26.4	100.0
States with below average maternal mortality						
Vermont	1.6	32.0	37.4	105.0	26.1	99.0
Oregon	1.9	38.0	33.7	95.0	24.1	91.0
Montana	2.3	46.0	30.9	87.0	25.0	95.0
Utah	2.5	50.0	28.3	79.5	20.4	77.0
Massachusetts	2.7	54.0	30.8	86.5	21.9	83.0

TABLE 26. *(cont.)*

State	Maternal mortality rate[a]	Percentage	Perinatal mortality rate[b]	Percentage	Infant mortality rate[c]	Percentage
Conn.	2.8	56.0	30.6	86.0	21.7	82.0
Wyoming	2.8	56.0	33.3	93.5	28.5	108.0
North Dakota	3.2	64.0	32.6	91.5	25.1	95.0
Washington	3.2	64.0	30.4	85.0	24.5	93.0
Wisconsin	3.2	64.0	31.2	88.0	23.7	90.0
Maine	3.3	66.0	35.6	100.0	24.7	93.5
South Dakota	3.3	66.0	33.9	95.0	26.1	99.0
Illinois	3.4	68.0	32.7	92.0	24.8	94.0
Indiana	3.4	68.0	33.5	94.0	25.0	95.0
Alaska	3.5	70.0	36.1	101.0	37.4	103.0
California	3.6	72.0	31.6	89.0	23.6	89.0
Minnesota	3.6	72.0	30.6	86.0	21.8	82.5
Rhode Island	3.6	72.0	33.4	94.0	23.4	89.0
Iowa	3.9	78.0	28.8	81.0	22.1	84.0
Michigan	3.9	78.0	34.0	95.5	24.9	94.0
Ohio	3.9	78.0	34.6	97.0	24.8	93.0
New Hampshire	4.0	80.0	36.5	102.5	25.7	97.0
Pennsylvania	4.0	80.0	36.7	103.0	24.6	93.0
Colorado	4.1	82.0	41.4	116.0	30.3	115.0
New York	4.1	82.0	38.6	108.0	24.3	92.0
Nebraska	4.3	86.0	32.0	90.0	23.7	90.0
Arizona	4.4	88.0	35.9	101.0	34.8	132.0
Delaware	4.4	88.0	34.2	96.0	25.0	95.0
Idaho	4.4	88.0	27.9	78.0	20.8	79.0
West Virginia	4.6	92.0	34.6	97.0	27.3	103.0
Maryland	4.6	92.0	36.3	102.0	27.6	104.0
New Jersey	4.6	92.0	34.6	97.0	24.3	92.0
States with above average maternal mortality						
Kansas	5.1	102.0	32.3	91.0	23.3	88.0
District of Columbia	5.2	104.0	45.5	128.0	32.2	121.0
Missouri	5.2	104.0	34.5	97.0	25.3	96.0
Oklahoma	5.6	112.0	34.4	97.0	26.7	101.0
Texas	5.6	112.0	35.7	100.0	30.3	115.0
Nevada	5.8	116.0	38.6	108.0	30.0	114.0
Tennessee	6.1	122.0	36.9	104.0	29.2	111.0
Virginia	6.1	122.0	40.2	113.0	29.5	112.0
Florida	6.3	126.0	39.0	109.5	29.7	112.0
Kentucky	6.3	126.0	35.3	99.0	30.4	115.0
Louisiana	6.7	134.0	40.4	113.0	31.6	120.0
Arkansas	7.4	148.0	34.2	96.0	26.7	101.0

TABLE 26. (*cont.*)

State	Maternal mortality		Perinatal mortality		Infant mortality	
	rate[a]	Percentage	rate[b]	Percentage	rate[c]	Percentage
North Carolina	7.7	154.0	39.2	110.0	30.3	115.0
North Mexico	8.4	168.0	39.9	112.0	43.0	163.0
Georgia	10.1	202.0	42.1	118.0	29.9	113.0
South Carolina	10.3	206.0	41.2	116.0	34.1	129.0
Alabama	11.8	236.0	43.4	122.0	32.0	121.0
Mississippi	14.1	282.0	50.1	141.0	37.0	140.0

[a] Maternal mortality rate as deaths per 10,000 live births.
[b] Perinatal mortality as stillbirths plus deaths in first four weeks (neonatal deaths) per 1,000 total births.
[c] Infant mortality as deaths under age of 1 year per 1,000 live births.
Data shown as mortality rates and also as the percentage (for each state) of the rates for the USA as a whole.
The data available for this table defined perinatal mortality as stillbirths and infant deaths in the first *month* rather than the first *week* of life.
Correlations between maternal mortality (MMR), perinatal mortality (PMR), and infant mortality (IMR)

States with below average maternal mortality
Product moment correlation (Pearson)
MMR and PMR: coefficient = 0.239: τ = 1.34: df = 30: $P > 0.1$ Not significant
MMR and IMR: coefficient = 0.189: τ = 1.05: df = 30: $P > 0.1$ Not significant
PMR and IMR: coefficient = 0.611: τ = 5.47: df = 30: $P < 0.001$ Highly significant

Rank correlation coefficient (Spearman's)
MMR and PMR: coefficient = 0.380: τ = 2.24: df = 30: $P < 0.05, > 0.02$ Just significant
MMR and IMR: coefficient = 0.174: τ = 0.96: df = 30: $P > 0.1$ Not significant
PMR and IMR: coefficient = 0.611: τ = 5.48: df = 30: $P < 0.001$ Highly significant

States with above average maternal mortality
Pearson's product moment:
MMR and PMR: coefficient = 0.715: τ = 4.09: df = 16: $P < 0.001$ Highly significant
MMR and IMR: coefficient = 0.556: τ = 2.67: df = 16: $P < 0.02, > 0.01$ Significant
PMR and IMR: coefficient = 0.653: τ = 3.34: df = 16: $P < 0.01, > 0.001$ Significant

Rank correlation coefficient
MMR and PMR: coefficient = 0.598: τ = 2.98: df = 16: $P < 0.01, > 0.001$ Significant
MMR and IMR: coefficient = 0.606: τ = 3.04: df = 16: $P < 0.01, > 0.001$ Significant
PMR and IMR: coefficient = 0.760: τ = 4.67: df = 16: $P < 0.001$ Highly significant

TABLE 27. *Distribution of Post-Partum Maternal Deaths by Cause of Death and by Interval between Birth of Child and Death of Mother. New York State (exclusive of New York City), 1936–1938*

Interval between birth of child and death of mother	All causes	Placenta praevia	Post-partum haemorrhage	Toxaemia	Puerperal Septicaemia[a]
Total cases (No.)	689	38	99	158	157
(under 1 hour) (%)	(3)	(16)	(7)	(13)	(< 1)
under 1 day (%)	37	60	79	44	2
1 day (%)	6	8	4	12	1
2 days (%)	5	3	4	8	2
3 days (%)	5	3	3	7	4
4 days (%)	5	—	2	2	8
5 days (%)	5	3	1	4	8
6 days (%)	4	8	2	2	8
1 week (%)	15	13	4	13	26
2–3 weeks (%)	9	5	1	4	19
4 weeks + (%)	9	—	—	6	21

[a] Puerperal septicaemia includes deaths from septic abortion as well as deaths from full-term puerperal fever.

Source: J. Yerushalmy, M. Kramer, and E. M. Gardiner, 'Studies in Childbirth Mortality: Puerperal Fatality and Loss of Offspring', *Public Health Reports*, 55 (1940), 1020.

TABLE 28. *Dates from which Vital Statistics First Became Available in Certain Countries*

Alphabetical		Chronological	
Austria	1819	Sweden	1749
Belgium	1830	Finland	1751
Denmark	1801	Denmark	1801
England and Wales	1838	Norway	1801
Finland	1751	France	1801
France	1801	Austria	1819
German Empire	1841	Belgium	1830
Ireland	1864	England and Wales	1838
Italy	1863	The Netherlands	1839
The Netherlands	1839	German Empire	1841
Norway	1801	Scotland	1851
Portugal	1886	Spain	1858

TABLE 28. (*cont.*)

Alphabetical		Chronological	
Russia (Europe)	1867	Italy	1863
Scotland	1851	Ireland	1864
Spain	1858	Russia	1867
Sweden	1749	Switzerland	1870
Switzerland	1870	USA	1880/1933[a]
USA	1880/1933[a]	Portugal	1886

[a] The two dates refer to the creation and the completion of the Death-Registration Area in the USA.

Source: Children's Bureau Publications, US Department of Labor, Washington, DC, Government Printing Office, No. 152, R. M. Woodbury, *Maternal Mortality: The Risk of Death in Childbirth and from all the Diseases Caused by Pregnancy and Confinement* (1926), 119.

TABLE 29. *Maternal Mortality Rate per 10,000 Births, and the Percentage of Deaths Due to Puerperal Sepsis and to other Causes in Certain Countries, 1920–1924*

Country	Maternal mortality rate	Percentage of deaths due to puerperal sepsis	Percentage of deaths due to other causes
The Netherlands	24.0	33	67
Sweden	24.6	46	54
Denmark	27.1	37	63
England and Wales	39.0	36	64
Australia	49.6	34	66
New Zealand	53.4	35	65
Belgium	57.6	46	54
USA	68.9	37	63

Source: Children's Bureau Publications, US Department of Labor, Washington, DC, Government Printing Office, No. 152, R. M. Woodbury, *Maternal Mortality: The Risk of Death in Childbirth and from all the Diseases Caused by Pregnancy and Confinement* (1926); A. Macfarlane and M. Mugford, *Birth Counts: Statistics of Pregnancy and Childbirth*, 2 vols. (London, 1984); *Sveriges Officiella statistik* (Stockholm, 1911–1950); U. Högberg, *Maternal Mortality in Sweden*, Umeå University Medical Dissertations, NS 156 (Umeå, 1985); *Statistiek van de sterfte naar den leeftid en de oorzaken van den dood*, Central bureau voor de statistiek (1911–38); *Summary of Causes of Death in the Kingdom of Denmark*, National Health Services of Denmark (1949); *Annuaire statistique de la Belgique et du Congo Belgique*, Office Central de Statistique, (Brussels, 1851–1951); *Official Statistics, Commonwealth of Australia*, Melbourne, Commonwealth Bureau of Censuses and Statistics: population and vital statistics (1907–50); *Infant, Fetal and Maternal Mortality, United States, 1963*, National Center for Health Statistics, Series 20, No. 3, US Department of Health, Education and Welfare (Washington, DC, 1966).

TABLE 30. *Rates of Version, Forceps Deliveries, and Craniotomy in Certain European Hospitals. Mid-Nineteenth Century (Rates per 1,000 deliveries)*

	Version	Forceps	Craniotomy
London, Guy's Hospital	5	6	3.0
Paris, Maternité	10	13	2.0
Leipzig, Maternité	10	100	1.6
Leipzig, Polyclinique	45	166	12.0
Munich, Maternité	12	20	4.0
Dresden, Maternité	11	66	4.0
Vienna, Première Clinique	9	23	0.5
Vienna, Deuxième Clinique	10	17	1.2
St Petersburg, Hebammen-Institut	12	30	2.0

Source: Léon le Fort, *Des maternités* (Paris, 1866).

TABLE 31. *Deaths per Million Persons Living from Various Diseases and Mortality Rate from Puerperal Fever per 1,000 live births, 1860–1879. England and Wales*

Year	Scarlet fever		Erysipelas		Puerperal fever		Mortality rate (per 1,000 births)	Percentage variation
	Annual death rate	Percentage variation[a]	Annual death rate	Percentage variation	Annual death rate	Percentage variation		
1860	493	−41	85	−7	50	−23	1.44	−20
1861	456	−46	78	−14	45	−30	1.27	−30
1862	738	−12	76	−16	47	−28	1.32	−27
1863	1,498	+78	94	+3	57	−12	1.56	−14
1864	1,443	+71	102	+12	72	+11	2.00	+10
1865	852	−1	95	+5	64	−1	1.78	−2
1866	556	−34	80	−12	57	−12	1.59	−12
1867	580	−31	68	−25	50	−23	1.39	−23
1868	1,020	+21	91	0	56	−14	1.52	−16
1869	1,275	+51	87	−5	54	−17	1.53	−15
1870	1,461	+73	96	+6	67	+3	1.88	+4
1871	822	−3	99	+9	65	0	1.81	0
1872	521	−38	78	−14	61	−5	1.70	−6
1873	567	−32	88	−3	75	+15	2.10	+12
1874	1,062	+26	144	+58	132	+103	3.63	+100
1875	857	+2	127	+39	105	+61	2.94	+62
1876	696	−17	97	+7	72	+11	1.97	+9
1877	587	−30	85	−7	59	−9	1.63	−10
1878	694	−18	76	−16	57	−12	1.59	−12
1879	677	−20	77	−15	58	−11	1.66	−8

Mean death rates for the period 1860–79:

	843		91		65		1.81	

[a] Percentage variation for each year above or below the mean value for the whole period of twenty years.

Source: Annual Reports of the Registrar General for England and Wales.

TABLE 32. *Some of Sulphonamides which became Available between 1936 and 1940*

Prontosil rubrum: available from 1936
Prontosil album: available from 1936
Streptoside (Evand, Lescher and Webb) (P. aminobenzene sulphonamide)
Sulphonamide-P (British Drug Houses) (P. aminobenzene sulphonamide)
Sulphonamide A & H (Allen and Hanbury's) (P. aminobenzene sulphonamide)
Sulphanilamide (Glaxo)
Sulphonamide (Wellcome)
Rubiazol (Roussel) (Carboxy-sulphamido-chrysodine)
Soluseptasine
Proseptasine
M&B 693 (May and Baker) (Sulphapyridine)
Sulphathiazole and sulphadiazine.

Sources: Various pharmacopoeias and notices of new drugs published in the journal *Practitioner*.

Select Bibliography

BRITAIN

Parliamentary Papers and Government Publications

Report of the Select Committee on Medical Education, PP. 1834, XIII.

Special Report from the Select Committee on the Medical Act (1858) Amendment (No. 3) Bill (Lords), PP. 1878–9, XII.

Report of the Select Committee on Midwives' Registration, PP. 1892, XIV.

Report of the Select Committee on Death Certification, PP. 1893, 373, 402.

Report of the Departmental Committee Appointed by the Lord President of the Council to Consider the Working of the Midwives Act, 1902, PP. 1909, XXXIII.

Reports of the Local Government Board on Public Health and Medical Subjects, 'Statistics of the Incidence of Notifiable Infectious Diseases in each Sanitary District in England and Wales during the Year 1911' (London, HMSO, 1912).

Local Government Board, 44th Annual Report, 1914–15, Supplement containing a Report on Maternal Mortality in Connection with Childbearing and its Relation to Infant Mortality, PP. 1914–16, xxv, Cd. 8085.

CAMERON, ISABELLA, 'Maternal and Infant Mortality in Maternity Hospital Practice', in *Local Government Board, 44th Annual Report, 1914–1915*, Supplement containing a Report on 'Maternal Mortality in Connection with Childbearing and its Relationship to Infant Mortality', PP. 1914–16, xxv, Cd. 8085, pp. 104–8.

LANE-CLAYPON, JANET, 'The Economic Aspects of Midwifery', in *Local Government Board, 44th Annual Report, 1914–1915*, Supplement containing a Report on 'Maternal Mortality in Connection with Childbearing and its Relationship to Infant Mortality', PP. 1914–16, xxv, Cd. 8085, pp. 85–101.

Ministry of Health, *Memorandum in Regard to Maternity Hospitals and Homes*, Memo, 15/Maternal and Child Welfare (London, HMSO, 1920).

CAMPBELL, JANET, 'The Training of Midwives', *Reports of Public Health and Medical Subjects*, 21, Ministry of Health (London, HMSO, 1923).

—— 'Maternal Mortality', *Reports of Public Health and Medical Subjects*, 25, Ministry of Health (London, HMSO, 1924).

KINLOCH, J. P., SMITH, J., and STEPHEN, J. A., *Report on Maternal Mortality in Aberdeen, 1918–1927, with Special Reference to Puerperal Sepsis*, Scottish Board of Health (Edinburgh, HMSO, 1928).

Ministry of Health, *Interim Report of Departmental Committee on Maternal Mortality and Morbidity* (London, HMSO, 1930), 32–293.

SMITH, J., *Causation and Source of Infection in Puerperal Fever*, Department of Health for Scotland (Edinburgh, HMSO, 1931), 49–216.

Ministry of Health, *Final Report of Departmental Committee on Maternal Mortality and Morbidity* (London, HMSO, 1932), 32–300.

CAMPBELL, JANET, CAMERON, ISABELLA D., and JONES, DILWYS M., 'High Maternal Mortality in Certain Areas', *Reports on Public Health and Medical Subjects*, 68, Ministry of Health (London, HMSO, 1924).

Ministry of Health, *Report of an Investigation into Maternal Mortality* (London, HMSO, 1937), Cmd. 5422.

—— *Report on Maternal Mortality in Wales* (London, HMSO, 1937), Cmd. 5423.

—— Lewiss-Fanning, E., 'A Study of the Trends in Maternal Mortality Rates in Urban Communities of England and Wales with Special Reference to "Depressed Areas"', *Reports on Public Health and Medical Subjects*, 86, Ministry of Health (London, 1937).

—— *Report of Interdepartmental Committee on Abortion* (London, HMSO, 1939).

Government of Ireland, Ministry of Home Affairs, *Report on Maternal Mortality and Morbidity in Northern Ireland* (Belfast, HMSO, 1943), Cmd. 219.

McKINLAY, P. L., *Maternal Mortality in Scotland, 1911–1945* (Edinburgh, HMSO, 1947). Extracted from the report of the Registrar General for Scotland.

Registrar General for England and Wales, *Annual Reports, Statistical Reviews*, and *Decennial Supplements* for various years.

Registrars General for Scotland and Ireland, *Annual Reports* for various years.

Public Record Office, Kew, London. Ministry of Health. Reports on maternal and child welfare for various years.

Pre-1900

ANDERSON, ELIZABETH GARRETT, 'Deaths in Childbed', *British Medical Journal* (1898), ii. 839–40, 927.

ANON., *The Danger and Immodesty of the Present too General Custom of Unnecessarily Employing Men-Midwives. Proved Incontestibly in the Letters of a Man-Midwife* (London, 1772).

—— 'Workhouse Death-Rate in Childbirth', *Journal of the Statistical Society*, 30 (1867), 171–3. Reprinted from the *Pall Mall Gazette* (25 Jan. 1867).

ARMSTRONG, J., *Facts and Observations Relative to the Fever Commonly Called Puerperal* (London, 1814).

—— 'Additional Facts and Observations Relative to the Puerperal Fever which Appeared at Sunderland and Several Places in 1813', *Edinburgh Medical and Surgical Journal*, 10 (1814), 444–50.

AVELING, J. H., *English Midwives: Their History and Prospects* (London, 1872), republished with an introduction and biographical sketch of the author by J. L. Thornton (London, 1967).

BAILEY, H. W., 'Statistics of Midwifery', *Transactions of the Obstetrical Society of London*, 2 (1860), 299–307.

BARNES, R., 'On the Use of Forceps and its Alternatives in Lingering Labour', *Transactions of the Obstetrical Society of London*, 21 (1879), 121–41.

—— *Lectures on Obstetric Operations* (London, 1886).

—— 'On the Causes, Internal and External, of Puerperal Fever', *British Medical Journal* (1887), ii. 1036–42.

BEALE, J., 'Review of 700 Cases in Midwifery', *Medical Times and Gazette*, 8 (1854), 315–16.

BEATTY, W. J., '1,000 Maternity Cases without a Death', *British Medical Journal* (1885), i. 1244.

BLACKMORE, E., 'Observations on Puerperal Fever', *Provincial Medical Journal*, 9 (1845), 173–8, 210–13, 228–30, 242–5, 321–4, 338–41, 353–5, 369–71, 387–90, 399–401, 638–9.

BLAND, R., 'Midwifery Reports of the Westminster General Dispensary', *Philosophical Transactions*, 71 (1781), 355–71.

BLUNT, J., *Man-Midwifery Dissected* (London, 1793).

BOXALL, R., 'Fever in Childbed', *Transactions of the Obstetrical Society of London*, 40 (1890), 219–43, 264–70, 275–303.

—— 'The Mortality of Childbirth', *Lancet* (1893), ii. 9–15.

BRAXTON HICKS, J., and PHILLIPS, J. J., 'Remarks on Tables of Mortality after Obstetric Operations', *Transactions of the Obstetrical Society of London*, 13 (1870), 55–87.

BRENAN, J., *Thoughts on Puerperal Fever Illustrated by Cases in the Lying-in Hospital, Dublin* (London, 1814).

BURTON, J. E., 'Out-door versus In-door Maternity Charities', *Medical Press and Circular* (1882), ii. 150–2, 172–4.

BYERS, J., 'The Prevention of Puerperal Fever in Private Practice', *British Medical Journal* (1887), ii. 1042–4.

CAMPBELL, W., *A Treatise on the Epidemic Puerperal Fever as it Prevailed in Edinburgh in 1821–22* (Edinburgh, 1822).

CHURCHILL, FLEETWOOD, *Essays on the Puerperal Fever* (London, Sydenham Society, 1849).

—— *On the Theory and Practice of Midwifery* (London, 1850).

—— 'Report of Private Obstetric Practice for Thirty-Nine Years', *Dublin Journal of Medical Sciences*, 53 (Jan.–June 1872), 525–40.

CLARKE, J., *Practical Essays on the Management of Pregnancy and Labour and on the Inflammatory and Febrile Diseases of Lying-in Women* (2nd. edn., London, 1806).

COGHILL, J. G. C., *Address in Obstetric Medicine* (London, 1888). Pamphlet: Address to the 49th annual meeting of the British Medical Association.

COPEMAN, E., 'Statistical and Practical Remarks on Consultation Midwifery in Private Practice, *Transactions of the Obstetrical Society of London*, 16 (1874), 103–10.

CULLINGWORTH, C. J., *Puerperal Fever: A Preventable Disease* (London, 1888).

—— 'On the Undiminished Mortality from Puerperal Fever in England and Wales', *Transactions of the Obstetrical Society of London*, 40 (1898), 91–114.

—— 'Biographical Notes on J. Braxton Hicks and Étienne Stéphane Tarnier', *Transactions of the Obstetrical Society of London*, 40 (1898), 39–111.

—— *The Registration of Midwives* (London, 1898; reprinted from the *Contemporary Review* (Mar. 1898)).

DAVIS, DAVID D., *The Principles and Practice of Obstetric Medicine* (London, 1836).

DAVIS, J. HALL, 'Introductory Lectures on Midwifery and Diseases of Children', *Lancet* (1842–3), ii. 209–16.

—— *Parturition and its Difficulties* (London, 1865).

'Deaths in Childbirth' (leading article), *London Medical Gazette*, NS 1 (1843–4), 747–9.

DENMAN, T., *Essay on Puerperal Fever* (London, 1773).

DENMAN, T., *An Essay on Natural Labours* (London, 1786).

—— *An Introduction to the Practice of Midwifery*, 2 vols. (London, 1795).

DOIG, C. D., 'Notes on Labours', *Medical Times and Gazette* (1863), i. 419–20.

DUNCAN, J. MATTHEWS, 'The Mortality of Childbed', *Edinburgh Medical Journal*, 15 (1869–70), 399–409.

—— *On the Mortality of Childbed and Maternity Hospitals* (Edinburgh, 1870).

—— 'Inaugural Address to the Obstetrical Society of London', *Transactions of the Obstetrical Society of London*, 23 (1881), 64–81.

EASTLAKE, D., 'On the Management of the Third Stage of Labour', *Transactions of the Obstetrical Society of London*, 7 (1865), 226–48.

Edinburgh Maternity Hospital, 'Second Annual Report of the Directors, 19th December 1845', *Monthly Journal of Medical Science*, 6 (1846), 265–70.

EDIS, A. W., 'The Forceps in Modern Midwifery', *Transactions of the Obstetrical Society of London*, 19 (1877), 69–92.

ELKINGTON, F., 'Observations on the Contagiousness of Puerperal Fever', *Provincial Medical Journal*, 7 (1844), 287–8.

ELLIS, H. W. T., 'Analysis of 2,157 Cases of Labour', *British Medical Journal* (1859), i. 64.

FAIRBANKS, W., 'Obstetric Practice in Rural Districts with Notes', *Edinburgh Medical Journal*, 33 (1887–8), 414–20.

FARR, WILLIAM, 'Letters to the Registrar General' published in the *Annual Reports of the Registrar General* especially for the years 1841, 1854, 1870, 1874, and 1876.

GLAISTER, J., *Dr. William Smellie and his Contemporaries: A Contribution to the History of Midwifery in the Eighteenth Century* (Glasgow, 1894).

GODSON, C., 'Midwifery Statistics of Thirty Five Years of Obstetric Practice', *Transactions of the Obstetrical Society of London*, 18 (1876), 223–38.

GOOCH, R., *An Account of some of the Most Important Diseases Peculiar to Women* (2nd edn., London, 1838).

GORDON, A., *A Treatise on the Epidemic Puerperal Fever of Aberdeen* (London, 1795).

GRANVILLE, A. B., *A Report on the Practice of Midwifery at the Westminster General Dispensary during 1818* (London, 1819).

—— 'A Report of the Midwifery Department of the Westminster General Dispensary', *Medical and Physical Journal*, 44 (1820), 231.

—— 'A Report of the Practice of Midwifery at the Westminster General Dispensary during 1819', *Medical and Physical Journal*, 47 (1822), 283–8 and 374–8.

—— 'Political Condition of Midwifery in the Metropolis', *Lancet* (1830–1), i. 301–2.

—— 'Phenomena, Facts and Calculations Connected with the Power and Act of Propagation in Females of the Industrial Classes in the Metropolis, Derived from Eleven Years' Experience of Two Lying-in Institutions', *Transactions of the Obstetrical Society of London*, 2 (1860), 139–96.

—— *Autobiography* (London, 1874).

GREENE, W. T., 'A Synopsis of One Thousand Five Hundred Consecutive Labours', *Transactions of the Obstetrical Society of London*, 19 (1877), 204–17.

HAMILTON, A., *A Treatise on Midwifery* (London, 1781).

—— *Outlines of the Theory and Practice of Midwifery* (London, 1791).

HARDY, GATHORNE, 'Workhouse Death Rate in Childbirth', *Journal of the Statistical*

Society, 30 (1867), 171–3.

HARRINSON, I., 'Statistics of 1,000 Cases of Obstetrics', *British Medical Journal* (1859), i. 908–9.

HARRIS, J. P., 'A Record of the Porro Caesarean Section Showing its Results in all Countries', *British Medical Journal* (1889), i. 708–9.

HEWITT, G., 'On Puerperal Fever in the British Lying-in Hospital', *Transactions of the Obstetrical Society of London*, 10 (1868), 69–92.

HEY, W., JR., *A Treatise on the Puerperal Fever* (London, 1815).

HIRSCH, A., *Handbook of Geographical and Historical Pathology*, 3 vols. (London, 1883).

'Husbands in Lying-in Room' (correspondence), *Lancet* (1841–2), i. 390–1, 421–2, 551–2, 759–60.

KEELING, J. H., 'An Address on Modern Obstetrics', *British Medical Journal* (1883), ii. 57–60.

KELLY, J. K., 'A Review of 13 Years Private Obstetric Practice, 1873–1885', *British Medical Journal* (1887), i. 284–5.

KENNEDY, E., *Hospitalism and Zymotic Diseases as More Especially Illustrated by Puerperal Fever or Metria...Also a Reply to the Criticisms of Seventeen Physicians upon this Paper* (2nd edn., London, 1869).

KIDD, G. H., 'On Puerperal Fever', *British Medical Journal* (1884), ii. 217–21.

LAWRENCE, S., 'Statistical Report of One Thousand Midwifery Cases', *Edinburgh Medical and Surgical Journal*, 8 (1862–3), 712–24 and 800–14.

LEAKE, J., *Introduction to the Theory and Practice of Midwifery* (London, 1782).

LEE, R., *Researches on the Pathology and Treatment of some of the Most Important Diseases of Women* (London, 1833).

—— 'Clinical Reports on Difficult Cases in Midwifery', *London Medical Gazette*, NS 2 (1838–9), 827–32.

—— 'Clinical Reports in Midwifery', *Lancet* (1841–2), ii. 334–6, 369–72, 408–9.

—— *Clinical Midwifery with Histories of Four Hundred Cases of Difficult Labour* (London, 1842).

—— *Lectures on the Theory and Practice of Midwifery* (London, 1844).

—— *Three Hundred Consultations in Midwifery* (London, 1864).

—— *Puerperal Fever: The Goulstonian Lectures* (London, 1875).

LEISHMAN, W., *A System of Midwifery* (2nd edn., Glasgow, 1876).

LEVER, J. C. W., 'Cases of Puerperal Convulsions with Remarks', *Guy's Hospital Reports*, NS 1 (1843), 495–517.

LONGSTAFF, G. B., 'On Some Statistical Indications of a Relationship between Scarlatina, Puerperal Fever and Certain other Conditions', *Transactions of the Epidemiological Society of London*, 4 (1875–81), 421–32.

MAUBRAY, J., *The Female Physician: To which is Added, the Whole Art of New Improved Midwifery* (London, 1724).

'Medical Practitioner', *An Important Address to Wives and Mothers on the Dangers and Unsuitability of Man-Midwifery* (London, 1830).

MENDENHALL, G., 'On the Mortality in the Lying-in Ward of the Cincinnati Hospital', *Transactions of the Obstetrical Society of London*, 12 (1871), 357–9.

MERRIMAN, S., 'Cases of Premature Labour Artificially Induced, in Women with Distorted Pelvis', *Medico-Chirurgical Transactions*, 3 (1812), 123–45.

MERRIMAN, S., *A Synopsis of the Various Kinds of Difficult Parturition* (London, 1814).

MILLER, A., 'Twenty Years' Obstetric Practice', *Glasgow Medical Journal*, 51 (1899), 216–27.

MOUAT, F. J., 'Note on the Statistics of Childbirth in the Lying-in Wards of the Workhouse Infirmaries of England and Wales for Ten Years, 1871–1880', *Transactions of the International Medical Congress of London*, 4 (1881), 392–4.

NEWSHOLME, A., 'A National System of Notification and Registration of Sickness', *Journal of the Royal Statistical Society*, 59 (1896), 1–37.

NIGHTINGALE, FLORENCE, *Introductory Notes on Lying-in Hospitals* (London, 1876).

NIHELL, ELIZABETH, *A Treatise of the Art of Midwifery* (London, 1760).

'Obstetric Medicine, Retrospect, 1888', *British Medical Journal* (1888), ii. 1457.

Obstetrical Society of London, Report of inaugural meeting, *Transactions of the Obstetrical Society of London*, 1 (1859), pp. XV–XXIV.

'Obstetricus', 'Proportion of Deaths in Child-bed to Births', *London Medical and Physical Journal*, 25 (1811), 213–15. (The anonymous author was probably Francis Henry Ramsbotham.)

OSBORN, W., *Essays on the Practice of Midwifery* (London, 1792).

PAGET, C. E., *Wasted Records of Disease* (London, 1897).

PATERSON, J., 'Analysis of One Thousand Cases of Labour, Occurring in Private Practice, with Remarks', *Glasgow Medical Journal*, 10 (1862–3), 259–72.

PATTERSON, J., 'Cases of Puerperal Peritonitis', *Dublin Journal of Medical Sciences*, 4 (1834), 170–80.

PLAYFAIR, W. S., 'Inaugural Address', *Transactions of the Obstetrical Society of London*, 21 (1879), 29–37.

—— 'Introduction to a Discussion on the Prevention of Puerperal Fever', *British Medical Journal* (1887), ii. 1034–6.

PRIESTLY, W. O., 'Notes on a Visit to some of the Lying-in Hospitals in the North of Europe, and Particularly of the Advantages of the Antiseptic System in Obstetric Practice', *Transactions of the Obstetrical Society of London*, 27 (1885), 197–222.

'Proprietas', *An Address to the Public on the Propriety of Midwives instead of Surgeons Practising Midwifery* (2nd edn., London, 1826).

RAMSBOTHAM, F. H., 'Table of Difficult Cases of Midwifery'. *London Medical Gazette*, 3 (1829), 284–6.

—— 'The Eastern District of the Royal Maternity Charity', *London Medical Gazette*, NS 2 (1843–4), 619–23.

—— *Principles and Practice of Obstetrics, Medicine and Surgery* (London, 1867).

'Report of the Infantile Mortality Committee of the Obstetrical Society of London', *Transactions of the Obstetrical Society of London*, 12 (1870), 132–49; ibid. 13 (1871), 388–403.

ROBERTON, J., *Essays and Notes on the Physiology and Diseases of Women* (London, 1851).

ROSE, H. C., 'A Contribution to the Statistics of Midwifery in General Practice', *Transactions of the Obstetrical Society of London*, 18 (1876), 147–59.

ROUTH, C. H. F., 'On the Causes of the Endemic Puerperal Fever of Vienna', *Medico-chirurgical Transactions*, 14 (2nd ser.) (1849), 27–39.

ROWLING, C. R., 'The History of the Florence Nightingale Lying-in Ward, King's College Hospital', *Transactions of the Obstetrical Society of London*, 10 (1869), 51–6.

Royal Maternity Charity (leading article and correspondence concerning its staff and management), *Lancet* (1853), ii. 147, 227, 323–4, and ibid. (1854), i. 22, 135.

SIDEY, C., 'Cases of Puerperal Fever', *Edinburgh Medical and Surgical Journal*, 51 (1839), 91–9.

SIMON, Sir JOHN, *Public Health Reports*, ed. Edward Seaton, 2 vols. (London, 1887).

SIMPSON, J. Y., *Answer to the Religious Objections Advanced against the Employment of Anaesthetic Agents in Midwifery and Surgery* (Edinburgh, 1848).

—— 'Report on the Early History and Progress of Anaesthetic Midwifery', *Monthly Journal of Medical Science*, 9 (1848), 209–51.

—— 'Report of the Edinburgh Royal Maternity Hospital, St John's Street', *Monthly Journal of Medical Science*, 9 (1848–9), 329–38.

—— *Anaesthesia, Hospitalism, Hermaphroditism and a Proposal to Stamp out Small-pox and other Contagious Diseases* (Edinburgh, 1871).

—— and RAMSBOTHAM, F. H. (correspondence (1844–52)), manuscript collection of the National Library of Medicine, History of Medicine Division, Bethesda, Md.

SMELLIE, W., *A Treatise on the Theory and Practice of Midwifery* (London, 1752).

—— *A Course of Lectures upon Midwifery* (London, 1753).

SMITH, A., '1300 Midwifery Cases Attended in Private Practice', *Lancet* (1859), i. 481.

SMITH, P., *Scriptural Authority for the Mitigation of the Pains of Labour by Chloroform and other Anaesthetic Agents* (London, 1848).

SMITH, W. T., 'Annual Address to the Obstetrical Society of London', *Transactions of the Obstetrical Society of London*, 5 (1864), 18–24.

SPENCER WELLS, T., 'On the Relation of Puerperal Fever to the Infective Diseases and Pyaemia', *Transactions of the Obstetrical Society of London*, 17 (1876), 90–165.

STEELE, A. B., *Maternity Hospitals, their Mortality, and What should be Done with them* (London, 1874).

STEPHENSON, W., 'A Criticism of Midwifery Forceps in General Use', *British Medical Journal* (1888), i., 684.

STEWART, J., 'A Contribution to the Statistics of Obstetrics', *London and Edinburgh Monthly Journal of Medical Sciences*, 4 (1844), 273–8.

STONE, SARAH, *A Complete Practice of Midwifery* (London, 1737).

TOOGOOD, J., 'On the Practice of Midwifery with Remarks', *Provincial Medical and Surgical Journal*, 7 (1844), 103–8.

WADDINGTON, J., 'Statistics of Midwifery', *London Medical Gazette*, NS 2 (1843–4), 144–5.

WALKER, J., 'On the Intended Surgeon's Bill, as far as it Relates to Midwifery', *London Medical and Physical Journal*, 36 (1817), 283–4.

WEATHERHEAD, G. H., *An Essay on the Diagnosis between Erysipelas, Phlegmon, and Erythema, with an Appendix Touching on the Probable Nature of Puerperal Fever* (London, 1819).

WEST, T., 'Observations on some Diseases, particularly Puerperal Fever, which Occurred in Abingdon and its Vicinity in 1813 and 1814'. *London Medical Repository*, 2 (1815), 103–5.

WILLIAMS, W., *An Epidemic of Puerperal Septicaemia*, Reprinted from Reports to the Sanitary Committee of Glamorgan County Council (1893).

—— 'Puerperal Mortality', *Transactions of the Epidemiological Society of London*, 15 (1895–6), 100–33.

WILSON, J., 'Report of the Glasgow Lying-in Hospital for the Year 1851–52 with an

Address to the Students Attending the Hospital', *Glasgow Medical Journal*, 1 (1853), 1–10.

Twentieth Century

BAIRD, D., 'Maternal Mortality in Hospital', *Lancet* (1936), i. 295–8.
—— 'The Evolution of Modern Obstetrics', *Lancet* (1960), ii. 557–64 and 609–14.
—— 'Environment and Reproduction', *British Journal of Obstetrics and Gynaecology*, 87 (1980), 1057–67.
BALFOUR, M. I., and DRURY, J. C., *Motherhood in Special Areas of Durham and Tyneside* (London, 1935).
BANKS, H. S., *Modern Practice in Infectious Fevers*, 2 vols. (London, 1951).
BELL, A. C., 'The Use of Antistreptococcal Preparations in Obstetrics', *Practitioner*, 139 (Jan.–June 1938), 673–9.
BONNEY, V., 'The Continued High Mortality of Childbearing', *Proceedings of the Royal Society of Medicine*, 12/3 (1918–19), 75–107.
BOURNE, ALECK, *A Doctor's Creed* (London, 1962).
BRACKENBURY, Sir HENRY, *Patient and Doctor* (London, 1835).
—— 'Maternity in its Sociological Aspects', *Social Service Review*, 18 (1937), 37–47.
British Medical Association (Report of annual conference), *Lancet* (1935), ii. 210–11. Discussion of midwifery.
—— 'An Urgent National Problem' (the problem of maternal mortality), *Lancet* (1936), i. 736–7.
BROOKES, B., *Abortion in England, 1900–1967* (London, 1988).
BROWNE, F. J., *et al.*, 'Team Work for Maternity', *Lancet* (1934), ii. 1198–9.
BURT-WHITE, H., 'Puerperal Sepsis and Sensitiveness to Streptococcal Toxins', *British Medical Journal* (1928), i. 975–6.
CAMPBELL, Dame JANET, 'Debate on Maternal Mortality', *Lancet* (1935), ii. 1254–5.
—— *Maternity Services* (London, 1935).
CAMPBELL, R., and MACFARLANE, A., 'Place of Delivery: A Review', *British Journal of Obstetrics and Gynaecology*, 93 (1986), 675–83.
—— —— *Where to be Born?* (Oxford, 1987).
CHALMERS, I., and RICHARDS, M., 'Intervention and Causal Inference in Obstetric Practice', in T. Chard and M. Richards, *Benefits and Hazards of the New Obstetrics* (London, 1977).
—— ENKIN, M., and KEIRSE, M. J. N. C., *Effective Care in Pregnancy and Childbirth*, 2 vols. (Oxford, 1989).
CLAYE, A. M., 'The Use and Abuse of Drugs in Midwifery', *Practitioner*, 138 (1937), 484–92.
—— and W. STANLEY SYKES, *The Evolution of Obstetric Analgesia* (Oxford, 1939).
COLEBROOK, L., 'Some Laboratory Investigations in Connexion with Puerperal Fever', *Proceedings of the Royal Society of Medicine*, 19 (1926), 31–42.
—— 'The Prevention of Puerperal Sepsis', *Journal of Obstetrics and Gynaecology of the British Empire*, 43 (1936), 691–714.
—— 'The Story of Puerperal Fever: 1800–1950', *British Medical Journal* (1956), i. 247–52.
—— and KENNY, M., 'Treatment with Prontosil of Puerperal Infections due to

Haemolytic Streptococci', *Lancet* (1936), ii. 1319–22.

COLEBROOK, V., 'Leonard Colebrook: Reminiscences on the Occasion of the 25th Anniversary of the Birmingham Burns Unit', *Injury: The British Journal of Accident Surgery*, 2/3 (1971), 182–4.

COLLIER, H. E., 'A Study of the Influence of Certain Social Changes upon Maternal Mortality and Obstetrical Problems, 1834–1927', *Journal of Obstetrics and Gynaecology of the British Empire*, 37 (1930), 27–47.

COLLINS, F. G., 'A Midwife as a Carrier of Infection', *Lancet* (1934), ii. 718.

CRAWFORD, M. D., 'The Obstetric Forceps and its Use', *Lancet* (1932), i. 1239–43.

CREIGHTON, C., *A History of Epidemics in Britain* (London, 1956; 1st edn., 1894).

CROOM, Sir J. HALLIDAY, 'The Teaching of Obstetrics to Undergraduates', *Edinburgh Medical Journal*, 21 (1918), 268–74.

CULLINGWORTH, C. J., *Oliver Wendell Holmes and the Contagiousness of Puerperal Fever* (London, 1906).

DAVIS, A., '2655 Cases of Abortion: A Clinical Survey', *British Medical Journal* (1950), ii. 123–30.

DINGWALL, R., RAFFERTY, A. M., and WEBSTER, C., *An Introduction to the Social History of Nursing* (London, 1988).

DONNISON, J., *Midwives and Medical Men* (London, 1977).

DORAN, ALBAN, 'Dusée: His Forceps and His Contemporaries', *Journal of Obstetrics and Gynaecology of the British Empire*, 22 (1912), 119–42.

—— 'Dusée, De Wind and Smellie: An Addendum', *Journal of Obstetrics and Gynaecology of the British Empire*, 22 (1912), 203–7.

—— 'Burton ("Dr Slop"): His Forceps and his Foes', *Journal of Obstetrics and Gynaecology of the British Empire*, 23 (1913), 3–24.

—— 'Burton: Part II', *Journal of Obstetrics and Gynaecology of the British Empire*, 23 (1913), 65–86.

—— 'Jointed Obstetric Forceps', *Journal of Obstetrics and Gynaecology of the British Empire*, 24 (1913), 197–211.

—— 'A Chronology of the Founders of the Forceps', *Journal of Obstetrics and Gynaecology of the British Empire*, 27 (1915), 154–72.

DOUGLAS, C. E., 'Some Observations on Seventy Years of Country Midwifery Practice', *Journal of Obstetrics and Gynaecology of the British Empire*, 31 (1924), 622–46.

DOUTHWAITE, A. H., 'The Use of Antistreptococcal Preparations in General Practice', *Practitioner*, 139 (1937), 661–72.

DOW, D., *The Rotten Row: The History of the Glasgow Maternity Hospital, 1834–1984* (Carnforth, 1984).

DUDFIELD, R., 'A Survey of the Mortality due to Childbearing in London from the Seventeenth Century', *Proceedings of the Royal Society of Medicine*, 17 (1924), 59–72.

ECCLES, A., 'Obstetrics in the 17th and 18th Centuries and its Implications for Maternal and Infant Mortality', *Bulletin of the Society for the Social History of Medicine*, 20 (1977), 8–11.

EDEN, T. W., 'Eclampsia', *Journal of Obstetrics and Gynaecology of the British Empire*, 29/3 (1922), 386–401.

EYLER, J. M., *Victorian Social Medicine: The Ideas and Methods of William Farr* (Baltimore, Md., 1979).

FAIRBAIRN, J. S., 'Clinical Teaching of Midwifery and Diseases of Women', *Edinburgh Medical Journal*, 21 (1918), 286–90.

—— 'The Medical and Psychological Aspects of Gynaecology', *Lancet* (1931), ii. 999–1004.

FERGUSON, J. H., 'The Teaching of Obstetrics and Gynaecology', *Edinburgh Medical Journal*, 21 (1918), 294–6.

FERGUSON, S., and FITZGERALD, H., *History of the Second World War: Studies in the Social Services* (London, 1954).

FITCH, W. K., 'The Nomenclature and Dosage of New Antistreptococcal Preparations', *Practitioner*, 139 (1937), 680–8.

FORBER, Lady (Dr Janet Lane-Claypon), 'The Independent Midwife', *British Medical Journal* (1935), i. 490.

—— 'The Economic Conditions of Midwifery Practice', *British Medical Journal* (1935), ii. 862–3.

FORD, J., *A Medical Student at St Thomas's Hospital, 1801–1802: The Weekes Family Letters, Medical History*, supplement no. 7 (London, 1987).

FOTHERGILL, W. E., 'Puerperal Pelvic Infection', *British Medical Journal* (1924), i. 773–4.

FOULIS, M. A., and BARR, J. B., 'Prontosil Album in Puerperal Sepsis', *British Medical Journal* (1937), i. 445–6.

FOX, E., 'Powers of Life and Death: Aspects of Maternal Welfare in England and Wales between the Wars', *Medical History*, 35 (1991), 328–52.

GARCIA, J., KILPATRICK, R., and RICHARDS, M. (eds.), *The Politics of Maternity Care: Services for Childbearing Women in Twentieth-Century Britain* (Oxford, 1990).

GEDDES, G., *Statistics of Puerperal Sepsis and Allied Infectious Diseases* (Bristol, 1912).

—— *Puerperal Septicaemia: Its Causation, Symptoms, Prevention and Treatment* (Bristol, 1926).

GERSON, H. M., 'Twilight Sleep', *Lancet* (1922), i. 428–9.

GIBBERD, G. F., 'Streptococcal Puerperal Sepsis', *Guy's Hospital Reports*, 81 (1931), 29–44.

—— 'Prontosil in Puerperal Infection', *British Medical Journal* (1937), ii. 229–30.

GILLIAT, Sir WILLIAM, 'Maternal Mortality', in A. W. Bourne and W. C. W. Nixon (eds.), *Transactions of the 12th British Congress of Obstetrics and Gynaecology* (London, 1949).

GREBENIK, E., and PARRY, D. J., 'The Maternity Services in England and Wales before the War', *Agenda*, 2 (1943), 133–46.

GUNN, A., 'Maternity Hospitals', in F. N. L. Poynter (ed.), *The Evolution of Hospitals in Britain* (London, 1964).

HALL, D. M. B., 'Birth Asphyxia and Cerebral Palsy', *British Medical Journal* (1989), ii. 279–82.

HAMILTON, W., 'Midwifery in General Practice', *Lancet* (1934), i. 242–3.

HAULTAIN, F. W. N., 'A Retrospect and Comparison of the Progress of Midwifery and Gynaecology', *Edinburgh Medical Journal*, NS 6 (1911), 17–37.

HAWKINS, F., and STEWART LAWRENCE, J., *The Sulphonamides* (London, 1950).

HOBBS, A. R., 'Puerperal Sepsis', *British Medical Journal* (1928), i. 971–4.

HOERLEIN, H., 'The Development of Chemotherapy for Bacteriological Diseases', *Practitioner*, 139 (1937), 645–9.

HOLLAND, E., 'Maternal Mortality', *Lancet* (1935), i. 936–7.

—— 'Obstetrics and Gynaecology', *Practitioner*, 139 (1937), 434–48.

HORROCKS, P., 'An Address on the Midwifery of the Present Day', *British Medical Journal* (1906), i. 541–5. Subsequent correspondence, ibid.: (F. Rees), 712–13; (W. W. Williams), 713; (F. E. Wynne), 773; (F. C. Mears), 773; (J. R. Leeson), 831; (J. Cameron), 831–2; (A. L. Scott), 892; (A. M. Thomas), 892; (J.M.M.), 949; ('Colliery Surgeon'), 949; (B. T. Lownes), 950; (F. J. Geoghegan), 1012; (B. Jordan), 1012–13; (C. E. Douglas), 1255.

—— 'Inaugural Address: A Century's Progress in Midwifery and Diseases of Women', *Transactions of the Obstetrical Society of London*, 43 (1901), 79–107.

HORWITZ, C. H. S., '"Twilight Sleep" and the General Practitioner', *Lancet* (1921), ii. 1154–5.

ILLINGWORTH, R. S., 'A Paediatrician Asks: Why is it Called Birth Injury?', *British Journal of Obstetrics and Gynaecology*, 92 (1985), 122–30.

JELLETT, H., *The Causes and Prevention of Maternal Mortality* (London, 1929).

JOHNSON, R. W., 'Prophylactic Use of Sulphonamide Preparations in Obstetric Practice', *British Medical Journal* (1938), i. 562–4.

JONES, O. V., 'Pre-eclamptic Toxaemia', *British Medical Journal* (1957), ii. 1341–3.

KEIRSE, M. J. N. C., 'Preterm Delivery', in I. Chalmers, M. Enkin, and M. J. N. C. Keirse, *Effective Care in Pregnancy and Childbirth*, 2 vols. (Oxford, 1989).

KEOWN, J., *Abortion, Doctors and the Law: Some Aspects of the Legal Regulation of Abortion in England from 1803 to 1982* (Cambridge, 1988).

KERMACK, W. O., MCKENDRICK, A. G., and MCKINLAY, P. L., 'Death Rates in Great Britain and Sweden', *Lancet* (1934), ii. 698–703.

KERR, J. M. MUNRO, *Maternal Mortality and Morbidity* (Edinburgh, 1933).

—— JOHNSTONE, R. W., and PHILLIPS, M. H., *Historical Review of British Obstetrics and Gynaecology* (London, 1954).

KITZINGER, J., 'Strategies of the Early Childbirth Movement: A Case-Study of the National Childbirth Trust', in J. Garcia, R. Kilpatrick, and M. Richards (eds.), *The Politics of Maternity Care: Services for Childbearing Women in Twentieth-Century Britain* (Oxford, 1990).

KNIGHT, P., 'Women and Abortion in Victorian and Edwardian England', *History Workshop Journal*, 4 (1977), 57–68.

LEA, A. W. W., *Puerperal Infection* (London, 1910).

LEWIS, J., *The Politics of Motherhood* (London, 1980).

—— 'Mothers and Maternity Policies in the Twentieth Century', in J. Garcia, R. Kilpatrick, and M. Richards (eds.), *The Politics of Maternity Care: Services for Childbearing Women in Twentieth-Century Britain* (Oxford, 1990).

LOGAN, D. DALE, 'The General Practitioner and Midwifery', *Lancet* (1934), ii. 1141–3.

LOUDON, I., 'Deaths in Childbed from the Eighteenth Century to 1935', *Medical History*, 30 (1986), 1–41.

—— *Medical Care and the General Practitioner: 1750–1850* (Oxford, 1986).

—— 'Obstetric Care, Social Class and Maternal Mortality', *British Medical Journal* (1986), ii. 606–8.

—— 'Puerperal Fever, the Streptococcus and the Sulphonamides, 1911–1945', *British Medical Journal* (1987), ii. 485–90.

LOUDON, I., 'Maternal Mortality, 1880–1950: Some Regional and International Comparisons', *Social History of Medicine*, 1 (1988), 183–228.

—— 'Puerperal Insanity in the Nineteenth Century', *Journal of the Royal Society of Medicine*, 81 (1988), 76–9.

—— 'Obstetrics and the General Practitioner', *British Medical Journal* (1990), i. 703–7.

—— 'On Maternal and Infant Mortality', *Social History of Medicine*, 4 (1991), 29–73.

—— 'Some Historical Aspects of Toxaemia of Pregnancy. A Review', *British Journal of Obstetrics and Gynaecology*, 98 (1991), 853–8.

LOWRY, C. G., 'Maternal Mortality', *Lancet* (1922), i. 158.

LUDOVICI, ANTHONY, *The Truth about Childbirth* (London, 1937).

MACFARLANE, A., and MUGFORD, M., *Birth Counts: Statistics of Pregnancy and Childbirth*, 2 vols. (London, 1984).

McGIBBON, J., 'On Caesarean Section and Repeated Caesarean Section for Contracted Pelvis, with Notes of a Case Successfully Performed for the Third Time on the Same Woman', *Edinburgh Medical Journal*, NS 7 (1911), 513–30.

McILROY, Dame LOUISE, 'Surgical Intervention in Obstetrical Practice', *British Medical Journal* (1937), i. 800–2.

MACKENZIE, E. K., 'Rural Midwifery Practice', *Practitioner*, 115 (1925), 264–73.

McKEOWN, T., *The Role of Medicine: Dream, Mirage or Nemesis?* (London, 1976).

McKINLAY, P. L., 'The Relations between Puerperal Septicaemia and Certain Infectious Diseases', *Journal of Hygiene*, 27 (1928), 186–96.

McLAREN, A., 'Women's Work and Regulation of Family Size', *History Workshop Journal*, 4 (1977), 70–81.

McQUAY, T. A. I., 'Childbirth Deaths in Shipton-under-Wychwood, 1565–1665', *Population Studies*, 42 (1989), 54–6.

'Maternal Mortality' (leading article by A. Farquhar Murray), *British Medical Journal* (1930), i. 294–5.

'Maternal Mortality' (leading article), *Lancet* (1937), i. 1125–9.

'Maternal Mortality in Wales' (leading article), *Medical Officer*, 57 (1937), 215.

Maternity in Great Britain: A Survey of Social and Economic Aspects of Pregnancy and Childbirth Undertaken by the Joint Committee of the Royal College of Obstetricians and Gynaecologists and the Population Investigation Committee (London, 1948).

Medical Research Council, London. Archives, files MRC 2060/2.

MURRAY, A. F., 'Whither Midwifery?', *British Medical Journal* (1936), i. 375–7.

NEWMAN, Sir GEORGE, *The Building of a Nation's Health* (London, 1938).

NICHOLSON, O., 'Some Physiological Aspects of Maternal Mortality', *British Medical Journal* (1935), i. 127.

NISSEL, M., *People Count: A History of the General Register Office* (London, 1987).

NIXON, W. C. W., 'Obstetrics', *Practitioner*, 141 (July–Dec. 1938), 785–8.

OAKLEY, A., *The Captured Womb* (Oxford, 1984).

OXLEY, W. H. F., 'Prevention of Puerperal Sepsis in General Practice', *British Medical Journal* (1934), i. 1017–19.

—— PHILLIPS, M. H., and YOUNG, J., 'Maternal Mortality in Rochdale: An Experiment in A Black Area', *British Medical Journal* (1935), i. 304–7.

PAINE, C. G., 'The Aetiology of Puerperal Infection', *British Medical Journal* (1935), i. 243–6.

PEACHEY, G. C., 'Note upon the Provision for Lying-in Women in London up to the

Middle of the Eighteenth Century', *Proceedings of the Royal Society of Medicine*, 17 (1924), 72–6.

PEEL, Sir JOHN, *William Blair-Bell: Father and Founder* (London, 1986).

PERETZ, E., 'The Professionalisation of Childcare', *Oral History*, 1 (1980), 22–8.

—— 'A Maternity Service for England and Wales: Local Authority Maternity Care in the Inter-War Period in Oxfordshire and Tottenham', in J. Garcia, R. Kilpatrick, and M. Richards (eds.), *The Politics of Maternity Care: Services for Childbearing Women in Twentieth-Century Britain* (Oxford, 1990), 30–46.

PHAFF, J. M. L. (ed.), *Perinatal Health Services in Europe* (London, 1986).

PHILLIPS, H. J., 'Treatment of Puerperal Infection by Intra-Uterine Injections of Glycerine', *Proceedings of the Royal Society of Medicine*, 19 (1926), 26–31.

PORTER, I. A., *Alexander Gordon, MD, of Aberdeen*, Aberdeen Studies, 139 (Edinburgh, 1958).

PRICHARD, P. V., 'Maternal Mortality: A Critical Review of the Statistical References in the Interim Report of the Department Committee on Maternal Mortality', MD thesis (University of Edinburgh, 1931).

REDMAN, C. W. G., 'Eclampsia Still Kills' (leading article), *British Medical Journal* (1988), i. 1209–10.

—— 'Hypertension in Pregnancy', in Sir Alec Turnbell and G. Chamberlain (eds.), *Obstetrics* (London, 1989).

RINGEN, S., *The Possibility of Politics* (Oxford, 1987).

ROGERSON, J. P. G., 'Midwifery in General Practice', unpublished paper.

ROSE, J. K., 'Notes on Haemolytic Streptococcal Puerperal Infection', *Journal of Obstetrics and Gynaecology of the British Empire*, 44 (1937), 278–88.

ROSENFIELD, A., and MAINE, D., 'Maternal Mortality: A Neglected Tragedy. Where is the M in MCH?', *Lancet* (1985), ii. 83–5.

ROUTH, A., *Caesarean Section in Great Britain and Ireland* (London, 1911).

RUSH, R. W., *et al.*, 'Contribution of Preterm Delivery to Perinatal Mortality', *British Medical Journal* (1976), ii. 965–8.

RUSSELL, J. K., 'Maternal Mortality', in S. L. Barron and A. M. Thomson (eds.), *Obstetrical Epidemiology* (London, 1983).

RYLE, J. A., and SMITH, R. E., 'The Natural History, Prognosis and Treatment of Streptococcal Fever', *Guy's Hospital Reports*, 81 (1931), 1–28.

SAUER, R., 'Infanticide and Abortion in Nineteenth-Century Britain', *Population Studies*, 32 (1978), 81–93.

SCHNORRENBERG, B. B., 'Is Childbirth any Place for a Woman? The Decline of Midwifery in Eighteenth Century England', *Studies in Eighteenth-Century Culture*, 10 (1981), 393–407.

SCHOFIELD, R., 'Did the Mothers Really Die? Three Centuries of Maternal Mortality in "The World we have Lost"', in L. Bonfield, R. Smith, and K. Wrightson (eds.), *The World we have Gained: Histories of Population and Social Structure* (Oxford, 1986).

SELIGMAN, S. A., 'The Royal Maternity Charity: The First One Hundred Years', *Medical History*, 24 (1980), 403–18.

—— 'The Lesser Pestilence: Non-Epidemic Puerperal Fever', *Medical History*, 35 (1991), 89–102.

SELWYN, S., 'Aseptic Rituals Unmasked' (leading article), *British Medical Journal* (1984), ii. 1642–3.

SEN, A., *Poverty and Famines* (Oxford, 1981).

SHORTER, E., *A History of Women's Bodies* (London, 1983).

SNODGRASS, W. R., 'Uses and Abuses of Chemotherapy in Streptococcal Diseases', *Practitioner*, 144 (1940), 16–24.

SPENCER, HERBERT, *The History of British Midwifery from 1650 to 1800* (London, 1927).

STERN, D. M., 'The Elderly Primipara', *Lancet* (1934), ii. 685–7.

STOOKES, Dr, 'Some Points in the Puerperal Mortality', *Journal of Obstetrics and Gynaecology of the British Empire*, 23 (1913), 174–6.

TAYLOR, W., 'Changing Patterns of Mortality in England and Wales: I. Infant Mortality', *British Journal of Preventive and Social Medicine*, 8 (1954), 1–9.

—— and DAUNCEY, M., 'Changing Patterns of Mortality in England and Wales: II. Maternal Mortality', *British Journal of Preventive and Social Medicine*, 8 (1954), 172–5.

TITMUSS, R. M., *Poverty and Population: A Factual Study of Contemporary Social Waste* (London, 1938).

—— *Birth, Poverty and Wealth: A Study of Infant Mortality* (London, 1943).

TOPLEY, W. W. C., and WILSON, G. S., *The Principles of Bacteriology and Immunity* (2nd edn., London, 1938; 3rd edn., 1946).

TOPPING, A., 'Maternal Mortality and Public Opinion', *Public Health*, 49 (1936), 342–9.

—— 'Prevention of Maternal Mortality: The Rochdale Experiment', *Lancet* (1936), i. 545–7.

TOTTENHAM, R. E., 'Some Observations on the Maternal Mortality of the USA', *Irish Journal of Medical Sciences*, 5th ser., no. 46 (1925), 516–29.

TOWLER, J., and BRAMALL, J., *Midwives in History and Society* (London, 1986).

TURNBELL, Sir ALEC, and CHAMBERLAIN, G. (eds.), *Obstetrics* (London, 1989).

TWEEDY, E. H., 'Reasons for the Present Defective Education in Obstetrics, with Suggested Remedies', *Edinburgh Medical Journal*, 21 (1918), 283–6.

'Twilight Sleep' (leading article), *Nursing Times* (4 Oct. 1919), 1041–2.

VAUGHAN, KATHLEEN, 'The Shape of the Pelvic Brim as the Determining Factor in Childbirth', *British Medical Journal* (1931), ii. 939–41.

WEBB, J., and WESTON-EDWARDS, P., 'Recent Trends in Maternal Mortality', *Medical Officer*, 86 (1951), 201–4.

WEBSTER, C., 'Healthy or Hungry Thirties?', *History Workshop Journal*, 13 (1982), 110–29.

—— 'Health, Welfare and Unemployment during the Depression', *Past and Present*, 109 (1985), 204–30.

WHITBY, L., 'The Assessment of the Efficiency of Chemotherapeutic Substances', *Practitioner*, 139 (1937), 650–60.

WILLIAMS, Lady, 'Malnutrition as a cause of Maternal Mortality', *Public Health*, 50 (1936–7), 11–19.

WILLIAMS, W., *Deaths in Childbed* (London, 1904), being the Milroy Lectures delivered at the Royal College of Physicians of London, 1904.

WILLMOTT DOBBIE, B. M., 'An Attempt to Estimate the True Rate of Maternal Mortality, Sixteenth to Eighteenth Centuries', *Medical History*, 26 (1982), 79–80.

WILSON, A., 'Participant or Patient? Seventeenth-Century Childbirth from the Mother's Point of View', in R. Porter (ed.), *Patients and Practitioners: Lay Perceptions of Medicine in Pre-Industrial Society* (Cambridge, 1985), 129–144.

WILSON, L. G., 'The Early Recognition of Streptococci as Causes of Disease', *Medical History*, 31 (1987), 403–14.

WINTER, J. M., 'Infant Mortality, Maternal Mortality and Public Health in Britain in the 1930s', *Journal of European Economic History*, 8 (1979), 439–62.

—— 'Public Health and the Extension of Life Expectancy in England and Wales, 1901–1960', in M. Keynes, D. Coleman, and N. Disdale (eds.), *The Political Economy of Health and Welfare* (London, 1988).

—— 'Unemployment, Nutrition and Infant Mortality in Britain, 1920–1950' in id. (ed.), *The Working Class and Modern British History* (Cambridge, 1983).

WOOD, J. L. M., and CAMPS, F. E., 'Puerperal Infection in Relation to Midwifery Attendants', *British Medical Journal* (1937), ii. 811–12.

WOOD, Sir KINGSLEY, 'Overcrowding and Maternal Mortality', *British Medical Journal* (1935), i. 697.

WOODS, R. I., WATTERSON, P. A., and WOODWARD, J. H., 'The Causes of the Rapid Infant Mortality Decline in England and Wales, 1861–1921', *Population Studies*, 42 (1988), 343–66; ibid. 43 (1989), 113–32.

YOUNG, J. H., 'Maternal Mortality from Puerperal Sepsis', *British Medical Journal* (1928), i. 967–71.

—— 'Maternal Mortality and Maternal Mortality Rates', *American Journal of Obstetrics and Gynaecology*, 31 (1936), 198–212.

—— *Caesarean Section: The History and Development of the Operations from the Earliest Times* (London, 1944).

UNITED STATES OF AMERICA
(SEE ALSO APPENDIX 3)

ACKERNECHT, E. H., FISCHER-HOMBERG, E., 'Five Made it—One Not: The Rise of Medical Craftsmen to Academic Status during the 19th Century', *Clio Medica*, 12 (1977), 255–67.

American Public Health Association, Vital Statistics Section, 'Stillbirth and Maternal Mortality Rates', *American Journal of Public Health*, 34 (1944), 889–93.

ANSPACH, B. M., 'The Drudgery of Obstetrics', *American Journal of Obstetrics and Gynaecology*, 2 (1921), 245–8.

ANTLER, J., and FOX, D. M., 'The Movement Toward a Safe Maternity: Physician Accountability in New York City, 1915–1940', *Bulletin of the History of Medicine*, 50 (1976), 569–95.

BACON, C. S., 'The Mortality from Puerperal Infection in Chicago', *American Journal of Obstetrics and Gynaecology*, 8 (1896), 429–46.

BAILEY, H., 'Maternal and Infant Mortality in 4488 Cases in an Out-door Clinic, 1922–25', *American Journal of Obstetrics and Gynaecology*, 12 (1926), 817–24.

BAKER, S. J., 'Schools for Midwives', *American Journal of Obstetrics*, 65 (1912), 256–70.

—— 'Maternal Mortality in the United States', *Journal of the American Medical Association*, 89 (1927), 2016–17.

BARD, S., *A Compendium on the Theory and Practice of Midwifery* (New York, 1808).

BARKER, F., *The Puerperal Diseases* (New York, 1880).

BARNES, F., 'Indications for Caesarean Section as compared with those for

Symphisiotomy, Craniotomy and Premature Inducution of Labor', *Medical Record of New York*, 56 (1899), 496–8.

BEARDSLEY, E. H., *A History of Neglect: Health Care for Blacks and Mill Workers in the Twentieth-Century South* (Knoxville, Tenn., 1987).

BERNARDY, E. P., 'Observations on Private Practice in the Past Decade', *Proceedings of the Philadelphia County Medical Society*, 13 (1892), 110–17.

BIGELOW, H. A., 'Maternity Care in Rural Areas by Public Health Nurses', *American Journal of Public Health*, 27 (1937), 975–90.

Birth, Stillbirth and Infant Mortality Statistics for the Birth Registration area of the USA, US Bureau of the Census, Department of Commerce (Washington, DC, 1924).

BLAKE, J. B., 'The Early History of Vital Statistics in Massachusetts', *Bulletin of the History of Medicine*, 29 (1955), 46–68.

BLAND, P. B., 'Puerperal Morbidity and Mortality', *Medical Journal and Record*, 129 (1929), 83–6, 135–6.

BLISS, J. C., 'Statistics of Private Obstetric Practice', *New York Journal of Medicine*, 8 (1847), 88–94.

BOLT, R. A., 'Maternal Mortality Study for Cleveland, Ohio', *American Journal of Obstetrics and Gynaecology*, 27 (1934), 309–13.

BORST, C. G., 'The Training and Practice of Midwives: A Wisconsin Study', *Bulletin of the History of Medicine*, 62 (1988), 606–27.

Boston Lying-in Hospital, *Annual Reports*, Boston, Countway Medical Library, Rare books department.

BRANDT, E. N., 'Infant Mortality: A Progress Report', *Public Health Reports*, 99 (1984), 284–8.

BRECKINRIDGE, MARY, 'The Nurse-Midwife, a Pioneer', *American Journal of Public Health*, 17 (1927), 1147–51.

—— 'A Frontier Nursing Service', *American Journal of Obstetrics and Gynaecology*, 15 (1928), 867–72.

—— *Wide Neighbourhoods: A Story of the Frontier Nursing Service* (New York, 1952).

BREMNER, R. H. (ed.), *Children and Youth in America* (Cambridge, Mass., 1971).

BRENNER, M. H., 'Fetal, Infant and Maternal Mortality during Periods of Economic Instability', *International Journal of Health Services*, 2 (1973), 145–59.

BRICKMAN, J. P., 'Public Health, Midwives and Nurses, 1880–1930', in E. C. Lagermann (ed.), *Nursing History: New Perspectives, New Possibilities* (New York, 1983).

BRINDLEY, A. A., 'How do we Attempt to do Scientific Obstetrics in General Practice?', *Ohio State Medical Journal*, 16 (1920), 660–2.

BROWN, C. B., 'Obstetrical Work by the Country Doctor', *Illinois Medical Journal*, 14 (1908), 552–66.

BROWN, W. S., 'Forty Years of Experience in Midwifery', *Boston Medical and Surgical Journal*, 112 (1885), 241–3.

BROWNE, H. E., and ISACCS, G., 'The Frontier Nursing Service: The Primary Care Nurse in the Community Hospital', *American Journal of Obstetrics and Gynaecology*, 121 (1976), 14–17.

BRUMBAUGH, C. G., 'The Present Standard of Obstetrical Practice in Rural Pennsylvania', *Pennsylvania Medical Journal*, 26 (1922–3), 283–4.

BURTENSHAW, J. H., 'The Fever of the Puerperium (Puerperal Infection)', *New York*

Journal and Philadelphia Medical Journal, 79 (1904), 1073–9, 1134–8, 1189–94, and 1234–8; ibid. 80 (1904), 20–5.

BYRNE, J. J., *A History of the Boston City Hospital, 1905–1964* (Boston, 1964).

CASSEDY, J. H., 'The Registration Area and American Vital Statistics', *Bulletin of the History of Medicine*, 39 (1965), 221–31.

—— *American Medicine and Statistical Thinking, 1800–1860* (Cambridge, Mass., 1984).

—— *Medicine and American Growth, 1800–1860* (Madison, Wis., 1986).

Children's Bureau Publications, US Department of Labor, Washington, DC, Government Printing Office, No. 19, Grace Meigs, *Maternal Mortality from all Conditions Connected with Childbirth in the United States and Certain other Countries* (1917).

—— No. 26, Elizabeth Moore, *Maternity and Infant Care in a Rural County in Kansas* (1917).

—— No. 34, Viola Paradise, *Maternity Care and the Welfare of Young Children in a Homestead County in Montana* (1919).

—— No. 46, Elizabeth Moore, *Maternity and Infant Care in Two Rural Counties in Wisconsin* (1919).

—— No. 88, Helen M. Dart, *Maternity and Child Care in Selected Rural Areas of Mississippi* (1921).

—— No. 95, *Promotion of the Welfare and Hygiene of Maternity and Infancy: The Text of Act of Nov. 23 1921* (1921).

—— No. 120, G. Steele, *Maternity and Infant Care in a Mountain County in Georgia* (1923).

—— No. 142, R. M. Woodbury, *Causal Factors in Infant Mortality* (1925).

—— No. 152, R. M. Woodbury, *Maternal Mortality: The Risk of Death in Childbirth and from all the Diseases Caused by Pregnancy and Confinement* (1926).

—— No. 221, *Maternal Deaths: A Brief Report of a Study Made in Fifteen States* (1933).

—— No. 223, *Maternal Mortality in Fifteen States* (1934).

—— No. 229, Elizabeth Tandy, *Comparability of Maternal Mortality Rates in the United States and Certain Foreign Countries* (1935).

—— No. 243, Elizabeth Tandy, *Infant and Maternal Mortality among Negroes* (1937).

—— No. 288, *Births, Infant Mortality and Maternal Mortality* (1945).

Children's Bureau, Statistical Series, No. 12, *Infant and Maternal Mortality in Metropolitan and Outlying Counties, 1944–1948*, Federal Security Agency, Social Security Administration, Children's Bureau (Washington, DC, 1950).

Commission on Medical Education, Final Report (New York, 1932).

CONDIE, Dr, 'Puerperal Fever', *Transactions of the College of Physicians of Philadelphia*, 1 (1841–6), 50–62.

CONVERSE, T. A., BUKER, R. S., and LEE, R. V., 'Hutterite Midwifery', *American Journal of Obstetrics and Gynaecology*, 116 (1973), 719–25.

COUDON, J., *An Inaugural Essay on Eclampsia* (Baltimore, Md., 1813).

Country Doctor, 'Leaves from the diary of a Country Doctor', *Country Practitioner*, 2 (1881), 326–30.

CREE, W. J., 'One Hundred Consecutive Obstetrical Cases', *American Lancet Detroit*, NS 12 (1889), 203–5.

CRITTENDEN, C. B., and SKAGGS, L., *Maternal Mortality in Kentucky: A Study of Puerperal Deaths, 1932–1939*, Kentucky State Department of Health (1949).

CROWELL, F. E., 'The Midwives of New York', *Charities and the Commons* (17 Jan. 1907), 557–677 (reprinted in J. B. Litoff, *The American Midwife Debate: A Sourcebook on its Modern Origins* (New York, 1986).

—— 'Supervision of Midwives', *Journal of the American Medical Association*, 48 (1907), 712.

CUSHING, BENJAMIN, Records of private obstetric practice of his uncle Robert Thaxter from 1801 to 1852, MSS Boston, Countway Medical Library.

DANFORTH, D. D., 'Contemporary Titans: Joseph Bolivar DeLee and John Whitridge Williams', *American Journal of Obstetrics and Gynaecology*, 120 (1974), 577–88.

DEAVITT, NEAL, 'The Statistical Case for the Elimination of the Midwife', *Women and Health*, 4 (1979), 81–96, 169–86.

DELEE, J. B., 'Theories of Eclampsia', *American Journal of Obstetrics*, 51 (1905), 325–30.

—— 'The Technique of the Chicago Lying-in Hospital and Dispensary', *Surgery, Gynaecology and Obstetrics*, 3 (1906), 805–15.

—— *The Principles and Practice of Obstetrics* (2nd edn., Philadelphia, Pa., 1915; 7th edn., 1938).

—— 'Progress toward Ideal Obstetrics', *American Journal of Obstetrics*, 73 (1916), 407–15.

—— 'The Prophylactic Forceps Operation', *American Journal of Obstetrics and Gynaecology*, 1 (1920–1), 34–44, 77–84.

—— and SIEDENTOPF, H., 'The Maternity Ward of the General Hospital', *Journal of the American Medical Association*, 100 (1933), 6–14.

Department of Agriculture, USA, *Domestic Needs of Farm Women*, Report No. 104 (Washington, DC, 1913).

Department of Health Education and Welfare, USA, *Infant, Fetal and Maternal Mortality*, National Center for Health Statistics, Ser. 20 (Washington, DC, 1966).

DEPORTE, J. V., *Maternal Mortality and Stillbirths in New York State: 1915–1925* (New York, 1928).

DE WEES, W., 'Obstetric Notes Based upon 1,000 Consecutive Cases in Town and Country Practice', *Kansas City Medical Index*, 9 (1888), 262–8.

DICKINSON, F. G., and WELKER, E. L., 'Maternal Mortality in the United States in 1949', *Journal of the American Medical Association*, 144 (1950), 1395–400.

DONEGAN, J. B., *Women and Men-Midwives: Medicine, Morality and Misogyny in Early America* (Westport, Conn., 1978).

DOWLING, J. D., 'Points of Interest in a Survey of Maternal Mortality', *American Journal of Public Health*, 27 (1937), 803–8.

DUBLIN, L. I., 'The Problem of Maternity: A Survey and a Forecast', *American Journal of Public Health*, 29 (1939), 1025–313.

DUGGAN, M., *Report on the Midwife Survey in Texas, January 2nd, 1925*, in J. B. Litoff, *The American Midwife Debate: A Source book on its Modern Origins* (New York, 1986), 67–81.

DUNHAM, E., et al., 'Problem of the Causes of Stillbirth', *American Journal of Public Health*, 28 (1938), 491–8.

DUNN, W. A., 'Report of 1168 Cases of Labor in Private Practice', *Boston Medical and Surgical Journal*, 124 (1891), 451–3.

DYE, N. S., 'Mary Breckinridge, the Frontier Nursing Service and the Introduction of

Nurse-Midwifery in the United States', *Bulletin of the History of Medicine*, 57 (1983), 485–507.

EASTMAN, N. J., 'Whither American Obstetrics', *New England Journal of Medicine*, 224 (1941), 89–93.

EBBS, J. H., TISDALL, F. F., and SCOTT, W. A., 'The Influence of Prenatal Diet on the Mother and Child', *Journal of Nutrition*, 22 (1941), 515–26.

ELDREDGE, J. H., 'Twelve Hundred and Forty-three Cases of Confinement in the Care of General Practitioners from March 23, 1811, to June 23, 1838, a Period of Twenty-seven Years', *Transactions of the Rhode Island Medical Society*, 4 (1889–93), 164–9.

EMERSON, G., 'Medical Statistics', *American Journal of Medical Sciences*, 9 (1831–2), 21–5.

ENGLEMANN, G. J., 'Pregnancy, Parturition and Childbed among Primitive People', *American Journal of Obstetrics*, 14 (1881), 602–18.

—— *Labor among Primitive Peoples* (2nd edn., St Louis, Ind., 1883).

—— 'Birth and Death Rate as Influenced by Obstetric and Gynecic [sic] Progress', *Boston Medical and Surgical Journal*, 146 (1902), 505–8, 541–4.

ENO, E., 'A Study in Puerperal Morbidity', *Surgery, Gynaecology, and Obstetrics*, 36 (1923), 797–801.

ERICKSON, G., 'Southern Initiative in Public Health Nursing: The Founding of the Nurses' Settlement and Instructive Nurses Association in Richmond, Virginia, 1900–1910', *Journal of Nursing History*, 3 (1987), 17–29.

FEINER, D., 'An Analysis of Maternal Mortality in Ten Thousand Obstetric Cases', *American Journal of Obstetrics and Gynaecology*, 29 (1935), 444–50.

FINDLEY, P., 'The Lost Art of Obstetrics', *Northwest Medicine*, 17 (1918), 67–70.

FITZGERALD, J. E., and WEBSTER, A., 'Nineteen-Year Survey of Maternal Mortality at Cook County Hospital', *American Journal of Obstetrics and Gynaecology*, 65 (1953), 528–33.

FLEXNER, A., *Medical Education in the United States and Canada: A Report for the Carnegie Foundation for the Advancement of Teaching*, Bulletin No. 4 (New York, 1910), 117–18.

FLINT, A., Account of Women Delivered 1785–1834. MSS Boston, Countway Medical Library.

—— 'Responsibility of the Medical Profession in Further Reducing Maternal Mortality', *American Journal of Obstetrics and Gynaecology*, 9 (1925), 864–6; discussion of paper, 704–8.

FULTON, A. L., 'An Experience of 25 Years in Midwifery Practice', *Kansas City Medical Record*, 11 (1894), 325–9.

GALDSTON, IAGO, *Maternal Deaths: The Way to Prevention* (New York, 1937).

GARDENER, A. K., *A History of the Art of Midwifery* (New York, 1852).

GARRIGUES, H. J., 'On Lying-in Institutions, especially those of New York', *Transactions of the American Gynaecological Society*, 2 (1878), 593–649.

GODDARD, J., *Medical and Nursing Services for the Maternal Cases of the National Health Survey*, United States Government Printing Office (1941).

GOLDSBOROUGH, F. C., 'Maternal Mortality in the First 5,000 Obstetrical Cases at the Johns Hopkins Hospital', *Johns Hopkins Hospital Bulletin*, 19 (1908), 12–19.

GRAY, R. H., 'Maternal Reproduction and Child Survival', *American Journal of Public*

Health, 74 (1984), 1080–1.

GREGORY, S., *Man-Midwifery Exposed and Corrected* (Boston, 1848).

GRIMES, D. A., and CATES, W., 'The Impact of State Maternal Mortality Committees on Maternal Deaths in the United States', *American Journal of Public Health*, 67 (1977), 830–3.

HAINES, B. M., and MARSH, E. T., 'Four Years of the Federal Maternal and Infancy Act', *Nation's Health*, 8 (1926), 729–32.

HAMBLEN, A. D., 'A Statistical Study of One Hundred Caesarean Cases', *Commonwealth*, 10 (1923), 111–19.

HARMON, G. E., 'Place Variations in Death Rates from Puerperal Septicaemia', *American Journal of Public Health*, 24 (1934), 732–8.

HARRIS, R. P., 'Which shall we Perform: Craniotomy, Caesarean Section, or Symphyseotomy?', *Medical Press and Circular*, NS 5 (1894), 561–2.

HEATON, C. E., 'The History of Anaesthesia and Analgesia in Obstetrics', *Journal of the History of Medicine and Allied Sciences*, 1 (1946), 567–72.

HINE, D. C., '"They shall Mount up with Wings as Eagles": Historical Images of Black Nurses, 1850–1950', in A. H. Jones, *Images of Nurses* (Philadelphia, Pa., 1988).

HIRST, B. C., 'The Death Rate of Lying-in Hospitals in the United States', *Medical News of Philadelphia*, 50 (1887), 253–6.

HOLBROOK, M. L., *Parturition without Pain* (Toronto, 1875).

HOLMES, O. W., 'On the Contagiousness of Puerperal Fever', *New England Quarterly Journal of Medicine*, 1 (1842–3), 503–30.

—— *Puerperal Fever as a Private Pestilence* (Boston, 1855).

HOLMES, R. W., *et al.*, 'The Midwives of Chicago', *Journal of the American Medical Association*, 50 (1908), 1346–50.

—— 'The Fads and Fancies of Obstetrics: A Comment on the Pseudo-Scientific Trend of Modern Obstetrics', *American Journal of Obstetrics and Gynaecology*, 2 (1920), 225–37.

IRVING, F. C., *Safe Deliverance* (Boston, 1942).

JANVIER, G. V., 'The More Important Obstetrical Emergencies Met by the General Practitioner', *Pennsylvania Medical Journal*, 26 (1922–3), 284–8.

JEWETT, C., 'The Question of Puerperal Self-Infection', *American Gynaecological and Obstetrical Journal*, 8 (1896), 417–29.

KAUNITZ, A. M., *et al.*, 'Perinatal and Maternal Mortality in a Religious Group Avoiding Obstetric Care', *American Journal of Obstetrics and Gynaecology*, 150 (1984), 826–32.

KLEIN, M. D., and CLAHR, J., 'Factors in the Decline of Maternal Mortality', *Journal of the American Medical Association*, 168 (1958), 237–42.

KNIPE, W. H. W., '"Twilight Sleep" from the Hospital Viewpoint', *Modern Hospital*, 3 (1914), 250–1.

KNODEL, J. E., *Demographic Behaviour in the Past: A Study of Fourteen German Village Populations in the Eighteenth and Nineteenth Centuries* (Cambridge, 1988).

—— and HERMALIN, A. J., 'Effects of Birth Rank, Maternal Age, Birth Interval and Sibship size on Infant and Child Mortality: Evidence from 18th and 19th Century Reproductive Histories', *American Journal of Public Health*, 74 (1984), 1098–106.

KOBRIN, F. E., 'The American Midwife Controversy: A Crisis of Professionalisation', in J. W. Leavitt and R. L. Numbers (eds.), *Sickness and Health in America* (Madison, Wis., 1978), 217–28.

KOSMAK, G. W., 'Results of Supervised Midwife Practice in Certain European Countries. Can we Draw a Lesson from this for the United States? *Journal of the American Medical Association*, 89 (1927), 2009–12.

KUHLMANN, A., 'Obstetrics of 1,000 Cases as Seen by a Country Practitioner', *Minnesota Medicine*, 6 (1923), 449–53.

LADD-TAYLOR, M., *Raising a Baby the Government Way: Mothers' Letters to the Children's Bureau, 1915–1932* (New Brunswick, 1986).

LANSING, D. I., PENMAN, W. R., and DAVIS, J. D., 'Puerperal Fever and the Group B haemolytic streptococcus', *Bulletin of the History of Medicine*, 57 (1983), 70–80.

LAPHAM, M. E., 'Study of Maternity Care in Gibson County', *Journal of the Tennessee Medical Association*, 28 (1935), 223–38.

LEAVITT, J. W., *Women and Health in America* (Madison, Wis., 1984).

—— *Brought to Bed: Childbearing in America, 1750–1950* (New York and Oxford, 1986).

—— 'The Growth of Medical Authority: Technology and Morals in Turn-of-Century Obstetrics', *Medical Anthropology Quarterly*, 1/3 (1987), 230–55.

—— 'Joseph B. DeLee and the Practice of Preventive Obstetrics', *American Journal of Public Health*, 78 (1988), 1353–9.

LEE, W. G., *Childbirth* (Chicago, 1928).

LEHMANN, D. K., *et al.*, 'The Epidemiology and Pathology of Maternal Mortality: Charity Hospital of New Orleans, 1965–1984', *Obstetrics and Gynaecology*, 69/6, (1987), 833–40.

LEISHMAN, W., *A System of Midwifery*, with additions by John S. Parry (Philadelphia, Pa., 1875).

LELAND, GEORGE ADAMS, Obstetric casebook for 1905 to 1909, MSS Boston, Countway Medical Library.

LESSER, A. J., 'The Origin and Development of Maternal and Child Health Programs in the United States', *American Journal of Public Health*, 75 (1985), 590–8.

LEVY, J., 'The Maternal and Infant Mortality in Midwifery Practice in Newark, N.J.', *American Journal of Obstetrics*, 77 (1918), 41–53.

—— 'Maternal Mortality and Mortality in the First Month of Life in Relation to Attendant at Birth', *American Journal of Public Health*, 13 (1923), 88–95.

LEWIS, D., 'Mutilating Operations in Obstetric Practice', *Clinical Review, Chicago*, 12 (1900–1), 12–26.

LITOFF, J. B., *American Midwives: 1860 to the Present* (Westport, Conn., 1978).

—— *The American Midwife Debate: A Sourcebook on its Modern Origins* (New York, 1986).

LOCK, F. R., and GEISS, F. C., 'The Anaesthetic hazards of Obstetrics', *American Journal of Obstetrics and Gynaecology*, 70 (1955), 861–75.

LUSK, W. T., 'The Genesis of an Epidemic of Puerperal Fever', *American Journal of Obstetrics*, 8 (1875), 369–99.

—— 'On Sudden Death in Labor and Childbed', *Journal of American Medical Association*, 3 (1884), 427–31.

MacDONALD, C. F., 'Puerperal Insanity: A Cursory View for the General Practitioner', *Transactions of the Medical Society of New York for the Year 1889* (1889), 138–68.

McGILLICUDDY, T. J., 'Operative Interference in the Second Stage of Labour', *Medical Record of New York*, 44 (1893), 517–22.

McKay, F., 'What New York State is Doing to Reduce Maternal Mortality', *American Journal of Obstetrics and Gynaecology*, 9 (1925), 704–8.

MacPHAIL, E. S., 'A Statistical Study in Maternal Mortality', *American Journal of Public Health*, 22 (1932), 612–26.

MARKOE, J. W., 'Modern Standards in Abnormal Cases and their Treatment', *Medical Record*, 94 (1919), 177–80.

MARMOL, J. G., SCRIGGINS, A. L., and VOLLMAN, R. F., 'History of the Maternal Mortality Study Committees in the United States', *Obstetrics and Gynaecology*, 34 (1969), 123–38.

MASON KNOX, J. H., 'Reduction of Maternal and Infant Mortality in Rural Areas', *American Journal of Public Health*, 25 (1935), 68–75.

Massachusetts, Commonwealth of Massachusetts Annual Reports to the State Board of Health. Boston, Countway Medical Library.

Maternal and Child Health, 'The Secret of Maternal and Child Health' (leading article), *American Journal of Public Health*, 75 (1985), 585–7.

Maternal Health and Diet (editorial), *American Journal of Public Health*, 32 (1942), 315–16.

MEIGS, C. D., *Females and their Diseases: A Series of Letters to his Class* (Philadelphia, Pa., 1848).

MEIGS, G. L., 'Rural Obstetrics', *Transactions of the American Association for the Study and Prevention of Infant Mortality*, 7 (1916), 46–61.

METCALF, J. G., Obstetric Cases, 1826–31. MSS Boston, Countway Medical Library.

Michigan, Bureau of Maternal and Child Health, *Maternal Mortality Survey, 1935–1939* (Pontiac, Mich., 1940).

—— *Maternal Care in Michigan: A Study of Obstetric Practices*, National Institute of Health, United States Public Health Service (Washington, DC, 1938). Bulletin No. 8 of Preliminary Reports of the National Health Survey, Sickness and Medical Care Series.

MINOR, T., 'Erysipelas and Child-bed Fever', *Practitioner*, 15 (1875), 158–60.

Mississippi, State Board of Health, *Annual Bulletins of Statistics* (1917–71).

MITCHELL, R. McNAIR, 'Maternal Mortality in the Pennsylvania Hospital: Tabular Review of Maternal Deaths, 1929–1953', *Obstetrics and Gynaecology*, 5 (1955), 123–36.

MONGEAU, B., SMITH, H., and MANEY, A., 'The "granny" Midwife: Changing Roles and Functions of a Folk Tradition', *American Journal of Sociology*, 66 (1961), 497–505, reprinted in R. Dingwall and J. McIntosh (eds.), *Readings in the Sociology of Nursing* (Edinburgh, 1978), 135–49.

MOORE, J. H., 'Maternal Mortality in North Dakota', *Journal of the American Medical Association*, 116 (1941), 1887–9.

MOSHER, G. C., 'Maternal Morbidity and Mortality in the United States', *American Journal of Obstetrics and Gynaecology*, 7 (1924), 294–8, 326–30.

MURRAY, R. A., 'The Limitations of the Caesarean Section', *Transactions of the Medical*

Society of the State of New York for 1893 (1893), 121–7.

National Academy of Sciences, *Maternal Nutrition and the Course of Pregnancy* (Washington, DC, 1970).

New York City Public Health Committee and New York Academy of Medicine, *Maternal Mortality in New York, 1930, 1931, 1932* (New York, 1933).

NEWMAN, H. P., 'The Specialty of Obstetrics', *American Journal of Obstetrics*, 80 (1919), 464–71.

Oklahoma, Maternal, Infant and Child Mortality, 1928–1950, Division of Maternal and Child Health, Oklahoma State Department of Health (n.d.).

OXORN, H., 'Maternal Mortality: A 40-Year Survey'. *Obstetrics and Gynaecology*, 39 (1967), 744–9.

PARRY, J. S., 'Description of a Form of Puerperal Fever which Occurred at the Philadelphia Hospital Characterised by Diphtheritic Deposits of Wounds of the Genital Passages and by other Peculiar Phenomena', *American Journal of Medical Sciences*, 69 (1875), 46–76.

PARVIN, T., 'A Contribution to Demography', *American Gynaecological and Obstetric Journal of New York*, 6 (1895), 393–8.

PECKHAM, C. H., 'Abortion: Statistical Analysis of 2787 Cases', *Surgery, Gynaecology and Obstetrics*, 63 (1936), 109–15.

—— 'A Survey of 447 Maternal Deaths Occurring in the Counties of Maryland during the Years 1930–1936 (inclusive)', *American Journal of Obstetrics and Gynaecology*, 36 (1938), 317–30.

Philadelphia County Medical Society, Committee on Maternal Welfare, *Maternal Mortality in Philadelphia, 1931–33* (Philadelphia, 1934).

PIPER, W. A., 'Rural Obstetrics and a Comparative Study of its Relation to Puerperal Mortality Statistics', *Minnesota Medicine*, 9 (1926), 489–99.

PLASS, E. D., 'Organisation, Supervision and Objectives of Prenatal Care', *American Journal of Public Health*, 31 (1941), 964–6.

—— and ALVIS, H. J., 'A Statistical Study of 129,539 Births in Iowa with Special Reference to the Method of Delivery and the Stillbirth Rate', *American Journal of Obstetrics and Gynaecology*, 28 (1934), 297–305.

PORGES, R. F., 'The Response of the New York Obstetrical Society to the Report by the New York Academy of Medicine on Maternal Mortality, 1933–34', *Obstetrics and Gynaecology*, 152 (1985), 642–9.

'Puerperal Fever' (discussion), *Transactions of the College of Physicians of Philadelphia*, 1 (1841–6), 50–61.

'Puerperal Infection in Private Practice' (leading article), *Journal of the American Medical Association*, 33 (1902), 1008–9.

RATNER, H., 'The Dehumanisation of American Obstetrical Practice', *Child and Family*, 16 (1977), 4–37.

REECE, M., 'The Use of Antiseptics in Puerperal Cases', *Journal of the American Medical Association*, 3 (1884), 120–1.

ROCHAT, R. W., 'Maternal Mortality in the USA', *World Health Statistics Quarterly*, 34 (1984).

ROHE, G. H., 'The Influence of Parturient Lesions of the Uterus and Vagina in the Causation of Puerperal Insanity', *Journal of the American Medical Association*, 19 (1892), 59–62.

ROSENBERG, C. E., *The Care of Strangers: The Rise of America's Hospital System* (New York, 1987).

ROSENTHAL, E., 'A Report of 1000 Obstetrical Cases', *Transactions of the Philadelphia County Medical Society*, 13 (1892), 118–30.

ROSS, J., 'Analysis of 6677 Cases of Midwifery Attended by James Ross MD, Toronto, between the Years 1852 and 1892', *American Journal of Obstetrics of New York*, 32 (1895), 380–7.

ROWLAND, J. M. H., 'Reduction of Mortality and Morbidity in Childbirth', *Journal of the American Medical Association*, 87 (1926), 2158–9.

RUBAN, G., *et al.*, 'The Risk of childbearing Re-evaluated', *American Journal of Public Health*, 71/7 (1981), 712–16.

RUCKER, M. P., 'The Relation of the Midwife to Obstetric Mortality, with Especial Reference to New Jersey', *American Journal of Public Health*, 13 (1923), 816–22.

—— 'An Eighteenth-Century Method of Pain Relief in Obstetrics', *Journal of the History of Medicine and Allied Sciences*, 5 (1950), 101–5.

SACHS, B. P., *et al.*, 'Maternal Mortality in Massachusetts', *New England Journal of Medicine*, 136 (1987), 667–72.

SANDELOWSKI, MARGARETE, *Pain and Pleasure in American Childbirth: From Twilight Sleep to the Read Method, 1914–1960* (Westport, Conn., 1984).

SCHAFFNER, W., *et al.*, 'Maternal Mortality in Michigan: An Epidemiologic Analysis', *American Journal of Public Health*, 67 (1977), 821–9.

SCHMIDT, W. M., 'The Development of Health Services for Mothers and Children in the United States', *American Journal of Public Health*, 63 (1973), 419–27.

SCHOLTEN, C. M., ' "On the Importance of the Obstetrick Art": Changing Customs of Childbirth in America, 1760–1825'. *William and Mary Quarterly*, 34 (1977), 426–45.

SCHOOLEY, A. H., 'Twenty Years Obstetrical Work in the Country', *Journal of the Iowa State Medical Society*, 14 (1924), 377–81.

SHAPIRO, S., SCHLESINGER, E. R., NESBITT, R. E. L., *Infant, Perinatal, Maternal, and Childhood Mortality in the United States* (Cambridge, Mass., 1968).

SMITH, J. L., *et al.*, 'An Assessment of the Incidence of Maternal Mortality in the USA', *American Journal of Public Health*, 74 (1984), 780–3.

South Carolina Medical Association, Committee on Maternal Welfare, *Maternal Mortality in South Carolina, 1934–5* (1936), Supplement for 1941–1 (1941).

STEVENS, R., *In Sickness and in Wealth: American Hospitals in the Twentieth Century* (New York, 1989).

STIX, R. K., and WIEHL, D. G., 'Abortion and Public Health', *American Journal of Public Health*, 28 (1938), 621–8.

STOECKLE, J. D., and WHITE, G. A., *Plain Pictures of Plain Doctoring: Vernacular Expression in New Deal Medicine and Photography* (Cambridge, Mass., 1985).

STOLLER, NANCY, *Forced Labor: Maternity Care in the United States* (New York, 1974).

STUDDIFORD, W. E., 'The Relation of Obstetrics to Preventitive Medicine', *Boston Medical and Surgical Journal*, 191 (1924), 617–30.

TAUSSIG, F. J., 'An Account of a Visit by American Physicians to the Soviet Union', *American Journal of Obstetrics and Gynaecology* (1931), 134–9.

—— *Abortion, Spontaneous and Induced: Medical and Social Aspects* (London, 1936).

TEMPLETON, J. S., 'Obstetrics in Country Practice', *Illinois Medical Journal*, 39 (1918), 90–3.

TUCKER, B. E., and BENARON, H. B., 'Maternal Mortality of the Chicago Maternity Center', *American Journal of Public Health*, 27 (1937), 33–6.

UNGERLEIDER, H. E., STEINHAUS, H. W., and GUBNER, R. S., 'Public Health and Economic Aspects of Pneumonia: A Comparison with Pre-Sulfonamide Years', *American Journal of Public Health*, 33 (1943), 1093–101.

US Department of Health, Education and Welfare, National Center for Health Statistics, *Vital Statistics Rates in the United States, 1940–1960* (Washington, DC, 1968).

VAN HOOSEN, BERTHA, 'The New Movement in Obstetrics', *Woman's Medical Journal*, 25 (1915), 121–3.

VARNER, M. W., DALY, K. D., GOPLERUD, C. P., and KEETEL, W. C., 'Maternal Mortality in a Major Referral Hospital, 1926–1980', *American Journal of Obstetrics and Gynaecology*, 143 (1982), 325–34.

WARD, G. G., 'Our Obstetric and Gynaecologic Responsibilities', *Journal of the American Medical Association*, 87 (1926), 1–3.

WARREN, S. P., 'The Prevalence of Puerperal Septicaemia in Private Practice at the Present Time Contrasted with that of a Generation ago', *American Journal of Obstetrics*, 51 (1905), 301–31.

WEDGEWOOD, H., 'Midwifery in Massachusetts', *Commonwealth*, 8 (1921), 71–96.

WEINBERG, E. D., 'Pregnancy-Associated Depression of Cell-Mediated Immunity', *Review of Infectious Diseases*, 6 (1984), 814–31.

WERTZ, R. W., and WERTZ, D. C., *Lying-in: A History of Childbirth in America* (New York, 1977).

WESTLEY, M. D., 'Obstetrics in a Rural Community', *Journal-Lancet*, 37 (1917), 181–5.

WHITACRE, F. E., and JONES, E. W., *Maternity Care in Two Counties, Gibson County, Tennessee and Pike County, Mississippi, 1940–41, 1943–44* (New York, 1950).

WHITCOMB, H. H., 'A Report of 616 Cases of Labor in Private Practice', *Medical and Surgical Reporter*, 56 (1887), 201–3.

White House Conference on Child Health Protection, *Fetal, Newborn and maternal morbidity and mortality* (New York, 1933).

WILKIE, K. E., and MOSELEY, E. R., *Frontier Nurse: Mary Breckinridge* (New York, 1969).

WILLIAMS, J. WHITRIDGE, 'Medical Education and the Midwife Problem in the United States', *Journal of the American Medical Association*, 58 (1912), 1–76.

—— 'Criticism of Certain Tendencies in American Obstetrics', *New York State Journal of Medicine*, 22 (1922), 493–9.

WILSON, L. G., 'The Early Recognition of Streptococci as Causes of Disease', *Medical History*, 31 (1987), 403–14.

WILTBANK, J., *A Plea for Obstetrics* (Philadelphia, Pa., 1848).

WOODBURY, R. M., *Infant Mortality and its Causes* (Baltimore, Md., 1926).

WORKMAN, W., Statistical Account of Obstetrical Cases, 1846–7, MSS Boston, Countway Medical Library.

WORMELY, W., '1000 Obstetrical Cases Occurring in General Practice', *Medical Times of New York*, 30 (1902), 231–4.

YERUSHALMY, J., 'Births, Infant Mortality and Maternal Mortality in the United States', *Public Health Reports*, 59 (1944), 797–809.

YERUSHALMY, J., 'Infant and Maternal Mortality in the Modern World', *Annals of the American Academy of Political and Social Sciences*, 237 (1945), 134–41.

——, KRAMER, M., and GARDINER, E. M., 'Studies in Childbirth Mortality. I. Puerperal Fatality and Loss of Offspring', *Public Health Reports*, 55 (1940), 1010–27. 'Studies in Childbirth Mortality. II. Age and Parity as Factors in Puerperal Fatality', *Public Health Reports*, 55 (1940), 1195–220.

—— PALMER, C. E., and KRAMER, M., &

YOUNG, J., 'Maternal Mortality and Maternal Mortality Rates', *American Journal of Obstetrics and Gynaecology*, 31 (1936), 198–212.

EUROPE

ACKERNECHT, E. H., FISCHER-HOMBERG, E., 'Five Made it—One Not: The Rise of Medical Craftsmen to Academic Status during the 19th Century', *Clio Medica*, 12 (1977), 255–67.

ANCELET, Gabriel-Paul, *Essai historique et critique sur le création et la transformation des maternités à Paris* (Paris, 1896).

BARDET, J.-P., *et al.*, 'La Mortalité maternelle autrefois: Une étude comparé (de la France de l'ouest à l'Utah)', *Annales de démographie historique* (1981), 31–48.

BIDEAU, A., 'Accouchement naturelle et accouchement à haut risque', *Annales de démographie historique* (1981), 49–66.

CAZEAUX, P., *A Theoretical and Practical Treatise on Midwifery, including the Diseases of Pregnancy and Parturition*, revised and annotated by S. Tarnier (5th American edn. from the 7th French edn. of 1868; Philadelphia, Pa., 1873).

CHAMPION, M. E., 'The Midwives of Holland', *American Journal of Public Health*, 17 (1927), 1290–1.

'Childbirth in Holland' (leading article), *Lancet* (1934), ii. 713–14.

CULLINGWORTH, C. J., 'Biographical Note on Étienne Stéphane Tarnier', *Transactions of the Obstetrical Society of London*, 40 (1898), 78–9.

DELAUNAY, P., *La Maternité de Paris* (Paris, 1909).

DEVRAIGNE, L., *L'Obstétrique à travers les âges* (Paris, 1939).

DROGENDIJK, A. C., *De Verloskundige in Dordrecht [Obstetric Provision in Dordrecht]* (Amsterdam, 1935).

GELFAND, T., 'Empiricism and Eighteenth-Century French Surgery', *Bulletin of the History of Medicine*, 44 (1970), 40–53.

—— 'The Hospice of the Paris College of Surgery (1774–1793)', *Bulletin of the History of Medicine*, 47 (1973), 375–93.

—— 'The Decline of the Ordinary Practitioner and the Rise of a Modern Medical Profession', in M. S. Staum and D. E. Larsen, *Doctors, Patients and Society* (Ontario, 1981).

GÉLIS, J., *A History of Childbirth: Fertility, Pregnancy and Birth in Early Modern Europe*, trans. Rosemary Morris (Cambridge, 1991). First published as *L'Arbre et le fruit* (Paris, 1984).

GUTIRREZ, H., and HOUDAILLE, J., 'La Mortalité maternelle en France au XVIIIème siècle', *Population*, 6 (1983), 974–94.

HEMMINKI, E., and PAAKKULAINEN, Y., 'The Effects of Antibiotics on Mortality from

Infectious Diseases in Sweden and Finland', *American Journal of Public Health*, 66 (1976), 1180–4.

HÖGBERG, U., 'The Decline in Maternal Mortality in Sweden 1750–1980: A Comparative Study', paper presented at the International Conference on Medical Education in the field of Primary Maternal Child Health Care, Egypt, December 1983.

—— *Maternal Mortality in Sweden*, Umeå University Medical Dissertations, NS 156 (Umeå, 1985).

—— and BROSTROM, G., 'The Impact of Early Medical Technology on Maternal Mortality Rate in late 19th Century Sweden', *International Journal of Obstetrics and Gynaecology*, 24 (1986), 251–61.

KNODEL, J. E., *Demographic Behavior in the Past: A Study of Fourteen German Village Populations in the Eighteenth and Nineteenth Centuries* (Cambridge, 1988).

KUHN, W., and TRÖHLER, U., *Armamentarium obstetricum Gottingense* (Göttingen, 1987).

LA BERGE, A. F., 'The Paris Health Council, 1802–1848', *Bulletin of the History of Medicine*, 49 (1975), 339–52.

LACOMME, 'New Results Obtained in the Trial of a Prophylactic Treatment of Puerperal Infections at the Baudelocque Clinic: Interpretation of Results', *Surgery, Gynaecology and Obstetrics*, 66 (1938), 164. Originally published in *Bulletin de Société d'Obstétriques et de Gynécologie de Paris*, 26 (1937), 459.

LAGET, MIREILLE, 'Childbirth in Seventeenth- and Eighteenth-Century France: Obstetrical Practices and Collective Attitudes', in R. Forster and O. Ranum (eds.), *Medicine and Society in France* (Baltimore, Md., 1980), 1–76.

LE FORT, LÉON, *Des maternités* (Paris, 1866).

—— *Étude sur l'organisation de la médecine en France et à l'étranger* (Paris, 1874).

League of Nations, Health Organization, *Memorandum Relating to the Causes and Prevention of Still-Births and Mortality during the First Year of Life: Austria, France, Germany, Great Britain, Italy, Netherlands, Norway* (Geneva, 1930).

LEWES, F., 'The Letters between Adolphe Quetelet and William Farr', *Bulletin de la classe des lettres et des sciences morales et politiques*, 5 ser. 49 (1983), 417–28.

LOUCHE, JEAN-LOUIS, 'La Maternité de Liège ou cent ans de l'évolution d'un hospice', *Annales de la société belge d'histoire des hôpitaux et de la santé publique*, 22 (1984), 5–25.

LUMEY, L. H., 'Obstetric Performance of Women after *in Utero* Exposure to the Dutch Famine', Ph.D. thesis (Columbia University, 1988).

McLAREN, A., 'Abortion in France: Women and the Regulation of Family Size', *French Historical Studies*, 10 (1978), 461–85.

MARLAND, H. (ed.), *Mother and Child were Saved: The Memoirs (1693–1740) of the Frisian Midwife, Catharina Schrader* (Amsterdam, 1987).

—— 'A Woman's Touch: Female Doctors and Maternal and Infant Care in the Netherlands in the Late Nineteenth and Early Twentieth Century', in V. Fildes, H. Marland, and L. Marks (eds.), *Women and Children First* (London, forthcoming).

MASUAY-STROOBANT, GODELIEVE, *Les Déterminants individuels et régionaux de la mortalité infantile: La Belgique d'hier et d'aujourd'hui*, Département de Démographie, Université Catholique de Louvain (1983).

MENDENHALL, D. R., *Midwifery in Denmark*, US Department of Labor, Children's

Bureau (Washington, DC, 1929).

Ministry of Health, 'The Maternity Services of the Netherlands, Denmark and Sweden', *Final Report of Departmental Committee on Maternal Mortality and Morbidity* (London, 1932).

Netherlands, Vital statistics, *Verslag van des Geneeskundig Hoofdinspecteur van de Volksgezondheid* (various years).

—— *Malnutrition and Starvation in Western Netherlands: Sept. 1944 to July 1945*, 2 vols. (The Hague, 1948).

—— 'The Hunger Winter', *Timewatch*, BBC 2 Television (29 June 1989).

OZANAM J. A. F., *Histoire médicale, générale et particulière des maladies contagieuses et épizootiques*, 4 vols. (Lyons, 1835).

PETRELLI, R. L., 'The Regulation of French Midwifery during the *ancien régime*', *Journal of the History of Medicine and Allied Sciences*, 26 (1971), 276–92.

PHAFF, J. M. L., 'The Organisation and Administration of Perinatal Services in the Netherlands', in Phaff, *Perinatal Health Services in Europe* (London, 1986).

ROMLID, CHRISTINA, 'The Swedish Maternal Mortality Rate in the 19th Century', unpublished paper (*c.*1989).

ROSEN, GEORGE, 'Hospitals, Medical Care and Social Policy in the French Revolution', *Bulletin of the History of Medicine*, 30 (1956), 124–49.

SAVONA-VENTURA, C., 'Reproductive Performance on the Maltese Islands during the Second World War', *Medical History*, 34/2 (1990), 164–77.

SCHOFIELD, R., REHER, D., and BIDEAU, A., *The Decline in Mortality in Europe* (Oxford, 1991).

SEMMELWEIS, IGNAZ, *The Etiology, Concept and Prophylaxis of Childbed Fever*, trans. K. Codell Carter (Madison, Wisconsin, 1983; originally published 1861).

SIEBOLD, E. G. J. DE, *Essai d'une histoire de l'obstétrice*, trans. from German by F. J. Herrgot (Paris, 1891).

STARMANS, J. H., *Verloskunde en Kindersterfie in Limburg [Midwifery and Child Deaths in Limburg]* (Maastricht, 1930).

'The Maternity Services in Holland' (leading article), *Lancet* (1936), i. 736–7.

VALLGARDA, S., 'Hospitals and the Poor in Denmark', *Scandinavian History*, 13 (1986), 93–105.

VAN GELDER, F., 'The Case of the Midwives: A Forgotten Profession', paper given at the third Anglo-Dutch Labour History Conference, Maastricht, 1982.

VAN LIEBURG, M. J., and MARLAND, H., 'Midwife Regulation, Education, and Practice in the Netherlands during the Nineteenth Century', *Medical History*, 33 (1989), 296–317.

VAN TUESSENBROOEK, CATHARINE, *De Ontwikkeling der Aseptische Verloskunde in Nederland [The Development of Aseptic Midwifery in the Netherlands]* (Haarlem, 1911).

WITKOWSKI, G.-J., *Histoire des accouchements chez tous les peuples* (Paris, 1887).

World Health Organization, Division of Family Health, *Maternal Mortality Rates* (Geneva, 1985).

—— *Having a Baby in Europe: Report of a Study*, Regional Office for Europe, World Health Organization, *Public Health in Europe*, 26 (Copenhagen, 1985).

World Health Statistics Report, 22/6 (1969). Maternal Mortality in various countries.

AUSTRALIA AND NEW ZEALAND

ALLEN, R. MARSHALL, 'Interim Report on Maternal Mortality and Morbidity in Victoria', *Medical Journal of Australia* (1927), i. 1–10.

—— 'Avenues of Progress in Maternal Welfare', *Medical Journal of Australia* (1936), i. 251–8.

ANDREWS, A., 'Notes of 800 Consecutive Midwifery Cases', *The Australasian Medical Gazette*, 12 (1883), 361–2.

Australia, Parliament of the Commonwealth of Australia, Department of Trades and Customs, Committee Concerning Causes of Death and Invalidity in the Commonwealth, *Report on Maternal Mortality in Childbirth* (Victoria, 1917), C.7867.

—— Report of puerperal fever, *British Medical Journal* (1875), ii. 354.

BENNETT, F. O., 'The Art of Obstetrics: A Century of Progress'. *New Zealand Medical Journal*, 41 (1942), 7–13, 17–19.

BRITTON, C. J. C., 'The Sulphanilamide Compounds: Their Value in Medicine', *New Zealand Medical Journal*, 37 (1938), 154–61.

BULL, W. H. B., 'Abortion and Contraception', *New Zealand Medical Journal*, 35 (1936), 39–44.

CHENHALL, W. T., 'Contracted Pelvis in Obstetric Practice', *Medical Journal of Australia* (1919), ii. 22–7.

CHESTERMAN, J., 'Puerperal Infections due to Haemolytic Streptococci', *Medical Journal of Australia* (1938), i. 237–42.

—— 'The Use of Sulphanilamide in some Clinical Conditions', *Medical Journal of Australia* (1938), ii. 1110–14.

CORKHILL, T. F., 'The Trend of Obstetric Practice in New Zealand', *New Zealand Medical Journal*, 32 (1933), 41–52.

D'ARCY, CONSTANCE, 'The Problem of Maternal Welfare' (The Anne Mackenzie oration), *Medical Journal of Australia* (1935), i. 385–99.

DAWSON, J. B., 'Comparability of International Statistics', *New Zealand Medical Journal*, 32 (1933), 13–18.

—— 'Doctor and Midwife, Colleagues or Rivals?' *New Zealand Medical Journal*, 32 (1933), 20–3.

GIBSON, A. J., 'Maternal Welfare', *Medical Journal of Australia* (1938), i. 761–5.

GORDON, DORIS, *Backblocks Baby-Doctor* (London, 1955).

—— *Doctor Down Under* (London, 1958).

HAYDEN, F. J., 'Maternal Mortality in History and Today', *Medical Journal of Australia*, 57 (1970), 100–9.

HILL, A. M., 'Modern Aspects of Puerperal Sepsis', *Medical Journal of Australia* (1941), i. 537–41.

HILL, G., 'The Teaching of Obstetrics', *Medical Journal of Australia* (1922), i. 610–12.

JACOBS, H., 'The Causes and Prevention of Maternal Mortality', *Medical Journal of Australia* (1926), i. 593–611, 627–44.

JAMIESON, J., 'Childbirth Mortality in the Australian Colonies', *Australian Medical Journal*, NS 9 (1887), 842–8.

LOWE, G., 'Puerperal and Post-Abortional Sepsis', *Medical Journal of Australia* (1940), ii. 550–1.

'Maternal Mortality', Correspondence in *Medical Journal of Australia*, 13 (1935), i. 34, 101, 163, 193, 414; ii. 469.

'Maternal Welfare: A Notable Advance' (leading article), *Medical Journal of Australia* (1939), i. 197–8.

MORRIS, E. S., 'An Essay on the Causes and Prevention of Maternal Morbidity and Mortality', *Medical Journal of Australia* (1925), ii. 301–45.

MYERS, E. S., 'Some Aspects of Puerperal Mortality and Morbidity', *Medical Journal of Australia* (1922), ii. 54–6.

PAGET, T. L., BEWART, I., 'Ante-natal Care in New Zealand', *New Zealand Medical Journal*, 34 (1935), 13–20.

'Puerperal Infection' (leading article), *Medical Journal of Australia* (1917), ii. 207–8.

PURDY, J. S., 'Maternal Mortality in Childbirth', *Medical Journal of Australia* (1921), i. 39–47, 56–8.

ROBB, D., 'The Future of General Practice', *New Zealand Medical Journal*, 43 (1944), 248–55.

SMITH, M. ELLIOT, 'Maternal Mortality: Some Practical Points in Prevention', *Medical Journal of Australia* (1935), ii. 285–8.

SMITH, P. M., *Maternity in Dispute: New Zealand, 1920–1939*, Wellington, New Zealand, Dept. of Internal Affairs, Historical Publications Branch (1986).

'Streptococcal Carriers', *Medical Journal of Australia* (1936), ii. 798–803.

TUCKER, C., 'Points from Practice: Obstetrical', *Medical Journal of Australia* (1926), ii. 416–19.

WEBSTER, H. W., 'The Teaching of Obstetrics', *Medical Journal of Australia* (1921), ii. 231–2.

WILSON, K., 'Notes on Maternal Mortality', *Medical Journal of Australia* (1935), ii. 281–5.

WORRALL, R., 'Some Common Faults in Midwifery Practice', *Medical Journal of Australia* (1918), ii. 386–8.

Index

abortion 107–29
  and abortionists 126–7
  and family limitation 124–6, 479–80
  incidence and mortality 109–16
  and infanticide 123–4
  mortality from non-septic abortion 270–1
  penalties for procuring 127
  spontaneous 108
  types of 108
abortion, Britain:
  and contribution to maternal mortality 107
  estimates of rate 115–16
  and illegitimacy in Second World War
    266–71
  Interdepartmental Committee on (1937)
    114
  marital status and social class
  and puerperal sepsis 60, 113–14
  and trend in maternal mortality 250–1
abortion, various countries:
  Australia, high level of 473–5
  Belgium (Liege) 438
  Europe 116–21
  France and involvement of midwives
    117–18
  Ireland 114
  Germany, Austria, and Poland 116
  New Zealand 479–80
  Scandinavia 118–19
  Scotland 114
  Soviet Union 119–21
  USA 121–3, 528–31
accidental haemorrhage, see obstetric
    haemorrhage
Amand, Phillipe 400
analgesia in childbirth:
  and Caesarean section 345
  chloroform, Simpson's method 346
  chloroform versus ether 286, 344–5
  large drug dosage 348–9
  and natural childbirth 349
  opium and morphine 343–4
  twilight sleep 223, 346–8
Anderson, Elizabeth Garrett 190, 229
antenatal care 90–1, 452
antisepsis:
  agents used 205
  in Australian practice 470
    effect on mortality of lying-in hospitals
      203–5
    introduction of 203–5
    neglect of in general practice 220–1, 251,
      289
Armstrong, John 60, 70
Association of Apothecaries and Surgeon-
    Apothecaries 425
Astruc, Jean 166
Aveling, J. H. 173, 183

Bacon, W. S. 36
Baird, Sir Dougald 459
Baker, Josephine 301, 365
Bardet, J-P. 404
Barker, Fordyce 57
Barnes, Robert 173, 183
Baudelocque, Jean-Louis 134
Beardsley, Edward H. 377
Bellevue School of Midwifery, New York 301
β-haemolytic streptococcus, Lancefield
    group A, see Streptococcus pyogenes
Blackmore, Edward 60
Bliss, Dr 286
blood transfusion 255, 257, 263, 271–2, 476
Bolt, Robert 45
Bonney, Victor 218, 223
Borst, C. 325
Bovin, Mme (midwife) 404
Boxall, Robert 37, 73, 75
Brackenbury, Sir Henry 44–5
Braxall, J. 173
Breckinridge, Mary 318–21, 339, 426
Brickman, Janet P. 302
Brown, Dr 286
Brown, J. 26
Brumbagh, C. G. 290
Burkhardt, H. 80
Butter, William 400
Button, Lt.-Col. Eardley 481

Caesarean section 134–7, 287, 320, 427
  for contracted pelvis 134–7, 447
  in Kentucky Nursing Service 320
  for placenta praevia 101–2
  for toxaemia 89
  in USA 357, 363, 380, 393, 529–31
Cairns, Sir Hugh 481

Cameron, Murdoch 102, 134–7
Campbell, Dame Janet 207, 210, 214, 252
Carlisle, Sir Anthony 190
Cassie, Ethel 227
Central Midwives Board and Certificate
  207–8, 212, 232, 319
certification of deaths, problems of
  methodology 28–9
Chamberlin, Neville 211
Channing, Walter 344
Chapelle, Mme la 404
Chapman, E. 400
Chassar Moir, John 257
childbirth in primitive and civilized
  peoples 340–3
Children's Bureau, Washington DC 278, 279
Churchill, Fleetwood 142–3
Clark, Sir Charles 98, 189
Clarke, John 21
Clement, Julian 167
Colebrook, Dora 81–3
Colebrook, L., and Kenny, M. and the trial of
  sulphonamides in puerperal fever 259–6
Colebrook, Leonard 81–4, 285–60
Condie, Dr 62
Confidential Inquiries into Maternal
  Deaths 506
contracted pelvis 130–43
  and Caesarean section 134–5
  in European countries 447
  incidence of 134–5
  and induction of labour 133–4
  and maternal deaths 506
  minor degrees of 142
  and Murdoch Cameron of Glasgow 136–7
  nature of 130–2
  and rickets 130, 446–8
  and surgical measures 132–5
  and symphysiotomy 132
Cooper, Thomas 83
Coudray, Mme du
craniotomy 133–4, 138–41, 338, 361, 447
Crosse, John Greene 176
Crowell, Elizabeth 305–7
Cullen, William 26
Cullingworth, Charles J. 173, 183, 203, 204,
  244

D'Arcy, Constance 470, 473, 475
Dart, Helen 315–16
Davis, A. B. 336
Davis, D. D. 183
Dawkes, T. 400
DeLee, Joseph Bolivar 88, 322, 337–8, 401
deliveries:
  proportion of by doctors and midwives
  175–8

proportion in home and hospital 155–6,
  282–5, 360–1
delivery, home, by nineteenth-century doctor
  185–6
Denman, Thomas 83, 400
Deventer, Hendrik van 400, 403
Dick-Read, Grantley 349–50
Dionis, Pierre 398
disproportion, cephalo-pelvic, *see* contracted
  pelvis
Döderlein, Albert 80
Domagk, Gerhard 258
Dowling, J. D. 380
Dublin, Louis I. 321, 336

Eccles, Audrey 159
Eden, Thomas W. 93
Eldredge, J. 287
Elkington, John 71
Elliott, J. S. 479
Englemann, George J. 331, 341–2
ergometrine 255, 272

Fairbairn, J. S. 319
Faith Assembly, Indiana, USA, and maternal
  mortality 395–7
Farr, William, 2, 21, 27, 97, 176, 179, 181,
  196, 206, 518, 525
fevers, nineteenth-century concepts of
  causation 69–70
Finer, Dr 221
Flexner, Abraham 296
Flinders, Matthew 170
Flint, Austin 297
Florey, Sir Howard 481
forceps delivery:
  Australia 469
  Britain 133, 137, 142, 161, 171, 186, 187,
    215, 219–21, 225, 345
  in early nineteenth century
  Europe 407
  introduced in Britain, 171 n. 15
  by Swedish midwives 407
  USA 341, 345, 354–7, 361, 393–4,
    529–31
Ford, Dr 194
Fothergill, W. E. 51
Fulton, A. L. 296

Gamp, Sarah (fictional) 403
Gardener, A. G. 344
Garrigues, Henry J. 327
Garrison, Fielding H. 342
Geddes, George 237–8
Gélis, Jacques 162
Gibberd, G. F. 83–4
Gibson, Joseph 183

Giffard, William 400
Goodell, A. 100
Gordon, Alexander 56–60, 68, 70–7, 83, 318, 400, 534
Gordon, Doris 478
Granville, Augustus Bozzi 173, 400–1
Greig, Dr 91–2
Grisar Monsieur 433
Guthrie, Sir James, PRCS 189
gynaecology, influence on obstetric practice 184

Haines, Nora 241–2
Halford, Sir Henry, PRCP 188
handywomen 216–18
  evidence concerning from Professor Blackburn, Drs Finer, Fuller, Walshe 217–18
Harrison, Edward 175
Haultain, F. W. N. 229
Hebra, Ferdinand von 65, 436
Hektoen, L. 536
Henry Street Settlement, New York 277
Hey William 60, 70
Hicks, Braxton 173
'hidden' maternal deaths 34–7, 369–71, 518–27
  estimates of 369, 519–24
  and peritonitis, pyaemia, septicaemia 519
Hirsch, August 57, 436
Hirst B. C. 327–8
Hobbs, Remington 83
Högberg, Ulf 410
Holland, Eardley 224
Holmes, Oliver Wendell 62–4, 70, 282, 433
Holmes, R. W. 89, 290, 348
Hoosen, Bertha van 347
Horrocks, Peter 219–20
hospitals:
  Hôtel Dieu, Paris 403
  Kings College, London 202
  Massachusetts General 332
  see also lying-in hospitals
Hull House Chicago 277
hunger-winter 1944/5, Netherlands, and maternal and infant mortality rates 455–9
Hutterites 395–6
hyperemesis gravidarum, high incidence in Scotland 247

induction of labour 88, 92, 133–4, 357–8
infant mortality 483–517
  definition of 485
  determinants of 485–8
  endogenous and exogenous 485
  in Kentucky 320

in late nineteenth- and early twentieth-century 206–7
main conclusions 516–8
in Malta 43, 460
and maternal age and parity 500–7
maternal mortality, relationship to 483–518
neonatal mortality and maternal age and parity 508–9
neonatal mortality and postneonatal mortality 488–9
in New Zealand 477
post neonatal mortality 485–6, 510
poverty and social class 492–5
rates of, international and regional comparisons 496–500
secular trends in 491–2
institutional deliveries:
  estimates of in 1880s 195–6
  in Manchester 227
  and maternal mortality rates 196–203
International Classification of Diseases 26–7

Jackson, Dr 63
Janvier, Dr 287
Jellett, Henry 478
Jewett, C. 80
Jex-Blake, Sophia 190
Johnson, J. 83
Jones, Evan 98
Jones, O. V. 88, 92

Kay, Richard 169
Kelly, Florence 277
Kennedy, Evory 202
Kerr, J. Munro 225–6
King, Truby 477
Knipe, W. 347
Knodel, J. E. 508
Kobrin, F. E. 325
Kolletchka, Dr 66
Kosmak, George 279, 321, 393, 406, 414

Laget, M. 167
Lamaze, F. 350
Lancefield, Rebecca 81
Lane-Claypon, Janet (Lady Forber) 213–14
Le Fort, Leon 429, 431–3
Lea, Arnold 36
Leavitt, Judith W. 325
Lee, Robert 183, 201
Leishman, William 56
Lever, John 86–7, 92, 183
Levy, Julius 307, 395
Leiburg, Mart van 416–19
Lister, Joseph (Lord Lister) 204, 436–7
Litoff, Judy B. 325
Logan, Dale 219

lying-in charities (out-patient):
  Birmingham 97
  Liverpool 202
  London, Guy's Hospital 141
  London, Royal Maternity Charity 68, 97,
    138, 194–5
  low maternal mortality rate of, 200–3,
    337–9
  Paris Bureau de bienfaisance 432, 434
  USA 335–9
  USA Chicago Maternity Center 337–8
  USA Johns Hopkins, Cornell, Boston 336
lying-in hospitals, Australia 464
lying-in hospitals, Britain:
  Birmingham 203
  Dublin (The Rotunda) 138–41, 202
  Edinburgh 102
  founded eighteenth century 169
  Glasgow 202
  London: East End Maternity 226–7;
    General Lying-In 195, 204; Queen
    Charlotte's Hospital, 138, 142, 195, 204,
    258; Westminster 196; Woolwich 319
  Manchester, St Mary's 195, 203
  and principle of referral 333
  question of closure in nineteenth
    century 201–3
  range in quality 156–7
lying-in hospitals, Europe:
  Budapest 428–9
  Copenhagen 422
  Denmark 446
  founded seventeenth century 169
  France 428–9; number of hospital
    deliveries 428; organization of staff 429
  Gothenberg 414
  and hospices des enfants trouvés 429
  Liège 437–8
  Lille, Munich, Dresden, Berlin,
    Brussels 428–9
  Netherlands, 439–42
  Paris, high maternal mortality rate in 434–6
  and private patients 429–30
  problem of puerperal fever 430–4
  puerperal fever and antisepsis in 438–44
lying-in hospitals, USA 327–39
  advantages to patients 329
  Boston Lying-In 330–1
  Chicago, Cook County 347
  Chicago Lying-In 353
  growth of after First World War 334–5
  high maternal mortality in 332–3
  Johns Hopkins 330
  Minnesota Maternity 327
  and private patients 332–3
  Sloane Hospitals for Women, New
    York 329

lying-in wards in general hospitals, danger
  of 196–7, 393

Mackenzie, Sir Leslie 319
McLaren, Angus 117, 405
McQuay, Thomas A. I. 159
MacPhail, E. S. 32
malnutrition and maternal mortality, *see*
  poverty
man-midwifery in eighteenth century 166–7
Manningham, Sir Richard 168, 399
Marland, Hilary 416–19
maternal care, Australia 464–6
  Maternity Allowance Act (1913) 466
  home versus hospital deliveries
maternal care, Britain:
  comparison with Continent of Europe
    423–7
  diversity of maternal care 231–3
  increasing demand for hospital care 223–4
  Maternal and Child Welfare Act (1918)
    209, 233
  standard of care in general practice
    218–23, 245, 249–50
maternal care, Europe:
  comparison with USA 398–401
  beginnings of man-midwifery 399
maternal care, New Zealand:
  concern over population 477
  home versus hospital deliveries 477
maternal care, USA:
  conservative phase of care 286
  emergency program of Second World
    War 283
  and home deliveries by general practitioners
    285–9
  in immigrant populations 275
  in isolated areas 275, 278, 308–11
  in Michigan 360–4
  national committee on maternal welfare
    (1920) 279
  phase of surgical interference in labors 279
  in Pontiac, Michigan 362–3
maternal deaths, classification of 525–7
maternal mortality:
  and antisepsis 238–40
  associated deaths 28–34
  avoidable maternal deaths 249–50
  and birth–death interval 22
  causes and determinants 43–4
  causes, *see also* contracted pelvis;
    haemorrhage; puerperal fever; puerperal
    insanity; toxaemia
  compared with other mortalities 162–5
  decline after 1935 by cause 257
  and duration of pregnancy 146–8
  genetic and cultural factors in 225–4

hidden maternal deaths 34–8, 518–27
indirect maternal deaths, *see* associated
    deaths
international comparisons and associated
    deaths 32–4
international comparisons, an overview
    151–7
international differences in rates of 152–3
in lying-in hospitals 196
measurement and definition of 11–18; and
    multiple births 21; and stillbirths 19–21,
    146–8; and postnatal period 21–2; rate,
    definition of, 17, 19; and statistical
    significance 532–3
and mortality crises 240–1
and standards of living 44–5
in terms of population 16–17
maternal mortality, Australia:
    high-level and preventable deaths 463–4
    secular trend in 464
maternal mortality, Britain:
    and birth registration 22–4
    decline after 1935, 255
    and fertility rate 242–3
    fluctuations in rate and the streptococcus
    238
    in general practice 186–7
    in home and hospital deliveries 227–8
    in lying-in charities 199–200
    in lying-in hospitals 197–200
    and Medical Research Council 222
    the peak of 1874, 235–7
    in pre-registration period 158–60
    regional variations 251–3
    the Rochdale 'experiment' 245–6
    secular trend England and Wales:
        1850–1980, 12–18; 1850–1950; 235;
        1850–1910, 234–40; 1910–34,
        240–51; 1935–50, 254–7
    secular trend, Ireland 235
    secular trend, Scotland 235, 246–50
    and social class 44–8, 243–6
maternal mortality, Europe:
    and abortion 443, 453
    in lying-in hospitals: European 431;
        Paris 431–2, 435; Liège 437;
        Netherlands 443–4
    in Malta 460–1
    and midwives, Sweden and Norway,
        409–12
    in Normandy 404
    in Second World War 454–62
    in towns, 432, 439–4
maternal mortality, USA:
    conclusions 392–5
    geographical factors 274–6
    and general practitioners 289–91

and 'hidden' deaths 369–70
high level of 279, 365
methodological problems 365–7
in Michigan 360–3
and midwives 323–4
in North Dakota 393
in non-white mothers 373–81
and poverty 379–81
regional variations 371–3
reports on 528–31
rural v. urban 291–5
secular trend 366–7
secular trend compared with other countries
    390
secular trend, regional variations 381–9
in Southern States 373–89
in two religious groups 395–7
in Virginia 385–9
Maternity Center Association, New York 301,
    336, 338
maternity hospitals, *see* lying-in hospitals
Maubray, J. 168, 400
Mauquest de la Motte, Guillame 400
Mauriceau, François 400
medical education in obstetrics:
    in Australia 471–3
    in England and Wales 188–92, 229–30
    in Scotland 192
    in USA 295–7
Medical Acts (1858) and (1886) 191
Medical Research Council 258
Meigs, Charles 49, 54, 64, 282
Meigs, Grace 37, 279–80, 308, 477, 528
Mein Smith, Phillipa 478
Mendenhall, Dorothy 343, 421–2, 446–7
Merriman, Samuel 173, 183
Metcalf, John 285
Michigan, maternal care and mortality
    in 360–4
Midwives Acts, England and Wales
    (1902) 207, 212–13, 464
    England and Wales (1918) and (1936) 207,
    209, 262
    Scotland (1918) and (1937) 207, 262
midwives, Australia:
    regulation and training 464
    untrained 465
midwives, Britain:
    'bona fide' midwives 208, 213–14
    and county nursing associations 213
    in eighteenth century 161, 168
    income in early twentieth century 213–14
    in nineteenth century 174–6, 178–82, 201
    in twentieth century 207–9, 212–18, 231
    numbers of in nineteenth century 174–5
    opposed by general practitioners 208–9,
    425

midwives, Britain (*cont.*)
  records of Queen's Institute nurse-midwife
    214–16
  stereotype of 425
  see also handywomen; monthly nurse
midwives, European 398, 423–7
  character, regulation, and licensing 401–3
  traditional midwives 408
midwives, Danish 421–3
  social status and income 422, 423
  standard of practice 422–3
midwives, Netherlands 415–21
  'baker' and 'kraamverzorgester' 402–1
  low maternal mortality achieved 417
  numbers compared with other countries
    420
  status and skills 418–19
  training and regulation 416–21
midwives, French 402–6
  and abortion 405
  training 403–5
  two classes of 405
midwives, Swedish 406–15
  high standard of 406
  the 'jordgumma' (traditional midwife) 408
  training and regulation from 1663, 406
  training, twentieth century 414–15
  use of forceps by 407
midwives, USA 298–326
  black midwives of the south 311–18;
    clientele 311; of Kentucky 317–18;
    of South Carolina 317; standards of
    313–16; of Texas 316; training of 317
  deliveries by 281, 298–9
  immigrant midwives 302–7; abortions
    by 305–7; nationality 302–4; social
    status 303–4; standards of 305–7
  Kentucky Frontier Nursing service
    318–21, 377
  licensing of 278, 300–2
  and maternal mortality 323–4
  in Newark 323–5
  numbers of 1930–35 298–9
  opposed by obstetricians 321–3
  range of women employed as midwives
    298–300
  rural midwives 307–11
  in Wisconsin 325
Millar, J. 83
Ministry of Health (England and Wales) 207,
  209, 262
monthly nurse 181–2
Morris, E. Sydney 466–8
Morton, William T. G. 344
Murray, Farquhar 207

neonatal mortality:
  and birth injury 512
  causes of 485
  definition 485
  and prematurity 510–1
New York Academy of Medicine 279
Newman, Sir George 211
Nightingale, Florence 197, 464
Nixon, John 81
North Western University Medical
  School 353
notification of infectious diseases 51

obstetric haemorrhage 97–106
  accidental haemorrhage 100
  antepartum haemorrhage 100
  Créde's method for retained placenta 99
  deaths due to, in nineteenth century 97
  forms of obstetric haemorrhage 99
  and 'grand multiparity' 98
  mortality from all forms of 102–6
  mortality from placenta praevia 106
  placental abruption, *see* accidental
    haemorrhage
  placenta praevia and Caesarean section 101
  postpartum haemorrhage 99
  prevention and treatment after 1935, 255,
    271
obstetric texts, growth of in eighteenth
  century 400
Obstetrical Society of London 173, 176, 400
obstetricians, Britain, distribution of 1900–35,
  227–9
obstetricians, USA, number of in early
  twentieth century 289
obstetrics in general practice, poor standard of,
  1930–5, 218–23
obstetrics, opposition to 189–90, 229–30
obstetrics, practised by physicians and
  surgeons 183
obstetrics, status of in nineteenth century
  172–3
obstructed labour, *see* contracted pelvis
Ogle, William 518, 525
Osborn, William 135
Osburn, Miss 464
out-patient maternity services, *see* lying-in
  charities
Oxley, W. H. F. 245–6

Paget, Rosalind 405
Paget, Thomas 477–8
Paine, C. C. 81
Paradise, Viola 309
Pasteur, Louis 78
Pasteur Institute, Paris 259

Paxton, R. 169
penicillin 255, 260, 272, 416
Peretz, Elizabeth 232
Peu, Philippe 400
Phillips, Miles 447
Pinel, Philippe 26
Piper, Dr 86
placenta, manual removal of, 99, 215, 354–5
placenta praevia 100–2
placental abruption, *see* accidental
   haemorrhage
Playfair, W. S. 184, 193, 204
Pomeroy Dr 357
poor law maternal care 193–4
Porro, E., and caesarean section 135
Portal, P. 400
Porter, Roy, and Porter, Dorothy, 162
Potter, Dr, and routine version 357
poverty, definitions, measurement and
   concepts of 45–7, 377–9
poverty and maternal mortality 45–8, 160,
   377–81
pregnancy and health 30–1
Prontosil rubrum 258
prophylactic forceps operation and J. B.
   DeLee 354–7
puerperal fever 49–84
   see also Colebrook, L. and D.; Gordon, A.;
     Hey, W.; Holmes, O. W.; Semmelweis, I.;
     Tarnier, E. S.; White, C.
   and asymptomatic carriers 81–3, 535
   bacteriology of 52–4, 77–9, 78: nn. 67, 68
   causes, ideas in nineteenth century 69–70
   clinical course 53–6
   contagiousness of 57, 58–70
   endogenous and exogenous infection
     79–81
   epidemics form 57
   epidemic in Norway 76
   epidermic of 1874, 73–6
   epidemics in various towns in England
     58–60
   fatality rate 51–2
   link with erysipelas 70–7
   notification of cases 51–2
   number of deaths from 49
   and peritonitis 55–6
   puerperal pyrexia, definition of 52
   puerperal sepsis and septic abortion 50
   and septicaemia 79, 84
   terminology 50, 525
   treatment of, before 1935, 83–4
   and venesection 59, 83
puerperal insanity 143–6
   categories of 143
   confused with other conditions 144–5

and maternal mortality 145–6
   nature of in nineteenth century 144
puerperal mania and depression, *see* puerperal
   insanity
Pulsford, Benjamin and William 169

Queen Victoria's Jubilee Nursing Institute 214,
   232, 426
Quetelet, Adolphe 27

Ramsbotham, Francis 138, 172, 182, 345
Rentoul, Robert 35
reports on maternal mortality in Britain 210
rickets, *see* contracted pelvis
Rigby, Edward 100
Roberton, John 60
Rockwell, Norman 285
Rokitansky, Carl 78
Roleau, J. 400
Romlid, Christina 411
Roosevelt, Theodore 277
Rosenberg, Charles 327, 333
Routh, C. H. F. 68
Royal College of Obstetricians and
   Gynaecologists 211–12, 232, 262
Rutter, Dr 62, 83

Sandelowski, Margarete 348
Sanger, Max 135
Sauvages, Bosissier de lacroix 26
Schofield, Roger 159, 162–4
Schrader, Catharina 416–7
Second World War, maternal care and
   maternal mortality:
   Britain 262–6, 454–62
   France 455
   Malta 460–2
   Netherlands 455–9
   USA 278, 385
Select Committee on Medical Education
   (1834) 189–90
Select Committee on Midwives Registration
   (1892) 191, 208, 405
Semmelweis, Ignaz 63, 65–8, 203, 318, 433,
   436–7
Sen, Amartya 377–8
serum, anti-streptococcal 84
Shapiro, S. 509–10
Shattock, Lemuel 277
Shepperd–Towner Act (1922), USA 277–8,
   335
Shorter, Edward 250
Simpson, Sir James Young 101–2
   and chloroform in childbirth 344–6
Sinclair, Sir William 49
Skoda, Josef 436

Smith, J. 81
Spence, D. 400
Steele, A. B. 202
Steinbüchel, Richard von 346
Stevens, Rosemary 334
stillbirth, definition of 19–20
Stone, Sarah 168
Stopes, Marie 479
Storer, Dr 63
streptococcal infection and puerperal
        fever 53–4, 77–79, 81–3, 534–40
    asymptomatic carriers of 81–3, 470–1
    fatality rates 51–2, 536–7
    identification of streptococcus 78
    mortality peak of 1874 75–7, 412, 539
    prevalence of in industrial areas 238–9
    relationship of virulence to prevalence
        538–9
    scarlet fever and erysipelas 70–77, 535–6
    streptococcal strains 535
    streptococcal virulence: decline in 261, 414;
        as factor in mortality trend 160, 238, 246,
        255, 451; the nature of 538–40
Streptococcus pyogenes, Streptococcus haemolyticus,
        see streptococcal infections
sulphonamides 84, 255, 258–61, 272, 454,
        476, 481
    'M & B 693' 260
    prontosil, discovery of 258
    sulphanilamide 258
    trials of in puerperal fever 259

Tait, Lawson 101
Tandy, Elizabeth 20, 33, 312, 380
Tarnier, Étienne 434–6
Taussig, F. J. 116, 119, 121, 126–7
Taylor, Alan J. P. 129
Thompson, F. M. L. 177
Thurtle, Mrs 115
Tonellé, W. 56
Topping, Andrew 245–6, 272, 318
Towers, J. 183
toxaemia of pregnancy and eclampsia 85–96
    and antenatal care 90–1
    and Bright's disease 87
    early ideas of causation 87–8
    incidence 85–6
    mortality decline after mid-1930s 255–7
    mortality rate due to 92–6

nature of 85–6
New Zealand, high rate of 478
synonyms 85
treatment and prevention 88–92
Virginia, high rate of 389
Tuessenbrook, Catharine van 439–44
Tunnicliff, Ruth 536

unnecessary surgical interference in labour:
    Australia 469
    Britain 184, 218–21
    USA 287–9, 351, 352, 358–6, 394;
        Michigan 361
    various countries compared 351

Valerie, Mme de la 167
van Blarcom, Caroline 301
Victoria, Queen 345
Virchow, Rudolf 436
vital registration:
    England and Wales 22–5
    Scotland 22
    USA, 25–6, 366–71, 572–3
    various countries, 25, 579
Wald, Lillian 277
Waltman, Vrouw 418
Ward, G. G. 281
Warren, S. P. 289
Weatherhead G. H. 71
Webster, Charles 224
West, Thomas 61, 433, 534
White House Conferences on Maternal and
        Child Health 277, 279, 529–30
White, Charles 58, 160, 400
Whitridge Williams, John 80, 84, 296–7, 322,
        352–4, 356–7, 401
Willmot-Dobbie, B. M. 159
Wilson, Andrew 167–8
Wiltbank, John 282
Women's Co-operative Guild 223
Wood, Sir Kingsley 211
Woodbury, Robert Morse 38, 280, 365–70,
        483, 529
Wright, H. D. 81
Wrigley, Anthony 160

Yerushalmy, J. 484
Young, J. H. 447
Young, James 128, 351, 415, 447